Jill Ker Conway

Written *by* Herself

AUTOBIOGRAPHIES
OF AMERICAN WOMEN:
AN ANTHOLOGY

Jill Ker Conway was born in Hillston, New South Wales, Australia, graduated from the University of Sydney in 1958, and received her Ph.D. from Harvard University in 1969. From 1964 to 1975 she taught at the University of Toronto and was vice president there before serving for ten years as president of Smith College. Since 1985 she has been a visiting scholar and professor in M.I.T.'s Program in Science, Technology, and Society, and she now lives with her husband in Boston, Massachusetts.

She is the author of *Merchants and Merinos* (1960), *The Female Experience in Eighteenth- and Nineteenth-Century America* (1982), *Women Reformers and American Culture* (1987), and *The Road from Coorain* (1989) and editor of (with Susan C. Bourque and Joan W. Scott) *Learning About Women* (1989) and (with Susan Bourque) *The Politics of Women's Education* (forthcoming).

Written *by* Herself

AUTOBIOGRAPHIES
OF AMERICAN WOMEN:
AN ANTHOLOGY

Edited and with an Introduction by
Jill Ker Conway

VINTAGE BOOKS
A DIVISION OF RANDOM HOUSE, INC.
NEW YORK

A VINTAGE ORIGINAL, NOVEMBER 1992
FIRST EDITION

Copyright © 1992 by Jill Ker Conway

All rights reserved under International and Pan-American Copyright Conventions. Published in the United States of America by Vintage Books, a division of Random House, Inc., New York, and simultaneously in Canada by Random House of Canada Limited, Toronto.

Library of Congress Cataloging-in-Publication Data
Written by herself: autobiographies of American women: an anthology / edited and with an introduction by Jill Ker Conway.
p.   cm.
"A Vintage original"—T.p. verso.
ISBN 0-679-73633-6
1. American prose literature—Women authors.   2. Women—United States—Biography.   3. Autobiography—Women authors.
I. Conway,
Jill K., 1934–   .
PS647.W6W75   1992
920.72′0973—dc20   92-50081
CIP

Page 674 constitutes an extension of this copyright page.

DESIGN BY ROBERT BULL DESIGN

Manufactured in the United States of America
10   9

CONTENTS

INTRODUCTION

Autobiography is a form of writing which fascinates modern readers. Because so much of modern cultural criticism teaches us about the fragility of identity and the difficulty of achieving a strong sense of self, we are interested in hearing many distinct "voices" explain their experience. Autobiographical narratives are fictions, in the sense that the narrator imposes her or his order on the ebb and flow of experience and gives us a false sense of certainty and finality about causation in life. Yet they are not fictions but accounts of real lives, lived in a specific time and place, windows on the past, chances to enter and inhabit the real world of another person, chances to try on another identity and so broaden our own.

Autobiographies by women excite particular interest today, because three important trends in late-twentieth-century culture intersect to heighten the resonance of this form of narrative. The rise of democracy has enlarged the focus of interest in the lives of other people—from monarch, great general, and political leader to the ordinary person—someone like ourselves. And, as feminists have insisted that battles for power, authenticity, moral stature, and survival occur as fiercely within the domestic as in the public arena of life, what was once seen as placidly domestic now offers the reader a world charged with great issues.

Moreover, once Freud's condescending notion that a woman does not develop beyond the age of thirty, remaining permanently childish into old age, was displaced by the work of feminist psychologists presenting their own compelling version of the female Oedipal story, we came to see the development of women as filled with drama and challenge, as much concerned with work as with love and as potentially instructive as any male life.

Postmodern thought, influenced by the notion of contingency in nature and the uncertainty of natural events, has made us obsessed with causal narrative and has heightened our curiosity about agency in life. While we know that no life flows along clear, logical lines of causation, we still crave such coherence, so that the well-written autobiographical narrative seems to free us momentarily from ambiguity. Since, in Western culture, women have been seen as persons without agency, the female narrative with its conception of agency has a powerful appeal, the more so as our view of nature, with which in Western culture women have been identified, becomes chaotic and random.

There are distinct differences between the traditions of male and female autobiography in the West. The male form derives from classical models. The plot, borrowed from the *Odyssey,* shows us the narrator being tested in an heroic journey, emerging victorious from his trials, ready to claim his rightful place and his faithful Penelope. As readers we can thrill to the trials of Odysseus, secure in the certainty that he will triumph and return to claim his birthright. We don't have the same comfort about the testing of women, for we are used to the archetypal romantic plot dealing with female lives, in which the heroine must die tragically.

Whether religious (St. Augustine's *Confessions*) or secular (Rousseau's *Confessions*), the standard forms of the male narrative give the reader the sense that the narrator's actions are decisive and that his life has metaphysical significance. Thus we see the fate of Christianity in the West in balance in the famous moment of Augustine's theft of the pears. And the form of Rousseau's narrative converts an essentially sleazy set of erotic encounters into a mythic quest for democratic spontaneity.[1]

Women's narratives are rare until the nineteenth century, and their plots concern inner spiritual journeys, accounts of a relationship with God. The Protestant Reformation was a spur to more frequent female narratives because of the convention which encouraged accounts of religious conversion. Thus we have Anne Bradstreet's poem "To My Dear Children" and the life story of Elizabeth Ashbridge, a Quaker woman missionary whose account of her conversion and call to preach is compelling.[2]

This plot form was expanded in the mid-nineteenth-century

---

1. St. Augustine, *Confessions,* translated with an introduction and notes by Henry Chadwick, Oxford University Press, New York, 1991; Jean Jacques Rousseau, *Confessions,* translated with an introduction, Gibbings, London, 1907.

2. Anne Bradstreet, *The Works of Anne Bradstreet,* ed. Jeannine Hensley (Cambridge, Mass.: Harvard University Press, 1967); Elizabeth Ashbridge, *Some Account of the Early Part of the Life of Elizabeth Ashbridge, Who Died in the Service of the Truth, at the House of Robert Lecky, in the County of Carlow, Ireland, 1755, Written by Herself* (Providence, R.I. / H. H. Brown, 1831).

United States by slave narratives, accounts by women of their sexual exploitation in slavery and their dramatic and heroic breaks for freedom. These narratives escape the bourgeois convention that a woman's story ends in marriage, because slavery allowed a woman no family and respected neither kinship nor bonds of affection. Slave narratives are heroic stories of survival, accounts of endurance and of inextinguishable identity which transcend the usual Western quest or romance. This gives them their formidable power and explains their dynamizing impact on white women abolitionists.

By midcentury white American women with access to education saw their experience as exemplary, something to be made available to others, to encourage fellow seekers after knowledge and to instruct skeptics who doubted the value of female learning. After the Civil War, the generation of white women who entered higher education followed three paths into adulthood. The first was toward the creative life of the artist, a trailblazing path for the pioneer sculptors, photographers, and scholars who pushed their way into the training needed to acquire the techniques of their trade, and a more conventional path for the writers who set out alone to learn their calling.

The second route was toward the life of the literal pioneer in new professions and occupations for women. These trailblazers created new styles of life and explored and challenged accepted social norms and values. There were no male enclaves in studios, workshops, or ivied colleges which contained the knowledge these women sought, so their lives and callings were more or less invented as they went along.

A third, much smaller group of educated white women elected the vocation of scientist, seeking to work at the most abstract core of the emerging science and technology which would shape the twentieth-century West. They too had to push their way into the training they sought and to deal with male bias against women at its most intense level, in elite professional schools for men.

For all three groups there was no literary plot convention, no archetypal pattern in the culture, which told what their lives were about. They could never appropriate the *Odyssey*, for their trials were too severe, the absence of an attendant male version of Penelope too obvious, and the chances of triumphant recognition too remote. The bourgeois romance, the great myth of nineteenth-century capitalism, was ill suited to a group of women who seriously resisted becoming male property and who found adventure, work, politics, art, letters all more fulfilling than the glowing hearth and patter of little feet assigned women in the nineteenth-century cult of domesticity. Nor did the inner religious quest of earlier women autobiographers fit the lives of such typical American activists, many of whom rejected traditional Christianity.

The stories they told about their lives therefore show us a culture under stress. The plots, the notions of causation, the self-presentation in their narratives literally show us individuals grappling with the problems of describing a life which can't be crammed into conventional cultural categories.

In general, the artists and scientists, along with black women, dealt most easily with their narrative problems. They knew that their lives didn't fit easily into conventional patterns, but, nonetheless, their vocations have long histories in Western culture. A woman artist may not have fit her generation's definitions of femininity yet may have seen herself a lineal descendant of Leonardo. A woman scientist could have looked back with comfort to Galileo and Newton, even as her contemporary male colleagues were harassing her. A black woman may have looked back to the history of slavery in the Old Testament and seen her journey to freedom as a reenactment of that sacred history. The life plot for such people exists supposedly independent of gender. One's life is a quest—to realize one's vision of beauty, to see more deeply into nature, to escape from Egypt into the Promised Land. As we will see from the narratives in this anthology, the role of artist or scientist or escaped slave is not independent of gender, but such lives are lived consciously outside the standard patterns of bourgeois culture.

By contrast, the problems of personal narrative were intense for white women writers, social reformers, political leaders, athletes, and foreign adventurers. There were no conventions setting them outside bourgeois norms. Most, needing an appreciative audience for their causes to prosper, had to present themselves as the embodiments of romantic femininity, women to whom things happened rather than people who shaped events. A close reading of their narratives will show them moving to the passive voice whenever they are really acting decisively (Jane Addams), or taking refuge in the convention of being drawn to act by forces of destiny outside their control (Margaret Sanger). The hard-driving athlete Babe Didrikson—who once won a national track meet serving as a one-woman team competing successfully in every event and who, when she took up golf, practiced her drive till her hands bled—let the reader think she was always led to a new sport or a new dream of excelling by a generous mentor, not by her own restless search for new challenges.

Addams needed public support for her efforts as an urban reformer and teacher of the American social conscience. Sanger, in reality a total rebel against bourgeois sexual norms for women, had to win popular support for her campaign for legal access to birth control information. And Didrikson, the pioneer of women's professional sports in the United States, had to be able to draw a crowd. The narratives they wrote cultivate the image of the romantic female, nurturant, peace loving, and swayed only by positive emotion, rather than the driven, creative, high achievers we see when we really study their behavior. By presenting themselves in terms consistent with romantic imagery they created their own myth about female achievement in America. In their stories achievement comes from the intersection of emotionally prepared women with events and causes, to which they respond but which they do not shape. Their stories are about conversion experiences, about being swept along by events as the romantic heroine is swept off her feet by her lover, about being carried by events toward moments of intuitive insight and emotional truth.

It is only when we read the memoirs of public women influenced by the feminist movement of the 1960s and '70s that we encounter a nonromantic view of the female life. For Maya Angelou, sex is purely instrumental, the noblest relationships are with other women, and rage at life's injustices inspires some of her most powerful rhetoric. Maxine Hong Kingston alternates bitter realism about an Asian American woman's life situation with her own lyrical myth adapted from the Chinese folk story of the Woman Warrior. And Gloria Steinem infuses her account of her mother's unhappy life with her own anger and grief at the society and the attitudes which turned her competent mother into a helpless woman, terrified of life to the point of insanity. In these stories we hear a new tone of voice, politically aware, energized by rage, alternating gritty realism with powerfully lyrical imagery of a better world. These women also aim to persuade their readers, but by employing polemics, not by accepting and manipulating cultural patterns they cannot confront.

The selections in this anthology are organized in four sections, chosen to exemplify the range of activities, occupations, and social situations which have prompted the autobiographical muse for American women. Because the black female voice is so powerful in American letters, the first section deals with black women, though each memoir could well appear in one of the other three sections, concerned with the writing of women scientists and physicians, women artists and scholars, and women pioneers and reformers. Each section is arranged chronologically so that the reader can trace the history of American women through the narratives presented, describing American women's lives from the 1840s to the 1960s and '70s. The only principle of selection has been the literary quality of the memoirs. A more representative approach would produce quite another type of anthology. The aim of this one has been to present the most powerful female voices commenting on the American experience over the century and a half since women began writing memoirs in significant numbers.

Each section is introduced by a brief essay commenting on the historical context surrounding the lives of the authors as a group, emphasizing both what is unique about them and the themes linking their collective experience. A brief biographical sketch introduces each work, the selections from which are presented as connected narrative, with as little editorial clanking of gears as possible. All but two are parts of full dress autobiographies. The excerpts of Louise Bogan's memoirs are drawn from a posthumous memoir edited by Ruth Limmer, who has interwoven passages from Bogan's diaries and letters with passages from Bogan's astonishingly powerful autobiographical essay, "A Journey Around My Room," originally written for *The New Yorker*. Gloria Steinem's essay about her mother, "Ruth's Song (Because She Could Not Sing It)," comes from a collection of Steinem's essays, only a few of which are autobiographical. The selections drawn from works out of print or available only in manuscript are deliberately longer than those taken from current autobiographies, readily available to the interested reader. The aim of the whole is to give the reader a feel for the texture and imagery of women's writing and a sense of the kinds of narrative problems which a woman autobiographer must resolve.

Naturally, the selections vary in quality, but all claim our attention because of the powerful motivations which led these writers to cast aside the convention of female "modesty" and set them to telling the world about their lives. When we finish, and imagine this cast of characters, now become our friends, instructing us about our lives, we know that they will continue to instruct while they are parts of our memory, and that they will make us both more reflective and more decisive about working on the inner script with which we construct the meaning of our own lives. For this, after all, is what links us to the authors, who have set down on paper what we all do, with more or less conscious artistry. It is valuable to examine our own inner texts with these powerful models in mind, for they can both instruct and call forth a more confident inner voice of our own.

Written *by* Herself

My Story Ends with Freedom

Black women's autobiography celebrates the determination of black women to survive, to nourish and shelter those they love, and to assert their will in a hostile and often dangerous world. It records the power of faith and offers an unblinking and unabashed view of sexuality.

The tradition of black women's narratives reaches beyond slavery, back to the role of women as storytellers and religious figures in African culture. Their mesmerizing storytelling has riveted readers' attention from the time the first slave narratives were given wide publicity by the abolition movement. Black women's narratives establish their hold on the reader because of the rich rhetoric of black folk culture and the cadences of the Old Testament, so cherished by the black church. Because, from girlhood, these women faced the dual injustices of racial hostility and male exploitation, their life histories are told with no hint of romantic conventions. They describe, instead, a quest for physical and psychological survival.

The narrative voice in these stories is by turns witty, ironic, heroic, outraged, and triumphant. We hear each woman as a formidable presence, unvanquished despite terrible hazards. Whether the child of black sharecroppers or of urban industrial workers, each of these women knew fear and exploitation but possessed the psychic resources to fight them. Beside their stories the tests and tribulations of white women's lives seem lived in a minor key.

Strength and the forced wanderings of exile are both characteristics of these stories. Whereas white women might struggle to free themselves from family and polite conventions, Harriet Jacobs (1813–1897), Zora Neale Hurston (1901?–1960), and Maya Angelou (1928–   ) have been wanderers from childhood. Angelou and her brother were shipped as children across the United States to the safe haven of their grandmother's home in Arkansas. Hurston's wanderings began when she was fourteen, cast out of her family home after the death of her mother and a violent quarrel with her father's second wife. Jacobs was the ultimate wanderer, a fugitive slave, condemned by a corrupt public authority to hiding and disguise. The journeys of Marian Anderson (1902–   ) were for artistic recognition; they were courageous travels, always as the first black performer her European audiences had seen.

Women who experience extreme sexual exploitation see sexuality, and sexual morality, in terms different from those of bourgeois society. Jacobs knew that slave women, unprotected by convention or law from white male sexual demands, could not be held accountable to conventional sexual morality. When Angelou became pregnant as a teenager, her surrogate father told her that women had been getting pregnant since Eve ate the apple, and that there was no cause for alarm. Violated as a child by one of her mother's lovers, Angelou sought her first voluntary sexual partner herself, to check out empirically the nature of her sexual preference. When the experience turned out to be unsatisfactory, she reflected wryly that *she* had had a man, in an encounter in which she had set the terms.

Physical strength, and its righteous expression in violence, are also recurring themes in these stories. Jacobs endured intense privation and solitary confinement in her quest for freedom for herself and her children. Hurston administered a physical beating to the woman who had replaced her dead mother in her father's affections and had spitefully ordered Hurston's sister out of the house. Angelou fought and was wounded by her father's mistress, after the mistress spoke disrespectfully of Angelou's mother. These are women who fight to protect honor and who expect no male protector.

Along with physical strength go moral courage and deep spirituality. The transforming figures in these stories are mothers or grandmothers. Jacobs's grandmother was respected and feared by black and white alike in Edenton. The faith of Anderson's mother inspired her daughter to great art. Angelou's Momma (her paternal grandmother) was a fierce but loving guardian angel who gave her grandchildren preternatural strength.

The men in these stories come and go, like Angelou's grandmother's third husband, who had to be watched closely on his infrequent visits lest he steal all her possessions. Only Anderson, a product of the northern black middle class, had a trustworthy father and husband, but because of her father's early death it was Anderson's mother who encouraged her genius. Brothers and sons were fiercely loved, but in three of these four lives adult males were uncertain quantities. The exception is Anderson, whose male teachers, accompanists, and mentors joined with her community in recognizing and encouraging her extraordinary talents.

Angelou tells us that black women are strong because to enter adulthood they must confront and defy both racial hatred and male hostility. These stories show us women's lives completely outside the myths of romanticism. Therein lies their compelling power.

Harriet Ann Jacobs

(1813–1897)

Harriet Ann Jacobs was born to slaves in Edenton, North Carolina, and raised by her parents and her deeply religious maternal grandmother. Her idyllic childhood ended when she was sent at the age of six to the household of her mistress. There she was gently treated until her owner's death, when Jacobs was bequeathed as a twelve-year-old to her owner's five-year-old niece.

In this household, given the name Flint in Jacobs's narrative, she quickly became the object of the sexual attentions of her new owner's father, though she was somewhat protected by the stature in the community of her maternal grandmother and her grandmother's watchful attention to her well-being. Hoping to forestall her eventual violation by her owner's father, Jacobs contracted an alliance with another white man and bore him two children. While her children were young they were left in the care of her grandmother, but the prospect that they would become plantation laborers and be "broken" by the brutal discipline of slavery prompted Jacobs to flee in 1835, when she was twenty-two years old.

Thereafter, she lived for seven years in extraordinarily confined hiding places in her native town, relying on friends and her grandmother for food and shelter. Even in disorienting solitary confinement, Jacobs remained strong and unshakably determined to secure freedom for herself and her children.

Escaping to New York in 1842, Jacobs made a home for her son and daughter, kept in slavery by their father even though he had pledged to grant their freedom. This home was threatened as much in New York as it would have been in the South after the passage of the Fugitive Slave Law in 1850.

In 1852 Jacobs was purchased by the Colonization Society and freed. Shortly thereafter she began to write *Incidents in the Life of a Slave Girl,* which was published under the pseudonym Linda Brent and "edited," following a practice that lent credence to the authenticity of slave narratives, by the abolitionist writer and editor Lydia Maria Child (1802–1880). In spite of Child's endorsement, the events of Jacobs's escape were long thought to be fictional because of the elegance of her prose style. Recent research has, however, established Jacobs's bona fides and substantiated the events described in her narrative.

INCIDENTS IN THE LIFE
OF A SLAVE GIRL:
Written by Herself

I was born a slave; but I never knew it till six years of happy childhood had passed away. My father was a carpenter, and considered so intelligent and skillful in his trade, that, when buildings out of the common line were to be erected, he was sent for from long distances, to be head workman. On condition of paying his mistress two hundred dollars a year, and supporting himself, he was allowed to work at his trade, and manage his own affairs. His strongest wish was to purchase his children; but, though he several times offered his hard earnings for that purpose, he never succeeded.

I was so fondly shielded that I never dreamed I was a piece of merchandise, trusted to them for safe keeping, and liable to be demanded of them at any moment. I had one brother, William, who was two years younger than myself—a bright, affectionate child. I had also a great treasure in my maternal grandmother, who was a remarkable woman in many respects. She was the daughter of a planter in South Carolina, who, at his death, left her mother and his three children free, with money to go to St. Augustine, where they had relatives. It was during the Revolutionary War; and they were captured on their passage, carried back, and sold to different purchasers. . . .

She was a little girl when she was captured and sold to the keeper of a large hotel. I have often heard her tell how hard she fared during childhood. But as she grew older she evinced so much intelligence, and was so faithful, that her master and mistress could not help seeing it was for their interest to take care of such a valuable piece of property. She became an indispensable personage in the household, officiating in all capacities, from cook and wet nurse to seamstress. She was much praised for her cooking; and her nice crackers became so famous in the neighborhood that many people were desirous of obtaining them. In consequence of numerous requests of this kind, she asked permission of her mistress to bake crackers at night, after all the household work was done; and she obtained leave to do it, provided she would clothe herself and her children from the profits. . . .

To this good grandmother I was indebted for many comforts. My brother Willie and I often received portions of the crackers, cakes, and preserves, she made to sell; and after we ceased to be children we were indebted to her for many more important services.

Such were the unusually fortunate circumstances of my early childhood. When I was six years old, my mother died; and then, for the first time, I learned, by the talk around me, that I was a slave. My mother's mistress was the daughter of my grandmother's mistress. She was the foster sister of my mother; they were both nourished at my grandmother's breast. In fact, my mother had been weaned at three months old, that the babe of the mistress might obtain sufficient food. They played together as children; and, when they became women, my mother was a most faithful servant to her white foster sister. On her death-bed her mistress promised that her children should never suffer for any thing; and during her lifetime she kept her word. They all spoke kindly of my dead mother, who had been a slave merely in name, but in nature was noble and womanly. I grieved for her, and my young mind was troubled with the thought who would now take care of me and my little brother. I was told that my home was now to be with her mistress; and I found it a happy one. No toilsome or disagreeable duties were imposed upon me. My mistress was so kind to me that I was always glad to do her bidding, and proud to labor for her as much as my young years would permit. . . .

When I was nearly twelve years old, my kind mistress sickened and died. As I saw the cheek grow paler, and the eye more glassy, how earnestly I prayed in my heart that she might live! I loved her; for she had been almost like a mother to me. My prayers were not answered. She died, and they buried her in the little churchyard, where, day after day, my tears fell upon her grave.

I was sent to spend a week with my grandmother. I was now old enough to begin to think of the future; and again and again I asked myself what they would do with me. I felt sure I should never find another mistress so kind as the one who was gone. She had promised my dying mother that her children should never suffer for any thing; and when I remembered that, and recalled her many proofs of attachment to me, I could not help having some hopes that she had left me free. . . .

After a brief period of suspense . . . we learned that she had bequeathed me to her sister's daughter, a child of five years old. So vanished our hopes. My mistress had taught me the precepts of God's Word: "Thou shalt love thy neighbor as thyself." "Whatsoever ye would that men should do unto you, do ye even so unto them." But I was her slave, and I suppose she did not recognize me as her neighbor. I would give much to blot out from my memory that one great wrong. As a child, I loved my mistress; and, looking back on the happy days I spent with her, I try to think with less bitterness of this act of injustice. While I was with her, she taught me to read and spell; and for this privilege, which so rarely falls to the lot of a slave, I bless her memory. . . .

Little attention was paid to the slaves' meals in Dr. Flint's house. If they could catch a bit of food while it was going, well and good. I gave myself no trouble on that score, for on my various errands I passed my grandmother's house, where there was always something to spare for me. I was frequently threatened with punishment if I stopped there; and my grandmother, to avoid detaining me, often stood at the gate with something for my breakfast or dinner. I was indebted to *her* for all my comforts, spiritual or temporal. It was *her* labor that supplied my scanty wardrobe. I have a vivid recollection of the linsey-woolsey dress given me every winter by Mrs. Flint. How I hated it! It was one of the badges of slavery. . . .

My grandmother's mistress had always promised her that, at her death, she should be free; and it was said that in her will she made good the promise. But when the estate was settled, Dr. Flint told the faithful old servant that, under existing circumstances, it was necessary she should be sold.

On the appointed day, the customary advertisement was posted up, proclaiming that there would be a "public sale of negroes, horses, &c." Dr. Flint called to tell my grandmother that he was unwilling to wound her feelings by putting her up at auction, and that he would prefer to dispose of her at private sale. My grandmother saw through his hypocrisy; she understood very well that he was ashamed of the job. She was a very spirited woman, and if he was base enough to sell her, when her mistress intended she should be free, she was determined the public should know it. She had for a long time supplied many families with crackers and preserves; consequently, "Aunt Marthy," as she was called, was generally known, and every body who knew her respected her intelligence and good character. Her long and faithful service in the family was also well known, and the intention of her mistress to leave her free. When the day of sale came, she took her place among the chattels, and at the first call she sprang upon the auction-block. Many voices called out, "Shame! Shame! Who is going to sell *you*, Aunt Marthy? Don't stand there! That is no place for *you*." Without saying a word, she quietly awaited her fate. No one bid for her. At last, a feeble voice said, "Fifty dollars." It came from a maiden lady, seventy years old, the sister of my grandmother's deceased mistress. She had lived forty years under the same roof with my grandmother; she knew how faithfully she had served her owners, and how cruelly she had been defrauded of her rights; and she resolved to protect her.

I now entered on my fifteenth year—a sad epoch in the life of a slave girl. My master began to whisper foul words in my ear. Young as I was, I could not remain ignorant of their import. I tried to treat them with indifference or contempt. The master's age, my extreme youth, and the fear that his conduct would be reported to my grandmother, made him bear this treatment for many months. . . .

I was compelled to live under the same roof with him—where I saw a man forty years my senior daily violating the most sacred commandments of nature. He told me I was his property; that I must be subject to his will in all things. My soul revolted against the mean tyranny. But where could I turn for protection? No matter whether the slave girl be as black as ebony or as fair as her mistress. In either case, there is no shadow of law to protect her from insult, from violence, or even from death; all these are inflicted by fiends who bear the shape of men. . . .

I know that some are too much brutalized by slavery to feel the humiliation of their position; but many slaves feel it most acutely, and shrink from the memory of it. I cannot tell how much I suffered in the presence of these wrongs, nor how I am still pained by the retrospect. My master met me at every turn, reminding me that I belonged to him, and swearing by heaven and earth that he would compel me to submit to him. If I went out for a breath of fresh air, after a day of unwearied toil his footsteps dogged me. . . .

Sometimes he would complain of the heat of the tea room, and order his supper to be placed on a small table in the piazza. He would seat himself there with a well-satisfied smile, and tell me to stand by and brush away the flies. He would eat very slowly, pausing between the mouthfuls. These intervals were employed in describing the happiness I was so foolishly throwing away, and in threatening me with the penalty that finally awaited my stubborn disobedience. . . .

I had entered my sixteenth year, and every day it became more apparent that my presence was intolerable to Mrs. Flint. Angry words frequently passed between her and her husband. He had never punished me himself, and he would not allow any body else to punish me. . . .

I knew nothing would enrage Dr. Flint so much as to know that I favored another; and it was something to triumph over my tyrant even in that small way. I thought he would revenge himself by selling me, and I was sure my friend, Mr. Sands, would buy me. He was a man of more generosity and feeling than my master, and I thought my freedom could be easily obtained from him. The crisis of my fate now came so near that I was desperate. I shuddered to think of being the mother of children that should be owned by my old tyrant. . . .

I know I did wrong. No one can feel it more sensibly than I do. The painful and humiliating memory will haunt me to my dying day. Still, in looking back, calmly, on the events of my life, I feel that the slave woman ought not to be judged by the same standard as others. . . .

I went to my grandmother. My lips moved to make confession, but the words stuck in my throat. I sat down in the shade of a tree at her door and began to sew. I think she saw something unusual was the matter with me. . . .

Presently, in came my mistress, like a mad woman, and accused me concerning her husband. My grandmother, whose suspicions had been previously awakened, believed what she said. She exclaimed, "O Linda! has it come to this? I had rather see you dead than to see you as you now are. You are a disgrace to your dead mother." . . .

When my babe was born, they said it was premature. It weighed only four pounds; but God let it live. I heard the doctor say I could not survive till morning. I had often prayed for death; but now I did not want to die, unless my child could die too. Many weeks passed before I was able to leave my bed. I was a mere wreck of my former self. For a year there was scarcely a day when I was free from chills and fever. My babe also was sickly. His little limbs were often racked with pain. Dr. Flint continued his visits, to look after my health; and he did not fail to remind me that my child was an addition to his stock of slaves. . . .

As the months passed on, my boy improved in health. When he was a year old, they called him beautiful. The little vine was taking deep root in my existence, though its clinging fondness excited a mixture of love and pain. When I was most sorely oppressed I found solace in his smiles. I loved to watch his infant slumbers; but always there was a dark cloud over my enjoyment. I could never forget that he was a slave. . . .

When Dr. Flint learned that I was again to be a mother, he was exasperated beyond measure. He rushed from the house, and returned with a pair of shears. I had a fine head of hair; and he often railed about my pride of arranging it nicely. He cut every hair close to my head, storming and swearing all the time. I replied to some of his abuse, and he struck me. Some months before, he had pitched me down stairs in a fit of passion; and the injury I received was so serious that I was unable to turn myself in bed for many days. He then said, "Linda, I swear by God I will never raise my hand against you again"; but I knew that he would forget his promise. . . .

When they told me my newborn babe was a girl, my heart was heavier than it had ever been before. Slavery is terrible for men; but it is far more terrible for women. Superadded to the burden common to all, *they* have wrongs, and sufferings, and mortifications peculiarly their own.

Dr. Flint had sworn that he would make me suffer, to my last day, for this new crime against *him*, as he called it; and as long as he had me in his power he kept his word. On the fourth day after the birth of my babe, he entered my room suddenly, and commanded me to rise and bring my baby to him. The nurse who took care of me had gone out of the room to prepare some nourishment, and I was alone. There was no alternative. I rose, took up my babe, and crossed the room to where he sat. "Now stand there," said he, "till I tell you to go back!" My child bore a strong resemblance to her father, and to the deceased Mrs. Sands, her grandmother. He noticed this; and while I stood before him, trembling with weakness, he heaped upon me and my little one every vile epithet he could think of. Even the grandmother in her grave did not escape his curses. In the midst of his vituperations I fainted at his feet. This recalled him to his senses. He took the baby from my arms, laid it on the bed, dashed cold water in my face, took me up, and shook me violently, to restore my consciousness before any one entered the room. Just then my grandmother came in, and he hurried out of the house. I suffered in consequence of this treatment; but I begged my friends to let me die, rather than send for the doctor. There was nothing I dreaded so much as his presence. My life was spared; and I was glad for the sake of my little ones. Had it not been for these ties to life, I should have been glad to be released by death, though I had lived only nineteen years. . . .

My grandmother belonged to the church; and she was very desirous of having the children christened. I knew Dr. Flint would forbid it, and I did not venture to attempt it. But chance favored me. He was called to visit a patient out of town, and was obliged to be absent during Sunday. "Now is the time," said my grandmother; "we will take the children to church, and have them christened." . . .

When my baby was about to be christened, the former mistress of my father stepped up to me, and proposed to give it her Christian name. To this I added the surname of my father, who had himself no legal right to it; for my grandfather on the paternal side was a white gentleman. What tangled skeins are the genealogies of slavery! I loved my father; but it mortified me to be obliged to bestow his name on my children.

[Jacobs and her children were sent to the Flint family's plantation as a punishment. The implication for her was that her children would be "broken" as field slaves.]

Early next morning I left my grandmother's with my youngest child. My boy was ill, and I left him behind. I had many sad thoughts as the old wagon jolted on. Hitherto, I had suffered alone; now, my little one was to be treated as a slave. As we drew near the great house, I thought of the time when I was formerly sent there out of revenge. I wondered for what purpose I was now sent. I could not tell. I resolved to obey orders so far as duty required; but within myself, I determined to make my stay as short as possible. Mr. Flint was waiting to receive us, and told me to follow him up stairs to receive orders for the day. My little Ellen was left below in the kitchen. It was a change for her, who had always been so carefully tended. My young master said she might amuse herself in the yard. This was kind of him, since the child was hateful to his sight. My task was to fit up the house for the reception of the bride. In the midst of sheets, tablecloths, towels, drapery, and carpeting, my head was as busy planning, as were my fingers with the needle. At noon I was allowed to go to Ellen. She had sobbed herself to sleep. I heard Mr. Flint say to a neighbor, "I've got her down here, and I'll soon take the town notions out of her head. My father is partly to blame for her nonsense. He ought to have broke her in long ago." The remark was made within my hearing, and it would have been quite as manly to have made it to my face. He *had* said things to my face which might, or might not, have surprised his neighbor if he had known of them. He was "a chip off the old block." . . .

The next morning the old cart was loaded with shingles for town. I put Ellen into it, and sent her to her grandmother. Mr. Flint said I ought to have asked his permission. I told him the child was sick, and required attention which I had no time to give. He let it pass; for he was aware that I had accomplished much work in a little time.

I had been three weeks on the plantation, when I planned a visit home. It must be at night, after every body was in bed. I was six miles from town, and the road was very dreary. I was to go with a young man, who, I knew, often stole to town to see his mother. One night, when all was quiet, we started. Fear gave speed to our steps, and we were not long in performing the journey. I arrived at my grandmother's. Her bed room was on the first floor, and the window was open, the weather being warm. I spoke to her and she awoke. She let me in and closed the window, lest some late passerby should see me. A light was brought, and the whole household gathered round me, some smiling and some crying. I went to look at my children, and thanked God for their happy sleep. The tears fell as I leaned over them. As I moved to leave, Benny stirred. I turned back, and whispered, "Mother is here." After digging at his eyes with his little fist, they opened, and he sat up in bed, looking at me curiously. Having satisfied himself that it was I, he exclaimed, "O mother! you ain't dead, are you? They didn't cut off your head at the plantation, did they?" . . .

Again and again I had traversed those dreary twelve miles, to and from the town; and all the way, I was meditating upon some means of escape for myself and my children. My friends had made every effort that ingenuity could devise to effect our purchase, but all their plans had proved abortive. Dr. Flint was suspicious, and determined not to loosen his grasp upon us. I could have made my escape alone; but it was more for my helpless children than for myself that I longed for freedom. Though the boon would have been precious to me, above all price, I would not have taken it at the expense of leaving them in slavery. Every trial I endured, every sacrifice I made for their sakes, drew them closer to my heart, and gave me fresh courage to beat back the dark waves that rolled and rolled over me in a seemingly endless night of storms. . . .

My plan was to conceal myself at the house of a friend, and remain there a few weeks till the search was over. My hope was that the doctor would get discouraged, and, for fear of losing my value, and also of subsequently finding my children among the missing, he would consent to sell us; and I knew somebody would buy us. I had done all in my power to make my children comfortable during the time I expected to be separated from them. I was packing my things, when grandmother came into the room, and asked what I was doing. "I am putting my things in order," I replied. I tried to look and speak cheerfully; but her watchful eye detected something beneath the surface. She drew me towards her, and asked me to sit down. She looked earnestly at me, and said, "Linda, do you want to kill your old grandmother? Do you mean to leave your little, helpless children? I am old now, and cannot do for your babies as I once did for you."

I replied, that if I went away, perhaps their father would be able to secure their freedom.

"Ah, my child," said she, "don't trust too much to him. Stand by your own children, and suffer with them till death. Nobody respects a mother who forsakes her children; and if you leave them, you will never have a happy moment. If you go, you will make me miserable the short time I have to live. You would be taken and brought back, and your sufferings would be dreadful." . . .

My mistress and I got along very well together. At the end of a week, old Mrs. Flint made us another visit, and was closeted a long time with her daughter-in-law. I had my suspicions what was the subject of the conference. The old doctor's wife had been informed that I could leave the plantation on one condition, and she was very desirous to keep me there. If she had trusted me, as I deserved to be trusted by her, she would have had no fears of my accepting that condition. When she entered her carriage to return home, she said to young Mrs. Flint, "Don't neglect to send for them as quick as possible." My heart was on the watch all the time, and I at once concluded that she spoke of my children. The doctor came the next day, and as I entered the room to spread the tea table, I heard him say, "Don't wait any longer. Send for them to-morrow." I saw through the plan. They thought my children's being there would fetter me to the spot, and that it was a good place to break us all in to abject submission to our lot as slaves. After the doctor left, a gentleman called, who had always manifested friendly feelings towards my grandmother and her family. Mr. Flint carried him over the plantation to show him the results of labor performed by men and women who were unpaid, miserably clothed, and half famished. The cotton crop was all they thought of. It was duly admired, and the gentleman returned with specimens to show his friends. I was ordered to carry water to wash his hands. As I did so, he said, "Linda, how do you like your new home?" I told him I liked it as well as I expected. He replied, "They don't think you are contented, and to-morrow they are going to bring your children to be with you. I am sorry for you, Linda. I hope they will treat you kindly." I hurried from the room, unable to thank him. My suspicions were correct. My children were to be brought to the plantation to be "broke in."

To this day I feel grateful to the gentleman who gave me this timely information. It nerved me to immediate action. . . .

I resolved to leave them that night. I remembered the grief this step would bring upon my dear old grandmother; and nothing less than the freedom of my children would have induced me to disregard her advice. I went about my evening work with trembling steps. Mr. Flint twice called from his chamber door to inquire why the house was not locked up. I replied that I had not done my work. "You have had time enough to do it," said he. "Take care how you answer me!"

I shut all the windows, locked all the doors, and went up to the third story, to wait till midnight. . . .

At half past twelve I stole softly down stairs. I stopped on the second floor thinking I heard a noise. I felt my way down into the parlor, and looked out of the window. The night was so intensely dark that I could see nothing. I raised the window very softly and jumped out. Large drops of rain were falling, and the darkness bewildered me. I dropped on my knees, and breathed a short prayer to God for guidance and protection. I groped my way to the road, and rushed towards the town with almost lightning speed. . . .

I tapped several times before she heard me. At last she raised the window, and I whispered, "Sally, I have run away. Let me in, quick." . . .

I told her I had a hiding-place, and that was all it was best for her to know. I asked her to go into my room as soon as it was light, and take all my clothes out of my trunk, and pack them in hers;

for I knew Mr. Flint and the constable would be there early to search my room. . . .

I went forth into the darkness and rain, I ran on till I came to the house of the friend who was to conceal me.

Early the next morning Mr. Flint was at my grandmother's inquiring for me. She told him she had not seen me, and supposed I was at the plantation. He watched her face narrowly, and said, "Don't you know any thing about her running off?" She assured him that she did not. He went on to say, "Last night she ran off without the least provocation. We had treated her very kindly. My wife liked her. She will soon be found and brought back. Are her children with you?" When told that they were, he said, "I am very glad to hear that. If they are here, she cannot be far off. If I find out that any of my niggers have had any thing to do with this damned business, I'll give 'em five hundred lashes." As he started to go to his father's, he turned round and added, persuasively, "Let her be brought back, and she shall have her children to live with her." . . .

The search for me was kept up with more perseverance than I had anticipated. I began to think that escape was impossible. I was in great anxiety lest I should implicate the friend who harbored me. I knew the consequences would be frightful; and much as I dreaded being caught, even that seemed better than causing an innocent person to suffer for kindness to me. A week had passed in terrible suspense, when my pursuers came into such close vicinity that I concluded they had tracked me to my hiding-place. I flew out of the house, and concealed myself in a thicket of bushes. There I remained in an agony of fear for two hours. Suddenly, a reptile of some kind seized my leg. In my fright, I struck a blow which loosened its hold, but I could not tell whether I had killed it; it was so dark, I could not see what it was; I only knew it was something cold and slimy. The pain I felt soon indicated that the bite was poisonous. I was compelled to leave my place of concealment, and I groped my way back into the house. The pain had become intense, and my friend was startled by my look of anguish. I asked her to prepare a poultice of warm ashes and vinegar, and I applied it to my leg, which was already much swollen. The application gave me some relief, but the swelling did not abate. The dread of being disabled was greater than the physical pain I endured. My friend asked an old woman, who doctored among the slaves, what was good for the bite of a snake or a lizard. She told her to steep a dozen coppers in vinegar, over night, and apply the cankered vinegar to the inflamed part. . . .

I had succeeded in cautiously conveying some messages to my relatives. They were harshly threatened, and despairing of my having a chance to escape. . . .

Among the ladies who were acquainted with my grandmother, was one who had known her from childhood, and always been very friendly to her. She had also known my mother and her children, and felt interested for them. . . .

She was unlike the majority of slaveholders' wives. My grandmother looked earnestly at her. Something in the expression of her face said "Trust me!" and she did trust her. She listened attentively to the details of my story, and sat thinking for a while. At last she said, "Aunt Martha, I pity you both. If you think there is any chance of Linda's getting to the Free States, I will conceal her for a time. But first you must solemnly promise that my name shall never be mentioned. If such a thing should become known, it would ruin me and my family. No one in my house must know of it, except the cook. She is so faithful that I would trust my own life with her; and I know she likes Linda. It is a great risk; but I trust no harm will come of it. Get word to Linda to be ready as soon as it is dark, before the patrols are out. I will send the housemaids on errands, and Betty shall go to meet Linda." The place where we were to meet was designated and agreed upon. My grandmother was unable to thank the lady for this noble deed; overcome by her emotions, she sank on her knees and sobbed like a child. . . .

I received a message to leave my friend's house at such an hour, and to go to a certain place where a friend would be waiting for me. . . .

My friend Betty was there; she was the last person I expected to see. We hurried along in silence. The pain in my leg was so intense that it seemed as if I should drop, but fear gave me strength. We reached the house and entered unobserved. Her first words were: "Honey, now you is safe. Dem devils ain't coming to search *dis* house. When I get you into missis' safe place, I will bring some nice hot supper. I specs you need it after all dis skeering." Betty's vocation led her to think eating the most important thing in life. She did not realize that my heart was too full for me to care much about supper. . . .

The mistress came to meet us, and led me up stairs to a small room over her own sleeping apartment. "You will be safe here,

Linda," said she; "I keep this room to store away things that are out of use. The girls are not accustomed to be sent to it, and they will not suspect any thing unless they hear some noise. I always keep it locked, and Betty shall take care of the key. But you must be very careful, for my sake as well as your own; and you must never tell my secret; for it would ruin me and my family. I will keep the girls busy in the morning, that Betty may have a chance to bring your breakfast; but it will not do for her to come to you again till night. I will come to see you sometimes. Keep up your courage. I hope this state of things will not last long." Betty came with the "nice hot supper," and the mistress hastened down stairs to keep things straight till she returned. How my heart overflowed with gratitude! Words choked in my throat; but I could have kissed the feet of my benefactress. For that deed of Christian womanhood, may God forever bless her! . . .

Opposite my window was a pile of feather beds. On the top of these I could lie perfectly concealed, and command a view of the street through which Dr. Flint passed to his office. Anxious as I was, I felt a gleam of satisfaction when I saw him. Thus far I had outwitted him, and I triumphed over it. Who can blame slaves for being cunning? They are constantly compelled to resort to it. It is the only weapon of the weak and oppressed against the strength of their tyrants.

[Jacobs's children were bought by their father and returned to their grandmother.]

Great surprise was expressed when it was known that my children had returned to their grandmother's. The news spread through the town, and many a kind word was bestowed on the little ones. . . .

I had my season of joy and thanksgiving. It was the first time since my childhood that I had experienced any real happiness. I heard of the old doctor's threats, but they no longer had the same power to trouble me. The darkest cloud that hung over my life had rolled away. Whatever slavery might do to me, it could not shackle my children. . . .

We all saw that I could not remain where I was much longer. I had already staid longer than was intended, and I knew my presence must be a source of perpetual anxiety to my kind benefactress. During this time, my friends had laid many plans for my escape, but the extreme vigilance of my persecutors made it impossible to carry them into effect. . . .

Alas, it was not an easy thing, for one in my situation, to go to the north. In order to leave the coast quite clear for me, she went into the country to spend the day with her brother, and took Jenny with her. She was afraid to come and bid me good by, but she left a kind message with Betty. I heard her carriage roll from the door, and I never again saw her who had so generously befriended the poor, trembling fugitive! Though she was a slaveholder, to this day my heart blesses her! . . .

I had not the slightest idea where I was going. Betty brought me a suit of sailor's clothes,—jacket, trowsers, and tarpaulin hat. She gave me a small bundle, saying I might need it where I was going. In cheery tones, she exclaimed, "I'se *so* glad you is gwine to free parts! Don't forget ole Betty. P'raps I'll come 'long by and by."

[Jacobs's first break for the North was aborted.]
They told me a place of concealment had been provided for me at my grandmother's. I could not imagine how it was possible to hide me in her house, every nook and corner of which was known to the Flint family. They told me to wait and see. We were rowed ashore, and went boldly through the streets, to my grandmother's. I wore my sailor's clothes, and had blackened my face with charcoal. I passed several people whom I knew. The father of my children came so near that I brushed against his arm; but he had no idea who it was.

"You must make the most of this walk," said my friend Peter, "for you may not have another very soon."

I thought his voice sounded sad. It was kind of him to conceal from me what a dismal hole was to be my home for a long, long time. . . .

A small shed had been added to my grandmother's house years ago. Some boards were laid across the joists at the top, and between these boards and the roof was a very small garret, never occupied by any thing but rats and mice. It was a pent roof, covered with nothing but shingles, according to the southern custom for such buildings. The garret was only nine feet long and seven wide. The highest part was three feet high, and sloped down abruptly to the loose board floor. There was no admission for either light or air. My uncle Phillip, who was a carpenter, had very skillfully made a concealed trap-door, which communicated with the storeroom. He had been doing this while I was waiting in the swamp. The storeroom opened upon a piazza. To this hole I was conveyed as soon as I entered the house. The air was stifling; the darkness total. A bed had been spread on the floor. I could sleep quite comfortably on one side; but the slope was so sudden that I could not turn on the other without hitting the roof. The rats and mice ran over my bed; but I was weary, and I slept such sleep as the wretched may, when a tempest has passed over them. Morning came. I knew it only by the noises I heard; for in my small den day and night were all the same. I suffered for air even more than for light. But I was not comfortless. I heard the voices of my children. There was joy and there was sadness in the sound. It made my tears flow. How I longed to speak to them! I was eager to look on their faces; but there was no hole, no crack, through which I could peep. This continued darkness was oppressive. It seemed horrible to sit or lie in a cramped position day after day, without one gleam of light. Yet I would have chosen this, rather than my lot as a slave, though white people considered it an easy one; and it was so compared with the fate of others. . . .

My food was passed up to me through the trap-door my uncle had contrived; and my grandmother, my uncle Phillip, and aunt Nancy would seize such opportunities as they could, to mount up there and chat with me at the opening. But of course this was not safe in the daytime. It must all be done in darkness. It was impossible for me to move in an erect position, but I crawled about my den for exercise. One day I hit my head against something, and found it was a gimlet. My uncle had left it sticking there when he made the trap-door. I was as rejoiced as Robinson Crusoe could have been at finding such a treasure. It put a lucky thought into my head. I said to myself, "Now I will have some light. Now I will see my children." I did not dare to begin my work during the daytime, for fear of attracting attention. But I groped round; and having found the side next the street, where I could frequently see my children, I stuck the gimlet in and waited for evening. I bored three rows of holes, one above another; then I bored out the interstices between. I thus succeeded in making one hole about an inch long and an inch broad. I sat by it till late into the night, to enjoy the little whiff of air that floated in. In the morning I watched for my children. The first person I saw in the street was Dr. Flint. I had a shuddering, superstitious feeling that it was a bad omen. Several familiar faces passed by. At last I heard the merry laugh of children, and presently two sweet little faces were looking up at me, as though they knew I was there, and were conscious of the joy they imparted. How I longed to *tell* them I was there! . . .

Autumn came, with a pleasant abatement of heat. My eyes had become accustomed to the dim light, and by holding my book or work in a certain position near the aperture I contrived to read and sew. That was a great relief to the tedious monotony of my life. But when winter came, the cold penetrated through the thin shingle roof, and I was dreadfully chilled. The winters there are not so long, or so severe, as in northern latitudes; but the houses are not built to shelter from cold, and my little den was peculiarly comfortless. The kind grandmother brought me bed-clothes and warm drinks. Often I was obliged to lie in bed all day to keep comfortable; but with all my precautions, my shoulders and feet were frostbitten. . . .

Dr. Flint and his family repeatedly tried to coax and bribe my children to tell something they had heard said about me. One day the doctor took them into a shop, and offered them some bright little silver pieces and gay handkerchiefs if they would tell where their mother was. Ellen shrank away from him, and would not speak; but Benny spoke up, and said, "Dr. Flint, I don't know where my mother is. I guess she's in New York; and when you go there again, I wish you'd ask her to come home, for I want to see her; but if you put her in jail, or tell her you'll cut her head off, I'll tell her to go right back."

Mr. Sands was elected [to Congress]; an event which occasioned me some anxious thoughts. He had not emancipated my children, and if he should die they would be at the mercy of his heirs. Two little voices, that frequently met my ear, seemed to plead with me not to let their father depart without striving to make their freedom secure. Years had passed since I had spoken to him. I had not even seen him since the night I passed him, unrecognized, in my disguise of a sailor. I supposed he would call before he left, to say something to my grandmother concerning the children, and I resolved what course to take.

The day before his departure for Washington I made arrangements, towards evening, to get from my hiding-place into the storeroom below. I found myself so stiff and clumsy that it was with great difficulty I could hitch from one resting place to another. When I reached the storeroom my ankles gave way under me, and I sank exhausted on the floor. It seemed as if I could never use my limbs again. But the purpose I had in view roused all the strength I had. I crawled on my hands and knees to the window, and, screened behind a barrel, I waited for his coming. The clock struck nine, and I knew the steamboat would leave between ten and eleven. My hopes were failing, but presently I heard his voice, saying to some one, "Wait for me a moment. I wish to see Aunt Martha." When he came out, as he passed the window, I said, "Stop one moment, and let me speak for my children." He started, hesitated, and then passed on, and went out of the gate. I closed the shutter I had partially opened, and sank down behind the barrel. I had suffered much; but seldom had I experienced a keener pang than I then felt. Had my children, then, become of so little consequence to him? And had he so little feeling for their wretched mother that he would not listen a moment while she pleaded for them? Painful memories were so busy within me, that I forgot I had not hooked the shutter, till I heard some one opening it. I looked up. He had come back. "Who called me?" said he, in a low tone. "I did," I replied. "Oh, Linda," said he, "I knew your voice; but I was afraid to answer, lest my friend should hear me. Why do you come here? Is it possible you risk yourself in this house? They are mad to allow it. I shall expect to hear that you are all ruined." I did not wish to implicate him, by letting him know my place of concealment; so I merely said, "I thought you would come to bid grandmother good by, and so I came here to speak a few words to you about emancipating my children. Many changes may take place during the six months you are gone to Washington, and it does not seem right for you to expose them to the risk of such changes. I want nothing for myself; all I ask is, that you will free my children, or authorize some friend to do it, before you go."

He promised he would do it, and also expressed a readiness to make any arrangements whereby I could be purchased.

I hardly expect that the reader will credit me, when I affirm that I lived in that little dismal hole, almost deprived of light and air, and with no space to move my limbs, for nearly seven years. But it is a fact; and to me a sad one, even now; for my body still suffers from the effects of that long imprisonment, to say nothing of my soul. . . .

My friend Peter came one evening, and asked to speak with me. "Your day has come, Linda," said he, "I have found a chance

for you to go to the Free States. You have a fortnight to decide."
The news seemed too good to be true; but Peter explained his
arrangements, and told me all that was necessary was for me to say
I would go. I was going to answer him with a joyful yes, when the
thought of Benny came to my mind. I told him the temptation was
exceedingly strong, but I was terribly afraid of Dr. Flint's alleged
power over my child, and that I could not go and leave him behind.
Peter remonstrated earnestly. He said such a good chance might
never occur again; that Benny was free, and could be sent to me;
and that for the sake of my children's welfare I ought not to hesitate
for a moment. I told him I would consult with uncle Phillip. My
uncle rejoiced in the plan, and bade me go by all means. He promised, if his life was spared, that he would either bring or send my
son to me as soon as I reached a place of safety. I resolved to go,
but thought nothing had better be said to my grandmother till very
near the time of departure. But my uncle thought she would feel it
more keenly if I left her so suddenly. "I will reason with her," said
he, "and convince her how necessary it is, not only for your sake,
but for hers also. You cannot be blind to the fact that she is sinking
under her burdens." I was not blind to it. I knew that my concealment was an ever-present source of anxiety, and that the older
she grew the more nervously fearful she was of discovery. My uncle
talked with her, and finally succeeded in persuading her that it was
absolutely necessary for me to seize the chance so unexpectedly
offered. . . .

I made all my arrangements to go on board as soon as it was
dusk. The intervening time I resolved to spend with my son. I had
not spoken to him for seven years, though I had been under the
same roof, and seen him every day, when I was well enough to sit
at the loophole. I did not dare to venture beyond the storeroom;
so they brought him there, and locked us up together, in a place
concealed from the piazza door. It was an agitating interview for
both of us. After we had talked and wept together for a little while,
he said, "Mother, I'm glad you're going away. I wish I could go
with you. I knew you was here; and I have been *so* afraid they
would come and catch you!"

I was greatly surprised, and asked him how he had found it
out.

He replied, "I was standing under the eaves, one day, before
Ellen went away, and I heard somebody cough up over the wood

shed. I don't know what made me think it was you, but I did think so." . . .

As the hour approached for me to leave, I again descended to the storeroom. My grandmother and Benny were there. She took me by the hand, and said, "Linda, let us pray." We knelt down together, with my child pressed to my heart, and my other arm round the faithful, loving old friend I was about to leave forever. On no other occasion has it ever been my lot to listen to so fervent a supplication for mercy and protection. It thrilled through my heart, and inspired me with trust in God.

Peter was waiting for me in the street. I was soon by his side, faint in body, but strong of purpose. I did not look back upon the old place, though I felt that I should never see it again.

When we arrived in New York, I was half crazed by the crowd of coachmen calling out, "Carriage, ma'am?" . . .

We had been recommended to a boarding-house in Sullivan Street, and thither we drove. . . . I sent for an old friend from my part of the country, who had for some time been doing business in New York. He came immediately. I told him I wanted to go to my daughter [Jacobs's children had been sent to New York by the Sands family], and asked him to aid me in procuring an interview.

I cautioned him not to let it be known to the family that I had just arrived from the south, because they supposed I had been at the north seven years. He told me there was a colored woman in Brooklyn who came from the same town I did, and I had better go to her house, and have my daughter meet me there. I accepted the proposition thankfully, and he agreed to escort me to Brooklyn. We crossed Fulton ferry, went up Myrtle Avenue, and stopped at the house he designated. I was just about to enter, when two girls passed. . . .

I turned, and there stood my Ellen! I pressed her to my heart, then held her away from me to take a look at her. She had changed a good deal in the two years since I parted from her. Signs of neglect could be discerned by eyes less observing than a mother's. My friend invited us all to go into the house; but Ellen said she had been sent on an errand, which she would do as quickly as possible, and go home and ask . . . to . . . come and see me. It was agreed that I should send for her the next day. Her companion, Sarah, hastened to tell her mother of my arrival. When I entered the house, I found the mistress of it absent, and I waited for her return. Before I saw her, I heard her saying, "Where is Linda Brent? I used to know her father and mother." Soon Sarah came with her mother. So there was quite a company of us, all from my grandmother's neighborhood. These friends gathered round me and questioned me eagerly. They laughed, they cried, and they shouted. They thanked God that I had got away from my persecutors and was safe on Long Island. It was a day of great excitement. How different from the silent days I had passed in my dreary den! . . .

The conversation I had with my child did not leave my mind at ease. When I asked if she was well treated, she answered yes; but there was no heartiness in the tone, and it seemed to me that she said it from an unwillingness to have me troubled on her account. Before she left me, she asked very earnestly, "Mother, when will you take me to live with you?" It made me sad to think that I could not give her a home till I went to work and earned the means; and that might take me a long time. When she was placed with Mrs. Hobbs, the agreement was that she should be sent to school. She had been there two years, and was now nine years old, and she scarcely knew her letters. There was no excuse for this, for there were good public schools in Brooklyn, to which she could have been sent without expense.

She staid with me till dark, and I went home with her. I was received in a friendly manner by the family, and all agreed in saying that Ellen was a useful, good girl. Mrs. Hobbs looked me coolly in the face, and said, "I suppose you know that my cousin, Mr. Sands, has *given* her to my eldest daughter. She will make a nice waiting-maid for her when she grows up." I did not answer a word. How *could* she, who knew by experience the strength of a mother's love, and who was perfectly aware of the relation Mr. Sands bore to my children—how *could* she look me in the face, while she thrust such a dagger into my heart? . . .

Mr. Sands had not kept his promise to emancipate them. I had also been deceived about Ellen. What security had I with regard to Benjamin? I felt that I had none. . . .

My greatest anxiety now was to obtain employment. My health was greatly improved, though my limbs continued to trouble me with swelling whenever I walked much. . . .

One day an acquaintance told me of a lady who wanted a nurse for her babe, and I immediately applied for the situation. The lady told me she preferred to have one who had been a mother, and accustomed to the care of infants. I told her I had nursed two babes of my own. She asked me many questions, but, to my great relief, did not require a recommendation from my former employers. She told me she was an English woman, and that was a pleasant circumstance to me, because I had heard they had less prejudice against color than Americans entertained. It was agreed that we should try each other for a week. The trial proved satisfactory to both parties, and I was engaged for a month. . . .

I was far from feeling satisfied with Ellen's situation. She was not well cared for. She sometimes came to New York to visit me; but she generally brought a request from Mrs. Hobbs that I would buy her a pair of shoes, or some article of clothing. This was accompanied by a promise of payment when Mr. Hobbs's salary at the Custom House became due; but some how or other the payday never came. Thus many dollars of my earnings were expended to keep my child comfortably clothed. That, however, was a slight trouble, compared with the fear that their pecuniary embarrassments might induce them to sell my precious young daughter. . . .

I usually went to Brooklyn to spend Sunday afternoon. One Sunday, I found Ellen anxiously waiting for me near the house. "O, mother," said she, "I've been waiting for you this long time. I'm afraid Mr. Thorne has written to tell Dr. Flint where you are. Make haste and come in. Mrs. Hobbs will tell you all about it!"

The story was soon told. While the children were playing in the grape-vine arbor, the day before, Mr. Thorne came out with a letter in his hand, which he tore up and scattered about. Ellen was sweeping the yard at the time, and having her mind full of suspicions about him, she picked up the pieces and carried them to the children, saying, "I wonder who Mr. Thorne has been writing to."

"I'm sure I don't know, and don't care," replied the oldest of the children, "and I don't see how it concerns you."

"But it does concern me," replied Ellen; "for I'm afraid he's been writing to the south about my mother."

They laughed at her, and called her a silly thing, but good-naturedly put the fragments of writing together, in order to read them to her. They were no sooner arranged, than the little girl exclaimed, "I declare, Ellen, I believe you are right."

The contents of Mr. Thorne's letter, as nearly as I can remember, were as follows: "I have seen your slave, Linda, and conversed with her. She can be taken very easily, if you manage prudently. There are enough of us here to swear to her identity as your property. I am a patriot, a lover of my country, and I do this as an act of justice to the laws." He concluded by informing the doctor of the street and number where I lived. The children carried the pieces to Mrs. Hobbs, who immediately went to her brother's room for an explanation. He was not to be found. The servants said they saw him go out with a letter in his hand, and they supposed he had gone to the post office. The natural inference was, that he had sent to Dr. Flint a copy of those fragments. When he returned, his sister accused him of it, and he did not deny the charge. He went immediately to his room, and the next morning he was missing. He had gone over to New York, before any of the family were astir.

It was evident that I had no time to lose; and I hastened back to the city with a heavy heart. Again I was to be torn from a comfortable home, and all my plans for the welfare of my children were to be frustrated by that demon Slavery! I now regretted that I never told Mrs. Bruce my story. I had not concealed it merely on account of being a fugitive; that would have made her anxious, but it would have excited sympathy in her kind heart. I valued her good opinion, and I was afraid of losing it, if I told her all the particulars of my sad story. But now I felt that it was necessary for her to know how I was situated. I had once left her abruptly, without explaining the reason, and it would not be proper to do it again. I went home resolved to tell her in the morning. But the sadness of my face attracted her attention, and, in answer to her kind inquiries, I poured out my full heart to her, before bed time. She listened with true womanly sympathy, and told me she would do all she could to protect me. How my heart blessed her!

Early the next morning, Judge Vanderpool and Lawyer Hopper were consulted. They said I had better leave the city at once, as the risk would be great if the case came to trial. Mrs. Bruce took me in a carriage to the house of one of her friends, where she assured me I should be safe until my brother could arrive, which would be in a few days. In the interval my thoughts were much occupied with Ellen. She was mine by birth, and she was also mine by Southern law, since my grandmother held the bill of sale that made her so. I did not feel that she was safe unless I had her with me. Mrs. Hobbs, who felt badly about her brother's treachery, yielded to my entreaties, on condition that she should return in ten days. I avoided making any promise. She came to me clad in very thin garments, all outgrown, and with a school satchel on her arm, containing a few articles. It was late in October, and I knew the child must suffer; and not daring to go out in the streets to purchase any thing, I took off my own flannel skirt and converted it into one for her. Kind Mrs. Bruce came to bid me good by, and when she saw that I had taken off my clothing for my child, the tears came to her eyes. She said, "Wait for me, Linda," and went out. She soon returned with a nice warm shawl and hood for Ellen. Truly, of such souls as hers are the kingdom of heaven.

My brother reached New York on Wednesday. Lawyer Hopper advised us to go to Boston by the Stonington route, as there was less Southern travel in that direction. Mrs. Bruce directed her servants to tell all inquirers that I formerly lived there, but had gone from the city. . . .

I could not feel safe in New York, and I accepted the offer of a friend, that we should share expenses and keep house together. I represented to Mrs. Hobbs that Ellen must have some schooling, and must remain with me for that purpose. She felt ashamed of being unable to read or spell at her age, so instead of sending her to school with Benny, I instructed her myself till she was fitted to enter an intermediate school. The winter passed pleasantly, while I was busy with my needle, and my children with their books. . . .

For two years my daughter and I supported ourselves comfortably in Boston. At the end of that time, my brother William offered to send Ellen to a boarding school. It required a great effort for me to consent to part with her, for I had few near ties, and it was her presence that made my two little rooms seem home-like. But my judgement prevailed over my selfish feelings. . . .

The next morning, she and her uncle started on their journey to the village in New York, where she was to be placed at school. It seemed as if all the sunshine had gone away. My little room was dreadfully lonely. I was thankful when a message came from a lady, accustomed to employ me, requesting me to come and sew in her family for several weeks. On my return, I found a letter from brother William. He thought of opening an anti-slavery reading room in Rochester, and combining with it the sale of some books and stationery; and he wanted me to unite with him. We tried it, but it was not successful. We found warm anti-slavery friends there, but the feeling was not general enough to support such an establishment. I passed nearly a year in the family of Isaac and Amy Post, practical believers in the Christian doctrine of human brotherhood. They measured a man's worth by his character, not by his complexion. The memory of those beloved and honored friends will remain with me to my latest hour. . . .

Mrs. Bruce and every member of her family, were exceedingly kind to me. I was thankful for the blessings of my lot, yet I could not always wear a cheerful countenance. I was doing harm to no one; on the contrary, I was doing all the good I could in my small way; yet I could never go out to breathe God's free air without trepidation at my heart. This seemed hard; and I could not think it was a right state of things in any civilized country.

From time to time I received news from my good old grandmother. She could not write; but she employed others to write for her. The following is an extract from one of her last letters:—

Dear Daughter: I cannot hope to see you again on earth; but I pray to God to unite us above, where pain will no more rack this feeble body of mine; where sorrow and parting from my children will be no more. God has promised these things if we are faithful unto the end. My age and feeble health deprive me of going to church now; but God is with me here at home. Thank your brother for his kindness. Give much love to him, and tell him to remember the Creator in the days of his youth, and strive to meet me in the Father's kingdom. Love to Ellen and Benjamin. Don't neglect him. Tell him for me, to be a good boy. Strive, my child, to train them for God's children. May he protect and provide for you, is the prayer of your loving old mother.

These letters both cheered and saddened me. I was always glad to have tidings from the kind, faithful old friend of my unhappy youth; but her messages of love made my heart yearn to see her before she died, and I mourned over the fact that it was impossible. Some months after I returned from my flight to New England, I received a letter from her, in which she wrote, "Dr. Flint is dead. He has left a distressed family. Poor old man! I hope he made his peace with God." . . .

His departure from this world did not diminish my danger. He had threatened my grandmother that his heirs should hold me in slavery after he was gone; that I never should be free so long as a child of his survived. . . .

I was well aware what I had to expect from the family of Flints; and my fears were confirmed by a letter from the south, warning me to be on my guard, because Mrs. Flint openly declared that her daughter could not afford to lose so valuable a slave as I was. . . .

This Mr. Dodge, who claimed me as his property, was originally a Yankee pedler in the south; then he became a merchant, and finally a slaveholder. He managed to get introduced into what was called the first society, and married Miss Emily Flint. . . .

Dr. Flint left him no property, and his own means had become circumscribed, while a wife and children depended upon him for support. Under these circumstances, it was very natural that he should make an effort to put me into his pocket. . . .

I had been told that Mr. Dodge said his wife had never signed away her right to my children, and if he could not get me, he would take them. . . .

The next day, baby and I set out in a heavy snow storm, bound for New England again. I received letters from the City of Iniquity, addressed to me under an assumed name. . . .

By the next mail I received this brief letter from Mrs. Bruce: "I am rejoiced to tell you that the money for your freedom has been paid to Mr. Dodge. Come home to-morrow. I long to see you and my sweet babe." . . .

I had objected to having my freedom bought, yet I must confess that when it was done I felt as if a heavy load had been lifted from my weary shoulders. When I rode home in the cars I was no longer afraid to unveil my face and look at people as they passed. I should have been glad to have met Daniel Dodge himself; to have had him seen me and known me, that he might have mourned over the untoward circumstances which compelled him to sell me for three hundred dollars.

When I reached home, the arms of my benefactress were thrown round me, and our tears mingled. As soon as she could speak, she said, "O Linda, I'm *so* glad it's all over! You wrote to me as if you thought you were going to be transferred from one owner to another. But I did not buy you for your services. I should have done just the same, if you had been going to sail for California tomorrow. I should, at least, have the satisfaction of knowing that you left me a free woman."

My heart was exceedingly full. I remembered how my poor father had tried to buy me, when I was a small child, and how he had been disappointed. I hoped his spirit was rejoicing over me now. I remembered how my good old grandmother had laid up her earnings to purchase me in later years, and how often her plans had been frustrated. How that faithful, loving old heart would leap for joy, if she could look on me and my children now that we were free! My relatives had been foiled in all their efforts, but God had raised me up a friend among strangers, who had bestowed on me the precious, long desired boon.

My grandmother lived to rejoice in my freedom; but not long after, a letter came with a black seal. She had gone "where the wicked cease from troubling, and the weary are at rest."

Reader, my story ends with freedom; not in the usual way, with marriage. I and my children are now free! We are as free from the power of slaveholders as are the white people of the north; and though that, according to my ideas, is not saying a great deal, it is a vast improvement in *my* condition. The dream of my life is not yet realized. I do not sit with my children in a home of my own. I still long for a hearthstone of my own, however humble. I wish it for my children's sake far more than for my own. But God so orders circumstances as to keep me with my friend Mrs. Bruce. Love, duty, gratitude, also bind me to her side. It is a privilege to serve her who pities my oppressed people, and who has bestowed the inestimable boon of freedom on me and my children.

It has been painful to me, in many ways, to recall the dreary years I passed in bondage. I would gladly forget them if I could. Yet the retrospection is not altogether without solace; for with those gloomy recollections come tender memories of my good old grandmother, like light, fleecy clouds floating over a dark and troubled sea.

Zora Neale Hurston

(1901?–1960)

Third daughter and seventh child of Alabama tenant farmers, Zora Neale Hurston was born in Eatonville, Florida, an all-black town which her father, a Baptist preacher, served as mayor. Her mother's death and her father's speedy remarriage when Hurston was nine ended her childhood and left her in charge of her own life. Her passion for education took her to Morgan Academy and, in 1918, to Howard University.

While at Howard, Hurston began to write and to make contact with some of the leading figures of the Harlem Renaissance. These experiences led to her move in 1925 to New York, where she found employment as secretary to the popular romantic writer Fannie Hurst and continued her studies at Barnard College, from which she graduated in 1928.

A student of Franz Boas, Hurston devoted the five years following her graduation to the collection of rural black folklore. Her ear for the rhythms of speech and her daring in seeking initiation into many voodoo cults resulted in ethnographic studies which convey the color and vigor of rural black culture. Hurston married twice but found the demands of marriage incompatible with her career. The recipient of Rosenwald and Guggenheim fellowships, she first undertook fieldwork in the Caribbean but eventually settled to her most cherished calling, that of fiction writer. *Jonah's Gourd Vine* (1934) and *Their Eyes Were Watching God* (1937) established her reputation as a black writer; they were followed by *Moses Man of the Mountain* (1939) and *Seraph on the Suwanee* (1948).

By the 1950s Hurston's conservative views on race relations, highlighted by her critical comments on the 1954 Supreme Court segregation decision, put her out of touch with the temper of the times. She argued (correctly, as events would demonstrate) that pressure for integration would undermine the values and vitality of black culture. She died in poverty and obscurity, although black militants of later generations were to rediscover and revere her celebrations of black culture and the black imagination.

DUST TRACKS ON A ROAD:
An Autobiography

We lived on a big piece of ground with two big chinaberry trees shading the front gate and Cape jasmine bushes with hundreds of blooms on either side of the walks. I loved the fleshy, white, fragrant blooms as a child but did not make too much of them. . . .

We had a five-acre garden with things to eat growing in it, and so we were never hungry. We had chicken on the table often; home-cured meat, and all the eggs we wanted. . . .

Our house had eight rooms, and we called it a two-story house; but later on I learned it was really one story and a jump. The big boys all slept up there, and it was a good place to hide and shirk from sweeping off the front porch or raking up the back yard. . . .

There were eight children in the family, and our house was noisy from the time school turned out until bedtime. After supper we gathered in Mama's room, and everybody had to get their lessons for the next day. Mama carried us all past long division in arithmetic, and parsing sentences in grammar, by diagrams on the blackboard. That was as far as she had gone. Then the younger ones were turned over to my oldest brother, Bob, and Mama sat and saw to it that we paid attention. You had to keep on going over things until you did know. How I hated the multiplication tables—especially the sevens! . . .

Mama exhorted her children at every opportunity to "jump at de sun." We might not land on the sun, but at least we would get off the ground. Papa did not feel so hopeful. Let well enough alone. It did not do for Negroes to have too much spirit. He was always threatening to break mine or kill me in the attempt. My mother was always standing between us. She conceded that I was impudent and given to talking back, but she didn't want to "squinch my spirit" too much for fear that I would turn out to be a mealy-mouthed rag doll by the time I got grown. Papa always flew hot when Mama said that. I do not know whether he feared for my future, with the tendency I had to stand and give battle, or that he felt a personal reference in Mama's observation. He predicted dire things for me. The white folks were not going to stand for it. I was going to be hung before I got grown. . . .

I discovered that I was extra strong by playing with other girls near my age. I had no way of judging the force of my playful blows, and so I was always hurting somebody. Then they would say I meant to hurt, and go home and leave me. Everything was all right, however, when I played with boys. It was a shameful thing to admit being hurt among them. Furthermore, they could dish it out themselves, and I was acceptable to them because I was the one girl who could take a good pummeling without running home to tell. . . .

So I was driven inward. I lived an exciting life unseen. But I had one person who pleased me always. That was the robust, gray-haired white man who had helped me get into the world. When I was quite small, he would come by and tease me and then praise me for not crying. When I got old enough to do things, he used to come along some afternoons and ask to take me with him fishing. . . .

He was always making me tell him things about my doings, and then he would tell me what to do about things. . . .

"Truth is a letter from courage. I want you to grow guts as you go along. So don't you let me hear of you lying. You'll get 'long all right if you do like I tell you. Nothing can't lick you if you never get skeered."

[Hurston's mother died when she was nine years old.]
Even though she had talked to me very earnestly one night, I could not conceive of Mama actually dying. She had talked of it many times. . . .

I had left Mama and was playing outside for a little while when I noted a number of women going inside Mama's room and staying. It looked strange. So I went on in. Papa was standing at the foot of the bed looking down on my mother, who was breathing hard. As I crowded in, they lifted up the bed and turned it around so that Mama's eyes would face the east. I thought that she looked to me as the head of the bed was reversed. Her mouth was slightly open, but her breathing took up so much of her strength that she could not talk. But she looked at me, or so I felt, to speak for her. She depended on me for a voice. . . .

But life picked me up from the foot of Mama's bed, grief, self-despisement and all, and set my feet in strange ways. That moment was the end of a phase in my life. I was old before my time with grief of loss, of failure, and of remorse. . . .

I have often wished I had been old enough at the time to look into Papa's heart that night. . . .

. . . the next day, Sam Moseley's span of fine horses, hitched to our wagon, carried my mother to Macedonia Baptist Church for the last time. The finality of the thing came to me fully when the earth began to thud on the coffin.

That night, all of Mama's children were assembled together for the last time on earth. The next day, Bob and Sarah went back to Jacksonville to school. Papa was away from home a great deal, so two weeks later I was on my way to Jacksonville, too. I was under age, but the school had agreed to take me in under the circumstances. My sister was to look after me, in a way.

The midnight train had to be waved down at Maitland for me. That would put me into Jacksonville in the daytime. . . .

Jacksonville made me know that I was a little colored girl. Things were all about the town to point this out to me. Streetcars and stores and then talk I heard around the school. I was no longer among the white people whose homes I could barge into with a sure sense of welcome. These white people had funny ways. . . .

In the classroom I got along splendidly. The only difficulty was that I was rated as sassy. I just had to talk back at established authority and that established authority hated backtalk worse than barbed-wire pie. My immediate teachers were enthusiastic about me. It was the guardians of study-hour and prayer meetings who felt that their burden was extra hard to bear.

School in Jacksonville was one of those twilight things. It was not dark, but it lacked the bold sunlight that I craved. I worshipped two of my teachers and loved gingersnaps with cheese, and sour pickles. But I was deprived of the loving pine, the lakes, the wild violets in the woods and the animals I used to know. . . .

My sister moped a great deal. She was Papa's favorite child, and I am certain that she loved him more than anything on earth. . . .

Papa arranged for her to leave school.

That had very tragic results for Sarah. In a week or two after she left me in Jacksonville, she wrote back that Papa had married again. That hurt us all, somehow. But it was worse for Sarah, for my stepmother must have resented Papa's tender indulgence for his older daughter. It was not long before the news came back that she had insisted that Papa put Sarah out of the house. That was terrible enough, but it was not satisfactory to Papa's new wife. Papa must go over and beat Sarah with a buggy whip for commenting on the marriage happening so soon after Mama's death. Sarah must be driven out of town. So Sarah just married and went down on the

Manatee River to live. She took Everett with her. She probably left more behind her than she took away. . . .

As for me, looking on, it made a tiger out of me. It did not matter so much to me that Sarah was Papa's favorite. I got my joys in other ways, and so, did not miss his petting. I do not think that I ever really wanted it. It made me miserable to see Sarah look like that. And six years later I paid the score off in a small way. It was on a Monday morning, six years after Sarah's heartbreak, that my stepmother threatened to beat me for my impudence, after vainly trying to get Papa to undertake the job. I guess that the memory of the time that he had struck Sarah at his wife's demand, influenced Papa and saved me. I do not think that she considered that a changed man might be in front of her. I do not think that she thought that I would resist in the presence of my father after all that had happened and had shown his lack of will. I do not think that she even thought that she could whip me if I resisted. She did think, if she thought at all, that all she had to do was to start on me, and Papa would be forced to jump in and finish up the job to her satisfaction in order to stay in her good graces. Old memories of her power over him told her to assert herself, and she pitched in. She called me a sassy, impudent heifer, announced that she was going to take me down a buttonhole lower, and threw a bottle at my head. The bottle came sailing slowly through the air and missed me easily. She never should have missed.

The primeval in me leaped to life. Ha! This was the very corn I wanted to grind. Fight! Not having to put up with what she did to us through Papa! Direct action and everything up to me. I looked at her hard. And like everybody else's enemy, her looks, her smells, her sounds were all mixed up with her doings, and she deserved punishment for them as well as her acts. The feelings of all those six years were pressing inside me like steam under a valve. I didn't have any thoughts to speak of. Just the fierce instinct of flesh on flesh—me kicking and beating on her pudgy self—those two ugly false teeth in front—her dead on the floor—grinning like a dead dog in the sun. Consequences be damned! If I died, let me die with my hands soaked in her blood. I wanted her blood, and plenty of it. That is the way I went into the fight, and that is the way I fought it.

She had the advantage of me in weight, that was all. It did not seem to do her a bit of good. Maybe she did not have the guts, and certainly she underestimated mine. She gave way before my first rush and found herself pinned against the wall, with my fists pounding at her face without pity. She scratched and clawed at me, but I felt nothing at all. In a few seconds, she gave up. I could see her face when she realized that I meant to kill her. She spat on my dress, then, and did what she could to cover up from my renewed fury. She had given up fighting except for trying to spit in my face, and I did not intend for her to get away.

She yelled for Papa, but that was no good. Papa was disturbed, no doubt of it, but he wept and fiddled in the door and asked me to stop, while her head was traveling between my fist and the wall, and I wished that my fist had weighed a ton. She tried to do something. She pulled my hair and scratched at me. But I had come up fighting with boys. Hair-pulling didn't worry me.

She screamed that she was going to get Papa's pistol [sic] and kill me. She tried to get across the room to the dresser drawer, but I knew I couldn't let that happen. So the fight got hotter. A friend of hers who weighed over two hundred pounds lived across the street. She heard the rumpus and came running. I visualized that she would try to grab me, and I realized that my stepmother would get her chance. So I grabbed my stepmother by the collar and dragged her to a hatchet against the wall and managed to get hold of it. As Mrs. G. waddled through the living-room door, I hollered to her to get back, and let fly with that hatchet with all that my right arm would do. It struck the wall too close to her head to make her happy. She reeled around and rolled down those front steps yelling that I had gone crazy. But she never came back and the fight went on. I was so mad when I saw my adversary sagging to the floor I didn't know what to do. I began to scream with rage. I had not beaten more than two years out of her yet. I made up my mind to stomp her, but at last Papa came to, and pulled me away. . . .

I was not at all pacified. She owed me four more years. Besides there was her spit on the front of her dress. I promised myself to pay her for the old and the new too, the first chance I got. Years later, after I had graduated from Barnard and I was doing research, I found out where she was. I drove twenty miles to finish the job, only to find out that she was a chronic invalid. She had an incurable sore on her neck. I couldn't tackle her under such circumstances, so I turned back, all frustrated inside. All I could do was to wish that she had a lot more neck to rot.

The five years following my leaving the school at Jacksonville were haunted. I was shifted from house to house of relatives and friends and found comfort nowhere. I was without books to read most of the time, except where I could get hold of them by mere chance. . . .

Gradually, I came to the point of attempting self-support. It was a glorious feeling when it came to me. But the actual working out of the thing was not so simple as the concept. I was about fourteen then.

For one thing, I really was young for the try. Then my growth was retarded somewhat so that I looked younger than I really was. Housewives would open the door at my ring and look me over. No, they wanted someone old enough to be responsible. No, they wanted someone strong enough to do the work, and so on like that. . . .

. . . at that time I received a letter from Bob, my oldest brother. He had just graduated from Medicine and said that he wanted to help me to go to school. He was sending for me to come to him right away. His wife sent love. He knew that I was going to love his children. He had married in his Freshman year in college and had three of them.

Nothing can describe my joy. I was going to have a home again. I was going to school. I was going to be with my brother! He had remembered me at last. My five haunted years were over!

I shall never forget the exaltation of my hurried packing. When I got on the train, I said goodbye—not to anybody in particular, but to the town, to loneliness, to defeat and frustration, to shabby living, to sterile houses and numbed pangs, to the kind of people I had no wish to know; to an era. I waved it goodbye and sank back into the cushions of the seat.

It was near night. I shall never forget how the red ball of the sun hung on the horizon and raced along with the train for a short space, and then plunged below the belly-band of the earth. There have been other suns that set in significance for me, but *that* sun! It was a book-mark in the pages of a life. I remember the long, strung-out cloud that measured it for the fall.

But I was due for more frustration. There was to be no school for me right away. I was needed around the house. My brother took me for a walk and explained to me that it would cause trouble if he put me in school at once. His wife would feel that he was pampering me. Just work along and be useful around the house and he would work things out in time. . . .

But I made an unexpected friend. She was a white woman and poor. She had children of my own age. Her husband was an electrician. She began to take an interest in me and to put ideas in my head. I will not go so far as to say that I was poorly dressed, for that would be bragging. The best I can say is that I could not be arrested for indecent exposure. I remember wanting gloves. I had never had a pair, and one of my friends told me that I ought to have on gloves when I went anywhere. I could not have them and I was most unhappy. But then, I was not in a position to buy a handkerchief.

This friend slipped me a message one day to come to her house. We had a code. Her son would pass and whistle until I showed myself to let him know I heard. Then he would go on and as soon as I could I would follow. This particular day, she told me that she had a job for me. I was delighted beyond words.

"It's a swell job if you can get it, Zora. I think you can. I told my husband to do all he can, and he thinks he's got it hemmed up for you."

"Oooh! What is it?"

"It is a lady's maid job. She is a singer down at the theater where he is electrician. She brought a maid with her from up North, but the maid met up with a lot of colored people and looks like she's going to get married right off. She don't want the job no more. The lady asked the men around the theater to get her somebody, and my husband thought about you and I told him to tell the rest of the men he had just the right girl for a maid. It seems like she is a mighty nice person."

I was too excited to sit still. I was frightened too, because I did not know the first thing about being a lady's maid. All I hoped was that the lady would overlook that part and give me a chance to catch on.

"You got to look nice for that. So I sent Valena down to buy you a little dress." Valena was her daughter. "It's cheap, but it's neat and stylish. Go inside Valena's room and try it on."

The dress was a navy blue poplin with a box-pleated skirt and a little round, white collar. To my own self, I never did look so pretty before. I put on the dress, and Valena's dark blue felt hat with a rolled brim. She saw to it that I shined my shoes, and then gave me car-fare and sent me off with every bit of advice she could think of.

My feet mounted up the golden stairs as I entered the stage door of that theater. The sounds, the smells, the backstage jumble of things were all things to bear me up into a sweeter atmosphere. I felt like dancing towards the dressing-room when it was pointed out to me. But my friend was walking with me, coaching me how to act, and I had to be as quiet and sober as could be.

The matinee performance of *H.M.S. Pinafore* was on, so I was told to wait. In a little while a tenor and a soprano voice quit singing a duet and a beautiful blond girl of about twenty-two came hurrying into the dressing-room. I waited until she went inside and closed the door, then I knocked and was told to come in.

She looked at me and smiled so hard till she almost laughed.

"Hello, little girl," she chanted. "Where did you come from?"

"Home. I come to see you."

"Oh, you did? That's fine. What did you come to see me about?"

"I come to work for you."

"Work for me?" She threw back her head and laughed. That frightened me a great deal. Maybe it was all a joke and there was no job after all. "Doing what?" she caroled on.

"Be your lady's maid."

"You? Why, how old are you?"

"Twenty," I said, and tried to look serious as I had been told. But she laughed so hard at that, till I forgot and laughed too.

"Oh, no, you are not twenty." She laughed some more, but it was not scornful laughter. Just bubbling fun.

"Well, eighteen, then," I compromised.

"No, not eighteen, either."

"Well, then how about sixteen?"

She laughed at that. Instead of frowning in a sedate way as I had been told, here I was laughing like a fool myself.

"I don't believe you are sixteen, but I'll let it go at that," she said.

"Next birthday. Honest."

"It's all right: you're hired. But let's don't bring this age business up again. I think I'm going to like you. What is your name?"

I told her, fearing all the time she was going to ask questions about my family; but she didn't.

"Well, Zora, I pay ten dollars a week and expenses. You think that will do?"

I almost fell over. Ten dollars each and every week! Was there that much money in the world sure enough? Com-press-ti-bility!! It wouldn't take long for me to own a bank at that rate.

"Yes, ma'am!" I shouted.

"Well, change my shoes for me."

She stuck out her foot, and pointed at the pair she wanted to put on. I got them on with her tickling me in the back. She showed me a white dress she wanted to change into and I jumped to get it and hook it up. She touched up her face laughing at me in the mirror and dashed out. I was crazy about her right then. I washed out her shoelaces from a pair of white shoes and her stockings, which were on the back of a chair, and wrung them out in a bath towel for quick drying, and sat down before the mirror to look at myself. It was truly wonderful! . . .

That night, she let me stand in the wings and hear her sing her duet with the tenor, "Farewell, my own! Light of my life, farewell!" It was so beautiful to me that she seemed more than human. Everything was pleasing and exciting. If there was any more to Heaven than this, I didn't want to see it.

I did not go back home, that is to my brother's house, at all. I was afraid he would try to keep me. I slept on a cot in the room with Valena. She was almost as excited as I was, had come down to see me every night and had met the cast. We were important people, she and I. Her mother had to make us shut up talking and go to sleep every night.

The end of the enchanted week came and the company was to move on. Miss M—— whom I was serving asked me about my clothes and luggage. She told me not to come down to the train with an old dilapidated suitcase for that would make her ashamed. So the upshot of it was that she advanced me the money to buy one, and then paid me for the week. I paid my friend the six dollars which she had spent for my new dress. Valena gave me the hat, an extra pair of panties and stockings. I bought a comb and brush and toothbrush, paste, and two handkerchiefs. Miss M—— did not know when I came down to the station that morning that my new suitcase was stuffed with newspapers to keep my things from rattling.

The company, a Gilbert and Sullivan repertoire, had its own coach. That was another glory to dazzle my eyes. The leading man had a valet, and the contralto had an English maid, both white. I was the only Negro around. But that did not worry me in the least.

I had no chance to be lonesome, because the company welcomed me like or as, a new play-pretty. It did not strike me as curious then. I never even thought about it. Now, I can see the reason for it.

In the first place, I was a Southerner, and had the map of Dixie on my tongue. They were all Northerners except the orchestra leader, who came from Pensacola. It was not that my grammar was bad, it was the idioms. They did not know of the way an average Southern child, white or black, is raised on simile and invective. They know how to call names. It is an everyday affair to hear somebody called a mullet-headed, mule-eared, wall-eyed, hog-nosed, 'gator-faced, shad-mouthed, screw-necked, goat-bellied, puzzle-gutted, camel-backed, butt-sprung, battle-hammed, knock-kneed, razor-legged, box-ankled, shovel-footed, unmated so and so! Eyes looking like skint-ginny nuts, and mouth looking like a dish-pan full of broke-up crockery! They can tell you in simile exactly how you walk and smell. They can furnish a picture gallery of your ancestors, and a notion of what your children will be like. What ought to happen to you is full of images and flavor. Since that stratum of the Southern population is not given to book-reading, they take their comparisons right out of the barnyard and the woods. When they get through with you, you and your whole family look like an acre of totem-poles.

I had been with her for eighteen months and though neither of us realized it, I had been in school all the time. I had loosened up in every joint and expanded in every direction.

I had done some reading. Not as much as before, but more discriminate reading. The tenor was a Harvard man who had traveled on the Continent. He always had books along with him, and offered them to me more and more. The first time I asked to borrow one, he looked at me in a way that said "What for?" But when he found that I really read it and enjoyed it, he relaxed and began to hand them to me gruffly. He never acted as if he liked it, but I knew better. That was just the Harvard in him.

Then there was the music side. They broke me in to good music, that is, the classics, if you want to put it that way. There was no conscious attempt to do this. Just from being around, I became familiar with Gilbert and Sullivan, and the best parts of the light-opera field. Grand opera too, for all of the leads had backgrounds of private classical instruction as well as conservatory training. Even the bit performers and the chorus had some kind of formal training in voice, and most of them played the piano. It was not unusual for some of the principals to drop down at the piano after a matinee performance and begin to sing arias from grand opera. Sing them with a wistfulness. The arias which they would sing at the Metropolitan or La Scala as they had once hoped actively, and still hoped passively even as the hair got thinner and the hips got heavier. Others, dressed for the street, would drift over and ease into the singing. Thus I would hear solos, duets, quartets and sextets from the best-known operas. . . .

And now, at last it was all over. It was not at all clear to me how I was going to do it, but I was going back to school.

One minute I felt brave and fine about it all. The wish to be back in school had never left me. But alone by myself and feeling it over, I was scared. Before this job I had been lonely; I had been bare and bony of comfort and love. Working with these people I had been sitting by a warm fire for a year and a half and gotten used to the feel of peace. Now, I was to take up my pilgrim's stick and go outside again. Maybe it would be different now. . . .

How . . . did I get back to school? I just went. I got tired of trying to get the money to go. My clothes were practically gone. Nickeling and dimeing along was not getting me anywhere. So I went to the night high school in Baltimore and that did something for my soul.

There I met the man who was to give me the key to certain things. In English, I was under Dwight O. W. Holmes. There is no more dynamic teacher anywhere under any skin. He radiates newness and nerve and says to your mind, "There is something wonderful to behold just ahead. Let's go see what it is." He is a pilgrim to the horizon. Anyway, that is the way he struck me. He made the way clear. Something about his face killed the drabness and discouragement in me. I felt that the thing could be done.

I turned in written work and answered questions like everybody else, but he took no notice of me particularly until one night in the study of English poets he read *Kubla Khan*. You must get him to read it for you sometime. He is not a pretty man, but he has the face of a scholar, not dry and set like, but fire flashes from his deep-set eyes. His high-bridged, but sort of bent nose over his thin-lipped mouth . . . well, the whole thing reminds you of some old Roman like Cicero, Caesar or Virgil in tan skin.

That night, he liquefied the immortal brains of Coleridge and let the fountain flow. I do not know whether something in my attitude attracted his attention, or whether what I had done previously made him direct the stream at me. Certainly every time he lifted his eyes from the page, he looked right into my eyes. It did not make me see him particularly, but it made me see the poem. . . .

This was my world, I said to myself, and I shall be in it, and surrounded by it, if it is the last thing I do on God's green dirtball.

But he did something more positive than that. He stopped me after class and complimented me on my work. He did something else. He never asked me anything about myself, but he looked at me and toned his voice in such a way that I felt he knew all about me. His whole manner said, "No matter about the difficulties past and present, step on it!"

I went back to class only twice after that. I did not say a word to him about my resolve. But the next week, I went out to Morgan College to register in the high-school department.

William Pickens, a Negro, was the Dean there, and he fooled me too. I was prepared to be all scared of him and his kind. I had no money and no family to refer to. I just went and he talked to me. He gave me a brief examination and gave me credit for two years' work in high school and assigned me to class. He was just as understanding as Dwight Holmes in a way.

Knowing that I had no money, he evidently spoke to his wife, because she sent for me a few days later and told me enthusiastically that she had a job for me that would enable me to stay in school. Dr. Baldwin, a white clergyman, and one of the trustees of Morgan, had a wife with a broken hip. He wanted a girl to stay at the house, help her dress in the morning, undress at night and generally look after her. There was no need for anyone except in the morning and at night. He would give me a home and two dollars a week. . . .

So I went to live with the Baldwins. The family consisted of the Minister, his wife and his daughter, Miss Maria, who seemed to be in her thirties and unmarried.

They had a great library, and I waded in. I acted as if the books would run away. I remember committing to memory, overnight—lest I never get a chance to read it again—Gray's *Elegy in a Country Churchyard*. Next I learned the *Ballad of Reading Gaol* and started on the *Rubaiyat*. . . .

Nobody shoved me around. There were eighteen people in my class. Six of them were boys. Good-looking, well-dressed girls from Baltimore's best Negro families were classmates of mine. . . .

And here I was, with my face looking like it had been chopped out of a knot of pine wood with a hatchet on somebody's off-day, sitting up in the middle of all this pretty. To make things worse, I had only one dress, a change of underwear and one pair of tan oxfords.

Therefore, I did not rush up to make friends, but neither did I shrink away. My second day at school, I had to blow my nose and I had no handkerchief with me. Mary Jane Watkins was sitting next to me, so she quickly shoved her handkerchief in my hand without saying a word. We were in chapel and Dr. Spencer was up speaking. So she kept her eyes front. I nodded my thanks and so began a friendship. . . .

My two years at Morgan went off very happily indeed. The atmosphere made me feel right. I was at last doing the things I wanted to do. Every new thing I learned in school made me happy. . . .

When it came time to consider college, I planned to stay on at Morgan. But that was changed by chance. Mae Miller, daughter of the well-known Dr. Kelly Miller of Howard University, came over to Morgan to spend the week-end with her first cousins, Bernice and Gwendolyn Hughes. So we were thrown together. After a few hours of fun and capers, she said, "Zora, you are Howard material. Why don't you come to Howard?"

Now as everyone knows, Howard University is the capstone of Negro education in the world. There gather Negro money, beauty, and prestige. It is to the Negro what Harvard is to the whites. . . .

I had heard all about the swank fraternities and sororities and the clothes and everything, and I knew I could never make it. I told Mae that.

"You can come and live at our house, Zora," Bernice offered. At the time, her parents were living in Washington, and Bernice and Gwendolyn were in the boarding department at Morgan. "I'll ask Mama the next time she comes over. Then you won't have any room and board to pay. We'll all get together and rustle you up a job to make your tuition."

So that summer I moved on to Washington and got a job. First, as a waitress in the exclusive Cosmos Club downtown, and later as a manicurist in the G Street shop of Mr. George Robinson. . . .

I shall never forget my first college assembly, sitting there in the chapel of that great university. I was so exalted that I said to the spirit of Howard, "You have taken me in. I am a tiny bit of your greatness. I swear to you that I shall never make you ashamed of me."

It did not wear off. Every time I sat there as part and parcel of things, looking up there at the platform crowded with faculty members, the music, the hundreds of students about me, it would come down on me again. When on Mondays we ended the service by singing Alma Mater, I felt just as if it were the "Star Spangled Banner.". . .

My joining *The Stylus* influenced my later moves. On account of a short story which I wrote for *The Stylus,* Charles S. Johnson, who was just then founding *Opportunity Magazine,* wrote to me for material. He explained that he was writing to all of the Negro colleges with the idea of introducing new writers and new material to the public. I sent on *Drenched in Light* and he published it. Later, he published my second story *Spunk.* He wrote me a kind letter and said something about New York. So, beginning to feel the urge to write, I wanted to be in New York. . . .

Being out of school for lack of funds, and wanting to be in New York, I decided to go there and try to get back in school in that city. So the first week of January, 1925, found me in New York with $1.50, no job, no friends, and a lot of hope.

The Charles Johnsons befriended me as best they could. I could always find something to eat out at their house. Mrs. Johnson would give me carfare and encouragement. I came to worship them really.

So I came to New York through *Opportunity* to Barnard. I won a prize for a short story at the first Award dinner, May 1, 1925, and Fannie Hurst offered me a job as her secretary, and Annie Nathan Meyer offered to get me a scholarship to Barnard. My record was good enough, and I entered Barnard in the fall, graduating in 1928. . . .

Because my work was top-heavy with English, Political Science, History and Geology, my adviser at Barnard recommended Fine Arts, Economics, and Anthropology for cultural reasons. I started in under Dr. Gladys Reichard, had a term paper called to the attention of Dr. Franz Boas and thereby gave up my dream of leaning over a desk and explaining Addison and Steele to the sprouting generations.

I began to treasure up the words of Dr. Reichard, Dr. Ruth Benedict, and Dr. Boas, the king of kings.

That man can make people work the hardest with just a look or a word, than anyone else in creation. He is idolized by everybody who takes his orders. We all call him Papa, too. One day, I burst into his office and asked for "Papa Franz" and his secretary gave me a look and told me I had better not let him hear me say that. Of course, I knew better, but at a social gathering of the Department of Anthropology at his house a few nights later, I brought it up.

"Of course, Zora is my daughter. Certainly!" he said with a smile. "Just one of my missteps, that's all." The sabre cut on his cheek, which it is said he got in a duel at Heidelberg, lifted in a smile. . . .

I had the same feeling at Barnard that I did at Howard, only more so. I felt that I was highly privileged and determined to make the most of it. I did not resolve to be a grind, however, to show the white folks that I had brains. I took it for granted that they knew that. Else, why was I at Barnard? Not everyone who cries, "Lord! Lord!" can enter those sacred iron gates. In her high scholastic standards, equipment, the quality of her student-body and graduates, Barnard has a right to the first line of Alma Mater. "Beside the waters of the Hudson, Our Alma Mater stands serene!" . . .

So I set out to maintain a good average, take part in whatever went on, and just be a part of the college like everybody else. I graduated with a *B* record, and I am entirely satisfied. . . .

Two weeks before I graduated from Barnard, Dr. Boas sent for me and told me that he had arranged a fellowship for me. I was to go south and collect Negro folklore. Shortly before that, I had been admitted to the American Folk-Lore Society. Later, while I was in the field, I was invited to become a member of the American Ethnological Society, and shortly after the American Anthropological Society.

. . . from what I heard around Miami, I decided to go to the Bahamas. I had heard some Bahaman music and seen a Jumping Dance out in Liberty City and I was entranced.

This music of the Bahaman Negroes was more original, dynamic and African, than American Negro songs. I just had to know more. So without giving Godmother a chance to object, I sailed for Nassau.

I loved the place the moment I landed. Then, that first night as I lay in bed, listening to the rustle of a cocoanut palm just outside my window, a song accompanied by string and drum broke out in full harmony. I got up and peeped out and saw four young men and they were singing Bellamina, led by Ned Isaacs. I did not know him then, but I met him the next day. The song has a beautiful air, and the oddest rhythm

Bellamina, Bellamina!
She come back in the harbor
Bellamina, Bellamina
She come back in the harbor
Put Bellamina on the dock
And paint Bellamina black! Black!
Oh, put the Bellamina on the dock
And paint Bellamina, black! Black!

I found out later that it was a song about a rum-running boat that had been gleaming white, but after it had been captured by the United States Coast Guard and released, it was painted black for obvious reasons.

That was my welcome to Nassau, and it was a beautiful one. The next day I got an idea of what prolific song-makers the Bahamans are. In that West African accent grafted on the English of the uneducated Bahaman, I was told, "You do anything, we put you in sing." I walked carefully to keep out of "sing."

This visit to Nassau was to have far-reaching effects. I stayed on, ran to every Jumping Dance that I heard of, learned to "jump," collected more than a hundred tunes and resolved to make them known to the world.

On my return to New York in 1932, after trying vainly to interest others, I introduced Bahaman songs and dances to a New York audience at the John Golden Theater, and both the songs and the dances took on. The concert achieved its purpose. I aimed to show what beauty and appeal there was in genuine Negro material, as against the Broadway concept, and it went over. . . .

The humble Negroes of America are great song-makers, but the Bahaman is greater. He is more prolific and his tunes are better. Nothing is too big, or little, to be "put in sing." They only need discovery. They are much more original than the Calypso singers of Trinidad, as will be found the moment you put it to the proof. . . .

I enjoyed collecting the folk-tales and I believe the people from whom I collected them enjoyed the telling of them, just as much as I did the hearing. Once they got started, the "lies" just rolled and story-tellers fought for a chance to talk. It was the same with the songs. . . . The subject matter in Negro folk-songs can be anything and go from love to work, to travel, to food, to weather, to fight, to demanding the return of a wig by a woman who has turned unfaithful. The tune is the unity of the thing. And you have to know what you are doing when you begin to pass on that, because Negroes can fit in more words and leave out more and still keep the tune better than anyone I can think of. . . .

While I was in the research field in 1929, the idea of *Jonah's Gourd Vine* came to me. I had written a few short stories, but the idea of attempting a book seemed so big, that I gazed at it in the quiet of the night, but hid it away from even myself in daylight.

For one thing, it seemed off-key. What I wanted to tell was a story about a man, and from what I had read and heard, Negroes were supposed to write about the Race Problem. I was and am thoroughly sick of the subject. My interest lies in what makes a man or a woman do such-and-so, regardless of his color. It seemed to me that the human beings I met reacted pretty much the same to the same stimuli. Different idioms, yes. Circumstances and conditions having power to influence, yes. Inherent difference, no. But I said to myself that that was not what was expected of me, so I was afraid to tell a story the way I wanted, or rather the way the story told itself to me. So I went on that way for three years. . . .

I had collected a mass of work-songs, blues and spirituals in the course of my years of research. After offering them to two Negro composers and having them refused on the ground that white audiences would not listen to anything but highly arranged spirituals, I decided to see if that was true. I doubted it because I had seen groups of white people in my father's church as early as I could remember. They had come to hear the singing, and certainly there was no distinguished composer in Zion Hope Baptist Church. The congregation just got hold of the tune and arranged as they went along as the spirit moved them. And any musician, I don't care if he stayed at a conservatory until his teeth were gone and he smelled like old-folks, could never even approach what those untrained singers could do. LET THE PEOPLE SING, was and is my motto, and finally I resolved to see what would happen.

So on money I had borrowed, I put on a show at the John Golden Theater on January 10, 1932, and tried out my theory. The performance was well received by both the audience and the critics. Because I know that music without motion is not natural with my people, I did not have the singers stand in a stiff group and reach for the high note. I told them to just imagine that they were in Macedonia and go ahead. One critic said that he did not believe that the concert was rehearsed, it looked so natural. I had dramatized a working day on a railroad camp, from the shack-rouser waking up the camp at dawn until the primitive dance in the deep woods at night.

In May, 1932, the depression did away with money for research so far as I was concerned. So I took my nerve in my hand and decided to try to write the story I had been carrying around in me. Back in my native village, I wrote first *Mules and Men*. That is, I edited the huge mass of material I had, arranged it in some sequence and laid it aside. . . .

I wrote *Their Eyes Were Watching God* in Haiti. It was dammed up in me, and I wrote it under internal pressure in seven weeks. I wish that I could write it again. In fact, I regret all of my books. It is one of the tragedies of life that one cannot have all the wisdom one is ever to possess in the beginning. Perhaps, it is just as well to be rash and foolish for a while. If writers were too wise, perhaps no books would be written at all. . . . You take up the pen when you are told, and write what is commanded. There is no agony like bearing an untold story inside you. You have all heard of the Spartan youth with the fox under his cloak.

Work was to be all of me, so I said. Three years went by. I had finished that phase of research and was considering writing my first book, when I met the man who was really to lay me by the heels. I met A.W.P.

He was tall, dark brown, magnificently built, with a beautifully modeled back head. His profile was strong and good. The nose and lip were especially good front and side. But his looks only drew my eyes in the beginning. I did not fall in love with him just for that. He had a fine mind and that intrigued me. When a man keeps beating me to the draw mentally, he begins to get glamorous.

I did not just fall in love. I made a parachute jump. No matter which way I probed him, I found something more to admire. We fitted each other like a glove. His intellect got me first for I am the kind of a woman that likes to move on mentally from point to point, and for my man to be there way ahead of me. Then if he is strong and honest, it goes on from there. Good looks are not essential, just extra added attraction. He had all of those things and more. It seems to me that God must have put in extra time making him up. He stood on his own feet so firmly that he reared back. . . .

In the midst of this, I received my Guggenheim Fellowship. This was my chance to release him, and fight myself free from my obsession. He would get over me in a few months and go on to be a very big man. So I sailed off to Jamaica. But I freely admit that everywhere I set my feet down, there were tracks of blood. Blood from the very middle of my heart. I did not write because if I had written and he answered my letter, everything would have broken down.

So I pitched in to work hard on my research to smother my feelings. But the thing would not down. The plot was far from the circumstances, but I tried to embalm all the tenderness of my passion for him in *Their Eyes Were Watching God*.

When I returned to America after nearly two years in the Caribbean, I found that he had left his telephone number with my publishers. For some time, I did not use it. Not because I did not want to but because the moment when I should hear his voice something would be in wait for me. It might be warm and eager. It might be cool and impersonal, just with overtones from the grave of things. So I went South and stayed several months before I ventured to use it. Even when I returned to New York it took me nearly two months to get up my courage. When I did make the call I cursed myself for the delay. Here was the shy, warm man I had left.

Then we met and talked. We both were stunned by the revelation that all along we had both thought and acted desperately in exile, and all to no purpose. We were still in the toils and after all my agony, I found out that he was a sucker for me, and he found out that I was in his bag. And I had a triumph that only a woman could understand. He had not turned into a tramp in my absence, but neither had he flamed like a newborn star in his profession. He confessed that he needed my aggravating presence to push him. He had settled down to a plodding desk job and reconciled himself. He had let his waistline go a bit and that bespoke his inside feeling. That made me happy no end. No woman wants a man all finished and perfect. You have to have something to work on and prod. That waistline went down in a jiffy and he began to discuss workplans with enthusiasm. He could see something ahead of him besides time. I was happy. If he had been crippled in both legs, it would have suited me even better.

What will be the end? That is not for me to know.

Well, that is the way things stand up to now. I can look back and see sharp shadows, high lights, and smudgy inbetweens. I have been in Sorrow's kitchen and licked out all the pots. Then I have stood on the peaky mountain wrappen in rainbows, with a harp and a sword in my hands.

What I had to swallow in the kitchen has not made me less glad to have lived, nor made me want to low-rate the human race, nor any whole sections of it. I take no refuge from myself in bitterness. To me, bitterness is the under-arm odor of wishful weakness. It is the graceless acknowledgement of defeat. I have no urge to make any concessions like that to the world as yet. I might be like that some day, but I doubt it. I am in the struggle with the sword in my hands, and I don't intend to run until you run me. So why give off the smell of something dead under the house while I am still in there tussling with my sword in my hand?

If tough breaks have not soured me, neither have my glory-moments caused me to build any altars to myself where I can burn incense before God's best job of work. My sense of humor will always stand in the way of my seeing myself, my family, my race or my nation as the whole intent of the universe. When I see what we really are like, I know that God is too great an artist for we folks on my side of the creek to be all of His best works. Some of His finest touches are among us, without doubt, but some more of His masterpieces are among those folks who live over the creek.

Marian Anderson

(1902–   )

The eldest daughter of an aspiring black family in Philadelphia, Marian Anderson and her two sisters were raised by their courageous mother following their father's death in their early childhood. Her mother supported the family by working as a cleaner in a department store. Through her thrift and her daughters' efforts, the family eventually bought a modest house close to the network of kin which had helped them survive the loss of Anderson's father.

The Union Baptist Church provided the focal point of the family's life, and the church's choir was the setting in which Anderson discovered her talents. Her first singing lessons were paid for by a church fund-raiser. Thereafter she helped support her family with her concert earnings. In 1925 she won recognition in a New York City competition held at Lewisohn Stadium, and the following year her public concert career was launched.

Anderson's reputation as a singer was established by her courageous determination to study and sing in Europe, where she could acquire the knowledge of languages necessary to sing the classical repertory. Once her European reputation was established, she was taken under the wing of the great concert impresario Sol Hurok. Her career as one of the world's leading contraltos was capped by her debut at the Metropolitan Opera in *Un Ballo in Maschera* in 1955.

Anderson was the first African-American woman to break the barriers which kept blacks from the concert stage and the first in a succession of black divas at the Metropolitan Opera. She encountered many racial slights, the most infamous being the refusal of the Daughters of the American Revolution to allow her to appear in Constitution Hall in Washington, D.C. This slight was publicly rebuffed by the Roosevelt administration when Anderson was invited to sing on Easter Sunday of 1939 from the steps of the Lincoln Memorial and to perform for King George VI and Queen Elizabeth when they dined at the White House shortly thereafter.

After her retirement from the concert stage, Anderson was showered with honors. Appointed U.S. delegate to the United Nations in 1955, she was awarded the Congressional Medal of Honor in 1977 and the National Medal of Arts in 1986. She has received twenty-four honorary degrees and decorations from Sweden, France, Japan, Liberia, and Haiti. At every stage in her career Anderson has seen herself as a pioneer in combating segregation and advancing the cause of African-Americans.

MY LORD, WHAT A MORNING:
An Autobiography

I don't know all the things my father did to earn a living. As a child I was not concerned. But I do know that for many years he was employed by day at the Reading Terminal Market, in the refrigerator room, and we looked forward to his homecoming every evening. . . .

I was born on Webster Street in South Philadelphia in a room my parents had rented when they were married. I was about two years old when we first moved to my grandmother's. She had a big house, and there was going to be more room for the three of us and the new baby. My earliest recollection is of the third-story room my parents occupied in that house. . . .

Father took pride in his work at the Union Baptist Church. He was a special officer there, and among other things had charge of the ushers. He received no pay for his service; it was something that a person did out of love for his religion and duty to his church. He loved this job and never missed a Sunday at church.

Even before I was six I was taken along to church every Sunday, partly, I suppose, to alleviate my mother's burden of taking care of three children. I would take part in the Sunday school and then sit through the main service. After my sixth birthday I was enrolled in the junior choir of the church. . . .

The man who led the junior choir was Alexander Robinson. He was not a voice teacher or professional musician, but another person who, out of sheer love for the church and out of a spirit of service, gave his time freely to help others. . . .

I remember the day when Mr. Robinson gave me a piece of music to take home, and another copy to Viola Johnson. It was a hymn, "Dear to the Heart of the Shepherd." Viola and I were to look it over, and then we would sing it together, she the upper and I the lower part. Mr. Robinson played the melody over for us, and after I had heard it enough I could remember it. Viola and I rehearsed it carefully and seriously. Then came the Sunday morning when we sang it in church—my first public appearance.

Mother was not there. It was not such a great event, and in any case she had my sisters to look after at home. On the way home from church, Father stopped at Grandmother's house, which was on the direct route from the church to our house, and he chatted for a while. By the time we got home Mr. Robinson had been there and gone. He had left word with Mother that he would like Viola and me to be in church earlier the next Sunday because he wanted us to rehearse the duet again, for the main service this time. . . .

All this time I kept on singing in the junior choir at church, mostly alto. The music we had to sing was not very high, and I could just as well have sung the soprano part but there were always more sopranos than altos, and I thought I would like to be where I was needed most. . . .

As I moved into my teens, singing at the church took on more importance. When I was thirteen I was invited to join the adult choir. I accepted gladly, and I continued my work with the junior choir. In fact, I sang with both groups until I was past twenty.

Singing was a serious business with me, and I had a deep sense of responsibility about my work with the choirs. Our church was large. The senior choir sang in the upper balcony at one end, and our minister was at the other end. Without knowing anything about the tricks of the trade, I sang naturally, free as a bird, with a voice of considerable size and wide range. There was no difficulty in filling the church auditorium. In my youthful exuberance I let myself go, and on several occasions it was suggested gently that my voice was a little too prominent.

I had no thought about technique or style. It may seem boastful to say so, but at that moment I did not need them. I had no difficulty with any music set before me, for I could sing any note in any of the registers. Usually I sang the alto part, but I could fill in for the soprano or tenor. . . .

The visitors who came to the Union Baptist Church were often responsible for invitations to the choir to sing elsewhere. When the distance was too great and traveling expenses were too steep for the whole choir to go, a double quartet, a quartet, or a duet might be sent. Sometimes it happened that one individual represented the church. I was frequently a member of the group that went, and eventually I was sent out as representative alone.

My first visit to New York was with a group from our senior choir. We sang at the Abyssinian Baptist Church; I believe it is the largest church in Harlem. The minister of the church is now Congressman Adam Clayton Powell, and its minister then was his father, who was a friend of our Reverend Parks.

Music meant a great deal to Reverend Parks. He saw to it that we had a big concert at the Union Baptist Church once a year, and this event drew people from all parts of the city, church people and music-lovers alike. . . .

I was fortunate to have so many opportunities to sing in public, and when I began to cultivate my voice seriously these appearances proved to be a useful backlog of experience. Having learned to accompany myself at the piano in a few songs, I dared to appear on my own. Some event was always taking place in one church or another, and I was often invited to sing. I would come home from school, try to scramble through my lessons and do whatever chores I was expected to attend to, and then I would run out to fill my engagements. . . .

Did I receive payment? Sometimes yes and sometimes no. It did not matter; it was a pleasure to sing. . . .

My voice at that time never wearied. I sang the contralto aria in *The Messiah,* "He shall feed His flock like a shepherd" and the one for soprano, "Come unto Him all ye that labor," tossing off trills and other gymnastics without the slightest vocal difficulties.

The more I did in church the more call there was for me to sing in other places. From the socials I went on, while still in high school, to bigger events. I was paid a little more for such appearances, and soon I was emboldened to establish a minimum of five dollars for an appearance. . . .

What did I do with the fee? I gave each of my sisters a dollar, two to Mother, and one I kept. In those days I was not dressed so grandly that I needed taxis to deliver me to the places where I sang. A trolley car sufficed, and the fare was my only expenditure. Mother insisted that the carfare must come out of the money I had turned over to her. And when my fees inched up beyond the five-dollar minimum she argued that I was entitled to keep a larger share for myself.

The opportunity to belong to the Philadelphia Choral Society came along and provided me with another musical outlet. The people in this Negro group sang for the love of it, as I did. With its excellent director, Alfred Hill, the society prepared major works for presentation to its large following. I remember that several years later, when I went to my second voice teacher, the members of this group raised money to help pay for my lessons. . . .

All this time I was singing from nature, so to speak, without any thought of *how*. My heart was filled when I sang, and I wanted to share what I felt. It slowly dawned on me that I had to have some training.

It was through a family acquaintance, John Thomas Butler, who gave public readings in his spare time and who had invited me to appear on his programs, that I met my first vocal teacher. He called on us and asked whether he could take me to sing for a friend of his. The lady he took me to see was Mary Saunders Patterson, a Negro who lived not too far from our house. She had a magnificent soprano voice, and she had studied uptown, as we called it, with a real vocal teacher. After listening to me, she told me that she would like to teach me what she knew. She charged a dollar a lesson, which Mr. Butler knew, and he had decided in his generosity that he would pay for the instruction out of his own pocket.

Mrs. Patterson waited until he was out of the room and asked whether my family was prepared to pay for the lessons. I was compelled to tell her that we could not afford them. She said she did not believe that young people just starting on what might be long careers should have obligations or strings attached to them, no matter how unselfish or noble the offer of help might be. She offered to give me the lessons free of charge. . . .

I sensed the need for a formal musical education when I was in my teens and was beginning to make my first modest tours. I decided, in fact, to see if I could not go to a music school. . . .

That music school no longer exists in Philadelphia, and its name does not matter. I went there one day at a time when enrollments were beginning, and I took my place in line. There was a young girl behind a cage who answered questions and gave out application blanks to be filled out. When my turn came she looked past me and called on the person standing behind me. This went on until there was no one else in line. Then she spoke to me, and her voice was not friendly. "What do *you* want?"

I tried to ignore her manner and replied that I had come to make inquiries regarding an application for entry to the school.

She looked at me coldly and said, "We don't take colored."

I don't think I said a word. I just looked at this girl and was shocked that such words could come from one so young. . . .

It was my first contact with the blunt, brutal words, and this school of music was the last place I expected to hear them. True enough, my skin was different, but not my feelings.

It must be remembered that we grew up in a mixed neighborhood. White and Negro lived side by side and shared joys and sorrows. At school and on the street we encountered all kinds of children. . . .

There were times when we heard our relatives and friends talking, and we knew we might come in contact with this, that, or the other thing. In some stores we might have to stand around longer than other people until we were waited on. There were times when we stood on a street corner, waiting for a trolley car, and the motorman would pass us by. There were places in town where all people could go, and there were others where some of us could not go. There were girls we played with and others we didn't. There were parties we went to, and some we didn't. We were interested in neither the places nor the people who did not want us.

I tried to put the thought of a music school out of my mind, for I could not help thinking of other music schools and wondering whether this would be their attitude too. I would not risk rejection again, and for some years the idea was not mentioned. . . .

I was still in high school when I took my first long trip to participate in a gala concert. Mother went with me. At Washington we changed trains, and this time our bags were taken to the first coach—the Jim Crow car!

The windows were badly in need of washing, inside and outside the car was not clean, and the ventilation and lighting were poor. When the air became much too stuffy and windows were raised it just might happen that you would get, along with your fresh air, smoke and soot from the train's engine. At mealtime containers of all shapes and sizes were brought down from the racks, and the train vendor had a sizable supply of soft drinks, fruit, and packaged cookies. . . .

Throughout our stay in Savannah my thoughts went often to that first coach. We returned to Washington under the same conditions, a bit wiser but sadder and so ashamed. I had looked closely at my people in that train. Some seemed to be embarrassed to the core. Others appeared to accept that situation as if it were beyond repair. . . .

In the next few years I had occasion to do much more traveling. My tours were modest, but the concerts were increasing in number, and many of these engagements were in the south. Billy King [Anderson's accompanist] still traveled with me, and we were giving full programs. I did not have the attention that a big managerial office can provide for a performer, and it was important to have travel conditions as convenient and comfortable as possible. I tried to make my own travel arrangements, but I found that often if I presented myself at a railroad ticket window, sometimes even in Philadelphia, there would be no reservations available. . . .

I tried to relax on these trips, but I could not help being tense at least part of the time. . . .

After a while we learned that it was wisest not to arrange for our own transportation. We began to rely on a man in Philadelphia to make as many advance arrangements as possible. He looked after the entire itinerary, and if he foresaw that some leg of a journey would not be comfortable for one reason or another, he warned us in advance, and we tried to make this part of the trip by auto. This we could afford to do only on short runs.

Shortly before I left high school I was introduced to Giuseppe Boghetti, who remained my teacher for many years, with breaks here and there, until he died. . . .

Mr. Boghetti was short, stocky, and dynamic. He could be pleasant, but there were times when he could be stern and forbidding. At that first meeting he was severe, even gruff. He began by declaring that he had no time, that he wanted no additional pupils, and that he was giving his precious time to listen to this young person only as a favor. . . .

My song was "Deep River." I did not look at Mr. Boghetti as I sang, and my eyes were averted from him when I had finished. He came to the point quickly. "I will make room for you right away," he said firmly, "and I will need only two years with you. After that, you will be able to go anywhere and sing for anybody." Then he began to talk about his fees as if the lessons would begin at once.

They could not begin at once. There was no money for lessons. . . . I might have known that my neighbors and the people at the Union Baptist Church would find a way to provide. Mrs. Ida Asbury, who lived across the street from us, and some other neighbors and friends arranged a gala concert at our church. The main presentation of the evening was "In a Persian Garden," and among the soloists was, I believe, Roland Hayes. After all expenses, about six hundred dollars were realized, and with that money Mr. Boghetti was engaged to be my teacher. . . .

With Mr. Boghetti I learned some of the songs I still sing today: Schubert and Brahms, and later Schumann and Hugo Wolf in German; songs by Rachmaninoff and other Russians, in English; Italian arias; songs in French, and songs in English by American and British composers. . . .

It was in Mr. Boghetti's studio, too, that I became aware of the meaning of professionalism for a public performer. There I learned that the purpose of all the exercises and labors was to give you a thoroughly reliable foundation and to make sure that you could do your job under any circumstances. . . .

During the years I stayed with Mr. Boghetti my tours increased. I went through all my programs for him, and he criticized and corrected. Toward the end of his life, by which time I was busy and away singing most of the time, I kept coming back to him, letting him check on what I was doing. . . .

There came a time when the money provided for the lessons by my friends and neighbors was exhausted, but Mr. Boghetti did not put me out of his studio. . . . Indeed, he carried me without payment of any kind for more than a year. . . .

Working with Mr. Boghetti gave added impetus to my secret desire to go to Europe. He had been trained there, and so much about his musical style had a flavor that attracted me.

By the time I was graduated from high school we were able to think of touring on a much larger scale than we had attempted before. Having Billy King as accompanist even before he added the duties of manager was helpful, for his name on a program carried weight. When it became more or less official that he would play for me, he visited my home and met my people and I was taken to his house to meet his parents. His family lived in a house that was detached on one side, and it was possible to practice there without disturbing other people. It was deemed all right for me to go to his house, for our people knew each other. . . .

Our tours were focused around Negro colleges in the South. In some places that did not have such institutions individuals got together and arranged special concerts, and in time a college might offer to arrange several other appearances in its vicinity. In return we would take a lower fee from this college, which was only fair. . . .

In addition to college auditoriums and churches, we also began to perform in theaters when local promoters had no other places in which to present us. These theater appearances gave me a personal sense of accomplishment. Theaters were places where people with well-known names gave their performances. I began to feel that this was turning into a career. . . .

I think it was at an appearance in Washington, sponsored by Howard University, that I had a sudden awareness of enlarged capacities. The audience was mixed. In the course of a group by Richard Strauss, I reached "Morgen." When I had started to learn this song it had not seemed too difficult. I had soon realized that there was a great deal to it, and in the studio it had been drummed into me that this was a test piece. When I launched into "Morgen" in Washington it took on new meaning. The mood was set. "Morgen" seemed mine to do with what I pleased.

There are such moments in a career, when you feel that you belong to a thing and it belongs to you. "Morgen" that afternoon in Washington was like that. Everything else I did caught fire from "Morgen." As I saw the faces of that audience—a pleasantly surprised look here, a faint smile there—I felt that here was compensation for everything that had happened in the years gone by. . . .

I became determined to make further sacrifices to push on to higher goals, not because I was proud or vainglorious but because I felt that my career thus far warranted such a decision. And so I committed myself to make the plunge and give a recital in New York's Town Hall. For this event I saved money whenever I could, and I worked hard with Mr. Boghetti to prepare a program.

The concert was arranged by a young man who lived in Harlem. I had appeared for him before at the Savoy and at Renaissance Hall. The last appearance had been a sell-out, and he recommended that we try downtown. I felt I had friends in New York; I had also sung in churches, at the Baptist Convention, and for the National Association for the Advancement of Colored People—Walter White, secretary of the association, had heard me in Philadelphia and had arranged an appearance in New York.

The promoter engaged Town Hall. Mr. Boghetti gave me four new songs, including Brahms's "Von ewiger Liebe," and he assured me that I was doing fine with them. I had a great desire to sing Lieder in such a hall because Roland Hayes had done them so movingly.

On the day of the concert there was much excitement. Mr. Boghetti gave me precise instructions, when to eat (four in the afternoon) and what. He warned me to be at the hall at seven that evening. We came in early from Philadelphia, and I stayed in a room at the Y.W.C.A. in Harlem. I followed Mr. Boghetti's orders. I got to the hall at seven, and we went through some vocal exercises. I felt for all the world like a prima donna.

The tickets had been on sale for quite a while, and I had been told that they were selling well. Billy King arrived at the hall, and I watched the clock expectantly for the starting time. I asked casually how everything was going in the auditorium and was assured that we would have a full house. Starting time came and passed, and the man who was to signal us to go out on the stage did not come. It got to be eight forty-five, and I began to feel uneasy. At nine the young man who was managing the concert advised us to begin. Billy and I walked out on the stage. My heart sank. There was only a scattering of people in the hall. I had been misled, and the enthusiasm drained out of me.

To make matters worse, the opening number was Handel's "Ombra mai fù," which we were to do with organ instead of piano. Billy King went to the organ at the side of the stage. I stood quite remote from him and felt miserably alone. I had had a lot of experience and had been foolish enough to think that I was prepared for anything, but I was only about twenty, and I had a great deal to learn.

I got to the Brahms songs. The first three were not easy, but "Von ewiger Liebe" was especially difficult. I sang the German as best I could, having learned it phonetically. . . . Somehow the program came to an end though I felt it had dragged on endlessly. And the next morning the newspaper comments were not complimentary. One writer said that the voice was good, but this and that were not so good. Another said, "Marian Anderson sang her Brahms as if by rote."

. . . I felt lost and defeated. The dream was over. . . .

I stopped going regularly to Mr. Boghetti's studio. I appeared once in a while, and things must have gone very indifferently. He realized how much the fiasco had shaken me, and he did not make an issue of my irregular attendance.

Mother and I talked about the whole thing, and with her patience and understanding she helped me out of my trouble. I knew that the criticism was right and that I should not have given the critics the opportunity to write as they did. I kept reiterating that I had wanted so very much to sing well enough to please everybody.

"Listen, my child," Mother said. "Whatever you do in this world, no matter how good it is, you will never be able to please everybody. All you can strive for is to do the best it is humanly possible for you to do."

As the months went by I was able again to consider singing as a career. "Think about it for a while," Mother advised, "and think of other things you might like to do."

I thought about it. It took a long time before I could confront singing again with enthusiasm, before the old conviction returned that nothing in life, not even medicine, could be so important as music.

One of my great comforts in this time of self-doubt and indecision was that Mother and my sisters and I were living in our own little house. We had taken the momentous step of buying it some time after I finished high school. It may seem that this was a chancy thing for us to do. We had stayed with Grandmother and my aunt for a number of years, moving with them from Fitzwater Street to other houses on Seventieth and Christian, on Carpenter Street, on Eighteenth Street, and on South Martin Street. Grandmother and my aunt had been kind and loving, but nothing could take the place of a home of one's own.

A small house on South Martin Street, across the way from Grandmother's, was put up for sale by an Irish family. We liked the street; it was well kept, quiet, quite desirable. Many of the people on it, Negro and white, owned their own homes. We decided to buy the little house. . . .

Mother's father had died some time before and had left her some money, and I had tried very hard to save something from my earnings. I think I had about six hundred dollars in the bank at that time, and it had taken me a long time to accumulate it. I remember that when I had gone to the bank to open my first savings account several years before I had been full of hope that my nest egg would grow with dazzling speed. When the bank informed me that the limit for a savings account was ten thousand dollars I thought that I would have to look around for a second bank in no time. My account, however, refused to shoot up and create such a problem for me. Whenever it seemed to be growing encouragingly some crisis developed, and money had to be withdrawn. I don't know how it had risen to as much as six hundred dollars when we bought the little house.

The signing of the deed and the payment of the cash that had to be put down were big events in our lives. We were incredibly happy. In the nights before the purchase became final I had visions that I would not live long enough to move into the house. After the occupants left I went into the empty house and looked around critically and fondly.

I met King—his full name is Orpheus H. Fisher, and another nickname he had was Razzle—in Wilmington, Delaware, when we were both still in school. . . .

. . . it was not long before King . . . became my boy friend. . . . King traveled up to Philadelphia to attend art school. He used to come over to our house after school, and we would play records on the phonograph he had borrowed for me.

The day came when King said he wanted me to meet his family. It was a well-known, quite social family, and I was excited and nervous. . . .

When we got to Wilmington he took me to his sisters first— each married and in her own home—and in the evening I had dinner at his parents' house. King did not say anything about the seriousness of this expedition, but once we were back in Philadelphia he made clear what he had on his mind—as if I did not suspect.

As a matter of fact, he had suggested earlier that we run away and get married. I was busy with the beginnings of my concert life, and I thought that there was no great hurry. . . .

We continued to see each other often. My concert work increased, and he completed art school and a few years later went off to New York to study and to work. I felt badly when he left town. . . .

One gets swept up in a career, and one has time for little else. I went to Europe, and, when I returned, another young man whom I admired came out in a tender to meet the boat, and King heard about it. King visited me only once in the months I remained in the United States, and our conversation was brief and cool. He left, and I could not tell whether I would ever see him again. But when I was back in Europe he sent me a long letter. Upon my return to the United States he came to see me often, and presently we knew that someday we would be married. What with King's busy career as an architect and mine with its recurrent long absences from home, our wedding did not take place until 1943. It was worth waiting for.

Things were going well again—not grandly, of course, but there were earnings, payments could be made on the installments, and a little money began to accumulate in the savings account. . . .

We had seen Mother going and coming from work all these years, and though we were preoccupied with our own affairs we would have been blind if we had not noticed how weary she was at times. It was borne in on me that she must be freed from her bondage, that the first thing we must do the moment we could afford it was to get her out of all this.

The day came unexpectedly, without preparation. She arrived home from work one evening, not feeling well. We had prepared dinner, but she did not eat. I was worried about her and, knowing that she would make little of her illness, I slipped out unseen and went down to the corner and rang the doorbell of Dr. Taylor, whom Mother had known when they had both lived in Virginia.

Dr. Taylor soon arrived at our house, and Mother was surprised and wanted to know how he had happened to come by. "Oh, I just thought I'd stop in," he said casually. "I see you're not well." Without asking her permission, he took her pulse, asked her questions, made an examination, and said, "I'll take a look at you tomorrow, and I think you ought to stay in for a few days."

The next morning Mother was up at her usual time. She was sneezing and coughing and looking miserable, but she was preparing to go to work. We reminded her of what the doctor had said, but she did not see how she could stay home for a few days, with her many obligations. We were just as determined as she, and because she was really shaky on her feet she submitted.

She stayed home for quite a few days. Though she was increasingly concerned about getting back to work, even she realized that she had been very ill and needed time to recuperate. I kept thinking about the problem and considering our financial position and possibilities, and I came to a very definite decision.

I went to the telephone and called Wanamaker's. I asked to speak to the supervisor, and as I waited for her to come to the phone I felt, I must say, a glowing satisfaction. I was primed for the lady. She was a big person on her job, and maybe she had a heart, but it remained at home when she went to work. It was a good and happy moment when she came to the phone and I could say, after identifying myself, "I just wanted to tell you that Mother will not be coming back to work."

I realize that this statement could not have been shattering to her. After all, she would be able to find some other poor soul on whom to load extra work. But to us it was an event of great joy—and another turning point. . . .

It is difficult to describe Mother's purity and simplicity of character, and she will find it embarrassing that I speak of her in print. But I must. A great deal of what I am and what I achieved I owe to her. Not once can I recall, from my earliest recollections, hearing Mother lift her voice to us in anger. Even after my father's death, when she was grief-stricken and sorely troubled, she was not short with us. . . .

I cannot remember a single complaint from Mother. Though she toiled incessantly, she did not spend money on personal things. Her first concern was our needs. . . . I no longer reprove her when she lets someone take unfair advantage of her, as I might have when I was younger. She is what she is, bless her. . . .

Mother gave balance to the home and led us into a rich spiritual life. We knew from earliest childhood that she prayed, and she saw to it that as little girls we said our prayers. . . .

Good habits can be fine things. If you say your prayers every night there comes a time when they grow more meaningful to you. The child who learns to repeat after his mother, "Now I lay me down to sleep," may get a little thrill out of just saying it, at the beginning. After a time he realizes that he can do nothing about keeping his own soul when he is asleep. . . .

And later, when Mother taught us the Lord's Prayer, she put her heart into it. You tried to say it as she did, and you had to put a little of your own heart into it. I believe that Mother, realizing that she was left alone to raise three girls, knew that she had to have a support beyond herself. . . .

I believe in the basic things Mother believes in. Her God is my God. I would not condemn people who do not believe as we do. I feel, however, that each one of us must have something in which he believes with all his heart, so that he need never be absolutely alone. . . .

My religion is something I cherish. I am not in church every Sunday, but I hope and believe that I am on good speaking terms with Him. I carry my troubles, and I don't sit back waiting for them to be cleared up. I realize that when the time is ripe they will be dissolved, but I don't mean that one should sit inert, waiting for all things to come from above. If one has a certain amount of drive, intelligence, and conscientiousness, one must use them. Having made the best effort, one is more likely to get a hearing in an extremity.

I believe that I could not have had my career without the help of the Being above. I believe, as Mother does, that He put it in the hearts of many people to be kind, interested, and helpful, and to do things that needed to be done for me and that I could not have done for myself. It would have happened anyhow, some might say. I don't believe that it would have happened anyhow.

It was a step up to come under the notice and management of Arthur Judson. I had high hopes that now steady advancement was assured. Arthur Judson, after all, represented the top in concert management, and when he showed an interest in my work I may have gone too far in imagining a future of unlimited rosiness. . . .

The first year under the new arrangement brought fewer engagements than I had had in the past, but with the higher fee the amount earned remained about the same. There was no question that I was on another level. When Billy King and I decided to give a concert all our own in the Academy of Music in Philadelphia, it was undoubtedly impressive to be presented by the Arthur Judson office. . . .

With the higher fee, Billy King had to be paid more for his services as accompanist, and this was only fair and reasonable. And I found that clothes became a bigger item: I had to have more than one evening dress. I remember that for the first Judson year I got a new dress—light blue—and I had a pair of white slippers tinted blue to match. Even in those days I tried to have clothes that were simple in design but made of good material and effective in appearance. I might add that I began to realize, particularly when I appeared in the South, how important one's appearance was. I think that my people felt a sense of pride in seeing me dressed well. I don't mean that they were unaccustomed to good clothes and a good appearance. Quite a few of them owned handsome things and knew how to dress attractively. But it made them feel good, I found out, to see one of their own pleasantly got up.

The change in my itinerary under the Judson direction was not especially marked, and it was some years before I was moved up to the supervision of Mr. Judson's main office and the fee rose to seven hundred and fifty dollars. I still appeared in churches. I still traveled as I always had.

... The great majority of the concerts were what might be called Billy King—Marian Anderson dates; they stemmed from our previous tours. Eventually there was a Judson concert, one that our card file had nothing to do with producing. Then there were a few others, but they were not many. The high hopes began to dwindle. Progress seemed to have stopped; I had substantially the same circuit of concerts but little more. I was beginning to feel that I was at a standstill. . . .

I have no doubt that the Judson office was encountering resistance in selling a young Negro contralto to its normal concert circuits, and I had no European reputation such as Roland Hayes had acquired. But all I knew at the time was that I was uneasy.

The decision to go to Europe was not taken lightly. There was, to begin with, the all-important question of money. We had some savings in the bank. We calculated that, after paying for the passage, I could take about fifteen hundred dollars with me. There would be some money left for the family, and, with the help my sisters could provide, it should suffice.

Mother and I discussed the matter at length. I went over all the arguments: I was going stale; I had to get away from my old haunts for a while; progress was at a standstill; repeating the same engagements each year, even if programs varied a little, was becoming routine; my career needed a fresh impetus, and perhaps a European stamp would help. . . .

The trip was pleasant, even though I was alone most of the time. I didn't make friends aboard ship. There may have been a few pangs of loneliness, but the experience was so new and exciting that the time went rapidly. There were a good many Americans on board, but I had the delightful feeling of being at least partly in a foreign environment. . . .

We reached England, and the boat train arrived at Paddington Station in London late in the evening. I went immediately to telephone Roger Quilter [the British voice teacher to whom Anderson had been directed]. As I understood the arrangements, he would tell me where to go, and if he were not home there would be a message. The phone rang for a long time, and finally there was an answer.

"This is Marian Anderson," I said. "I have just arrived."

The voice replied, "Who?"

I repeated my name slowly. The voice at the other end had never heard it before.

"Is this Roger Quilter?"

"No, madam."

"Well, who is it?"

"The butler, madam."

"May I speak to Mr. Quilter?"

"He's in a nursing home, madam." . . .

Roger Quilter did not remain long in the nursing home, and a few days later I got to see him. He was a tall, thin, sensitive man, an English-looking Englishman, as I put it to myself. He had a fine home, always open to musicians. It was not uncommon to go there and find his music room occupied by someone who needed a quiet place to work and study. Mr. Quilter was a cultivated man, a patron of the arts, and a fine musician in his own right. He played very well, and he had a number of charming songs to his credit.

After some days in London I took a train to a town in Sussex called Steyning, where I hoped to begin work with Raimund von Zur Muhlen. I made arrangements for lodgings at the home of Vicky Newburg, a young printer, and his wife. . . .

I got to see Master, as Raimund von Zur Muhlen was called. Having been assured that he was the best man in England for Lieder, I felt a sense of excitement and almost fear. I was shown into a large room with a piano at the far end. Master was old, and he remained seated in a big chair with a red rug over his knees. He had a cane at his side, and when he wanted your attention he pounded the floor with it. He talked to me for a few minutes and then requested that I sing something. A young Englishman who was the accompanist went to the piano, and we began. I sang "Im Abendrot," and when I was finished Master said, "Come here."

It seemed like a long walk from the piano to a chair beside him.

"Do you know what that song means?" he demanded.

"Not word for word," I said, "and I'm ashamed that I don't."

"Don't sing it if you don't know what it's about."

"I know what it's about," I explained, "but I don't know it word for word."

"That's not enough," he said with finality.

He asked me to sing something else. This time I did a song in English, with which I felt secure.

Master pounded his cane on the floor before I was finished. "Wait a minute," he called. "You're singing like a queen, and I have not crowned you yet."

He was not unkind, however, and we sat and talked for a while. When I left he lent me a book of Schubert songs and suggested that I learn the first one in it, "Nahe des Geliebten." It had several verses in German, and the book contained no English translation. Fortunately, Vicky-bird knew some German. Ordinarily he and his wife spent a lot of time cutting the pages of books just off the press, but that evening they abandoned their favorite pastime to help me with the German. Vicky-bird was stumped by some phrases, and went out and called in a friend who also knew some German. Together, we all tried to puzzle out the subtle meanings of the German poetry. It was obvious to me that even if they succeeded in doing a fair job on this song I could not possibly learn enough German overnight to be at home with the language. I thought that Master must be merely testing my capacities to work.

I did not see Master again for almost a week. He was recovering from a thrombosis, and some days he did not feel well enough to see anyone. Nor could he devote much time to me. After I had sung a part of "Nahe des Geliebten" he stopped me, though he was not too displeased with what I had accomplished. I went way from that lesson feeling that this was really right for me. . . .

A few days later I hopefully telephoned Vicky-bird and got the sad news that Master had been obliged to stop all teaching.

It was a keen disappointment. After only two visits with Master, I had felt that he represented the answer to my most urgent artistic problems. Now I had to start looking for a teacher again. Roger Quilter suggested Mark Raphael, a pupil of Raimund von Zur Muhlen. I went to Raphael, who was a good teacher, and the lessons with him were beneficial. . . .

. . . having entree to Roger Quilter's home and his circle was an agreeable thing. There I met English people, composers and performers as well as society folk. Mr. Quilter did what he could to introduce me musically. Several times I sang for the gatherings in his spacious music room, with Mr. Quilter accompanying me at the piano. His visitors were warm in their reception. I sang a full program once, songs in German, Italian, and English, including several by Mr. Quilter. His friends suggested that I should appear in a concert at Wigmore Hall, and, thanks to Mr. Quilter, it was arranged. Then he and his friends were good enough to obtain an engagement for me with the Promenade Concerts under Sir Henry Wood. . . .

It should be made clear that I appeared in London not as an artist of consequence but almost as a student. When I returned to the United States I had no big achievements to show for my absence of about a year. If I had done something noteworthy such as singing for the king and queen, that might have made a difference. But a recital at Wigmore Hall? That was just another appearance by an American aspirant. To people who wanted to know what had been accomplished abroad there was not a great deal to tell. . . .

The return home was necessary. Money was running low, and I had concert engagements which had been arranged on the understanding that I would be back. I wanted to see my family and friends.

I was disappointed that there were not more dates booked for me, and yet I had feared in my heart it would not be otherwise. Though there was more money per concert, there were far fewer engagements than in the days when Billy King and I had done our own bookings. I have a copy of a letter sent by a secretary in the management office, dated August 27, 1930, and addressed to Billy King, which lists the tour that was then ahead of me. In five months nineteen concerts are scheduled. Two of these dates are not definite because contracts have not yet been signed. Other concerts are subject to change of time, though the contracts are signed.

This could not be called a bad tour for a young artist, though I felt I had been before the public long enough not to be considered a newcomer. The sensation that I was standing still, which had led to my going to England, returned. I had not been home too long before I decided that I ought to go back to Europe. . . .

I happened to be singing in Chicago at a concert under the auspices of the Alpha Kappa Alpha sorority, of which I had been made an honorary member. The appearance was not in one of the regular concert halls, but in a high school auditorium. During the performance a message came backstage that a man whose name sounded like Raphael would like to see me. I was as excited as could be. What was Mark Raphael doing in Chicago?

At the end of the concert the man arrived. His name turned out to be Ray Field. He was accompanied by Mr. George Arthur, and they were both representatives of the Julius Rosenwald Fund. They were friendly and interested in my work and aspirations. They wanted to know what plans I had for the future, and I told them that what I wanted and needed was to go to Germany. They invited me to come to the Fund offices two days later. Of course the regular questionnaire had to be filled out.

When we met again they told me that they thought the Fund would be able to offer me a fellowship. If I decided to go to Germany they assured me that a grant would be forthcoming for the trip. This was heartening. As Mother would say, a way had been found, and I made up my mind to go. . . .

My primary objective in Berlin was musical guidance in the field of German Lieder. The name most often recommended had been that of Michael Raucheisen, and I went to him for coaching. Before and during that time I had a few lessons with Sverre Jordan, who played a part in drawing the attention of a Norwegian manager to me.

One day while I was in Raucheisen's studio two strangers were admitted by my coach's mother, and they sat quietly while we finished the song we were working on. The men introduced themselves to Raucheisen, and he turned and made formal introductions to me. The two were Rule Rasmussen, a Norwegian manager, and Kosti Vehanen, a Finnish pianist. They were traveling together, looking for new talent.

Rasmussen wanted to know whether I would be available for some concerts. I said that I might be. "If you come to Norway to sing, this man will play for you," he said, pointing to Kosti. But before they would commit themselves they wished to be sure that I could sing an aria.

I had promised to sing that evening at a small concert arranged by Sverre Jordan at the high school where he taught, and Mr. Rasmussen and Mr. Vehanen could hear me there under something like normal performance conditions. They came to the recital, I sang an aria, and Mr. Rasmussen was now certain that he wanted me to go to Norway. . . .

Shortly after the Bachsaal concert there came a letter from Mr. Rasmussen, announcing that arrangements had been made for concerts in the north. There was a promise of six appearances, in pairs, with the understanding that the second of two in Norway, for example, would take place only if the first had been a success. I was to start with a pair in Oslo, follow with a pair in Stockholm, and end with a pair in Helsinki. Mr. Rasmussen decided, however, that it would do no harm, en route to Oslo, to stop and sing in

Stavanger. That did not go too badly, and a concert was arranged for Bergen, where there was a similar reception. In Oslo the first concert was so well received that the second was called for immediately.

The reaction in Norway, I think, was a mixture of open-mindedness and curiosity. These audiences were not accustomed to Negroes. One of the newspaper reports described the singer as being "dressed in electric-blue satin and looking very much like a chocolate bar." Another paper made the comparison with *café au lait*. And so it went. The comments had nothing to do with any prejudice; they expressed a kind of wonder.

This sense of surprise seemed to affect the listeners at the first concert in Oslo. I recall that there was an unexpected demonstration of applause at the end of the first group, and at the end of the first half it was almost impossible to stop for the intermission. After the first concert, the second was quickly sold out. People wrote to the manager and to me at my hotel, making special requests for things to be included in the program.

A lot of Norwegians spoke English. They kept the phones at my hotel busy, and some arrived in person to chat for a few minutes. They came to talk about their own country and mine. Some were anxious to discuss conditions for me and my people in the United States. Others wanted to speak about music; one or two persons brought flowers, and others songs which they hoped I would sing. Possibly a few came, as they might in any land, because they had nothing better to do.

I went on to Stockholm, where my appearance was to be managed by Helmer Enwall, to whom Rasmussen had delegated the chore. Director Enwall, as he is called, was younger than Rasmussen. He had vigor, enthusiasm, and vision. He felt that the name Anderson would be an asset in his country as well as in the other Scandinavian countries, particularly since I did not look in the least like a Scandinavian, and he made careful plans for my first concert in Stockholm. Because of his reputation for introducing interesting performers the concerts he managed usually attracted a knowledgeable public.

The reaction of the first Swedish audience was, to put it mildly, reserved. Director Enwall assured me that the concert had been a success. However, I had my doubts. Compared with Norwegian responses, this had been pallid. To prove that he meant what he said, Director Enwall swiftly arranged my second concert, and it drew a large audience. Again the reaction was not too impressive. It took me some time to discover that what Director Enwall claimed for Sweden was true: its people were slow to manifest their warmth, but it would build up into something durable. . . .

From Stockholm I went to Helsinki. The reaction there, comparable with the enthusiasm of Norway, made me feel that I would like to sing a great deal in Finland. I even tried a very simple folk song in Finnish. It was no great feat, but the audience appreciated the gesture no end. Kosti Vehanen was my accompanist. To Kosti, Finland was home; he helped to make me welcome there, and some Finns who spoke English came on their own for a visit. The second concert followed the first in Finland as a matter of course.

Kosti Vehanen played for me for the rest of that rather brief tour, and later, when I returned to Scandinavia, he became my regular accompanist. He was a well-trained musician, had studied in Germany, and spoke German fluently, and he could help me with Lieder. . . . A man of culture and a gentleman, Kosti Vehanen was an invaluable aid to me. It is not too much to say that he helped me a great deal in guiding me onto the path that led to my becoming an accepted international singer.

From Helsinki we went to Copenhagen, pausing in Stockholm on the way for a third concert. The news of what success I had had in Norway, Sweden, and Finland preceded me to Denmark, and the audiences were larger at the very outset. In Copenhagen nearly everyone I met seemed to speak English, and there were a good many English and American people there. One felt as if it could be an audience in America. After the first concert some Americans came backstage to say hello.

I felt very much at home in Copenhagen. Even at the hotel I was made as welcome and comfortable as if I were among my own people and closest friends. People seemed happy to be with you; they sought you out. They accepted you as an individual in your own right, judging you for your qualities as a human being and artist and for nothing else. Even the first curiosity about my outward difference was in no way disturbing or offensive, and it seemed only a moment before that dropped away. . . .

That first trip to the Scandinavian countries was an encouragement and an incentive. It made me realize that the time and energy invested in seeking to become an artist were worth while, and that what I had dared to aspire to was not impossible. The acceptance by these audiences may have done something for me in another way. It may be that they made me feel that I need not be cautious with such things as Lieder, and it is possible that I sang with a freedom I had not had before. I know I felt that this acceptance provided the basis for daring to pour out reserves of feeling I had not called upon. I tried to remember reactions to specific songs and even to passages in songs. After a performance I would go back to my hotel room and examine the music to see where this place or that could be done more effectively. If these people believed in me as an artist, then I could venture to be a better one. I could face the challenge of bigger things. . . .

The first visit to the north took only a few weeks, but it made a tremendous difference in my life. The full six months allotted for this European trip were soon up, and I was on my way to the United States. Some news of the success in the Scandinavian countries had reached my own country. I suppose I expected it to be of use in my tour schedule. It is possible that there would have been some such effect if the news had come from successes in Paris or London or Vienna. But American managers did not seem too impressed with what had been accomplished in Scandinavia. In any event, my tour schedule was essentially what it had been before. After completing it, I began to think of returning to Europe. . . .

I went back to Europe in 1933. My return was speeded by Director Enwall. One day he sent me a cable: CAN OFFER YOU TWENTY CONCERTS WHEN CAN YOU COME? I did not answer immediately. While I was deliberating there came another message from him: CAN OFFER FORTY CONCERTS. I replied that I expected to have a certain number of concerts at home that year. As a matter of fact, I knew that there would be about the usual twenty, and I did not want to give them up. Mr. Enwall answered with another cable: CAN OFFER SIXTY CONCERTS. If I had not known him to be utterly reliable and if I had not had the warm memories of the first Scandinavian tour, I might have thought that he was going wild with a kind of personal numbers game. But I was fairly sure that if he said sixty he would have sixty dates for me. Nevertheless, I decided to fulfill my American commitments and wrote to Mr. Enwall that I could accept only twenty concerts. He agreed, and after I finished my schedule at home I returned to Scandinavia.

This time I remained in Europe for more than two years, and for a considerable part of the time I was kept busy entirely in the Scandinavian countries. I had not expected to remain so long, thinking I would come home for my usual tour, whatever its size. As work kept piling up in Europe, I wrote to the Judson office to inquire whether my American dates could be postponed. The answer came back that they could not. . . .

Director Enwall was ready for me not only with the sixty concerts he had mentioned in his maximum offer, but with a lot of additional ones. Before I was through I had done more than a hundred concerts—I think the exact number was one hundred and eight—within a twelve-month period. I sang nearly everywhere in Sweden, Norway, Finland, and Denmark. I sang in the remote north of Sweden and Finland in churches of small communities. In some towns there were two and three concerts; in Stockholm there were more.

The houses were full, and the enthusiasm of the public was what it had been the first time. The only difference was in Sweden, where the reserve seemed to have melted. . . .

As a guest of the Scandinavian peoples, I felt I ought to learn and sing some of the songs of their composers. Time was short on our crowded itinerary, but Kosti and I managed to work on new things now and then. He was particularly eager that I should learn some songs by Jean Sibelius, Finland's great and beloved composer. We worked on several, and I was fascinated and puzzled by one called "Norden." It was beautiful, but it was also strange and so foreign to me that I could not quite grasp it. . . .

[Kosti Vehanen arranged for Anderson to meet Sibelius.] We were greeted warmly by Sibelius and his family. I was surprised to find that he was not so tall as his photographs had indicated, but with his strong head and broad shoulders he looked like a figure chiseled out of granite. I sang one of his songs that had a German text, "Im Wald ein Mädchen singt," "Norden," and several other pieces. When I was finished he arose, strode to my side, and threw his arms around me in a hearty embrace. "My roof is too low for you," he said, and then he called out in a loud voice to his wife, "Not coffee, but champagne!"

Kosti beamed, and I could hardly speak. We spent much more than the fixed half-hour. With Kosti serving as interpreter, we discussed the songs. Sibelius came to the piano to make certain points. I left feeling a glow from the meeting with so great a man, and also a rewarding knowledge that I had caught a deeper glimpse of the meaning of such a song as "Norden." It was as if a veil had been lifted, and whenever I sang the songs of Sibelius again I sensed that I was approaching them with fresh understanding. . . .

I went on to Paris, appearing in the Salle Gaveau. . . . The program was very much like those I had been singing in Scandinavia. In the spot usually reserved for an aria, I had a French operatic excerpt; otherwise, there were Italian classics, songs in German and English, and a group of spirituals. . . .

The first Paris program was well received. Mr. Horowitz, who had been a leading figure in Berlin before the Hitler regime took over, was the manager, and he suggested a second program. This one was almost a sell-out, and Mr. Horowitz was emboldened to propose a third for the middle of June. Mr. Enwall and his wife had come to Paris for my debut in France, but they had returned home by this time, and I had to decide the question of a third concert myself. My first reaction was against it.

"Out of the question," I told Mr. Horowitz. "It's too late in the season."

Mr. Horowitz listened to this excuse and others I could think of, and ended by persuading me. He proved his point by doing so good a job that the house was sold out the day before the concert. I was overjoyed. Other places in Europe were important, but Paris was still Paris, and its influence was not to be undervalued. And that third concert produced such flattering notices that I was certain of being "on my way." It was a "tremendous success."

I had not gone to Paris with the thought that this would be a voyage of conquest. I had gone to do my best. I had been singing long enough not to expect any miracles from any one appearance. I did not realize that this third Paris concert, which Mr. Horowitz had forced me into giving, was to produce a big change in my career. It was this concert that led Mr. Sol Hurok to me, or vice versa.

Before I had left the United States, several years before, I had tried to arrange a meeting with Mr. Hurok. I had known his reputation for daring and constructive management, had admired the boldness with which he did things, and had hoped that I could interest him in my work. But I had been unable to see him.

There I was in Paris, resting during the intermission, when Mr. Horowitz walked in with Mr. Hurok. I learned later that Mr. Hurok had happened to be spending several days in Paris, had seen the posters announcing the concert as he walked along the boulevards, and had decided to attend on the spur of the moment. This, too, was fortunate. It would not, however, be surprising to find him any place in this wide world on a given evening, examining a new attraction. So there he was in Paris at my concert, quite by chance.

Mr. Hurok said casually that he would like to see me. Could I meet him at Mr. Horowitz's office the next day? Could I! I don't know how I got through the rest of the program, but, like all programs, this one also came to an end.

With Kosti I went to Mr. Horowitz's office the next day. I still have a vivid picture of the scene in my mind. Mr. Horowitz sat at one side of his big desk, while Mr. Hurok occupied the chair behind it. Kosti and I took seats in front of it. In those days Mr. Hurok was built along generous lines. In recent years he has slimmed himself down so that he looks like the dapper man about town, but in June 1935 he had the impressive bulk befitting the grand impresario. I cannot tell you how big and important he seemed to me; Kosti and I felt inadequate in his presence. As Mr. Hurok slowly lifted his cane, which he held at his side, and placed it before him on the desk, his shoulders seemed to broaden. I think I would have run away if I had dared.

Mr. Hurok's tone was calm. He wanted to know how many concerts I had been getting each season in the United States and how much I received for them. There were many other questions. As I recall it, he made no mention of his reaction to my concert the previous night. At last he spoke the words that I had been hoping to hear! "I might be able to do something for you."

He proceeded to spell out the offer. He would guarantee fifteen concerts at a certain fee, which was less than I had hoped for. There was a disappointing moment, but it went quickly. I was convinced in my heart that he could do something unusual for a performer if he took a notion to do so. . . .

Kosti and I left the office. I felt like a marathon runner at the end of his race. Evidently Kosti was excited too. "Marian," he said as we reached the street, "the only thing to do now is to have a schnapps and come to life once more." . . .

I continued my appearances in Europe that fall, and then began to prepare for my return to the United States to sing under Mr. Hurok's management. I have been asked on occasion why I was so glad to return to America. Some people have wondered why I did not decide to make my permanent home in Europe, which had accepted me, as others of my group had done on occasion. No such thought ever entered my mind. . . . I had gone to Europe to achieve something, to reach for a place as a serious artist, but I never doubted that I must return. I was—and am—an American.

It might have been playing it safe to remain where things were going well, but I was more eager than ever to return. I wanted to come home, and I knew that I had to test myself as a serious artist in my own country. . . .

A difficult, even painful decision had to be made before the return home. Kosti Vehanen had been my accompanist in Europe, appearing with me in Scandinavia and other European countries. Billy King had been my accompanist in the United States. Who should be my accompanist when I came back? Because I had been working most recently with Kosti, I felt more at home with him in the new programs. With his help I had made considerable progress in the weaker phases of my repertory. On the other hand, Billy also had been a good and faithful friend when I needed one.

The issue went deeper, and I was aware that, whatever the decision, it would be open to misunderstanding and would be criticized by some. If I did not use Billy King some of my own people might be offended. And particularly in the South, where I knew I would be singing, people might take offense that a white man was serving as my accompanist.

I knew in my heart that the right decision would be the one taken on musical grounds. I put the matter to Kosti, feeling that he should be prepared if he came. He was eager for the assignment. Indeed, he was troubled that he might not have it.

"Marian," he said, "if I can come and play only the first pieces on the program, I will charm them so that they will want me to stay."

And so it was. Kosti Vehanen came, and he stayed. I think he did charm people, and he remained with me for the next five years during my American as well as European tours.

We knew several months before the return that the date fixed for the first homecoming concert was December 30 at New York's Town Hall, and we began preparing the program in September while we were still in Europe. . . . We worked with concentration and diligence. Kosti gave a lot of thought to every detail of program arrangement, trying to balance each group for maximum effect. He selected certain songs which he called the *Schlagers,* those that would make the biggest impression, the knockouts. He made suggestions for songs that would begin each group and for the pieces that should come in the middle. He wanted nothing left to chance. I agreed with him, of course, and before we sailed we had the program for the New York concert prepared.

We continued to work on board the ship. We applied to the

purser for the use of a room with a piano and discovered that another passenger who was a singer had made a similar request. Fixed times were allotted to each of us.

On the third day of the voyage I was relaxing out on deck when I noticed that it was almost time for my rehearsal. I hastened to the stairway, intent on getting down to my room to pick up my music. The sea was rough that day, and as I started down, my hands touching the rail very lightly, the ship lurched. I lost my balance, stumbled, reached for the rail, and tumbled down the stairs. My ankle seemed to buckle under me, and I actually saw stars. I had always believed that such stars were things seen only in the comic strips, but I saw them. The first thought that entered my mind was, I wonder if I can do that concert? And the next was, Why not? . . .

On the day of arrival I took off the bandages, and the ankle did not feel too bad when I stood up and walked about. I had a pair of elegant brown sport shoes, which I had purchased in Stockholm, and I was as fond of them as of any shoes I had ever had, including the Buster Brown pair of my girlhood. In any case, I had to wear them that day, and I had a costume that went well with them. I had not been home for a long time; I knew that there would be many special people to meet me at the pier, and I did not wish to alarm anyone. Oh, yes, there was vanity in it, too.

I walked off the pier, went through customs, and had all the excitement of seeing my family again. . . .

The next morning—it was a day or two before Christmas—I awoke and looked at my foot. There was no swelling around the ankle, but my toes had turned blue and green, and there was numbness in the foot. I became frightened; my sister called a cab, and we went to the hospital, where the foot and ankle were X-rayed. There was a break in the ankle, and I was outfitted with a cast that covered the leg up to the calf and left the toes sticking out.

"Is that my foot?" I asked the doctor as I looked at the X-ray pictures.

"There's no reason why it shouldn't be," he said.

Then he told me that the cast would have to stay on for six weeks. I returned home, feeling a gnawing sense of desperation. I was equipped with a pair of crutches, and learning how to get around with them was difficult and did not add to my tranquillity. I realized that this New York concert after the long European sojourn was most important, and I knew that Mr. Hurok had made careful plans to launch me under his management. I did not want to sing unless I was in perfect shape physically, and yet I did not see how I could not sing. As I hobbled about I realized that there was no great pain. I could manage if I wanted to. The cumbersome crutches were a nuisance, but there seemed to be nothing to do but make the best of the situation.

I drove in to New York two days before the concert. We hired a heated automobile for the trip, which took almost five hours because the weather was stormy. A registered nurse accompanied me. The doctor had recommended that the toes and upper leg should be massaged regularly to keep the circulation moving, and the nurse was to attend to this task.

I went to the Y.W.C.A. in Harlem and tried to rest. The next morning there was an interview with the press in Mr. Hurok's office, and I came down for that. I was careful to get myself seated comfortably behind a desk before the visitors entered, for I did not see why it was relevant to have them know of my accident.

On the day of the concert I wanted very much to be staying somewhere near the hall. There was a young woman I knew who occupied a suite at the Algonquin Hotel. She had phoned me in Philadelphia and had asked when I would be coming to New York. I had been vague at that moment, and she had said that she would be leaving her suite for some days and I would be welcome to use it. I did not know that she had broached the idea to someone in authority but had not received approval, and when I arrived at the hotel I got a cool reception. I should say that Frank Case, the owner of the Algonquin, later changed all that, and for some years I had a suite of my own there whenever I was in New York.

I remained at the Algonquin the night of the concert and the following night. The nurse stayed with me and helped me to move about as I dressed. I wore a black and gold brocade evening dress, which reached the floor so that no one in the audience would know there was anything amiss.

We were at Town Hall early, and a good deal of time was spent discussing the problem of how to get on and off the stage without causing undue excitement. It was decided that the curtains should be kept drawn as I was wheeled on stage. When I stood up and took my place in the bend of the piano, putting my weight on my feet without the aid of crutches, there was little difficulty. The pain was not intense, but there was some. I would not agree that an announcement should be made to the public, explaining my difficulty. To tell the audience I was singing despite a broken ankle would smack of searching for pity, and I was not there for pity that night. I was there to present myself as an artist and to be judged by that standard only.

As the curtains were pulled apart I looked out apprehensively, fearful of what the public might be thinking of these dramatics. I could not tell. At the end of the concert many people came backstage—not only my family but also such musical friends as Mr. Boghetti and other persons from my city, as well as other men and women. Those who didn't know the reason for my apparent immobility had found out from others who did know, and I realized that many in the audience had not taken offense at the ostentation of the drawing and parting of the curtains. But when I began to sing I had no such comforting knowledge. I was both fearful and hopeful.

We began with Handel's "Begrüssung." A friend of Kosti's had given it to me in Europe, and I knew that it was rarely sung in concert. It begins with a long, sustained tone that builds to a crescendo. To do it properly you must be a rather calm person. To start a program with it you must be sure of yourself. The first tone of your first number can make a decisive first impression. I had no reason to fear it, for I had done it often in Europe, and if I had not had a nagging feeling that the plaster cast might impede my freedom I would have sung that tone without any restraint at all. Having decided to give the concert, I did not think I should change the carefully arranged program just because of this tone. I had gone over the music before going out on the stage to immerse myself in the mood, and I was as ready as I could be.

The opening tone and the rest of "Begrüssung" might have been freer. But when I was finished with the song I had the feeling that I had done it worse on other occasions.

I felt, too, after that song, that the audience was with me. I cannot stress too strongly how significant a role the audience plays in any concert. Although I sing with my eyes closed, I have a picture of the audience out front. The lights on the stage carry well into the front rows, and you can make out the expressions on the faces of your listeners before you start and after each number. After many years of singing in public you develop a knack of finding the people who are with you, and you are able, you think, to pick out those who stand apart from you, determined to be shown. Often you choose an individual or a group, strangers all, to whom you sing.

Of course you sing to and for all, but there may be one person who is unlike the other ninety-nine. This person, you sense, wants to be brought back into the fold and you can help bring him back. And so as you sing you have to be so deeply convinced of what you are doing that the person for whom you are singing will be convinced.

It was like that at Town Hall that night. I do not recall what the particular person I was trying to reach looked like. I do not know what the full program was, number by number . . . it is only the mood that needs to be remembered. When I reached the intermission—by which time I had sung my Schubert songs and had not been too uncomfortable with them—I had mingled feelings. Part of what I had done had gone as I had hoped; part had not. On average, I would have said that it was more right than wrong. There was a responsiveness in the audience that lifted the spirit, and I did not worry so much about the drawing and pulling apart of the curtains at the end of the first half and the beginning of the second.

I will make no bones about the fact that the program was devised so that there would be opportunity to show whatever I was capable of doing, including low notes and high. In Schubert's "Der Tod und das Mädchen" there is a low D that I felt to be effective when done well. In the spiritual "The Crucifixion" there are several low F's. But the program was not put together to make an impression with individual notes. It was selected to include music I liked, music about which I had a conviction. "The Crucifixion," for example, was more than a song. It contained a spiritual message. Maybe there was something extra in "The Crucifixion" that night; maybe there was something extra in all the spirituals at the end of the program. I do not know. When I reached them I felt as if I had come home, fully and unreservedly—not only because they were the songs I had sung from childhood but also because the program was almost finished, and I had survived.

After the visitors left the artist's room backstage I felt a sense of weariness and repose. People had been generous in their comments. There were words of praise from some who had not needed to utter them. But I did not delude myself. I knew that this was not the end of the quest to be an artist. It was, I felt, a beginning—a new beginning.

There was exhilaration in the flattering reviews the next day, but there was also the weight of greater responsibility. When I returned to Philadelphia and several days had passed, taking the keen edge off the excitement, I got out my music. I studied the songs

I had sung at Town Hall, examining my singing in retrospect to check where I had not done as I would have liked and where a point had been exaggerated or undervalued. Here was a song that should have begun more softly and ended more powerfully. There was another that had not been all of a piece. I thought back to the spirituals, and I felt that in some places I had touched too lightly on the essential feeling, missing its depth. Had I given passages in them the character of art songs, which is not their nature at all? I feared that I might have. I resolved to be more careful. . . .

Mr. Hurok had planned my first season under his management with great care. He hoped to have about fifteen dates for me that year. He also arranged an extra concert at Carnegie Hall to take advantage of the excitement generated by the Town Hall appearance. Though the plaster cast still encumbered me, I filled my engagements. Curtains were drawn and parted in halls that had them. In auditoriums where there were no curtains I managed to hobble on, and this was worse than the business of the curtains. The public knew of the shipboard accident and was kind enough to make allowances, but I could not get it out of my mind that it looked a bit as though I were "putting on."

As events developed, the fifteen concerts Mr. Hurok had hoped for did not pan out, but this did not worry him. I have since learned from another source, not from Mr. Hurok, that when he returned to America and reported that he had signed me a person who knew the concert business had told him, "You won't be able to give her away."

Mr. Hurok was not disturbed. He had faith in his own judgements, and he did not hesitate to take big risks in support of them. The normal thing in the music world is for the performer to defray the costs of a New York concert, but Mr. Hurok did not follow routine. He met all the expenses himself. He never bothered to tell me how he made out on the event, but I learned later that the gross receipts at the box office were about nine hundred dollars, a good deal less than the amount he spent.

He and his staff went to great pains in arranging the next New York concert at Carnegie Hall. Again there was no discussion of who would pay what bills; he met them all. There may have been a profit from this one; I never knew. What counted was that Mr. Hurok was satisfied that things were progressing well.

I cannot thank him too much for the consideration and taste with which he handled everything. There was dignity in all things, in the publicity that was sent out and in the auspices he approved for appearances. He did not care if he took a loss on the first season. He knew, by the way, that I was planning to go back to Europe several months after my return because I had commitments there. He was not worried that this might mean passing up dates we could have. He was building for the future. He did not accept any offer that came along, simply because it meant a quick fee. He was concerned whether a concert would be right for me. If he arranged for an appearance in a concert course, he made sure it was one of the best. If I was billed outside of a regular concert series, he saw to it that much was made of the fact that this was to be a special attraction.

Best of all, Mr. Hurok brought a deep personal interest to my career. There was the kind of friendship that you do not look for in managers. Mr. Hurok, of course, is not just a manager. He is an impresario who takes chances whenever he believes in the artist or in the ensemble. . . .

He made a determined effort to get certain doors opened to me. I remember that I had always wanted to appear at the Philadelphia Forum. Mr. Hurok turned the trick. It was gratifying that after my appearance the Forum asked for my return the next season, of its own accord.

In later years Mr. Hurok may have held up a date for me with some series because he hoped to get an opportunity for a young artist. If he did, I do not mind; indeed, I am flattered. It would be only justice that my success should be used to help others as I had been helped. . . .

Mr. Hurok's aim was to have me accepted as an artist worthy to stand with the finest serious ones, and he sought appearances for me in all the places where the best performers were expected and taken for granted. The nation's capital was such a place. I had sung in Washington years before—in schools and churches. It was time to appear on the city's foremost concert platform—Constitution Hall.

As it turned out, the decision to arrange an appearance in Constitution Hall proved to be momentous. I left bookings entirely to the management. When this one was being made I did not give it much thought. Negotiations for the renting of the hall were begun while I was touring, and I recall that the first intimation I had that there were difficulties came by accident. Even then I did not find out exactly what was going on; all I knew was that something was amiss. It was only a few weeks before the scheduled date for Washington that I discovered the full truth—that the Daughters of the American Revolution, owners of the hall, had decreed that it could not be used by one of my race. I was saddened, but as it is my belief that right will win I assumed that a way would be found. I had no inkling that the thing would became a *cause célèbre*.

I was in San Francisco, I recall, when I passed a newsstand, and my eye caught a headline: MRS. ROOSEVELT TAKES STAND. Under this was another line, in bold print just a bit smaller: RESIGNS FROM D.A.R., etc. I was on my way to the concert hall for my performance and could not stop to buy a paper. I did not get one until after the concert, and I honestly could not conceive that things had gone so far.

As we worked our way back East, continuing with our regular schedule, newspaper people made efforts to obtain some comment from me, but I had nothing to say. I really did not know precisely what the Hurok office was doing about the situation and, since I had no useful opinions to offer, did not discuss it. I trusted the management. I knew it must be working on every possible angle, and somehow I felt I would sing in Washington.

Kosti became ill in St. Louis and could not continue on tour. Here was a crisis of immediate concern to me. I was worried about Kosti's well-being and we had to find a substitute in a hurry. Kosti had had symptoms of this illness some time before and had gone to see a physician in Washington, who had recommended special treatment. It was decided now that Kosti should be taken to Washington and hospitalized there.

Franz Rupp, a young man I had never met before, was rushed out to St. Louis by the management to be the accompanist. I had a piano in my hotel room, and as soon as Franz, who is now my accompanist, arrived, we went over the program. . . .

Mr. Rupp and I gave the St. Louis concert, and then we filled two other engagements as we headed East. Our objective was Washington. We knew by this time that the date in Constitution Hall would not be filled, but we planned to stop in Washington to visit Kosti. I did not realize that my arrival in Washington would in itself be a cause for a commotion, but I was prepared in advance when Gerald Goode, the public-relations man on Mr. Hurok's staff, came down to Annapolis to board our train and ride into the capital with us.

Mr. Goode is another person who made a contribution to my

career the value of which I can scarcely estimate. He was with Mr. Hurok when I joined the roster, and I am sure that he labored devotedly and effectively from the moment of my return from Europe for that first Hurok season in America. His publicity efforts were always constructive, and they took account of my aversion to things flamboyant. Everything he did was tasteful and helpful. And in the Washington affair he was a tower of strength.

Mr. Goode filled me in on developments as we rode into Washington, and he tried to prepare me for what he knew would happen—a barrage of questions from the newspaper people. They were waiting for us in the Washington station. Questions flew at me, and some of them I could not answer because they involved things I did not know about. I tried to get away; I wanted to go straight to the hospital to see Kosti. There was a car waiting for me, and the reporters followed us in another car. I had some difficulty getting into the hospital without several reporters following me. They waited until I had finished my visit, and they questioned me again—about Kosti's progress and his opinion of the Washington situation. Finally we got away and traveled on to New York.

The excitement over the denial of Constitution Hall to me did not die down. It seemed to increase and to follow me wherever I went. I felt about the affair as about an election campaign; whatever the outcome, there is bound to be unpleasantness and embarrassment. I could not escape it, of course. My friends wanted to discuss it, and even strangers went out of their way to express their strong feelings of sympathy and support.

What were my own feelings? I was saddened and ashamed. I was sorry for the people who had precipitated the affair. I felt that their behavior stemmed from a lack of understanding. They were not persecuting me personally or as a representative of my people so much as they were doing something that was neither sensible nor good. Could I have eased the bitterness, I would have done so gladly. I do not mean that I would have been prepared to say that I was not entitled to appear in Constitution Hall as might any other performer. But the unpleasantness disturbed me, and if it had been up to me alone I would have sought a way to wipe it out. I cannot say that such a way out suggested itself to me at the time, or that I thought of one after the event. But I have been in this world long enough to know that there are all kinds of people, all suited by their own natures for different tasks. It would be fooling myself to think that I was meant to be a fearless fighter; I was not, just as I was not meant to be a soprano instead of a contralto.

Then the time came when it was decided that I would sing in Washington on Easter Sunday. The invitation to appear in the open, singing from the Lincoln Memorial before as many people as would care to come, without charge, was made formally by Harold L. Ickes, Secretary of the Interior. It was duly reported, and the weight of the Washington affair bore in on me.

Easter Sunday in 1939 was April 9, and I had other concert dates to fill before it came. Wherever we went I was met by reporters and photographers. The inevitable question was, "What about Washington?" My answer was that I knew too little to tell an intelligent story about it. There were occasions, of course, when I knew more than I said. I did not want to talk, and I particularly did not want to say anything about the D.A.R. As I have made clear, I did not feel that I was designed for hand-to-hand combat, and I did not wish to make statements that I would later regret. The management was taking action. That was enough.

It was comforting to have concrete expressions of support for an essential principle. It was touching to hear from a local manager in a Texas city that a block of two hundred tickets had been purchased by the community's D.A.R. people. It was also heartening; it confirmed my conviction that a whole group should not be condemned because an individual or section of the group does a thing that is not right.

I was informed of the plan for the outdoor concert before the news was published. Indeed, I was asked whether I approved. I said yes, but the yes did not come easily or quickly. I don't like a lot of show and one could not tell in advance what direction the affair would take. I studied my conscience. In principle the idea was sound, but it could not be comfortable to me as an individual. As I thought further, I could see that my significance as an individual was small in this affair. I had become, whether I liked it or not, a symbol, representing my people. I had to appear.

I discussed the problem with Mother, of course. Her comment was characteristic: "It is an important decision to make. You are in this work. You intend to stay in it. You know what your aspirations are. I think you should make your own decision."

Mother knew what the decision would be. In my heart I also knew. I could not run away from this situation. If I had anything to offer, I would have to do so now. It would be misleading, however, to say that once the decision was made I was without doubts.

We reached Washington early that Easter morning and went to the home of Gifford Pinchot, who had been Governor of Pennsylvania. The Pinchots had been kind enough to offer their hospitality, and it was needed because the hotels would not take us. Then we drove over to the Lincoln Memorial. Kosti was well enough to play, and we tried out the piano and examined the public-address system, which had six microphones, meant not only for the people who were present but also for a radio audience.

When we returned that afternoon I had sensations unlike any I had experienced before. The only comparable emotion I could recall was the feeling I had had when Maestro Toscanini had appeared in the artists' room in Salzburg. My heart leaped wildly, and I could not talk. I even wondered whether I would be able to sing.

The murmur of the vast assemblage quickened my pulse beat. There were policemen waiting at the car, and they led us through a passageway that other officers kept open in the throng. We entered the monument and were taken to a small room. We were introduced to Mr. Ickes, whom we had not met before. He outlined the program. Then came the signal to go out before the public.

If I did not consult contemporary reports I could not recall who was there. My head and heart were in such turmoil that I looked and hardly saw, I listened and hardly heard. I was led to the platform by Representative Caroline O'Day of New York, who had been born in Georgia, and Oscar Chapman, Assistant Secretary of the Interior, who was a Virginian. On the platform behind me sat Secretary Ickes, Secretary of the Treasury Morgenthau, Supreme Court Justice Black, Senators Wagner, Mead, Barkley, Clark, Guffey, and Capper, and many Representatives, including Representative Arthur W. Mitchell of Illinois, a Negro. Mother was there, as were people from Howard University and from churches in Washington and other cities. So was Walter White, then secretary to the National Association for the Advancement of Colored People. It was Mr. White who at one point stepped to the microphone and appealed to the crowd, probably averting serious accidents when my own people tried to reach me.

I report these things now because I have looked them up. All I knew then as I stepped forward was the overwhelming impact of that vast multitude. There seemed to be people as far as the eye could see. The crowd stretched in a great semicircle from the Lincoln Memorial around the reflecting pool on to the shaft of the Washington Monument. I had a feeling that a great wave of good will poured out from these people, almost engulfing me. And when I stood up to sing our National Anthem I felt for a moment as though I were choking. For a desperate second I thought that the words, well as I knew them, would not come.

I sang, I don't know how. There must have been the help of professionalism I had accumulated over the years. Without it I could not have gone through the program. I sang—and again I know because I consulted a newspaper clipping—"America," the aria "O mio Fernando," Schubert's "Ave Maria," and three spirituals— "Gospel Train," "Trampin'," and "My Soul Is Anchored in the Lord."

I regret that a fixed rule was broken, another thing about which I found out later. Photographs were taken from within the Memorial, where the great statue of Lincoln stands, although there was a tradition that no pictures could be taken from within the sanctum.

It seems also that at the end, when the tumult of the crowd's shouting would not die down, I spoke a few words. I read the clipping now and cannot believe that I could have uttered another sound after I had finished singing. "I am overwhelmed," I said. "I just can't talk. I can't tell you what you have done for me today. I thank you from the bottom of my heart again and again."

It was the simple truth. But did I really say it?

There were many in the gathering who were stirred by their own emotions. Perhaps I did not grasp all that was happening, but at the end great numbers of people bore down on me. They were friendly; all they wished to do was to offer their congratulations and good wishes. The police felt that such a concentration of people was a danger, and they escorted me back into the Memorial. Finally we returned to the Pinchot home.

I cannot forget that demonstration of public emotion or my own strong feelings. In the years that have passed I have had constant reminders of that Easter Sunday. It is not at all uncommon to have people come backstage after a concert even now and remark, "You know, I was at that Easter concert." In my travels abroad I have met countless people who heard and remembered about that Easter Sunday.

In time the policy at Constitution Hall changed. I appeared

there first in a concert for the benefit of China Relief. The second appearance in the hall, I believe, was also under charitable auspices. Then, at last, I appeared in the hall as does any other musical performer, presented by a concert manager, and I have been appearing in it regularly. The hall is open to other performers of my group. There is no longer an issue, and that is good.

It may be said that my concerts at Constitution Hall are usually sold out. I hope that people come because they expect to hear a fine program in a first-class performance. If they came for any other reason I would be disappointed. The essential point about wanting to appear in the hall was that I wanted to do so because I felt I had the right as an artist.

I wish I could have thanked personally all the people who stood beside me then. There were musicians who canceled their own scheduled appearances at Constitution Hall out of conviction and principle. Some of these people I did not know personally. I appreciate the stand they took.

May I say that when I finally walked into Constitution Hall and sang from its stage I had no feeling different from what I have in other halls. There was no sense of triumph. I felt that it was a beautiful concert hall, and I was happy to sing in it. . . .

I do not recall meeting Mrs. Franklin D. Roosevelt on that Easter Sunday. Some weeks later in 1939 I had the high privilege of making her acquaintance. It was on the occasion of the visit to this country of King George VI and his Queen, and I was one of those honored with an invitation to perform for the royal guests.

While waiting to sing I was in Mrs. Roosevelt's room in the White House. There was a traveling bag on a chair, and the tab on it indicated that she would soon be off again. I can still see it plainly.

Knowing that I would be introduced to the President, I tried to prepare a little speech suitable for such an occasion. When I met him, he spoke first. "You look just like your photographs, don't you?" he said, and my pretty speech flew right out of my head. All I could say was, "Good evening, Mr. President." . . .

Thanks to the skill and thoughtfulness of my manager and his staff, I have been spared and shielded. They have not told me every hazard they have encountered and overcome in arranging things for me. They have not told me of difficulties in making reservations. They have not let me in on all the problems they have met with local managers or committees. And I am grateful.

I know, of course, that there have been difficulties and problems.

I look at the itinerary, see that I am scheduled to stay at a certain hotel in a certain city, and sense that an exception has been made. It is better not to know for sure. It is more comfortable not to think about it if I can avoid it. I have a performance to give, and if my feelings are divided I cannot do my best. If my mind dwells even partly on the disconcerting thought that I am staying where I am not really welcome, I cannot go out and sing as though my heart were full of love and happiness. . . .

I was never very happy about singing in halls where segregation was practiced. Some years ago I decided that I had had enough, and I made it a rule that I would not sing where there was segregation. I am aware that this decision made it difficult for the sponsors of local concerts in some cities where I had appeared. They did not feel that they could venture to present concerts on any basis other than the old one—with an invisible line marking off the Negro section from the white, from orchestra to topmost balcony. One could not expect them to take a poll of their patrons. This was their business, and there are plenty of other artists. For myself it meant the loss of several engagements a year. I am sorry to give up warm and enthusiastic audiences. I do not feel, however, that these audiences are irretrievably lost because I am standing on principle. I may be able to go back someday and sing to nonsegregated audiences. If not I, someone else surely will.

In the meantime there have been at least four communities— one in Virginia, one in Kentucky, and two in Florida—where I could appear before nonsegregated audiences. In Florida the concerts took place in the auditoriums of Negro colleges, but in both these gatherings there was a high percentage of white persons. Some of the latter called to ask whether there were reserved seats, which is the expression used to connote segregation. They were told that they could sit anywhere they wished, and they ordered tickets anyhow. . . .

My own people always streamed backstage almost triumphantly. They were so delighted at the recognition I was getting that they felt the auditorium was theirs for an evening. Even as I was finishing my last number they started backstage. They were not accustomed to coming backstage, and some who came from the balconies wandered around, trying to find their way. Parents, I discovered, made great sacrifices to have their children hear me. They brought them backstage, and some did not bother to ask for autographs. "This is the lady we were telling you about," one would say. "This is Marian Anderson," another would tell his children. "Shake hands with her, and you can always say that you shook hands with Marian Anderson." I have heard of one woman who scrimped, saved, and borrowed so that she could take her children to my concert. What could be more touching and humbling?

In September 1954 Mr. Hurok brought the Old Vic production of *A Midsummer Night's Dream* to America from England, and he was thoughtful enough—he is unbelievably thoughtful about such things—to invite my husband and me to the New York opening at the Metropolitan Opera House, where the show played. Following the opening there was to be one of those fabulous parties that Mr. Hurok knows so well how to give, and we were invited to that also. The party was for the entire company, and I knew that there would be many, many guests and that Mr. Hurok would be so busy he would not miss us if we did not go.

"It was grand of Mr. Hurok to invite us," I told my husband outside the theater, "but he'll have plenty of guests to take care of. Let's go home."

We have a little apartment uptown because there are many evenings when I must perform in and around New York and it becomes difficult to travel to the country. My husband agreed to my suggestion.

"I'll telephone Mr. Hurok from the apartment," I said, trying to assure myself that this was the right thing to do, "and make our apologies."

My husband turned the car north. "If that's what you want, all right," he said amiably.

We rode some distance, and I said, "I have a strange feeling that we should go to the party and say hello. Then we can leave immediately. I'm sure that's best."

"I don't see why we have to leave right away," he said as he turned the car around.

We got to the party, met some people we knew, and soon were having a good time. Presently I saw Mr. Rudolf Bing, general manager of the Metropolitan Opera, coming toward me. He did not stand on ceremony but drew me aside and came to the point immediately.

"Would you be interested in singing with the Metropolitan?" he asked.

I looked at him with some surprise. I could not be sure that he was serious.

"Would you be interested?" he repeated. He was not urgent. Indeed, his tone was casual.

"I think I would," I said, trying also to be casual.

"Do you really think you would?"

"Yes, I would."

"Would you call me tomorrow morning?" Mr. Bing asked.

"Yes, I will."

"Oh, just a moment," he said. "Here comes Max Rudolf." And he introduced me to his artistic administrator.

"Didn't Mr. Hurok say anything to you about this?" Mr. Rudolf wanted to know.

"He mentioned it, but I thought it was all very vague."

"We spoke to Mr. Hurok a year ago," said Mr. Bing.

Mr. Rudolf mentioned the part they had in mind—Ulrica, the old sorceress in Verdi's *Un Ballo in Maschera* (*A Masked Ball*).

"Do you know it?" he asked.

"No," I said, and I surely did not. I could have answered in the same way about any other opera. I did not know any role from beginning to end. I had never had a pressing need to learn operatic roles. . . .

The next morning the Metropolitan Opera phoned the Hurok office. There was a question of whether my concert schedule could be rearranged to make time available for rehearsals and appearances at the Opera, and the Hurok office thought that it could be done. The Metropolitan then sent over a score of *A Masked Ball*, and the Hurok office got it up to my apartment immediately.

I glanced through the part of Ulrica. My first impression was that it lay too high for my voice, and I felt like saying no at once. But by this time I had agreed to spend some time working on the part. The understanding was that after I had studied it a bit I would have an audition with Dimitri Mitropoulos, who was to be the conductor, and then we would give our opinions as to whether I would do the role. . . .

The rehearsals moved up to the roof stage. . . . Hearing those magnificent voices and working on a fixed schedule in a theater that could afford no other way of operation were unbelievably stimulating. Some people know how to order their lives so that they do things on schedule. I do not have that gift, but I had to adapt myself to the way the Metropolitan did things. I had become so saturated with my concert life that I found I scarcely had time for anything but getting my work done. At the Metropolitan I had to stretch my hours to crowd more activity into them, and somehow all this caused the blood to race through me with new meaning. I felt incredibly alive, able to do any amount of extra tasks. I even managed to get some of my letters answered, and that's really something.

There was a wonderful family feeling in all the preparations. I was not wholly unfamiliar with the Metropolitan Opera stage, for I had sung concerts from it on a number of Easter Sundays. And yet it looked entirely different when the sets were up and we were assembled for the dress rehearsal. . . .

The night of the performance arrived—January 7, 1955. My husband drove me down early in the afternoon. . . . My family had come up from Philadelphia and were put up at our apartment; they were in their box at the Met early. The leading members of the cast came to my dressing room to wish me well in various languages. . . . I could hear other singers doing their warm-up exercises, and for once I did not feel hesitant about doing mine. . . . Then there was a tap on the door, and a voice said, "We're beginning now. Your call will come in twenty minutes. Good luck."

The curtain rose on the second scene, in which Ulrica appears, and I was there on the stage, mixing the witch's brew. I trembled, and when the audience applauded and applauded before I could sing a note I felt myself tightening into a knot. I had always assured people that I was not nervous about singing, but at that moment I was as nervous as a kitten. I was terribly anxious that this of all things should go well, but there were things that happened to my voice that should not have happened. With all the experience I had behind me, I should have been firm and secure, but my emotions were too strong. I suppose it is well not to be so blasé that nothing will affect you. I know I tried too hard; I know I overdid. I was not pleased with the first performance; I know it was not the best I could do.

The audience was unbelievably sympathetic. So were my colleagues. I was given a little push at curtain-call time so that I would be on the stage a moment by myself, although this is against Metropolitan policy. And Miss Milanov embraced me on the stage in full view of the audience.

. . . Mother arrived, and she threw her arms around me and whispered in my ear, "We thank the Lord." Her only words before the performance had been, "Mother is praying for you," and after it she just stood there, and though she is not outwardly demonstrative I could see that there was a light around her face. She did not know much about opera, but she knew the significance of what was going on that night and she was profoundly moved by it. If she had said more she would have said, "My cup runneth over."

. . . the company brought *A Masked Ball* to Philadelphia and I sang as a member of the Metropolitan in my native city. . . . There was a lift in seeing the big sign, MET OPERA, in Penn Station at the entrance to the special train. For the others in the troupe it was perhaps a matter of routine; to me every aspect of the trip was exciting. . . .

The chance to be a member of the Metropolitan has been a highlight of my life. It has meant much to me and to my people. If I have been privileged to serve as a symbol, to be the first Negro to sing as a regular member of the company, I take greater pride from knowing that it has encouraged other singers of my group to realize that the doors everywhere may open increasingly to those who have prepared themselves well. . . . I will never forget the wholehearted responsiveness of the public. I may have dreamed of such things, but I had not foreseen that I would play a part in the reality.

Maya Angelou

(1928–   )

The second child and only daughter of urban black parents, Maya Angelou, like many children of the first generation of black families outside the South, was sent, along with her brother, to be raised by her paternal grandmother, a storekeeper in Stamps, Arkansas. Her formal education in segregated southern schools and in San Francisco was paralleled by her instruction in life by her grandmother, her mother, who was an entertainer, and her mother's friends. Rooted in both the rich folk tradition of rural black culture and the faster-paced world of San Francisco, Angelou acquired the command of language and imagery which make her a writer of compelling power.

Her first public recognition came with the publication in 1970 of her memoir *I Know Why the Caged Bird Sings*. A prolific writer, Angelou has produced *Just Give Me a Cool Drink of Water 'fore I Die* (1971), *Georgia Georgia* (1972), *Gather Together in My Name* (1974), *Oh Pray My Wings Are Gonna Fit Me Well* (1975), *Singin' and Swingin' and Gettin' Merry Like Christmas* (1976), *And Still I Rise* (1978), *The Heart of a Woman* (1981), *Shaker, Why Don't You Sing?* (1983), *All God's Children Need Traveling Shoes* (1986), *Now Sheba Sings the Song* (1987), and *I Shall Not Be Moved* (1990).

Since 1991 Angelou has held the Reynolds professorship of American Studies at Wake Forest University. Now recognized as one of the most powerful black voices in America, she served on the Bicentennial Commission, which oversaw the commemoration of the two hundredth anniversary of the Revolution. Named one of the One Hundred Most Influential American Women in 1983, she continues a career of writing and lecturing, and has received honorary doctorates from Smith College, Mills College, and the University of Kansas.

I KNOW WHY
THE CAGED BIRD SINGS

When I was three and Bailey four, we had arrived in the musty little town, wearing tags on our wrists which instructed—"To Whom It May Concern"—that we were Marguerite and Bailey Johnson Jr., from Long Beach, California, en route to Stamps, Arkansas, c/o Mrs. Annie Henderson.

Our parents had decided to put an end to their calamitous marriage, and Father shipped us home to his mother. A porter had been charged with our welfare—he got off the train the next day in Arizona—and our tickets were pinned to my brother's inside coat pocket.

I don't remember much of the trip, but after we reached the segregated southern part of the journey, things must have looked up. Negro passengers, who always traveled with loaded lunch boxes, felt sorry for "the poor little motherless darlings" and plied us with cold fried chicken and potato salad. . . .

The town reacted to us as its inhabitants had reacted to all things new before our coming. It regarded us a while without curiosity but with caution, and after we were seen to be harmless (and children) it closed in around us, as a real mother embraces a stranger's child. Warmly, but not too familiarly.

We lived with our grandmother and uncle in the rear of the Store (it was always spoken of with a capital S), which she had owned some twenty-five years. . . .

The formal name of the Store was the Wm. Johnson General Merchandise Store. Customers could find food staples, a good variety of colored thread, mash for hogs, corn for chickens, coal oil for lamps, light bulbs for the wealthy, shoestrings, hair dressing, balloons and flower seeds. Anything not visible had only to be ordered. . . .

When Bailey was six and I a year younger, we used to rattle off the times tables with the speed I was later to see Chinese children in San Francisco employ on their abacuses. Our summer-gray potbellied stove bloomed rosy red during winter, and became a severe disciplinarian threat if we were so foolish as to indulge in making mistakes.

Uncle Willie used to sit, like a giant black Z (he had been crippled as a child), and hear us testify to the Lafayette County

Training Schools' abilities. His face pulled down on the left side, as if a pulley had been attached to his lower teeth, and his left hand was only a mite bigger than Bailey's, but on the second mistake or on the third hesitation his big overgrown right hand would catch one of us behind the collar, and in the same moment would thrust the culprit toward the dull red heater, which throbbed like a devil's toothache. . . .

During these years in Stamps, I met and fell in love with William Shakespeare. He was my first white love. Although I enjoyed and respected Kipling, Poe, Butler, Thackeray and Henley, I saved my young and loyal passion for Paul Laurence Dunbar, Langston Hughes, James Weldon Johnson and W. E. B. Du Bois' "Litany at Atlanta." But it was Shakespeare who said, "When in disgrace with fortune and men's eyes." It was a state with which I felt myself most familiar. I pacified myself about his whiteness by saying that after all he had been dead so long it couldn't matter to anyone any more. . . .

Weighing the half-pounds of flour, excluding the scoop, and depositing them dust-free into the thin paper sacks held a simple kind of adventure for me. I developed an eye for measuring how full a silver-looking ladle of flour, mash, meal, sugar or corn had to be to push the scale indicator over to eight ounces or one pound. When I was absolutely accurate our appreciative customers used to admire: "Sister Henderson sure got some smart grandchildrens." If I was off in the Store's favor, the eagle-eyed women would say, "Put some more in that sack, child. Don't try to make your profit offa me." . . .

Until I was thirteen and left Arkansas for good, the Store was my favorite place to be. Alone and empty in the mornings, it looked like an unopened present from a stranger. Opening the front doors was pulling the ribbon off the unexpected gift. . . .

Throwing scoops of corn to the chickens and mixing sour dry mash with leftover food and oily dish water for the hogs were among our evening chores. Bailey and I sloshed down twilight trails to the pig pens, and standing on the first fence rungs we poured down the unappealing concoctions to our grateful hogs. They mashed their tender pink snouts down into the slop, and rooted and grunted their satisfaction. We always grunted a reply only half in jest. We were also grateful that we had concluded the dirtiest of chores and had only gotten the evil-smelling swill on our shoes, stockings, feet and hands.

Late one day, as we were attending to the pigs, I heard a horse in the front yard (it really should have been called a driveway, except that there was nothing to drive into it), and ran to find out who had come riding up on a Thursday evening when even Mr. Steward, the quiet, bitter man who owned a riding horse, would be resting by his warm fire until the morning called him out to turn over his field.

The used-to-be sheriff sat rakishly astraddle his horse. His nonchalance was meant to convey his authority and power over even dumb animals. How much more capable he would be with Negroes. It went without saying.

His twang jogged in the brittle air. From the side of the Store, Bailey and I heard him say to Momma, "Annie, tell Willie he better lay low tonight. A crazy nigger messed with a white lady today. Some of the boys'll be coming over here later." Even after the slow drag of years, I remember the sense of fear which filled my mouth with hot, dry air, and made my body light.

The "boys"? Those cement faces and eyes of hate that burned the clothes off you if they happened to see you lounging on the main street downtown on Saturday. Boys? It seemed that youth had never happened to them. Boys? No, rather men who were covered with graves' dust and age without beauty or learning. The ugliness and rottenness of old abominations.

If on Judgement Day I were summoned by St. Peter to give testimony to the used-to-be sheriff's act of kindness, I would be unable to say anything in his behalf. His confidence that my uncle and every other Black man who heard of the Klan's coming ride would scurry under their house to hide in chicken droppings was too humiliating to hear. . . .

Immediately, while his horse's hoofs were still loudly thudding the ground, Momma blew out the coal-oil lamps. She had a quiet, hard talk with Uncle Willie and called Bailey and me into the Store.

We were told to take the potatoes and onions out of their bins and knock out the dividing walls that kept them apart. Then with a tedious and fearful slowness Uncle Willie gave me his rubber-tipped cane and bent down to get into the now-enlarged empty bin. It took forever before he lay down flat, and then we covered him with potatoes and onions, layer upon layer, like a casserole. Grandmother knelt praying in the darkened store.

It was fortunate that the "boys" didn't ride into our yard that evening and insist that Momma open the Store. They would have surely found Uncle Willie and just as surely lynched him. He moaned the whole night through as if he had, in fact, been guilty of some heinous crime. The heavy sounds pushed their way up out of the blanket of vegetables and I pictured his mouth pulling down on the right side and his saliva flowing into the eyes of new potatoes and waiting there like dew drops for the warmth of morning.

. . . our father came to Stamps without warning. It was awful for Bailey and me to encounter the reality one abrupt morning. We, or at any rate I, had built such elaborate fantasies about him and the illusory mother that seeing him in the flesh shredded my inventions like a hard yank on a paper chain. He arrived in front of the Store in a clean gray car (he must have stopped just outside of town to wipe it in preparation for the "grand entrance"). Bailey, who knew such things, said it was a De Soto. His bigness shocked me. His shoulders were so wide I thought he'd have trouble getting in the door. He was taller than anyone I had seen, and if he wasn't fat, which I knew he wasn't, then he was fat-like. His clothes were too small too. They were tighter and woolier than was customary in Stamps. And he was blindingly handsome. Momma cried, "Bailey, my baby. Great God Bailey." And Uncle Willie stuttered, "Bu-Buh-Bailey." My brother said, "Hot dog and damn. It's him. It's our daddy." And my seven-year-old world humpty-dumptied, never to be put back together again.

His voice rang like a metal dipper hitting a bucket and he spoke English. Proper English, like the school principal, and even better. Our father sprinkled *ers* and even *errers* in his sentences as liberally as he gave out his twisted-mouth smiles. His lips pulled not down, like Uncle Willie's, but to the side and his head lay on one side or the other, but never straight on the end of his neck. He had the air of a man who did not believe what he heard or what he himself was saying. He was the first cynic I had met. "So er this is Daddy's er little man? Boy, anybody tell you errer that you er look like me?" He had Bailey in one arm and me in the other. "And Daddy's baby girl. You've errer been good children, er haven't you? Or er I guess I would have er heard about it er from Santa Claus." I was so proud of him it was hard to wait for the gossip to get around that he was in town. Wouldn't the kids be surprised at how handsome our daddy was? And that he loved us enough to come down to Stamps to visit? Everyone could tell from the way he talked and from the car and clothes that he was rich and maybe had a castle out in California. (I later learned that he had been a doorman at Santa Monica's plush Breakers Hotel.) Then the possibility of being compared with him occurred to me, and I didn't want anyone to see him. Maybe he wasn't my real father. Bailey was his son, true enough, but I was an orphan that they picked up to provide Bailey with company. . . .

Then one day he said he had to get back to California. I was relieved. My world was going to be emptier and dryer, but the agony of having him intrude into every private second would be gone. And the silent threat that had hung in the air since his arrival, the threat of his leaving someday, would be gone. I wouldn't have to wonder whether I loved him or not, or have to answer "Does Daddy's baby want to go to California with Daddy?" Bailey had told him that he wanted to go, but I had kept quiet. Momma was relieved too, although she had had a good time cooking special things for him and showing her California son off to the peasants of Arkansas. But Uncle Willie was suffering under our father's bombastic pressure, and in mother-bird fashion Momma was more concerned with her crippled offspring than the one who could fly away from the nest.

He was going to take us with him! The knowledge buzzed through my days and made me jump unexpectedly like a jack-in-the-box. Each day I found some time to walk to the pond where people went to catch sun perch and striped bass. The hours I chose to go were too early or late for fishermen, so I had the area to myself. I stood on the bank of the green dark water, and my thoughts skidded like the water spiders. Now this way, now that, now the other. Should I go with my father? Should I throw myself into the pond, and not being able to swim, join the body of L.C., the boy who drowned last summer? Should I beg Momma to let me stay with her? I could tell her that I'd take over Bailey's chores and do my own as well. Did I have the nerve to try life without Bailey? I couldn't decide on any move, so I recited a few Bible verses, and went home. . . .

Momma cut down a few give-aways that had been traded to her by white women's maids and sat long nights in the dining room sewing jumpers and skirts for me. She looked pretty sad, but each time I found her watching me she'd say, as if I had already disobeyed, "You be a good girl now. You hear? Don't you make people think I didn't raise you right. You hear?" She would have been more surprised than I had she taken me in her arms and wept at losing me. Her world was bordered on all sides with work, duty, religion and "her place." I don't think she ever knew that a deep-brooding love hung over everything she touched.

To describe my mother would be to write about a hurricane in its perfect power. Or the climbing, falling colors of a rainbow. We had been received by her mother and had waited on the edge of our seats in the overfurnished living room (Dad talked easily with our grandmother, as whitefolks talk to Blacks, unembarrassed and unapologetic). We were both fearful of Mother's coming and impatient at her delay. It is remarkable how much truth there is in the two expressions: "struck dumb" and "love at first sight." My mother's beauty literally assailed me. Her red lips (Momma said it was a sin to wear lipstick) split to show even white teeth and her fresh-butter color looked see-through clean. Her smile widened her mouth beyond her cheeks beyond her ears and seemingly through the walls to the street outside. I was struck dumb. I knew immediately why she had sent me away. She was too beautiful to have children. I had never seen a woman as pretty as she who was called "Mother." . . .

Our father left St. Louis a few days later for California, and I was neither glad nor sorry. He was a stranger, and if he chose to leave us with a stranger, it was all of one piece. . . .

Mother's boyfriend, Mr. Freeman, lived with us, or we lived with him (I never quite knew which). He was a Southerner, too, and big. But a little flabby. His breasts used to embarrass me when he walked around in his undershirt. They lay on his chest like flat titties.

Even if Mother hadn't been such a pretty woman, light-skinned with straight hair, he was lucky to get her, and he knew it. She was educated, from a well-known family, and after all, wasn't she born in St. Louis? Then she was gay. She laughed all the time and made jokes. He was grateful. I think he must have been many years older than she, but if not, he still had the sluggish inferiority of old men married to younger women. He watched her every move and when she left the room, his eyes allowed her reluctantly to go. . . .

Because of the lurid tales we read and our vivid imaginations and, probably, memories of our brief but hectic lives, Bailey and I were afflicted—he physically and I mentally. He stuttered, and I sweated through horrifying nightmares. He was constantly told to slow down and start again, and on my particularly bad nights my mother would take me in to sleep with her, in the large bed with Mr. Freeman.

Because of a need for stability, children easily become creatures of habit. After the third time in Mother's bed, I thought there was nothing strange about sleeping there.

One morning she got out of bed for an early errand, and I fell asleep again. But I awoke to a pressure, a strange feeling on my left leg. It was too soft to be a hand, and it wasn't the touch of clothes. Whatever it was, I hadn't encountered the sensation in all the years of sleeping with Momma. It didn't move, and I was too startled to. I turned my head a little to the left to see if Mr. Freeman was awake and gone, but his eyes were open and both hands were above the cover. I knew, as if I had always known, it was his "thing" on my leg.

He said, "Just stay right here, Ritie, I ain't gonna hurt you." I wasn't afraid, a little apprehensive, maybe, but not afraid. Of course I knew that lots of people did "it" and that they used their "things" to accomplish the deed, but no one I knew had ever done it to anybody. Mr. Freeman pulled me to him, and put his hand between my legs. He didn't hurt, but Momma had drilled into my head: "Keep your legs closed, and don't let anybody see your pocketbook."

"Now, I didn't hurt you. Don't get scared." He threw back the blankets and his "thing" stood up like a brown ear of corn. He took my hand and said, "Feel it." It was mushy and squirmy like the inside of a freshly killed chicken. Then he dragged me on top of his chest with his left arm, and his right hand was moving so fast and his heart was beating so hard that I was afraid that he would die. Ghost stories revealed how people who died wouldn't let go of whatever they were holding. I wondered if Mr. Freeman died holding me how I would ever get free. Would they have to break his arms to get me loose?

Finally he was quiet and then came the nice part. He held me so softly that I wished he wouldn't ever let me go. I felt at home. From the way he was holding me I knew he'd never let me go or let anything bad happen to me. This was probably my real father and we had found each other at last. But then he rolled over, leaving me in a wet place and stood up.

"I gotta talk to you, Ritie." He pulled off his shorts that had fallen to his ankles, and went into the bathroom.

It was true the bed was wet, but I knew I hadn't had an accident. Maybe Mr. Freeman had one while he was holding me. He came back with a glass of water and told me in a sour voice, "Get up. You peed in the bed." He poured water on the wet spot, and it did look like my mattress on many mornings.

Having lived in Southern strictness, I knew when to keep quiet around adults, but I did want to ask him why he said I peed when I was sure he didn't believe that. If he thought I was naughty, would that mean that he would never hold me again? Or admit that he was my father? I had made him ashamed of me.

"Ritie, you love Bailey?" He sat down on the bed and I came close, hoping. "Yes." He was bending down, pulling on his socks, and his back was so large and friendly I wanted to rest my head on it.

"If you ever tell anybody what we did, I'll have to kill Bailey." What had we done? We? Obviously he didn't mean my peeing in the bed. I didn't understand and didn't dare ask him. It had something to do with his holding me. But there was no chance to ask Bailey either, because that would be telling what we had done. The thought that he might kill Bailey stunned me. After he left the room I thought about telling Mother that I hadn't peed in the bed, but then if she asked me what happened I'd have to tell her about Mr. Freeman holding me, and that wouldn't do. . . .

On a late spring Saturday, after our chores (nothing like those in Stamps) were done, Bailey and I were going out, he to play baseball and I to the library. Mr. Freeman said to me, after Bailey had gone downstairs, "Ritie, go get some milk for the house."

Mother usually brought milk when she came in, but that morning as Bailey and I straightened the living room her bedroom door had been open, and we knew that she hadn't come home the night before.

He gave me money and I rushed to the store and back to the house. After putting the milk in the icebox, I turned and had just reached the front door when I heard, "Ritie." He was sitting in the big chair by the radio. "Ritie, come here." I didn't think about the holding time until I got close to him. His pants were open and his "thing" was standing out of his britches by itself.

"No, sir, Mr. Freeman." I started to back away. I didn't want to touch that mushy-hard thing again, and I didn't need him to hold me any more. He grabbed my arm and pulled me between his legs. His face was still and looked kind, but he didn't smile or blink his eyes. Nothing. He did nothing, except reach his left hand around to turn on the radio without even looking at it. Over the noise of music and static, he said, "Now, this ain't gonna hurt you much. You liked it before didn't you?"

I didn't want to admit that I had in fact liked his holding me or that I had liked his smell or the hard heart-beating, so I said nothing. And his face became like the face of one of those mean natives the Phantom was always having to beat up.

His legs were squeezing my waist. "Pull down your drawers." I hesitated for two reasons: he was holding me too tight to move, and I was sure that any minute my mother or Bailey or the Green Hornet would burst in the door and save me.

"We was just playing before." He released me enough to snatch down my bloomers, and then he dragged me closer to him. Turning the radio up loud, too loud, he said, "If you scream, I'm gonna kill you. And if you tell, I'm gonna kill Bailey." I could tell he meant what he said. I couldn't understand why he wanted to kill my brother. Neither of us had done anything to him. And then.

Then there was the pain. A breaking and entering when even the senses are torn apart. The act of rape on an eight-year-old body is a matter of the needle giving because the camel can't. The child gives, because the body can, and the mind of the violator cannot.

I thought I had died—I woke up in a white-walled world, and it had to be heaven. But Mr. Freeman was there and he was washing me. His hands shook, but he held me upright in the tub and washed my legs. "I didn't mean to hurt you, Ritie. I didn't mean it. But don't you tell . . . Remember, don't you tell a soul."

I felt cool and very clean and just a little tired. "No, sir, Mr. Freeman, I won't tell." I was somewhere above everything. "It's just that I'm so tired I'll just go and lay down a while, please," I whispered to him. I thought if I spoke out loud, he might become frightened and hurt me again. He dried me and handed me my bloomers. "Put these on and go to the library. Your momma ought to be coming home soon. You just act natural."

Walking down the street, I felt the wet on my pants, and my hips seemed to be coming out of their sockets. I couldn't sit long on the hard seats in the library (they had been constructed for children), so I walked by the empty lot where Bailey was playing ball, but he wasn't there. I stood for a while and watched the big boys tear around the dusty diamond and then headed home.

After two blocks, I knew I'd never make it. Not unless I counted every step and stepped on every crack. I had started to burn between my legs more than the time I'd wasted Sloan's Liniment on myself. My legs throbbed, or rather the insides of my thighs throbbed, with the same force that Mr. Freeman's heart had beaten. Thrum . . . step . . . thrum . . . step . . . STEP ON THE CRACK . . . thrum . . . step. I went up the stairs one at a, one at a, one at a time. No one was in the living room, so I went straight to bed, after hiding my red-and-yellow-stained drawers under the mattress.

When Mother came in she said, "Well, young lady, I believe this is the first time I've seen you go to bed without being told. You must be sick."

I wasn't sick, but the pit of my stomach was on fire—how could I tell her that? Bailey came in later and asked me what the matter was. There was nothing to tell him. When Mother called us to eat and I said I wasn't hungry, she laid her cool hand on my forehead and cheeks. "Maybe it's the measles. They say they're going around the neighborhood." After she took my temperature she said, "You have a little fever. You've probably just caught them."

Mr. Freeman took up the whole doorway, "Then Bailey ought not to be in there with her. Unless you want a house full of sick children." She answered over her shoulder, "He may as well have them now as later. Get them over with." She brushed by Mr. Freeman as if he were made of cotton. "Come on, Junior. Get some cool towels and wipe your sister's face."

As Bailey left the room, Mr. Freeman advanced to the bed. He leaned over, his whole face a threat that could have smothered me. "If you tell . . ." And again so softly, I almost didn't hear it—"If you tell." I couldn't summon up the energy to answer him. He had to know that I wasn't going to tell anything. Bailey came in with the towels and Mr. Freeman walked out.

Later Mother made a broth and sat on the edge of the bed to feed me. The liquid went down my throat like bones. My belly and behind were as heavy as cold iron, but it seemed my head had gone away and pure air had replaced it on my shoulders. Bailey read to me from *The Rover Boys* until he got sleepy and went to bed.

That night I kept waking to hear Mother and Mr. Freeman arguing. I couldn't hear what they were saying, but I did hope that she wouldn't make him so mad that he'd hurt her too. I knew he could do it, with his cold face and empty eyes. Their voices came in faster and faster, the high sounds on the heels of the lows. I would have liked to have gone in. Just passed through as if I were going to the toilet. Just show my face and they might stop, but my legs refused to move. I could move the toes and ankles, but the knees had turned to wood.

Maybe I slept, but soon morning was there and Mother was pretty over my bed. "How're you feeling, baby?"

"Fine, Mother." An instinctive answer. "Where's Bailey?"

She said he was still asleep but that she hadn't slept all night. She had been in my room off and on to see about me. I asked her where Mr. Freeman was, and her face chilled with remembered anger. "He's gone. Moved this morning. I'm going to take your temperature after I put on your Cream of Wheat."

Could I tell her now? The terrible pain assured me that I couldn't. What he did to me, and what I allowed, must have been very bad if already God let me hurt so much. If Mr. Freeman was gone, did that mean Bailey was out of danger? And if so, if I told him, would he still love me?

After Mother took my temperature, she said she was going to bed for a while but to wake her if I felt sicker. She told Bailey to watch my face and arms for spots and when they came up he could paint them with calamine lotion.

That Sunday goes and comes in my memory like a bad connection on an overseas telephone call. Once, Bailey was reading *The Katzenjammer Kids* to me, and then without a pause for sleeping, Mother was looking closely at my face, and soup trickled down my chin and some got into my mouth and I choked. Then there was a doctor who took my temperature and held my wrist.

"Bailey!" I supposed I had screamed, for he materialized suddenly, and I asked him to help me and we'd run away to California or France or Chicago. I knew that I was dying and, in fact, I longed for death, but I didn't want to die anywhere near Mr. Freeman. I knew that even now he wouldn't have allowed death to have me unless he wished it to.

Mother said I should be bathed and the linens had to be changed since I had sweat so much. But when they tried to move me I fought, and even Bailey couldn't hold me. Then she picked me up in her arms and the terror abated for a while. Bailey began to change the bed. As he pulled off the soiled sheets he dislodged the panties I had put under the mattress. They fell at Mother's feet. . . .

In the hospital, Bailey told me that I had to tell who did that to me, or the man would hurt another little girl. When I explained that I couldn't tell because the man would kill him, Bailey said knowingly, "He can't kill me. I won't let him." And of course I believed him. Bailey didn't lie to me. So I told him.

Bailey cried at the side of my bed until I started to cry too. Almost fifteen years passed before I saw my brother cry again.

The barrenness of Stamps was exactly what I wanted, without will or consciousness. After St. Louis, with its noise and activity, its trucks and buses, and loud family gatherings, I welcomed the obscure lanes and lonely bungalows set back deep in dirt yards. . . .

For an indeterminate time, nothing was demanded of me or of Bailey. We were, after all, Mrs. Henderson's California grandchildren, and had been away on a glamorous trip way up North to the fabulous St. Louis. Our father had come the year before, driving a big, shiny automobile and speaking the King's English with a big city accent, so all we had to do was lie quiet for months and rake in the profits of our adventures. . . .

People, except Momma and Uncle Willie, accepted my unwillingness to talk as a natural outgrowth of a reluctant return to the South. And an indication that I was pining for the high times we had had in the big city. Then, too, I was well known for being "tender-hearted." Southern Negroes used that term to mean sensitive and tended to look upon a person with that affliction as being a little sick or in delicate health. So I was not so much forgiven as I was understood.

For nearly a year, I sopped around the house, the Store, the school and the church, like an old biscuit, dirty and inedible. Then I met, or rather got to know, the lady who threw me my first life line.

Mrs. Bertha Flowers was the aristocrat of Black Stamps. She had the grace of control to appear warm in the coldest weather, and on the Arkansas summer days it seemed she had a private breeze which swirled around, cooling her. She was thin without the taut look of wiry people, and her printed voile dresses and flowered hats were as right for her as denim overalls for a farmer. She was our side's answer to the richest white woman in town.

Her skin was a rich black that would have peeled like a plum if snagged, but then no one would have thought of getting close enough to Mrs. Flowers to ruffle her dress, let alone snag her skin. She didn't encourage familiarity. She wore gloves too. . . .

She was one of the few gentlewomen I have ever known, and

has remained throughout my life the measure of what a human being can be. . . .

She acted just as refined as whitefolks in the movies and books and she was more beautiful, for none of them could have come near that warm color without looking gray by comparison. . . .

One summer afternoon, sweet-milk fresh in my memory, she stopped at the Store to buy provisions. Another Negro woman of her health and age would have been expected to carry the paper sacks home in one hand, but Momma said, "Sister Flowers, I'll send Bailey up to your house with these things."

She smiled that slow dragging smile, "Thank you, Mrs. Henderson. I'd prefer Marguerite, though." My name was beautiful when she said it. "I've been meaning to talk to her, anyway." They gave each other age-group looks.

Momma said, "Well, that's all right then. Sister, go and change your dress. You going to Sister Flowers'." . . .

There was a little path beside the rocky road, and Mrs. Flowers walked in front swinging her arms and picking her way over the stones.

She said, without turning her head, to me, "I hear you're doing very good school work, Marguerite, but that it's all written. The teachers report that they have trouble getting you to talk in class." We passed the triangular farm on our left and the path widened to allow us to walk together. I hung back in the separate unasked and unanswerable questions.

"Come and walk along with me, Marguerite." I couldn't have refused even if I wanted to. She pronounced my name so nicely. Or more correctly, she spoke each word with such clarity that I was certain a foreigner who didn't understand English could have understood her.

"Now no one is going to make you talk—possibly no one can. But bear in mind, language is man's way of communicating with his fellow man and it is language alone which separates him from the lower animals." That was a totally new idea to me, and I would need time to think about it.

"Your grandmother says you read a lot. Every chance you get. That's good, but not good enough. Words mean more than what is set down on paper. It takes the human voice to infuse them with the shades of deeper meaning."

I memorized the part about the human voice infusing words. It seemed so valid and poetic.

She said she was going to give me some books and that I not only must read them, I must read them aloud. She suggested that I try to make a sentence sound in as many different ways as possible.

"I'll accept no excuse if you return a book to me that has been badly handled." My imagination boggled at the punishment I would deserve if in fact I did abuse a book of Mrs. Flowers'. Death would be too kind and brief. . . .

She said that I must always be intolerant of ignorance but understanding of illiteracy. That some people, unable to go to school, were more educated and even more intelligent than college professors. She encouraged me to listen carefully to what country people called mother wit. That in those homely sayings was couched the collective wisdom of generations. . . .

When I finished the cookies she brushed off the table and brought a thick, small book from the bookcase. I had read *A Tale of Two Cities* and found it up to my standards as a romantic novel. She opened the first page and I heard poetry for the first time in my life.

"It was the best of times and the worst of times . . ." Her voice slid in and curved down through and over the words. She was nearly singing. I wanted to look at the pages. Were they the same that I had read? Or were there notes, music, lined on the pages, as in a hymn book? Her sounds began cascading gently. I knew from listening to a thousand preachers that she was nearing the end of her reading, and I hadn't really heard, heard to understand, a single word.

"How do you like that?"

It occurred to me that she expected a response. The sweet vanilla flavor was still on my tongue and her reading was a wonder in my ears. I had to speak.

I said, "Yes, ma'am." It was the least I could do, but it was the most also.

"There's one more thing. Take this book of poems and memorize one for me. Next time you pay me a visit, I want you to recite."

I have tried often to search behind the sophistication of years for the enchantment I so easily found in those gifts. The essence escapes but its aura remains. To be allowed, no, invited, into the private lives of strangers, and to share their joys and fears, was a chance to exchange the Southern bitter wormwood for a cup of mead with Beowulf or a hot cup of tea and milk with Oliver Twist. When I said aloud, "It is a far, far better thing that I do, than I have ever done . . ." tears of love filled my eyes at my selflessness. . . .

Childhood's logic never asks to be proved (all conclusions are absolute). I didn't question why Mrs. Flowers had singled me out for attention, nor did it occur to me that Momma might have asked her to give me a little talking to. All I cared about was that she had made tea cookies for *me* and read to *me* from her favorite book. It was enough to prove that she liked me.

Momma told us one day that she was taking us to California. She explained that we were growing up, that we needed to be with our parents, that Uncle Willie was, after all, crippled, that she was getting old. All true, and yet none of those truths satisfied our need for The Truth. The Store and the rooms in back became a going-away factory. Momma sat at the sewing machine all hours, making and remaking clothes for use in California. Neighbors brought out of their trunks pieces of material that had been packed away for decades in blankets of mothballs (I'm certain I was the only girl in California who went to school in water-marked moire skirts and yellowed satin blouses, satin-back crepe dresses and crepe de Chine underwear). . . .

Our transportation was Momma's major concern for some weeks. She had arranged with a railroad employee to provide her with a pass in exchange for groceries. The pass allowed a reduction in her fare only, and even that had to be approved, so we were made to abide in a kind of limbo until white people we would never see, in offices we would never visit, signed and stamped and mailed the pass back to Momma. My fare had to be paid in "ready cash." That sudden drain on the nickel-plated cash register lopsided our financial stability. Momma decided Bailey couldn't accompany us, since we had to use the pass during a set time, but that he would follow within a month or so when outstanding bills were paid. Although our mother now lived in San Francisco, Momma must have felt it wiser to go first to Los Angeles where our father was. She dictated letters to me, advising them both that we were on our way.

And we were on our way, but unable to say when. Our clothes were washed, ironed and packed, so for an immobile time we wore those things not good enough to glow under the California sun. Neighbors who understood the complications of travel, said good-bye a million times. . . .

Mother's beauty made her powerful and her power made her unflinchingly honest. When we asked her what she did, what her job was, she walked us to Oakland's Seventh Street, where dusty bars and smoke shops sat in the laps of storefront churches. She pointed out Raincoat's Pinochle Parlor and Slim Jenkins' pretentious saloon. Some nights she played pinochle for money or ran a poker game at Mother Smith's or stopped at Slim's for a few drinks. She told us that she had never cheated anybody and wasn't making any preparations to do so. Her work was as honest as the job held by fat Mrs. Walker (a maid), who lived next door to us, and "a damn sight better paid." She wouldn't bust suds for anybody nor be anyone's kitchen bitch. The good Lord gave her a mind and she intended to use it to support her mother and her children. She didn't need to add "And have a little fun along the way." . . .

With all her jollity, Vivian Baxter had no mercy. There was a saying in Oakland at the time which, if she didn't say it herself, explained her attitude. The saying was, "Sympathy is next to shit in the dictionary, and I can't even read." Her temper had not di-minished with the passing of time, and when a passionate nature is not eased with moments of compassion, melodrama is likely to take the stage.

World War II started on a Sunday afternoon when I was on my way to the movies. People in the streets shouted, "We're at war. We've declared war on Japan."

I ran all the way home. Not too sure I wouldn't be bombed before I reached Bailey and Mother. Grandmother Baxter calmed my anxiety by explaining that America would not be bombed, not as long as Franklin Delano Roosevelt was President. He was, after all, a politician's politician and he knew what he was doing.

Soon after, Mother married Daddy Clidell, who turned out to be the first father I would know. He was a successful businessman, and he and Mother moved us to San Francisco. Uncle Tommy, Uncle Billy and Grandmother Baxter remained in the big house in Oak-land. . . .

Although my grades were very good (I had been put up two semesters on my arrival from Stamps), I found myself unable to settle down in the high school. It was an institution for girls near my house, and the young ladies were faster, brasher, meaner and more prejudiced than any I had met at Lafayette County Training School. Many of the Negro girls were, like me, straight from the South, but they had known or claimed to have known the bright lights of Big D (Dallas) or T Town (Tulsa, Oklahoma), and their language bore up their claims. They strutted with an aura of invincibility, and along with some of the Mexican students who put knives in their tall pompadours they absolutely intimidated the white girls and those Black and Mexican students who had no shield of fearlessness. Fortunately I was transferred to George Washington High School.

The beautiful buildings sat on a moderate hill in the white residential district, some sixty blocks from the Negro neighborhood. For the first semester, I was one of three Black students in the school, and in that rarefied atmosphere I came to love my people more. Mornings as the streetcar traversed my ghetto I experienced a mixture of dread and trauma. I knew that all too soon we would be out of my familiar setting, and Blacks who were on the streetcar when I got on would all be gone and I alone would face the forty blocks of neat streets, smooth lawns, white houses and rich children.

In the evenings on the way home the sensations were joy, anticipation and relief at the first sign which said BARBECUE or DO DROP INN or HOME COOKING or at the first brown faces on the streets. I recognized that I was again in my country.

In the school itself I was disappointed to find that I was not the most brilliant or even nearly the most brilliant student. The white kids had better vocabularies than I and, what was more appalling, less fear in the classrooms. They never hesitated to hold up their hands in response to a teacher's question; even when they were wrong they were wrong aggressively, while I had to be certain about all my facts before I dared to call attention to myself.

George Washington High School was the first real school I attended. My entire stay there might have been time lost if it hadn't been for the unique personality of a brilliant teacher. Miss Kirwin was that rare educator who was in love with information. I will always believe that her love of teaching came not so much from her liking for students but from her desire to make sure that some of the things she knew would find repositories so that they could be shared again. . . .

I was prepared to accept Daddy Clidell as one more faceless name added to Mother's roster of conquests. I had trained myself so successfully through the years to display interest, or at least attention, while my mind skipped free on other subjects that I could have lived in his house without ever seeing him and without his becoming the wiser. But his character beckoned and elicited admiration. He was a simple man who had no inferiority complex about his lack of education and, even more amazing, no superiority complex because he had succeeded despite that lack. He would say often, "I been to school three years in my life. In Slaten, Texas, times was hard, and I had to help my daddy on the farm."

No recriminations lay hidden under the plain statement, nor was there boasting when he said, "If I'm living a little better now, it's because I treats everybody right."

He owned apartment buildings and, later, pool halls, and was famous for being that rarity "a man of honor." He didn't suffer, as many "honest men" do, from the detestable righteousness that diminishes their virtue. He knew cards and men's hearts. So during the age when Mother was exposing us to certain facts of life, like personal hygiene, proper posture, table manners, good restaurants and tipping practices, Daddy Clidell taught me to play poker, blackjack, tonk and high, low, Jick, Jack and the Game. He wore expensively tailored suits and a large yellow diamond stickpin. Except for the jewelry, he was a conservative dresser and carried himself with the unconscious pomp of a man of secure means. Unexpectedly, I resembled him, and when he, Mother and I walked down the street his friends often said, "Clidell, that's sure your daughter. Ain't no way you can deny her."

Proud laughter followed those declarations, for he had never had children.

My education and that of my Black associates were quite different from the education of our white schoolmates. In the classroom we all learned past participles, but in the streets and in our homes the Blacks learned to drop s's from plurals and suffixes from past-tense verbs. We were alert to the gap separating the written word from the colloquial. We learned to slide out of one language and into another without being conscious of the effort. At school, in a given situation, we might respond with "That's not unusual." But in the street, meeting the same situation, we easily said, "It be's like that sometimes."

Without willing it, I had gone from being ignorant of being ignorant to being aware of being aware. And the worst part of my awareness was that I didn't know what I was aware of. I knew I knew very little, but I was certain that the things I had yet to learn wouldn't be taught to me at George Washington High School.

I began to cut classes, to walk in Golden Gate Park or wander along the shiny counter of the Emporium Department Store. When Mother discovered that I was playing truant, she told me that if I didn't want to go to school one day, if there were no tests being held, and if my school work was up to standard, all I had to do was tell her and I could stay home. She said that she didn't want some white woman calling her up to tell her something about her child that she didn't know. And she didn't want to be put in the position of lying to a white woman because I wasn't woman enough to speak up. That put an end to my truancy, but nothing appeared to lighten the long gloomy day that going to school became.

To be left alone on the tightrope of youthful unknowing is to experience the excruciating beauty of full freedom and the threat of eternal indecision. Few, if any, survive their teens. Most surrender to the vague but murderous pressure of adult conformity. It becomes easier to die and avoid conflicts than to maintain a constant battle with the superior forces of maturity. . . .

The Black female is assaulted in her tender years by all those common forces of nature at the same time that she is caught in the tripartite crossfire of masculine prejudice, white illogical hate and Black lack of power.

The fact that the adult American Negro female emerges a formidable character is often met with amazement, distaste and even belligerence. It is seldom accepted as an inevitable outcome of the struggle won by survivors and deserves respect if not enthusiastic acceptance.

The Well of Loneliness was my introduction to lesbianism and what I thought of as pornography. For months the book was both a treat and a threat. It allowed me to see a little of the mysterious world of the pervert. It stimulated my libido and I told myself that it was educational because it informed me of the difficulties in the secret world of the pervert. I was certain that I didn't know any perverts. . . .

A classmate of mine, whose mother had rooms for herself and

her daughter in a ladies' residence, had stayed out beyond closing time. She telephoned me to ask if she could sleep at my house. Mother gave her permission, providing my friend telephoned her mother from our house.

When she arrived, I got out of bed and we went to the upstairs kitchen to make hot chocolate. In my room we shared mean gossip about our friends, giggled over boys and whined about school and the tedium of life. The unusualness of having someone sleep in my bed (I'd never slept with anyone except my grandmothers) and the frivolous laughter in the middle of the night made me forget simple courtesies. My friend had to remind me that she had nothing to sleep in. I gave her one of my gowns, and without curiosity or interest I watched her pull off her clothes. At none of the early stages of undressing was I in the least conscious of her body. And then suddenly, for the briefest eye span, I saw her breasts. I was stunned.

They were shaped like light-brown falsies in the five-and-ten-cent store, but they were real. They made all the nude paintings I had seen in museums come to life. In a word they were beautiful. A universe divided what she had from what I had. She was a woman.

My gown was too snug for her and much too long, and when she wanted to laugh at her ridiculous image I found that humor had left me without a promise to return.

Had I been older I might have thought that I was moved by both an esthetic sense of beauty and the pure emotion of envy. But those possibilities did not occur to me when I needed them. All I knew was that I had been moved by looking at a woman's breasts. . . .

I somersaulted deeper into my snuggery of misery. After a thorough self-examination, in the light of all I had read and heard about dykes and bulldaggers, I reasoned that I had none of the obvious traits—I didn't wear trousers, or have big shoulders or go in for sports, or walk like a man or even want to touch a woman. I wanted to be a woman, but that seemed to me to be a world to which I was to be eternally refused entrance.

What I needed was a boyfriend. A boyfriend would clarify my position to the world and, even more important, to myself. A boyfriend's acceptance of me would guide me into that strange and exotic land of frills and femininity. . . .

I believe most plain girls are virtuous because of the scarcity of opportunity to be otherwise. They shield themselves with an aura of unavailableness (for which after a time they begin to take credit) largely as a defense tactic.

In my particular case, I could not hide behind the curtain of voluntary goodness. I was being crushed by two unrelenting forces: the uneasy suspicion that I might not be a normal female and my newly awakening sexual appetite.

I decided to take matters into my own hands. (An unfortunate but apt phrase.)

Up the hill from our house, and on the same side of the street, lived two handsome brothers. They were easily the most eligible young men in the neighborhood. If I was going to venture into sex, I saw no reason why I shouldn't make my experiment with the best of the lot. I didn't really expect to capture either brother on a permanent basis, but I thought if I could hook one temporarily I might be able to work the relationship into something more lasting.

I planned a chart for seduction with surprise as my opening ploy. One evening as I walked up the hill suffering from youth's vague malaise (there was simply nothing to do), the brother I had chosen came walking directly into my trap.

"Hello, Marguerite." He nearly passed me.

I put the plan into action. "Hey." I plunged, "Would you like to have sexual intercourse with me?" Things were going according to the chart. His mouth hung open like a garden gate. I had the advantage and so I pressed it.

"Take me somewhere."

His response lacked dignity, but in fairness to him I admit that I had left him little chance to be suave.

He asked, "You mean, you're going to give me some trim?"

I assured him that that was exactly what I was about to give him. Even as the scene was being enacted I realized the imbalance in his values. He thought I was giving him something, and the fact of the matter was that it was my intention to take something from him. His good looks and popularity had made him so inordinately conceited that they blinded him to that possibility.

We went to a furnished room occupied by one of his friends, who understood the situation immediately and got his coat and left us alone. The seductee quickly turned off the lights. I would have preferred them left on, but didn't want to appear more aggressive than I had been already. If that was possible.

I was excited rather than nervous, and hopeful instead of frightened. I had not considered how physical an act of seduction would be. I had anticipated long soulful tongued kisses and gentle caresses. But there was no romance in the knee which forced my legs, nor in the rub of hairy skin on my chest.

Unredeemed by shared tenderness, the time was spent in laborious gropings, pullings, yankings and jerkings.

Not one word was spoken.

My partner showed that our experience had reached its climax by getting up abruptly, and my main concern was how to get home quickly. He may have sensed that he had been used, or his disinterest may have been an indication that I was less than gratifying. Neither possibility bothered me.

Outside on the street we left each other with little more than "Okay, see you around."

Thanks to Mr. Freeman nine years before, I had had no pain of entry to endure, and because of the absence of romantic involvement neither of us felt much had happened.

At home I reviewed the failure and tried to evaluate my new position. I had had a man. I had been had. I not only didn't enjoy it, but my normalcy was still a question. . . .

Three weeks later, having thought very little of the strange and strangely empty night, I found myself pregnant. . . .

The world had ended, and I was the only person who knew it. People walked along the streets as if the pavements hadn't all crumbled beneath their feet. They pretended to breathe in and out while all the time I knew the air had been sucked away in a monstrous inhalation from God Himself. I alone was suffocating in the nightmare.

The little pleasure I was able to take from the fact that if I could have a baby I obviously wasn't a lesbian was crowded into my mind's tiniest corner by the massive pushing in of fear, guilt and self-revulsion. . . .

. . . this time I had to face the fact that I had brought my new catastrophe upon myself. How was I to blame the innocent man whom I had lured into making love to me? . . .

All my motions focalized on pretending to be that guileless schoolgirl who had nothing more wearying to think about than mid-term exams. Strangely enough, I very nearly caught the essence of teenage capriciousness as I played the role. Except that there were times when physically I couldn't deny to myself that something very important was taking place in my body. . . .

School recovered its lost magic. For the first time since Stamps, information was exciting for itself alone. I burrowed myself into caves of facts, and found delight in the logical resolutions of mathematics.

I credit my new reactions (although I didn't know at the time that I had learned anything from them) to the fact that during what surely must have been a critical period I was not dragged down by hopelessness. Life had a conveyor-belt quality. It went on unpursued and unpursuing, and my only thought was to remain erect, and keep my secret along with my balance. . . .

As my sixth month approached, Mother left San Francisco for Alaska. She was to open a night club and planned to stay three or four months until it got on its feet. Daddy Clidell was to look after me but I was more or less left on my own recognizance and under the unsteady gaze of our lady roomers.

Mother left the city amid a happy and cheerful send-off party (after all how many Negroes were in Alaska?), and I felt treacherous allowing her to go without informing her that she was soon to be a grandmother. . . .

Two days after V-Day, I stood with the San Francisco Summer School class at Mission High School and received my diploma. That evening, in the bosom of the now-dear family home I uncoiled my fearful secret and in a brave gesture left a note on Daddy Clidell's bed. It read: *Dear Parents, I am sorry to bring this disgrace on the family, but I am pregnant. Marguerite.*

The confusion that ensued when I explained to my stepfather that I expected to deliver the baby in three weeks, more or less, was reminiscent of a Molière comedy. Except that it was funny only years later. Daddy Clidell told Mother that I was "three weeks gone." Mother, regarding me as a woman for the first time, said indignantly, "She's more than any three weeks." They both accepted the fact that I was further along than they had first been told but found it nearly impossible to believe that I had carried a baby, eight months and one week, without their being any the wiser.

Mother asked, "Who is the boy?" I told her. She recalled him, faintly.

"Do you want to marry him?"

"No."

"Does he want to marry you?" The father had stopped speaking to me during my fourth month.

"No."

"Well, that's that. No use ruining three lives." There was no overt or subtle condemnation. She was Vivian Baxter Jackson. Hoping for the best, prepared for the worst, and unsurprised by anything in between.

Daddy Clidell assured me that I had nothing to worry about. That "women been gittin' pregnant ever since Eve ate the apple." He sent one of his waitresses to I. Magnin's to buy maternity dresses for me. For the next two weeks I whirled around the city going to doctors, taking vitamin shots and pills, buying clothes for the baby, and except for the rare moments alone, enjoying the imminent blessed event.

After a short labor, and without too much pain (I decided that the pain of delivery was overrated), my son was born. Just as gratefulness was confused in my mind with love, so possession became mixed up with motherhood. I had a baby. He was beautiful and mine. Totally mine. No one had bought him for me. No one had helped me endure the sickly gray months. I had had help in the child's conception, but no one could deny that I had had an immaculate pregnancy. . . .

Totally my possession, and I was afraid to touch him. Home from the hospital, I sat for hours by his bassinet and absorbed his mysterious perfection. His extremities were so dainty they appeared unfinished. Mother handled him easily with the casual confidence of a baby nurse, but I dreaded being forced to change his diapers. Wasn't I famous for awkwardness? Suppose I let him slip, or put my fingers on that throbbing pulse on the top of his head?

Mother came to my bed one night bringing my three-week-old baby. She pulled the cover back and told me to get up and hold him while she put rubber sheets on my bed. She explained that he was going to sleep with me. . . .

I lay on the edge of the bed, stiff with fear, and vowed not to sleep all night long. But the eat-sleep routine I had begun in the hospital, and kept up under Mother's dictatorial command, got the better of me. I dropped off.

My shoulder was shaken gently. Mother whispered, "Maya, wake up. But don't move."

I knew immediately that the awakening had to do with the baby. I tensed. "I'm awake."

She turned the light on and said, "Look at the baby." My fears were so powerful I couldn't move to look at the center of the bed. She said again, "Look at the baby." I didn't hear the sadness in her voice, and that helped me to break the bonds of terror. The baby was no longer in the center of the bed. At first I thought he had moved. But after closer investigation I found that I was lying on my stomach with my arm bent at a right angle. Under the tent of blanket, which was poled by my elbow and forearm, the baby slept touching my side.

Mother whispered, "See, you don't have to think about doing the right thing. If you're for the right thing, then you do it without thinking."

She turned out the light and I patted my son's body lightly and went back to sleep.

Research Is a Passion with Me: Women Scientists and Physicians

The women scientists and physicians whose narratives appear here displayed all the characteristics identified as typical of the life formation of male scientists. Their narratives describe their unusually precocious early intellectual life and their sense of closeness to, and wonder about, nature. Margaret Morse Nice (1883–1974), for instance, described keeping the first field notes of her observations of birds at the age of eight.

Cecilia Payne Gaposchkin (1900–1979) recalled her first sense of discovery at the age of eight, on seeing and recognizing a plant her mother had described earlier as growing wild.

These women's narratives show the sense of being set apart—and socially isolated—reported by male scientists. Margaret Mead (1901–1978), for instance, described her feelings of "specialness" as arising from her unusual education, her parents' expectations, and her own craving for intellectual intensity.

These narratives often describe unusually liberal or innovative early schooling as a shaping force in their authors' intellectual development. The Poughkeepsie school of S. Josephine Baker (1873–1945) in the 1880s had no graded classes, no marks, reports, or examinations, and allowed each student to proceed according to her ability to complete a particular course. Mead's mother and grandmother played critical roles in her early education. Her paternal grandmother set her to observing and keeping notes on the development of Mead's two younger sisters, a task she began at the age of eight.

While precocious intellectual development, closeness to nature, and unconventional schooling are recurring themes in the lives of male scientists, there are many aspects of experience unique to gifted women with scientific ambitions. A common theme in these stories is the drive to make up to a loved parent for not being a boy. Baker knew her father craved a son. She wrote, "Trying to make it up to Father for being a girl, which went right on even after the next arrival delighted the household by being a boy, did turn me into a tomboy type in the early days." In her sixteenth year, Baker's younger brother, followed shortly by her father, died in a typhoid epidemic. Nice described a similar loss when aged thirteen and attributed her increased interest in ornithology to the loneliness that followed her brother's death.

Most of these narratives report countless examples of discrimination, although Margaret Floy Washburn (1871–1939) and Margaret Mead stoutly denied the experience in working relationships with male colleagues. Washburn's narrative is less than candid in its account of her year at Columbia, where the trustees delayed her admission for an entire semester before agreeing that she could audit graduate courses in psychology, though she could not earn credit toward a degree. Her decision to enroll at Cornell the following year was prompted by the discovery that she could be admitted as a degree candidate there. Her memoir makes the reader think her transfer was a matter of curricular choice rather than the response to discrimination she preferred not to acknowledge.

Both Mead and Washburn stressed their strongly positive experience with mentors and colleagues. In her first encounter with the great Columbia experimental psychologist Dr. James McKeen Cattell, Washburn impressed him with her seriousness as a researcher. Yet, when Washburn completed her Cornell doctorate, no job was waiting for her as they were for her male colleagues. When she finally found one, it paid half the salary of her male counterparts. Nonetheless, her friendships with male colleagues were sustaining. When Washburn fell ill during her first years as a faculty member at Wells College in upper New York State, two senior male colleagues from Cornell volunteered to teach her courses until her health was restored, thereby retaining her job for her.

Mead stressed her ease with being a woman and the pattern of strong women in her family as factors which outweighed her father's reluctance to meet the cost of her education and the hostility she encountered as an intellectual in the philistine, sorority-dominated world of her early undergraduate years at DePauw University. At Barnard and Columbia, it was Ruth Benedict's presence and capacity to interpret the distant Franz Boas that attracted Mead into anthropology.

Both Mead and Hortense Powdermaker (1896–1970) were restricted in their choice of sites for fieldwork because they were women. Boas thought that Mead's interest in cultural change was misplaced and that Polynesia, the fieldwork site for which she was best prepared, was too dangerous an environment for a young woman alone. Mead was stubbornly persistent about her wish to work there; Boas insisted that she study adolescence among American Indians. In the end Mead persuaded him to let her work in Polynesia but on his subject, adolescence, and at a site of Boas's choice. Nice dealt with her parents' fears about a young college girl exploring bird-watching sites on the Holyoke range by buying a revolver and learning how to use it, ignoring maternal complaints that shooting was "not an appropriate pastime for young women."

Powdermaker had a similar experience in 1929, as a student of Bronislaw Malinowski at the London School of Economics. Malinowski was willing to accept her chosen site in the mountains of New Guinea, but the government of the Australian mandate refused to permit the visit because they did not want to accept responsibility for a woman studying at so remote a location. Powdermaker, like Mead, was directed to a site where ships called regularly, in her case, a village on the island of New Ireland.

Both Baker and Nice described periods of depression during their girlhoods because of the restrictions placed on their ambitions and intellectual interests by family and friends opposed to women's education and distrustful of women's careers. Baker met the conventional opposition to a woman seeking medical training and, after her graduation, struggled mightily to overcome the popular prejudice against being treated by a woman doctor. Her low spirits were raised by friendship with other women physicians and by the lively cultural life of New York City.

Nice had no such support. Her parents opposed their daughter's intellectual aspirations, and her early marriage to Leonard Blaine Nice obliged her to abandon further formal education in science following the birth of the first of her four children in 1910. She made a virtue of necessity and trained as a child psychologist so that she could do research on the acquisition of speech, using her children as subjects. Nonetheless, she was subject to crippling bouts of depression until her decision in 1920 to return to the study of ornithology. "Research is a passion with me," she wrote in her diary in 1919, "it drives me; it is my relentless master."

Nice could practice her profession as a solitary housewife, untroubled by dress codes and utterly removed from daily encounters with her predominantly male profession. Baker, working in New York, first in private practice and then as a department head in the New York Department of Health, was conscious of the need to camouflage her femininity and blend easily with the male world in which she operated virtually alone. She was grateful for the Gibson Girl style of dress, which permitted her to wear mannishly tailored suits in dark colors so as, in her words, "not to draw much attention to my femininity."

Most of these narratives show us women who eventually succeeded in transcending the constraints of genteel female mores and attitudes. Baker was capable of knocking a drunk down a flight of stairs in order to concentrate on delivering a slum woman's baby. Powdermaker found joyful escape from polite Jewish society in her fieldwork in the village of Lesu. Nice eventually turned her husband and children into aides for her ornithological research. Payne Gaposchkin found the place in her profession of which she had dreamed as a young researcher and eventually wrested from a reluctant Harvard administration the recognition which was her due.

Mead's three marriages represented the cheerful flaunting of the constraining view of women against which she had been obliged to struggle in her father and her censorious fellow students at DePauw. So did her lesbian relationships, unavowed in her memoir but hinted at in her descriptions of the powerful women in her family and of the important friendships forged with women in her college and graduate student years. Washburn alone remained enmeshed in her family of birth, grateful that her appointment at Vassar, in no sense a research institution, allowed her to spend every weekend with her parents. Yet her energy and passion for research led to significant contributions to the study of animal behavior during every one of her years as a teacher of undergraduates.

These narratives are remarkable for the degree to which each tells its story as a journey unconstrained by conventional romantic notions of women's lives. All seven women showed a childhood interest in philosophy and abstract reasoning and had an early sense of involvement in issues larger than personal happiness as conventionally understood. Each voice conveys a strong sense of agency, so that the reader is left in no doubt that these women made their careers happen, surmounting many forms of discrimination along the way.

The quest for scientific truth or the adventure of applying scientific knowledge to transform the human environment has traditionally been seen as an odyssey. These women took the journey on its preestablished terms, though they felt no pining for a faithful Penelope. Dorothy Reed Mendenhall (1874–1964), Nice, Mead, and Payne Gaposchkin wanted children and established the relationships which made forming a family possible. Washburn and Baker, products of a pre-Freudian age, were unself-consciously content with surrogate families and the excitement of their work. Neither essentialist nor assimilationist, they were adventurers, interested in charting new territory as women but motivated principally by the life of the mind.

Margaret Floy Washburn

(1871–1939)

Born in New York City of Quaker heritage, Margaret Floy Washburn was the only child of a prosperous Methodist and then Episcopalian minister. Intellectually precocious, she went to Vassar College at age sixteen and received her A.B. in 1891. Her college life offered the chance to study science and philosophy, and to become an agnostic, freedoms she thought priceless. Her decision to pursue experimental psychology led her to seek admission to Columbia, where she was allowed to attend classes but not to seek a degree. Advised by James McKeen Cattell, her Columbia mentor, Washburn enrolled at Cornell in 1892 to work with E. B. Titchener. There she earned her Ph.D. in 1894 for a study of the influence of visual imagery on judgments of distance and direction.

Washburn taught at Wells College, unhappily at Cornell, where she was invited as an administrator, not a scientist, and at the University of Cincinnati before moving to Vassar in 1903. She produced some sixty scholarly articles of which she was sole author and a further seventy as joint author. Her major publication was her book *The Animal Mind* (1908), reviewing the current state of knowledge about animal behavior. A rooted individualist, Washburn disagreed with the European psychologists' exclusive focus on consciousness and the American preoccupation with behavior. Her leadership in American psychology was recognized by her election to the National Academy of Sciences in 1931; she was the second woman to be so recognized.

A HISTORY OF PSYCHOLOGY IN AUTOBIOGRAPHY

I was born in New York City on July 25, 1871, in a house built for my mother's father. It stood surrounded by a large garden. . . .

I was an only child, and the first eight years of my life were spent in the Harlem house; my father then entered the Episcopal ministry and for two years had a parish at Walden, an Orange County village. We next moved to the small Hudson River city of

Kingston, where I got my high-school training and whence I went to Vassar.

It seems to me that my intellectual life began with my fifth birthday. I remember a few moments when I was walking in the garden; I felt that I had now reached an age of some importance, and the thought was agreeable. Thinking about myself was so new an experience that I have never forgotten the moment.

I was not sent to school until I was seven, but, like many other persons, I cannot remember the time when I could not read, nor when I learned. The first school was a private one kept by the Misses Smuller, the three accomplished daughters of a retired Presbyterian minister who lived in the next house. It would be hard to find better teaching anywhere at the present time. In my year and a half there I gained, besides the rudiments of arithmetic, a foundation in French and German that saved me several years in later life, and the ability to read music and play all the major and minor scales from memory, a musical grounding that has been the chief aid to one of my greatest sources of enjoyment.

When we left New York for the two-years' sojourn in Walden, my school was, though still a private one, much like the district-school type, housed in a single-room building. I learned very little there: some American history and a little elementary physics. . . .

The removal to Kingston came when I was eleven; here I entered a public school. By a blunder I was put into a grade too high for me, and suffered much anguish with arithmetic; in the spirit of M. Aurelius, however, it may be said that this was a piece of good fortune, for, managing somehow to scramble through the Regents' examinations, I entered the high school at twelve. New York State's system of Regents' examinations is, I believed, considered by all enlightened educators as below contempt, but I had much reason for gratitude to it. The terrifying formalities attending these examinations where one's teachers with trembling fingers broke the seals on the packages of question papers sent from Albany, and one signed at the end of one's production a solemn declaration of having neither given nor received help, made all subsequent examinations in college and university seem trivial. . . .

The curriculum at Ulster Academy covered three years and would deeply distress a modern authority. It consisted of short-term courses in a large variety of subjects, each of which supplied a certain number of "Regents' credits." This method gave very poor results in the sciences, and my entire class failed twice to pass the

Regents' examination in chemistry, having had no laboratory work. Our teacher performed some demonstration experiments, of which I can remember only sodium scurrying over the surface of water as a little silver ball and potassium bursting into flame under similar circumstances; also Prince Rupert's drop falling into dust when its tip was pinched; why, we had not the slightest idea. However, the course in "political economy" firmly fixed in one's mind the rudiments of the theory of supply and demand, and that in "civil government" equipped one with some lasting idea of the structure of state, county, township, and city. We had to learn the Constitution of the United States thoroughly, and a few years ago I was able to impress my colleague of the Department of Political Science at Vassar by answering test questions on it. Passing Regents' examination in Latin had somewhat the nature of a sporting event. Having read four books of Virgil, we tried the examination on all six, reading at sight the passages from the last two. Several of us got over this hurdle, and the *Aeneid* knew us no more. What we lost in literary appreciation was gained in confidence for sight reading. . . .

In the spring of 1883 my parents and I made a memorable trip down the Mississippi from St. Louis to New Orleans by one of the old "palatial" steamers, which took a week for the run. I can still hear the call of the man with the lead, repeated from an upper deck and from the pilot-house. "Mark three!"; when it was "Mark twain!" a deep bell sounded once, the slow alternating puffs of the two engines stopped, and the great boat floated softly on over the shoal. . . .

I entered Vassar in the fall of 1886 as a preparatory student, for I lacked some Latin and had had no French since my earliest school days. Miss Smuller had laid so good a foundation that I needed only a semester at Vassar to secure admission to freshman French.

At this time there were no "majors" in the Vassar curriculum. English, mathematics, Latin, a moden language, physics and chemistry, were required through the sophomore year; psychology, so-called, and ethics in the senior year; there was no requirement of continuity in any other subject. So far as there was continuity in my own studies it lay in chemistry and French. Professor LeRoy Cooley taught chemistry and physics in crystal-clear lectures: his favorite word was "accurate," which he pronounced "ackerate," and I have loved, though by no means always attained, "ackeracy" ever since. Particularly delightful was quantitative analysis, with the excitement of adding up the percentages of the different ingredients in the hope that their sum might approach one hundred; though the faint suspicion always remained that a particularly "ackerate" result was due to losing a trace of something here and getting in a grain or two of dust there. French was admirably taught by two alternately kindly and ferocious sisters, Mlle. Achert and Mme. Guantieri, known to the students as Scylla and Charybdis. . . .

I am rather glad that I took no courses in English literature. When I was sixteen I began to love poetry, especially Keats, who absolutely bewitched me. Later, through a growing interest in philosophy, Matthew Arnold, with his matchless combination of classic beauty, clear thinking, and deep feeling became my favorite; I wrote my Commencement oration on "The Ethics of Matthew Arnold's Poetry," tracing the Stoic elements in it. For the love of poetry and philosophy I found in my sophomore year a strong stimulus in an older student who had been a senior in my preparatory year and had returned to college to work for a master's degree. She had been the leader of a brilliant group of girls in the class of '87, whose religious radicalism had distressed President Taylor in his first year of office. I now experienced the mental expansion that comes with dropping orthodox religious ideas, an expansion accompanied by exhilaration. . . .

A wonderful new field was opened in my junior year by a course in biology whose teacher was a young Bryn Mawr Ph.D., Marcella O'Grady. She later married Theodor Boveri, the great authority on cytology, and has now, some years after his death, returned to America and to teaching. She lectured admirably and drew beautiful figures on the board. In this year, too, I began the study of Greek: Professor Abby Leach was a skillful teacher of its grammar, and brought the little group of my classmates in two semesters to the point where they could join the incoming freshmen who had had two years' preparation. I cherish proudly the scraps that remain, and pity the person who has to master scientific terms with no knowledge of Greek.

It was, I think, the summer after my junior year that I read in my father's library Arthur Balfour's *Defence of Philosophic Doubt* and acquired for a lifetime the conviction that no one has ever succeeded in constructing a logic-proof system of monistic metaphysics.

President Taylor's course in psychology, required in the first semester of all seniors, was based on James Clark Murray's *Handbook of Psychology* and lectures on the history of philosophy by Dr. Taylor. Murray's book was directed against the associational school, Dr. Taylor's lectures against materialism. Murray's argument was that association could not explain the process of active relating, which he called comparison: "association can merely associate." This was a sound position: James had expressed the same thing the year before in pointing out the neglect of "selective attention" by the associational school. The problem is focal in psychology at the present time, with the believers in "creative mind," vitalism, voluntarism, and so forth on one side and the mechanists on the other: I firmly believe that it can be solved by mechanism, but not that of the old associative type. . . . Dr. Taylor (whom, by the way, we regarded with great affection) had no idea of presenting metaphysical systems to us impartially: he wished to preserve our religious convictions by saving us from materialism in the one direction and pantheistic idealism in the other. . . .

At the end of my senior year I had two dominant intellectual interests, science and philosophy. They seemed to be combined in what I heard of the wonderful new science of experimental psychology. Learning of the psychological laboratory just established at Columbia by Dr. Cattell, who had come a year before from the fountain-head, the Leipzig laboratory, I determined to be his pupil, and my parents took a house in New York for the year. But Columbia had never admitted a woman graduate student: the most I could hope for was to be tolerated as a "hearer," and even that would not be possible until after Christmas when the trustees had met. I solaced myself by taking the School of Mines course in quantitative chemical analysis at the Barnard laboratory, the second floor of a brownstone house on Madison Avenue. President Butler was then the amazingly efficient young dean of the department of philosophy, and, at his suggestion, I read Wundt's long article on psychological methods in the first volume of *Philosophische Studien;* having had only a year of German I began by writing out a translation of it, an excellent way of getting the vocabulary. After Christmas I was allowed to present myself to Dr. Cattell for admission as a hearer. The psychological laboratory was the top floor of the old President's House on Forty-ninth Street close to the New York Central tracks. "What do you think is done in psychological laboratories?" asked Dr. Cattell, who looked then just as he does now, barring the grey hair. I blessed the hours I had spent on W. Wundt's article: instead of speaking as I am sure I was expected to do, of hypnotism, telepathy, and spiritism, I referred to reaction-time, complication experiments, and work on the limens and Weber's Law, and was rewarded by the remark that I seemed to have some knowledge of the matter.

From that time Dr. Cattell treated me as a regular student and required of me all that he required of the men. A lifelong champion of freedom and equality of opportunity, it would never have occurred to him to reject a woman student on account of her sex. The four men students, seniors, and I listened to his lectures, prepared reports on experimental work, and at least one paper on a theoretical subject. He assigned to me the experimental problem of finding whether Weber's Law held for the two-point threshold on the skin. I improvised apparatus, used a metronome to keep the duration of the stimuli constant, and found observers among my Barnard associates. Incidentally, it may be mentioned that Weber's Law does not hold for the two-point threshold. . . .

Dr. Cattell raised me to the height of joy after I had read a paper on the relation of psychology to physiology by writing me a note to suggest that I sent it to the *Philosophical Review*. Nothing would have induced me to do anything so daring. At the end of the year, since there were no fellowships at Barnard he advised me to apply for a graduate scholarship at the newly organized Sage School of Philosophy at Cornell. . . .

While I was thus being initiated into Cattell's objective version of the Leipzig doctrine, the influence of William James's *Principles* was strong. His enthusiasm for the occult was unattractive; it seemed that in his zeal to keep an open mind he kept it open more widely to the abnormal than to the normal. But his description of the stream of consciousness, and the consistently analytic rather than synthetic point of view which he maintained in holding that simpler mental states are products of analysis, and in developing all spatial relations by analysis from a primitive space instead of compounding them like Wundt out of non-spatial elements, never lost their effect even though the prestige of the Leipzig school increased.

I went in the fall of 1892 to Cornell, where Titchener had just arrived from Oxford and Leipzig. He was twenty-five, but seemed older at first sight because of his square-cut beard; the illusion of age vanished on acquaintance. There was nothing about him at that time to suggest either his two greatest gifts or his chief failing in later life. The gifts, in my opinion, were his comprehensive scholarship, shown conspicuously in his *Instructor's Manuals of Experimental Psychology;* and his genius as a lecturer. In his first two years at Cornell his lectures were read, and were frankly after the German fashion: we regarded him as a brilliant young man who would give us the latest news from Leipzig, rather than as one to be heard for his own sake. The failing that later grew upon him was that of remaining isolated so far as his immediate surroundings were concerned from all but subordinates. In these first years he was entirely human. . . .

I was his only major graduate student, and experimental psychology was so young that he did not quite know what to do with me. Appointments for planning laboratory work would be made which often ended in his telling stories of Oxford life for an hour or two. He finally suggested that since I had some experience in work on tactual space perception, I should make an experimental study of the method of equivalents. I wrote up the results in a paper which was accepted in June at Vassar for an M.A. *in absentia,* Titchener having given me a written examination lasting three hours, of which I do not recall a single question. . . .

The Sage School of Philosophy was an inspiring place to work, for the members of its faculty were nearly all young. I chose as my minor subjects philosophy and ethics. President Schurman taught the advanced course in ethics. He had visited Vassar in my senior year and given several lectures on Herbert Spencer, which it was my privilege to report as a college editor. They were models of clearness and force. . . .

At the end of this year I was asked to take the Chair of Psychology at the Woman's College of Western Reserve University, and went to Cleveland to look it over. The opportunity was a good one, but I think I was wise in deciding to finish my work for the doctorate at Cornell although Dr. Schurman disapproved of the decision. In my second year at Cornell I was no longer Titchener's only major student, being joined by Walter Pillsbury from Nebraska; this is an association of which I have always been proud. I had, during my work with the method of equivalents, thought of a subject for a doctor's thesis: the influence of visual imagery on judgments of tactual distance and direction. Much of my time this year went to the thesis. I had also a course in Lotze's metaphysics with F. C. S. Schiller, who had come from Oxford for a year's stay in the wilderness and was even then a very distinguished man. The thesis was finished by the spring vacation, and Dr. Titchener sent it to Wundt, who had it translated into German and published in *Philosophische Studien,* where the Leipzig theses appeared. On this occasion my translator enriched the German language with a new verb: *visualisiren.*

Examinations for the doctorate at that time were wholly oral. . . . The occasion was a pleasant one. I received the doctor's degree in June, 1894.

No position was waiting for me, and I even considered teaching psychology in a New York finishing school. The elderly gentleman at its head impressed me with its high standards: all the members of his senior class in astronomy the last year had attained the mark of 100 per cent. Before I committed myself to this institution a telegram asked me to come to Wells College. Its new president, Dr. William E. Waters, being a classical scholar, preferred to teach Greek instead of the psychology and ethics required of a college president; in this emergency they could offer me little money, but I gladly accepted the Chair of Psychology, Philosophy, and Ethics (not to mention logic), at a salary of three hundred dollars and home. (The arrangement with my family was that when I visited them they paid the expenses of importation, but I must pay my own way back.) Wells was, and I hear still is, though much grown, a delightful place; I spent six years there that left not a single unpleasant memory. The salary, by the way, had by the last two years reached the maximum for women professors, seven hundred dollars and home; the men were paid fifteen hundred. What money meant in those days is shown by the fact that at the end of the six years I had saved five hundred dollars without any effort at all. . . .

During this period I accepted the general point of view of what Titchener called structural psychology. To a person with a liking for chemistry the idea of introspectively analyzing mental states into irreducible elements had attraction, yet one could not forget James's conception of consciousness as a stream and the impossibility that it should be at once a stream and a mosaic. I never followed Titchener when he developed his elaborate, highly refined introspective analysis, and not one of the doctor's theses produced at Cornell and later at Clark (under Baird) by the use of this method had any real appeal for me. It is worth while to describe conscious states, but not, in describing them, to turn them into something unrecognizable. . . .

In my sixth year at Wells I became restless, and felt that a year at the Harvard laboratory would be a refreshing change. I was granted leave of absence for this purpose in the spring of 1900, but a telegram from President Schurman changed my plan. He asked me to come to Cornell as Warden of Sage College, with plenty of opportunity for my psychological work and what then seemed the enormous salary of fifteen hundred dollars and home. So I returned to Cornell for two years. In the first, I tried to work out in the physics laboratory the problem of the flight of colors, but did not succeed in obtaining good results from any controllable source of light. I had to spend too much time and energy at social functions, which, however, gave much profitable experience in other directions. In the physics laboratory I served as an observer for Frank Allen's research on the fusion rate of retinal impressions from different regions of the spectrum, and got a further glimpse of the futility of elaborate introspection. As I observed and reported on the visual phenomena, I accompanied my judgments of fusion by introspective accounts of variations in my general state of mind which would undoubtedly make the curves in one experiment quite different from those in another. I mentally congratulated Mr. Allen in having for the first time an observer skilled in introspective sources of error. Much surprise resulted when the curves proved highly uniform; the sources of error had not influenced the sensory judgments at all. . . .

Being a "warden" and having to concern oneself with the behavior of other people was highly uncongenial, and when, at the end of two years, I was offered an assistant professorship in full charge of psychology at the University of Cincinnati, where Dr. Howard Ayers was president, I eagerly accepted it, though I disliked going so far from my parents. I was the only woman of professorial rank on the faculty, and President Ayers took especial pains to treat me, as we sat around a long table at faculty meetings, on a footing of perfect equality with the men. . . . The place offered . . . many opportunities, but it is hard for a deeply rooted Easterner to be transplanted. When I sat in the station and heard the train called for "Buffalo-Rochester-Syracuse-Albany," the sound was sweet in my ears, and I can still remember the thrill of happiness that came with the first stir of the car wheels on their eastward journey. I was thankful when President Taylor in the spring of 1903 called me to Vassar as Associate Professor of Philosophy. There I could spend every Sunday with my parents, who were living only sixteen miles away. . . .

The genetic point of view was much in my mind during these years, and so were kinaesthetic processes. To the Stanley Hall *Festschrift* in 1903 I contributed the suggestion that the social reference of certain conscious states, e.g., the thought of another's suffering, had as its nervous basis kinaesthetic processes from certain incipient reactions, for instance the impulse to help. . . .

If this were an emotional instead of an intellectual autobiography, an almost morbidly intense love of animals would have to be traced to its occult sources. Animal psychology began to occupy me when I gave a course on it at Cornell. During a six-weeks' stay at Ithaca in the summer of 1905, I collaborated with Dr. Bentley in some experiments on color vision in a brook fish which he captured from a neighboring stream. The chub learned with great speed, in spite of lacking of cortex; it discriminated both dark and light red from green. Our method of eliminating the brightness error by varying the brightness of the red was inadequate, but later investigators have confirmed our results. Shortly after this, I began to collect and organize literature on animal behavior. The Animal Behavior Series, which the Macmillans published under Dr. Yerkes's editorship, brought out the first edition of *The Animal Mind* in 1908. While the objective school of interpretation, represented in America chiefly by Loeb, had long urged that much animal conduct should be regarded as unaccompanied by mind, no one had then suggested that all animal behavior, still less that all human behavior, is unconscious, and the patterns of animal consciousness seemed to me then, as they do now, well worth investigating and perfectly open to investigation. . . .

I had for some time been collecting the results of all the German and French experiments on the higher mental processes. Vassar celebrated in 1915 the fiftieth anniversary of its founding, and the trustees decided to publish a commemorative series of volumes by alumnae, books of a scholarly rather than popular nature, which might not readily find a publisher in the ordinary way. For this series I wrote *Movement and Mental Imagery*, trying to interpret the experimentally obtained data on the higher mental processes

by the motor principles I had been evolving, and developing the
doctrine that thinking involves tentative or incipient movements. . . .

Watson's radical behaviorism was of course the favorite topic
of discussion in the years from 1915 to 1922 or thereabouts. It will
be remembered that his first attack on the existence of conscious
processes consisted in denying that of mental imagery. A critic could
easily point out that his principles required also denial of the existence of all sensation qualities. In fact, the existence of sensation
qualities is irreconcilable with any materialistic monism. My presidential address before the 1921 meeting of the Psychological Association tried, while rejecting the Watsonian metaphysics, to show
that introspection itself is an objective method and one necessarily
used by the behaviorist. . . .

A second edition of *The Animal Mind* had appeared in 1917,
nine years after the first, and a third one seemed to be due in 1926;
this time the book was very considerably rewritten. Reviewing
Woodworth's *Dynamic Psychology* in 1918, I began to realize how
completely my motor theory had ignored the explanatory function
of the *drive*. Of course, one had taken for granted that an animal
would not learn without a motive, but, as I analyzed in 1926 the
recent literature on learning, especially the work of Szymanski, it
became clear that the drive explains the formation of successive
movement systems by being present throughout the series, and by
setting in readiness its own consummatory movements. A paper on
"Emotion and Thought," written for the Wittenberg Conference
on Feelings and Emotions, discussed some relations between the
passage of drive energy into visceral and non-adaptive muscular
movements, as in emotion, and into tenative movements and the
"activity attitude," as in thinking. In my address as retiring Chairman of Section I of the American Association for the Advancement
of Science, December, 1927, I used the passage of a drive into the
activity attitude as a mechanistic explanation of purposive action,
and urged that vitalism and emergent evolution, in general, are too
ready to adopt the primitive mind's recourse to unknown forces.
The address also suggested that a precursor of the activity attitude
might be the "orientation towards a goal" observed in animals
learning a maze path. . . .

The enthusiasm with which the *Gestalt* psychology was being
preached in America during these years by Köhler and Koffka was
far from being unwelcome; it was a real pleasure to have the patterns
of consciousness, surely among the most fascinating objects in the

universe, made the subject of thorough study and experiment instead of being stupidly ignored after the behaviorist fashion. . . .

The results of experimental work, if it is successful at all, bring more lasting satisfaction than the development of theories. Some of the small studies from the Vassar laboratory which have covered a period of twenty-five years do give me a measure of such satisfaction, to wit: certain observations on the changes occurring in printed words under long fixation; the fact that the movements of the left hand are better recalled than those of the right, probably because they are less automatized; the fact that movement on the skin can be perceived when its direction cannot; observations on the perception of the direction in which sources of sound are moving; observations on retinal rivalry in after-images; a study of the trustworthiness of various complex indicators in the free association method; experiments on the affective value of articulate sounds and its sources; the concept of affective sensitiveness or the tendency to feel extreme degrees of pleasantness and unpleasantness, and the fact that it appears to be greater in poets than in scientific students; the first experiments on affective contrast; the fact that the law of distributed repetitions holds for the learning of series of hand-movements; the study of revived emotions. In 1912, Miss Abbott and I proved red color-blindness in the rabbit, and, incidentally, that the animal reacts to the relative rather than the absolute brightness of colors, a fact later exploited by the configurationists. A student, Edwina Kittredge, proved that a bull-calf also was red color-blind; this coincided in time with Stratton's disproof of the notion that red angers bulls.

The Ninth International Congress of Psychology, September 1–8, 1929, is still fresh in our memories; in mine it lingers as a recollection of talks with old and new friends, whether sitting on benches in the beautiful Harkness Quadrangle or at tables where we enjoyed the super-excellent food of the Yale cafeteria. I am sure our foreign friends will never forget the revelation of democracy in action which they obtained from standing in line and collecting their own sustenance at that cafeteria. I was elected to the International Committee at this meeting, an honor I appreciated the more because of the other Americans chosen at the same time.

One of the difficulties in writing these recollections has been that the present is so much more interesting than the past. It is hard to keep one's attention on reminiscence. Scientific psychology in

America—though not, alas! in Germany, its birthplace—seems fuller of promise than ever before. The behaviorists have stimulated the development of objective methods, while configurationism is reasserting the importance of introspection; and, best of all, pure psychology is enlisting young men [sic] of excellent ability and a far sounder general scientific training than that possessed by any but a few of their predecessors.

S. Josephine Baker

(1873–1945)

The third daughter of wealthy Quakers, S. Josephine Baker had a happy childhood until the death of her father and brother in her sixteenth year. Prompted by financial reverses brought on by her father's death, Baker assumed responsibility for earning her own living and, backed by her mother, who had been a member of the first class at Vassar College, selected the career of physician. Graduating in 1898 from New York Infirmary for Women and Children, she entered private practice in New York, only to discover that a woman physician faced such prejudice that she could not earn enough to support herself. An appointment as medical inspector for the New York City Health Department supplemented her meager earnings and brought her into contact with the public health problems of New York's black, Italian, and Irish immigrant populations. Troubled by their infant mortality rate, which climbed to 1,500 a week in the summers, Baker designed an experimental program of education on the value of breast feeding, ventilation, and sanitation. Recognizing her achievement in lowering the infant death rate, in 1908 the city established the Division of Child Hygiene with Baker as chief. Thereafter she pioneered in the delivery of health education, the provision of uncontaminated milk, and the operation of popularly accepted vaccination programs for contagious diseases of infancy. Troubled by the difficulty of making eye medications available at birth, she invented a foolproof container readily used by midwife and physician alike, thereby nearly eliminating widespread cases of avoidable infant blindness.

Baker combined her practical administration in public health with lecturing and research when she began to teach child hygiene at the New York University–Bellevue Medical School in 1916. Accepting the position on condition that she be enrolled in the doctoral program in public health, she earned her degree in 1917 with a dissertation on the effects of classroom ventilation on rates of respiratory disease in children. She persevered with this teaching assignment for fifteen years, although she hated the unrelenting hazing to which she was subjected by the all-male student body.

The author of five books—*Healthy Mothers, Healthy Babies* and *Healthy Children* (1920), *The Growing Child* (1923), and *Child Hygiene* (1925)—and more than fifty articles for the *American*

Journal of Public Health, Baker was an important figure in the development of public health in America and a moving force in the establishment of federal and state programs of child welfare. Drawn into the suffrage movement by her experience of discrimination and by her concern for women's political participation, she was a lively speaker and campaigner and a skilled user of the media.

FIGHTING FOR LIFE

I know that women of my generation who struck out on their own are supposed to have become rebellious because they felt cramped and suppressed and unhappy as children in an alien environment. It is a convenient formula and no doubt perfectly applicable in many cases. But it does not fit mine. I was reared in a thoroughly conventional tradition and took to it happily. I understood that after I left school I would go to Vassar, and then, I supposed, I would get married and raise a family and that would be that. . . .

It would have taken a pretty demanding, not to say peevish, kind of child to fail to adjust to the family environment in which I was reared. We were reasonably well to do as wealth went in Poughkeepsie, so I had none of that precocious sense of responsibility which children often derive from straitened family incomes. Father was one of the most eminent lawyers in town; so eminent that, when I was making a speech in Poughkeepsie several years ago, I received a large basket of flowers with a card: "From the members of the Dutchess County Bar to the daughter of O. D. M. Baker." That was about thirty years after his death and it went straight to the heart of a daughter one of whose earliest resolves was to make it up to Father for having been born a girl. There is no particular point in emphasizing that ambition or its cause. Father was not one of those childish people who take disappointment out on children. But I did happen to arrive in the world as the third daughter in a row and I heard family legends about Father's remarks when the nurse congratulated him on Daughter Number Three. . . .

Of course I can find a few special characteristics creeping out, if I look for them. Trying to make it up to Father for being a girl, which went right on even after the next arrival delighted the household by being a boy, did turn me into a tomboy type in the early days. I was an enthusiastic baseball player and trout-fisher and still like both of these amusements fifty years later. . . .

I was extremely fond of the school to which I was sent. . . . It was a highly unusual school, of a type practically unheard of fifty years ago, although some of its peculiarities have much in common with the most advanced of modern educational methods. The school was the private effort of the Misses Thomas, two extremely large ladies who much resembled the late Elisabeth Marbury, in a lovely, peaceful old house on Academy Street, full of exquisite old furniture and a sense of overwhelming calm which impressed the most rambunctious little girl the moment she entered. . . .

So far as the academic side went, the school itself was strangely modern in its plan of study. There were no graded classes, no marks or reports, no examinations, not even any commencement exercises. When Miss Sarah was satisfied that you knew enough mathematics, Latin, French, English, or the elementary sciences, she told you so and all of the women's colleges of that time took her certificate of a student's preparation as sufficient for entrance requirements without a shadow of question. The classes were small and rather informal affairs with only three or four girls in each group, usually held around a table in some upstairs room. You progressed strictly according to your ability to master that particular course. If you had a special piece of work to do, you took your own time to master it, without urging. The teachers were nearly all college-bred women and the instruction was fine and thorough. Discipline was hardly needed, so beautifully did this pair of fine, shrewd women manage their charges. . . .

It was splendid preparation for a child who would presently have to study on her own. By the time I was sixteen I was prepared to enter any women's college in the country and in Latin and mathematics could have been eligible for entrance to the sophomore year.

There had never been any question about my entering Vassar, which was already as familiar to me as my own face in the mirror. But then things began to happen with devastating swiftness. That was just my private calamity out of a series of calamities which went far toward shattering our family and jarred me out of the life I was apparently destined to lead.

When I was sixteen my brother died suddenly. He was only thirteen years old but a fine and promising lad and the one boy in a family of girls. Three months later Father died of typhoid. In those days typhoid was the scourge of Poughkeepsie and no wonder, since the town water supply was drawn from the Hudson just below the outlet of the sewer from the large Asylum of the Insane above the town. . . . Father's typhoid was serious enough, but we all knew it was rather a lack of will to live that killed him. My brother's death had taken all the zest for life from him. We were an understanding trio—my father, my brother, and myself—and when they died so close together there seemed very little left to live for.

Perhaps it was just as well that financial troubles appeared so soon after Father's funeral to make us all think of something else. We had always had a comfortable home and enough money, and Father had saved too. But when the estate came to be settled, a recent series of losses and bad investments told the inevitable story of practically nothing left. It was immediately evident that somebody would have to get ready to earn a living for all three of us— my mother, my sister, who had always been delicate and a semi-invalid, and myself. I considered myself elected. It was a hard struggle to give up Vassar but there was not enough money left to pay for that and for any additional preparation for a professional life. . . . in the end it was decided that Mother and Mary should live at home and I should take five thousand of the few precious dollars remaining, go to New York and study to be a doctor. . . .

I wish I could remember what made me choose medicine as a way of earning my living—for that is the conscious commercial attitude I had toward it at that time. I expect that even then I did not know my motive very clearly. Many years afterward, a newspaper reporter interviewed me for hours in an effort to get a story which would give some definite starting point to my career. . . . His conclusion was that an injury to my knee, which kept me on crutches for over two years, had developed in me a tremendous respect for the profession of medicine and a not-to-be-denied yearning for a medical education. To be exact he wrote: "If little Josephine Baker had not hurt her knee, 90,000 babies now alive would have died." I have the utmost respect for the Fourth Estate and in my years of Health Department work learned to know intimately many of those splendid fellows—of both sexes—and I know what "copy" means to a reporter. But I have a profound conviction that he was wrong. . . .

But in my sheltered life medical women were such rare and unusual creatures that they could hardly be said to exist at all. There was no medical tradition on either side of my family. There were lawyers but no doctors. And both sides of the family were aghast at the idea of my spending so much money in such an unconventional way. It was an unheard of, a harebrained and unwomanly scheme. At first my mother too was rather overwhelmed at the idea, but she trusted me and she made a gallant surrender. "If you really think you should, Jo," she said, "go ahead. I'll try not to fret too much about it." . . .

My only explanation of the mental process that led me to my decision is that the study of medicine did occur to me, rather casually, from my long association with the Doctors Sayre, and that later, when I encountered only argument and disapproval, my native stubbornness made me decide to study medicine at all costs and in spite of everyone. . . .

It took about six weeks of unaccustomed and unpleasant work for me to be transformed to the place where I could honestly say to myself: "This is the one thing of all others that I will and must do." I have never regretted it. Long hours of work both day and night, discouragement and rebuffs all seemed just part of a natural life and if it has been a difficult road to travel it has also been a deeply satisfying one.

When I began my bashful and inefficient inquiries as to the way of getting a medical education my ignorance was colossal. Finally some courageous good angel . . . told me that there was a women's medical college in New York attached to the New York Infirmary for Women and Children. . . . It was a pleasant building, on the corner of Stuyvesant Square at East Fifteenth Street, and, when I summoned up my courage to go in and ask questions, they treated me very well. It was a brisk, and yet a serious institution. I liked it and found with great relief that the people in charge—all women too—seemed to consider the study of medicine a reasonable career for a girl. But they made it clear that I should have to earn my opportunity. The certificate from Miss Thomas which would enable me to enter Vassar College was of no value here. This college required a certificate from the State Board of Regents covering a series of subjects which included elementary chemistry and biology. . . .

So back home I went and for the next year I studied continuously and renewed my acquaintance with arithmetic, geography and even spelling (which continues to be one of my weakest points). I was near enough to studies like Latin, French and the higher mathematics to have them cause me no difficulty. . . . During this whole year I was encouraged and stimulated by a running fire of sarcasm from my numerous relatives—all, that is, except my mother, who stood by me without a word once her mind had been made up. . . . At the end of this year of cramming I passed the Regents' examinations, packed my bag and set out on my rather lonely great adventure. I knew that I had finally left my home and that I would never go back except for short visits. It was hardly comforting knowledge, but I could not let anyone know how little confidence I felt in myself or the possibility of my ever justifying the expenditure of that precious $5,000. . . .

. . . the one subject I failed in medical school was to be the foundation of my life-work. This was related to a course, during my sophomore year, on "The Normal Child," given by Dr. Annie Sturges Daniel, a pioneer woman physician who is loved and honored by every student who came under her influence. Dr. Daniel's course was an uncharted sea and I had no interest in it; neither had anyone else so far as I could discover except Dr. Daniel herself. . . .

That was my first, and only, failure. It not only gave a severe jolt to my pride but roused in me a fierce anger at having to take the course over again the following year. I made up my mind that, stupid as it might seem, I intended to learn all there was to know about the normal child. I took voluminous notes on the lectures; I read everything I could find that had the slightest relation to the subject. . . . The lectures, I discovered . . . were very fine; the bits of sought-out information most intriguing. As a result, that little pest, the normal child, made such a dent on my consciousness that it was he, rather than my lame knee, who is undoubtedly responsible for the survival of those 90,000 babies the reporter mentioned. The whole procedure of preventive hygiene which I was later to install in modern child care certainly had its inspiration in that half-year of pique and hard work.

The privilege and honor of writing M.D. after his name is always a great spiritual comfort to the newly graduated medical student. It was a particular joy to me because so many inhabitants of Poughkeepsie had prophesied that I would never go through with it; and were now greeting the news that I had done so with rather scant appreciation. In spite of all the impressive Latin on the sheepskin, however, "M.D." in itself does not mean much. A student fresh out of medical school is no more a doctor than a man who has taught himself to go through swimming motions across a chair is a swimmer. That, of course, is why experience either as interne in a hospital or other graduate experience is almost an essential before beginning actual practice. . . .

So I became an interne, addressed as Dr. Baker for the first time, wearing a white uniform and doing actual work in a hospital. Since I had graduated second in a class of eighteen (the rest of the thirty-five had fallen by the wayside), I was offered a fine interneship in the New York Infirmary for Women and Children, the hospital in connection with the college where I had taken my degree. But I felt that I needed to cut away from this familiar environment, to which I had devoted four whole years, that I needed new associates and a new point of view. That idea took me to Boston where I applied for, and obtained, a position as interne in the New England Hospital for Women and Children. There was no question of getting into a large general hospital. At that time no such institution admitted women in any capacity. . . .

For the first time in my life I was really up against facts. No student, whether in law or medicine, is living a real life. An academic atmosphere is necessarily artificial. Here, in Boston, submerged in the hectic life of a big clinic, I was abruptly forced to translate what I had studied into actuality, to realize that the luridly colored pictures in ponderous medical texts meant actual fever and pain and delirium and mutilation, and that those crisp summaries of what to do about this or that physical ailment, which had sounded so reassuring on the printed page, were of distressingly little help to an inexperienced beginner. It was all the more discouraging because the raw material we worked with on Fayette Street was anything but pretty. We were dealing with the dregs of Boston, ignorant, shiftless, settled irrevocably into surly degradation. Just to make sure they would be hopeless, many of them drank savagely. Having borne children and lived and fought and made love regardless, they took that method of dodging the consequences. Nothing admirable about it, but one could not honestly blame them for making use of alcohol as an anaesthetic.

In time I got used to it, if not hardened to it. But, for the first few weeks at the clinic, my inexperienced and still reasonably girlish soul was aghast at the discovery that, with these people, any and every calamity was such a matter of course. There was the Irish-woman who came to the Hospital to be delivered of a baby. She looked much too old for motherhood, but then you get wrinkled and bent quickly under the conditions she had always known. On admission she proved to have both feet badly burned in addition to her other difficulties. I asked her how the burns happened. "Well, deary," she said, "I come in a night or two ago with my feet wet and I stuck thim in the oven to dry thim and forgot thim." Drunk, no doubt, drifting peacefully off into an alcoholic fog with a new life in her waiting to be born, and much too numb to know that her feet were blistering in the oven. Numb—that seems to be the right word for all of them.

Presently I signalized my new acquaintance with reality by committing murder—to all intents and purposes. That came about with appalling naturalness. It was another obstetrical case, a routine hurry call to come to a woman who was about to have a baby. A man with a long beard brought the message. He silently guided me through snow-choked alleyways to an old frame house hidden in a court. As soon as he saw me started up to the top floor, he went away; I had the idea that he was afraid to accompany me for some reason. But I went on up the stairs, feeling with my feet for loose boards and holes in the enveloping darkness, and found my patient at last.

I thought I already knew something about how filthy a tenement room could be. But this was something special, particularly in the amount of insect life. One dingy oil lamp, by the light of which I could barely make out the woman in labor, lying on a heap of straw in one corner. Four stunted children, too frightened to make any noise, huddled together in a far corner. The floor was littered with scraps of food, too old to be easily identifiable, but all contributing to the odor of the place. Cockroaches and bedbugs crawled about everywhere. The only thing to wash up in was, as usual, an old tin basin, rusted and ragged at the edge. All of it was the nth power of abject, discouraged squalor. But the ugliest detail was a man, also lying on the floor because he was apparently too drunk to get up. But he was all too capable of speech.

The moment I approached my patient I discovered that her back was one raw, festering sore. She said that her husband had thrown a kettle of scalding water over her a few days before. That accusation brought him to his feet crazy with rage, threatening me and her, toppling and lurching all over the place.

I knew that could not go on. I had to get him out of the way. As he wavered toward me, waving his clenched fist and uttering verbal filth, I ran out into the hall. He followed me as I intended. I had thought of running in quickly again and seeing if the door would lock. But then, as he lurched after me, he crossed the stair-

head and, with instinctive reaction, I doubled my fist and hit him.
It was beautifully timed. I weighed hardly half as much as he, but
he was practically incapable of standing up, and this frantic tap of
mine was strategically placed. He toppled backward, struck about
a third of the way down the rather long stair and slid to the bottom
with a hideous crash. Then there was absolute silence. I had taken
my opportunity and the result was evident. I went back into the
room, pushed a piece of furniture against the closed door and delivered the baby undisturbed. . . .

   At the end of our year as internes, Dr. Laighton and I went
back to New York to seek what advice we could get about the
chance of our starting to practice in that city. . . . We thanked all
of our advisers and rented an apartment on West Ninety-first Street,
near Central Park, took a few weeks off to pass our State Regents'
examinations, hung out our shingles and, with inexplicable equa-
nimity, had no fear at all for the future. Dr. Laighton's family gave
us enough money to furnish the place and equip our office and we
had every intention of staying. . . .

   Paradoxically, our only asset was that we were women doctors.
We were almost the only ones established on the west side of New
York above Fifty-ninth Street. For many years women came to us
because we were women and the competition in that line was small.
But we deserved to starve and I do not know why we did not. My
first year's proceeds amounted to exactly $185.00. And, except that
I was paid for it, my first case was a sample of the whole year. In
those days, Amsterdam Avenue, which has since experienced both
a feverish building-boom and a period of gradual decline, was filled
with squatters' shacks made of hammered-out tin cans and waste
lumber, inhabited by ne'er-do-wells and swarming with goats. I
began my practice by delivering a baby in one of those shacks.
Again it was a hurry call and they had sent for me much too late;
it was a difficult and abnormal case. Even with Dr. Laighton's
assistance, saving the mother and keeping the baby alive for an hour
or two was the best I could do. . . .

   A dollar bill should have been saved out of that first ten, to
frame and hang in my office. But that was economically impossible.
A dollar was such a rare object. On one occasion when I was down
to my last two dollars in the world, I defiantly spent it on a grand
lunch at the old Waldorf Hotel and a magazine to read on the
trolley car going home. Rent day was just around the corner too.
But when I reached our apartment, there was a patient waiting who

paid me in cash and enabled me to carry on a little longer. . . .

Being young, we were incapable of worrying. But we did have to use our mother-wit to find ways of supplementing our incomes. For that purpose a call from a much too persistent life-insurance agent proved accidentally helpful. In order to get rid of him, we asked if the company had a woman doctor to examine us if we did take out insurance. He said no, certainly not—he had never heard of such a thing. Our tones were shocked as we said that we would never think of being examined by a man doctor and we showed him to the door with well-simulated indignation. . . .

Having plenty of time in which to pursue the idea, Dr. Laighton and I went down town the next day, she to visit the New York Life Insurance Company while I went to the Equitable. Each of us had the same experience. In both places the Chief Medical Examiner was mildly amused at the idea. But we went on stubbornly pointing out the advantages in the scheme and eventually persuaded the companies to inform their agents that, when a prospective client wanted one, a woman examiner would be available in our persons. We came away enrolled as special medical examiners. That brainstorm of ours brought us a steady stream of profitable fees and opened up that whole field of medical activity for women.

I was in general practice for a number of years. . . . I was hardly well started when another accident, the mere catching sight of an item in the morning paper, diverted me into taking the first step toward my real career. The paper said that civil service examinations for the position of medical inspector of the Department of Health would be held at such a time and place; the salary to be thirty dollars a month. A dollar a day: about double my first year's rate of income. It was tempting enough to make me take the examination and I came out high enough on the passed list for a possible appointment. Ordinarily I would have supposed that this would guarantee me the job. But by this time I was vaguely aware that there was corruption in city politics and that people sometimes had to use pull to get city appointments. That really was the innocent extent of my knowledge of what I was getting into. So I asked a lawyer patient of mine to give me a letter of recommendation to a justice of the New York Supreme Court who was, of course, right in the middle of politics and the justice passed me on with another letter to one of the, then, three Commissioners of Health. . . .

The Department headquarters were at that time in a forlorn

old building at the corner of Sixth Avenue and Fifty-fifth Street which had formerly housed the New York Athletic Club and had obviously been neither cleaned nor painted since the athletes had vacated it. As the central focus of the sanitary and medical services of a great city, it was a shock; the Commissioner was another. I do not remember his name, but he could have sat as a cartoon for the public idea of a typical Tammany henchman. He was paunchy with a fat blue-jowled face and sat with his feet on the desk, his hat on the back of his head and the last two inches of a disorganized cigar in the corner of his mouth. I had supposed he would ask me some questions but he did not deign to do that. He did not even look at me twice. He just opened my letter, glanced through it, rang a bell and, when a clerk appeared, he jerked his thumb at me over his shoulder and said: "Give the lady her appointment." . . .

When Mayor Seth Low came into office in 1902 and Dr. Ernest J. Lederle was appointed Commissioner of Health, the whole department shuddered at the shake-up and house-cleaning that occurred. At the beginning, I knew little or nothing of that for I had no interest in the administrative side of my job. But I did know that in the shaking-up process I was sent for by a new assistant sanitary superintendent and offered a summer position in hunting out and looking after sick babies. This new appointee, Dr. Walter Bensel, my chief for years afterwards, was about the only reason I had yet seen for changing my opinion of the Health Department and its works. He had every appearance of being energetic, clean-cut and honest; all of which proved true and all of which was a novelty. I liked him, and his attitude, so much that I changed my mind and took the offered job at an increase in salary to one hundred dollars a month.

This time I had let myself in for a really gruelling ordeal. Summer anywhere in New York City is pretty bad. In my district, the heart of old Hell's Kitchen on the west side, the heat, the smells, the squalor made it something not to be believed. Its residents were largely Irish, incredibly shiftless, altogether charming in their abject helplessness, wholly lacking in any ambition and dirty to an unbelievable degree. At the upper edge of Hell's Kitchen, just above Fifty-ninth Street, was the then largest colored district in town. Both races lived well below any decent level of subsistence. My job was to start in this district every morning at seven o'clock, work until eleven, then return for two hours more—from four to six. I climbed stair after stair, knocked on door after door, met drunk after drunk, filthy mother after filthy mother and dying baby after dying baby. It was the hardest physical labor I ever did in my life: just backache and perspiration and disgust and discouragement and aching feet day in and day out. . . .

It was an appalling summer too, with an average of fifteen hundred babies dying each week in the city; lean, miserable, wailing little souls carried off wholesale by dysentery. . . . Babies always died in summer and there was no point in trying to do anything about it. It depressed me so that I branched out and went looking for healthy babies too and tried to tell their mothers how to care for them. But they were not interested. I might as well have been trying to tell them how to keep it from raining. . . .

. . . if I was to be the only woman executive in the New York City Department of Health, I badly needed protective coloring. As it was, I could so dress that, when a masculine colleague of mine looked around the office in a rather critical state of mind, no feminine furbelows would catch his eye and give him an excuse to become irritated by the presence of a woman where, according to him, no woman had a right to be. My man-tailored suits and shirtwaists and stiff collars and four-in-hand ties were a trifle expensive, but they more than paid their way as buffers. They were also very little trouble. I could order a suit and another dozen shirtwaists and collars with hardly a tenth of the time and energy that buying a single new frock would have required. . . . I wore a standard costume—almost a uniform—because the last thing I wanted was to be conspicuously feminine when working with men. . . .

I was assigned to the office of Dr. Darlington and given the official title of "Assistant to the Commissioner of Health." And during nearly all of these years I was what might be called a "trouble shooter." Anything which did not fit into the assignments of the regular staff of inspectors fell to me. It was a fine idea. For one thing, it kept life from anything like monotony. And for another, it showed me that this field of public health was far removed from anything that had been comprised in my conventional medical training. . . . We were dealing with the problems of a community, and the individual became important only when he contributed to the problem as a whole.

And so the odds and ends of experience began to take form in my eyes. There was a great deal that was rather rough. Invading Bowery lodging-houses, the ten-cents-a-night kind, for instance, to vaccinate the patrons against small-pox in the very early hours of the morning. It had to be done between midnight and six since the Bowery floaters were up and away by the time dawn broke and that was the only time to find them in any numbers. Few of them were nature's noblemen, so I always had a Health Department policeman by my side when I marched in; the usual picture being a huge, airless room in a decrepit old building that shook every time the elevated went by, filled with fully dressed men sleeping in musty blankets. The policeman would wake a man up and tell him to put out his arm. Then I would vaccinate him and pass on to the next. They were usually too far gone from bad whiskey to know very much about what was going on.

Things were exciting in another way when New York developed a spectacular and tragic epidemic of cerebrospinal meningitis and I became the temporary Department expert on the subject; not by merit, but because I happened to be the only member of the staff who had ever had much experience with this peculiarly horrible disease which then killed the majority of its victims and left the remainder maimed for life....

At that time health departments went entirely on the principle that there was no point in doing much until something had happened. If a person fell ill with a contagious disease, you quarantined him; if he committed a nuisance you made him stop doing it or made him pay the penalty. It was all after-the-fact effort—locking the stable door after the horse was stolen; pretty hopeless in terms of permanent results. No, there was no preventive medicine in public health. The term "Public Health Education" had not been invented. Perhaps something might be done; I was not sure but I hoped it could be tried.

The Bureau of Municipal Research group and I saw this at the same time. They had authority; I had none. And then they recommended to the Department that a division should be established to deal with the matter.... I [became] the proud and bewildered Chief of the newly created Division of Child Hygiene. I had no staff; I had no money; all I had was an idea. It was clear to the Commissioner that it was going to be a struggle to convince the Board of Estimate and Apportionment that money could be legally appropriated to care for well people. I could see that myself. A large part of being a successful government administrator consists of being able to keep the political powers-that-be appropriating funds for your pet projects.... You have to be a salesman as well as an executive. As a salesman I was going to need an impressive sample before I could get into our budget a sum large enough to pay for any such experiment. . . .

After several consultations as to how this approach might be made, I was allowed a trial experiment. The closing of schools in June would mean that the thirty-odd nurses on school inspection duty would be at liberty. June also meant the beginning of the diarrhoeal season which, if this summer of 1908 was going to be anything like its predecessors, would kill its 1,500 babies each week all through the hot weather. The Commissioner and Dr. Bensel let me have those nurses to use in an experiment in preventive child hygiene.

In order to make our experiment count for something, the scheme had to be tried out first in a district with a very high baby death rate. So I selected a complicated, filthy, sunless and stifling nest of tenements on the lower east side of the city. If we could accomplish anything in the face of living conditions like these, we would go far toward proving our point. This neighborhood was largely populated by recently landed Italians, willing to learn new things in a new country. . . .

How to reach the newborn babies without any waste effort was a problem. But it was not too difficult to solve. The Registrar of Records in the Department was cooperative and used to each day send me the name and address on the birth certificate of every baby whose birth had been reported on the previous day. It was essential to reach these babies while they were still very young and this proved to be the ideal way to find them. . . . Within a few hours, a graduate nurse, thoroughly instructed in the way to keep a well baby well, visited the address to get acquainted with the mother and her baby and go into the last fine detail of just how that baby should be cared for. Nothing revolutionary; just insistence on breast-feeding, efficient ventilation, frequent bathing, the right kind of thin summer clothes, out-of-door airing in the little strip of park around the corner—all of it common place enough for the modern baby . . . all of it new in public health. Many of these mothers were a little flattered to have an American lady take all that trouble about little Giovanni, and were likely to go out of their way to learn and to cooperate. . . .

From the first I was pretty sure that we were getting results. I was not prepared, however, for the impressiveness of the facts when the results of the summer's campaign in that corner of the east side were tabulated. During that summer there were 1,200 fewer deaths in that district than there had been the previous summer; we had saved more babies than there were men in a regiment of soldiers and I had learned one certain thing: heat did not necessarily kill babies. Everywhere else in town the summer death rate of babies had been quite as bad as ever. We had found out how to save babies on a large scale. But it was far more important that we had proved that prevention paid far beyond our wildest hopes. There, if we have to be dramatic about it, was the actual beginning of my life work.

It was never quite clear in my mind whether in pioneering in child hygiene being a woman was more of an asset than a liability. There were many times when a man might bury himself under the anonymity of his sex in such a position and thus contrive to get many things done without comment or criticism. But for a woman, this was more difficult. There were many stumbling blocks and the first one came early. It is difficult to realize now, but at that time the appointment of a woman as an executive was an upturning of procedure that brought out trouble all along the way. On the other hand, it had its compensations. From the point of view of publicity, it was superb. I have a well-defined feeling that if a man had been given this position, it would have been just another bureau; but for a woman to get this job, well, that was news. The Bureau needed publicity; my sex offered a challenge that provided good copy for the reporters and one of my real problems was how to avoid publicity instead of seeking it. That challenge was met immediately.

The start came when I was assigned a staff. Naturally they were all men. I had previously worked with all of them; we were good friends in our lowly capacity of inspectors. The picked few who were to help me from the Bureau were doctors; all splendid men, able, conscientious and adjustable. But evidently not adjustable enough to take kindly to the idea of working for a woman. They had hardly received notice of their appointments when all six of them walked solemnly into my office and told me that they had submitted their resignations. It was nothing personal, they assured me, but they could not reconcile themselves to the idea of taking orders from a woman. This was an impasse that I had not thought about but it was a serious one. I had to think quickly. I needed those particular doctors; I wanted them to work with me. It was a rather tense moment and I asked them to sit down and talk it over with me. "See here," I said; "you are really crying before you are hurt. I quite realize that you may not like the idea of working under me as a woman. But isn't there another side of this question? I do not know whether I am going to like working with you. None of us know how this is going to turn out. But if I am willing to take the responsibility of our success or failure, I think you might take a sporting chance with me."

They looked thoughtful for a long moment but no one said anything. I had to go on. "Let's try it this way. Give the arrangement a month's trial. If at the end of a month you still do not like it, go ahead and resign, and I will not say anything about it. But, if all goes well and you want to stay, I shall be glad. Is that agreed?"

They pondered again for a few moments and then, not too enthusiastically, said they would stay and hold up their resignations for a month. That month went by and I reminded them that the time had come for their decision. All of them told me that they had withdrawn their resignations. They had completely recovered from their distressful doubts and sensibilities. By that time we were all in the midst of an interesting and enthralling job and, as I had hoped, they were much too keen about its possibilities to leave it for a moment. Besides, with what now seems almost like Machiavellian subtlety, I had given each one a title and placed him at the head of a division in the Bureau. All six of those men stayed with me during the critical years of organization. . . .

The fact that the politicians and I mutually liked one another helped a great deal, of course. At bottom they were thoroughly corrupt and cynical, a sort of government cancer, but my occasional half-hour chats with these bosses were almost invariably very pleasant occasions. . . .

Sometimes I went to Tammany for the help I could not get from the city government. We would often find a baby in a family completely on the ragged edge, starving and freezing. Organized charity acted too slowly in such cases. So here was the cue for dropping in on the local Tammany district leader, who kept up his political fences by handing out help wherever it was needed. Two minutes of description, then: "Sure, ma'am, he'll get a sack of coal and enough money to eat on right away." Naturally the family so assisted meant another vote for the Tammany candidate in the next election, but that was not my business in such an emergency. . . .

To be quite honest, I must confess that I would rather work

with a Tammany administration than with a reform administration. I know, and knew then, that the organization meant graft and wholesale corruption. In the shameful conditions in the Health Department in my early days I had seen at close range where that sort of thing led. But, as the head of a Bureau trying to get things done, I inevitably had to depend upon the administration in power, and Tammany's methods, in my case, were a comfort. When I took a new idea to a reform administration, they were always very gentlemanly about it. But it was a long and arduous road to follow. They would, of course, ask how much it would cost and then, after they had studied my carefully worked out statement which went into meticulous detail, they would send me word that it would be considered in due course. Months later, they would let me know that although the idea was fundamentally sound, the state of the city's finances made it inadvisable at the moment. I did not want things considered; I wanted them done. Their caution appeared to be in the taxpayers' interest, of course, but from my point of view it was not the way to get things accomplished, and in the long run the taxpayers were bound to suffer too. I knew my work was important and I knew that it would always be an up-hill fight to put it over. . . .

I was by no means the logical person for the job of constructing an organization for saving babies. It should have been in the hands of a person with all the theory and practice of governmental administration right at his fingers' ends. And I was just a harmless young woman from a small town who had been forced by circumstances into becoming a doctor for lack of any career that attracted her more. On the face of it I am still a doctor. In fact, when I took my degree as Doctor of Public Health in 1917, I became a doctor for the second time. But, largely by accident, I was forced into becoming an executive and having less and less to do with the practice of medicine. It is queer how, after the necessary jostling and shaking, you usually end up in the right spot. I was probably cut out to manage things, although it took me a long time to find it out. Whether I had started in a biscuit factory or a profession or a suburban kitchen, I would probably have ended up behind a desk somewhere making the telephone and a staff of assistants jump around in the interests of some wide-spread scheme or other. Perhaps that was why I so welcomed this venture into uncharted seas. . . .

The work itself occasionally suffered from the blundering of doctors to whom it had never occurred that, if you went about things with insufficient preparation, you were likely to provoke riots among parents and children who would have been amiable enough if intelligently handled. In our tonsil-and-adenoid riot, for instance, I found myself in accord with the rioters. That was the culmination of several years of trying to make operable tonsil-and-adenoid cases in the public schools fit into our limited facilities for taking care of them. Hospital clinics were being swamped with cases referred by school medical inspectors, and post-operative treatment was out of the question; time and again I was called up in the middle of the night to reassure a frightened nurse about another case of post-operative septic sore throat or haemorrhage. It was not my line— I was a pediatrician, not a nose-and-throat specialist—but anyone working with a Bureau of Child Hygiene has to know a good deal about everything that can go wrong with human beings, except possibly senile dementia.

Since the clinics were so overworked, a brilliant staff member in a big hospital suggested that the doctors would do far better to go around and perform tonsil-and-adenoid operations *en masse* in the schools themselves instead of cluttering up the clinics. The Bureau knew nothing about this decision. I first heard of it when I got a 'phone call that there was serious trouble at one of the public schools on the lower east side and went down to investigate. The school yard was clogged with a mob of six or seven hundred Jewish and Italian mothers wailing and screaming in a fine frenzy and aparently just on the point of storming the doors and wrecking the place. Every few minutes their hysteria would be whipped higher by the sight of a child ejected from the premises bleeding from mouth and nose and screaming with sheer panic. In view of what I saw when I had fought my way inside, I would not have blamed the mothers if they had burned the place down. For the doctors had coolly descended on the school, taken possession, lined the children up, marched them past, taken one look down each child's throat, and then two strong arms seized and held the child while the doctor used his instruments to reach down into the throat and rip out whatever came nearest to hand, leaving the boy or girl frightened out of a year's growth and bleeding savagely. No attempt at psychological preparation, no explanation to the child or warning to the parents. In ten seconds I was in the middle of it, shouting that it must stop at once. When that point was carried, and it required a good deal of pointed language to carry it, I turned to pacifying the mob of mothers and getting them to go home. It was an out-rage—as cruel and as stupid as an initiation ceremony in an African tribe. You would have thought these children were so many fox-terriers having their ears and tails clipped, and that does not mean I approve of clipping them either.

It was stopped all right—stopped so short that there were no more of these operations done in school buildings. But with the overcrowded conditions in the clinics, the next move was up to me. I brought the matter up at the next meeting of the Section on Laryngology of the Academy of Medicine. What I wanted was assurance that, instead of this wholesale slaughter of innocents which, I shrewdly suspected, included many cases which did not need operations at all, the hospitals would take all justifiable school cases, give them a skilled operator, use approved anaesthetics and supply twenty-four hours of post-operative care before sending the child home. I said that, if they would not cooperate to that rea-sonable extent, I would open our own hospitals. The assembled laryngologists took that for mere bluster and said "No."

So I bided my time, caught the city fathers in a melting mood and obtained an appropriation for six small hospitals, city-run, specializing in nose-and-throat operations, staffed by men from our own medical force who were sent to get special training in this sort of work. They were beautiful little hospitals, with the latest equip-ment and surpassing technical standards. Then we started sending to them all school cases that were really operable, bringing in the children the evening before, operating under nitrous oxide gas and oxygen in the morning, keeping them all day surrounded by toys and ice cream and sending them home fit and cheerful that night. In six years we removed thousands upon thousands of adenoids and tonsils without a single fatality or a single instance of septic sore throat or post-operative bleeding—that last due in no small measure to our routine use of the new "thromboplastin" which had just been perfected by Dr. Alfred Hess. Our one difficulty was of a gratifying kind: the children had such a good time that it was sometimes a task to get them to go home. These hospitals were maintained for about five years. Then the general hospitals of the city agreed to follow the same procedure and we gladly turned the work back to them. . . .

There was the time when I grew quite bothered about the open-air classrooms in the schools. Not that they were bad in themselves: far from it. They were almost too good. The difficulty seemed to be that there were too few of them and that they were set apart as a sort of shrine not to be approached by the common herd. Why, I pondered, should we limit the advantage of fresh air to a chosen few? Why should we select only the most tragic cases for life in the out-of-doors? Why should we breed more candidates for fresh-air classes than we could possibly accommodate?

In going about the schools, I was struck with the pale and anaemic appearance of the children kept in badly ventilated classrooms with closed windows and then contrasted their appearance with the twenty or thirty children who were in the one open-air classroom in the same building. Only the most undernourished children, the most anaemic and the most fragile children were considered candidates for the open-air class. Once established in it, their cheeks became redder, their appetites improved, they gained weight and made miraculous recoveries. It was all very dramatic but wholly wrong from the point of view of one who had to think in terms of the masses. Indoors, there would be too many small bodies, too closely contained in their clothes, perhaps not literally sewn in for the winter, but semi-permanently garbed just the same. The empty desks where children were absent with colds were numerous, the children's faces were pale, their eyes dull. Mine would have been the same way if I had had to stay in such a room six hours each day for five days each week. The Elizabeth McCormick Memorial Foundation in Chicago used to publish a poster which went to the heart of the matter, although I always suspected that much of the irony in it was by no means intended by the artist. It was a picture of a ragged, undersized, shivering boy looking up into the face of a healthy man standing outside of a door labelled "Open Air School." "Mister," he was saying, "how sick do I have to be to get in there?"

I had the privilege, shared with a great many other women, of being suspected of mildly radical sympathies which during the war [1917–18] were, of course, synonymous with giving aid and comfort to the enemy. I was no pacifist whatever. I would hardly have received that major's commission if I had been. But I did belong to a luncheon club for women active in various social and economic movements, and that was apparently enough. The name of the club was, and still is, Heterodoxy. Perhaps it was the name that alarmed the spy-chasers. Perhaps it was true, as legend said, that a worried member of Heterodoxy had written a letter calling on the secret service men to keep an eye on the club's weekly meetings because its rolls contained so many pacifists and radicals. The fantastic result was that we really did have to shift our meeting-place every week to keep from being watched. It was just like an E. Phillips Oppenheim novel. All except the characters, that is. My colleagues in treason were not sloe-eyed countesses with small pearl-handled revolvers in their pocketbooks but people like Crystal Eastman, Fannie Hurst, Rose Pastor Stokes, Inez Haynes Irwin, Fola La Follette and Mabel Dodge Luhan. . . .

It may have been my connection with Heterodoxy that offended the Daughters of the American Revolution. Or perhaps it was my connection with the Federal Children's Bureau, which, for some reason or other, struck the stupider kind of conservatives as vaguely subversive when it was first started. I did not know I was on the D.A.R. blacklist until I received an invitation from a committee, headed by Heywood Broun, for a dinner given by and for all people who were not to be allowed to address meetings of the D.A.R., wherever found. I went to the dinner and had a very fine time in the very best of company—that list was the cream of American intellectuals with a slightly liberal leaning, for it was at the time when the Red-hunt was at its hottest.

Up to 1914 I think I could conscientiously have testified on oath that, in my opinion, I was leading a fairly active life. The foregoing pages merely summarize and actually give very little idea of the amount of skirmishing about, plus omnipresent, desk-confining detail, that goes into the organization and management of an undertaking like the Bureau of Child Hygiene. During the next five or six years, however, I began to look back on the pre-war period as a period of dignified relaxation. And I am not speaking merely of the war. Everything started whirling at once that year; why I do not know. Suffrage, for instance. Once I start talking suffrage and the general crisis in the cause of women's rights with which the height of American suffrage agitation coincided, I indulge in another period of marveling at the difference twenty years has made.

In the spring of 1914 I received a letter from the Philadelphia College of Physicians asking me to read a paper before them on some aspect of my child health work. I assumed that the Philadelphia College of Physicians was about the same as the New York Academy of Medicine, an institution with which I have had many contacts, both friendly and otherwise. When I reached Philadelphia, however, there was a note waiting for me at my hotel asking me to dine with twelve of the College doctors at the Union League. I was the only woman in the clubhouse. From the way the place felt and the way the members' faces froze into paralytic astonishment as I passed, I suspect I was the only woman who ever *had* been in the clubhouse. The dinner was a highly formal, extremely enjoyable, but definitely stately occasion. I could not understand why they were making so much social fuss over the mere reading of a paper before a first-rate medical society, or why I had been honored with this exclusively male society.

After dinner, my twelve hosts formed up in a column and escorted me in an impressive procession of motor cars to the College itself. There were no women in the audience there either. Then the President of the college rose to introduce me to this solemn assemblage of medical men, and they *were* an impressive-looking group.

"Gentlemen," he said, "this is a remarkable occasion. For the first time since the Philadelphia College of Physicians was founded in 1787, a woman has been allowed to enter its premises." I learned privately afterwards that it was only after months of debate that the College had decided to invite me at all.

That was more than half a century after Dr. Blackwell had started women in medical practice in America. The name of Pankhurst was already a household word wherever newspapers were read and periodicals of all kinds had been talking about the New Woman for thirty years.

[Dr. William H. Park, dean of the NYU Medical School, and lab director in the] New York Department of Health, asked me to lecture on child hygiene in a new course the school was giving to lead up to the new degree of Doctor of Public Health. I reflected that presently I would be taking into the Bureau new men who could write Dr.P.H. after their names, whereas I would be without that extremely pertinent degree. So, in the interests of discipline, I offered Dr. Park a bargain: I would give those lectures on child hygiene at Bellevue if he would let me enroll in the course myself, so I could take a Dr.P.H. degree too. He refused. The idea of letting me take the same course in which I was lecturing was not what bothered him. It was the college regulations forbidding women in any courses whatever. I can hardly be accused of acting unreasonably because I declined to act as teacher in an institution that considered me unfit for instruction.

Dr. Park tried for some time to find someone to lecture in that part of the course. No one would. Child hygiene was not as well known a subject then as it has since become. So he returned to me and again I refused except on that one condition and the argument went back and forth until we were all heartily sick of it. Finally the college surrendered. I was to be allowed to take the two-year course in public health and get my degree. Naturally they could not admit me and deny entrance to other women, so another set of long-barred doors opened to the female of the species.

With that farcical beginning, I lectured to Bellevue students for fifteen years. They never allowed me to forget that I was the first woman ever to impose herself on the college. Their method of keeping me reminded derived directly from my first lecture, which was a nerve-racking occasion. I stood down in a well with tiers of seats rising all around me, surgical-theater fashion, and the seats were filled with unruly, impatient, hardboiled young men. I looked them over and opened my mouth to begin the lecture. Instantly, before a syllable could be heard, they began to clap—thunderously, deafeningly, grinning and pounding their palms together. Then the only possible way of saving my face occurred to me. I threw back my head and roared with laughter, laughing at them and with them at the same time—and they stopped, as if somebody had turned a switch. I began to lecture like mad before they changed their minds, and they heard me in dead silence to the end. But, the moment I stopped speaking at the end of the hour, that horrible clapping began again. Frightened and tired as I was from talking a solid hour against a gloweringly hostile audience I fled at top speed. Every lecture I gave at Bellevue, from 1915 through to 1930, was clapped in and clapped out that way; not the spontaneous burst of real applause that can sound so heart-warming, but instead the flat, contemptuous whacking rhythms with which the crowd at a base-ball game walk an unpopular player in from the outfield.

By that time I was in the middle of the suffrage fight, as I should have been as a conspicuous woman in government service. I have explained before that I did not start out as a feminist at all. But it was impossible to resist the psychological suction which gradually drew you into active participation in the great struggle to get political recognition of the fact that women are as much human beings as men are. Fundamentally that was what we were all after. We suffrage agitators talked a great deal about how women's votes would clean up political corruption and encourage legislation and discourage wars, high-sounding hopes which seemed plausible enough at the time. But most of that was no more than strategic special pleading before the court of public opinion. Deep down what held us together was our sense of how unfair and absurd it was that the male half of the world should possess responsibilities from which we were excluded.

My early indifference to the suffrage issue broke down soon enough for me to be one of the five or six original members of the College Equal Suffrage League, an organization of college women working for the vote. We tried particularly to emphasize the absurdities of denying to well-educated women a privilege accorded to semi-illiterate men. . . .

The annual suffrage parade up Fifth Avenue . . . which eventually became one of the most impressive shows in American life, had only five hundred marchers the first time it braved public scorn. I was one of the five hundred, all of us about as excited and apprehensive as if we had been early Christian martyrs lining up for the grand march into the Colosseum. When I heard the command to march, I was literally not at all sure that the nerves and muscles in my quivering legs would meet their assignment. None of us had any idea how the public would react to the idea of a group of women making a public show of themselves, and that was pretty certainly the way the man in the street was going to look at it those days. So our orders were to march straight ahead, eyes front, no matter what happened.

A group of some fifty courageous men, headed by Oswald Garrison Villard, marched with us and carried banners and placards boosting our cause as fervidly as we were boosting it ourselves. When this men's section swung into line and stepped out into Fifth Avenue, we all heard a roar of laughter go up and pursue them like a vanishing wave. Here it comes, we thought, glancing out of the corners of our eyes at the grinning, sniggering crowd. But they had a respectable reason for their mirth. Somebody had been in too much of a hurry handing out the placards, and one of the men, striding along conspicuously in the van of the men's section, was carrying a large sign that read: "Men can vote—why can't we?"

When we got that away from him, the spectators quieted down somewhat. There was plenty of jeering, but there was also a fair amount of encouragement for us. The chief danger was from the sheer bulk of the crowd. Police protection was most inadequate and presently the spectators were pressing inquisitively in from the sidewalks, as crowds always will when there is nothing to hold them back, threatening to smother the parade without trying to. But we stepped right ahead, chins up and out, and our immediate path was kept clear by a kind of psychological right of eminent domain.

Every year after that experiment, the suffrage parade was bigger, more impressive and more picturesque, and every year we drew larger and more friendly crowds. Different units in the parade had special costuming both to work up morale among their members and to increase the spectacular aspects of the show; we college women, for instance, did our parading as a solid phalanx of academic caps and gowns—and there were masses of brilliant scarves and magnificent women-riders dashing up and down on horseback, acting as marshals and incidentally demonstrating to the crowd that a female creature, for all this weaker sex talk, could sit a horse like a cavalry colonel. . . . The whole thing was a grand show in the bright sunshine of early fall when the parade was usually held; the air just a little crisp, the bands playing and thousands on thousands of determined and disciplined women steadily marching from Union Square to 59th Street in a demonstration of solidarity that made each individual in the line of march feel like a giantess in her own right. What a thrill we did get out of it! I am not much of a walker, but every time we got to the Plaza and were ordered to disband, I felt childishly disappointed because we could not go right back to Union Square and start over again.

In writing an autobiography, one has the great advantage of occupying the center of the stage. It is much the same feeling that came over me during those long years when I taught. . . . For that brief moment you are there to be listened to, and in a sense, your word is law. . . . So now, I assume the right to give my reactions to my life as I have lived it. . . .

Years ago, when the work for saving babies started, there was little or no doubt in my mind that it was a great humanitarian project and that no effort, no matter how great, could be counted wasted if it accomplished this purpose. Not that I was ever even mildly sentimental about working for and with children. There were many times when it seemed quite clear to me that I might as well have been part of any business that involved mass production. It brought into play all of the administrative and executive functions that might be applied to any large business. Once in a while, it seemed actually necessary for me to make trips throughout the city and to visit the baby health stations and the schools so that the necessary human touch would come back to me. On the whole, my work was strangely impersonal; simply an intriguing proposition that had enough difficulties to make it worth doing. . . . Here was a great waste: my problem was how to prevent it. . . .

In the earliest years it was practically all struggle. There were, no doubt, many mistakes. That seemingly could not be helped. No one liked a woman in an executive job in a city department. Few tried to help. Later, when insults began to come, my friends were many and of the right sort. First among them were the pediatricians of the city, although in the very beginning they too had held themselves very much aloof. . . . No one could have asked for better support than I had among the professional groups. Though we had our differences of opinion, they were loyal and stalwart champions of our common cause.

I presume I have always had the spirit of the pioneer, and at first, had the gay and gorgeous buoyance of youth. Not that I have recognized it; life has been too busy for that. But as I look back over the years, there seem to have been a surprising number of "firsts" in my life. I suspect that was because women were then making an effort to get out of the shadow-land where they had dwelt for so long, and the enormous vitality and strength of youth made almost anything seem possible. I was young and active during the years when women began to be emancipated and to find their place. . . . The pioneer aspect of my work—that I could have been the first woman to earn the degree of Doctor of Public Health, the first woman to hold an executive governmental position, the first woman to be appointed in the professional rank in the League of Nations and above all, the first woman (or man for that matter) to act on the idea that preventive medicine in baby and child care was a function of government—seems very strange and unreal now. But it has left me with a special interest in the achievements of my sex. Today women are everywhere in public life. Not that they have made the strides that I had hoped for them thirty years ago. It seemed for a time—certainly after they received the right to vote— as though the way were clear and open before them. For several years, women went constantly forward. Today, there are many signs that they are content with a lower level of attainment. Possibly the economic condition of the world is responsible, but the fact remains.

I know that in the profession of medicine women are still a long way from their goal and, moreover, that they have been losing their higher grade positions and failing to get anywhere near the "top." Hospitals still do not open their doors to women in staff positions; clinics still relegate them to the lower ranks and, on the whole, they have not held their hardly won gains of twenty, or even fifteen years ago. . . .

I hold no brief for women as women. There are good and bad in their ranks. But I have a strong suspicion that the same holds true for men, and I do not think that many women have been the success that they might well be. It is still a man's world. The vote did not bring us either full emancipation or full opportunity. We still have plenty of indirect influence but little that is direct. We have made some gains but we have also suffered many losses. During the suffrage days I had no great illusion about my sex; I wanted the vote as a matter of common justice. But I still believe that women have something to offer this sick world that men either do not have or have not offered.

It seems to me that women could make a real contribution in the field of medicine. In the course of my lifetime that profession has, I fear, become less human. The general practitioner is passing. Today, a patient has virtually to make his own diagnosis of his ailment before knowing what doctor to choose to treat him. Specialism is rampant among both men and women doctors, although women, still at a disadvantage in the profession, increase the hazard if they decide to specialize. It is true today, as always, that the general practitioner could care for, with adequate and good results, at least eighty percent of all the ailments of mankind. The need for highly specialized knowledge is not frequent. . . . It is true that the laboratory and the X-ray have added much that is valuable to our knowledge of diagnosis, but in this change of tactics the average doctor has lost much of his basic skill. Thirty years ago, we had to depend upon our sense of touch, sight and hearing to make a diagnosis, and experience developed an alertness that is not completely replaced by routine laboratory reports. . . .

. . . sick people need immediate help, understanding and humanity almost as much as they need highly standardized and efficient practice. The medical profession is mostly composed of high-minded men, but organized medicine as it exists today in the United States has surrounded the profession with too many taboos and too strong a cult for success to allow it to meet the everyday needs of the mass of the people. I have a great sense of pride in my profession. I know it is moving forward. But I regret the road it has chosen to take.

Dorothy Reed Mendenhall

(1874–1964)

Second daughter and youngest child of a prosperous midwestern manufacturing family descended from seventeenth-century American pioneers, Dorothy Reed Mendenhall was educated at home by governesses and her maternal grandmother. A graduate of Smith College, class of 1895, she entered Johns Hopkins Medical School in 1896 after having prepared in physics and chemistry at M.I.T. After receiving her M.D. in 1900, Reed worked at Johns Hopkins in the laboratories of two noted medical scientists, William Osler and William H. Welch. Her research in pathology in Welch's laboratory established conclusively that Hodgkin's disease, hitherto thought a form of tuberculosis, is a distinct disorder characterized by a specific blood cell, thereafter known as the Reed cell. Despite the promise of her research, Reed left Johns Hopkins in 1902, discouraged by the lack of opportunities for women. Settling at Babies Hospital in New York in 1903, she began to develop what was to be a lifelong interest in maternal and child health.

Marriage in 1906 to Charles Elwood Mendenhall took Reed to the Univerity of Wisconsin, where for almost a decade she remained at home as the mother of young children. Only two of the couple's four children survived infancy, sons Thomas Corwin (b. 1910) and John Talbot (b. 1912). In 1914 Mendenhall returned to professional life as a lecturer in the Department of Home Economics at the University of Wisconsin. Her principal concerns were collecting epidemiological data about maternal and child health and preparing correspondence courses for new mothers. When war duty took her husband to Washington in 1917, Mendenhall became a medical officer for the U.S. Children's Bureau, extending her concerns for maternal and child health to the war orphans of France, Belgium, and England in 1919. She carried out an influential study in Denmark in 1929, concluding that maternal and child health in the United States was damaged by the American propensity for technological intervention in the natural process of birth. In *Midwifery in Denmark* (1929) she advocated greater reliance on midwives and a greater trust in natural processes.

Mendenhall's career interests were reshaped by the requirements of marriage and her passion for research redirected to epidemiology rather than laboratory science. A deeply reflective woman whose favorite reading was Marcus Aurelius, she speculated toward the end of her life about whether this rechanneling of her intellectual energy had been at too great a cost. She concluded that she could not imagine life without husband and sons, though she hoped for a future when marriage need not end a career of laboratory research.

UNPUBLISHED MEMOIR

I have determined to make a beginning—long deferred—of putting down my recollections of the past sixty years as clearly and as honestly as I can, though there will be omissions and unexplained passages—for I am a woman and a Victorian but I shall write for my great granddaughter of the way my world was made, and what happened to me in the making and unmaking of it. . . .

I have lived a long time—and to show how my braid has been plaited I shall go back to my earliest recollection—a house on E. Town St., Columbus, Ohio—next to the corner east of the Deaf and Dumb Asylum. I was taken out of that home before I was four years old—to live at my grandmother Kimball's on the edge of town—while my mother and father sought cures for his diabetes and long-standing tuberculosis. It was a small two story brick house between two large mansions occupied by friends of my mother. There was the usual back and front parlor, hall to the west and stairs going up, dining room back of the parlors, but upstairs the room over the dining room went from east to west, had windows on both sides of the room, a short step up into my mother's bedroom, and a door out to a stair going down to the kitchen. My brother slept in what was a hall bedroom—the space left over the front hall by the stairs, which ran up to our nursery door. A woman, Mrs. Adams, was our nurse at this time and my sister Elizabeth and I slept in the nursery with her. Clearly do I remember waking when I turned over in my crib in one corner to see Mrs. Adams sewing by a lamp at a table in the center of the room. Also I remember a light from my mother's bedroom illuminating for a brief instant our darkness, when my parents would come to the door for a word with Mrs. Adams or to see if all were well with us before they retired. I have a vivid recollection of falling down the steps leading from my mother's room and of a nightmare or dream when I rolled out of my low crib and into the open closet door on the opposite side of the room, to be found there sleeping quietly when our nurse rose to get us up in the morning. These impressions were all made in my third year—for I was not born in this house, but lived there from the time I was two until nearly four when my father's health was so poor that he retired from business and tried in vain for the few remaining years of his life to stem the rush of oncoming oblivion.

The Kimball place in Columbus . . . was the usual red brick, with high ceilings and long narrow windows set in twos in the rooms on either side of the front hall which was wide enough for tables, chairs, large hatrack—and lined with large pictures—steel engravings of Washington crossing the Delaware, Lincoln and his cabinet, the ten first Presidents of the United States (I own this), ran from the front portico to end in a wide porch which covered the entire length of kitchens and pantries which extended from the right side (on entering) of the house and led into the dining room. The stairs emptied into the back part of the hall, a landing at the end of the hall over the back door was lighted by a large window which gave light to the hall as well as the long narrow glass windows on either side of the wide front door. To me this is the most admirable type of stairs—one descending at the back of the hall with a landing from which a second flight or preferably two, reach the second story. The passing of the front hall, and the loss of beauty of stairways, landings, and railings have followed the trend to cities, to apartment life, and to economy of space. Family life was less dependent on halls than on fireplaces or porches for welding the lives of the individual members together—but if "a room of one's own" is necessary for individual development, I wonder if space of hallways and rooms were not necessary for the uncramped growth of large families. Children in utero may have deformities brought on and maldevelopment from too little space to move about caused by abnormally little "liquor animi." Physical and mental growth come best where the individual is not hampered by the pressure of other personalities. The trend today of the nursery school to socialize the child may in the future turn back a hundred years to giving the young organism an untrammeled place to develop without outside pressure. At least one of my firm convictions is that my life was allowed free development in a most unusual way, because of my father's illness and death and my sister's disease and my early sicknesses which prevented our going to public school and induced by mother to keep us at large half the year in the wilds of Talcottville and most of the winter on the Kimball place, when we were not in New York City to see the surgeons in charge of Elizabeth. I am unconvinced of the value of grade schooling. It seems to me all the pre-college education or even preparation for a simple vocation or work could well be put in six years, leaving the first ten for physical development, handicraft and organized play. As I never had any formal education before I was thirteen, I know it can be managed for the more fortunate.

Before my marriage in 1906—my mother had had, from the mid-'90s, more than half my income: after 1903—practically all my income, as I could live on my salary as Resident of the Babies Hospital.

These years of my mother's dependence on me, and the responsibility of the Furbish children [Mendenhall's deceased sister's children], and the sorrow of my sister's unhappy life and tragic last illness, forged my character into iron. Any sweetness I may have once had—turned to strength. It made a woman of me in my teens— sent me into a profession—and gave me many worthwhile responsibilities. One bad thing it gave me was a fear of being left in want. For years I would wake in the night—afraid of poverty. (Kipling: "Whatever comes or does not come, the children of man must not be afraid.")

The year after my first trip to Europe—my last in 1936 was my seventh—my mother was brought to realize that my formal education had to begin. I was 13½ years old and had never been in school. I could read and write and draw and paint, but as for arithmetic and grammar, I had never more than seen the books. . . . A most remarkable woman was chosen to teach me. Anna C. Gunning, an Irish woman of real culture and educational values, had been in the high school at Mansfield, Ohio, where Uncle Henry lived. She was a gaunt, frail woman, with skin the color of yellow parchment. I presume my mother paid her well and that she needed an easier job than the daily public school grind that she had followed for many years to support herself. At any rate, she came to Columbus and started to lighten my abysmal ignorance. She stayed with me three years and three months, prepared me for college, and by her unflinching rules of doing well what was to be done and at the required time, she ground into me habits of study which made it possible for me not only to go to college, but later to take up graduate work. Miss Gunning and my mother were at opposite poles of femininity. Homely, badly dressed, caring only for intellectual interests, this quiet, naturally rather timid woman, set herself against my superficial, pleasure-loving mother, in relentless opposition as far as my training was concerned. Why she stayed in such an uncongenial household, I cannot imagine. I am sure that my mother paid her generously, as was her custom, but she must have had a real interest in and affection for me, to stand some of the scenes and insist on study hours being kept and work being well done in a home where everyone did what he or she pleased and when the spirit moved. And yet I never remember a word from her to me in criticism of mother or her ways. I shudder to think what might have become of me without Miss Gunning's mental discipline and standards of accomplishment. The first months she was with me we were still living in Columbus. Elizabeth was in Berlin, Will in Boston. I had never been caged in a school room, so Miss Gunning proposed that we study out of doors. Old Brown carried table and chairs out in the cow pasture, next to our Columbus house, and we began study the spring of 1888 under a huge oak tree. Keeping me still and at work was the great problem. Finally Miss Gunning evolved the plan that if I studied or recited for 25 minutes I could have 5 minutes to run off my bottled-up spirits. It must have been a queer scene for anyone looking on. A big girl, with two pigtails below her waist, bent over a book or paper, with one eye on an adjacent alarm clock. When 5 minutes before the half or the hour was reached, off the pupil went with a whoop to tear around the lot, climb a tree, or raid the kitchen, while the undisturbed teacher went on quietly reading until the hour or half hour was reached, when a bell was sounded and the child recalled. My studies began with Latin grammar, arithmetic, and English. For the latter I chose a poem, or just a page or so from Shakespeare, which had been read from book to book by me long before I was twelve.

Years after, Miss Gunning told me that she was in despair this spring of being able to handle me. She had never attempted to guide an utterly untrained mind, and though she said no word of criticism, I realized even then that she not only had a hard job to do, but had to do it without any help from the family, and even against mother's thoughtless opposition. I shall always feel Anna Gunning saved me from being an ignorant nonentity. Thinking over this period in my life, I cannot be grateful enough to this quiet, austere, unattractive woman who came into my life at the crucial moment. Another year, or with a less determined guide, my chance of being a really well educated woman would have passed. She literally set my feet solidly on the paths of higher learning and inspired me with her real love of knowledge and respect for mental attainment. She was the most impersonal in her relations with youth of any teacher I had ever known. . . . She expected the best of me, and insisted that once planned the work should be accomplished. My number work was the poorest. That year I finished arithmetic, the next plane geometry, the third year algebra—all under protest. I remember clearly my wail—"Why do I have to learn this stuff—what does it have to do with life?" Latin I thoroughly enjoyed and finally read all of Virgil with her, at sight, in order to finish the Latin requirement for college—our last spring in Germany. Through Miss Gunning's guidance my English reading became wider and more worthwhile. My natural taste for poetry was developed. The required reading for college entrance was covered a hundred fold.

The curriculum my first year [at Smith] was quite prescribed. We took Latin with Dr. Brady and Miss Norcross, English with Miss Jordan and Miss Czarnomska, mathematics with Miss Eleanor Cushing, history with Miss Lord, German with Frau Kopp, and French with a variety of weaklings. All the rest were good teachers— but none of them great as far as I was concerned.

Probably my taking biology my second year under Harris Wilder settled for me the field of my future work. Dr. Wilder, a small, pint-sized, red-haired man, was a great teacher. He knew his subject thoroughly, was a brilliant lecturer, and had such an unusual dexterity, coupled with artistic ability, that he illustrated his talks by drawing most unusual pictures of any animal form he was describing. He was ambidextrous and would stand in front of the blackboard and draw the details of an intricate organism using both hands and moving from a central line both right and left so rapidly that it was difficult to follow him until the entire picture, complete and whole, was on the board.

Harris Wilder was the first great teacher I had ever had. I well remember my feeling after his first lecture in general biology. During the entire hour I sat spellbound. I was not conscious of my surroundings and was oblivious of the passage of time. At the end of the lecture I gasped, sat up, and said to myself, "This is it, this makes sense—this is what I have been waiting for all these years." When most study, though pleasant, was drudgery, naturally I took all of the biology offered and did well in all of the courses. I took honors in biology, but I was so absorbed in filling my curriculum with his courses that I took no chemistry. Though a good course was offered in this science, oddly enough there was no physics offered at Smith during my stay or for a number of years afterwards.

Looking back as I now can on sixty years of life, I find three pleasures have been paramount to me. First in its appearance, if not in strength, was love of woods, hills, plant life—especially paths leading in and out of hilly places such as at Talcottville in my youth, or Tryon today. A voyage of discovery—even if only a few miles as in Montreat this winter—offers the greatest pleasure left to me. Then I should put love of art—started by my grandmother Kimball in my childhood, and which still, especially for the love of color, gives me joy and has always been my favorite resource. Mental activity—mastering an intellectual subject in order to make it your own, and be able to give it out in recitation, lecture, or in written form—though less frequently resorted to—especially in later years, has afforded me the highest emotional outlet. Creative energy has been the most exciting experience in my life. Music has meant little to me. I regret that I have not cultivated my knowledge of music for the great resource it offers as age advances—especially since I have had great musical opportunities, and it would have meant so much to Charles if I had been able to share his talent and interest.

Perhaps at Smith, more than actual study, my contact with girls my own age and the making of a few close friends, were the most valuable part to me. My childhood was spent largely with people much older than I was, so that when I went to college I had never had a close girl friend and had known only a few of my sister's friends, casually. As I look back on these college days, I realize how awkward I was in making new contacts—not especially from shyness or any inhibitions on my part—but mostly from sheer ignorance and lack of experience in meeting adolescents. It was as if because of not going to school, travelling a good deal, and living with adults, I had skipped the between stage from childhood to womanhood—and yet I lacked maturity and the experience girlhood builds on childhood. At any rate, I was allowed a period to fill out and a fine normal place for development.

[Reed's first journey to Johns Hopkins Medical School]
There was only one passenger in the car besides myself, and I soon was aware that I was an object of interest to him. Almost opposite my seat on the bench that ran lengthwise of the car, sat a

distinguished gentleman dressed in grey oxford morning coat, striped trousers, and wearing a silk hat. He was short, but so finely built and slender that he did not seem small. I noticed immediately the sallow, ivory-colored tone of his skin and the small hands with tapered fingers folded over a cane which he held between his knees. My appearance seemed to interest him for he literally stared me out of countenance—seeming to go over me from head to foot, as if he were cataloguing every detail for future reference. I decided that he was an oriental—this conclusion brought about by his color and the long, thin rattail moustache that he kept pulling as he inventoried my charms. I knew that he was a gentleman, so I was embarrassed but not alarmed. Thinking to avoid him as soon as possible, when the car stopped at Broadway I hopped out first, and walked quickly in the direction of the hospital gates a block away. He soon caught up with me, and walking along side of me, said very casually, "Are you entering the medical school?" I managed to gasp out that I intended to. "Don't," said he, "go home." And to my amazement without another word walked on ahead of me and went up the long flight of steps leading to the hospital door. Well, thought I, he must be crazy. How would he know that I was going into medicine, or why should he advise me not to? I think this incident dampened my interest in the unprepossessing brick buildings of the hospital and the medical school, for after a very short stay, I found a return street car and took myself back to Miss Conway's and my little room. No other incidents of my first day in Baltimore remain in my memory. I was decently housed in a home of gentle women who gave me excellent meals and looked after my comfort in every possible way. That night I must have read my Marcus Aurelius, which I had acquired some years before, and which I have read as a daily help for 50 years, using the 12 chapters for the different months of the year, and finding unfailing guidance from the wise words written by the great Roman Emperor nearly 1,900 years ago. There is an annotation of my year at Tech [M.I.T.] in this little volume of the Jeremy Collier translation that has been my constant companion since 1894, and a number of quotations written in that I recognize as emanating from my years in medical school. In Book VIII, a pencil date, Sept. 21, 1896, the night before my 22nd birthday my first week in Baltimore, marks the verse, "All conditions are subject to revolution, so that you need not be afraid of anything new." Certainly in my life, the greatest influence and the greatest comfort has been the words of this pagan follower of the Greek philosophers, who, to me at least, seems to have so much more of a personal message than his Greek masters. . . .

The next day at the appointed hour in the morning I went over to the University buildings, then in the city itself—I think, on Howard Street. I found the floor with no difficulty and a dozen or more men waiting in an ante-room. I remember no women being there. Possibly we had appointments alphabetically, because the men I grew to know well, as Glanville Rusk and Dick Rand, were waiting with me. At last, my name—Dorothy Reed—was called and with my heart thumping until I thought it would break my chest, I entered a long, impressive room. Around an enormous table sat a distinguished gathering of men, representing, I presume, the faculty of the new medical school. Only two of the group became definite personalities to me. I was too scared to do more than take the chair offered me. The chairman, or at least the man sitting at the head and next to whom my chair was placed, was the Dean, Dr. Welch. I think that he introduced himself. He asked questions of me, referring to the credentials I had sent to him. Then he said, "I think Miss Reed has fulfilled all our requirements." One man I cannot place, possibly Dr. Remsen, asked me about the number of chemistry laboratory hours I had taken. When I looked up to answer him, to my amazement, next to him was the man of the street car incident. I mumbled a reply. Dr. Welch rose and bowed and intimated that the interview was over, telling me to be at the medical school the next morning at 9 o'clock. I got up and—not knowing what to do—*backed out* of the room until I reached the door—feeling that this group represented to me—royalty.

Once again in the ante-room, I said to a man waiting there—later known to me as my good friend Dr. Rusk—"Who was the gentleman sitting on the left of Dr. Welch?" He answered, "Why, that is the great Dr. Osler." I do not think that I had then ever heard of the man, who later became my teacher and the kindest of friends. Of all the men I have ever known, or even met, William Osler has always seemed to me to have the most vivid personality as well as the finest mind and character. He was the greatest teacher I have ever known; an inspiration to his pupils and colleagues, one of the great gentlemen and influences of his age in the profession of medicine. . . .

There is one more incident that I must give of my 2nd year in Baltimore—an experience that nearly sent me out of medicine. As at any medical school there was a hospital medical society besides many other evening meetings and lectures. We heard the other students talking about going to the monthly meetings, and as I was very eager to grasp every opportunity that would give me a better chance to do well in medicine, I proposed to Mabel Austin walking down to the monthly meeting. She wouldn't or couldn't go and I induced Margaret Long to companion me. We arrived before the crowd and took front seats in a lecture room on the ground floor under one of the public wards. It was a large room but soon filled. I think that we were the only women present. The one woman interne and the women upper classmen, few in number, knew better than to attend this meeting. Simon Flexner presided, sitting at a table just in front of us. The speaker of the evening—Dr. Mackenzie of the nose and throat department—was introduced after some preliminary business. He talked an hour on some disease of the nose. But from the start he dragged in the dirtiest stories I have ever heard, read, or imagined, and when he couldn't say it in English he quoted Latin from sources not usually open to the public. Unfortunately, I had majored in Latin at Smith, and 7 years study made most of his quotations understandable to me. Nearly 50 years has passed since this night, but much he said is branded in my mind and still comes up like a decomposing body from the bottom of a pool that is disturbed. It seems impossible that on such a harmless subject a specialist could make it so pornographic. Of course, the diseases of the nose and throat were not taken up before our 4th year and the entire lecture would have been over our heads had he limited himself to his subject. However, I did know my anatomy, and Dr. Mackenzie spent most of his hour discussing the cavernous tissue present in the nasal passages and comparing it with the corpus spongiosa [sic] of the penis. We sat just opposite the speaker and the chairman, so that the flushed, bestial face of Dr. MacKenzie, his sly pleasure in making his nasty points, and I imagine the added fillip of doing his dirt before two young women, was evident. I knew that we could not go out—not only should not, but I doubted that I could make the distance to the door without faltering. The decision to sit it through was the right one, so I fastened my gaze on Simon Flexner and prayed that he would not laugh. Roars of laughter filled the room behind us at every dragged-in joke of Dr. Mackenzie and at every allusion to the similarity of the nose to the male reproductive system. Through it all Simon Flexner sat like a graven image, his face absolutely impassive like the profile of an old Roman coin. All my life I have been grateful for this man's decency, which at the time seemed to be an anchor to buoy me through this ordeal. Somehow the talk came to a close. I got up, and followed by Margaret, made for the door through a sea of leering, reddened faces. We got outside and started to walk down the parkway in the center of Broadway. I cried all the way home—hysterically—and Margaret swore. When we made the Pill Box, I went to our room, leaving Margaret to explain my disturbed condition to the girls. This was the first of the week. The next few days I stayed at home, spending most of my time in Clifton Park—debating with myself whether or not to leave the medical school. Such mud as had been flung at me stuck, and I couldn't make up my mind as to whether or not I was strong enough to rise above such defilement. The girls discussed it at night, and I prayed for help. It is characteristic that Margaret Long was untouched—she put it down to the natural bestiality of man and ignored it entirely. Part of my trouble was that I couldn't face my class, many of whom I had seen thoroughly enjoying themselves at the lecture. Some of them I knew well, liked, and had thought of them as friends. Finally on Saturday I made myself try it. I went down to the Pathological Laboratory to make up the work I had lost. I had Mabel's notes and the girls of my class had collected my slides for me. I was bending over my microscope with only a few students in the laboratory when Dr. Carter—an assistant in the laboratory—the son of the President of Williams College, remarkable to us as the tallest man in the medical school, came up to me. He asked if I needed any help and then hung around a few minutes. When we were quite alone, he said, "Miss Reed, I want to say every decent man at the meeting Monday night felt the way you looked. I want to apologize for being at such a meeting." Then he left and I felt purged of all pitch that had been thrown at me. A few minutes later Paul Woolley in my class came in—said he had to make up the week's work and it finally came out that he, too, had been at the medical meeting. It had made him violently sick at his stomach, and he had taken to the woods, literally, and had been studying birds. He was quite an ornithologist, and the son of the prohibitionist candidate for President. I went home calm and in control of myself. Simon Flexner, Dr. Carter, and Paul had felt as I did—there were probably many others. All was right with the world. Several years after I spoke to Dr. Osler about such a lecture being permitted to be given at the Hospital. He replied that the real speaker of the evening had been prevented from coming and the program committee had heard of a good paper of Dr. Mackenzie's—and had substituted it. Dr. Osler said that Dr. Flexner was sick about it, and he himself would never have permitted any talk of Dr. Mackenzie.

This hideous experience, added to unpleasant practical jokes from the class ahead of us (my own class was essentially quiet and gentlemanly), made me consider carefully my relation to those surrounding me, as it affected my actions and feeling. I decided after much thought, that as long as I was in medicine that I would never object to anything a fellow student or doctor did to me or in my presence if he would act or speak the same way to a man. If he were a boor, he would act like one—be loose in his conversation or jokes, slam a door in your face, hog the best of everything, be oblivious of any of the niceties of life or the courtesies—but if he discriminated against me because I was a woman—tried to push me around, was offensive in a way he wouldn't be to a man, I would crack down on him myself—or take it up with the authorities if he proved too much for me alone. On the whole, this was the right way to take the position of woman in medicine in the 19th century. It made life bearable, allowed me to make friends with some men who were not very pleasant persons—but knew no better, and earned me the respect and friendship of many of my associates. It didn't endear me to one or two I fell afoul of, and undoubtedly I developed an independence, even an arrogance, which was foreign to my original nature. I was distinctly not such a "nice" person, but a stronger one, after Johns Hopkins.

As I have said, in the '90s there were relatively few women in medicine and no other first-rate school admitting women. . . .

Ours, the class of 1900, was the largest class ever entered, around 50, and the 4th regular class to graduate from Johns Hopkins Medical School. We entered, I think, with 12 women. Four from Smith—Florence Sabin, Rose Fairbank, Hannah Myrick, and Dorothy Reed; Ellen Stone from Brown University; Clara Meltzer from Barnard; three Leland Stanford graduates—Clelia Mosher, Evelyn Briggs, and Ellen Lowell; Alma Beale, Eleanor Chace, and Mary Marvell from Wellesley; and an unfortunate dumbbell from Vassar who dropped out during the first year along with Evelyn Briggs, a psychotic.

[On graduation Reed was offered research positions but no regular hospital appointment.] I went into a huddle with myself and went back to Dr. Welch with my decision. I thanked him very much for his interest, and Dr. Halsted and Dr. Williams for their offer to give me a place in their services, but I wanted medicine and if I couldn't have medicine at Hopkins, I should have to go up to New York and see what offered itself there. Dr. Welch was disturbed, but he took my decision as final, asking only that I do nothing without first telling him of my plan. So it rested during the last weeks of our year. The examinations came and went. Everyone was very jittery about grades. I remember Dick Rand who took second place in the entire class assuring me solemnly that he had flunked and disgraced himself. Commencement day came and went. We medical students, with the other university graduates, sat in a big circle on the stage back of the faculty and facing the audience in the amphitheater of one of the Baltimore theaters. It was terribly long, hot, and tiresome. Finally the President, Dr. Gilman, came to the medical school, and the names of those taking honors were read. Florence and I were the only women. . . .

. . . when it was all over the ranking medical students were told to appear the next morning at the hospital to meet the attending physicians and to be assigned their interneships and other positions. So the suspense was still kept up.

We were all together at nine o'clock with Dr. Osler, Dr. Halsted, and others of professional rank. All I remember was Dr. Osler speaking and saying that John MacCallum, first of all in our class, was too ill to take a hospital post or any other position. John had lived in a private room in the hospital most of his last year, going to such classes as he was allowed to and having a rest cure most of the time. . . . Then Dick Rand's name was read. What service do you take, Dr. Rand? Surgery of course. Then a man named Allen— who took medicine. Then 4th in the class, Florence Sabin. "Medicine" faltered Dr. Sabin. To my surprise Bill Sowers and I tied for 5th place with the same average of 97. Dr. Osler explained this and asked, "Miss Reed, what is your choice?" I looked him in the eye and said, "Medicine, sir." Dr. Sowers took medicine too and the crisis was past. . . . After it was over Dr. Osler spoke to his 4 medical appointees. Boys, he said to Dr. Allen and Dr. Sowers, these girls will have a hard time and I expect you both to give them any help you can to make it easier. Dr. Sabin and I were of course to have the white women's ward, or the colored wards—men, women, and children. There was apparently quite a lot of bad feeling brought about by my being given medicine. Henry Christian, later Dean at Harvard Medical School, wrote me a very courteous letter asking if I were quite certain that I wanted and was going to take my medical appointment, ending that if he couldn't have medicine under Dr. Osler, he would not stay in Baltimore. I felt very indignant at his intimating that I should make way for him. It is difficult to realize how anyone could bring themselves to ask such a favor, even indirectly, from a classmate. One day in the library Paul Woolley brought up the subject, saying that it seemed very hard that he had to take obstetrics and I be given medicine. Dr. Rusk who was with us countered immediately, "Miss Reed deserves what she was given—she was a better student than you every year." This animosity was a blow to me. It was the first time that I personally was made to feel that I was not wanted in the medical profession and my first realization of the hard time any woman has to get recognition for equal work. I left for a summer in Talcottville, still somewhat elated but not dreaming of what was to come from this situation.

In June of 1900, I left Baltimore with high hopes. It seemed that God had given me the things I had asked for. Also I had the satisfaction of having worked hard and really done my best for 5 years so the reward of an interneship under Dr. Osler seemed deserved. . . . So it was a shock to me, after the announcement of our appointments, to meet some bad feeling in my classmates as I have described. In spite of a good deal of talk about the unfairness of giving 2 women honors though we were 1/4th of the entire class, and knowing from Dr. Welch that there had been strong objection in the medical faculty, I went home with the conviction that all was well with my world.

Until I returned in September, I had not realized what we faced. After 3 months at home, with mother, my sister, and her children—a rather dispiriting time as the Berlin Falls Mills had burned and Elizabeth was home until Willard could find something to do. My mother had her hands full with the housekeeping and the care of 3 little children, for my sister was already sick with the infection which caused her death three years later. It was a hard summer for everyone, but September finally came and I was on my way back to Baltimore filled with joyful anticipation. I reached the hospital on the last day of August and was met by a very upset Dr. Sabin. She had arrived earlier and had been sent for by Dr. Hurd, the Superintendent of the Johns Hopkins Hospital—who had been a psychiatrist until this appointment some ten years before. Dr. Osler was in England, Dr. Futcher, my very good friend, the resident, had just left for his vacation, and Tom McCrae the assistant resident—

a dour personality always—was in charge. Dr. Hurd had not minced words with Florence—"It was unheard of for a woman to be in charge of the Negro wards. It would end in disaster, it couldn't be done—he wouldn't stand for it, etc., etc., etc." Florence, always a timid character, had listened to him and had talked to Dr. McCrae and it was the consensus of opinion that only one of us should have an internship in medicine. Her plan—and I think suggested by them—was for her to take a fellowship in anatomy and to leave me the hospital appointment. I was very tired—24 hours travelling over night in a sleeper always wrecks me—but I had no intention of assenting to any such disposition. I said plainly if anyone went— I would be the one—but after all Dr. Osler had given me the post and Dr. Welch had congratulated me on it—and I would talk to Dr. Hurd. Unsuspectingly I saw him that very afternoon. To my horror he said that he understood that it was I who wanted the colored wards. He had had experience with a similar woman physician, Anita Newcomb Magee—the only daughter of the distinguished astronomer, Simon Newcomb—who had a resident-ship at Hopkins before my day. He told me of her abnormal sex interests and of what he considered sex perversions. He said that of course he thought—and all my classmates and the medical staff would think the same thing—that only my desire to satisfy sexual curiosity would allow me or any woman to take charge of a male ward. When it came to negroes, did I realize that the white nurses were always in danger on the male colored wards and that if anything happened to them by word or deed that I would be held responsible. The man interne was all that kept them and the colored orderlies from insulting the nurses and women students—or worse. How about rectal and genital examinations, catheterization, and other unpleasant duties which might devolve on the interne. Finally he said so much that my anger came to my rescue. "Dr. Hurd," I replied, "I came to Baltimore to learn a profession in order to earn my living. I have worked hard and fulfilled every requirement in the medical school for a degree. During my four years I never was given G.U.—ever taught to catheterize a male or make the examinations for which you think I have a repressed desire. I have spent 6 months as clerk on the colored wards, male and female, surgical and medical. In that time I took all the histories, made most of the physicals, and certainly did any examinations not left to an orderly by an interne. As far as I know I gave satisfaction. Dr. Osler gave me this appointment and said that Dr. Sabin and I would share the white and colored wards. He evidently considered both of us capable of running these wards to his satisfaction. Until he returns, sir, I shall be the interne of the colored wards, and I shall do my best. If in October I find that I cannot successfully perform my duties, I shall tender Dr. Osler my resignation." Then I got up, and the anguish he had caused me boiled over. I said, "Dr. Hurd, it was a difficult decision for me to go into medicine—there were unpleasantnesses that I was told might occur, but I waited four years to be treated unfairly, and the first insult I have received was from the Superintendent of the Johns Hopkins Hospital." I got myself out of his office and found the tears of rage were rolling down my cheeks. Florence was in the corridor and I said, "Come with me to Dr. McCrae." I stalked ahead of her to his office where I told them both what had taken place. "Dr. McCrae," I said, "until Dr. Osler returns I shall do my best to give satisfaction and to perform all the duties of an interne, as I have been taught them on these wards." All he said was, "Miss Reed, call on me any time—in an emergency." I thanked him and left, still boiling inside and with the unpleasant thought that my fellow internes and the staff considered me, as Dr. Hurd had pictured me—"a sex pervert."

This interview with Dr. Hurd was a body blow. In my anger with him and my indignation at his conception of a woman doctor, I had mapped out a course which seemed impossible when the reaction to my fatigue and rage overwhelmed me. The first month as interne at Johns Hopkins Hospital was an agony long drawn out. Every day I was on the ward at 6 a.m. before there was a shift of nurses to see what had occurred during the few night hours during which I was absent. I stayed on the ward until after the resident made midnight rounds and often, if there was a very sick case, I slept on the ward, rolled up in a clean sheet on an unused bed in the room for special cases on each floor. For 5 weeks I never averaged 6 hours sleep—3 to 4 at night and a nap in the afternoon if things were quiet and Florence was on duty. The service was heavy, and my work would have been arduous for any interne since there were no clerks as the school hadn't opened and September was one of the heavy typhoid months. The weather was oppressive—hot and humid. Many of my duties were new, even if I had been on the wards before. But the weight of my spirit, and the fear in my heart, was put there by Dr. Hurd. Could I acquit myself well, protect the nurses, and earn the respect of the other internes and residents?

Florence and I had adjacent rooms on the 3rd floor, right hand side as you went up the stairs and facing the yard, which was then grass and trees—the old almshouse green. Our bathroom was on the floor above the rear, while in front on this floor was the doctors' lounge. Because of the cloud over our start at the hospital, neither Florence nor I entered this common room as we should have done. We went to the nurses' home for a sitting room and recreation. This seems a silly decision in the light of the present free and easy intercourse of sexes in any hospital nowadays, but 46 years ago we still felt on sufferance and wished to be unobtrusive.

After I had completed nearly six months on the colored wards, Florence Sabin came to me and said she would like to change services with me—since the white woman's ward was so uninteresting. It amused me to have her ask for my wards, for in September when we were being bullied by Dr. Hurd she declared that she could never attempt running the negro service.

On the whole, we women at Johns Hopkins were treated very well. Some over-attention while in the school, and a little horse play not especially directed at us by the boisterous men of the 3rd class and boring to the serious men of our class as well as to the women, a disagreeable boorish interne, Dr. Luetscher, and my bout with Dr. Hurd, and the indecent talk of Dr. Mackenzie my 2nd year— covered the hardships I, as a medical woman student, had to bear. As interne, there was no discrimination against us. After the following incident was past, I learned that Jack Yates had had a bout with Dr. McCrae even more serious than the episodes I shall relate.

Early in the fall, Florence Sabin had had a very young girl—a child—on her ward with typhoid. Dr. Osler had been interested in her case because typhoid before puberty was rare. One afternoon there were some serious symptoms which suggested perforation and Florence spent the early evening on the ward counting the leucocytes which rise invariably when perforation is imminent. Nothing showing in the blood count, she left a note of the symptoms and her findings on the ward for the resident and went to bed after her midnight rounds. Unfortunately for her, Dr. Futcher, our fine senior resident, was out that night and Dr. Thomas McCrae came on the ward between 1 and 2 a.m. Finding the child awake and in pain, he did not call Dr. Sabin, as should have been done by the nurse, but made a blood count and sent the child to the operating room. It happened that I had been sent for on my ward, and around 3 a.m. in going front through the corridors connecting the different wards, I passed a window from which I could see the surgical operating rooms on Monument Street. One of the rooms was lighted and out of curiosity I wandered over to see what was the emergency. To my great surprise, I saw it was the little girl from Florence's ward. I waited a few minutes and went over to a group of internes standing around Dr. McCrae and asked him directly what had happened. He answered in a disagreeable tone that it was evidently a typhoid perforation. I asked "Where is Dr. Sabin" at which he very cuttingly said he presumed, "asleep, but as she had neglected to report the child's symptoms he hadn't been interested in having her called." He added that "if the child died he should consider Dr. Sabin responsible." I was aghast and very indignant at the unwarranted and public accusation. So I crossed the room to the telephone and asked front to send Dr. Sabin to the operating room. She came in a few minutes, and we had one of the most embarrassing hours of my life. Dr. McCrae refused to notice Florence, the surgeons were full of glee at the row of the medical staff, and I am afraid none of them were sorry to see a woman put in the wrong. It was true, we were tolerated and on the whole treated well—but we were distinctly not wanted. In medicine as in every profession then and now a woman has to stand head and shoulders above a man to expect equal preferment. Poor Florence, always conscientious and hard working, scarcely left the child for days and managed to pull her through and she recovered entirely. Nothing further was said, and on the whole she was lucky it was Dr. McCrae who was the cause of her trouble for he was thoroughly disliked. Still the garbled story went around the school and nothing could be done about it.

Some weeks afterwards, I happened to be on the ward one evening when a young negro had similar symptoms. I immediately went through the routine treatment and counted the blood repeatedly, finally getting almost a continuous slow rise in the leucocyte count. There was no doubt that the case was progressing badly. A little after 12 midnight, after I had rung for a resident repeatedly to be told all were out, Dr. McCrae came on the ward. I met him at the outer door—not wanting my anxiety to be noticed in the ward. He brushed rudely by me not heeding my "Dr. McCrae, sir?" and went in to the nurse and asked her to make rounds. I followed, literally boiling. When we came to the bed of the bad typhoid, I stepped forward with my blood counts and again said, "Dr. McCrae, I wish to report . . ." The boy was sleeping and without another word or any notice of my sheet of figures, he brushed by me and left the ward. The nurse and I were speechless. She, as furious as I was, said, "He wouldn't let you say a word." I answered, "Please remember I tried repeatedly to speak to him." After thinking it over, I decided I would wait for Dr. Futcher's return. I left word front that I wanted Dr. Futcher the moment he returned, and went back to blood counting. After hours, it seemed to me, of waiting while I comforted myself with Dr. Osler's statements that operation should only be attempted in absolutely *positive* cases, Dr. Futcher appeared. I quickly told him of the symptoms, my treatment, and showed him my leucocyte chart which gave a steady rise for the past 6 hours. In a few seconds he ordered operation, called up the surgical resident, and in a short time we were on our way to the operating table. Perforations were enough of a rarity so that all present wanted to hear all about the case. Just as the anaesthetic was begun, Dr. Futcher turned around to me and asked where is Dr. McCrae. I knew that the showdown had come and I was prepared for it. With as innocent a face as I could manage I answered, "Dr. McCrae came on the ward at midnight, sir. He didn't seem himself for I tried to speak to him 3 times about the case, but as the nurse will tell you, he refused to speak to me or listen to what I had to say, and so I waited until you returned and made my report to you." Dr. Futcher was startled and called Dr. McCrae who appeared at once in a coat over his pajamas. He came up to me pale with anger and in a bullying tone asked what I meant by not making the report to him. I again said, that as the nurse would corroborate I had followed him all around the ward with my notes on the case and that he either couldn't or wouldn't hear me. Then I said that there seemed nothing for me to do but to wait for Dr. Futcher. The entire operating room laughed. Dr. McCrae was disliked, he was a hard drinker and in his cups disagreeable to everyone. There was nothing to do then. He went to Dr. Osler about it, but Dr. Futcher must have said a good word for me, because I heard no more of the incident. My patient got well promptly and all of us enjoyed Dr. McCrae's discomfiture. Two can play at a game.

When summer came, most of the internes dropped out, finding a 4th year student, just graduated, and willing to take the service temporarily. For some reason, I felt that I should stick out my 12 months service. Even Florence got sick and went off in August, as she was to return in September as Fellow in Anatomy in the Medical School and begin her life work in that science. The weather was torrid, the nights unbearable. I never went to my room until 2 or 3 o'clock and then watched the men internes chasing each other up and down the top of the corridor outside of my window with the fire hose. If it hit a man squarely it knocked him over from the force of the water. When I went to bed I tied either long braid to a bedpost in the attempt to dry them out before morning. At 8 o'clock in the morning as I went to my ward, the thermometer in the shaded corridor stood over 100° F. These were trying days. The attending physicians were all away and the service was tiresome and monotonous. I didn't leave until the last day—something Dr. Hurd had said of a woman's being irresponsible, and not to be trusted to see things through, kept me at my post. One lesson that I had learned, that it is not enough to work and to be industrious—but stick-to-itiveness, lasting to the last ditch is imperative. I had enjoyed my interneship, I had made a number of good friends and had an interesting life—and worked very hard. I think that I had given satisfaction. As internes went, both Florence and I were far above the average, both in ability and conscientiousness. To me the contact and friendship of Dr. Osler was the high spot of the year. Not wanting women in the school, which he finally admitted, he was scrupulous in seeing fair play, and even included us in social activities and in gifts and remembrances at Christmas. I felt that he was my friend and to me William Osler has always stood for the greatest personality and the soundest medical teaching possible at that time.

From the very first my research went swimmingly. None of the animals came down with tuberculosis which was a great surprise to Dr. Welch, who had visualized Hodgkin's disease as an unusual form of this dread disease. My slides, especially the serial sections, demonstrated the appearance of the disease in different organs and the eosinophiles usually accompanying the growth and the peculiar form of giant cell, which Steinberg had mentioned.

Finally, I was ready, in the beginning of 1902, to publish. Dr. Welch, Dr. Flexner visiting us from New York, and Dr. MacCallum had all gone over my work and were satisfied that Hodgkin's disease was not a form of tuberculosis, that the growth had a definite cellular structure of which a peculiar form of giant cell was the prominent feature. Later the name "Dorothy Reed cell" was given to this distinctive diagnostic feature of the disease. I never felt that I was the discoverer of this cell—though previously it had been seen and considered a form of giant cell seen in tuberculosis, it had not been considered a destructive [sic] feature. I think that Dr.

Longcope was the indirect reason for my name being attached to
the giant cell of Hodgkin's. Dr. Longcope, later professor of medicine at Hopkins, whom I never liked, had gone up to Philadelphia,
where in the year 1902–1903 Jack Yates followed him. Knowing
my work, he apparently decided that he would publish on the disease, and, as I understood from the anger aroused in my colleagues
in pathology, giving me little, if any, credit for my work. Dr.
MacCallum then put the name "Dorothy Reed" in his textbook on
pathology and my friends so kept my work in the public eye. . . .

During the early part of 1902, it is evident when I look back
on these months, that I was undecided as to my future plans. I was
very upset in my soul—and there was literally no one I could go
to for advice. In my life I have had a great many good women
friends—fine individuals whom I admired immensely—but not one
of whom I ever felt like unburdening myself to. Mary Strong, whom
I learned to know in Baltimore, was perhaps my closest friend but
I never thought of going to her for advice. In fact, I would not have
considered it worth taking. Men friends I had too, but the problems
of a man's life are so essentially different from those facing a woman
that it would be difficult for him to put himself in her place and
see the straight path. It certainly is "one man's hand on the lonely
plough." The decision I had to make this year was momentous for
my whole life—I slept on it—looked into various temporary
fields . . . prayed a lot, and tried to use my reason and judgement
for my own problems. Always much harder to do for yourself than
others. Dr. Welch had asked me to stay another year as University
Fellow in Pathology. He was extremely pleased with my work on
Hodgkin's and in the department and gave me carefully measured
praise and promise of a future in the work. He even offered, if I
could not accept the small stipend of $500 a year, to get me a
Rockefeller Fellowship at $900 and the assurance that I could hold
it as long as I wished. Pathology was the work I had liked best in
medicine, and the one I felt a real interest in following. The pay
seemed inadequate, and difficult for me to be content with, as it
was evident mother would need practically all of my income, then
$1,800 a year. Finally I asked Dr. Welch what prospect for pro-
motion would there be in the Medical School. He looked puzzled
and then embarrassed. I explained that the man who had had the
fellowship just before me had done no research but had been made
an assistant in pathology the next year and both he and Jack Yates
could look forward to promotion in the Medical School—if they

wished it. Why not I? After a moment's pause, he answered that no woman had ever held a teaching position in the School and that he knew there would be great opposition to it. There were a very few women employed at all in the Medical School—Florence Sabin, Fellow in anatomy, and Elizabeth Hendon, assistant to Dr. Kelly. Dr. Hendon, blocked for promotion, returned to England. Florence starved 10 years as Fellow, was finally promoted to Assistant Professor—as good a teacher and as distinguished an anatomist as the country afforded, but, on Dr. Mall's sudden death, a man was promoted over her to fill the chair who was her inferior in age, experience, brains, and ability to succeed. She left after 20 years service to take a $10,000 position at the Rockefeller Foundation. One has to accept that women were blocked, and are still not given equal opportunity for promotion in the medical profession.

Suddenly, as I saw what I had to face in acceptance of injustice and in being overlooked—I knew that I couldn't take it. And I told Dr. Welch that, if I couldn't look forward to a definite teaching position even after several years of apprenticeship, I couldn't stay. I just couldn't take it. He seemed to feel my point and immediately began to make suggestions, and bring me offers in medical fields outside my ken. It has always amused me to remember that I turned down an offer that he was very anxious for me to consider—pathologist to a new clinic in Rochester, Minnesota—the Mayo Clinic. My reason was, largely, its situation, so far from my mother and sister who were needing my support more and more. Also, I remember a position in pathology at the New England Hospital for Women and Children, that I think offered too little and also a job at the Women's Medical School at Philadelphia. Finally, after a trip to New York, Dr. Welch told me that Dr. L. Emmett Holt, even then the leading pediatrist of the country, had approached him at a board meeting and explained his need of a woman resident to be in charge of the new Babies Hospital then being built at 55th and Lexington Avenue in New York City—and now a part of the Medical Center in upper New York. Apparently Dr. Welch had impressed my value on Dr. [Holt] for he brought a definite offer from him which carried with it room, board, uniform washing, and $1000 a year salary. After I came to know Dr. Holt, I realized how hard Dr. Welch had had to argue to get the money from him. Dr. Holt was the meanest man God ever made, and I'm sure that his first thought would have been that a resident should pay him for the privilege of being associated with him. As I have said, Dr. Welch realized perfectly my needs, and I think that he sold me to Dr. Holt because Dr. Holt was anxious to adopt Hopkins standards, and Dr. Welch made him offer me what I could afford to accept. Anyway, the chance for me seemed to be either going into pediatrics or general practice, and the former had always appealed to me as one of the best fields in medicine for women. I accepted it almost at once— realizing that I must leave Baltimore and that if I were to go into any active medical field I needed more training and time to decide where I should locate. Dr. Holt would not be ready for me for 6 months, as the hospital was not finished. Shortly after I had closed with Dr. Holt the arrangments for me to take charge of the Babies Hospital on January 1, 1903, I received an offer to be a temporary resident, starting June 1, 1902, at the New York Infirmary for Women and Children—the Elizabeth Blackwell project, famous in the annals of medical history. The incumbent had been sent west with tuberculosis and it was necessary to bridge over the months until 1903, when the new appointee would take over. Looking back on this necessary stop gap to keep me going these intervening 7 months, I am sure that it was brought about by Dr. Welch, though as I remember the offer came through Whitridge Williams, then Dean of Johns Hopkins Medical School. I certainly had good friends who interested themselves in my welfare. This left me a few weeks only to finish up my work, to pack up and leave for my new job. It was one of the saddest periods of my life. May 30th, the very day I left Baltimore, was the lowest point of my life of nearly 28 years. Memorial Day has always had a special significance to me. On that day I turned my back on all I wanted most and started to make a new life for myself. My house had come down on my head.

My decision to give up my profession and to marry Charles Mendenhall came about gradually and through a number of years. In my days as a student in Baltimore, I had known him as a friend who shared my love of country and life outdoors. We spent many Sundays walking in the lovely country around the city and became good friends. Our tastes were not similar. Charles was deeply musical and had a wide knowledge of music. He disliked poetry and was not imaginative, while I had little if any knowledge or appreciation of music, though I had heard a lot in my early days in Berlin. I loved poetry and romantic imaginings of every sort. I am naturally a dramatic character and willing to attempt any forlorn hope, while Charles was essentially cautious and disliked the strange or unusual.

It is difficult for me to portray him adequately, for to be fair to anyone in such a close relationship is difficult and I am further hampered by the consciousness of not having loved him as much, or in the way he loved me, and also because when the tragedies and hardships of my early married life bore in on me, I was often heedless of his wishes and dominated his life at home, because if I didn't assert myself, I should have succumbed to the overwhelming pressure of unhappiness of those years of misery.

Charles had a repressed, stifled nature. His father's influence in his early life must have been terrific. His mother—as she once told me—never expressed an opinion until she found how her husband felt about the subject, and then she agreed with him. She herself was gentle and sweet and she loved her only child. . . .

. . . With Father Mendenhall it was a different matter. . . . I think that I should have always disliked his concept of women. I had, as he knew, taken a degree at the best medical school in the country and had made something of a name for myself in my profession. He always ignored these facts. In the years I knew him he never alluded to my being a physician or even introduced or spoke of my profession to me or to anyone else. For him a woman's place was in the home and her position should always be subservient to her husband. Perhaps I could have ignored his attitude towards even higher education for women, but his treatment of Charles infuriated me.

I wanted children. In fact, all the 4 children I have had were wanted, and two of them, Richard and John, were planned for. As I was nearly 32 when I married and as I had married to have a family and normal home life, I never used any birth control, but my pregnancies were all desired and welcome.

[Mendenhall's first child died after a botched delivery, leaving her deeply depressed.] Undoubtedly I was hard to live with and Charles had much to put up with. A man is seldom devoted to a child until it shows signs of intelligence. Charles felt deeply our loss and my suffering, but he became more rather than less inarticulate. In fact, we were so estranged at this time that I longed to give up our life together and go back east and take up the practice of medicine. I thought of it every day and made all sorts of plans, but always came back to the fact that it would be throwing up the sponge, breaking a promise, and giving up while there was still a possibility of making a success of our marriage. I think that I always realized the devotion Charles really felt, though unexpressed, and I couldn't bear to hurt him. At any rate, we went north in the summer for a canoe trip, and fishing and nature did much to heal my body and hurt spirit. We returned to the same apartment for the next year and I went to Dr. De Lee and found out from him when I could have another child. The repairs which I was so much in need of had to wait until I was through child bearing for there was little tissue left to make a new perineal floor from, and Dr. De Lee would not chance a further injury of what was left. The following spring (1908) I was again pregnant, and we went with Mary Strong for a summer in Nova Scotia. In spite of continuous nausea, I was better in every way for the trip. Feeling a great responsibility for the child I carried, I took good care of myself and didn't allow the depression I had been suffering from to overwhelm me. Dr. De Lee saw me in the fall and pronounced me in excellent shape but insisted that I must be down in Chicago under his care *one month* before my expected delivery. (He felt that with the injuries I had received at my first delivery I might have a precipitous labor!) So shortly after the first of the year I left home and stayed in the apartment of the nurse I had engaged for my confinement. The loneliness and discomfort of these stays in Chicago preliminary to 2 weeks in the old Lying-in Hospital remain vividly in my memory as far more unpleasant than the 3 hard labors that ended my vigils. In the case of Richard, Dr. De Lee finding that I apparently would not have 2nd stage labor pains at all and that the 1st stage pains were too weak to fully dilate the cervix, resorted to every device that I had learned under Dr. Williams to bring on labor—Bainer Bags, forcible dilation, etc. Four days went by in agony. Given food on one side of the bed, I brought it up when I turned over. I remember saying to Dr. De Lee, "I should think that you would be afraid to do so many things to me." He asked what I meant and I said, "Afraid of infection." He said, "If you get any infection it will be my fault and I should not like it." I decided then that a man who weighed every chance, sterilized his own gloves, and brought them dated to the delivery room, was to be trusted. On the 5th day, he gave me full anesthesia, did a high forceps, and delivered a fine boy over 8 pounds in weight. . . .

Last night I tried to sum up for myself whether or not my marriage had been a success for me and for Charles. Thinking it over dispassionately—for myself, in spite of the tragic start with

Margaret's death and Richard's loss, it turned out better than I should have expected. I have had a full, useful, and after the first unhappy years, a full and pleasant life. If it had started more smoothly both Charles and I would have suffered less but it is through suffering that one develops. The effort I had to make the first ten years to go on at all hardened me and gave me an unpleasant drive that must have been *hard* for others to live with. Charles had been so repressed, as a child, that it is difficult for me to evaluate what marriage brought him. He always loved me, but we had few interests in common other than a real joy in outdoors. I do not think my plans in regard to the family or carrying on my work were always agreeable to him. He would have had me stay home and do the usual thing, but he never objected seriously to any decision of mine. . . . If he hadn't married me, I do not think that his life would have been as full or varied as it was, nor that he would have been as happy as he was in his silent, undemonstrative way, in his family. . . .

Both Thomas and John are men that I am proud of—four square and true. They have never given me a sleepless night, and I feel that both have made the most of their capabilities. Charles was proud of them too—and satisfied. Perhaps our two sons are the best answer to was our marriage a success.

I must say that I have been impressed both by the variety of my activities as well as the extent of my knowledge. It has answered one question for me. I can say proudly that there is evidence to claim that my medical accomplishment over 40 years was worthwhile and something to be proud of. Alice Hamilton told me that when the subject of opening Harvard Medical to women was brought up at faculty meetings, I was cited as an able woman who had married and failed to use her expensive medical education. It always hurt, but now I know it was a damn lie, and I can claim honestly that I think that I can give evidence of the use of medical knowledge much wider and deeper than that shown by the average physician, whether in practice or in teaching. This is why I am writing this section on my work after marriage.

When I look back over the past 60 years of my life, it seems as if my end was shaped slowly but surely in the years of my preparation, life abroad, family responsibility, research, obstetrical training, and pediatrics—all of which enabled me to go back to work after my children were born and to make a worthwhile contribution to the city, the state, and the nation. Some of the hardest experiences of my life gave me the training requisite for the work

I was dropped into. Probably one determining cause of my taking up work was needing money to help with the care and education of my sister's children—especially Dorothy Sharp who had just entered Smith College in 1912. When these three were little—in the 9 years from their mother's death in 1903—I had been able to supply their extra medical or vacation needs out of my own income. Their father gave them a home, helped by the income of their mother's estate—around $1,200 a year—and I robbed Peter to pay Paul when extra demands were made on me. . . .

In the fall of 1913—when John was less than 6 months old, and I was comparatively free since, because of his early illness, I had had to employ a nurse for his care—I was asked by the University of Wisconsin if I would be willing and able to give some lectures on the care and feeding of children in neighboring small towns. This feature of extension work had been started in 1912. In Madison at this time, there was neither an obstetrician or a pediatrist, and outside of Milwaukee, this was true of the whole state. The rural districts were worse off. There were entire counties, as I found out later, without any regular physician, without hospitals, and there were no county or visiting nurses in the entire state. Charles and I talked it over, and it seemed to be the kind of opening that I was looking for. As I remember, I was paid $15 and expenses for a single lecture, not entailing staying over night. Later I went out on Monday and returned on Friday for $100 a week and expenses, and I earned every cent of it. My first extension lecture was given on an afternoon in the fall of 1913 at Stoughton, Wisconsin, to a rural audience of women gathered at a so-called community institute. As I remember, there was a fairly large audience of stolid young women, wives of farmers, agricultural workers, and small tradesmen of the town and the vicinity. Knowing nothing of the extension movement which had been begun in this country at the University of Wisconsin, and which had added health teaching to the curriculum it offered, nor appreciating the level of intelligence, opportunity, or education that such an audience would offer, the lecture I presented was totally inappropriate. Since we usually put the cart before the horse, I had been commissioned to talk on the care and feeding of infants in the hope of benefitting the health of the mothers of the community, and giving them the knowledge to bring up their children to be healthier and to lower the infant death rate. Also from my inexperience, the talk I had prepared was too scientific, too complete and high brow to be understood by the average woman. Also, it was written and read, which took away from the spontaneity and insured it going over the heads of my audience. I soon learned to write out a talk, but never to read it if I wished to reach my listeners. Talking from headlines on one card became my practice early in this work. When I returned to Madison, I frankly told the extension people that my subject had been wrong. What the women wanted was how to get better obstetrics and the principles of prenatal care—since in the discussions after the lecture, all questions had been along these lines—how to prevent miscarriage, what caused childbed fever, etc. This fall I gave several such talks in the vicinity of Madison, and my opinion of what the rural health needs were was confirmed. The health of the mother, prenatal care, better obstetric care, possibility of hospitalization, post partum rest, and the importance of breast feeding. Our death rate in infancy was due to intrinsic causes and not primarily to the care and feeding in infancy or to impure milk. . . .

The way that I was introduced through the health extension movement . . . to the U.S. Children's Bureau, seems, looking back on it, to have been prepared for by my obstetrics with J. Whitridge Williams and 3 years at the Babies Hospital under L. Emmett Holt. Certainly unless I had been grounded in obstetrics and pediatrics and had the social experience 5 or 6 years of hospital wards gave me, handling the very poor, I could never have succeeded in the rural health work I built up in the next 4 years in Wisconsin, or in my writing for the Children's Bureau, or in the establishing of the Health Center of Madison, and work I have done for the State Board of Health of Wisconsin, and later teaching "Care of the Mother and Child" at the University of Wisconsin.

. . . in 1914 I was working for the University of Wisconsin. I talked on health, a home economics instructor on food and nutrition, and usually there was another speaker on a subject especially needed by that community—water supply, sewage disposal, or infectious diseases. Travel was usually in the daytime, the train service poor, the cars always the common day coach—dirty and unventilated in those days. The hotels we had our meals in were small, always on the American plan, the food scanty and badly cooked. The improvement since the general use of the automobile in paving of roads and hotel accommodations is unbelievable. If we had to spend the night, the rooms were cold, the beds hard, the food inadequate. As we usually went out in the winter time because this is the leisure time on the farm and of drawing greater audiences from the rural districts—our travel and living conditions were never comfortable. . . .

Once we were snowed up in a village near Waupaca for 3 days, and had a miserable time—of cold and near starvation diet, as no one could get out of the house we were supposed to stay in only one night. On the whole, however, the trips were so full of interest, the audience so eager for information, and always presenting some unusual person who made a deep impression. . . .

Shortly after I began extension work in Wisconsin—probably in 1914—in calling on Dr. Harper, the head of the State Board of Health of Wisconsin, he asked me to report back to him whenever I found especially bad or unusual health conditions in the rural areas I visited. He finally appointed me a deputy State Health Officer and asked me to call on the local health authorities *for him* and find out—if I could—what were the problems and needs of each place. In those early days health officers were not even physicians or men [*sic*] with any public health training, and were often woefully ignorant and oblivious of any but the most superficial of their duties. Public health was largely concerned with control of nuisances, inspection of slaughter houses, and water pollution, although Wisconsin was far ahead of most of the states and has gradually developed a very adequate service extending to every county—a far cry from a barber health officer whom I once visited in a serious epidemic of scarlet fever in a small town in an upper county. . . .

As far as I know, Wisconsin was first in the field in putting emphasis on prenatal care and the instruction of the mother in the care she should have and her care of the child. It is well done and I am proud of it, though in the advance we have made in the last 40 years it may now seem inadequate or old fashioned. I owe the ability to have developed this work to my sound training in obstetrics by Whitridge Williams and my experience in pediatrics . . . under L. Emmett Holt. The importance of a sound foundation and the influence of early interests is exemplified in the work I did from 1914 to 1934, when professional activity stopped for me—with Charles' illness when I was 60 years old.

Margaret Morse Nice

(1883–1974)

Fourth child of an academic family, Margaret Morse had a childhood that combined the idyllic rural setting of the Connecticut Valley with the rich intellectual environment of Amherst, Massachusetts. Her interest in natural sciences, prompted by a childhood of love of birds, was shaped by scientific work at Mount Holyoke College, from which she graduated in 1906. Two years as a research fellow in biology followed at Clark University in Worcester, where she met and married Leonard Blaine Nice. Her work thereafter was dictated by the progress of her husband's medical career. They moved first to Cambridge, where he attended Harvard Medical School, then to Norman, Oklahoma, where he became chairman of the Department of Physiology in 1913. In 1927 he joined the faculty of Ohio State University, settling finally, in 1936, on the faculty of the Medical School of the University of Chicago.

Between 1910 and 1923 the couple had four daughters, requiring Nice's constant attendance at home. Deeply depressed by the emptiness of household routine and the care of four toddlers, she attempted to satisfy her love of research by studying language acquisition in infants, work for which she was awarded an M.A. by Clark University in 1915. In the 1920s, after the birth of the family's last child and the purchase of their first automobile, Nice resumed work in ornithology, producing the first of some 250 research publications in the field.

The move to Columbus, Ohio, resulted in the purchase of a house on the banks of the Olentangy River, situated in low, marshy land frequented by many species of birds. Here Nice was able to band individual birds and chart their life histories. Her research made her one of the leading students of bird behavior, documenting territorial behavior in small birds, courtship rituals, and patterns of sexual dominance. Her two-volume *Studies in the Life History of the Song Sparrow* (1937, 1943) established her world reputation and made her the leading influence in ornithology in America. Predecessors had studied flocks of birds; Nice studied individuals and reported on their life cycles.

A fluent linguist, Nice translated the work of European ornithologists for her American colleagues and maintained lively correspondence with German, Dutch, and English colleagues. Her contributions to professional associations were recognized by her election as president of the Wilson Ornithological Society in 1938, making her the first woman to head a major American ornithological organization.

Unhappy unless engaged in research, Nice was a prodigious field-worker, prolific writer, and committed scientist. Her autobiography makes clear that the early years of her married life were bitterly unhappy, but the physical, moral, and financial support of her husband eventually allowed her career to flourish, despite her lack of a university appointment and accompanying institutional support for her research.

RESEARCH IS A PASSION WITH ME

Our family alternated—boy, girl, boy, girl—till there were seven of us. I was the middle child, born December 6, 1883. I like to think that the same year saw the birth of the American Ornithologists' Union, although it was a long time before I, in my ignorance, became aware of the existence of that august body.

We were an enterprising lot of youngsters in the large house set in the two-acre orchard and garden at 28 Northampton Road in the village of Amherst, Massachusetts. My father, Anson Daniel Morse, professor of history at Amherst College, had a deep love for the wilderness, yet at the same time was a devoted gardener, delighting in fine flowers and choice fruits. We learned of nature at first hand, planting and weeding in our own small gardens. . . .

Amherst lies in a broad valley; to the east are the Pelham Hills, to the north wild Mount Toby and rugged Mount Sugarloaf, to the west the Connecticut River, and to the south the Holyoke Range lying like a couchant dragon. It is fascinating country, with its woods and meadows, its clear streams and friendly mountains. Many were the family trips into the countryside . . . usually afoot.

My mother, inspired by her course in botany at Mount Holyoke Seminary, taught us the names of the wild flowers. Happy memories come to me of Sunday afternoon walks in the woods with the whole family, and of late April trips for flowers for our May baskets to Mill Valley—the only place in the neighbourhood where we knew that spring beauty grew. One spring, two ladies conducted Saturday morning walks for children. On one never-to-be-forgotten May morning I had helped my brothers escort our cow, Daisy, to her pasture in Daisy's Woods, a mile to the west of our home. On this radiant day of buttercups and daisies, bluets and dandelions, we startled a Song Sparrow[1] from her eggs; and when we reached home the flaming flowers of Japanese quince were glorified by another flame—the first Ruby-throated Hummingbird[2] of the season. . . .

The first real bird book with which I became acquainted was John B. Grant's *Our Common Birds and How to Know Them*, published in 1891 by Scribner's. In it, the males of ninety species are described, with sixty-four of them illustrated by photographs of stuffed specimens. Mr. Grant's aim was simplification. "Do not attempt," he writes, "to identify any bird which presents puzzling characteristics or, rather, any which does *not* present some striking mark either of song or plumage." Unfortunately, birds with puzzling characteristics insisted on calling attention to themselves instead of always skulking in the bushes. With no hint as to the plumages of females and young, and with no emphasis on the locality covered— the New York City region, some one hundred and fifty miles south-west of Amherst—one small girl was badly led astray.

Our cherry trees were full of birds whose colouring best matched the description of Yellow-breasted Chats.[3] I thought it strange that they did not seem the least bit shy and I looked in vain for clownish actions; nevertheless, I can remember that as "Y.b Chats" they were listed in my earliest records and it was some time before I discovered that they were really female and immature Baltimore Orioles.[4] One notable summer an Indigo Bunting[5] sang persistently in our great blackberry patch, but we could locate no mate, looking as we did for another blue bird. We believed him to be a bachelor until we happened upon the nest and thus discovered his plain brown wife.

One June day, by the little alder-bordered brook in the tangle we called Song Sparrow Jungle, I stumbled upon a tiny yellow bird with a black mask across his face. He was quite unbelievable; it

---

1. *Melospiza melodia.*
2. *Archilochus colubris.*
3. *Icteria virens.*
4. Northern Oriole, *Icterus galbula.*
5. *Passerina cyanea.*

was almost as if I had found a fairy! I remembered the name "Hooded Warbler"[6] from our book. Neither it nor the Maryland Yellowthroat (nor the chat, by the way) was illustrated. I jumped to the conclusion that here was a pair of Hooded Warblers and how proud I was of my discovery! But search as I would, I never could find the nest of the indignant pair, which long afterwards I found had been *Yellowthroats*. Thirty years were to pass before I at last beheld a Hooded Warbler.

Although *Our Common Birds* misled me in some respects, in others it should have served as a trustworthy starting point. Looking at it now, it is gratifying to find under the Northern Shrike[7] a good statement of the modern view of the role of predators; namely, that by removing the old and sickly, they actually *benefit* the prey species. As to my "Yellow-breasted Chats" and "Hooded Warblers," they were indeed strangers to the township of Amherst.

I used to say that I kept my first notes on birds when I was eight, but no records have survived earlier than the spring of 1893, when I was nine years of age. In this first of my extant diaries, the Song Sparrow, prophetically enough, is the first bird mentioned. Robins and hummingbirds also appear, as well as spring flowers; but most items tell of Harold's and my expeditions to get inhabitants for our dishpan aquariums. . . .

The most cherished Christmas present of my life came in 1895—Mabel Osgood Wright's *Bird-Craft* (1895). For the first time, I had coloured bird pictures. Many of these were adapted from Audubon's *Birds of America* (1827); single birds, or occasionally a pair, sometimes in surprising attitudes, were depicted. In later years, when looking at the reproductions of Audubon's original plates, every now and then a picture has given me a little tug at the heart, recalling my childhood years of eager search. The simple descriptions, the charming discussions, the enthusiastic introductory chapters of *Bird-Craft*—all these I pored over and all but learned by heart.

Sometimes an author captures the imagination and so stirs anticipation over a particular species that when the bird is finally met there is a glow of satisfaction, a realization that here is a very special

---

6. *Wilsonia citrina.*
7. *Lanius excubitor.*

character. Thanks to *Bird-Craft*, those were stirring events, when I met my first Magnolia[8] and Blackburnian Warblers[9] and, many years later in Oklahoma, the Yellow-breasted Chat and White-eyed Vireo.[10] That these two loud-voiced species had been absent from our haunts in Lyme may well have been due to the close pasturing of the hillsides by the cattle and Angora goats of our neighbour, Kansas Nebraska Bill; in 1931 these croppers were gone, shrubs had flourished, and both of these beguiling species were at home.

Bird-Craft had been the first great step in my ornithological education; some months afterwards came the second. Playing in our attic on a rainy afternoon, I chanced upon a ragged, coverless, undated, and apparently anonymous pamphlet whose first page announced "An Artificial Key to the Birds of Amherst." Beyond this, I found to my wonderment and delight an annotated list of our local birds, and a notation as to whether each was beneficial or injurious. Part I treated "Birds of Regular and Certain Appearance in Amherst at the Proper Seasons," and this I studied with loving care. Part II, "Birds of Irregular and Uncertain Appearance in Amherst," and Part III, "Birds Extremely Rare or Accidental in the Country," I consulted only occasionally. My parents told me that the author was Hubert L. Clark, son of Colonel William S. Clark, a former president of the Massachusetts Agricultural College, which was situated a mile to the north of our home. Later I discovered that *Birds of Amherst and Vicinity* had been published by J. E. Williams in 1887, when the author was only seventeen.

Bird-Craft gave me descriptions and habits and pictures: *Birds of Amherst* told me what to expect and when. I took my precious copy apart, interleaved it with my own observations, fixed up a cover, and fastened it all together again. Following the dictates of *Bird-Craft*, I corrected Hubert Clark's ideas on economic status of various species. I also recorded notes on nests I had found. My chief interest, however, was in outdoing the book in the matter of dates of earliest arrivals; it was always with a glow of pride when I beat *Birds of Amherst*. This local list, although based on inadequate work, was of the greatest value to me in narrowing my field

---

8. *Dendroica magnolia.*

9. *Dendroica fusca.*

10. *Vireo griseus.*

by showing me what species to expect, and in stimulating me to add my mite to the knowledge of our local birds. . . .

In August, 1896, our family received a cruel blow in the death of my best-beloved brother, Harold; of all of us children it fell heaviest on me. When we drove to Wildwood to choose a plot in the woods, my instant thought on seeing some migrating warblers was, "I must tell Harold." And then I remembered I never again could tell him anything.

This bereavement threw me on my own resources, and I turned to birds with a passion that was not to be matched for many years.

My second surviving diary (from October 25 to December 6, 1896) is full of notes on fall migrants, on nests, the weather, and on my pair of canaries. By this time, I had a good acquaintance with the local birds. I wrote:

Oct. 29 Juncos abundant.[11] Kinglets have come. Warblers have passed.

Nov. 7 Driving up to Wildwood I counted 54 nests in the trees we passed. Coming home, 21 Oriole nests, all built so we could not get them; 29 other nests, including Chippies[12], Robins, Cedar Birds[13] and 1 Vireo's nest.

Nov. 8 Going to church found 5 Vireos' nests and 1 Yellow Warbler's nest. (These must have been all Red-eyed Vireo[14] nests.)

Nov. 9 This is the time to find nests. Saw 47 of them from school to home. Climbed up a maple and got Vireo's nest.

My "personally taken" collection of nests was augmented by a windfall. My mother had taken me to call upon two elderly ladies who had a number of nests; upon seeing my admiration, they then and there presented them to me. I arranged all my best nests on a shelf above my bed—the greatest prizes being a bunch of glued twigs of a Chimney Swift[15] and a few straws laid by a Mourning Dove on top of an old Robin's nest. I gloated over my treasures,

---

11. Dark-eyed Junco, *Junco hyemalis.*

12. Chipping Sparrow, *Spizella passerina.*

13. Cedar Waxwing, *Bombycilla cedrorum.*

14. *Vireo olivaceus.*

15. *Choetura pelagica.*

and every evening, for fear I might forget their identity, I recited their names. . . .

Two lectures that I heard made lasting impressions. John Tyler, Professor of Zoology at Amherst College, talked to the High School Girls' Club on "Weeds"; he told us that to call a plant a weed is to give it the greatest of compliments for it has shown itself hardy and successful in the struggle for existence. This was a new viewpoint for me who had been taught to hate weeds as pests; who had pulled them up in the family garden at the stipend of three cents an hour, and under the spur of my Grandfather Ely's detestation of the graceful Queen Anne's lace had uprooted "lace weeds" at the rate of one cent for fifty.

On my fifteenth birthday Dr. G. Stanley Hall, President of Clark University at Worcester, Massachusetts, lectured at Amherst on "Love and Study of Nature." In my diary I find these quotations: "Science, art, literature, religion (except Christianity) originate in love of nature. Nature is the backbone of all education. Love is the great principle of nature and life." Little did I imagine that one day I would study nature at Clark University. . . .

My childhood had been a very happy one, with wonderful parents, a flock of congenial brothers and sisters, and the glories of nature at Lyme and Amherst. In my teens, however, I often felt depressed. Our parents were old-fashioned and over-protective; my mother perpetuated the attitudes of her parents, while my father was determined to spare us the struggles of his own childhood. They did not believe that their daughters should prepare themselves for professions. To be a "perfect housekeeper and homemaker" was the ideal held before us and how dreary it did seem (although I never imagined then that in adult life I would have to do much housework myself)! We three girls all wished we had been boys, since boys had far more freedom than girls did to explore the world and to choose exciting careers.

My college course was interrupted by almost a year in Europe [with Morse's grandmother]. . . . We spent an unhurried winter in Naples and Rome, and spring in the hill towns with visits to all the major and some of the minor places in Italy. We studied in leisurely fashion the Italian language, art, architecture, and history. In summer we visited the Tyrol, Switzerland, Germany, Holland, and England.

The European trip was a happy, rich experience with art, architecture, scenery, alpine flowers, and interesting people, but as far as birds were concerned, my eyes and ears were sealed. . . .

In September I returned eagerly to college with an enriched background for study and a new appreciation of my opportunities. . . .

. . . I found another comrade, Lucy Day, an expert canoeist and enthusiastic horseback rider; she was glad to spend Wednesday exploring the countryside. After all, had not Mary Lyon established Wednesday as Recreation Day?

New possibilities were now open. We explored the woods and mountains—Holyoke, Tom, and Norwottuck—on foot and horseback, too, for one winter I had Rex in South Hadley, and the next winter, Dolly, the mare belonging to our good friend, Malleville Emerson. Lucy hired horses from the livery stable.

One galling prohibition of our youth was that against the girls going walking in the woods and fields without a brother; our suggestion that we protect ourselves with a revolver met with strong disapprobation. During my sophomore year I had written home that I would like to purchase a .22 rifle; my father objected as follows: "(1) it is exceedingly dangerous; (2) it brings upon a young woman who is addicted to it the name of being eccentric." In my junior year I bought the rifle and blithely wrote home of Lucy's and my practice with it; we were re-enacting the current Russo-Japanese War in a ravine to the west of College with paper targets on tree stubs. Mother wrote, "I cannot smile I fear, on your rifle practice; it seems to be dangerous, and not an appropriate pastime for young women."

I did not tell my parents that I had also bought a revolver. Although I never had any excuse for using it—except in our so-called War—it was a great comfort to me in my solitary explorations of the Holyoke Range on horseback and also on foot with Lucy. And the same was true many years later on my eight-mile bird censuses in Oklahoma. . . .

The academic courses that were to be of use to me in ornithological research in later years were those in modern languages—French, German, and Italian—and in the natural sciences—geology, botany, and, particularly, zoology.

In my five courses in zoology . . . I received an excellent foundation, both practical and theoretical. For the bird study portion of first-year zoology, I bought Frank M. Chapman's *Handbook of the Birds of North America* (1895), a book which did not arouse my enthusiasm. We all kept lists of spring arrivals on the black-board; thanks to horseback rides through the countryside, my list headed all the others, until at last Miss Wallace got busy and out-distanced me.

Yet this bird study in class, chiefly identification, failed to awaken my former zeal. I felt I knew it all. I was unaware of any problems remaining to be solved, at any rate, any problems that held an appeal to me. I could see very little connection between the courses in college and the wild things I loved. I benefited from the knowledge acquired of varied forms of life, but the approach seemed to me a dead one. I did not like to cut up animals.

The four years at Mount Holyoke College were very happy for me, with excellent courses under stimulating teachers, the companionship of true friends, and carefree exploration of the lovely country. I was fortunate in making real friendships with two of my teachers—Miss Mary Young of the Romance Language Department and Miss Mignon Talbot, Geologist, who had many congenial out-door interests. Dr. Clapp was a delightful person, full of fun, over-flowing with kindness and high spirits. Our president, Mary Woolley, was a constant inspiration to us in her poise, her graciousness, her vision, and her ideals. The majority of the faculty were noble women, primarily interested in things of the mind, vital, and eager for the betterment of the world.

I believe that I was the only one of my class of 150 who graduated without a definite plan for earning her living, either at once or in the future. I did not want to teach school, nor had I taken the courses necessary for this occupation. I saw no future in laboratory zoology. I was not expert in any foreign language. I was to return to Amherst to be a daughter-at-home as my parents wished. . . .

. . . home in May to the burning question of escape from the toils of home, I was desperately dissatisfied with the aimless life of a daughter-at-home. I thought I would like to teach nature study somewhere, but there seemed to be no such opportunities. I toyed with the idea of social work, for which my only qualifications were a smattering of languages and a kind heart. And then fate took a hand.

The Massachusetts Agricultural College started a summer school that year and I attended. It was in Amherst a mile from home, and I rode my bicycle there and back. The various nature and gardening courses that I took made little impression on me, but a visitor who gave two lectures had a profound effect on me and gave direction to my whole life. Dr. Clifton F. Hodge of Clark University, Worcester, Massachusetts, told us about studying *live* animals, with the toad as chief example, how much and what they ate, how they affected man. If I could study such things in a university, life would have a real purpose for me. I talked with Dr. Hodge about this possibility and he was most encouraging. He had a problem all ready for me: he had plenty of farm-raised Bob-whites,[16] and I could study their food. This was an exciting possibility to me, but my parents were full of doubts.

. . . on August 17 [at] breakfast I found a note from my father: "I am verging to the conclusion that in view of all your talents, proclivities, likings and dislikings and accomplishments, it may be advisable for you to specialize in the field of Biology with the purpose of teaching and writing."

My intention on going to Clark University had been to get an M.A. on "The Food of the Bobwhite." I was so happy there that I decided to use this subject for a Ph.D. thesis; this in spite of strong family opposition, for my parents urged me unceasingly to return and again be a daughter-at-home. . . .

These plans were changed. Instead of raising Bobwhites, I was married; instead of working for a Ph.D., I kept house. Sometimes I rather regretted that I had not gone ahead and obtained this degree, as we stayed in Worcester for two more years until Blaine got his Ph.D. But no one had ever encouraged me to study for a doctor's degree; all the propaganda had been against it. My parents were more than happy to have me give up thoughts of a career and take up home-making, and in every way they helped us in this new venture.

After a simple wedding in August at my home in Pelham, Massachusetts . . . Blaine and I travelled to his home on a farm in south-eastern Ohio. He was the second son in a family of five boys and four girls. . . .

Blaine had attended, off and on, the ungraded country school, after which he spent a year at the New Marshfield High School, four miles distant from his home. The next year he taught at the country school and had among his pupils his four sisters and two

16. *Colinus virginianus.*

of his younger brothers. . . . His salary was $180 for the six-month term and now with money in his pockets, he entered the preparatory school of Ohio University at Athens, eight miles from his home. . . .

One of his teachers, Frank Copeland, had received his Ph.D. under Dr. Hodge in 1907, and it was through Frank's suggestion that Blaine received his assistantship in physiology at Clark University.

My first project was to work up my material on the food of the Bobwhite. Dr. Hodge wrote an introduction to it in which he said my paper "presented the most complete and convincing statement of the food of any bird," and he pointed out the dangers confronting this valuable species, especially from the cat. . . .

About this time Mr. E. P. Felt, editor of the *Journal of Economic Entomology,* called on Dr. Hodge, saw the paper, and offered to publish it in full. It appeared in June, 1910. Shortly thereafter, Mr. Felt sent Dr. Hodge a letter from Mr. W. L. McAtee, economic entomologist of the Biological Survey, which began: "I must protest against the undue praise given by Dr. Hodge" to the paper. He pointed out the fallacy of drawing conclusions about the food of a wild species by what a captive individual will eat; for instance, anteaters in zoos live upon hard-boiled eggs. . . .

I agree with much of McAtee's criticism, but when he wrote that the experiments on the *quantity* of food consumed were "even more disappointing" than those on the objects eaten, he could not have noticed how closely my results tallied with those of Dr. Judd. I must confess that it gave me considerable satisfaction to realize that these strictures were safely buried in a journal read by few bird enthusiasts, while my paper spread its message far and wide through the 300 reprints I had purchased for $8.00. They went to friends, relatives, and to state and government game departments.

"Food of the Bobwhite" made quite a stir. Whenever I read that these birds eat 129 different kinds of weed seeds, and as many as 12,000 to 30,000 seeds in a single day; whenever I saw that a Bobwhite ate 568 mosquitoes at a meal and 5,000 plant lice in a day, I knew that my studies had borne fruit. Dr. Hodge quoted my most spectacular feeding tests in a Nature Study pamphlet on *The Bobwhite* and in an article in the *Nature Study Review* (1910); Edward H. Forbush did likewise in an Audubon Bulletin. *Forest and Stream* ran two articles on the subject; Col. G. O. Shields of New York City quoted liberally from my article in his speeches on conservation; and William T. Hornaday gave a page and a half to my findings in his book *Our Vanishing Wild Life* (1913).

After two years in Cambridge, where Blaine had an instructorship in physiology at the Harvard Medical School, it was a pleasant adventure for us in September, 1913, to settle in the prairie town of Norman, Oklahoma, where Blaine had been appointed Professor of Physiology and Pharmacology in the University of Oklahoma. We were enchanted with the new, open country, the clear air, the prairie wild flowers, the Scissor-tailed Flycatchers,[17] Mockingbirds, and Cardinals,[18] with the friendliness of the people, and the mild winter weather. At that time there was no gas in town; the streets were largely unpaved and only two members of the faculty possessed automobiles.

For three years we were most fortunate in the student who lived with us in the roomy rented house we called the Yellow Pumpkin. Gladys Hilsmeyer was a fine and loyal friend. Besides helping with the housework, on Sunday afternoons she stayed with Marjorie and Constance so Blaine and I could explore the country. The favourite goal of these walks was the South Canadian River, three to four miles distant. This usually meandered as a small stream over its immense bed of sand, but on occasion it became a mighty flood. In our big backyard we installed hens, bees, and a garden, while pets from the laboratory came and went—frogs, guinea pigs, and a procession of rabbits. . . .

In 1917 we moved from a rented house to a bungalow which we owned. In 1918 we moved next door to another bungalow, slightly larger, with three bedrooms and sleeping porch. However in the fall of 1918, with four children aged six months to eight years, in what seemed to be cramped quarters, no one enjoying housework, and much of the time without even a college girl to come in an hour a day to wash the dishes, with no means of transportation but our own legs and the baby carriage, and no free Sunday afternoon for tramps to the river, I was truly frustrated. I resented the implication that my husband and the children had brains, and I had none. He taught; they studied; I did housework.

Even though our meals were simple, the washing and ironing

17. *Muscivora forficata.*
18. *Richmondena cardinalis.*

always sent out, and though I averaged an hour a day on research on speech development, my life became so cluttered with mere *things* that my free spirit was smothered. My desires were modest enough, inexpensive enough—an occasional walk to the river.

I decided it would be better to be a bird. Birds are very busy at one period each year caring for babies, but this lasts only a few weeks with many of them, and then their babies are grown and gone. Best of all, they leave their houses forever and take to camping for the rest of the year. No wonder they are happy.

On March 10, 1919, I wrote in my notebook:

Research is a passion with me; it drives me; it is my relentless master. Ten days ago I finished and sent off "A Child's Imagination" (1919), and then turned to my mussed-up house and clamoring neglected duties. Many of these odds and ends I have done. Yet now I find myself longing, yea pining, to begin on my paper on Constance and nature.

Relief came through three channels: my finding birds again; Eleanor's growing out of babyhood; and in the spring of 1920 our purchase of an ancient car. . . .

Until 1919 we had always travelled each summer to Grey Rocks. But that year the railroads markedly increased their fares so, for the first time, we resolved to spend the summer in Oklahoma. This decision proved of signal importance to our family.

A newspaper item that summer was responsible for my becoming an ornithologist. Mourning Doves, protected entirely in the state from 1913 to 1917, for the last two years had not been mentioned in the State game laws, and Federal game laws fixed the start of the open season in Oklahoma on September 1. On a morning in early August the *Daily Oklahoman* reported that Ben Watts, State Game Warden, advocated an open season on doves from August 1 or "even August 15 when all the young doves are off the nest and strong fliers."

I felt that he was wrong on his facts; surely I had read that Mourning Doves nest through August. So that evening we packed our supper into the carriage with the baby and trundled off to the campus. Sure enough we located three doves on nests. A week later we found three more. At once I wrote protesting letters to the Oklahoma City and Norman newspapers entitled, "Doves Must

Not be Shot in August." I also told the story to the Oklahoma Game Department and to the United States Biological Survey.

August 20 chanced to be cool, and I escaped by myself to the river along one of our favourite paths with its tangled vines and bushes, its mistletoe-laden elms, its Cardinals, orioles, and gnat-catchers,[19] its display of wayside flowers. Many of these flowers were armed with spines—the exquisite great white prickly poppy, the rosin weeds, golden prionopsis, weedy horse nettle, and fierce tread-softly with its coarse spotted leaves. A large hawk flew to shelter in some cottonwoods pursued by six kingbirds[20] and a dashing Scissor-tailed Flycatcher. One of the kingbirds was so excited that he attacked an inoffensive Turkey Vulture.[21]

At Low Brook, just east of the river bed, myriads of little moths rose around me, while a great black and white beetle with antennae two inches long buzzed as it flew by. It seemed like fairyland with new flowers at every step. Many of these belonged to the pulse family—partridge pea, wild creeping pea with long narrow pods poking out under the bright pink bonnet of the flower, tick trefoil, pink and yellow bird's foot trefoil. There was a little pink fog fruit and, loveliest of all, a wonderful deep blue gentian, *Estoma Russellianum,* far larger than the fringed gentian of the East, and as stately as a wood lily. And for the last touch of enchantment, the hauntingly sweet refrain of the Field Sparrow.[22]

Under the great elms and cottonwoods on the river bank I watched the turbulent Canadian River and dreamed. The glory of nature possessed me. I saw that for many years I had lost my way. I had been led astray on false trails and had been trying to do things contrary to my nature. I resolved to return to my childhood vision of studying nature and trying to protect the wild things of the earth.

I thought of my friends who never take walks in Oklahoma, "for there was nothing to see." I was amazed and grieved at their blindness. I longed to open their eyes to the wonders around them; to persuade people to love and cherish nature. Perhaps I might be a sort of John Burroughs for Oklahoma.

This August walk was a turning point in my life. It was a day

---

19. Blue-gray Gnatcatcher, *Polioptila coerulea.*
20. Eastern Kingbird, *Tyrannus tyrannus.*
21. *Cathartes aura.*
22. *Spizella pusilla.*

of vision and prophecy. But what the future really held in store for me would have seemed to me utterly fantastic.

I now turned seriously to learning the local birds, a somewhat difficult matter since information was scattered and some of it unreliable. I bought Florence Merriam Bailey's *Birds of the Western United States* (1902), and studied it. I asked the Professor of Zoology which meadowlark nested with us. "The Western," he replied. The next spring we found it was the Eastern[23]. . . .

I had become a collaborator of the Biological Survey, keeping migration records for them and taking a nesting census of Snail Brook.

Life was full of happiness for all of our family. Bluebirds had adopted our box as soon as we had put it up. Bewick's Wrens were nesting in the children's play house—a former chicken house. Four pairs of Purple Martins[24] had settled in the new house Blaine had put up for them. As for Flower and Daisy, they both proved to be males, so as soon as we could get bands from the Biological Survey we released them, and that was the last we ever heard of them. Meanwhile the children and I were busy with our study of Mourning Doves nesting on the campus; here maps of the campus, given us by the University, were a help in keeping the multitudes of nests distinct from one another in my records.

At length I had found my vocation, and life held endless opportunities of discovery. What had converted me? The high railroad fares that kept us in Oklahoma that summer, Ben Watts' iniquitous demand to shoot doves in August, and that memorable walk when the beauty of nature engulfed me—all these had played a part.

The dove problem had presented a challenge: did these birds nest in August? We found they nested well into October. So we hastened to the defense of truth and the helpless birds. It is curious how all the pleasant, positive stimuli had proved unavailing, and that it was finally the determination to refute error and save the young doves from a lingering death that aroused me to action. Perhaps it was that no *problem* in regard to wild birds had ever really been posed to me until then. The keen interest in the doves awakened me to interest in all the birds, and the impact of my lone

---

23. Eastern Meadowlark, *Sturnella magna*.
24. *Progne subis*.

walk to the river gave me the determination to fight to preserve some wildness on the earth. . . .

In April 1920 our next door neighbour wished to build himself a garage; he proposed to construct a double one with such help as Blaine could provide in his spare time. A garage calls for an occupant, and promptly we had a Dodge, an open touring car, second hand to be sure, but said to be in the pink of condition. That very day we made an expedition, and I received my first lesson in driving. Prophetically enough, we had a flat tire.

The car was a boon to us, accustomed as we were to travelling on foot with the two youngest in the baby carriage or wagon. Two-year-old Eleanor could hardly be extracted at the end of a trip, for she would hurry to the far end of the seat and bury her face in the upholstery. Our range of operations was much increased, for we could now explore the countryside to the east with its black jack oaks, and also to the south farther than we had ever walked. Our greatest adventure was finding a Barred Owl's[25] nest with two eggs along Rock Creek east of Norman. Constance shinnied up a pole next the tree and reported on the contents. At our last visit she let down the two owlets by means of ropes so that the rest of us could admire and photograph them before she returned them to their home.

Our longest trip that spring was 60 miles northwest to King-fisher to visit two families of Blaine's relatives; here we were delighted with absurd Burrowing Owls[26], handsome Western King-birds[27] and abundant Grasshopper Sparrows[28] and Dickcissels[29]. As these last birds tirelessly chanted their unmusical *jig-jig-jig-jig* from barbed wire fences or telephone wires, Constance suggested we play a new kind of roadside euchre by counting them on a five-mile stretch. We found six to eight Dickcissels per mile. Constance's ambitions grew; she proposed that we count *all* the birds as we chugged and bumped along at less than 20 miles an hour. So our roadside census started—a technique that in those days of slow

25. *Strix varia.*
26. *Athene cunicularia.*
27. *Tyrannus verticalis.*
28. *Ammodramus savannarum.*
29. *Spiza americana.*

cars, unpaved roads, and blessedly "unimproved" roadsides, provided information on the commoner, more conspicuous birds in each region in Oklahoma which we later visited.

Now that we had a car our thoughts turned to camping. One day Blaine came home saying that Mr. Charles W. Shannon wished he could find someone to work on the birds of the state. This sounded like an exciting prospect, and we went to talk to Mr. Shannon. He told us that the original name of his bureau had been the Department of Geological and Natural History, and that two bird projects had already been sponsored: one in 1901–02, the other from 1913 to 1914. He would be glad to lend us camping equipment, help us with advice, and pay our expenses. So here was an opportunity for a camping trip with a serious and important goal. . . .

We now had two incomplete lists (Barde's and Van Vleet's) of the birds of Oklahoma and two partial collections of specimens in the University Museum. What seemed to be most needed was information on what birds occurred where in this far-flung state with its astonishing diversity of physiography, rainfall, and flora. Mr. Shannon suggested we go southwest to the Wichita Mountains, then to the Arbuckle Mountains in south-central Oklahoma, then to the Kiamitia Mountains in the southeast, and finally to the northwestern corner of the state. Since considerable collecting had already been done, and since we much preferred live birds to dead ones, we planned to depend as much as possible upon our eyes and ears rather than on the shotgun lent us by Mr. Shannon.

Our books were Mrs. Bailey's *Birds of the Western United States,* Frank Chapman's *Color Key to North American Birds* (1903), and my old Reed's *Guides,* purchased when the colours of the plates were still unworn. Mr. Shannon lent us a heavy, awkward tent that had to be put up with poles. He also lent us cots and cooking utensils, besides a supply of elegant notebooks. We purchased the rest of our outfit at army stores, prepared blanket sleeping bags, put bars on one side of the car to provide storage place in lieu of a car trunk, nonexistent in those days, and made countless other preparations. We had planned to leave the two- and four-year-olds with our good neighbour, Mrs. Hedley, who watched the flock and *mended* for them when we went out in the evening, but at the last minute she was called to Texas to care for sick relatives. So we decided on a trial trip to the Wichitas; if the children throve, we would start out again on the rest of our itinerary.

And then began our perfect week in the Wichita National Forest. We were welcomed by our friend Frank Rush, Chief Forester, who showed us the colony of Barn Swallow under the bridge by Headquarters and a Bewick's nest in a cow's skull. He also promised to supply us with milk. We set up camp on Elm Island and went to sleep under the stars.

The Wichita Mountains rise abruptly 700 to 900 feet above the plateau; they are jumbles of grey granite boulders with scattered black jack and post oaks and red cedars pushing through the rocks. Scarlet gilia lighted the scanty woods, while the close-cropped cattle range was clothed with showy gaillardia and several kinds of coreopsis. On the rocks by the roadside lay brilliant lizards—little blue-sided swifts and gorgeous "mountain boomers" (collared lizards) with yellow heads and brilliant green-blue bodies and tails.

It was a new world to all of us—the strangeness and wildness of the mountains and plains with the flowers, beasts, and birds. We, too, were part of it, living in it and seeking to understand it. We had a burning zeal to learn all we could, especially of the birds, and to share our knowledge with others. At last I was camping again and this time with an earnest purpose.

So earnest, indeed, that at the last cry of the Chuck-will's-widow[30] just before dawn we pulled on our shoes and canvas leggings (worn as protection from rattlesnakes) and started out to seek birds. Two hours later we would return to camp and the children, and cook bacon and eggs for all of us. Blaine was chief fire-maker and cook, the children were the wood-gatherers and dishwashers. They liked to scrub the tin plates with sand in the creek, for as seven-year-old Marjorie explained, "the fish are just delighted with our crumbs." Four-year-old Barbara decided she wanted "to camp always," even in winter. "Why don't we move here?" she asked. "Move really?" We swam in Cache Creek while Eleanor watched with astonishment and amusement. Blaine and I rode on Mr. Rush's buffalo horses in the tall blue stem of the pasture to visit the bison herd; we clambered up Elk Mountain, Bat Cave Mountain, and Little Baldy, and we met two rattlesnakes. My army breeches were my pride; I was amazed to find with what agility I could leap from rock to rock. By this time women in America were beginning to don male attire for outdoor activities.

---

30. *Caprimulgus carolinensis.*

The most abundant bird, both in the woods and on the prairie, was the Lark Sparrow. Woodpeckers were uncommon, but Great Crested Flycatchers,[31] Tufted Titmice, Carolina Chickadees, and bluebirds were all abundant; apparently they found favourable nesting sites in the knot holes of oaks. Each morning there was a chorus of Wood Pewees[32] uttering their beautiful twilight songs. This species was on the western edge of its range; we found none here on later visits—in 1923, 1926, 1929, 1937, and 1955.

As we explored the boulders at the foot of the mountains we soon discovered our first Rock Wrens,[33] absurd little things with their harsh, graty vocalizations, so appropriate to their environment. But what was this large, olive-grey, sparrow-like bird with its chestnut crown and black line down its throat? "This ought to be a Rock Sparrow,"[34] said I. Lo and behold, according to Mrs. Bailey's *Handbook,* Rock Sparrow it was! We had never before even heard of the existence of such a bird. We were very proud to think we had discovered a new bird for the Oklahoma list. Later, however, I found the Wichita Mountains included in the breeding range in the 1910 A.O.U. *Check-List of North American Birds.* . . .

We came home to a different bird world—to a morning chorus of Robins, Brown Thrashers, Catbirds, Mockingbirds, Orchard Orioles,[35] and Cardinals. When we started out again I felt pity for everyone who could not go camping to study the birds of Oklahoma. And then I remembered that, strange as it might seem, hardly anyone in Norman but ourselves would *want* to do it.

Sixty miles south of Norman lie the ancient, deeply eroded Arbuckle Mountains. Here matchless streams dashed over water-carved travertine rocks where every nook and cranny were filled with ferns. Stately sycamores stood along the streams while in the water grew parrot-feather and watercress, and where rapids flowed over step-like rocks, myriads of caddis fly larvae wove their tiny nets.

Situated 100 miles east of the Wichitas, less elevated and less arid, these more genial conditions were reflected in the bird life. We had found no warblers in the Wichitas; here there were four

---

31. *Myiarchus crinitus.*

32. Eastern Wood Pewee, *Contopus virens.*

33. *Salpinctes obsoletus.*

34. *Aimophila ruficeps.*

35. *Icterus spurius.*

species. Rock Sparrows frequented the stony tops of the eroded "mountains," but the country was not rugged enough for Rock Wrens. A new bird for us was the engaging little Black-capped Vireo.[36] We came upon a nest three feet up in a redbud; in it were three new infants and a partly hatched egg. The parents protested my presence, but the father came to the nest and gently billed his babies.

From our camp at Price's Falls one day we trundled across the high pastures where the strata are all on end as regular as furrows in a plowed field. Turner's Falls on Honey Creek was a noble sight.

A wood rat adopted our car as its den; each morning when we opened the hood there it sat looking at us with its bright eyes, surrounded by the stuff it had brought in during the night—scraps of wood and string, acorns, and even some of my hairpins. . . .

In Pushmataha County, 17 miles north of Antlers, we set up our tent in a wild and beautiful spot beneath the great yellow pines. Milk and water we obtained from a friendly family at a nearby cabin; they told us that we wouldn't be troubled by "varmints," although "timber wolves" (perhaps red wolves *Canis niger*) had carried off half their hogs. . . .

Birds were everywhere in the primeval forests of pine and oaks, hickories, winged elms and sweet gums. Old friends—Wood Pewees, Blue-grey Gnatcatchers, Red-eyed Vireos, Summer Tanagers,[37] and Carolina Wrens. And new friends, too: Chipping Sparrows, familiar door-yard birds in Massachusetts, and migrants in Norman, were here nesting in the deep woods. Warblers were a wonder and a delight—no less than nine species! Two exciting finds were birds of the southeastern pine forests here at the western limit of their range; several Red-cockaded Woodpeckers[38] and a single Brown-headed Nuthatch[39]—the first record for Oklahoma! Day and night there was song—the beauty of the Wood Thrush,[40] the earnestness of the Indigo Bunting, the absurdity of the White-eyed Vireo, the lullaby of the Chuck-will's-widow, and finally the deafening din of Katydids in the dark. . . .

36. *Vireo atricapillus.*
37. *Piranga rubra.*
38. *Picoides borealis.*
39. *Sitta pusilla.*
40. *Hylocichla mustelina.*

After we had recuperated a little from this fantastic trip, I went to consult with Mr. Shannon. Our plan had been to write a report on the birds we had found, comparing them with those in our home county and correlating distribution with geography, altitude, latitude, longitude, rainfall, and vegetation. I was dumbfounded to have Mr. Shannon cheerily talk of our writing a bulletin on *The Birds of Oklahoma*. I protested that we knew hardly anything of the birds of the state. He reassured me by telling of his proposed auto trip through northwestern Oklahoma and the Panhandle on which he would keep notes on the birds encountered. At length we agreed on a preliminary report on *Summer Birds* of the state, designed to arouse interest in bird study and protection. He urged us to prepare it at once for publication that fall. . . .

Mr. Shannon, home from his trip that had proved singularly unproductive so far as bird records went, asked us for a mimeographed list of the summer birds of Oklahoma to be distributed at the State Fair in Oklahoma City in September. Accordingly we prepared an unannotated list of 131 species and subspecies with both common and scientific names. It proved useful to send out to collaborators for their comments.

My absorbing occupation was the preparation of the bulletin. With state lists of Arkansas, Louisiana, Kansas, and Texas, all my books and government bulletins, some of them dating back to Clark University days and with my pile of *Bird-Lores,* we set to work. We pointed out the most glaring gaps in our knowledge of the breeding birds and encouraged readers to keep records of transients and winter residents. Each bird was briefly described, its status and known range given, its notes and nest mentioned; then followed a leisurely discussion of characteristics and life history anecdotes, largely gleaned from *Bird-Lore.* . . .

We had achieved accounts of 92 species when a notice of the A.O.U. meeting to be held in early November in Washington, D.C. [the 38th Stated Meeting of the American Ornithologists' Union, November 8–11, 1920], arrived with an invitation to all classes of members to read papers. Here was my chance; if only I could make Mr. Shannon see the necessity of consulting with Dr. Oberholser in person as to our "Summer Birds," then I could go to the meeting, give a paper on our Mourning Dove study, and incidentally see something of the Morse family. Mr. Shannon was agreeable and promised to pay half my expenses. I invited my mother to be my guest at Washington, and I dropped "Summer Birds" and turned feverishly to dove problems. This trip proved to be of crucial influence in making me into an ornithologist.

I found Dr. Oberholser at the end of a large room housing a number of workers in the Biological Survey; he welcomed me and sent me to the meetings in the National Museum in charge of Miss May T. Cooke of the Biological Survey. She was the daughter of the eminent student of migration, the late Wells W. Cooke. There were 35 papers scheduled for the three days, only one of them by a woman. . . .

At the exhibition of paintings in the Library of Congress I was intrigued with pictures by Althea Sherman, particularly of a cat creeping up on a nestful of Robins. I asked Dr. Palmer about Miss Sherman and he said she wrote a good deal for the *Wilson Bulletin*. This was the first time I had heard of this journal and of the Wilson Ornithological Club.

My own speech, "The Nesting of Mourning Doves at Norman, Oklahoma," came on the last afternoon when there was no time left for discussion. Mr. McAtee and Dr. Palmer hung up my charts on the blackboard, but the colours did not show up well. I was so over-awed that I read rapidly in a faint voice, and I fear the A.O.U. benefited little from my discoveries.

The next week Dr. Oberholser generously spent a whole day helping me with my problems, and this proved the most important pat of the entire trip to me. He showed me the bibliography which the Survey had on Oklahoma birds; this was a revelation to me, particularly in the matter of early explorers. He gave me the names of Oklahoma collaborators, and had books and maps brought me to study. He showed me portions of his great manuscript on *The Bird [Life] of Texas* (1974) with splendid maps indicating the range of each species in the state. Through him I purchased a complete set of the *Nuttall Bulletin* and *Auk* (1876–1919) that had belonged to Henry W. Henshaw, one of the Founders of the Nuttall Ornithological Club, the parent of the A.O.U. . . .

Carefully, we went through our State Fair List of *Summer Birds,* and what a field day Dr. Oberholser did have in changing scientific names and adding subspecific labels! Seven of our birds he rejected but later all but one were reinstated. As the day wore on I grew more and more conscious of our appalling ignorance and of our presumption in attempting to treat of the "Summer Birds of Oklahoma." I resolved then and there that no bulletin would be written by us without a great deal more field work.

I owe a great debt to Dr. Oberholser for starting me on the straight and narrow path in ornithology and in giving me a different viewpoint from that which I had acquired from *Bird-Lore*. But his magnification of the importance of the subspecies was unfortunate for us and for those who followed us, for it diverted attention from the species and made matters unduly confusing for the field student. . . .

Deeply impressed with my heavy responsibility in attempting a book on the breeding birds of Oklahoma, I devoted my energies to studying ornithology.

I joined the Wilson Ornithological Club, the association primarily of middlewestern bird watchers, and purchased the volumes of the *Wilson Bulletin*, beginning with 1912. Those contained many life history studies which I eagerly read. J. R Pemberton, Tulsa oologist, proposed my name for membership in the Cooper Ornithological Club, founded in 1889. In March 1921 I purchased a complete set of the *Condor*—the last set possessed by the Club. "This file of the *Condor*," wrote the business manager, W. Lee Chambers from Eagle Rock, California, "will give you the best working library on western birds obtainable." I also invested in a set of the *Oologist*, edited by R. M. Barnes of Lacon, Illinois, not for its ornithology, but to go through it page by page for references to Oklahoma birds. The money earned in girlhood by labours on the hens had now been put to worthy use.

I settled down to study the *Auk* and the *Condor*, going through them from beginning to end, reading the articles that most interested me and paying special attention to the editorials, correspondence, and book reviews. . . .

I absorbed techniques and standards besides learning much about birds and ornithologists.

The University Library subscribed to no ornithological journal, nor do I remember that it had any bird books. I built up my own library by sending for all the paper-bound State lists I could procure and many Biological Survey bulletins on migration and on the food of birds. Dr. Oberholser had my name placed on the list of the National Museum so that I would receive the current volumes of Arthur Bent's *Life Histories of North American Birds*. Fortunately, I was able to buy the early numbers of this notable set. . . .

Our new baby kindly timed her arrival after the fall migration and before the Christmas census. On December 23, leaving Janet with her sisters, Blaine and I spent an afternoon looking for birds, incidentally getting our only winter records for the county for Belted Kingfisher[41] and White-throated Sparrow.[42]

April 24, 1924, marked the attainment of the goal for which we had been striving for nearly four years. *The Birds of Oklahoma* by Margaret Morse Nice and Leonard Blaine Nice appeared as a University of Oklahoma Bulletin; University Study, No. 286. It is a small, paper-bound publication of 124 pages, starting with a physiographic map which shows the 77 counties in the state and ending with four of our photographs of scenes from the southeastern, southwestern, and northwestern corners of Oklahoma.

In the Introduction we had tried to fire the reader's imagination and to arouse enthusiasm for the protection of birds. An historical sketch gives vivid quotations from the early explorers. . . . Others also described the incredible wealth of wild life they found—the Passenger Pigeons, Carolina Parakeets,[43] Ivory-billed Woodpeckers,[44] Whooping Cranes,[45] and Swallow-tailed Kites. Brief sections are concerned with physical features and faunal areas of the state, with the game laws, the economic value of birds, and the attraction and protection of birds. The main body of the bulletin is devoted to the 361 species and subspecies we accepted; here we gave what we knew about the occurrence of each form—its status and its range with records according to counties, with dates and authorities. Errata were minimal: four misspellings of names.

The University printed 2,500 copies and distributed them widely without cost, sending up to 100 copies to the Zoology Departments of the numerous colleges in the state. . . .

We had letters from twenty-six appreciative ornithologists; three of these especially pleased us. Charles N. Gould, Director of the Oklahoma Geological Survey, called our bulletin "something from which to date Oklahoma ornithology." Ed Crabb, then at the Public Museum in Milwaukee, wrote: "You certainly exhausted about every possible bit of source material that is to be had and condensed it into the minimum amount of space. I consider your book the first important step that has been taken in putting Okla-

---

41. *Megacerlye alcyon.*

42. *Zonotrichia albicollis.*

43. *Conuropsis carolinensis.*

44. *Campephilus principalis principalis.*

45. *Grus americana.*

homa in the ornithological world." And finally a postcard from W. L. McAtee gave his approval to this piece of work: "It seems *sound* and well done."

Rain in the fall had brought destruction to some of our best bird haunts, but rain in the winter and spring formed "Shorebird Pond" in a low spot a half mile south of Norman where in other years we had found Wilson Snipe[46] and brightly coloured LeConte's Sparrows.[47] Hardly was our bulletin out before we began making exciting discoveries as to shorebirds. Day after day we saw species we had included on the basis of one or two reports—White-rumped[48] and Stilt Sandpipers[49] and Long-billed Dowitchers.[50] Semipalmated Sandpipers[51] of which we had found records of two specimens were amazingly abundant for two months. The Semipalmated Plover,[52] included on a sight record, became substantiated by a specimen. Two species were additions to the state list—the spectacular Hudsonian Godwit[53] and the handsome Dunlin.[54]

It was clear we would have to write a second *Birds of Oklahoma*. Although we had worked faithfully to learn all we could about the birds of this great state, Shorebird Pond had shown us we had only made a beginning on this happy, wonderful enterprise. . . .

A welcome letter came from Ernst Mayr: "I consider your Song Sparrow work the finest piece of life-history work, ever done." And for the entire study he offered publication in the Linnaean Society of New York. "Even if it runs to three volumes." This promised to be a most welcome solution for the publication of my great study. . . .

In [1937] the *Population Study of the Song Sparrow* was published. It made quite an impression. Mr. Whittle wrote me, "Your monumental Song Sparrow paper has come and has been read with

---

46. Common Snipe, *Capella gallinago*.
47. LeConte's Sparrow, *Ammospiza leconteii*.
48. *Calidris fuscicollis*.
49. *Micropalama himantopus*.
50. *Limnodromus scolopaceus*.
51. *Calidris pusillus*.
52. *Charadris semipalmatus*.
53. *Limosa hoemastica*.
54. *Calidris alpina*.

pleasure and wonder too at the wealth of data you have so pains-takingly gathered; it's really an ornithological epic." . . .

Mr. E. M. Nicholson wrote in *British Birds* (1939):

> This modestly presented paper includes at least as much original and significant observations of the essential facts of bird behaviour as almost any dozen ordinary bird books . . . a fundamental and orig-inal study of how birds live, worked out in the field in the terms of one species, but checked and illuminated by frequent references to work on the same problems with many species in many countries.

For the opportunity to follow my career, which has involved much more outlay of money than income derived from it, I am deeply indebted to a most understanding and sympathetic husband, who earned the living for us and who shared in many trips to see birds and attend meetings. I am also grateful to four enthusiastic and helpful daughters, and I rejoice in our seven fine grandsons. Finally, my brother Ted [Edward S. Morse], with his editorial ex-perience, and his enthusiasm, has given me fresh courage as I strug-gled on with this story of my life with birds.

Although in my long life, I have visited only a fraction of this wonderful world, yet I have been able to see many choice things and to study some of them, intensively.

It is true that I deplore much in the present situation in the world—basically due to overcrowding—yet for many of the features of civilization I am profoundly thankful: for instance, the compar-ative freedom of women, the advances in medical science, the avail-ability of classical music over FM radio, the great improvements in photographic techniques, paperback books printed in America, electric refrigerators, electric and gas stoves, frozen foods, and for transportation—the convenience of the automobile, and the mar-vellous experience of flying over the earth.

The study of nature is a limitless field, the most fascinating adventure in the world. I feel that ornithology is a splendid pursuit in which strong sympathy and fellowship reign among the majority of serious participants; we are friends, and we are glad to help one another.

We who love nature, who see and try to understand and inter-pret, are following the true goal. We have a talisman against the futil-ity of the lives of many people. We must try to open the eyes of the unseeing to the beauty and wonder of the earth and its wild life.

Hortense Powdermaker

(1896–1970)

The second child of German Jewish immigrants to Philadelphia, Hortense Powdermaker was the granddaughter of two affluent Jewish business families. Because her father's business success was sometimes uncertain, she grew up acutely conscious of money and class, which she rejected while a college student.

A history major in the class of 1919 at Goucher College, Powdermaker was excluded from college social life because she was Jewish. Influenced by socialism while an undergraduate, she worked in a men's shirt factory during one spring break and moved to New York to become an organizer for the Amalgamated Clothing Workers upon graduation. Her success as an organizer did not ease her sense of "not belonging" to the union movement, and in 1925 she sought a fresh start as a student at the London School of Economics. Enrolling in Bronislaw Malinowski's anthropology class, Powdermaker found her intellectual home and became one of Malinowski's early graduate students. His theory of functionalism and interest in the relationship between psychoanalytic concepts and anthropology became major themes in Powdermaker's work, inspiring her own extensive analysis.

Receiving her Ph.D. in 1928, Powdermaker left her student life in Bloomsbury for fieldwork at Lesu, a tiny village on the southwest Pacific island of New Ireland. *Life in Lesu* (1933), a classic in anthropology, was the product of this research, which launched her on an academic career in the United States. Funded by the Social Science Research Council, Powdermaker began a study of the community of Indianola, Mississippi, published as *After Freedom* (1939). She founded the department of anthropology and sociology at Queens College in New York in the late 1930s and taught there until her retirement.

Her most celebrated research, carried out in Hollywood in 1946–47, was published as *Hollywood: The Dream Factory,* in 1950. In this work Powdermaker criticized the crassness of Hollywood values, described the extent to which the structure of the film community shaped what was produced, and expressed concern about the impact of mass media on society. Her study of media and their effects in the troubled colonial society of Northern Rhodesia (later Zambia) was published as *Copper Town* (1962). Her autobiography, *Stranger and Friend: The Way of an Anthropologist*, published in 1966, became a classic in the field, conveying more vividly than other accounts the intellectual challenge of anthropology, the excitements and disappointments of fieldwork, and the perspective on an individual's life and personality gained from work in comparative social science.

Never a major theorist, Powdermaker made important contributions to anthropology through her sense of social justice, her demonstration of the value of fieldwork in analyzing social systems under stress, and the flair for locating the timely topic demonstrated in her studies of the media.

STRANGER AND FRIEND:
The Way of an Anthropologist

As a child, I did not accept the norms of my upper-middle- and middle-class German Jewish background. (A paternal grandmother was English Jewish.) I was second generation born in the United States. Grandparents on both sides seem to have been prosperous before migrating to Philadelphia, where the grandfathers were successful businessmen. I was early aware of the subtleties of class distinctions within the extended family. The business background was much the same for all, but levels of success varied. Actually these differences were not very large, but they were symbolically significant. My family was in the middle-middle group, though its fortunes went up and down. We moved away from Philadelphia when I was about five, and after seven or eight years of living in Reading, Pennsylvania, we settled in Baltimore.

I never had a sense of much real religious feeling in the family, although there was a definite sense of being Jewish, particularly for my mother. Her father had been president of a reform synagogue in Philadelphia and active in Jewish civic affairs. In Baltimore we belonged to a reform synagogue with a congregation of German descent, and I was confirmed in it. My family, other relatives, and their friends completely accepted the then current belief in the alleged social superiority of German Jews over more recent Jewish immigrants from eastern Europe. Knowledge of the social distinctions between these two groups preceded my awareness of the general social position of Jews in American culture. During childhood and adolescence, my friends were not restricted to any religious group.

My identity was polarized against this background, rebelling against the business values and the social snobbery. At the age of fourteen, after visiting an uncle and aunt, I wrote a poem called "Things," expressing scorn for the stress on acquiring and taking care of material things. School was a major interest in adolescence, and favorite subjects were literature, history, and Latin. I read omnivorously, and the fictional worlds created by Romain Rolland, Hawthorne, Dostoevski, Thackeray, and many others provided a way of stepping outside of my immediate environment. Later, I went out of my way to meet recent Jewish working-class immigrants from eastern Europe, whom my family scorned. I liked them. They seemed to have a feeling of what I now call cultural roots, which I envied. They sang Russian songs, spoke Yiddish, and ate Jewish foods. Most of those I knew had a socialist ideology, and a few had intellectual interests. Their style of life seemed more definitive than the Americanized business culture of my family, which bored me.

Goucher College strengthened the tendency to step in and out of my social group. My participation in college life through extracurricular activities was rather perfunctory. The detachment from college social life occurred partly because as a day-student, living at home, I did not have the in-group feeling of dormitory life. But there was another reason. In my freshman year I was surprised at not being invited to join a sorority and belatedly discovered that sororities were not open to Jews. I was not sure that I wished to join one, but I wanted to be invited. (Sororities ceased to exist at Goucher College in 1950.) A relatively unimportant snub by college sororities was thus my first awareness of social restrictions on Jews, or at least, the first I remember.

Interested in learning more about society, and, probably, wanting to understand my position in it, I thought of majoring in sociology. But it was not well developed at the Goucher of that time, and the two courses I took contributed little to my understanding and left me dissatisfied. (Anthropology was nonexistent in most undergraduate colleges then.) I changed to history, one of the top departments with a number of scholarly and stimulating teachers. From their courses I gained some sense of the comparative nature of civilizations and of historical depth. The Middle Ages and the Renaissance were my favorite periods. I read widely for other courses and on my own: literature, poetry, and philosophy. The humanistic bent was apparent. Fun and frivolity were part of life, too: parties, picnics, candy-pulls, canoeing on the Potomac river, walking trips through western Maryland, tennis, and other such doings.

At college I developed socialistic interests, shared by only a few fellow students. For several weeks, three of us debated with great seriousness whether it was right to accept inherited wealth. I took the negative position. I "discovered" the Baltimore slums and the trade-union movement. My belief in the latter was naive, simple, and ardent: poverty could be eradicated and the world would be better, if all workers joined unions. I had little concern with Marxian theory, or the political party. My interest in the labor movement was in part an expression of rebellion from the family, which made it no less socially legitimate.

In dilettantish fashion I began to explore the world of the workers, and spent a spring vacation working in a small unorganized men's shirt factory. Never having used even a hand-operated sewing machine, and being totally ungifted in sewing, I was scared by the power machine, as well as by the forelady. My body rebelled against sitting at a machine all day. In urgent need of exercise, I often went dancing in the evenings and played tennis over weekends. The physical sensation of sitting continuously at a machine and the memory of the unending boredom of sewing one seam on the back yoke of shirts have never left me.

A pleasant memory of my stint at the shirt factory is of the friendly girls. A particular friend was an Italian, working next to me. She helped me when I got into trouble with the machine, and we often ate lunch together. Before long she decided that her brother, who owned a tobacco and newspaper shop in a small town between Baltimore and Washington, and I should marry. Accordingly, I was invited to a family dinner to meet him. Unable to go through with the deception that I had any intention of marrying her brother and helping him run his shop, I disappeared from the factory a couple of days before the dinner. But I was pleased that it had been easy to make friendly contacts in the first excursion outside of my own environment.

I helped to revive the local Women's Trade Union League and became its representative to the Baltimore Federation of Labor, where I observed delegates playing politics in their bid for power. My first public speech was made in a campaign of the Federation to organize women. Terrified, I stood in a truck, parked in a working-class neighborhood; a large Irish man from the Machinists' Union, whose deep voice made my girlish one seem silly, did his best to quiet my fears. Somehow I spoke, and survived. During this period I knew the local officers and some members of the International Ladies' Garment Workers' Union and the Amalgamated Clothing Workers of America, or more colloquially, the I.L.G.W.U. and A.C.W. of A.

After college, eager to leave home and Baltimore, I went to New York and applied for a position (any position) at the headquarters of the Amalgamated Clothing Workers. I became an assistant to the director of education, J. B. Salutsky (later known as J. B. S. Hardman), who ran what he called the "intellectual backyard" of the organization, including its publications. He was an interesting Russian intellectual with a quick imaginative brilliance. But it was not my idea of changing the world to sit in an office and write, edit, and pound a typewriter; I wanted a more direct experience.

So, after five or six months, I went to see the president, Sidney Hillman, and told him that I was dissatisfied with my job and wanted to organize workers. Hillman looked at me, inquired about my experience, thought a while, and asked if I could be ready to go to Cleveland by the end of the week and conduct an organizing campaign there. Eager, but scared, I mentioned my lack of experience. Hillman seemed unconcerned and said he was sure I could do the job.

In retrospect, the few years spent as a labor organizer seem not to have been without value for an anthropologist-to-be. They provided a knowledge of social realities not gained through text books. I saw and experienced the operation of power within the union and in the struggle between workers and employers. Active participation in the lives of factory workers helped me understand a segment of the American class system to which I did not belong—what it was not, as well as what it was. A social movement became a complex living force rather than an abstraction. I stepped into a part of society I had not known, and, after a time, I stepped out of it. . . .

The Amalgamated . . . led by Sidney Hillman . . . developed new concepts of labor-management relations and expanded the functions of the union to include unemployment insurance, banks to serve the financial needs of members, adult education, cooperative housing, medical and other services. These benefits were centered primarily in New York, Chicago, and Rochester. In the hinterlands the union was weak or nonexistent, employers were hostile, agencies of government unfriendly, liberals and intellectuals indifferent. . . .

While my role as an organizer for the Amalgamated Clothing Workers of America was decidedly different from that of the anthropologist's participant observation, similarities were not altogether lacking. Aside from the couple of weeks in the shirt factory this was my first experience in a sub-culture different from my own, in a limited sense, a kind of fieldwork. I tried to understand people whose backgrounds were unlike mine and I participated—to some degree—in their lives. But the goals and methods were completely dissimilar. As an organizer, I endeavored to induce change: to give workers, some of them indifferent or apathetic, a sense of their own interests which I thought could best be served by belonging to a collectivity—the union—and to spot potential leaders and develop them. Later, as an anthropologist, I tried, as far as possible, to make no change in the society I studied. But even in the labor movement days, I seem to have been a "natural" observer and recorder. I kept a diary. It has long been lost, but excerpts from it, published in *The Amalgamated Illustrated Almanac,* have helped me to recall my work in the labor movement.[1]

In Cleveland a number of small shops in the men's clothing industry were in the union, but the largest one was still unorganized. It paid higher wages than the union shops, had a big welfare department, and was owned and run by two men who considered themselves liberals. When Hillman described the situation to me, he said he wanted the campaign conducted on a "high" level and, if possible, without antagonizing the liberal employers.

Feeling uncertain and yet confident, I arrived in Cleveland. First, I met the manager of the local Amalgamated organization and the members of their joint board. Hillman came a day or so later. Unconventionally, we called on the two men who were owners and managers of the large factory we hoped to organize. It was large, modern, with big windows, and in sharp contrast to small dingy

---

1. Hortense Powdermaker, "From the Diary of a Girl Organizer," *The Amalgamated Illustrated Almanac,* Amalgamated Clothing Workers of America, prepared by the Education Department under the direction of J. B. Salutsky (New York: 1924).

union shops in the city. The two gentlemen proudly escorted us through their factory. The workers thus saw two people, later to be identified as the president of the union and an organizer, within the shop escorted by the owner-managers. Hillman had hoped this would be an outcome of the visit. After the tour of the factory, we chatted pleasantly with the owners in their office. They said that of course, they would not organize their employees for us, but they would recognize the union if we succeeded in forming an organization in their shop. It was obvious that they considered this impossible and, as they looked at me, they appeared amused at the idea of my trying to do it. I remember how I looked: a young "flapper," dressed in a brown and white checked wool suit, and a brown upturned felt hat, perched a bit coquettishly on one side, over my bobbed hair.

The majority of the employees in the shop were young girls, many of Bohemian and Italian immigrant background, and the remainder American-born. The skilled cutters were usually of eastern European background and, of course, men. I do not remember just how I began and the published excerpts from the diary do not describe this. But quite early in the campaign, I began writing short one-page circulars, printed in different colors. Each circular contained a message about unionism, simply written, and generally based on a quotation from Abraham Lincoln, George Washington, Thomas Jefferson, or another "father" of the country. I was trying to break the image of the union as a radical European organization and to stress its advantages to American workers. Standing in front of the factory exit at closing time I passed out the circulars, and chatted with some of the workers. Almost no one refused the circular, and quite a few stopped to talk and said they would be glad to see me at home when I suggested a visit in the evening.

One cutter gave us a lead to his group. He had been an active socialist in Bohemia and believed in unions as a matter of principle. He was our first member, and through him we had access to other cutters. The girls were more difficult. They had never heard of Karl Marx, and were unaware of the concept of working-class solidarity. Like most girls, they were interested in beaus, clothes, having a good time, getting married; the younger ones hoped marriage would end their factory days. But they had their complaints—speeding up of work being a major one. The factory's elaborate welfare department seemed to have little meaning for them. As we became better acquainted, I was invited to some of their parties, or to go with them to the movies on a Sunday afternoon. We rented a hall and gave dances for them some Saturday evenings.

The [first union] meeting was a dismal failure. The day it was to take place, many of those who had joined the union, and all those who had shown leadership, were fired. In the almost empty hall, I wept. Hillman, however, did not seem surprised and tried to comfort me. He said the campaign had been a great success. Through my tears I asked how he could say that. He went on: it would take at least three or four campaigns before the shop would be organized; every other organizer whom he had asked to undertake the first campaign had refused, because they said the job was impossible.[2] Hillman had been quick to see that in my naivete I did not know the job was impossible; so, in a sense, I had done it.

But I was depressed. I had worked for almost a year and had built an organization. Following Hillman's instructions I had carefully avoided any attack on the two men who headed the firm. I really had believed they would recognize the union, if we succeeded in getting a sufficient number of their workers to join. In spite of Hillman's comforting words about the "success" of this initial campaign, I felt low. My earlier naivete was no comfort now. I had lost it.

Hillman thought I needed a change and sent me to Rochester, where the men's clothing industry was fully organized. My job was to develop activity and leadership in the women's local. Its membership was apathetic and meetings were poorly attended. I became friends with the girls, spotted the most likely new leaders, and planned interesting programs for the meetings. They became lively and well attended. In the next election a new leader was made chairman. The previous longtime chairman was chagrined and surprised. But she shook hands with me, remarking wryly, but in a tone of respect, that she had never expected to be defeated by a college girl. She was an astute and experienced politician. I seem to have played the game intuitively.

Then came a struggle between the "ins" and "outs" for control of the Rochester organization. The "ins" represented responsible administration, whom the General Office in New York wanted to keep in power. The "outs" were irresponsible, but avid for power.

---

2. Hillman's prophecy of several campaigns before the factory would be successfully organized turned out to be true.

It was not, however, a left-right struggle. I fought on the side of the "ins." We lost. The "outs" took office and, to my surprise, once in power they were as responsible as the former "ins." I wondered what the fight had really been about, and why I had put so much energy into it.

The emotional wave on which I had entered the labor movement seemed to have spent itself. I still believed in the workers' cause and the necessity of union organization. My social values had not changed. But I shuddered as I looked at the middle-aged organizers—holding on to a job. I was considered a successful organizer, but where was I to go from there? Tired of trying to get people to do something or to change, of being in the labor movement but as an outsider, I wanted the more normal social life of a young woman and hungered both for gaiety and intellectual companionship. I was bored. It was time for me to step out of the labor movement.

I went to New York and saw Hillman. When I told him I was resigning, he was surprised and offered to change my locale, to raise my salary, or to do anything else within reason to make me content. I thanked him, but said I had to leave. To his question "why," I answered that the reasons were complex and that I wasn't sure I knew all of them, but I was convinced I should resign, adding as an afterthought, "while my heart is in the right place." Hillman seemed to understand and complimented me on my work. I told him that I had learned much and that I was glad that I had worked for his union. . . .

Before beginning to study anthropology, I had experienced stepping in and out of my own society—in the family, in college, and in the labor movement.

I went to England partly because I wanted to go there and partly to put an ocean between me and many personal ties in the labor movement. After visiting London, Oxford, and Cambridge, I decided to stay in London. Oxford and Cambridge were beautiful, but too secluded for me; London I loved at sight.

I wanted to study, but had no thought of a graduate degree or of an academic career. I registered for two courses at the University of London, one in geology and the other in social anthropology, although I had done no previous work in either. Rocks and primitive peoples, I thought, would be pleasantly and totally unrelated to social causes and to my recent activities in the labor movement. The geology course turned out to be boring, and I soon dropped it. But anthropology happened to be taught by Bronislaw Malinowski, who was then—in the fall of 1925—a Reader at the London School of Economics. (Two years later he was appointed to the Chair of Anthropology.)

The anthropology course opened new doors. I had found a discipline which, more than any other I knew, provided an understanding of man and his society about which I was so curious. Malinowski's functional theory was a sharp instrument for social analysis and I was attracted by the breadth of the discipline and by his stimulating teaching. Anthropology was what I had been looking for without knowing it.

A young anthropologist on the staff of the L.S.E. (as the School is called colloquially) referred, in a recent conversation, to the late twenties there as "the Golden Age." Perhaps it was. . . . I try [here] only to recall the mood of that period, to give the flavor of Malinowski's personality, and to mention those theories and ideas which left their mark on my thinking. His work has been discussed at length, evaluated, and criticized by many anthropologists and other social scientists.[3]

Malinowski was an exciting teacher and person, as well as a distinguished anthropologist. As is well known, he received a Ph.D. in physics and mathematics from the University of Cracow in 1908.[4]

---

3. See, particularly, Raymond Firth ed., *Man and Culture, An Evaluation of the Work of Bronislaw Malinowski* (London: Routledge & Kegan Paul, 1957); Max. Gluckman, "Malinowski's Analysis of Social Change," *African Studies,* Vol. VI, 1947; "Malinowski's Contribution to Social Anthropology," *Africa,* Vol. XVII, 1947 (Reprinted together as "Malinowski's Sociological Theories," *The Rhodes-Livingstone Papers,* No. 16, Manchester University Press, 1949); E. A. Hoebel, "The Trobriand Islanders: Primitive Law as Seen by Bronislaw Malinowski," in *The Law of Primitive Man* (Cambridge, Mass.: Harvard University Press, 1954), pp. 177–210; Clyde Kluckhohn, "Bronislaw Malinowski 1884–1942," *Journal of American Folklore,* Vol. LVI, pp. 208–219; Harold Lasswell, "A Hypothesis Rooted in the Preconceptions of a Single Civilization Tested by Bronislaw Malinowski," Analysis 34 in *Methods in Social Science: A Case Book,* ed. Stuart A. Rice (Chicago: University of Chicago Press, 1931), pp. 480–88; E. R. Leach, "A Trobriand Medusa," *Man,* No. 158, 1954, London; Dorothy Lee, "A Primitive System of Values," *Philosophy of Science,* Vol. VII (1940), pp. 355–78; G. P. Murdock, "Malinowski, Bronislaw," *American Anthropologist,* Vol. XLV, pp. 441–51.

4. Most of the "fathers" of cultural anthropology were trained originally in the natural sciences: Boas in physics and geography; Haddon in marine zoology; Rivers in physiology; Radcliffe-Brown in experimental psychology, although his degree was in the moral sciences.

His health was bad and the doctor ordered him to discontinue his studies. While recuperating, he read Frazer's *The Golden Bough* and he told us that reading this many-volumed book made him decide to be an anthropologist. The explanation always sounded overly simple to me. Whatever the other influences may have been, when healthy enough to resume his studies, he went for a short time to Leipzig where he studied under Karl Bucher. In 1910 he came to London and worked with C. G. Seligmann, receiving a D.Sc. in 1916 with his publications on the Australian aborigines and the Mailu.

When I arrived at the L.S.E. in 1925, he had done his lengthy fieldwork in the Trobriand Islands and had published the *Argonauts of the Western Pacific*. He was passionately involved in anthropology, and his enthusiasm and earnestness were contagious. Nor was his thinking restricted to the "savages"; in lectures he often gave comparative examples from modern civilizations, and in conversations he made amusing allusions to contemporary British tribal rites and customs. He was a cultivated humanist as well as a scientist, and my impression is that he saw no conflict between the two views.

The lectures Malinowski gave in the classroom were not polished statements of a completed theory. He prepared them carefully—detailed charts and outlines on long yellow sheets of paper—but as he lectured one could almost hear him continuing to think. In the small seminars he made *us* think. If any one of the students had only half an idea, he encouraged and almost forced him, with kindly persistence, to follow through with it. He was at his best in Socratic discussion, and better at it than anyone I have ever met. We had to pursue a point until it led somewhere, or abandon it. This was a new experience for me and a good antidote to intellectual laziness.

Although his health was not always good, he had great vitality and was deeply involved with life—the minutiae and the general, whether in the Trobriand Islands or in London. He was also a man of paradoxes: kind and helpful as well as cruel and sarcastic. Keen perception and sharp wit helped make his barbs effective. Belligerence characterized many arguments with his peers. Then, too, he delighted in shocking people, particularly those he considered bourgeois and conventional. It was my impression that his relationships with women were easier than those with men. With women he was a continental gentleman, somewhat in the well-known gallant and flirtatious tradition, which, however, did not prevent him from being completely serious when it came to discussing their work. He tended to see men as rivals and I think there was, in general, more ambivalence on both sides in these relations than in those with women.

During my first year at the L.S.E. only three graduate students were in anthropology. The other two were E. E. Evans-Pritchard and Raymond Firth. Isaac Schapera came the second year and we were soon joined by Audrey Richards, Edith Clarke, the late Jack Driberg, Camilla Wedgwood, and Gordon and Elizabeth Brown. Strong personal bonds developed between us and with Malinowski; it was a sort of family with the usual ambivalences. The atmosphere was in the European tradition: a master and his students, some in accord and others in opposition. Many other students came later, and their relations with Malinowski may have differed from ours.

The School, known as a brain-child of Fabians such as Beatrice and Sidney Webb and Bernard Shaw, was still "pink" politically. Required courses, written examinations, and grades did not exist. The attendance at some of Malinowski's lecture courses was mixed—undergraduates as well as graduate students. The first year his courses were my introduction to anthropology. Later I still went to some of the lectures, because I continued to learn from them and because Malinowski liked his graduate students to attend, partly, perhaps, because he was then surer of a response when he asked a Socratic type of question. The lectures were usually in the late afternoon, and most of my days were spent reading in the library of the British Museum[5] . . .

Malinowski was in a particularly creative mood during this period, as he worked out his concept of institutions and his functional theories as they applied to magic, kinship, and primitive law. It is difficult now when much of Functionalism is an accepted part of anthropological and social science thinking to convey the tone of that early period when we felt we were striding along intellectual frontiers. An enemy was the diffusionist theories of that era, particularly those of Elliot Smith and W. J. Perry at University College. Their theory that all of culture originated in Egypt and fanned out over the world has been forgotten and discarded. But in my student days the members of the two schools were belligerent and Mali-

---

5. Anthropology was limited to social anthropology; archeology, physical anthropology, and linguistics (all part of the American curriculum) were absent.

nowski and Elliot Smith publicly damned each other's work. The term "evolution" was a bad word, whether referring to the Elliot Smith and Perry concept or to the oversimplified social theories which had followed publication of Darwin's theory of biological evolution. The concept of evolution has long since come out of the realm of historical fantasy, and is a significant and powerful theory rooted in physical anthropology and archeology, as well as in ethnology.

I learned much from my fellow students, particularly Evans-Pritchard, Raymond Firth, and Isaac Schapera. We spent long hours in pubs or in the inexpensive restaurants of Little Soho, discussing and arguing. I felt decidedly inferior to them, and was also envious. Each had "a people" while I had none. Evans-Pritchard would hold forth about the Azande, among whom he did fieldwork while still a student. Firth told us about the Maori, whom he knew before he came to London. Schapera already had an extensive knowledge of the Bushmen and other South African tribes. Theories were argued back and forth. Gossip about our teachers was told and retold gleefully. We talked of the need to keep the natives pure and undefiled by missionaries and civil servants. Missionaries were an enemy, except for Edwin Smith and H. A. Junod, who apparently were more interested in learning about the tribal peoples than in converting them.[6] British civil servants on leave came to Malinowski's lectures, and we accepted his point that training could make them more respectful and less disruptive of native life. Now, with the sociological interest in social change and with the knowledge of the significant roles played by missionaries and civil servants in it, our hostile attitude seems indeed biased. . . .

Life in London outside the anthropological circle was also amusing. With the exception of one winter in Hampstead, I lived in Bloomsbury, and had friends in the Bloomsbury circle as well as among the anthropologists and other L.S.E. people; some overlapping occurred between the two groups. I went to gay parties, was interested in contemporary art and frequented the galleries, had one season of intense interest in the ballet, and, in general, enjoyed

---

6. The books of these two men are still highly regarded: Edwin W. Smith, *The Golden Stool* (London: Holborn Publishing House, 2nd ed., 1927) and H. A. Junod, *Life of a South African Tribe* (London: MacMillan Co., 2nd ed., 1927).

London life. But most days I could be found at my desk in the reading room of the British Museum. This vast vaulted room, with its strange combination of readers—distinguished scholars, students, and "cranks"—was home to me. To return to my desk and to the uninterrupted hours of reading on a Monday morning after a gay weekend was steadying. Life during these student days had its ups and downs; but happy or unhappy, I felt as if I belonged. There was no stepping in and out of this society. I was an indigenous part of it.

After three years I was awarded a Ph.D. degree. This had not been my reason for coming to London and I originally planned to stay only one year. Towards the end of the first semester, Malinowski had suggested that I pick a subject for my Ph.D. thesis. He was shocked when I told him I did not plan to take a degree, and that I was studying for "fun." I had "principles" against higher degrees, and seriously argued what higher goal could there be than studying merely for enjoyment. I seem to have been without ambition for a career or the drive to make practical plans for the future. (Marriage was a possibility.) Malinowski was irritated and said he was not giving his time and energy to training students for their "fun." I walked along the Thames, debating whether or not to give up my "principles" and take a degree. Anthropology fascinated me. I wanted to continue studying and to be part of the L.S.E. group. I would be excommunicated if I did not work toward a degree. By the end of the first semester I registered retroactively for it and went on to become an anthropologist. I have never regretted the decision.[7]

Lesu is a village on the east coast of New Ireland, an island in the southwest Pacific. About two degrees from the equator and part

7. After returning to the United States, I was influenced by a number of anthropologists. The most significant for me was Edward Sapir, in whose department at Yale University I was a research associate. Others included Clark Wissler, Ralph Linton, Alfred Kroeber, and Ruth Benedict. Later I came to Robert Redfield's work, which strengthened my humanistic point of view. The work of A. I. Hallowell and of Abraham Kardiner and of course, of Edward Sapir, helped make a bridge between anthropological and psychoanalytic thinking. Analysis and, later, Erik Erikson's writings were major influences in that no-man's land. Twenty-five years of teaching have also been part of the learning process.

of the Bismarck Archipelago (southeast of New Guinea), it is under an Australian mandate.[8] The island is about two hundred miles long with an average width of twenty miles; a low range of mountains, three thousand feet at the highest altitude, runs through the center. Lesu, approximately eighty miles from the northern end of the island, had a population of 232 at the time of my fieldwork, April 1929 to February 1930.[9] The village was part of a linguistic unit of four other villages (Ambwa, Langania, Libba, and Tandis) which I visited to attend rites and secure ethnographic information. Occasionally I went to a village in an adjacent linguistic unit for a special ceremony. The people were Melanesian—tall, black, with bushy hair—members of the Oceanic Negroid race. Their homogenous society belonged to a late Stone Age culture.

I was the first anthropologist to study this society, then relatively uninfluenced by modern civilization. German Catholic missionaries had been in the southern part of New Ireland, as well as in other parts of the archipelago, and had written about the religion and the *Malanggans,* ritual carvings connected with mortuary rites. But no missionary had lived in the linguistic unit where I worked. A few people in the village were technically members of a Methodist mission (Australian in origin), but appeared unaffected by its teachings in any significant way. A "mission boy" in his teens held services on Sundays, but was without influence. Writing was unknown; no one had been to school, and pidgin English, spoken mainly by young men and children, was the only language other than Melanesian. Technological influence from outside was slight and implements were primitive—stone axes, wooden digging sticks and spears, sharp sea shells for scraping taro (a tuber vegetable). Rituals were performed in traditional manner and native customs were followed. The exceptions to the latter were cannibalism and murder, both forbidden by the Australian Mandated Government. Occasionally a few men left their villages to "sign on" for three years of work on a coconut plantation on New Ireland or a nearby island, but they brought little cultural innovation back with them. At the time

8. Before World War I, New Ireland was called Neu Mecklenburg and belonged to Germany. The spelling of the village name on old government maps and publications is Lossu. Lesu approximates the native pronunciation of the word more phonetically.

9. The fieldwork was financed by the Australian National Research Council.

of my study, none of the men were away from Lesu. Government patrols made infrequent brief visits to the villages. In general, native life was traditional and had a coherence and logic of its own. I was able to participate rather fully in it.

This was my first night in Lesu alone. As I sat on the veranda of my thatched-roof, two-room house in the early evening, I felt uncertain and scared, not of anything in particular, but just of being alone in a native village. I asked myself, "What on earth am I doing here, all alone and at the edge of the world?"

I had arrived two weeks earlier, accompanied by the Australian government anthropologist and a young English anthropologist (working on another island), who had met my boat in Rabaul, the capital of the Mandated Territory of New Guinea; they had generously offered to help me get settled in Lesu. When we met, the expression on their faces was, "Oh, my God!" I was a young woman, essentially urban, and obviously knew nothing about how to live in a primitive village. Their help in setting up my housekeeping was invaluable. The introduction by the government anthropologist was good because he was known to the natives through his occasional patrols, and he was well liked. The Englishman, an expert in pidgin English, gave me daily lessons in it. Pidgin is not bad English, but is a limited combination of English and native words, with a construction of its own. In this area a few German words were also in the vocabulary. My teacher was good, and I was able to practice immediately.

Both men supervised the finishing of my house (begun before my arrival for visiting government patrols), the building of a privy, the making of a primitive shower, adding a room to the cook-house for a servant's bedroom, and all the other details of settling in. Compared to the one-room village huts whose floor was the ground, my house seemed luxurious. It was raised from the ground and had two windowless rooms with a wide veranda between them and a narrow one around the sides of the house. One room was for sleeping and the other for keeping supplies. I worked, received company, and ate on the wide section of the veranda. The thatched roof was an advantage in the tropics.

Ongus, the *luluai*, an Australian-appointed chief, was a well-built, intelligent-looking man, obviously in command as he directed the unloading of my boxes and bales and the finishing of my house. I was lucky that he was well respected by the Lesu people. I knew that in the past there had been no chiefs and that authority had rested with the important elders. The Australian Mandated Government had appointed a chief in each village, in order to have a representative with whom to deal when they made patrols.

During these first days I was busy unpacking and settling in. Almost everyone in the village was in and around the house gazing with wonder, admiration, or amusement at my folding army cot, kitchen equipment, sewing basket, a ring of safety pins which particularly fascinated two old men, an oil lamp with a gas mantle, a portable typewriter, and all the other odds and ends which I thought necessary to existence. When I unrolled a thin mattress for the army cot, the English anthropologist was scornful. I replied serenely that I belonged to the comfort school of anthropology. I could see no reason for being more uncomfortable than necessary. He seemed to believe that discomforts were essential. During this time I made no real contacts with the native peoples, although I had a feeling that they were friendly. We smiled at each other, exchanged greetings in pidgin English, and I played a little with two babies. One responded with delighted coos; the other wailed loudly.

I had two servants, selected in Rabaul by the government anthropologist to accompany me to Lesu. The man, nick-named Pau, was a short, middle-aged Papuan with an unusual characteristic of extensive baldness. He came highly recommended as a cook and his experience included cooking for the Germans before World War I, as well as recently for Australians. He was responsible for the kitchen and for the shooting of birds for dinner. Taiti, the woman, a Melanesian, about thirty-five years old, had lived and worked in Rabaul for many years. She took care of my house, did the laundry, mending, and other such chores. Their wages, fixed by the Mandated Government, were, by Western standards, ridiculously little: two dollars a month plus a blanket and rations. Taiti had appeared willing to leave her half-caste Chinese husband in Rabaul. I knew nothing about Pau's marital life, but he seemed not to have any wife at this time. Both servants were still strangers to me.

My real contacts were limited to the two anthropologists; we talked about anthropology and gossiped about anthropologists. I was still primarily in my own modern world. In a couple of weeks, when my house was finished, Ongus, the *luluai*, and my anthropologist friends knew that a feast must be held to mark the occasion. The people in each hamlet of the village contributed piles of yams, taro, and bananas which they placed on the ground in front of the house. I noted that the women and small children sat together on one side and the men on the other side. Ongus made a speech about how the house was "finished good" and then distributed the food and my contribution of Virginia Emu Twist tobacco to the men. Fortunately, an anthropologist in Sydney had told me tobacco would be my best currency, and I had purchased a hundred dollars' worth of it.

A day or two later, my anthropologist friends left me to return to their own work. As I waved good-bye, I felt like Robinson Crusoe, but without a man Friday. That evening as I ate my dinner, I felt very low. I took a quinine pill to ward off malaria. Suddenly I saw myself at the edge of the world, and *alone*. I was scared and close to panic. When I arrived I had thought the place was lovely. Every-thing seemed in harmonious accord: the black natives, the vividness of the sea and of the wild flowers, the brightly plumed birds, the tall areca palm and coconut trees, the delicate bamboo, the low thatched-roofed huts, the beauty of the nights with the moon shin-ing on the palm trees. But now the same scene seemed ominous. I was not scared of the people, but I had a feeling of panic. Why was I here, I asked myself repeatedly.

There seemed to be no adequate reason: anthropology, curi-osity, career—all seemed totally unimportant. *Why* had I come? I began to think of all the events which had preceded my arrival here. I had been envious of fellow students in London who had done fieldwork, who had their people, while I had none. Towards the end of my studies, I had selected the Mafulu who lived on top of a mountain in New Guinea to become "my" people, partly because I liked the idea of being perched on a mountain top and partly because an adventurous solicitor, Robert Williamson, had published in 1912 a grammar of their language and some ethnographical data, both superficial but of potential usefulness to a beginning field worker. Malinowski had then arranged that the Australian National Research Council invite me to make the study. Their grant included the payment of all expenses, plus £100 (then the equivalent of about $500) as a personal stipend, for such items as cigarettes, toothpaste, and so forth.

Many months of preparation followed. First, I made a long, detailed outline—forty odd pages—of all I wanted to find out, and this was discussed in a small graduate seminar. I went to see a doctor at the School of Tropical Medicine (to whom Seligmann gave me an introduction) to learn a few simple rules about how to maintain good health in the tropics; the important ones were to see *always* that water was boiled, to sleep under a mosquito net, and to take the nightly quinine pill as a prophylactic against malaria. I shopped for mosquito boots and other appropriate clothes. Farewell parties were given. I had gone home the preceding summer to say "good-bye" to the family. Finally in December, 1928, I boarded a P. and O. ship.

Just before leaving I had received a cable from Radcliffe-Brown, chairman of the Australian National Research Council, to postpone my arrival in Sydney for a month because he would not be back from the field until then. Having kissed everyone good-bye I felt it would be an anticlimax to wait in London, and decided to sail as planned and stop over in Ceylon for a month. India seemed too vast for a month's visit.

When I arrived there [in Sydney], I went immediately to the anthropology department at the university to see Radcliffe-Brown, the chairman, and pick up mail. I found a letter from the government anthropologist advising (which meant commanding) me not to go to the Mafulu, because of the difficulties of securing porters to carry boxes and other luggage to the mountain top. Later I learned that the Mandated Government also feared the isolation of the Mafulu and was anxious about its responsibility for the first woman to work alone in its territory. The government anthropologist suggested in his letter that I go to Lesu, a village in New Ireland, and I duly accepted his suggestion.

Lesu sounded like a good place and actually, I had no alternative, since I knew I should be dependent on the Government for practical help in transportation after I reached the islands. The next boat did not leave Sydney for a month and I settled in a one-room apartment, with an efficiency kitchen which looked very American. Much of my time was spent in the university library reading everything I could find on the Bismarck Archipelago, all written in German by missionaries.

A daily tea in Radcliffe-Brown's office brought me in touch with him and the other members of his department. I had great respect and admiration for him, but could not play the worshiping role which he seemed to need. Ian Hogbin, who had returned from his first fieldwork in the Solomons, taught me how to use a Graflex camera that the department was lending me, and helped me shop, mostly at Woolworth's, for a year's supply of gifts for the Melanesians, whose pattern of reciprocal gift-giving was well known. Camilla Wedgwood, whom I had known in London, Lloyd Warner, and a few others were in the small anthropology group at the university. Some one in Baltimore had written to distant cousins in Sydney who were most hospitable. I enjoyed the company of my new friends, but, again, I was marking time. Occasionally I had a horrible feeling that I might go on traveling forever, arriving places, meeting pleasant people, and shopping for equipment. Fieldwork seemed to recede further and further away. I was truly glad when the *S.S. Montoro* of the Burns Philip Line was ready to sail. It was a small cargo boat carrying supplies to the islands and copra (dried coconuts) from them, and a few passengers.

I shall never forget the day the *Montoro* sailed from Sydney. It was supposed to leave at 9:00 A.M.; three friends who had come to see me off stayed until it actually left at four in the afternoon. The waiting was exhausting; I begged my friends to leave, but they insisted on staying. Radcliffe-Brown sent roses, and a note cautioning me not to forget to type my notes in duplicate and to send the extra copies to him as often as possible, just in case anything happened to me. One of the Australian Council's field workers had died in the field and another anthropologist was then writing up his notes. . . .

Finally, after eight days, came Rabaul, situated in a cove and hemmed in by mountains. The heat was oppressive. When I complained, the English anthropologist, who had met my boat, said sternly that people there did not talk about the heat. He took me shopping and I bought oil lamps, gallons of kerosene, tinned butter, jars of marmalade, many other grocery staples, a dutch oven, and a few cooking utensils. Shopping was sociable, as if I had met the store keepers on a big picnic, but had not been formally introduced. Tea parties, drinks, and dinners with government officials and their wives were more formal. Everyone gave me advice, and I tried to conceal that I was falling asleep and not hearing all of it. I had started taking quinine daily and it had the usual first effect of causing sleepiness and partial deafness. The Melanesians I saw were most disappointing. The servants looked sullen and furtive. The police boys with white caps perched on top of their bushy hair seemed slightly ridiculous.

After four days of Rabaul I was glad to go back to the *S.S. Montoro*, which had finished its unloading and loading and was ready to proceed to Kavieng, the capital of New Ireland. Soon we were there and for the first time I felt that I might be approaching the end of my traveling. Kavieng was small, not hemmed in as Rabaul was, and cool breezes were blowing. We were met by the District Officer, who invited us to stay at his home for a few days while we arranged for transportation by lorry over the rough road to Lesu. I spent much time in a hot warehouse, collecting my many bales, boxes, trunks, and so forth, and added to them by doing still more shopping. The small group of Australians in Kavieng were hospitable, but I had the feeling of being inspected. . . .

Finally we were off. The road followed the winding curves of the east coast, up hill and down hill. Miles without any sign of human habitation, and then suddenly we would pass through a village and I would have a glimpse of tall black men in their loin cloths at a feast, and a group of women sitting on the ground chatting and playing with their babies. They looked attractive and quite different from the Melanesians I had seen in Rabaul. Sometimes the road passed through a plantation with its orderly rows of coconut trees, owned by an Australian. Always there was the sea on one side and the bush on the other. After eighty miles, we arrived at Lesu. About four months had passed since I had left England.

Now I was sitting on my veranda, presumably ready to begin work, yet in a panic. I asked myself again, why am I here alone? I had to admit that no one had compelled me to come, that the expedition was not only voluntary but intensely desired. There could be only one explanation: I must have been mad. I quickly decided that although I may have been mad, I did not have to remain so. I would go home on the next boat which would leave Kavieng in six weeks. This brought some relief and I felt I could stick it out for that short time. The newspapers had publicized my being the first woman to go alone into the field in this area, and I now saw future headlines, "Anthropologist Leaves Field After Six Weeks Because She Is Scared!" But even that was better than being mad.

While I was immersed in gloom, visitors arrived: Ongus, the *luluai*, who had competently directed the finishing of my home, with his wife Pulong, and their adolescent daughter Batu. With Pulong and Batu I had only previously exchanged greetings. They presented me with a baked taro, and I asked them to sit down. Ongus and his daughter spoke pidgin English but Pulong did not. As we talked, Ongus gave me some words of the native language which I wrote down, and he told me a few stories about the former German administration (before World War I), which had been hated. He also told me a little about himself—how, when young, he had gone away to work for a few years on a plantation in New Guinea, where he had learned his pidgin English. He added that now he would never leave Lesu again. At the end of a few hours he said that he would soon call all the people together so that I could explain to them what I planned to do. He mentioned that they were very curious. At the end of the evening I felt at home not only with Ongus, but also with Pulong and Batu, who had said very little. When they were leaving Ongus said that I should "sing out" if I needed anything and he would come immediately. Their house was directly opposite mine.

I was no longer alone. I had friends. I went to bed and fell asleep almost immediately. No more thoughts of madness or leaving entered my mind. Several years later I learned that a definition of panic is a state of unrelatedness.

Cecilia Payne Gaposchkin

(1900–1979)

The third child of a cultivated British family, Cecilia Payne Gaposchkin began her education in the extensive library of her father, a
lawyer. Her love of nature and passionate interest in the natural
world were manifested in early childhood, as was a talent for mathematics. Educated at a series of proper English girls' boarding
schools, Payne had difficulty finding mathematics and science teachers who could keep up with their brilliant pupil. Because a *serious*
interest in science was not thought becoming for the daughters of
the English upper middle class, Payne worked against the grain of
the institutions that taught her until she arrived at Newnham College, Cambridge, in 1918.

Exposed there to the atomic theories of Rutherford, Bohr, and
Einstein, Payne quickly regretted her decision to read botany, a
choice she could not reverse as an undergraduate even though most
of her time was spent attending lectures in physics and astronomy.
An early visit to the Cambridge Astronomy Department's telescope
fulfilled her deep longing for a scientific vision of the heavens. Once
friends had helped her restore and operate the observatory and
telescope of Newnham College, during her second year as a student,
Payne was free to observe on her own.

Immediately after earning her undergraduate degree and a small
fellowship from Newnham in 1923, Payne left for postgraduate
work at the Harvard College Observatory, where she earned a Radcliffe College Ph.D. in 1925. Her thesis used concepts still not published, but available to Rutherford's Cambridge circle, to analyze
the statistical mechanics of atomic energy states as a means of
interpreting stellar spectra, which had previously been classified
empirically.

As an astronomer in her twenties, Payne used ionization theory
to determine the relative abundance of elements in stellar atmospheres. Her observations showed that natural bodies—the earth,
the stars, the sun—have similar compositions and that ninety stable
chemical elements of matter are manifest everywhere humans could,
in her day, observe. Using data from twenty of the twenty-five most
abundant elements in the earth's crust, she determined in 1926 that
helium is more abundant in the stars than on earth, a result which
contradicted received knowledge of the time but was confirmed by

later research. Payne's brilliance was established by the six papers she published before she was twenty-five and the two major books she published before her thirtieth birthday.

In the 1940s Payne applied the same aspects of atomic theory to study variable stars, focusing on the brightest stars in the Milky Way and in distant spiral nebulas. Her analysis enabled the determination of distance between the earth and galaxies as far away as 30 million light-years.

Despite her record of achievement, Payne faced serious discrimination throughout her early career. Her salary at the Harvard Observatory was paid out of the supplies budget of her mentor, Harlow Shapley, and for the first twenty years of her teaching career her courses were not listed in the catalog, nor was she paid appropriately. When James Bryant Conant became president of Harvard in 1933, Payne finally received a regular academic appointment, just one year before her work earned her election to the National Academy of Sciences. In 1956 she became professor and chairman of the Department of Astronomy, serving at that rank until her retirement in 1965.

As Payne's autobiography movingly demonstrates, she wanted to have children and the happiness of family life. Her meeting in 1933 with Sergei Gaposchkin, a political refugee facing certain reprisals in Europe, led to her successful effort to sponsor his entry into the United States. Their marriage in 1934 gave her a congenial colleague and the family she sought. As her narrative makes clear, there was no question in Payne's mind that her career came first; it was the ultimate ground of her life. However, as a woman of established scientific reputation, she set about demonstrating that her commitment to research was compatible with maternity and other human fulfillments.

AN AUTOBIOGRAPHY
AND OTHER RECOLLECTIONS

The Bee Orchis was growing in the long grass of the orchard, an insect turned to a blossom nestled in a purple star. Instantly I knew it for what it was. My Mother had told me of the Riviera—trapdoor spiders and mimosa and orchids—and I was dazzled by a flash of recognition. For the first time I knew the leaping of the heart, the sudden enlightenment, that were to become my passion. I think my life as a scientist began at that moment. I must have been about eight years old. More than 70 years have passed since then, and the long garnering and sifting has been spurred by the hope of such another revelation. I have not hoped in vain. These moments are rare, and they come without warning, on "days to be marked with a white stone." They are the ineffable reward of him who scans the face of Nature.

My first sight of the spectrum of Gamma Velorum, the realization that planetary nebulae are expanding and not rotating, the fact that U Gruis and RY Scuti are eclipsing stars, the true nature of T Ceti, the period of AE Aquarii, the bright-line nature of the supernova spectrum, these are some of the moments of ecstasy that I treasure in retrospect.

And yet none of these revelations was original. Agnes Clerke had described the spectrum of Gamma Velorum before I was born. Ejnar Hertzsprung, leaning over my shoulder and putting his finger on a wrong subtraction, solved the mystery of U Gruis. The nature of RY Scuti was my husband's discovery, not mine. I could never have understood T Ceti without de Sitter's photographs, nor AE Aquarii without Alfred Joy's velocities and Merle Walker's hint. The spectrum of the supernova had been surmised to be in emission before my day, but it was only a surmise. In a moment of enlightenment I *knew*. As I looked at the famous spectrum of Z Centauri (classified at Harvard many years before as a carbon absorption star), I suddenly saw it reverse, as one sees the craters of the Moon suddenly turn into hillocks, and absorption translated itself into emission. There is nothing personal in the thunderclap of understanding. The lightning that releases it comes from outside oneself.

I did not pluck the Bee Orchis. I stood and gazed at it; I see it now, rising in the long grass under the apple and hazel trees. I ran into the house to bring the news, and my Mother could not believe me. I must be mistaken: such a flower could not be growing in our homely Buckinghamshire soil—here she was mistaken; it is a characteristic plant of the chalk—but when she saw it she was convinced. Deering, the old gardener, was called to transplant it to the garden under the little spruce tree.

Orchis and spruce tree became a little shrine. I made a secret cult of the transplanted Christmas tree, and I well remember standing before it and taking a vow to devote myself to the study of Nature. . . .

Nature was very close. After a summer rainstorm I found the garden crawling with black slugs, and wept bitterly that the world could contain anything so horribly repulsive. Winter brought rare, beautiful snowstorms. I shall never forget my first encounter with snow. My Mother was wheeling me in my pram—I must have been about three years old—and I looked at the lovely, fluffy white carpet. It must be as warm and caressing as my swansdown pelisse. Nothing would satisfy me but to feel it round my feet. At last (in exasperation, I fear, for I was a most determined child) my Mother lifted me down. Instead of the gentle warmth I had pictured, I felt an icy chill. . . .

One winter evening my Mother was wheeling me in my pram, and we saw a brilliant meteorite blaze across the sky above Boddington Wood. She told me what it was, and taught me the right name for it by making a little rhyme

As we were walking home that night
We saw a shining meteorite.

It was my first encounter with astronomy. Soon I learned to look for "Charles' Wain" in the northern sky, and to recognize Orion's belt. When I was 10 years old I was taken out to look at Halley's Comet, a most disappointing sight! It could not compare with the great "Daylight Comet" that had blazed its tail across the western sky earlier in the year, a truly awesome experience.

It did not take me long to feel that I lived in a man's world. A brother and a sister joined me in the nursery. I felt from the first that my brother was the one who really mattered. My first reaction to my brilliant, warm-hearted brother Humfry was one of jealousy.

What a godlike figure my Father was! Every evening we used to watch for his return from London, where he had a legal practice. He came home over the fields in winter, swinging an enormous lantern with a tallow candle in it. He would bring us chunks of maple sugar, and would sit with us on the nursery floor, building "rude stone momuments," miniature Stonehenges, with the wooden bricks that he had had specially made for us.

He was a gifted musician and the house was full of music in my earliest years. When I was two weeks old he began to play scales to me on the recorder, "to educate your ear." I think he must have succeeded only too well, for I have perfect pitch, and such a fastidious ear that most singers and many string players seem to me woefully out of tune. . . .

When I was four years old, my Father died suddenly. I shall say nothing of that traumatic experience, which I remember only too well. My Mother could never afterwards speak of him without tears. For the rest of my childhood I felt I was not like other children, for I had *two* fathers in heaven.

I had been introduced to education at the age of about six. By a piece of extraordinary good fortune, a small school was opened, just across the street by Elizabeth Edwards. She was Welsh by descent and education, and had a remarkable gift for teaching. "A good education," she used to say, "will make you do a thing you do not like, willingly and well."

The first joy of school was learning to read. "Shall I be able," I remember asking, "to read the *Encyclopaedia Britannica*?" Assured that I should be able to read *anything*, I fell to with a will. I remember the pages of the primer as if it were yesterday—the vowels, labials, gutturals, sibilants, and silent letters printed in different colors, red, black, blue, green, and yellow. Reading became my joy and relaxation, and has been so ever since. Our house was full of books, not ony my Father's library, but legacies from many forbears—Latin, Greek, French, German, Spanish, Icelandic books, waiting to be explored. . . .

At school we were trained in memory and observation. We seldom used books, and even the long poems that we learned to recite in unison were taught by word of mouth. . . .

School discipline was strict. When we went for a walk, we marched. During our oral lessons we sat with backboards (thin slats of wood placed behind the shoulders and grasped with the hands). I think we enjoyed the military discipline rather than otherwise, and referred to Miss Edwards affectionately as "Tom," short for "Tommy Atkins," the archetypal British soldier. . . .

In six years that I spent at her school, Miss Edwards gave me a rich education. I sometimes think she taught me all I needed to know. At 12 I could speak French and German, had a basic knowledge of Latin and a full command of arithmetic. Geometry and algebra were part of our studies, and I delighted especially in the solution of quadratic equations. Even more important, we had been taught the principles of accurate measurement. The one piece of fine equipment in the school was a chemical balance, which we learned to use with precision and reverence. This is the program of education that I should choose for the young: languages and mathematics and a sense of accuracy. Besides these things, we had received memory training, and our powers of observation had been sharpened to a fine point.

When I was 12, my Mother decided to move to London, particularly for the sake of my brother Humfry, who must be prepared for Public School. Miss Edwards wrote me a letter of farewell and advice. "You will always be hampered," she said, "by your quick power of apprehension." She was one of the wisest people I have ever known. I cannot count how often those words have served as a warning against hastily jumping to conclusions. . . .

We exchanged the free enquiring spirit of our country school for a stronghold of the Church of England, large, highly organized, and very religious. The school had its own Chapel, with services at the beginning and end of the day. There was daily instruction in the Bible, the Catechism, and the history of the Christian Church. I felt the atmosphere to be stifling from the first, and these observances had little effect in bending an unregenerate twig. I did succeed in getting excused from the Chapel by fainting during the service, a technique that I had already discovered in connection with attendance at Church in Wendover. . . .

Learning at the new school was not the delight it had been under Miss Edwards. Mathematics was the subject I loved best, and it was a deep disappointment. I was placed in a class that still had to grapple with long division, and algebra was still a year away (alas, for my beloved quadratic equations!). We learned French and Latin, but not German (another sore point). And in the first year there were no science lessons at all; with so many hours devoted to religion, something had to go.

And I knew, as I had always known, that I wanted to be a scientist. I resolved to concentrate on the studies that would help me to reach that goal. In the atmosphere of that school it was uphill work. Nor did I find much help at home. My forbears had been historians, not scientists, and though we had thousands of books, few were devoted to science. At last I found two that helped to fill the void. One was an old treatise on botany, using the Linnaean System of classification, with text in German and French. The other was Newton's *Principia*. With the aid of a dictionary I laboriously translated the botany into English, under the impression that its contents were up-to-date, and I absorbed the Propositions of the *Principia,* though of course I could not follow the proofs. Here were beliefs that I could accept whole-heartedly.

Two other groups of books offered some help. One was the works of Emmanuel Swedenborg, especially the volume entitled *Chemistry, Physics, Philosophy,* which gave me a mystical view of Science that I never lost. The other was the collected essays of Thomas Huxley, a complimentary copy (sent to my Father?), decidedly out of place *dans cette galère.* Huxley quickly became one of my idols. I still read his essays periodically. If I learned to develop the spirit of a scientist, it is largely due to his influence.

Incredible as it may seem in the atomic age, the neglect of science teaching in a Church school in 1912 was a reflection of the nineteenth-century feeling that science is in conflict with religion. . . .

But by this time I had, in a sense, converted the laboratory into a chapel. On the top floor of the school (a town house, high and narrow) was a room set aside for the little science teaching conceded to the upper classes. The chemicals were ranged in bottles round the walls. I used to steal up there by myself (indeed I still do it in dreams) and sit conducting a little worship service of my own adoring the chemical elements. Here were the warp and woof of the world, a world that was later to expand into a Universe. As yet I had caught but few glimpses of it—the meteorite, Halley's Comet, the Daylight Comet of 1910. I had yet to realize that the heavenly bodies were within my reach. But the chemical elements were the stuff of the world. Nature was as great and impressive to me as it had seemed when I stood under the spruce tree and vowed myself to its service. . . .

In the second year of school things grew brighter. We began to study algebra and Euclid. And for the first time I found a friend and mentor. Dorothy Dalglish came to the school to teach science. A radiant personality, an inspired teacher, from the first she filled a unique place in my life. I am impatient now, as I was then, of the gross and cynical interpretations that are put upon the love of pupil for teacher. It is but one of the many forms of love (I shall have occasion to speak of others in their place), and it can be a strong and beautiful thing. Here, for the first time, I found someone who recognized my passion for science and sympathized with it. In the first year she taught us botany, and in the second, chemistry. I learned to my chagrin that the Linnaean System was obsolete, and

I gained a healthy respect for atoms. When she saw my interests burst the narrow bounds of the hours grudgingly accorded to science, she lent me books on physics and took me to museums. One Christmas she lent me a book on astronomy, and adroitly converted it into a Christmas present with the words "you can keep it if you like." Adoration ripened into friendship. For many years we met when we could, and took long country walks together. Forty years later I had the joy of presenting my daughter to her, then of the same age as mine when I first knew her. . . .

Intellectual preoccupations were fortified in another way. At about this time it became evident that I was developing a growth of facial hair. I turned for help to the family doctor, only to be told that there was nothing to be done about it. I burst into tears. "Never mind, Cecilia," he said kindly, "you've got brains. Make something of them." It was not much comfort, but it stiffened my resolve to become a scientist.

So I sought an outlet in active scientific work. My new-found interest in botany led me to begin to amass a herbarium, collecting and drying the plants that I found on my holiday walks. Miss Dalglish took a dim view of my collection, which she described as "dried hay." "Why," she asked, "did I not make a collection of drawings instead?" So I began to keep careful records of my finds, both drawings and dissections. I did not realize at the time what a valuable discipline I was developing. . . .

I continued the uphill fight for a scientific education. The school's strong suit was classical languages, and the powers above decided that I was to be trained as a classical scholar. During those years I was thoroughly drilled in Cicero (and learned to love his terse incisiveness), and went through the whole of the *Aeneid,* which I did not love at all, though the Georgics are still my delight. Then came the study of Greek—Plato, Euripides, Sophocles. Much as I wished I were learning botany and physics and chemistry, I could not be insensitive to this greatest of all literature. Antigone became, and has remained, the greatest of my heroines.

But still I fought for science. When I won a coveted prize at the end of the year I was asked what book I would choose to receive. It was considered proper to select Milton, or Shakespeare, or some writer of similar prestige. I said I wanted a textbook on fungi. I was deaf to all expostulation: that was what I wanted, and in the end I got it, elegantly bound in leather as befitted a literary giant.

I followed up this little victory with another. The first of two nationwide examinations, preparatory to College entrance, covered the usual subjects—mathematics, languages, literature. I asked to be entered also for botany, a subject that I had studied for the most part by myself, with the help of books borrowed from Miss Dalglish. The school demurred, and I had difficulty in persuading them. I remember with a glow of pride that I was placed at the top of the list in botany. By this time I had decided to become a botanist. . . .

A kindly teacher tutored me in German. I undertook the study of calculus and coordinate geometry by myself, and mathematics took on a kind of mystical significance. At last I was reluctantly turned over to a stern ascetic teacher of mathematics, who saw in my passion for the subject a passion for herself, which I certainly did not feel. She drove me into a nervous frenzy, and produced a block about the subject that I have never completely overcome. She sneered at me: "You will never become a scholar." It was then that the school gave me up. I was told that I must leave, must transfer to another school, that they could do no more for me. . . .

It seemed like the end of the world. I was almost 17. My one desire was to go to Cambridge, and to do so I must win a full scholarship, for there was no money with which to send me; and now the school had washed its hands of me. I wanted to be a scientist, and the only subjects I really knew were Latin and Greek. Mathematics had been my hope, and that had failed me. Yet if I had but known it, the powers that decided my fate had done me the greatest possible service.

The move to St. Paul's Girls' School seemed like a step from medieval to modern times. There were laboratories for biology, physics, and chemistry, and teachers who were specialists in their sciences. I was not only permitted, but actually encouraged, to study science. As I look back I see that life began for me when I entered the doors from Brook Green, Hammersmith. It was a time of dynamic happiness. I remember saying to myself: "I shall never be lonely again; now I can think about science." . . .

There was little more than a year in which to prepare for the fateful scholarship examination. Chemistry and physics had to be attacked almost from the beginning; in botany I had a better start. Chemistry seemed to be an exercise in memory and manual dexterity, but physics opened up a new world. At 13 I had been taught by a radiant, dynamic character; at 17 I first came under the influence of a scientist. Ivy Pendlebury did not teach, she elicited. She allowed me to unfold the subject for myself, drawing conclusion from premise, basing premise on observed fact. . . .

Miss Pendlebury led me through mechanics and rigid dynamics, electricity and magnetism, light and thermodynamics and the rudiments of astronomy. It is hard to believe, now, how much was crammed into that ecstatic time. She told me that she had never had a pupil with my power of sustained application. It was in fact the releasing of years of pent-up, unsatisfied desire. By the end of my schooldays, physics was replacing botany in my affections.

All motion, I had learned, was relative. Suddenly, as I was walking down a London street, I asked myself: "relative to *what*?" The solid ground failed beneath my feet. With the familiar leaping of the heart I had my first sense of the Cosmos. When I tried to tell Miss Pendlebury of the experience, she remarked calmly that I should find Relativity very interesting. She was wiser than she knew—it was Relativity that finally impelled me into the path I was to follow. Or was she? Of all the people I have known, she is the only one that I credit with Second Sight. On the fateful day when I left for Cambridge and the scholarship examination, she looked at me with her grave, penetrating brown eyes and said: "You'll get that scholarship." And I did. Perhaps she really knew. The previous day she had instructed me in the theory and construction of an air thermometer. I was not in the least surprised when the examiners made the air thermometer the basis of my laboratory test. It had been foreseen.

Beyond all hope and expectation I was able to go to College. I had won the only open scholarship large enough to pay my expenses. I was ready to enter Newnham College, Cambridge. . . .

In September 1919 . . . the atmosphere was euphoric. The "War to end war" was over. Few among us young people doubted that the Millennium was upon us. As we entered College, we were swept up by the surge of politics. We women, of course, had no votes (even had we been old enough), but that did not prevent us from conducting spirited debates. A new world was opening before mankind. We declared almost unanimously for Labour. . . .

The intellectual atmosphere was equally heady. Ernest Rutherford had come to the Cavendish Laboratory from Manchester as Professor of Physics, and the New Physics was gaining momentum.

As a student in natural sciences I had to select three subjects for the first part, and (if one proceeded to the second part, which many did not) a single one for the second. Officially I was still destined for botany, which would normally have been combined with zoology and chemistry, but I insisted on physics and was allowed the unusual combination of botany, physics, and chemistry. The lure of the Cavendish Laboratory was irresistible.

From the first I found botany disillusioning. My recent reading had been concentrated on paleobotany. Unable to afford to buy books, I had transcribed Scott's *Fossil botany* into a notebook during my last year at school. I knew that the Professor of Botany, A. C. Seward, was a leading paleobotanist, and hoped great things, but I had to attend the elementary lectures, whose content was familiar and boring. We were not encouraged to go beyond their limits. I found a fascinating group of desmids among the more humdrum algae that we were set to study under the microscope, and I told the demonstrator that I was having difficulty in identifying them. He turned me off relentlessly: "They don't come into your course." Poor man, desmids were probably not his subject. But I felt cheated. There were no lectures on paleobotany and when I actually met the Professor he furnished neither encouragement nor inspiration.

There had been other rebuffs. By now I was an avid collector, fascinated by the ramifications of systematics. I tried to convince my teachers that *Adoxa* belonged with the Saxifragaceae. I found a remarkable rose on the cliffs of Cornwall, and carried a drawing of it to the Herbarium of the Natural History Museum in London, convinced that I had found a new species. The Curator, kindly, peppery old Dr. Baker, examined my drawing and remarked that the genus *Rosa* is "very difficult." Then he added: "I suppose you tagged the bush?" I was crushed by the enormity of my inexperience. . . .

For I had a lot to learn about the nature of research, and I have been learning it gradually all my life. At a very early age (still in Wendover days, for I remember the locale clearly) I made up my mind to do research, and was seized with panic at the thought that everything might be found out before I was old enough to begin! . . .

For a year I persevered with botany, attended lectures, drew anatomized plants under the microscope, wrote essays for my tutor. I was fortunate to be tutored by Agnes Arber, beautiful, scholarly, withdrawn. I never came to terms with her view of the subject. I still find her *opus magnum, The natural philosophy of plant form,* to be beyond my understanding. She wrote of "the facile Darwinian view—so easy to understand, and therefore so fatally easy to accept." What had Aristotle, Theophrastus, Goethe, Boethius, and Spinoza to do with the panorama of the plant world, so neatly classified, so convincingly understood in terms of Natural Selection? Already I had the makings of a closed mind.

The lectures spread before us an array of intricately classified plant species, products of organic evolution (which I equated with Natural Selection). Mendelian heredity was well entrenched, with Bateson as its prophet; the mutation theory was gaining momentum. The physiology of plants was burgeoning into biochemistry. Hopkins was credited with having discovered "the chemical basis of species." The spirit of a new, rational biology was in the air, and the old picture seemed as démodé as the Ptolemaic system.

Mrs. Arber was patient with me, but she could not curb my passion for speculation, for simplistic ideas, "so fatally easy to accept." A crisis came when I submitted to her an essay on the evolution of root structures, of which I had a high opinion. She made the crushing comment that my ideas were neither original nor of much significance. I took the criticism very seriously. If I did not know a good idea from a bad one, I was probably studying the wrong subject. This was, of course, barefaced rationalization. I was eager to be off with the old love and to embrace the new, my beloved physics.

I finally saw the writing on the wall in the shape of the structural formulae of the anthocyanin pigments. The study of plant physiology led to a course in biochemistry. I was not ready for it; my knowledge of organic chemistry was rudimentary, and Willstatter's treatise on the anthocyanin pigments defeated me. I saw before me a science based on an intricate empirical foundation, which seemed to be utterly unreal. Were these structural formulae mere parables? Could we ever know what complex organic molecules were really like? Many years later, when I saw Stanley's electron microscope pictures of the tobacco virus molecule, I looked back ruefully at the day when I had decided to turn from an empirical science to one in which one knew what one was talking about. And of course I was wrong; the outer structure of the atom and of the atomic nucleus are an exact parallel, even more elusive than the structure of the organic molecule. But the process of rationalization ran its course, and I made up my mind to turn to physical science.

The most stimulating lectures that I heard at Cambridge were those of physical chemistry by H. J. H. Fenton. He began at the point where most instructors stopped. He laid the facts before us and outlined and accepted theories. Then with almost derisive eloquence, he proceeded to demolish the elaborate facade. He pointed out other facts, for which the theories did not account, and other theories that covered the facts equally well. . . .

The study of physics was pure delight. The Cavendish Laboratory was peopled with legendary figures. The great J. J. Thomson hovered in the background; there were Aston with his mass spectrograph, C. T. R. Wilson with his cloud chamber; there were visiting lecturers such as Niels Bohr and Irving Langmuir; and, looming over all, was the figure of Ernest Rutherford. We first-year students saw little of him, but he was always on the horizon, a towering blond giant with a booming voice.

At first we were soaked in classical physics, lectures and laboratory work. There was Alexander Wood of the golden voice, revered as a Muscular Christian. "I canna believe," he declaimed with his Paisley accent, "that the Univairse is a colossal prractical jooke on the parrt of the Creatorr." The laboratory work was the province of Dr. Searle, an explosive bearded Nemesis who struck terror into my heart. If one made a blunder one was sent to "stand in the corner" like a naughty child. He had no patience with the women students. He said they disturbed the magnetic equipment, and more than once I heard him shout, "Go and take off your corsets!" for most girls wore these garments then, and steel was beginning to replace whalebone as a stiffening agent. For all his eccentricities, he gave us excellent training in all types of precise measurement and in the correct handling of data.

In spite of his brusque manner, Dr. Searle was a kindly man, as I found to my embarrassment. When I felt that I was not keeping up with the heavy program of work, I appealed to him for help. "There's nothing wrong with your mind," he assured me, "it's your *soul* that needs attention." And he carried me off there and then to a Christian Science healer. It was a very strange confrontation. I sat through the ordeal in silence and thanked her politely, but I never appealed to Dr. Searle for help again.

Physics was at the parting of the ways. The classical branches of the subject were indeed enough to fill the student's time if he pursued them in their lapidary symmetry and elegance through mechanics, electromagnetic theory, and thermodynamics, but radioactivity was in the air. It dominated the Cavendish Laboratory, for Rutherford was beginning his attack on the atomic nucleus. The legendary J. J. Thomson, discoverer of the electron, was very much alive. James Chadwick, who was to discover the neutron, was a demonstrator in the advanced laboratory. The Bohr atom was introduced to us by Bohr himself. I still have the notes I took during his lectures on atomic structure, my first introduction to the subject that was to dominate many years of my work. His discourse was rendered almost incomprehensible by his accent; there were endless references to what I recorded as "soup groups," only later amended to "sub-groups." We heard rumors, at first little more, of the Quantum Theory. The word went around that a student could attain a First Class without studying classical physics at all.

The stress was on observation. "One thoroughgoing experiment," Rutherford thundered in one of his lectures, "is worth all the theories in the world—even if those theories are those of a Bohr." Years later, Eddington uttered the dictum that he would not believe an observation unless it was supported by a good theory. I was an astronomer by that time and knew him well. I told him that I was shocked by his pronouncement. He smiled gently. "I thought it would be good for Rutherford," he said.

Such was the scientific panorama as I saw it at the end of 1919. I was standing before the door through which I was soon to enter that world for myself. Suddenly, dramatically, it swung open.

There was to be a lecture in the Great Hall of Trinity College. Professor Eddington was to announce the results of the eclipse expedition that he had led to Brazil in 1918. Four tickets for the lecture had been assigned to students at Newnham College and (almost by accident, for one of my friends was unable to go) a ticket fell to me.

The Great Hall was crowded. The speaker was a slender, dark young man with a trick of looking away from his audience and a manner of complete detachment. He gave an outline of the Theory of Relativity in popular language, as none could do better than he. He described the Lorenz-Fitzgerald contraction, the Michelson-Morley experiment and its consequences. He led up to the shift of the stellar images near the Sun as predicted by Einstein and described his verification of the prediction.

The result was a complete transformation of my world picture. I knew again the thunderclap that had come from the realization that all motion is relative. When I returned to my room I found that I could write down the lecture word for word (as I was to do for another lecture a couple of years later). For three nights, I think,

I did not sleep. My world had been so shaken that I experienced something very like a nervous breakdown. The experience was so acute, so personal that I felt a stir of surprise when I read an account of this same lecture in James Hilton's *Random Harvest*.

The upshot was, perhaps, a foregone conclusion. I was done with biology, dedicated to physical science, forever. The next day I confronted the College authorities with the statement that I was going to "change my shop" and read physics.

It would have been impossible for me to transfer to astronomy, which was, and still is, treated at Cambridge as a branch of mathematics, to be approached by way of the Mathematical Tripos. But I could attend all the lectures on astronomy, and I fell on them with avidity at the beginning of the next year. Meanwhile I applied myself to completing the first part of the Natural Sciences Tripos, which I did in two years instead of three, and attained the desired First Class. The rest of my time at Cambridge was to be devoted to physics, with all the astronomy I could pick up on the side.

The advanced course in physics began with Rutherford's lectures. I was the only woman student who attended them and the regulation required that women should sit by themselves in the front row. There had been a time when a chaperone was necessary but mercifully that day was past. At every lecture Rutherford would gaze at me pointedly, as I sat by myself under his very nose, and would begin in his stentorian voice: "*Ladies* and Gentlemen." All the boys regularly greeted this witticism with thunderous applause, stamping with their feet in the traditional manner, and at every lecture I wished I could sink into the earth. To this day I instinctively take my place as far back as possible in a lecture room.

The laboratory work of the advanced course was exacting and I think the demonstrators shared Rutherford's scorn for women. At this point I needed a good tutor, but Newnham did not provide one in advanced physics, and I was passed from one reluctant young physicist to another, never getting the advice I needed. I was still agonizingly shy, and quite unaccustomed to dealing with men. I was afraid to ask questions, made many blunders, and learned very little about experimental physics.

Rutherford's daughter Eileen, then a student at Newnham, became one of my friends. She was a lovable, spontaneous girl, without an ounce of science in her makeup. When she invited me to her home for tea, I found her Father quite as alarming in private as in public. I was horrified by the zest with which he told a story of "the man whose life was saved by Swedish Punch." During the recent War he had dined too well with friends in Sweden and spent the night in the gutter as a consequence. Meanwhile, the ship to which he belonged had sailed without him and was torpedoed in the North Sea. It did not strike me as an amusing story.

Later Eileen reported to me that her Father had remarked: "She isn't interested in *you*, my dear; she's interested in *me*." I was outraged, for I was in fact very fond of her. There may have been a grain of truth in his remark, nevertheless. This did not allay my anger. Never, never would I rely on private influence, or enter their house again!

By this time I was reading all the astronomical books I could lay my hands on. Eddington's *Stellar movements and the structure of the Universe* introduced me to stellar motions; I did not know that the "Universe" of that work was the tiny province that Walter Baade later described as the "local swimming hole." I discovered Henri Poincaré. I remember finding *Science and hypothesis* in the library at Newnham, sitting down on the floor, and reading it from cover to cover on the spot. This was followed by *Science and method, The value of science,* and finally *Hypothèses cosmogiques,* a perennial source of inspiration.

Presently I learned that there was to be a public night at the Observatory. I bicycled up Madingly Road and found the visitors assembled in the Sheepshanks Telescope, that curious instrument which, in the words of William Marshall Smart, "combined all the disadvantages of a refractor and a reflector." He himself was there when I arrived and I heard him say: "Avoid the measuring machine with care"—advice that I did not follow later on! The gruff, kindly Second Assistant, Henry Green, was adjusting the telescope, and presently I had a view of a double star whose components (as he pointed out) differed in color. "How can that be," I asked him, "if they are of the same age?" He was at a loss for an answer and when I persisted in my questions he gave up in despair. "I will leave you in charge," he said, and fled down the stairs. By that time he had turned the instrument to the Andromeda Spiral. I began to expatiate on it (Heaven forgive my presumptuousness!) and was standing with a small girl in my arms, telling her what to look for. I heard a soft chuckle behind me, turned round, and found Eddington standing there.

As I heard him tell it later, when I had come to know him, Henry Green had gone to "The Professor's" study and told him:

"There's a woman out there asking questions," and asked for help. The moment had come and I wasted no time. I blurted out that I should like to be an astronomer. Was it then or later that he made the reply that was to sustain me through many rebuffs? "I can see no *insuperable* objection." I asked him what I should read. He mentioned several books, and I found that I had read them all. So he referred me to the *Monthly Notices* and the *Astrophysical Journal*. They were available in the library of the Observatory which he said I was welcome to use. To paraphrase Herschel's epitaph, he had opened the doors of the heavens to me.

I began to attend Eddington's lectures. Those on Relativity revived the interest first stimulated in the Great Hall of Trinity College. The Determination of Orbits and the Reduction of Observations proved to be of more lasting value. Under his eye we computed the orbits of several comets—all, of course, with the use of logarithms. These computational sessions were topped off by the special treat of tea at the Observatory, at the invitation of old Mrs. Eddington and her sweet and gentle daughter Winifred. There were only three or four students at these sessions and we were warmly received in the family atmosphere. It came as a slight shock to me to learn that Eddington's favorite composer was Humperdinck, and that the music he liked best included the songs of Harry Lauder, especially *Roamin' in the gloaming*. He was a very quiet man and a conversation with him was punctuated by long silences. He never replied immediately to a question; he pondered it, and after a long (but not uncomfortable) interval would respond with a complete and rounded answer.

There were other lectures too: Smart on Celestial Mechanics and Lunar Theory (of which I did not get the full import, for he was not one to temper the wind to the shorn lamb). Stratton lectured on astrophysics, introduced us to stars, the Russell diagram (as we called it in those days), variable stars, and novae. Stratton was the Director of the Solar Physics Observatory, and here too I was made welcome. When I spoke to him of my desire to become an astronomer, he was less than encouraging. "You can never hope," he said, "to be anything but an amateur."

One afternoon I bicycled up to the Solar Physics Observatory with a question in my mind. I found a young man, his fair hair tumbling over his eyes, sitting astride the roof of one of the buildings, repairing it. "I have come to ask," I shouted up at him, "why the Stark effect is not observed in stellar spectra." He climbed down and introduced himself as E. A. Milne, second in command at the Observatory. Later he became a good friend and a great inspiration to me. He did not know the answer to my question, which continued to exercise me. . . .

At about this time I discovered that Newnham College had an Observatory, which had long stood unused in the grounds. There was a small visual telescope, and I began to explore the sky for myself. The clock would not run but I set that to rights by removing a chrysalis from the works. I discovered the beauties of the planets— who can ever forget his first sight of the moons of Jupiter and the rings of Saturn? I organized public nights and began to observe variable stars and record their changes, and I installed an observing book, with a notice that anyone who observed with the telescope must make a record in the book, and sign and date the entry. I wonder how many records have been made in it since I left it?

A very real friend appeared in the shape of L. J. Comrie, who was working in Cambridge for an advanced degree. He was an extraordinary man. Crippled and deafened by war wounds, he was still extremely active and played a formidable game of tennis in spite of having lost a leg. He had just performed the remarkable feat of making a correct prediction of the eclipse of one of Saturn's satellites by the shadow of another. He gave me valuable lessons in computing, and helped me to acquire a library of mathematical tables. He persuaded me to join the amateur computing section of the British Astronomical Association, which carried on predictions of stellar occultations. Here I found to my chagrin that I was an inaccurate computer and learned, painfully, to check my calculations—an invaluable training that has stood me in good stead.

I began to keep a notebook in which I listed the problems that I should like to study. My first flight was an attempt to interpret Cepheid variables in terms of the oscillations of a star between an oblate and a prolate spheroid. I did not learn of Plummer's work on this program until many years later. More important, I noted that the absorption of light in space should be studied by discussing separately the colors of stars of all spectral types. I realized that this problem was then unsolved. I did not know that at the end of my scientific life I should still be concerned with it.

The time had come when learning from others was not enough. I wanted to explore the frontiers for myself. I went to Eddington and asked him to introduce me to research. At the time he was working on stellar interiors, and he gave me the problem of integrating the properties of a model star, starting from initial conditions at the center and working outwards, layer by layer. I fell to with enthusiasm; the problem haunted me day and night. I recall a vivid dream that I was at the center of Betelgeuse, and that, as seen from there, the solution was perfectly plain; but it did not seem so in the light of day. After a time it occurred to me that it would be interesting to take the rotation of the star into account, and I rushed in where angels might have feared to tread. As I should have foreseen, I ran into insoluble problems at the stellar surface. Finally I took my incomplete solution to Eddington and asked him how to overcome the difficulty. He smiled. "I've been trying to solve that problem for years," he said.

There was no future for me in England other than teaching. It was Mr. Comrie who came to my rescue. He was soon to go to a position at Swarthmore College in the United States, and he told me that a woman would have a better chance to be an astronomer in that country. He offered to take me to a lecture to be given in London by Harlow Shapley, newly appointed Director of the Harvard College Observatory.

It was a memorable lecture. The name of the speaker was not new to me, for I had read the papers on globular clusters that he had written at Mount Wilson Observatory. But I had not been prepared for his youth or his style. Eloquence it could not be called, for he had none of Eddington's classic polish. He spoke with extraordinary directness, conveyed the reality of the cosmic picture in masterly strokes. Here was a man who walked with the stars and spoke of them as familiar friends. They were brought within reach; one could almost touch them. He even descended to levity, but it was a levity that spoke of intimacy. The next day I found I could write down all that he had said, word for word.

Dr. Comrie introduced me to Harlow Shapley. I came immediately to the point. "I should like," I said, "to come and work under you." He answered that he would be delighted: "When Miss Cannon retires, you can succeed her." Knowing him as I did later, I doubt whether he took me seriously, or gave me a second thought. But I took *him* seriously. I bent all my efforts to getting the support needed, and collected enough money in fellowships and grants to finance a year in the United States.

Meanwhile I passed my final examinations, not too creditably. But when I remember how I neglected my studies for work at the

Observatory, it is surprising that I secured even a Second Class in the Tripos.

In the fall of 1923, I prepared to leave my native land, to sail to the west as more than one of my ancestors had done. The time for dreaming was over. I was about to enter the real world. . . .

As a graduate student at Radcliffe College I was assigned a room, and a roommate, at a graduate dormitory. The atmosphere was very different from that of Newnham, and I found the freedom novel and intoxicating. At Cambridge we had had rooms of our own. Permission had been required for leaving College after the evening meal. Lights had to be turned off at 11; in scholastic emergencies we were allowed to work later—by candlelight. Now I came and went as I pleased, could work at the Observatory all night if I so desired.

The climate of the New England fall was so stimulating that I found I could work prodigiously long hours. In Cambridge, by contrast, I had always been tired. The damp chill of the fenland air seemed to penetrate my bones, and I think I ached physically all the time I was there. In the heady atmosphere of New England in October, nothing seemed impossible. Once I worked for 72 hours without sleep. It was indeed a new world, a new life.

My fellow students were kind and friendly, and at first they found me hilarious. They ran around in all stages of *déshabillé*. I do not think that I had been undressed before anybody since I was a baby, and I suppose they found me ridiculously prudish. When they found that I wore layer upon layer of underwear, they used to watch me disrobe with shrieks of incredulous delight. It was not long before their laughter, and the climate, weaned me from my native wardrobe. To dress like the other girls conveyed yet another sense of freedom. . . .

The day after I arrived in the United States I was installed at a desk in the "Brick Building," then the newest structure in the Observatory grounds, now the only survivor of the buildings I first knew. It had been built to house the great collection of photographic plates that had been amassed by the previous Director, Edward C. Pickering. Here also were the offices of those who worked with the plates.

In Pickering's days all this work had been done by women. It was respectable work at the end of the nineteenth century, work that conferred a distinction, and the old Director had taken full advantage of the fact. The college-trained scientists Henrietta Leavitt, Annie Jump Cannon, and Antonia Maury were at the top of the hierarchy. The work of examining the plates, identifying the stars on them, of recording, of proofreading, of computing, of keeping half a million photographs in order in the plate stacks, employed a large team of women, nearly all of whom dated back to the Pickering era when I first came. Someone quoted to me an ancient joke: "Why is the Brick Building like Heaven? Because there is neither marrying nor giving in marriage there." Indeed in Pickering's day there had been no men there. Professor Bailey had an office under the dome of the 15-inch telescope (the "Great Telescope," in its day the largest in the world), Leon Campbell was even farther away, and Professor King and Professor Gerrish occupied another building on the far side of the grounds. But in 1922 the new Director had broken with tradition, and the young Dutchman Willem Luyten had an office on the lower floor of the plate stacks.

The Brick Building as I first knew it must have retained much of the flavor of Pickering's day. Miss Cannon reigned supreme, she was "Curator of the Astronomical Photographs." Much has been written about Miss Cannon; she was a legend in her own day. . . . When I think of her as a person I am at a loss for words to convey her vitality and charm. She had lost her hearing in youth, but she had none of the suspicious pessimism so often associated with the deaf. She wore her hearing aid with an air, and made a virtue of necessity by unshipping it when she wanted to be undisturbed or to do concentrated work. She was warm, cheerful, enthusiastic, hospitable. Like many people who are hard of hearing she had a sharp metallic voice, and often broke into a characteristic, resounding laugh.

Miss Cannon was extraordinarily kind to me. She might well have resented a young and inexperienced student who was presumptuous enough to attempt to interpret the spectra that had been her own preserve for many years. She never gave sign of doing so. "Do you realize," Shapley asked me later, "how easily Miss Cannon could throw a monkey-wrench into the works for you?" With the arrogance of youth I had not thought of it; I had even permitted myself to wonder how anyone who had worked with stellar spectra for so long could have refrained from drawing any conclusions from them. She was a pure observer, she did not attempt to interpret. As I look back I see how her work has outlasted my early efforts at interpretation. The *Henry Draper Catalogue* is a permanent monument. . . .

I make no apology for taking time to look back on the history of the great repository of data that was Edward C. Pickering's legacy. Hitherto I have written of my own small struggles. Now my theme has broadened, and I am concerned with the birth and development of a new science, a drama in which I was privileged to play a modest supporting role.

It is not to deny the contribution of earlier Directors of the Harvard College Observatory to say that Pickering gave a crucial impetus to twentieth-century astronomy. He saw the importance of observations, and set himself to supply those that were crucial to the astronomy of his day. Facts may seem like dry bones to the soaring imagination of the theorist. They are bones indeed, for they constitute the skeletal framework of the science, without which she could neither stand, nor walk, nor take the great leaps that have marked her progress in the last half century. . . .

During the nineteenth century the emphasis of stellar astronomy was on position and motion. It was the era of parallax and proper motion, of double stars and of the great *Durchmusterungen* which located and catalogued the brighter stars in both hemispheres. In the twentieth century the emphasis shifted to the star as an individual.

Pickering's work placed stellar photometry, stellar spectra, and the study of variable stars on a completely new footing. When we look at what he projected and what he achieved, we cannot but marvel at his foresight and his performance. . . .

. . . The *Henry Draper Catalogue* was not yet completely off the press, the first pigeonholing of 250,000 stellar spectra. Saha and Fowler and Milne had brought the spectral sequence into a physical order for the first time, but only in the most general terms. I followed Milne's advice, and set out to make quantitative the qualitative information that was inherent in the Henry Draper system.

A few weeks after I had begun to examine the spectra of the stars for the first time, Shapley called me into his office. I found him looking rueful and apologetic. "Menzel has come," he said. Henry Norris Russell had sent his student, Donald Menzel, to obtain material for his doctoral thesis (on the very same subject as the one I had chosen) in the Harvard plate collection. Russell, who was to have a great influence on my own work, had of course seen the enormous possibilities of the Saha theory, and it was natural that he should direct his ablest student to the fountain-head of the facts on stellar spectra.

Here a great mistake was made, a great opportunity missed. This should have been the occasion for a spirited and fruitful collaboration, for Donald Menzel had been trained at Princeton with a basic knowledge of laboratory spectroscopy. I, on the other hand, knew almost nothing about spectra, for the training at the Cavendish had stressed the physics of the nucleus, rather than the external properties of the atom. (I had heard Rutherford refer to the latter in disparaging terms as "descriptive botany," and the phrase grated on me, for I still had a respect for descriptive botany: the study of systematics has left a mark on my approach to the stars.)

Shapley could have brought Menzel and me together as friends and fellow-scientists. But that was not his way. He operated in the spirit by which Kipling described the British rule in India: "Strict supervision, and play them off one against the other." Not for over 20 years did I realize that he was practising this technique. Not until Donald Menzel succeeded him as Director of the Observatory did I see that we had been deliberately kept apart. I was never to be a Director—my sex debarred me (and I am grateful for that). But if such had been my fate I would have made it my business to promote collaboration and not to fan hostility. How could I have been blind for so long to these divisive tactics? I looked on Shapley in those early days with uncritical adoration; perhaps, with my natural tendency to masochism, I subscribed to his idea that one does one's best work when one is miserable. "Work," he used to say, "kills the pain." I ought to have remembered the precept inculcated at the religious school: "The words 'thy will be done' should not suggest a mourning widow, but a young person rushing out into the world to do good." It would have served me better than Shapley's gloomy philosophy. He used to say that no one could earn a Doctor's degree unless he had suffered a nervous breakdown in the process. I told him stoutly that this was a wrong. He rejected one excellent candidate for the Ph.D. on the grounds that the latter was not a serious person—he was always laughing. "Well," the boy replied, "it's better than weeping." He told me this many years later; he was a loss to astronomy. . . .

There followed months, almost a year as I remember, of utter bewilderment. Often I was in a state of exhaustion and despair, working all day and late into the night. Every evening I would listen for Dr. Shapley's light step, as he ran across from his residence to the Brick Building. He would stop at my desk and speak the words of encouragement that were the breath of life to me. Once, after I had toiled for many months, he asked me whether I did not think I ought to publish something, to give some evidence of the work I was doing. "No," I said, "I haven't solved the problem yet. I should regard it as a confession of failure." He accepted it, and I think he was pleased.

Finally some light dawned in the darkness. The intensities of the lines of silicon, in four successive stages of ionization, made some sense at last, and I made my first determination of the temperatures of the hotter stars. He encouraged me to write my first paper on stellar spectra. I wanted to sign it C. H. Payne, but he insisted on the full name: "Are you ashamed of being a woman?" he asked. Silicon had broken the ice for me; it is still one of my favorite atoms. Now I saw my way clear. . . .

Disillusionment was rarer than exaltation. As the work progressed, and the relation between line intensity and temperature began to take shape, the ionization potentials of the atoms took on great importance. In those far-off days, the analysis of laboratory spectra was only at the beginning, and this quantity was unknown for many of the metallic elements, even for iron. It occurred to me that one could infer the ionization potential of an atom from the behavior of its lines in the spectral sequence, when the scale had been established by means of other atoms of known properties. Donald Menzel hit on the same thing at about the same time—the idea was in the air—and published it too. Would that we had put our heads together! But this was not to be. When I brought my result to Dr. Shapley his enthusiasm was kindled: I must write it up at once and send it to the *Proceedings of the National Academy*. But the deadline was next day. "Write it up at once!" he exlaimed, "and I'll type it for you." What a glorious evening! I wrote, he typed, far into the night. Into the mail it went. And I walked back to my room in the dormitory in a dream. My feet did not seem to touch the ground. "I never knew before," I thought, "what it means to walk on air." Never again have I experienced that feeling; it was almost like flying. I had not wanted to tell him that I was quite a good typist myself. When still at Cambridge I had accustomed myself to compose on the typewriter. But he did not find that out until much later.

Two years of estimation, plotting, calculation, and the work I had planned was done. I had determined a stellar temperature scale and had measured the astrophysical abundance of the chemcial elements. It was to be a Ph.D. thesis (though . . . I cared little about the degree). Dr. Shapley said I must make it into a book, which I wrote, in a kind of ecstasy, in six weeks. It was called *Stellar atmospheres*, but I added a sub-title: *A contribution to the observational study of matter at high temperatures*. Two years earlier I had learned that this was to be the subject of the Adams Prize Essay at Cambridge, and that it was aimed at Ralph Fowler (who indeed received the Prize). I wanted to show that I had my contribution to make to the topic of the hour. Probably nobody even noticed that hubristic sub-title. . . .

Two years of daily contact with stellar spectra had brought one idea to the front. The composition of the stars was amazingly uniform. The years have modified this conclusion, but even today I find the uniformity more striking than the diversity.

My days as a student and a free agent were over. Fellowships had supported me for two years. Now I must find a place in the world. Dr. Aitken, Director of the Lick Observatory, asked me to go there and take a Research Fellowship. What would my future have been, I wonder, if I had accepted? When I told Dr. Shapley, he was indignant. Dr. Aitken, he said, should have consulted him first. He offered me a position at Harvard Observatory. In my innocence I did not ask how much he was going to pay me, or realize how little it would be. Nor, I think, should I have cared very much. I accepted the offer, and settled down to work at Harvard College Observatory, which was to be my home for more than 50 years. . . .

The position that I held at the Observatory was a very indefinite one, and I never succeeded in getting my duties defined. Dr. Shapley suggested that I follow up *Stellar atmospheres* with another book about supergiants, and he also asked me to undertake the editing of the Observatory publications. No restrictions were placed on anything else I felt like doing. . . .

The study of the high-luminosity stars opened up two vistas that have been expanding before my eyes ever since. The first was the grand array of Wolf-Rayet stars. Never shall I forget my first sight of the spectrum of Gamma Velorum! Among stellar spectra the Wolf-Rayet stars remain my first loves. Forty years later, when I was asked to speak at the opening of a conference on these still enigmatic objects, I likened them to the figure of the Nymph on the Grecian Urn: "Forever shalt thou love, and she be fair." Still fair, still elusive, the Wolf-Rayet stars continue to attract and puzzle us. I first met that great astronomer J. S. Plaskett at the 1925 meeting of the International Astronomical Union; he had just published his classic paper on their spectra. How did I summon up the courage to defy him in public, and maintain stoutly, in the face of his opposition, that some Wolf-Rayet stars show absorption lines? It was like a puppy defying an elephant. . . .

A second vista, even wider, opened up in the shape of the variable stars. In those distant days all variable stars seemed to be of high luminosity. But they were regarded rather in the light of second-class citizens of the heavens. Shapley did not hesitate to call them pathological stars. They are recognized today as the representatives of definite stages of stellar development, but in the 1920s there was a tendency to think of them as the province of the amateur. . . .

In the 1920s the requirements seemed to be more modest. Except for the North Polar Sequence and the brighter stars in a number of standard regions, there were few reliable photographic standards. Over most of the sky there were no such standards fainter than the thirteenth magnitude. Without them the survey of Milky Way variables could be no more than qualitative. With this in mind, Shapley recurred to his original suggestion that I should turn my attention to the determination of photographic magnitudes and standards. Alas for my beloved spectra! It was hard to leave them, and to turn to the arid field of standard photometry. . . .

I do not think that I could have made good contributions in the field of standard photometry. It calls for qualities that I do not possess. If my work has been of any value, the value has consisted in bringing together facts that were previously unrelated, and seeing a pattern in them. Such work calls for memory and imagination, neither of which has much to contribute to standard photometry. I am a field naturalist, not a surveyor. I wasted much time on this account. . . .

My change in field made the end of the decade a sad one. But it led to another activity that would occupy me for many years. I began to explore the potentialities of the Harvard photographs, not for the discovery of variable stars, but for the study of variables already known. The impetus was provided by a published catalogue of stars suspected to be long-period variables (Mira stars), about which little was known save their variability. The search led to some surprising results: one of the subjects, for example, turned out to be an eclipsing star. We determined the elements of no less than 100 previously unstudied, bright long-period variables. Thus I came upon a lode that was in future years to yield much precious metal, and occupy me, off and on, for the rest of my scientific life.

[Payne Gaposchkin traveled to the northern observatories of Europe in 1933 and then to Göttingen: Her travels were sad because of the treatment of scientists by both Soviet and Nazi regimes.]

Then I was in Göttingen, at the meeting of the Astronomische Gesellschaft. Everyone was kind, but there was a feeling of tension and distance. I knew none of the German astronomers, and though Eddington was there, his place was among the great. I took my seat shyly in the big auditorium, and someone brought me my mail, pronouncing my name as he did so. A young man sitting near by looked up in surprise. "Sind Sie Miss Payne?" he asked. I admitted as much. He introduced himself. His name was Gaposchkin, and he had come, he said, in the hope of seeing me. I do not think we spoke much, but he put into my hand a statement of his history, and asked me to read it. (He had expected, as I learned afterwards, that Miss Payne would be a little old lady, and was surprised to find her no older than himself.)

When I got back to my quarters I read the history he had given me, and I learned that here was one who had resolved, as I had resolved, to be an astronomer, and against what terrible odds he had achieved what had come so easily to me. Of course I knew I must help him to escape the last of the many disasters that had overtaken him, Nazi persecution, and to establish himself in a new world. I have not spent many sleepless nights, but that one was sleepless. Perhaps this, I thought, is my one chance to do something for someone who needs and deserves it. When I saw him the next day I told him that I could make no promises, but I would do what I could.

When I tried to talk to the German astronomers about the subject, they were anxious and evasive—always looking over their shoulders lest someone should overhear. I had seen the gesture in Russia too. Yes, they could recommend him; yes, he was a good astronomer. But it was impossible for him to stay. . . . I began to understand the political climate. He had been born in Russia; that was enough. (Who is your enemy? I had asked Gerasimovic; the picture fitted together.) . . .

Only when I was back in the United States did I feel I could breathe freely. And here it was possible to act freely too. I had never tried to exert any influence before, but I tried it now. A place was found at Harvard; I went to Washington to expedite the granting of a visa to a stateless man. Between August and November the thing was done, and Sergei Gaposchkin set foot in the New World.

What was the turning point? . . . Perhaps it was all ordained from the beginning. It led to the uniting of two lives, the flowing of two rivers, bound for the same goal, into one channel. In March 1934 I became Cecilia Payne Gaposchkin . . .

It was the beginning of a new life. We set off on a honeymoon trip across the country, retracing the steps I had taken four years before towards the great observatories of the West. In the interval I had settled down to the serious business of life. From now on the effort must be systematic and coordinated. I felt I was no longer a freelance, but a member of a team.

My husband had produced a doctoral thesis on eclipsing stars, truly remarkable for its thoroughness and scope. It had been the right moment for bringing together the enormous body of existing data on this group of variable stars. The time had come to consider what was known about them, and what was still needed for their interpretation.

Some years earlier, in the course of my survey of the stars of high luminosity, I had had occasion to survey the knowledge of intrinsic variables, and had made a beginning in my own understanding of their relationships. My early impression, that all intrinsic variables are luminous, had long given way to the recognition that they occur at many levels—the highly luminous supernovae and novae, the luminous Cepheids, the less luminous Mira stars and RR Lyrae stars. A synthesis of our knowledge of the low luminosity of novae and U Ceminorum stars at minimum was still to come, but variable stars were emerging as having a great variety of properties. It began to seem possible to classify them in a coherent scheme. No longer could they be regarded as "pathological stars." They clearly occupied definite domains in the range of stellar properties. Nor were they the province of the amateur astronomer, as they had seemed to be a few decades earlier. Miss Leavitt's discovery of the period-luminosity relation in the Magellanic clouds, and

Shapley's work on the globular clusters, had put an end to that. Variable stars were serious business in astronomy now. In the hands of Henrietta Swope, the Harvard programs on variable stars in the Milky Way were bearing fruit in enormous quantities.

It seemed to us that the time had come to put together what was known about variable stars. Together we undertook a survey of the subject, my husband covering the eclipsing variables, and my own domain being all the rest. Our goal was the arrangement of variable stars in a coherent scheme, with an attempt to cover the known species, and *Variable Stars* was the outcome of our efforts.

. . . Twenty years earlier the data would have been too sparse. Now, more than 30 years later, they would be unmanageable, and the subject calls for specialized treatments. In 1935 the picture could be sketched in broad outline, and in its main features it is still valid. It furnished us with a game plan for further exploration, a project for new researches.

Not only was the time ripe, but the place was right for a synthesis. The Harvard plate collection lay ready to our hands. In those days the Harvard Observatory was the scene of a weekly meeting, called by Shapley the "Hollow Square" because we were ranged around tables placed side by side in square formation. It was the occasion of free-for-all discussion of timely scientific topics. One afternoon Shapley was expatiating on the riches of the collection of photographs when a thought struck me. "Yes," I said, "but are we making full use of it?" He challenged me to make good my criticism, and at that moment an idea was born. Why not use the Harvard plates to get all possible information about all the known variable stars? I had already tried my apprentice hand on a couple of hundred Mira stars (and alleged Mira stars that turned out to be something else). It was an obvious plan, an ambitious plan, but feasible. We undertook to present an outline for the project.

Of course we could not investigate *all* known variable stars. I had not forgotten my first essay in systematic photometry. The plan had been to measure photographic magnitudes on extrafocal plates over the whole sky down to a given limit. . . .

Clouds were gathering on the international scene, and Dr. Richard Prager, renowned for his catalogue of variable stars, had left Germany and come to work at Harvard. His reaction to our plan was that it would take us 90 years to complete. It is pleasant to relate that we completed it in five. Funds were provided, and half a dozen people were hired to do the measuring. Even so, the task was a formidable one. A bright star in the northern hemisphere could be studied on at least 5,000 plates, and (except for stars with brief outbursts) most could be found on at least several hundred. The secret of the efficiency and success with which the program was carried out was the method of estimation devised by Sergei Gaposchkin. Everything was done systematically and objectively; the assistants made the estimates and the Gaposchkins did the reductions.

The material on which this survey of the brighter variable stars was carried out had its strengths and its weaknesses. The strength lay in the large number of available photographs and in the long time base; the first plates dated from 1889. One weakness lay in the fact that the photographs were part of a routine program, not geared to particular problems. The brightest stars were too bright to be accurately studied, for the exposures had been aimed at maximum coverage. The lengths of exposure set a limit too, on the study of very rapid variations or very short periods. The plates were taken with a variety of instruments, and color equation introduced problems, especially for stars of extreme color. Most serious of all, the establishment of magnitude scales presented great difficulties, and the most that could be claimed for the final magnitudes was that they were internally consistent.

The fruit of our five years' labor, then, was primarily the accurate determination of periods, and of changes of period. The forms of the light curves were well enough determined to be significant, and the magnitudes were at best approximate. We were able to clarify the type of variation for many stars and to classify many others for the first time. . . .

The book on variable stars that was our first collaborative work made no pretense to finality. It could truly have been entitled "Prolegomena," indeed that was the title we originally wished to give it. The study of variable stars on plates of the Harvard collection is of the same nature, and can claim to be no more. Here we can pick out star after star that is worthy of intensive study. This is no place for final and definitive work; it is what Pickering intended it to be, the domain of the pioneer.

A woman knows the frustration of belonging to a minority group. We may not actually be a minority, but we are certainly disadvantaged. Early experience had taught me that my brother was valued above me. His education dictated the family moves. He must go to Oxford at all costs. If I wanted to go to Cambridge I must manage it for myself. Early I learned the lesson that a man could choose a profession, but a girl must "learn to support herself." Presumably this would be until she found a husband. But it was early impressed upon me that I could scarcely hope to do that, as I had "no money of my own." Such was the Victorian social code in which I grew up.

In my case the real obstacle to marriage was that I met no men at all. There was an unwritten law in our house that if my brother should bring any of his friends home, his sisters must make themselves scarce. This was part of the social code of the contemporary Public School boy—another aspect of sex discrimination.

Once or twice I was asked to a dance, given for some school friend as a "coming-out party." This was a concentrated agony. I did not know how to dance. My clothes, too, were an embarrassment, for they were hand-me-downs from the daughter of a wealthy friend. I still remember my horror when I learned that one of my dancing partners knew her, and thought with crimson shame that he probably recognized the dress I was wearing. Even when I fell back on conversation it was a disaster. A friend of my brother, whom I had tried thus to entertain, remarked to him later: "Fancy! A girl who *reads Plato for pleasure*!" I simply did not know how to behave at a dance.

Matters did not improve when I went to Cambridge. Women were segregated in the lecture room. Even in the laboratory they were paired off, if possible, and (did I imagine it?) treated as second-class students. It might have been different if I had been gay and attractive and had worn pretty clothes. But I was dowdy and studious, comically serious and agonizingly shy. The Demonstrator in the Advanced Physics Laboratory told someone (who kindly repeated it to me) that I was "slow." It did not occur to me to protest. Ignorant and uncouth I might be, but not *slow*! I decided to pay no more attention to anything Henry Thirkill said: he was simply not noticing. Unluckily for me, he was one of the final Examiners in the Tripos, and I believed him responsible for placing me in the second class. I heard through the grapevine that the other Examiner, William Bragg whom I adored, had wished to place me higher. Henry Thirkill had put my back up; had I produced the same effect on him?

The attitude to women that oppressed my childhood and youth was typical in England at the time. Fifty years have not mended matters much. Although my work was well known by the time I was 30, I am sure that I stood not the slightest chance of obtaining a position in England between the time I went to Harvard to the time I retired in 1965. And how I would have jumped at the chance! But though I had gone to the Right University, I had read the wrong subject. One could not have become an astronomer in England without having obtained a First Class in the Mathematical Tripos. And, of course, I was a woman. The Royal Observatory was administered by the Admiralty. The redoubtable H. H. Turner recorded that when a candidate for the position of Chief Assistant at Greenwich was asked what qualifications he had had for the job, he replied: "Among other things I had to climb a rope." I should have failed the test; rope-climbing has never been my strong point. A restriction to the male sex no longer dominates the Royal Observatory, but something else still has a stranglehold on Astronomy in England.

We manage things better in the United States. Even 50 years ago a woman might do astronomical research and even make a name by publication. She might hold a position—without a title and ill-paid, it is true—and she could meet on equal terms with any astronomer in the world. In my early days at Harvard, everyone who was anybody (and many more besides, who were going to be somebody in the future) came through, and argued, and fraternized. Those were glorious days. We got to know Lundmark, Milne, and Unsold, Hund, Caratheodory, and ten Bruggencate. How we argued, how we walked about the streets and sat talking in restaurants until the manager turned off the lights in despair! We met as equals; nobody condescended to me on account of sex or youth. Nobody ever thought of flirting. We were scientists, we were scholars (neither of these words has a gender). In that heady atmosphere a woman did not degenerate into the abominable stereotype of the *Femme savante,* that combination of conscious erudition and affected coyness that suggests "It's really not *womanly* to know as much as I do." How different from the attitude described by one of my English friends: "With my education, I never could expect to marry." Yes, we do things better here.

There are those—and I am one of them—who rebel at having to deal with an intermediary. They want to go to the fountain-head. Someone who knows me well says that science, to me, has been a religious experience. He is probably right. If my religious passion had been turned towards the Catholic Church I should have wanted to be a priest. I am sure that I should never have settled for being a nun. If it had been directed towards medicine, I should have wanted to be a surgeon; nothing would have persuaded me to be content to be a nurse. As I look over the world of science, I picture most of the many women who are working in that field today in the role of nuns and nurses. They are not allowed—they are not supposed to be fit—to be in direct touch with the fountain-head, whether you call it God or the Universe. (But even as I write, this situation is changing.) Here I have had no cause for complaint. I have always been in direct touch with the fountain-head. No other mortal has made my intellectual decisions for me. I may have been underpaid, I may have occupied subordinate positions for many years, but my source of inspiration has always been direct.

I spent many years at Harvard, researching and writing my main interests, with an undercurrent of editing that gradually took more and more of my time, and incidentally taught me much about the craft of writing. I had no official status, as little as that of the students who provided the "girl-hours" in which Shapley counted his research expenditures. I was paid so little that I was ashamed to admit it to my relations in England. They thought I was coining money in a land of millionaires. But I had the run of the Harvard plates, I could use the Harvard telescopes (a dubious boon, this, in the climate of Cambridge), and I had the library at my fingertips.

Then came the time when Shapley organized the Department of Astronomy, and began to attract doctoral candidates. The first of these students was Frank Hogg, and (with or without status) I was to direct his research. Lectures began, informally at first, then more organized, and of course I had to lecture. The new Department called for a Chairman, a Professor. I could have done it; who knew the ropes better? But it was "impossible"; the University would never permit it. Only a few years earlier, Theodore Lyman had refused to accept a woman as candidate for the Ph.D. and Shapley had somehow circumvented the difficulty. But this time it was not to be. I do not know what he tried to do, but he reported to me that President Lowell had said that "Miss Payne should never have a position in the University while he was alive." Perhaps Shapley did make an attempt. But my nameless status remained nameless. Harry Plaskett was brought from Victoria to head the new Department.

As I look back, I see that this was a turning point in my career at Harvard. Plaskett had not expected to like me. Had I presumed to argue too vehemently with his father, the great J. S. Plaskett? Shapley had already paved the way for a difficult relationship by asking me "how much it would disturb me" if Harry Plaskett were to come to Harvard Observatory? What did he say, I wonder, when he "mentioned me to him"?

I remember the day when Plaskett arrived. Prompted by who knows what impulse, I had dressed with extra attention and put a blue ribbon in my hair. I remember his greeting: "You're not at all like what I expected." What *had* he expected? I wondered.

As it turned out, my relationship with him was not to be the same as with the visiting astronomers with whom I used to argue through the night. We became warm friends, but we never discussed astronomy. Scientifically we were on different wavelengths. He treated me as a woman, not as a scientist. I was not jealous of him, although the students assigned to me soon transferred their allegiance to him. I was sorry but I considered that it was their loss; and it left me more time for research. Meanwhile I spent many happy hours in the Plaskett home, playing with their children and chatting with Mrs. Plaskett. It was the first family I had got to know since I was grown up; I had very few human contacts in those days.

Only some years later, when Harry Plaskett was called to Oxford to succeed H. H. Turner, did I feel jealous of him. Of course I had no right to aspire to the Savilian Professorship, but I felt that I should have been as well qualified as he. Not for the first time, I felt I had been passed over because I was a woman.

When Plaskett left Harvard there was a search for a successor. Shapley said to me at this time: "What this Observatory needs is a spectroscopist." I replied indignantly that *I* was a spectroscopist, though I was being pushed against my will into photometry. I protested to no avail: a spectroscopist must be imported.

Another lapse of years, another President of the University, and the time came for Shapley to retire as Director of the Observatory. After an agonizing time of indecision, Donald Menzel finally succeeded him. To Donald I owe the advancement that was finally accorded me. The finances of the Observatory had been a closely guarded secret, and when he learned what salary I had been getting, he told me that he was shocked. He promptly raised it, and soon doubled it. Moreover, he succeeded where Shapley had failed (though I shall never know how hard he had actually tried): I was made Phillips Professor and Chairman of the Department of Astronomy. Such was the generous treatment I was accorded by the man from whom I had been systematically estranged for many years. He did not let my sex, or my less-than-cooperative attitude, stand in my way.

The new position was no sinecure. I inherited a heavy teaching load and the responsibility for a large graduate school. There was literally no time for research, a setback from which I have never fully recovered. But as a mother sees her life renewed in her children, I saw my scientific efforts perpetuated in my students. There is no greater reward for an instructor than that of seeing students, whom we began by teaching, grow into fellow-scientists who end by teaching us. A few of the young men and women who were my responsibility during those hard years have given me this reward, and I thank them for it. . . .

As I look back I ask myself what difference it has made to me as a scientist that I was born a woman. As concerns the intellectual side of the matter, I should say that it has made very little. I am not conscious of having used any feminine wiles in connection with my scientific work; in fact I do not see how I could have done so. In that sense scientific work is inhuman. I will not accept the conclusions of another astronomer simply because I am fond of him, or reject them because I dislike him (though I admit there is a temptation here). Neither do I expect others to accept my arguments or praise my work because they like me, or to attack me because they do not. Some charming people do slipshod work, and some disagreeable people have made great contributions. I have said elsewhere that I wish that all scientific work might be anonymous.

On the material side, being a woman has been a great disadvantage. It is a tale of low salary, lack of status, slow advancement. But I have reached a height that I should never, in my wildest dreams, have predicted 50 years ago. It has been a case of survival, not of the fittest, but of the most doggedly persistent. I was not consciously aiming at the point I finally reached. I simply went on plodding, rewarded by the beauty of the scenery, towards an unexpected goal.

Young people, especially young women, often ask me for advice. Here it is, *valeat quantum*. Do not undertake a scientific career in quest of fame or money. There are easier and better ways to reach them. Undertake it only if nothing else will satisfy you; for nothing else is probably what you will receive. Your reward will be the widening of the horizon as you climb. And if you achieve that reward you will ask no other.

Margaret Mead

(1901–1978)

The second of five children (four daughters and a son) of an academic family in Philadelphia, Margaret Mead was educated in progressive schools and through the efforts of her mother and paternal grandmother. Her mother arranged creative work in arts and crafts to supplement her children's formal education, while her grandmother taught Mead and her sisters mathematics, classical languages, and history at home whenever the local schools were deemed not sufficiently demanding.

Mead was trained in observation from early childhood, when her grandmother taught her to keep the detailed record of daily observations on the infant development of her two younger sisters which Mead's mother had maintained for Mead's first years of life. These two strong women were clearly important models for Mead, whose father, a professor of business at the University of Pennsylvania, acceded only reluctantly to her desire for a college education. He selected DePauw, his alma mater, for a daughter who was brilliant but the product of a highly individualistic education. Knowing nothing of the concerns with dress and social success becoming standard for the American sorority girl of her generation, Mead was miserable at DePauw and was a social outcast, considered unfit for membership in a sorority.

When she transferred to Barnard College in her sophomore year, Mead found herself among intellectual equals, and she was fascinated by the brilliance of Ruth Benedict, then teaching anthropology at Columbia in partnership with Franz Boas. Although majoring in psychology, Mead decided to do graduate work in anthropology under Boas's direction. She began in her junior year her close friendship with Benedict, which later became a powerful lesbian relationship.

Before setting out for DePauw, Mead had met and become engaged to a young Lutheran, Luther Cressman, intent on entering his church's ministry. The two were married in 1923, shortly before Mead set out to pursue her first fieldwork assignment in Samoa. This study resulted in her famous *Coming of Age in Samoa* (1928) and in an appointment beginning in 1926 to the anthropology staff of the American Museum of Natural History in New York; she was to hold this affiliation until her retirement in 1964.

Always volatile emotionally, Mead was troubled by medical advice that convinced her (mistakenly) that she could not bear a child. Her resulting determination to pursue her anthropological career to the maximum of her ability led to a gradual weakening of her ties to Cressman, whom she divorced in order to marry, in 1928, the New Zealand anthropologist Reo Franklin Fortune, whom she had met in Samoa.

This marriage also ended in divorce, principally because Mead found her partnership with Fortune less than satisfactory intellectually and because she found the fieldwork partner she had always sought in the British anthropologist Gregory Bateson, whom she met while in the field with Fortune, studying sexual mores and cultural patterns in New Guinea. The trio's collaborative work resulted in Mead's epoch-making *Sex and Temperament in Three Primitive Societies* (1935), which asserts the primacy of culture in gendered behavior, thereby predating the modern feminist interest in gender and culture by some thirty-five years.

Mead also anticipated the feminist critique of marriage and the Western preoccupation with heterosexual relationships by maintaining throughout her life concurrent erotic and emotional relationships with male and female partners, a pattern she discussed frankly with her one child, Mary Catherine Bateson, when Mead deemed her sufficiently adult.

A woman of prodigious energy and engaging openness to new issues, new technologies for research, and new media of communication, Mead published ten major works between 1928 and 1977, moving from studies of child rearing in the Pacific to the cultural and biological bases of gender, the nature of cultural change, the meaning of cultural pluralism, the structure and functioning of complex societies, race relations, and the origins of the drug culture.[1] While she became more conservative in her view of the family and of sexual norms, Mead remained a pioneer in the subjects she chose to address and in her willingness to think of new ways her discipline could serve society.

---

1. *Coming of Age in Samoa* (1928), *Growing Up in New Guinea* (1930), *Sex and Temperament in Three Primitive Societies* (1935), *And Keep Your Powder Dry* (1942), *Male and Female: A Study of the Sexes in a Changing World* (1949), *Childhood in Contemporary Cultures* (1955), *People and Places* (1959), *Blackberry Winter: My Earlier Years* (1972), *Ruth Benedict: An Autobiography* (1972), *Letters from the Field* (1977).

Though her approach to her fieldwork has been savagely criticized, most notably in Derek Freeman's *Margaret Mead and Samoa* (1983), in which the author claims that she misrepresented her data to permit the overemphasis of cultural influences on gender behavior, no critic has been able to undermine the extent of Mead's contribution to anthropology, her intellectual courage, and her willingness to tackle large subjects of major intellectual consequence for her own and succeeding generations. Her readiness to comment and her interest in all aspects of contemporary society made her something of a culture heroine for the English-speaking world in the post–Second World War era.

BLACKBERRY WINTER:
My Earlier Years

I think it was my grandmother who gave me my ease in being a woman. She was unquestionably feminine—small and dainty and pretty and wholly without masculine protest or feminist aggrievement. She had gone to college when this was a very unusual thing for a girl to do, she had a firm grasp of anything she paid attention to, she had married and had a child, and she had a career of her own. All this was true of my mother, as well. But my mother was filled with passionate resentment about the condition of women, as perhaps my grandmother might have been had my grandfather lived and had she borne five children and had little opportunity to use her special gifts and training. As it was, the two women I knew best were mothers and had professional training. So I had no reason to doubt that brains were suitable for a woman. And as I had my father's kind of mind—which was also his mother's—I learned that the mind is not sex-typed. . . .

Throughout my childhood she talked a great deal about teachers, about their problems and conflicts, and about those teachers who could never close the schoolhouse door behind them. The sense she gave me of what teachers are like, undistorted by my own particular experience with teachers, made me want to write my first book about adolescents in such a way that the teachers of adolescents would understand it. Grandma always wanted to understand things, and she was willing to listen or read until she did. There was only one subject, she decided rather fastidiously, that she did not wish to pursue. That was birth control. At eighty, she said, she did not need to know about it. . . .

Grandma . . . set me to work taking notes on [my sister's] behavior—on the first words Priscilla spoke and on the way one echoed the other. She made me aware of how Priscilla mimicked the epithets and shouts hurled up and down the back stairs by the Swedish nurse and the Irish cook and of how Elizabeth was already making poetry of life. Told that her dress was ragged, she replied happily, "Yes, I's the raggedy man." I learned to make these notes with love, carrying on what Mother had begun. I knew that she had filled thirteen notebooks on me and only four on Richard; now I was taking over for the younger children. In many ways I thought of the babies as my children, whom I could observe and teach and cultivate. . . .

Mother thought about every place we lived not only in terms of its schools, but also as a more or less promising source of "lessons." Whatever form such lessons took—drawing, painting, carving, modeling, or basketry—she thought of them as a supplement to formal education within the context of the most advanced educational theories. In Hammonton I had music lessons and also lessons in carving, because the only artist the town boasted was a skillful wood-carver. In Swarthmore we were taught by an all-round manual training teacher under whose tutelage I even built a small loom. In Bucks County I had painting lessons from a local artist and later from an artist in New Hope. And one year Mother had a local carpenter teach Dick and me woodworking. She was completely eclectic about what we were taught in these lessons provided the person who was teaching us was highly skilled.

Looking back, it seems to me that this way of organizing teaching and learning around special skills provided me with a model for the way I have always organized work, whether it has involved organizing a research team, a staff of assistants, or the available informants in a native village. In every case I try to find out what each person is good at doing and then I fit them together in a group that forms some kind of whole. . . .

Living on the farm—and we were told that we lived there because Grandma believed every child had a right to grow up on a farm—opened our eyes to great diversity of experience. There was always another family in the farmer's house, and we often had maids with little children. When the threshers came, there were twenty to sit down in the farmer's kitchen, and we all helped. My father taught me how to top off shocks of wheat as it was done in Ohio and then left me with the task of showing the men how to do it without making them mad. . . .

In school I always felt that I was special and different, set apart in a way that could not be attributed to any gift I had, but only to my background—to the education given me by my grandmother and to the explicit academic interests of my parents. I felt that I had to work hard to become part of the life around me. But at the same time I searched for a greater intensity than the world around me offered and speculated about a career. At different times I wanted to become a lawyer, a nun, a writer, or a minister's wife with six children. Looking to my grandmother and my mother for models, I expected to be both a professional woman and a wife and mother.

In some ways my upbringing was well ahead of my time— perhaps as much as two generations ahead. Mother's advanced ideas, the way in which all children in our home were treated as persons, the kinds of books I read—ranging from the children's books of my grandmother's generation to the most modern plays that my mother sent for to read with a group of friends—and the way all I read was placed in historical perspective, and above all, the continuous running commentary by my family on schools, on education, on the way teachers were treated by the community, and on the relationship between good schools and much-needed higher taxes—for I never heard taxes mentioned except in terms of their being too low—all these things represented an extraordinary sophistication and a view of children that was rare in my childhood.

But in other ways those years in Bucks County gave me a view of a much earlier life-style, one that corresponded with my grandmother's girlhood. There was the beautiful old eighteen-room house in which we lived, with its low windows under the eaves, deep cellar to keep the milk cool, and woodshed where the kerosene was kept to light the lamps for the eighteen rooms. When we bought the house, it was innocent of plumbing, and we spent the first year making it over so that we had a kitchen and bathroom with running water, and a furnace, and the old fireplaces were opened again. We saw it all, the way it was and the way it became.

Moreover, nothing was taken wholly for granted. Opening up the old fireplaces, or making butter, which Grandma had to learn to do, or setting out a great iron kettle to make apple butter in the fall—all this was part of an experience of a way of life that was compared and commented upon, on the one hand, against the background of my grandmother's childhood and, on the other, in the light of our experience of living in a modern city where people drove cars and rode in power-driven streetcars. The farm represented one way of living, but only one of many ways.

Quite early I also became aware of great discrepancies of attitude. At home the facts of life were presented to me seriously and realistically, but in a very abstract way. At the same time, in school, I continually heard about the startling and brutal events in the lives of our neighbors. At about the time my mother explained to me why it was that many readers had discontinued their subscription to a magazine when a statue of a white slave was pictured on the cover, I also learned from my schoolmates how a hired girl had been savagely raped within the hearing of her blind mistress, a woman held in high esteem in the community, and how she had not lifted a hand to help the girl. Listening to my mother's outspoken, modern views and to the crude, open gossip of the countryside left me little to find out in books. But I did discover through reading novels what an abortion was and what illegitimacy meant. . . .

In June . . . my science teacher, George Cressman, was asked to give the graduation address at the high school in Buckingham. I asked Mother to invite him to dinner, and when he explained that his younger brother Luther was visiting him, she invited him, too. I drove all the way to Furlong to meet them at the Interurban station. That night we danced and danced at the high school. . . .

Luther was four years older than I and a senior in college. He was studying Latin and Greek, and he gave me books of poetry with dedications in verse that he himself wrote. He was tall and slender and well built. He could drive a car and shoot a gun with great skill and he took beautiful photographs. He danced magnificently. He had an engaging grin and a wry sense of humor, yet he took life seriously and, like my mother, was willing to see life whole.

At Christmas, on another visit, Luther and I became engaged. And at this time his tentative plan to enter the ministry began to crystallize—it was what his mother had always wanted him to do, and a minister's wife was what I wanted to be. . . .

In the autumn of 1918, the whole family moved again, this time to New Hope, where the Holmquist School, a new and very special school, had opened. . . . There were almost as many teachers as students, and we had a precious diet of exciting teaching and religious exploration under one of the founders who also taught religion at Bryn Mawr. As the only help we had at home was a high-school girl, I did the cooking and, in between, learned trigonometry and worked my way through three years of French. When the war was over, Luther came home from camp and I told my parents that I was engaged to him. This was, of course, kept a deep secret from the other girls in school, who were still living out their romantic daydreams by reading forbidden books.

In the spring my father suffered a lot of losses in one of his private business ventures. This precipitated a crisis over my going to college. Hoping to get someone to back up his new view that I need not go to college, he called in our local physician, who said, "Look at those useless little hands! Never did a day's work in their life and never will! You'd maybe make a good mistress, but a poor wife. You'd better study nursing!" Hearing this, I exploded in one of the few fits of feminist rage I have ever had. At that moment I was not only carrying a heavy school program and making all the costumes for a play, but was also keeping house for the whole family. However, what really infuriated me was the totally contradictory notion that although I was not strong enough to study for a degree, I was strong enough to become a nurse.

In the end, using tactics that were wholly alien to her transparent honesty, Mother persuaded Father to send me to DePauw. This was his college, and the idea captured his interest. I was accepted at DePauw—and all my studying that year had been unnecessary. Luther, who had taught the half year after he was demobilized, was accepted at the General Theological Seminary in New York. . . .

Although I was tired at the end of the summer, I had my mother's stories of the free and democratic "West"—the West she had known in her girlhood—to buoy me up, and I packed for DePauw with enthusiasm. Mother let me plan my own clothes for a dressmaker who came to the house to make them. I designed an evening dress that was to represent a field of wheat with poppies against a blue sky with white clouds. The skirt, made of a stiff silver-green material, was accordion pleated and decorated with poppies; the blouse was made of blue and white Georgette crepe. The idea was romantic, but the dress was dreadful. However, Mother had done her duty by letting me plan it for myself. The dressmaker also made me little smocked-over blouses in crepe de Chine to wear for dinner. But I did not have a single garment that resembled anything the girls at DePauw actually wore.

I also planned my college room carefully. I picked the material for the curtains—the room was to be done in old rose and blue—and chose pictures to go on the walls, among them a picture of Rabindranath Tagore and a portrait of Catherine Bushkova, the "little grandmother" of the Russian Revolution. (Mother had danced for joy at the outbreak of the Revolution, when word came that the Russians, who had been enslaved by the evil czars, were free at last.) And of course I packed many boxes of books—poetry, novels, and essays.

My father said, "Of course you will be a Theta." Several of his fraternity brothers were on the campus at Greencastle. They had married Thetas, and he would write them. I found this all quite mysterious. I knew that Mother had belonged to Shakespeare at Wellesley and that Aunt Beth had been Mortarboard at the University of Chicago, but I had never heard of Greek-letter societies. During the summer I began to receive letters from an effusive girl who lived in the town where Aunt Beth, married to a very successful businessman, was living as a young social matron. The girl explained that she was a Kappa from DePauw and that she was looking forward to inviting me to a Kappa party when I arrived at college.

I was seventeen. I was engaged to be married. But above all else I was eager to enter the academic world for which all my life had prepared me. . . .

In the intellectual community to which my parents belonged, college was as necessary as learning to read. It was an intellectual experience and the gateway to the rest of life. All my life I expected to go to college, and I was prepared to enjoy it. . . .

. . . the overriding academic ethos shaped all our lives. This was tempered by my mother's sense of responsibility for society, by my father's greater interest in real processes than in theoretical abstractions, and by my grandmother's interest in real children, in chickens, and in how to season stewed tomatoes with toasted bread. But at the heart of their lives, the enjoyment of the intellect as mediated by words in books was central, and I was the child who could make the most of this—the child who was not asked to constrain or distort some other gift.

And so, even though it was decided that I was to go to DePauw rather than Bryn Mawr or Wellesley, I approached the idea of college with the expectation of taking part in an intellectual feast. I looked forward to studying fascinating subjects taught by people who understood what they were talking about. I imagined meeting brilliant students, students who would challenge me to stretch my mind and work instead of going skating with my lessons done well enough so that I led my classmates who hated what they were studying. In college, in some way that I devoutly believed in but could not explain, I expected to become a person.

At DePauw in 1919 I found students who were, for the most part, the first generation to go to college and whose parents appeared at Class Day poorly dressed while their daughters wore the raccoon or the muskrat coats that were appropriate to the sorority they had made. It was a college to which students had come for fraternity life, for football games, and for establishing the kind of rapport with other people that would make them good Rotarians in later life and their wives good members of the garden club.

I arrived with books of poetry, portraits of great personalities to hang on the wall, and the snobberies of the East, such as the expectation that one dressed in the evening for the members of one's own family. And I was confronted by the snobbery and cruelty of the sorority system at its worst, with rules against rushing that prevented the women who had gone to college with my father and who had married my father's fraternity brothers from ever speaking to me or inviting me to their homes—rules made by the Panhellenic Association in order to control competition that was so harsh and so unashamed that the very rules designed to control it made it even worse. This was my first and only real experience of discrimination—mild enough in all conscience. . . .

When I arrived at DePauw, I found that I had two roommates. One was a girl who had come to college to join a sorority, and this had been arranged in advance; the other expected to be rushed by a sorority that had little prestige. I soon learned that no one belonging to a sorority could speak to an unpledged freshman. This, of course, explained why I heard nothing from the effusive girl who had written me so many letters during the summer. When the invitations came out, I was invited to the Kappa rushing party. But when I arrived wearing my unusual and unfashionable dress that was designed to look like a wheat field with poppies blooming in it, my correspondent turned her back on me and never spoke to me again. I found the whole evening strangely confusing. I could not know, of course, that everyone had been given the signal that inviting me had been a mistake. Afterward, my two roommates got the bids they expected, but I did not get a bid.

It still took a little time for me to realize the full implications of what it meant to be an unpledged freshman in a college where everything was organized around the fraternities and sororities. For one thing, I had no dates; these were all arranged through commands to the freshman pledges of certain fraternities to date the freshman pledges of certain sororities. Although all freshmen had to live in dormitories, it meant also that there was a widening gulf between the pledges, who spent a lot of time at their sorority houses being disciplined and shaped up, and the unpledged freshmen and the few upperclassmen in the dormitories. . . .

During the year I studied at DePauw, I did not deny that I was hurt, nor did I pretend to myself that I would have refused the chance to be accepted by a sorority. The truth is, I would not have known enough to refuse. And once inside, it is quite possible that I would have been as unseeing as the rest. As it was, what particularly offended me as the year wore on was the contrast between the vaunted democracy of the Middle West and the blatant, strident artificiality of the Greek-letter societies on that midwestern campus, the harshness of the rules that prevented my father's classmates from ever addressing a hospitable word to me, and, more than anything else, the lack of loyalty that rejection engendered among the unchosen. . . .

My unusual clothing was not all that was held against me. There was my room with its carefully planned color scheme, my books and pictures, and, above all, my tea set. And I did not chew gum. Then, as if these things were not enough, there was my accent. . . .

And, although the sorority rejection was the sharper blow, there was another. I found out that I was also ineligible to belong to the Y.W.C.A. because, as an Episcopalian, I did not belong to an Evangelical religion. There were five of us at DePauw who were religious rejects—myself, one Roman Catholic, one Greek Orthodox, one Lutheran, and one Jew. The Jew was David Lilienthal. On one occasion he was asked to give a talk to the Methodist Sunday School on the Jewish conception of Jesus. The rest of us were simply beyond the pale. . . .

The teaching at DePauw was far less disappointing than the college social organization. In my catalogue I had marked courses totaling over 200 hours, even though 120 hours was all that a student could take in four years. I thoroughly enjoyed the magnificent teaching given by men who were first and foremost teachers, interested in their students and unharassed by the demand that they "publish or perish," an attitude that later came to haunt even small colleges like DePauw. The training in writing given me by Professor Pence was never equaled by anyone else. At DePauw I was introduced to discussions of the Old Testament prophets and the Social Gospel, and this firmly established association between the Old and the New Testament and the demands of social justice provided me with an ethical background up to the time of the development of ecumenicism and Vatican II. These courses were taught by deeply religious men who regarded it a privilege to be teaching where they were.

At DePauw, too, I took a course in History as Past Ethics, to which I still refer. However, there were only two girls and a couple of dozen boys in that class, and the two girls received the highest marks. As long as I was in high school, the greater maturity of adolescent girls had not struck me. But in the setting of this coeducational college it became perfectly clear both that bright girls could do better than bright boys and that they would suffer for it.

This made me feel that coeducation was thoroughly unattractive. I neither wanted to do bad work in order to make myself attractive to boys nor did I want them to dislike me for doing good work. It seemed to me that it would be much simpler to go to a girls' college where one could work as hard as one pleased.

This preference foreshadowed, I suppose, my anthropological field choices—not to compete with men in male fields, but instead to concentrate on the kinds of work that are better done by women. Actually, there are two kinds of fieldwork that women can do better than men. One is working with women and children in situations in which male investigators are likely to be suspected and resented by the men of a society. The other is working with both men and women as an older woman, using a woman's postmenopausal high status to achieve an understanding of the different parts of a culture, particularly in those cultures in which women past the reproductive period are freed from the constraints and taboos that constrict the lives of younger women. The first choice can be effectively exercised only in a situation in which the culture is being studied by a male-female pair or a team. For when a woman explicitly classifies herself with excluded women and uninitiated children, she does not have access to the rest of the culture. The second role is very practical for an older woman who is working alone in a culture that has already been explored by a male and female pair.

Nevertheless, as long as I remained at DePauw, I felt I was an exile. I used to sit in the library and read the drama reviews in *The*

New York Times. Like so many other aspiring American intellectuals and artists, I developed the feeling that American small towns were essentially unfriendly to the life of the mind and the senses. . . .

And so, at the end of the year, I persuaded my father to let me leave DePauw and enter Barnard College. . . .

By the very contrast that it provided, DePauw clarified my picture of the kind of college at which I wanted to be a student—a place where people were intellectually stirred and excited by ideas, where people stayed up all night talking about things that mattered, where one would meet one's peers and, still more important, people with different and superior minds, and, not least, where one would find out what one could do in life. . . .

In the autumn of 1920, I came to Barnard, where I found—and in some measure created—the kind of student life that matched my earlier dreams. In the course of those three undergraduate years friendships were founded that have endured a lifetime of change, and by the end of those years I knew what I could do in life.

At that time Barnard had only one large dormitory, and during preceding years one group of students had been permitted to live in an apartment and do cooperative housekeeping. They were unusual girls, most of whom became well known in later life—Margaret Mayer, Dorothy Swaine Thomas, Betsy Anne Selhayes, Agnes Piel, and Leonie Adams. When I arrived on the scene the group had dispersed and the Coop had been abolished, but the overflow of students still was housed in apartments. Although the space in which we lived was usually very confined, the fact that the cost of rooms varied—the kitchen and the maid's room were the least expensive—meant that a group with unequal financial resources could live together.

In our group Leonie Adams provided a link to the old Coop group and their ethos; out of this we developed our own ideas of unity, based on common tastes and a respect for diversity. Most of the group we formed lived together, in three successive apartments, throughout college. . . .

Each year we adopted as a group name some derogatory and abusive phrase that was hurled at us in particular or at the students at large. . . . "Ash Can Cats," the name that finally stuck, was an epithet bestowed on us by our most popular professor, the vivid, colloquial, contemporary-minded Minor W. Latham, after whom Barnard's theater is named. We all took the course in drama in which she brought together, with a fine human relevance and a contempt for historical sequence, Greek plays, the contemporary Broadway theater, and miracle plays, and we were her partisans against the more conventional members of the English Department, critics ever, who admired creativity only when the creator was dead. . . .

. . . we knew about Freud. Agnes Piel was being analyzed and, although overnight visitors were not allowed and had to be hidden when Miss Abbott pounced, Ag occasionally spent the night with us. The first time she came, I made up her bed for her. Accustomed to being the eldest, that was the kind of thing I always did. Ag looked at me and said, "Well, the man you marry will certainly have an Oedipus fixation on you, which will be all right if it isn't joined to an incest complex."

We learned about homosexuality, too, mainly from the covert stories that drifted down to us through our more sophisticated alumnae friends, through the Coop group, and through Leonie's older sister, who was close to some members of the faculty. Allegations were made against faculty members, and we worried and thought over affectionate episodes in our past relationships with girls and wondered whether they had been incipient examples. . . .

Our group was half Jewish and half Gentile. Looking back, it seems to me that the Gentile families were, on the whole, a little more receptive to their daughters' friendships than were the more tightly knit Jewish families. I had enjoyed the few Jewish children I had known earlier, and during college summers I often got very bored with the slower intellectual pace of the Gentile world. . . .

When we first began living together I invented a kinship system for the group. Deborah Kaplan, Leonie Adams, and I were the "parents," and Viola Corrigan and Eleanor Pelham Kortheuer—who had an extraordinary gift for sensitive and humorous insights—were the "children." In 1922 we added "grandchildren," only one of whom, Louise Rosenblatt, has remained part of the group, and finally, in 1923, we added a "great-grandchild." . . .

Although we were bound together by ties of temperament and congeniality and by a common interest in literature, some—but not all—of us also were children of our period and true descendants of the group of girls who had lived in the Coop. We belonged to a generation of young women who felt extraordinarily free—free from the demand to marry unless we chose to do so, free to postpone marriage while we did other things, free from the need to bargain and hedge that had burdened and restricted women of earlier generations. We laughed at the idea that a woman could be an old maid at the age of twenty-five, and we rejoiced at the new medical care that made it possible for a woman to have a child at forty.

We did not bargain with men. Almost every one of us fell in love with a much older man, someone who was an outstanding figure in one of the fields in which we were working, but none of these love affairs led to marriage. Schooled in an older ethic, the men were perplexed by us and vacillated between a willingness to take the love that was offered so generously and uncalculatingly and a feeling that to do so was to play the part of a wicked seducer. Later most of us married men who were closer to our own age and style of living, but it was a curious period in which girls who were too proud to ask for any hostage to fate confused the men they chose to love.

At the same time we firmly established a style of relationships to other women. "Never break a date with a girl for a man" was one of our mottoes in a period when women's loyalty to women usually was—as it usually still is—subordinate to their possible relationships to men. We learned loyalty to women, pleasure in conversation with women, and enjoyment of the way in which we complemented one another in terms of our differences in temperament, which we found as interesting as the complementarity that is produced by the difference of sex. Throughout extraordinarily different career lines we have continued to enjoy one another, and although meeting becomes more difficult as we scatter in retirement, we continue to meet and take delight in one another's minds. . . .

When I went to DePauw, I intended to be a writer and when I transferred to Barnard I continued to major in English. But the experience was disappointing. . . . So, although I had been deeply bored by my course in Introductory Psychology, I went on to take the necessary hours for a second major, in psychology.

In a curious way this [being twice divorced] has both protected me and permitted me a kind of single-minded pursuit of the things I have valued, just as being a woman has protected me from having to accept administrative posts. Otherwise, with my propensity for letting life call the shots, I might easily have been diverted by the argument that it was necessary for me to play a political role. As it was, as long as I did not put myself in the position of being a political target, my private life was not a liability and, in fact, rapidly faded from most people's memories. . . .

I wanted to make a contribution. It seemed to me then—as it still does—that science is an activity in which there is room for many degrees, as well as many kinds, of giftedness. It is an activity in which any individual, by finding his own level, can make a true contribution. So I chose science—and to me that meant one of the social sciences. My problem then was which of the social sciences?

I entered my senior year committed to psychology, but I also took a course on psychological aspects of culture given by William Fielding Ogburn, one of the first courses in which Freudian psychology was treated with respect. I had also to choose between the two most distinguished courses open to seniors—a philosophy course given by William Pepperell Montague and the course in anthropology given by Franz Boas. I chose anthropology.

I had absorbed many of the premises of anthropology at home as they lay back of what my mother had learned at Bryn Mawr under Caseby and what both my parents had learned from Veblen. I was accustomed to regard all the races of man as equal and to look at all human cultures as comparable. What was new to me was the vista that was opened up by discussions of the development of men from their earliest beginnings. The reconstructions of Stone Age men with bundles of sticks in their arms had a tremendous power to move me, as they evoked a sense of the millennia it had taken man to take the first groping steps toward civilization and of the many thousands of years the slender flakes from the cores men made into hammerstones had lain unused in paleolithic workshops.

Boas was a surprising and somewhat frightening teacher. He had a bad side and a good side of his face. On one side there was a long dueling scar from his student days in Germany—an unusual pursuit for a Jewish student—on which his eyelid drooped and teared from a recent stroke. But seen from the other side, his face showed him to be as handsome as he had been as a young man. His lectures were polished and clear. Occasionally he would look around and ask a rhetorical question which no one would venture to answer. I got into the habit of writing down an answer and nodding when it turned out to be right. At the end of the semester I and another girl whom I did not know but whose name rhymed with mine were excused from taking the examination for "helpful participation in class discussion."

Ruth Benedict was Boas' teaching assistant. She was tentative and shy and always wore the same dress. She spoke so hesitatingly that many students were put off by her manner, but Marie Bloomfield and I were increasingly fascinated. On Museum trips we would ride down and back on the Broadway streetcar with her. Her comments humanized Boas' formal lectures, as she would remark how like a communist state the Inca Empire had been or satirize the way the Crow Indians invested in visions. She invited Marie and me to the graduate seminar, where we were embarrassed by her shy, inarticulate report on John Dewey's *Human Nature and Conduct*. But we kept on going to the seminar. By the end of the first term I had decided to attend everything Boas taught, as Ruth Benedict said he might retire at the end of the year. I also propagandized the course so thoroughly at Barnard that it doubled in size the second semester and this made it possible for Boas to persuade the Barnard administration to appoint an instructor rather than paying Columbia for each student.

By the spring I was actively considering the possibility of entering anthropology, but I was already launched on my Master's essay in psychology. Then one day, when I was at lunch with Ruth Benedict and was discussing with her whether to go into sociology, as Ogburn wanted me to do, or into psychology, as I had already planned to do, she said, "Professor Boas and I have nothing to offer but an opportunity to do work that matters." That settled it for me. Anthropology had to be done *now*. Other things could wait. . . .

By electing anthropology as a career, I was also electing a closer relationship to Ruth, a friendship that lasted until her death in 1948. When I was away, she took on my varied responsibilities for other people; when she was away, I took on hers. We read and re-read each other's work, wrote poems in answer to poems, shared our hopes and worries about Boas, about Sapir, about anthropology, and in later years about the world. When she died, I had read everything she had ever written and she had read everything I had ever written. No one else had, and no one else has.

So I came at the end of my years at Barnard. I was engaged to be married in the fall. I was committed to taking my Master's degree in psychology and to finishing the work for this during the summer. I had accepted an assistantship to Ogburn in economics and sociology for the next autumn, when I would also begin my graduate work in anthropology.

At the senior dance Luther and I danced all night and in the damp dawn, which took all the curl out of my small ostrich feather fan, we walked along Riverside Drive, watching the sky brighten over the river.

I knew that I wanted to do field work as soon as I had my degree. Fortunately, the library work for my dissertation was already well under way. Luther proposed working out an adaptation that would allow him to pursue further studies that were open to him and, at the same time, allow me to go to the field. He would get a European travel fellowship for the next year, 1925–1926, and I would get a fellowship to take me to the field. . . .

The choice of a field and a people and a problem on which to start work—all this was much more difficult. I wanted to work on change: on the way in which new customs in a new country or new ways of life in an old country were related to older ones. . . .

The choice of where I went to the field and what problem I would work on was not mine alone to make. The final decision rested with Boas, and he wanted me to study adolescence.

He had reached one of those watersheds that occur in the lives of statesmen-scientists who are mapping out the whole course of a discipline. He felt that sufficient work had gone into demonstrating that peoples borrowed from one another, that no society evolved in isolation, but was continually influenced in its development by other peoples, other cultures, and other, differing, levels of technology. He decided that the time had come to tackle the set of problems that linked the development of individuals to what was distinctive in the culture in which they were reared. In the summer of 1924, when Ruth Bunzel said she wanted to go to Zuni, he suggested that she work on the role of the individual artist. Now he wanted me to work on adolescence, on the adolescent girl, to test out, on the one hand, the extent to which the troubles of adolescence, called in German *Sturm und Drang* and *Weltschmerz*, depended upon the attitudes of a particular culture and, on the other hand, the extent to which they were inherent in the adolescent stage of psychobiological development with all its discrepancies, uneven growth, and new impulses.

Scientists who are building a new discipline have to keep in mind the necessary next steps. In Boas' case, there were two additional considerations: first, the materials on which the new science depended were fast vanishing, and forever. The last primitive peoples were being contacted, missionized, given new tools and new ideas. Their primitive cultures would soon become changed beyond recovery. Among many American Indian groups the last old women who spoke a language that had developed over thousands of years were already senile and babbling in their cups; the last man who had ever been on a buffalo hunt would soon die. The time to do the work was *now*. And secondly, there were few sources of funds and very few people to do the work. In 1924 there were four graduate students in anthropology at Columbia and a mere handful in other universities. He had to plan—much as if he were a general with only a handful of troops available to save a whole country—where to place each student most strategically, so that each piece of work would count and nothing would be wasted and no piece of work would have to be done over.

Boas had a keen eye for the capabilities of his students although he confounded them by devoting his time to those whom he found least promising. As long as a student was doing well, he paid almost no attention to him at all. This was a loss. For good students it meant little person-to-person contact with Boas, and in some cases it led to serious errors in a student's self-estimate. With the exception of an occasional course taught by an outsider from another institution, Boas taught everything. This meant that I saw him in classes every day. But I had only a few rare interviews with him. The first was when I told him that I wanted to do graduate work in anthropology and he advised me to go to Harvard. The second took place when I chose my thesis subject and he suggested that I compare different cultures within an area: I could work on Siberia (that would mean learning Chinese and Russian), or on the Low Countries (for which I would have to have a command of French, Dutch, German, and medieval Latin), or on Polynesia ("which you could do with only French and German"). I chose Polynesia. I gave a seminar report on one section of my work, and when I turned in my dissertation I was told to add another paragraph or so to the introduction. That was all. But now there was the question of field work. . . .

I wanted to go to Polynesia, the area on which I had read so extensively. He thought it was too dangerous, and recited a sort of litany of young men who had died or been killed while they were working outside the United States. He wanted me to work among American Indians.

I wanted to study culture change, a subject that was not yet on his agenda, although it was soon to be. He wanted me to study adolescence.

Today a student would chafe against the restrictions with which we had to contend. Even then, some of my older contemporaries did chafe when Boas wanted them to work on the problems he thought came next, instead of following their own interests, like will-o'-the-wisps, wherever they led. But going to the field at all depended on his approval, for the only way to do it was to get one of the newly inaugurated graduate fellowships.

I was determined to go to Polynesia, but I was willing to compromise and study the adolescent girl, especially as the technology I had hoped to use in studying change had proved to be disappointingly inadequate. So I did what I had learned to do when I had to work things out with my father. I knew that there was one thing that mattered more to Boas than the direction taken by anthropological research. This was that he should behave like a liberal, democratic, modern man, not like a Prussian autocrat. It was enough to accuse him obliquely of exercising inappropriate authority to have him draw back. So I repeated over and over that by insisting that I work with American Indians he was preventing me from going where I wanted to work. Unable to bear the implied accusation that he was bullying me, Boas gave in. But he refused to let me go to the remote Tuamotu Islands; I must choose an island to which a ship came regularly—at least every three weeks. This was a restriction I could accept. . . .

At the same time, while I was bargaining with Boas, I told my father that Boas was trying to make me work with American Indians, already heavily contacted, instead of letting me go where things were interesting. My father, rivalrous as men often are in situations in which someone else seems to be controlling a person whom they believe they have the right—and may also have failed—to control, backed me up to the point of saying he would give me the money for a trip around the world. . . .

. . . in 1925, when both Boas and my father let me have my way, I was simply gleeful. That was the year in which I wrote "Of So Great Glee," a verse in which I expressed the sense I had of being invulnerable as long as I was moving in the right direction. . . .

The summer was given over to preparations. . . . most of my time was given over to getting inoculations and frantically assembling my field equipment—spare glasses, cotton dresses, a camera, pencils, and notebooks. . . .

. . . it is necessary to survive all kinds of hazards—having the inoculations that make you feel clumsy and feverish (in 1971, I had five sets all in one day, and afterward crushed my finger in a door and bruised my knee getting out of a taxi); breaking your glasses;

falling in love or having someone fall in love with you; trouble about passports and funds (in 1925, the Committee for the Biological Sciences of the National Research Council held a special meeting to decide whether they could advance $450 of my stipend, because communications with Samoa were so difficult); clothes that do not get finished and things that have been ordered but have not come.

[Mead divorced Luther Cressman to marry Reo Franklin Fortune in 1928. Shortly thereafter she met Gregory Bateson while in the field in Samoa.]

After we returned to Australia from the Sepik River in the spring of 1933, Reo and Gregory and I went separate ways. I returned to America to take up my job at the Museum and reopen the apartment that Reo and I had shared. Reo went to England by way of New Zealand, where he again met Eileen, the girl with whom he had originally been in love. Gregory went home to Cambridge on a freighter, and it was many weeks before I heard from him.

The developments that followed on our first theoretical formulations about temperament took several forms. Beginning with the contrast between expected male and female behavior and the way in which this contrast was institutionalized and made theatrical in Iatmul, Gregory wrote a first paper on the ethos of the Iatmul *naven* ceremony for an international congress in London.

I spent a summer month at a multi-disciplinary seminar organized by Lawrence K. Frank and held at Dartmouth, in the course of which I learned from John Dollard a much firmer way to describe cultural character. Afterward I began to write *Sex and Temperament*, a book in which I took into account only the different ways in which the behavior of the two sexes was stylized in Arapesh, Mundugumor, and Tchambuli. Although I had in mind the whole problem of temperament as a crosscutting type of differentiation, I did not discuss it in this book. In the summer of 1934, Gregory, C. H. Waddington, Justin Blanco-White, and I met briefly in Ireland. Here again we discussed the problem of temperamental types and attempted to further clarify the original formulations. That summer I finished *Sex and Temperament*, and the book was published in the spring of 1935.

How very difficult it was for Americans to sort out ideas of innate predispositions and culturally acquired behavior was evident in the contradictory responses to the book. Feminists hailed it as a demonstration that women did not "naturally" like children, and recommended that little girls should not be given dolls to play with. Reviewers accused me of not recognizing the existence of any sex differences. Fourteen years later, when I wrote *Male and Female*, a book in which I dealt carefully with cultural and temperamental differences as these were reflected in the lives of men and women and then discussed characteristics that seemed to be related to primary sex differences between men and women, I was accused of anti-feminism by women, of rampant feminism by men, and of denying the full beauty of the experience of being a woman by individuals of both sexes. . . .

In the spring of 1935 Gregory came to the United States. Working together with Radcliffe-Brown, we made a further attempt to define what is meant by society, culture, and cultural character. By then it seemed clear to us that the further study of inborn differences would have to wait upon less troubled times. On his return to England, Gregory completed the manuscript of *Naven*, his magnificent study of Iatmul culture.

In London, Reo had repudiated any psychological formulations. We were now divorced, and from England he had gone to China to teach. Gregory was awarded a new fellowship at Cambridge, and he and I were at last free to meet in Java and begin field work in Bali.

I was always glad that I was a girl. I cannot remember ever wanting to be a boy. It seems to me this was because of the way I was treated by my parents. I was a wanted child, and when I was born I was the kind of child my parents wanted. This sense of satisfying one's parents probably has a great deal to do with one's capacity to accept oneself as a kind of person. As a girl, I knew that someday I would have children. My closest models, my mother and my grandmother, had both had children and also had used their minds and had careers in the public world. So I had no doubt that, whatever career I might choose, I would have children, too. . . .

And then, in 1926, when I was told that I could never have children, I took this as a kind of omen about my future life. I had married Luther with the hope of rearing a houseful of children in a country parish. But now he was giving up the ministry and I was told that I could not have a child. I believed he would make a wonderful father, but this was no longer a possibility—for us.

On the other hand, I did not think that Reo, who wanted to

marry me, would make an ideal father. He was too demanding and jealous of my attention; he begrudged even the attention I gave to a piece of mending. I had always felt that my father demanded too much of my mother and took her away from us to satisfy his own immediate and capricious requests to do something or find something for him. I did not want a marriage that repeated this pattern. But without children, the future looked quite different, and I decided to choose a life of shared fieldwork and intellectual endeavor. I do not remember being terribly disappointed. There had always been the alternative of another kind of life. But Ruth was not pleased. Even though neither she nor anyone else questioned the doctor's verdict, she felt that I was somehow making an ascetic choice, a choice against the fullness of life.

So I married Reo. And, having made a commitment to work, I wrote to Professor Boas that he could send us anywhere he would send a man, since I would no longer need any special protection. I had accepted the need to give potentially childbearing women greater protection in the field than men. I still accept it, for the illness or death of a woman in the field makes for far more trouble for everyone—the people one is working with and the officials who have to deal with the situation. But this stricture no longer applied to me.

However, when we went to Mundugumor, I saw for the first time what the active refusal of children could do to a society. . . . among the Mundugumor both men and women actively disliked children. They are the only primitive people I have ever known who did not give an infant the breast when it cried. Instead, the child was hoisted up on the mother's shoulder. Sleeping babies were hung in rough-textured baskets in a dark place against the wall, and when a baby cried, someone would scratch gratingly on the outside of the basket.

The Mundugumor presented a harsh contrast to the Arapesh, whose whole meager and hardworking lives were devoted to growing their children. . . .

But it was the Mundugumor attitude toward children that was decisive. I felt strongly that a culture that rejected children was a bad culture. And so I began to hope—not very logically, but with a kind of emotional congruence—that perhaps after all I could have a child, perhaps I could manage it. . . .

A little later, while we were in Tchambuli, I had a miscarriage, but this did not weaken my renewed belief that somehow I was going to have a child.

Later, when Gregory and I were married and working in Bali, I continued to hope for a child, but once again I had several early miscarriages. Then, in 1938, when we went to the Sepik, it appeared that I might be having a premature menopause—again a doctor's theory. I was sad, but it was the kind of sadness that accompanies a hope that has been sustained. I wanted a child, but I did not feel, as Ruth had felt, that there was no possible compensation for not having a child. If I was now reaching a stage in my life in which it was certain that I could never have a child, I could face that, not with remorse or guilt, but only with regret.

Something very special sometimes happens to women when they know they will not have a child—or any more children. It can happen to women who have never married when they reach the menopause. It can happen to widows with children who feel that no new person can ever take the place of a loved husband. It can happen to young wives who discover they they never can bear a child. Suddenly, their whole creativity is released—they paint or write as never before or they throw themselves into academic work with enthusiasm, where before they had only half a mind to spare for it. . . .

When we returned to Bali for a brief stay in 1939, it appeared that I was, after all, pregnant. And so I was carried up and down the muddy, steep mile from the main road to Bajoeng Gede. The villagers had rigged up a kind of sedan from one of our old bamboo chairs. But the bamboo had dried out, and in the middle of the trip the chair suddenly collapsed on itself and held me as in a vise. That night, in the guesthouse in which we were staying in Kintamani, I had a rather bad miscarriage and the Dutch doctor was summoned. In those days Dutch doctors—indeed all the Dutch—strongly believed in having children. Every hotel room in the Indies had at least one crib, sometimes more. Instead of advising me not to try again for a while, the Dutch doctor said, "You want a child, yes?" and continued with homely advice.

By the time we reached Chicago, on our way back to New York, I thought I was pregnant again. One of the complications in the field is the difficulty of knowing whether you are, or are not, pregnant. But now it was possible to find out and to take precautions. However, we were visiting friends at the University of Chicago and had little time to ourselves; and so, instead of consulting a physician, I asked the secretary of the Anthropology Department to arrange for a test. The result was negative. I was heartbroken. Hope deferred was quite a different thing from resignation to what could not be changed.

Nevertheless, the first few weeks in New York were inexplicably peculiar. Without any good explanation for my mood, I was fretful, irritable, and cantankerous. I even had a sudden attack—the only one I ever had—of morning sickness. But I knew I was not pregnant. Finally, because I felt so strange, we went to a doctor, who said that either I was very pregnant or else I had a tumor and would have to be operated on immediately. The danger of a little knowledge! No one had warned me not to touch alcohol before taking a pregnancy test—and in Chicago, on the night before, we had gone to a big, gay party given by the Ogburns.

From the moment it was certain that I was pregnant, I took extreme precautions. I took a leave of absence from the Museum and gave up riding on streetcars, trains, and buses. I was given vitamin E as an aid to nidification, and I kept the baby.

We had planned to stay in the United States only briefly and then to go to England. There we intended to live in Cambridge, where Gregory held a fellowship in Trinity College. Now it appeared that I might have to have the baby in America and cope with all the tiresome regulations of hospitals and doctors that made breast feeding difficult and prevented a mother from keeping the baby in the room with her. . . .

And so it came about that at thirty-eight, after many years of experience as a student of child development and of childbirth in remote villages—watching children born on a steep wet hillside, in the "evil place" reserved for pigs and defecation, or while old women threw stones at the inquisitive children who came to stare at the parturient woman—I was to share in the wartime experience of young wives all around the world. My husband had gone away to take his wartime place, and there was no way of knowing whether I would ever see him again. We had a little money, a recent bequest from Gregory's aunt Margaret, so I would not have to work until after the baby was born. But that was all. . . .

Mary Catherine Bateson was born on December 8, 1939, and looked very much herself.

But I did have malaria, and the day after the baby's birth my fever shot up. Now my original choice of an obstetrician, as someone who would support what I wanted for the baby, paid off in the mysterious way that a correct choice so often determines that the outcome will be felicitous. For Dr. Heaton, who was open-minded beyond most men of his day, believed me when I said that this was an ordinary attack of tertian malaria, with familiar timing. He said reasonably, "She's had it, and none of us knows anything about it." And he found an ancient book in which quinine was prescribed as a postpartum drug and let me have the thirty grains a day I was accustomed to taking. Someone else might well have diagnosed the malaria as puerperal fever. I would then have been banished from the birth pavilion and my baby would have been put into a nursery to learn the lazy habits of bottle-fed babies and perhaps would never have learned to feed from the breast.

. . . whatever I write is, in a sense, an intrusion into [the] lives [of my family] and their own memories. Yet to ask each one of them to pass judgment on what I am writing would involve all of us in the curious unrealities of a committee approach to work without any of its rewards.

The alternative has been to resolve the difficulties in my own mind as best I could. As I also have resolved the way in which I have been publicly discussed, lambasted and lampooned, lionized and mythologized, called an institution and a stormy petrel, and cartooned as a candidate for the Presidency, wearing a human skull around my neck as an ornament. I have taken the stand, in my own mind and replying to others, that I have no right to resent the public expression of attitudes that I arouse in those whom I do not know and who know me only through what I have written or said and through the words that the mass media, correctly or incorrectly, have attributed to me.

Those whose lives I have touched—and still touch—have to deal with all this also. It is not as if I were a quiet and private person who has suddenly stepped into public view. All those about whom I write here, as well as many people who are closely connected with those about whom I am writing, have already had to put up with me in one way or another.

. . . even now, when for fifty years intensive fieldwork on living primitive societies has been carried out with sophisticated methods, relatively few human scientists understand what our aims have been—and still are—or the nature of the materials that are available to them. Instead of making use of these beautiful materials, materials incorporating the fine details made possible by modern techniques of filming and taping, some of the most brilliant synthesizers still write about a kind of mythical primitive man, much as nineteenth-century armchair philosophers did, as Freud did. When I am given manuscripts to read, brilliant discussions organized with the intention of breaking through the limits of current social science theory, I find, for example, first-class biology but only rags and tatters of what is known and has been well recorded about primitive cultures and the people who embody them. . . .

When I was a graduate student I used to wake up saying to myself, "The last man on Raratonga who knows anything about the past will probably die today. I must hurry." That was when I still dimly understood anthropology as a salvage operation, and knew that we must get to the old men and old women who alone knew about the old way which, once destroyed, could never be reconstructed.

But I did not go to Samoa in 1925 to record the memories of old people about the way titles had once been distributed or how hieroglyphic taboos had been put on trees or to collect still other versions of the tales of Polynesian gods. I did not go as an anti-quarian or as a representative of a discipline whose members were chiefly preoccupied with the peculiarities of kinship systems or with constructions based on primitive myths in which primitive peoples, treated as fossilized ancestors, served to prop up contemporary beliefs about the superiority or degeneration of Western society.

I went to Samoa—as, later, I went to the other societies on which I have worked—to find out more about human beings, human beings like ourselves in everything except their culture. Through the accidents of history, these cultures had developed so differently from ours that knowledge of them could shed a kind of light upon us, upon our potentialities and our limitations, that was unique. No amount of experimental apparatus, however complex, can simulate what it is to be reared as a Samoan, an Arapesh, a Manus, or a Balinese. We can carry out innumerable carefully con-trolled experiments with university students and still know nothing about the kind of thing that studying peoples in different living cultures can teach us. But most people prefer to carry out the kinds of experiments that allow the scientist to feel that he is in full control of the situation rather than surrendering himself to the situation, as one must in studying human beings as they actually live.

Arts and Letters

The seven narratives in this section represent four generations of American women, starting with the earliest able to pursue professional careers in the opening decades of the nineteenth century. Teachers, artists, and writers, these women seem, with one exception, to have been entirely self-made. The inherited southern elite position of Ellen Glasgow (1873–1945) sets her apart from the other women professionals, who had to forge their careers and to support themselves. Yet Glasgow, too, briefly lives a secret life in which she creates her own entirely satisfactory world.

The women of the first two generations remained single in order to be independent, although Glasgow is a transitional figure who cheerfully followed a sexual morality unthinkable for her strict southern Presbyterian father and genteel mother. The women of the later two generations—inhabitants of the twentieth century, inheritors of new ideas about female sexuality—expected marriage to be easily compatible with their driving careers and were obliged to learn, with some pain, that it was not.

Lucy Larcom (1824–1893), the sole representative of the first generation, demonstrates the influence of the early industrial revolution on women's lives. The provision of a life and a source of income outside the domestic sphere gave her both constraints and priceless opportunities. Larcom's progression from impoverished seafaring family through factory work and school teaching to her final role of college professor and editor is unique. She is a transitional figure in her aspiration for personal independence, her educational aims for women, and her religious sensibility, formed by the stern Calvinism of her childhood.

Vida Scudder (1861–1954), Janet Scudder (1869–1940) (a distant cousin of Vida Scudder), and Ellen Glasgow were members of the generation of women shaped by a new feminine consciousness. Whether inheritors of traditional New England or southern culture or of the uncertainties of mercantile life in burgeoning midwestern cities, these women, products of a society that had seen women serve the country in the Civil War, expected to be educated and to have access to higher education. For several of them, influenced by Darwinian ideas, religious faith was of minor or no importance. Janet Scudder found her artistic métier in decorating the houses of America's eastern elites, northern beneficiaries of the war's profits. Vida Scudder and Ellen Glasgow were radical or liberal critics of their society, formed in ways unthinkable for Lucy Larcom by access to nineteenth-century radical and liberal ideas. All these three were markedby the battle for suffrage, in which they were active participants.

Louise Bogan (1897–1970) and Margaret Bourke-White (1904–1971) began their working lives in the late 1920s, a period of liberated life-styles for American women and a time of openness to their professional aspirations. This openness was to be destroyed by the Great Depression, but by then both Bogan and Bourke-White were established in their work. Both ignored Freud's denigration of women as enemies of culture, and both lived as inheritors of the political and sexual rights won by women of the Progressive era. They were beneficiaries unconcerned with advancing those rights further. Bogan, gifted with a bitterly sardonic Irish sense of humor, could mock humorless women's rights advocates. Bourke-White made a place for herself in a world of men and found her important friendships among them.

Maxine Hong Kingston (1940–) is a product of American society after the Second World War. Hers is a voice from the Asian immigrant community, which has played an increasing role in American culture since the 1950s. She too creates herself, remarking bitterly about the choices she must make between conventional American culture and the culture of rural village China, which her redoubtable parents passed on to her. Hers is a strongly feminist voice, politicized by her understanding of the subjection of women in China and by the Chinese countermyths of female avengers, which are lacking in the American culture she seeks to understand.

Each of these women, whatever her generation, educated herself. Their parents could not participate in their worlds. Each, precociously intellectual, taught herself through reading, experiments with technique, travel, and an unquenchable curiosity. In the first two generations, we hear the voice of American sentimental culture, bourgeois and evangelical, at war with the inner voices of women who were forced, in order to be their creative selves, to live in opposition to its comfortable pretenses. By the generation of Bogan and Bourke-White, these pretenses were gone, replaced by apparently unblinking realism. Kingston's weaving of myth and cold reality is postmodern in its complexity and a stark comment on how limited the realist point of view is in understanding women's lives.

Lucy Larcom

(1824–1893)

Millworker, editor, teacher, and poet, Lucy Larcom was the seventh daughter of ten children born to a seafaring Yankee family in Beverly, Massachusetts. Her life history illustrates the extent to which this New England culture was eroding before the forces of the industrial revolution. The death of her father, a sea captain, when she was eleven left her family impoverished. Her widowed mother moved the family to Lowell, where she kept a boardinghouse for millworkers and where her children worked in the textile mills.

Larcom wrote about the idyllic beauty of her coastal village life, but it is clear that she throve in the world of female sociability in the Lowell mills. Although she found the work tedious and the hours long, her excellent education (she was mainly self-taught) enabled her to sustain her intellectual interests and to join in the literary and artistic life of other mill women, who were temporarily working in the mills to finance further education. These interests led Larcom and a group of friends to collaborate in founding the *Lowell Offering*, a literary magazine.

Larcom's religious experience gave meaning and pattern to her life, shaping her response to nature, to other people, to economic forces. Her love of the Old and New Testaments, her childhood reading in Samuel Johnson's dictionary, and her early efforts to teach herself English prosody gave her a powerful prose style, so that her autobiography speaks vividly today, even when its moralizing sentiments seem saccharine.

Moving west in 1846 with her sister Emmeline and her family, Larcom taught school for three years before entering Monticello Seminary, in Illinois, where she was a brilliantly successful student. Returning to Massachusetts after graduation, she taught English literature and rhetoric at Wheaton Seminary in Norton. During her eight years on the faculty, Larcom broadened the curriculum and breathed new life into the school's unusually regimented teaching methods. After 1862 she pursued an independent career in journalism, editing and writing for magazines for children, living part of the year in Boston and part in Beverly.

A NEW ENGLAND GIRLHOOD

It is hardly possible for an author to write anything sincerely without making it something of an autobiography. Friends can always read a personal history, or guess at it, between the lines. . . .

Whatever special interest this little narrative of mine may have is due to the social influences under which I was reared, and particularly to the prominent place held by both work and religion in New England half a century ago. The period of my growing-up had peculiarities which our future history can never repeat. . . .

The religion of our fathers overhung us children like the shadow of a mighty tree against the trunk of which we rested, while we looked up in wonder through the great boughs that half hid and half revealed the sky. Some of the boughs were already decaying, so that perhaps we began to see a little more of the sky than our elders; but the tree was sound at its heart. . . .

We learned no theories about "the dignity of labor," but we were taught to work almost as if it were a religion; to keep at work, expecting nothing else. It was our inheritance, handed down from the outcasts of Eden. And for us, as for them, there was a blessing hidden in the curse. . . .

My "must-have" was poetry. From the first, life meant that to me. And, fortunately, poetry is not purchasable material, but an atmosphere in which every life may expand. I found it everywhere about me. . . .

There were only two or three houses between ours and the main street, and then our lane came out directly opposite the finest house in town, a three-story edifice of brick, painted white, the "Colonel's" residence. There was a spacious garden behind it, from which we caught glimpses and perfumes of unknown flowers. . . .

Beyond the garden were wide green fields which reached eastward down to the beach. It was one of those large old estates which used to give to the very heart of our New England coast-towns a delightful breeziness and roominess. . . .

. . . my father's shop was just at the head of the lane, and we went to school up-stairs in the same building. After he left off going to sea,—before my birth,—my father took a store for the sale of what used to be called "West India goods," and various other domestic commodities.

The school was kept by a neighbor whom everybody called

"Aunt Hannah." It took in all the little ones about us, no matter how young they were, provided they could walk and talk, and were considered capable of learning their letters. . . .

I began to go to school when I was about two years old, as other children about us did. The mothers of those large families had to resort to some means of keeping their little ones out of mischief, while they attended to their domestic duties. Not much more than that sort of temporary guardianship was expected of the good dame who had us in charge.

But I learned my letters in a few days, standing at Aunt Hannah's knee while she pointed them out in the spelling-book with a pin, skipping over the "a b abs" into words of one and two syllables, thence taking a flying leap into the New Testament, in which there is concurrent family testimony that I was reading at the age of two years and a half. Certain it is that a few passages in the Bible, whenever I read them now, do not fail to bring before me a vision of Aunt Hannah's somewhat sternly smiling lips, with her spectacles just above them, far down on her nose, encouraging me to pronounce the hard words. . . .

The Sabbath mornings in those old times had a peculiar charm. They seemed so much cleaner than other mornings! The road and the grassy footpaths seemed fresher, and the air itself purer and more wholesome than on week-days. . . .

The Saturday's baking was a great event, the brick oven being heated to receive the flour bread, the flour-and-Indian, and the rye-and-Indian bread, the traditional pot of beans, the Indian pudding, and the pies; for no further cooking was to be done until Monday. . . .

It was Sabbath in the house, and possibly even on the doorstep; but not much farther. The town itself was so quiet that it scarcely seemed to breathe. The sound of wheels was seldom heard in the streets on that day; if we heard it, we expected some unusual explanation.

I liked to go to meeting,—not wholly oblivious to the fact that going there sometimes implied wearing a new bonnet and my best white dress and muslin "vandyke," of which adornments, if *very* new, I vainly supposed the whole congregation to be as admiringly aware as I was myself. . . .

It was from Aunt Hannah that I received my first real glimpses of the beautiful New Testament revelation. In her unconscious wisdom she chose for me passages and chapters that were like openings into heaven. They contained the great, deep truths which are simple because they are great. . . .

I distinctly remember the day of my christening, when I was between three and four years old. My parents did not make a public profession of their faith until after the birth of all their children, eight of whom—I being my father's ninth child and seventh daughter—were baptized at one time. . . .

Almost the first decided taste in my life was the love of hymns. Committing them to memory was as natural to me as breathing. I followed my mother about with the hymn-book ("Watts' and Select"), reading or repeating them to her, while she was busy with her baking or ironing, and she was always a willing listener. She was fond of devotional reading, but had little time for it, and it pleased her to know that so small a child as I really cared for the hymns she loved. . . .

Usually, the hymns for which I cared most suggested Nature in some way,—flowers, trees, skies, and stars. When I repeated,—

There everlasting spring abides,
And never-withering flowers,—

I thought of the faintly flushed anemones and white and blue violets, the dear little short-lived children of our shivering spring. They also would surely be found in that heavenly land, blooming on through the cloudless, endless year. . . .

We were allowed to take a little nosegay to meeting sometimes: a pink or two (pinks *were* pink then, not red, nor white, nor even double) and a sprig of camomile; and their blended perfume still seems to be a part of the June Sabbath mornings long passed away. . . .

As I think back to my childhood, it seems to me as if the air was full of hymns, as it was of the fragrance of clover-blossoms, and the songs of bluebirds and robins, and the deep undertone of the sea. . . .

The field-paths were safe, and I was allowed to wander off alone through them. I greatly enjoyed the freedom of a solitary explorer among the sea-shells and wild flowers. . . .

The tide itself was the greatest marvel, slipping away so noiselessly, and creeping back so softly over the flats, whispering as it reached the sands. . . .

I listened, and felt through all my little being that great, surging word of power, but had no guess of its meaning. . . .

And the dry land, the very dust of the earth, every day revealed to me some new miracle of a flower. . . .

The busy people at home could tell me very little about the wild flowers, and when I found a new one I thought I was its discoverer. I can see myself now leaning in ecstasy over a small, rough-leaved purple aster in a lonely spot on the hill, and thinking that nobody else in all the world had ever beheld such a flower before, because I never had. I did not know then, that the flower-generations are older than the human race. . . .

Violets and anemones played at hide-and-seek with us in shady places. The gay columbine rooted herself among the bleak rocks, and laughed and nodded in the face of the east wind, coquettishly wasting the show of her finery on the frowning air. Bluebirds twittered over the dandelions in spring. In midsummer, goldfinches warbled among the thistle-tops; and, high above the bird-congregations, the song-sparrow sent forth her clear, warm, penetrating trill,—sunshine translated into music. . . .

The book that I loved first and best, and lived upon in my childhood, was *Pilgrim's Progress*. It was as a story that I cared for it, although I knew that it meant something more,—something that was already going on in my own heart and life. Oh, how I used to wish that I too could start off on a pilgrimage! It would be so much easier than the continual, discouraging struggle to be good! . . .

The lot I most envied was that of the contented Shepherd Boy in the Valley of Humiliation, singing his cheerful songs, and wearing "the herb called *Heart's Ease* in his bosom"; but all the glorious ups and downs of the "Progress" I would gladly have shared with Christiana and her children, never desiring a turn aside into any "By-Path Meadow" while Mr. Great-Heart led the way, and the Shining Ones came down to meet us along the road. . . .

The history of the early martyrs, the persecutions of the Waldenses and of the Scotch Covenanters, I read and reread with longing emulation! Why could not I be a martyr, too? It would be so beautiful to die for the truth as they did, as Jesus did! . . .

One result of my infantile novel-reading was that I did not like to look at my own face in a mirror, because it was so unlike that of heroines always pictured with "high white foreheads" and "cheeks of a perfect oval." Mine was round, ruddy, and laughing with health; and, though I practiced at the glass a good deal, I could not lengthen it by puckering down my lips. . . .

It was fortunate for me that I liked to be out of doors a great deal, and that I had a brother, John, who was willing to have me for an occasional companion. Sometimes he would take me with him when he went huckleberrying, up the rural Montserrat Road, through Cat Swamp, to the edge of Burnt Hills and Beaver Pond. He had a boy's pride in explaining these localities to me, making me understand that I had a guide who was familiar with every inch of the way. . . .

A tattered copy of Johnson's large Dictionary was a great delight to me, on account of the specimens of English versification which I found in the Introduction. I learned them as if they were so many poems. I used to keep this old volume close to my pillow; and I amused myself when I awoke in the morning by reciting its jingling contrasts of iambic and trochaic and dactylic metre, and thinking what a charming occupation it must be to "make up" verses. . . .

My fondness for books began very early. At the age of four I had formed the plan of collecting a library. Not of limp, paper-covered picture-books, such as people give to babies; no! I wanted books with stiff covers, that could stand up side by side on a shelf, and maintain their own character as books. . . .

I regard a love for poetry as one of the most needful and helpful elements in the life-outfit of a human being. It was the greatest of blessings to me, in the long days of toil to which I was shut in much earlier than most young girls are, that the poetry I held in my memory breathed its enchanted atmosphere through me and around me, and touched even dull drudgery with its sunshine. . . .

After my father's death, our way of living, never luxurious, grew more and more frugal. Now and then I heard mysterious allusions to "the wolf at the door"; and it was whispered that, to escape him, we might all have to turn our backs upon the home where we were born, and find our safety in the busy world, working among strangers for our daily bread. Before I had reached my tenth year I began to have rather disturbed dreams of what it might soon mean for me to "earn my own living." . . .

A child does not easily comprehend even the plain fact of death. Though I had looked upon my father's still, pale face in his coffin, the impression it left upon me was of sleep; more peaceful and sacred than common slumber, yet only sleep. My dreams of him were for a long time so vivid that I would say to myself, "He was here yesterday; he will be here again to-morrow," with a feeling that amounted to expectation. . . .

It was hardest of all for my mother, who had been accustomed to depend entirely upon him. Left with her eight children, the eldest a boy of eighteen years, and with no property except the roof that sheltered us and a small strip of land, her situation was full of perplexities which we little ones could not at all understand. . . .

I knew that she believed in God, and in the promises of the Bible, and yet she seemed sometimes to forget everything but her troubles and her helplessness. I felt almost like preaching to her, but I was too small a child to do that, I well knew; so I did the next best thing I could think of—I sang hymns as if singing to myself, while I meant them for her. . . .

That it was a hard world for my mother and her children to live in at present I could not help seeing. The older members of the family found occupations by which the domestic burdens were lifted a little; but, with only the three youngest to clothe and to keep at school, there was still much more outgo than income, and my mother's discouragement every day increased. . . .

During my father's life, a few years before my birth, his thoughts had been turned towards the new manufacturing town growing up on the banks of the Merrimack. . . . From the beginning, Lowell had a high reputation for good order, morality, piety, and all that was dear to the old-fashioned New Englander's heart.

After his death, my mother's thoughts naturally followed the direction his had taken; and seeing no other opening for herself, she sold her small estate, and moved to Lowell, with the intention of taking a corporation-house for mill-girl borders. Some of the family objected, for the Old World traditions about factory life were anything but attractive; and they were current in New England until the experiment at Lowell had shown that independent and intelligent workers invariably give their own character to their occupation. My mother had visited Lowell, and she was willing and glad, knowing all about the place, to make it our home.

The change involved a great deal of work. "Boarders" signified a large house, many beds, and an indefinite number of people. Such piles of sewing accumulated before us! A sewing-bee, volunteered by the neighbors, reduced the quantity a little, and our child-fingers had to take their part. But the seams of those sheets did look to me as if they were miles long!

My sister Lida and I had our "stint,"—so much to do every day. It was warm weather, and that made it the more tedious, for we wanted to be running about the fields we were so soon to leave. One day, in sheer desperation, we dragged a sheet up with us into an apple-tree in the yard, and sat and sewed there through the summer afternoon, beguiling the irksomeness of our task by telling stories and guessing riddles.

It was hardest for me to leave the garret and the garden. In the old houses the garret was the children's castle. The rough rafters,— it was always an unfinished room, otherwise not a true garret,— the music of the rain on the roof, the worn sea-chests with their miscellaneous treasures, the blue-roofed cradle that had sheltered ten blue-eyed babies, the tape-looms and reels and spinning-wheels, the herby smells, and the delightful dream corners,—these could not be taken with us to the new home. . . .

To go away from the little garden was almost as bad. Its lilacs and peonies were beautiful to me, and in a corner of it was one tiny square of earth that I called my own, where I was at liberty to pull on my pinks and lady's delights every day, to see whether they had taken root, and where I could give my lazy morning-glory seeds a poke, morning after morning, to help them get up and begin their climb. Oh, I should miss the garden very much indeed! . . .

One sunny day three of us children, my youngest sister, my brother John, and I, took with my mother the first stage-coach journey of our lives, across Lynnfield plains and over Andover hills to the banks of the Merrimack. We were set down before an empty house in a yet unfinished brick block, where we watched for the big wagon that was to bring our household goods.

It came at last; and the novelty of seeing our old furniture settled in new rooms kept us from being homesick. One after another they appeared,—bedsteads, chairs, tables, and, to me most welcome of all, the old mahogany secretary with brass-handled drawers, that had always stood in the "front room" at home. With it came the barrel full of books that had filled its shelves, and they took their places as naturally as if they had always lived in this strange town. . . .

Most of my mother's boarders were from New Hampshire and Vermont, and there was a fresh, breezy sociability about them which made them seem almost like a different race of beings from any we children had hitherto known.

We helped a little about the housework, before and after school, making beds, trimming lamps, and washing dishes. The heaviest work was done by a strong Irish girl, my mother always attending to the cooking herself. She was, however, a better caterer than the circumstances required or permitted. She liked to make nice things for the table, and, having been accustomed to an abundant supply, could never learn to economize. At a dollar and a quarter a week for board (the price allowed for mill-girls by the corporations) great care in expenditure was necessary. It was not in my mother's nature closely to calculate costs, and in this way there came to be a continually increasing leak in the family purse. The older members of the family did everything they could, but it was not enough. I heard it said one day, in a distressed tone, "The children will have to leave school and go into the mill."

There were many pros and cons between my mother and sisters before this was positively decided. The mill-agent did not want to take us two little girls, but consented on condition we should be sure to attend school the full number of months prescribed each year. I, the younger one, was then between eleven and twelve years old.

I listened to all that was said about it, very much fearing that I should not be permitted to do the coveted work. For the feeling had already frequently come to me, that I was the one too many in the overcrowded family nest. Once, before we left our old home, I had heard a neighbor condoling with my mother because there were so many of us, and her emphatic reply had been a great relief to my mind:—

"There isn't one more than I want. I could not spare a single one of my children."

But her difficulties were increasing, and I thought it would be a pleasure to feel that I was not a trouble or burden or expense to anybody. So I went to my first day's work in the mill with a light heart. The novelty of it made it seem easy, and it really was not hard, just to change the bobbins on the spinning-frames every three quarters of an hour or so, with half a dozen other little girls who were doing the same thing. When I came back at night, the family began to pity me for my long, tiresome day's work, but I laughed and said,—

"Why, it is nothing but fun. It is just like play."

And for a little while it was only a new amusement; I liked it better than going to school and "making believe" I was learning when I was not. And there was a great deal of play mixed with it.

We were not occupied more than half the time. The intervals were spent frolicking around among the spinning-frames, teasing and talking to the older girls, or entertaining ourselves with games and stories in a corner, or exploring, with the overseer's permission, the mysteries of the carding-room, the dressing-room, and the weaving-room.

I never cared much for machinery. The buzzing and hissing and whizzing of pulleys and rollers and spindles and flyers around me often grew tiresome. I could not see into their complications, or feel interested in them. But in a room below us we were sometimes allowed to peer in through a sort of blind door at the great water-wheel that carried the works of the whole mill. It was so huge that we could only watch a few of its spokes at a time, and part of its dripping rim, moving with a slow, measured strength through the darkness that shut it in. It impressed me with something of the awe which comes to us in thinking of the great Power which keeps the mechanism of the universe in motion. . . .

When I took my next three months at the grammer school, everything there was changed, and I too was changed. The teachers were kind, and thorough in their instruction; and my mind seemed to have been ploughed up during that year of work, so that knowledge took root in it easily. It was a great delight to me to study, and at the end of the three months the master told me that I was prepared for the high school.

But alas! I could not go. The little money I could earn—one dollar a week, besides the price of my board—was needed in the family, and I must return to the mill. It was a severe disappointment to me, though I did not say so at home. . . .

I began to reflect upon life rather seriously for a girl of twelve or thirteen. What was I here for? What could I make of myself? Must I submit to be carried along with the current, and do just what everybody else did? No: I knew I should not do that, for there was a certain Myself who was always starting up with her own original plan or aspiration before me, and who was quite indifferent as to what people generally thought.

Well, I would find out what Myself was good for, and what she should be! . . .

In the older times it was seldom said to little girls, as it always has been said to boys, that they ought to have some definite plan, while they were children, what to be and do when they were grown up. There was usually but one path open before them, to become good wives and housekeepers. And the ambition of most girls was to follow their mothers' footsteps in this direction; a natural and laudable ambition. But girls, as well as boys, must often have been conscious of their own peculiar capabilities,—must have desired to cultivate and make use of their individual powers. When I was growing up, they had already begun to be encouraged to do so. We were often told that it was our duty to develop any talent we might possess, or at least to learn how to do some one thing which the world needed, or which would make it a pleasanter world. . . .

All my thoughts about my future sent me back to Aunt Hannah and my first infantile idea of being a teacher. I foresaw that I should be that before I could be or do anything else. It had been impressed upon me that I must make myself useful in the world, and certainly one could be useful who could "keep school" as Aunt Hannah did. I did not see anything else for a girl to do who wanted to use her brains as well as her hands. So the plan of preparing myself to be a teacher gradually and almost unconsciously shaped itself in my mind as the only practicable one. I could earn my living in that way,—an all-important consideration. . . .

I liked the thought of self-support, but I would have chosen some artistic or beautiful work if I could. I had no especial aptitude for teaching, and no absorbing wish to be a teacher, but it seemed to me that I might succeed if I tried. What I did like about it was that one must know something first. I must acquire knowledge before I could impart it, and that was just what I wanted. . . .

I knew I should write; I could not help doing that, for my hand seemed instinctively to move towards pen and paper in moments of leisure. But to write anything worth while, I must have mental cultivation; so, in preparing myself to teach, I could also be preparing myself to write.

This was the plan that indefinitely shaped itself in my mind as I returned to my work in the spinning-room, and which I followed out, not without many breaks and hindrances and neglects, during the next six or seven years,—to learn all I could, so that I should be fit to teach or to write, as the way opened. And it turned out that fifteen or twenty of my best years were given to teaching. . . .

We had also with us now the sister Emilie, . . . who had grown into a strong, earnest-hearted woman. We all looked up to her as our model, and the ideal of our heroine-worship; for our deference to her in every way did amount to that.

She watched over us, gave us needed reproof and commendation, rarely cosseted us, but rather made us laugh at what many would have considered the hardships of our lot. . . .

. . . she was determined that we should not be mentally defrauded by the circumstances which had made it necessary for us to begin so early to win our daily bread. This remark applies especially to me, as my older sisters (only two or three of them had come to Lowell) soon drifted away from us into their own new homes or occupations, and she and I were left together amid the whir of spindles and wheels. . . .

One thing she planned for us, her younger housemates,—a dozen or so of cousins, friends, and sisters, some attending school, and some at work in the mill,—was a little fortnightly paper, to be filled with our original contributions, she herself acting as editor. . . .

It was a cluster of very conscious-looking little girls that assembled one evening in the attic room, chosen on account of its remoteness from intruders (for we did not admit even the family as a public; the writers themselves were the only audience); to listen to the reading of our first paper. We took Saturday evening, because that was longer than the other work-day evenings, the mills being closed earlier. . . .

Our little home-journal went bravely on through twelve numbers. Its yellow manuscript pages occasionally meet my eyes when I am rummaging among my old papers. . . .

At this time I had learned to do a spinner's work, and I obtained permission to tend some frames that stood directly in front of the river-windows, with only them and the wall behind me, extending half the length of the mill,—and one young woman beside me, at the farther end of the row. She was a sober, mature person, who scarcely thought it worth her while to speak often to a child like me; and I was, when with strangers, rather a reserved girl; so I kept myself occupied with the river, my work, and my thoughts. And the river and my thoughts flowed on together, the happiest of companions. Like a loitering pilgrim, it sparkled up to me in recognition as it glided along, and bore away my little frets and fatigues on its bosom. When the work "went well," I sat in the window-seat, and let my fancies fly whither they would,—downward to the sea, or upward to the hills that hid the mountain-cradle of the Merrimack.

The printed regulations forbade us to bring books into the mill, so I made my window-seat into a small library of poetry.

One great advantage which came to these many stranger girls through being brought together, away from their own homes, was that it taught them to go out of themselves, and enter into the lives of others. Home-life, when one always stays at home, it necessarily narrowing. That is one reason why so many women are petty and unthoughtful of any except their own family's interests. We have hardly begun to live until we can take in the idea of the whole human family as the one to which we truly belong. To me, it was an incalculable help to find myself among so many working-girls, all of us thrown upon our own resources, but thrown much more upon each others' sympathies. . . .

And I was every day making discoveries about life, and about myself. I had naturally some elements of the recluse, and would never, of my own choice, have lived in a crowd. I loved quietness. The noise of machinery was particularly distasteful to me. But I found that the crowd was made up of single human lives, not one of them wholly uninteresting, when separately known. . . .

I discovered, too, that I could so accustom myself to the noise that it became like a silence to me. And I defied the machinery to make me its slave. Its incessant discords could not drown the music of my thoughts if I would let them fly high enough. Even the long hours, the early rising, and the regularity enforced by the clangor of the bell were good discipline for one who was naturally inclined to dally and to dream, and who loved her own personal liberty with a willful rebellion against control. Perhaps I could have brought myself into the limitations of order and method in no other way.

Like a plant that starts up in showers and sunshine and does not know which has best helped it to grow, it is difficult to say whether the hard things or the pleasant things did me most good. But when I was sincerest with myself, as also when I thought least about it, I know that I was glad to be alive, and to be just where I was. . . .

I found that I enjoyed even the familiar, unremitting clatter of the mill, because it indicated that something was going on. I liked to feel the people around me, even those whom I did not know. . . . I felt that I belonged to the world, that there was something for me to do in it, though I had not yet found out what. Something to do; it might be very little, but still it would be my own work. . . .

The girls who toiled together at Lowell were clearing away a few weeds from the overgrown track of independent labor for other women. They practically said, by numbering themselves among factory girls, that in our country no real odium could be attached to any honest toil that any self-respecting woman might undertake.

I regard it as one of the privileges of my youth that I was permitted to grow up among those active, interesting girls, whose lives were not mere echoes of other lives, but had principle and purpose distinctly their own. Their vigor of character was a natural development. The New Hampshire girls who came to Lowell were descendants of the sturdy backwoodsmen who settled that State scarcely a hundred years before. Their grandmothers had suffered the hardships of frontier life, had known the horrors of savage warfare when the beautiful valleys of the Connecticut and the Merrimack were threaded with Indian trails from Canada to the white settlements. Those young women did justice to their inheritance. They were earnest and capable; ready to undertake anything that was worth doing. My dreamy, indolent nature was shamed into activity among them. They gave me a larger, firmer ideal of womanhood. . . .

Perhaps the difficulties of modern housekeepers did begin with the opening of the Lowell factories. Country girls were naturally independent, and the feeling that at this new work the few hours they had of every-day leisure were entirely their own was a satisfaction to them. They preferred it to going out as "hired help." It was like a young man's pleasure in entering upon business for himself. Girls had never tried that experiment before, and they liked it. It brought out in them a dormant strength of character which the world did not previously see, but now fully acknowledges. Of course they had a right to continue at that freer kind of work as long as they chose, although their doing so increased the perplexities of the housekeeping problem for themselves even, since many of them were to become, and did become, American housemistresses. . . .

It is the first duty of every woman to recognize the mutual bond of universal womanhood. Let her ask herself whether she would like to hear herself or her sister spoken of as a shop-girl, or a factory-girl, or a servant-girl, if necessity had compelled her for a time to be employed in either of the ways indicated.

The two magazines published by the mill-girls, the *Lowell Offering* and the *Operatives' Magazine,* originated with literary meetings in the vestry of two religious societies, the first in the Universalist Church, the second in the First Congregational, to which my sister and I belonged.

On account of our belonging there, our contributions were given to the *Operatives' Magazine,* the first periodical for which I ever wrote, issued by the literary society of which our minister took charge. He met us on regular evenings, read aloud our poems and sketches, and made such critical suggestions as he thought desirable. This magazine was edited by two young women, both of whom had been employed in the mills, although at that time they were teachers in the public schools—a change which was often made by mill-girls after a few months' residence at Lowell. A great many of them were district-school teachers at their homes in the summer, spending only the winters at their work.

The two magazines went on side by side for a year or two, and then were united in the *Lowell Offering,* which had made the first experiment of the kind of publishing a trial number or two at irregular intervals. My sister had sent some verses of mine, on request, to be published in one of those specimen numbers. . . .

I suppose I should have tried to write,—perhaps I could not very well have helped attempting it,—under any circumstances. My early efforts would not, probably, have found their way into print, however, but for the coincident publication of the two mill-girls' magazines, just as I entered my teens. I fancy that almost everything any of us offered them was published, though I never was let in to editorial secrets. The editors of both magazines were my seniors, and I felt greatly honored by their approval of my contributions. . . .

When a Philadelphia paper copied one of my little poems, suggesting some verbal improvements, and predicting recognition for me in the future, I felt for the first time that there might be such a thing as public opinion worth caring for, in addition to doing one's best for its own sake. . . .

And, indeed, what we wrote was not remarkable,—perhaps no more so than the usual school compositions of intelligent girls. It would hardly be worth while to refer to it particularly, had not the Lowell girls and their magazines been so frequently spoken of as something phenomenal. But it was a perfectly natural outgrowth of those girls' previous life. For what were we? Girls who were working in a factory for the time, to be sure; but none of us had the least idea of continuing at that kind of work permanently. Our composite photograph, had it been taken, would have been the representative New England girlhood of those days. We had all been fairly educated at public or private schools, and many of us were resolutely bent upon obtaining a better education. Very few were among us without some distinct plan for bettering the condition of themselves and those they loved. For the first time, our young women had come forth from their home retirement in a throng, each with her own individual purpose. . . .

Many of them were supporting themselves at schools like Bradford Academy or Ipswich Seminary half the year, by working in the mills the other half. Mount Holyoke Seminary broke upon the thoughts of many of them as a vision of hope,—I remember being dazzled by it myself for a while,—and Mary Lyon's name was honored nowhere more than among the Lowell mill-girls. Meanwhile they were improving themselves and preparing for their future in every possible way, by purchasing and reading standard books, by attending lectures and evening classes of their own getting up, and by meeting each other for reading and conversation.

My return to mill-work involved making acquaintance with a new kind of machinery. The spinning-room was the only one I had hitherto known anything about. Now my sister Emilie found a place for me in the dressing-room, beside herself. It was more airy, and fewer girls were in the room, for the dressing-frame itself was a large, clumsy affair, that occupied a great deal of space. Mine seemed to me as unmanageable as an overgrown spoilt child. It had to be watched in a dozen directions every minute, and even then it was always getting itself and me into trouble. I felt as if the half-live creature, with its great, groaning joints and whizzing fan, was aware of my incapacity to manage it, and had a fiendish spite against me. I contracted an unconquerable dislike to it; indeed, I had never liked, and never could learn to like, any kind of machinery. And this machine finally conquered me. It was humiliating, but I had to acknowledge that there were some things I could not do, and I retired from the field, vanquished.

The two things I had enjoyed in this room were that my sister was with me, and that our windows looked toward the west. When the work was running smoothly, we looked out together and quoted to each other all the sunset-poetry we could remember. . . .

Then she would tell me that my nature inclined to quietness

and harmony, while hers asked for motion and splendor. I wondered whether it really were so. But that huge, creaking framework beside us would continually intrude.

A native professor had formed a class among young women connected with the mills, and we joined it. We met, six or eight of us, at the home of two of these young women,—a factory boarding-house,—in a neat little parlor which contained a piano. The professor was a music-teacher also, and he sometimes brought his guitar, and let us finish our recitation with a concert. More frequently he gave us the songs of Deutschland that we begged for. He sang the "Erl-King" in his own tongue admirably. We went through Follen's German Grammar and Reader:—what a choice collection of extracts that "Reader" was! We conquered the difficult gutturals, like those in the numeral *"acht und achtzig"* (the test of our pronouncing abilities) so completely that the professor told us a native really would understand us! At his request, I put some little German songs into English, which he published as sheet-music, with my name. . . .

A botany class was formed in town by a literary lady who was preparing a school text-book on the subject, and Eliza and I joined that also. The most I recall about that is the delightful flower-hunting rambles we took together. The Linnaean system, then in use, did not give us a very satisfactory key to the science. But we made the acquaintance of hitherto unfamiliar wild flowers that grew around us, and that was the opening to us of another door towards the Beautiful.

Our minister offered to instruct the young people of his parish in ethics, and my sister Emilie and myself were among his pupils. We came to regard Wayland's *Moral Science* (our text-book) as most interesting reading, and it furnished us with many subjects for thought and for social discussion.

Carlyle's *Hero-Worship* brought us a startling and keen enjoyment. It was lent me by a Dartmouth College student, the brother of one of my room-mates, soon after it was first published in this country. The young man did not seem to know exactly what to think of it, and wanted another reader's opinion. Few persons could have welcomed those early writings of Carlyle more enthusiastically than some of us working-girls did. The very ruggedness of the sentences had a fascination for us, like that of climbing over loose boulders in a mountain scramble to get sight of a wonderful land-scape. . . .

So the pleasantly occupied years slipped on, I still nursing my purpose of a more systematic course of study, though I saw no near possibility of its fulfillment. It came in an unexpected way, as almost everything worth having does come. I could never have dreamed that I was going to meet my opportunity nearly or quite a thousand miles away, on the banks of the Mississippi. . . .

The event which brought most change into my own life was the marriage of my sister Emilie. It involved the breaking up of our own little family, of which she had really been the "house-band," the return of my mother to my sisters at Beverly, and my going to board among strangers, as other girls did. I found excellent quarters and kind friends, but the home-life was ended.

My sister's husband was a grammar school master in the city, and their cottage, a mile or more out, among the open fields, was my frequent refuge from homesickness and the general clatter. Our partial separation showed me how much I had depended upon my sister. I had really let her do most of my thinking for me. Henceforth I was to trust to my own resources. I was no longer the "little sister" who could ask what to do, and do as she was told. It often brought me a feeling of dismay to find that I must make up my own mind about things small and great. And yet I was naturally self-reliant. I am not sure but self-reliance and dependence really belong to-gether. They do seem to meet in the same character, like other extremes.

The health of Emilie's husband failing, after a year or two, it was evident that he must change his employment and his residence. He decided to go with his brother to Illinois and settle upon a prairie farm. Of course his wife and baby boy must go too, and with the announcement of this decision came an invitation to me to accompany them. I had no difficulty as to my response. It was just what I wanted to do. I was to teach a district school; but what there was beyond that, I could not guess. I liked to feel that it was all as vague as the unexplored regions to which I was going. My friend and room-mate Sarah, who was preparing herself to be a teacher, was invited to join us, and she was glad to do so. It was all quickly settled, and early in the spring of 1846 we left New England. . . .

The exhilaration of starting off on one's first long journey, young, ignorant, buoyant, expectant, is unlike anything else, unless it be youth itself, the real beginning of the real journey—life. Annoyances are overlooked. Everything seems romantic and dreamlike. . . .

The breaking-up of our little company when the steamboat landed at Saint Louis was like the ending of a pleasant dream. We had to wake up to the fact that by striking due east thirty or forty miles across that monotonous greenness, we should reach our destination, and must accept whatever we should find there, with such grace as we could.

What we did find, and did not find, there is not room fully to relate here. Ours was at first the roughest kind of pioneering experience; such as persons brought up in our well-to-do New England could not be in the least prepared for, though they might imagine they were, as we did. We were dropped down finally upon a vast green expanse, extending hundreds of miles north and south through the State of Illinois, then known as Looking-Glass Prairie. The nearest cabin to our own was about a mile away, and so small that at that distance it looked like a shingle set up endwise in the grass. Nothing else was in sight, not even a tree, although we could see miles and miles in every direction. There were only the hollow blue heavens above us and the level green prairie around us,—an immensity of intense loneliness. We seldom saw a cloud in the sky, and never a pebble beneath our feet. If we could have picked up the commonest one, we should have treasured it like a diamond. Nothing in nature now seemed so beautiful to us as rocks. We had never dreamed of a world without them; it seemed like living on a floor without walls or foundations.

After a while we became accustomed to the vast sameness, and even liked it in a lukewarm way. And there were times when it filled us with emotions of grandeur. Boundlessness in itself is impressive; it makes us feel our littleness, and yet releases us from that littleness.

The grass was always astir, blowing one way, like the waves of the sea; for there was a steady, almost an unvarying wind from the south. It was like the sea, and yet even more wonderful for it was a sea of living and growing things. The Spirit of God was moving upon the face of the earth, and breathing everything into life. We were but specks on the great landscape. . . .

For myself, I know that I was sent in upon my own thoughts deeper than I had ever been before. I began to question things which I had never before doubted. I must have reality. Nothing but transparent truth would bear the test of this great, solitary stillness. As the prairies lay open to the sunshine, my heart seemed to lie bare beneath the piercing eye of the All-Seeing. . . .

I had many peculiar experiences in my log-cabin school-teaching, which was seldom more than three months in one place. Only once I found myself among New England people, and there I remained a year or more, fairly reveling in a return to the familiar, thrifty ways that seem to me to shape a more comfortable style of living than any under the sun. "Vine Lodge" (so we named the cottage for its embowering honey-suckles), and its warm-hearted inmates, with my little white schoolhouse under the oaks, make one of the brightest of my Western memories.

Only a mile or two away from this pretty retreat there was an edifice towards which I often looked with longing. It was a seminary for young women, probably at that time one of the best in the country, certainly second to none in the West. It had originated about a dozen years before, in a plan for Western collegiate education, organized by Yale College graduates. It was thought that women as well as men ought to share in the benefits of such a plan, and the result was Monticello Seminary. The good man whose wealth had made the institution a possibility lived in the neighborhood. Its trustees were of the best type of pioneer manhood, and its pupils came from all parts of the South and West.

Its Principal—I wonder now that I could have lived so near her for a year without becoming acquainted with her,—but her high local reputation as an intellectual woman inspired me with awe, and I was foolishly diffident. One day, however, upon the persuasion of my friends at Vine Lodge, who knew my wishes for a higher education, I went with them to call upon her. We talked about the matter which had been in my thoughts so long, and she gave me not only a cordial but an urgent invitation to come and enroll myself as a student. There were arrangements for those who could not incur the current expenses, to meet them by doing part of the domestic work, and of these I gladly availed myself. The stately limestone edifice, standing in the midst of an original growth of forest-trees, two or three miles from the Mississippi River, became my home—my student-home—for three years. . . .

The course of study at Monticello Seminary was the broadest, the most college-like, that I have ever known; and I have had experience since in several institutions of the kind. The study of mediaeval and modern history, and of the history of modern philosophy, especially, opened new vistas to me. In these our Principal was also our teacher, and her method was to show us the tendencies of thought, to put our minds into the great current of human affairs, leaving us to collect details as we could, then or afterward. We came thus to feel that these were life-long studies, as indeed they are. . . .

I believe that the postponement of these maturer studies to my early womanhood, after I had worked and taught, was a benefit to me. I had found out some of my special ignorances, what the things were which I most needed to know. I had learned that the book-knowledge I so much craved was not itself education, was not even culture, but only a help, and adjunct to both. As I studied more earnestly, I cared for fewer books, but those few made themselves indispensable. It still seems to me that in the Lowell mills, and in my log-cabin schoolhouse on the Western prairies, I received the best part of my early education. . . .

The great advantage of a seminary course to me was that under my broad-minded Principal I learned what education really is: the penetrating deeper and rising higher into life, as well as making continually wider explorations; the rounding of the whole human being out of its nebulous elements into form, as planets and suns are rounded, until they give out safe and steady light. This makes the process an infinite one, not possible to be completed at any school.

Vida Dutton Scudder

(1861–1954)

Vida Dutton Scudder, literary scholar, the only child of New England missionary parents, was born in India but brought back to her mother's Auburndale, Massachusetts, home following her father's death by drowning in 1862. Scudder's maternal family possessed means, so her childhood education was directed by her mother during extended travels in Europe, especially in the Italian and French Mediterranean. Scudder then entered the first class at Girls' Latin School in Boston, going on to enroll in the class of 1884 at Smith College. In the autumn following her graduation from Smith, Scudder spent a term at Oxford, where she attended and reveled in John Ruskin's last lectures. She returned to life in polite Boston on fire with Ruskin's social radicalism and overwhelmed by her inherited privilege.

In 1887 Scudder began teaching English literature at Wellesley College, choosing the teaching post that allowed her to continue to live with her mother, the one individual of whom she was incapable of radical criticism. Here she found a satisfactory setting in which to pursue her intense intellectual life, but her quest for commitment to social justice remained unsatisfied. In 1887 she joined with other women's college alumnae to establish the College Settlement Association. In 1893 she took leave from Wellesley to join in the launching of Denison House, Boston's first settlement, for which she provided dynamic leadership for the next nineteen years.

Scudder also joined the major Christian Socialist organizations of her day, encouraged labor groups to meet at Denison House, and served as a delegate to the council of the Boston Central Labor Union. These affiliations brought her into conflict with her mother and with the trustees of Wellesley College, many of whom demanded her resignation when she opposed the acceptance of what she saw as "tainted money" proffered by the Rockefeller family and when she addressed the striking textile workers of Lawrence, Massachusetts, in 1912.

Clearly torn by the conflict between her social convictions and her sense of responsibility toward a socially conservative mother, Scudder found her release in Anglo-Catholic prayer and meditation. Her religious interests led to her scholarly focus on the history of the Franciscan order and the life of St. Catherine of Siena. These concerns, developed in midlife, flowered after her retirement from Wellesley, when, following a life of literary publications, she established herself as one of the leading Franciscan scholars of her day with her *Franciscan Adventure* (1931). She became a regular lecturer and teacher on religion and social ethics, earning a fresh scholarly reputation.

A prolific writer, sought after speaker, and regular social activist, Scudder also lived an intense contemplative life through her affiliation with the Society of the Companions of the Holy Cross, a group of Episcopalian women dedicated to prayer and intercession for social justice, which she joined in 1889.

Her autobiography reveals both her inner conflicts and the progression of her religious awareness. Her gift for scene and imagery, her lightly conversational tone, and her swift movement from action to reflection give Scudder's memoir the beginnings of a modern, fragmented structure, as though the contending forces in her life could not be woven into a seamless narrative. Yet we see the inner coherence of a life which led her in her mideighties to address a group at the Episcopal Theological Seminary on the topic "Anglican Thought on Property."

ON JOURNEY

I was born in Madura, India, December 15, 1861. But my relations with India were brief. My father, David Coit Scudder, a young missionary under the Congregational Board of Foreign Missions, was drowned when I was a baby. . . .

My mother brought me home at once to her parents, then living in Auburndale, Massachusetts, and I have never been to India since. . . .

. . . the . . . three and a half years spent in Europe, till I was nearly ten years old, were my real childhood. . . .

I was not a very good little girl. I did love to argue, and they called me impertinent, and I was shut in the closet to sob, and I regret to say sometimes to kick; for I never meant to be impertinent, I only wanted—wanted forever, exhaustingly to my poor relatives—to know WHY? . . .

First we were on the Riviera, . . . but the child's memory . . . was awakening slowly to cathedrals, to far shining heights, to the great Italian art, to the world of history, one for her with romance and fairy tale. All these things became part of her before she was nine years old, and they have never ceased to be so. . . .

The Rome of 1869–1870: it was better than any fairy tale to a child. . . .

. . . the Rome of Hawthorne, of Shelley; the Baths of Caracalla were still the awesome shrine of the past, in which "Prometheus Unbound," that glorious vision of the future, was born. . . .

They ended, those happy European years—my sixth to my tenth; and I know, looking back, that they determined what sort of person I should be. Two influences had pervaded me which were always to control my instincts and in large measure to shape my conduct: devotion to beauty, and awed intuition of the human past. Contemporary folk were shadowy to that little girl; but blue gentians on Alpine slopes were real. So were the aqueducts of the Roman Campagna, and the chanting that filled the English cathedrals. Also, the Sistine Madonna.

I am fifteen. I am safely confirmed, and quite serious about it, though entirely bewildered. I have been graduated from Miss Sanger's school, and we are going abroad again, my mother, . . . [my aunt,] . . . and I. . . . this time we stayed a year and a half. . . .

The months were spent mainly in France. We lived with a charming French family, the De Coppets, and I picked up a French which stands me in good stead to this day. We studied the tongue assiduously, till we grew able to chatter in it, and I read with avidity all the French books on which I could lay my hands. My dear mother was equally pleased to have me do so, whatever the nature of the book; and I certainly did browse in queer pastures. "Mélange mine own," as Whitman remarked about the United States.

Novels mainly, of course: all George Sand; Eugène Sue's *Juif Errant*, in cheap blue paper, fine print, and many volumes; *Les Misérables* and *Notre Dame de Paris*, but these did not affect me much, except for the awakening of my incipient medievalism by the latter. . . .

Somehow—I know not how, in that ultra-Protestant family— I came across the *Life of Lacordaire*, written, if I mistake not, by the Père Chocarne. I can not remember much about the book now, and I have never seen it since; but I can almost say that it decided the future direction of my inner life. . . .

From that time, Catholic experience possessed me with that

strange deep sense of home-coming which this experience alone can offer those to whom it belongs. . . .

I did not at that time seriously contemplate becoming a Roman Catholic. But I did think that it might sometime become necessary for me to take the step. The necessity has never arisen, though I have often thought it imminent; for within my own Anglican communion I have been able, once surrendered to its disciplines, to breathe the air I craved. . . .

Even European episodes come to an end, and homeward we wended in the late autumn of 1876. What was the girl like, who returned?

Under much surface eagerness, and keen power of enjoyment in anything and everything life offered, she was not wholly a happy young creature. For she was unable to find reality anywhere. The most solid phenomena disappeared as she encountered them. This sounds absurd, and people may think I am talking nonsense. . . .

It is dreadful to feel the universe evading you wherever you meet it. And as I say, I fancy the experience is not uncommon among children. . . .

On my return to America . . . I became externally a much more normal young person. School and College: the Boston Latin School, and Smith College; 1878–1884, sixteen to twenty-two. . . .

I honor my mother for entering me, in the autumn of 1878, at the much heralded and just organized Girls' Latin School in Boston. She made her decision, so far as I remember, without consulting me; for her daughter never had confided to anyone the private fairy tale wherein, disguised as a boy, she crept into Harvard. My mother used as usual her own judgement; but how gladly I acquiesced! . . .

Time passed; and we went, five of us, to Smith College, entering in 1880, the autumn after the first class, 1879, had been graduated. The institution seemed venerable to us. . . .

. . . to tell the truth, Smith College did not educate me much. I look back at the four years spent there as the period in my whole life during which I was least interested in the things of the mind. This was not wholly the fault of Smith. . . .

I can not quite account for my lapse. It was due perhaps at the outset to the fact that we Latin School girls were exceptionally well prepared. We found freshman studies too easy. There was none of the severe discipline from which we had profited; no marks were given, prospective examinations had, for me at least, no terrors. I took my place easily and casually as a competent student, and that was that. . . .

In those four years I discovered my fellow-beings; one personality after another among these young folks of twenty or under emerged before me as a miracle. . . .

But whether enthusiastic or critical, I was initiated through these contacts into some reality at last. And reality hurt; it always hurts; but it was ecstasy also. One grows under its impact.

Then there was the country. Few regions are lovelier than the Connecticut River valley, uninvaded in those days by the industrialism which has here and there taken possession of it now. It breathed the perfume of old New England. . . . There was joy in the walks across the meadows, in climbs up those miniature mountains, Tom and Holyoke, so tiny yet so full of character; in the dignity and homely peace of the broad elm-shaded streets. . . .

. . . two teachers claimed my chief allegiance. One was Stuart Phelps; his tragic death at the outset of my senior year deflected my intellectual purpose. Under his brilliant guidance, I had had a tantalizing glimpse of what philosophic studies might mean, but no other guidance of quality was offered when the emergency of his death arose, and I turned away. The other, the man I most honored after President Seelye, was Professor J. B. Clark, later of Columbia. This true, gentle scholar, fresh from Germany, presenting those strange subjects, economics and sociology, opened, had I known it, vistas into a new world. . . .

But when the death of Professor Phelps changed the set of my interests, I turned, as I might have done in any case, to English studies. . . .

A specialist called to examine us all at the outset of senior year, said that this young lady—meaning me—was suffering from double curvature of the spine. . . .

I was discouraged from attending class appointments; and I resigned myself to a luxurious senior year. The college was generously lenient as to "the academic"; I wrote a lot of papers which proved acceptable—one or two even got printed; and I did attend some classes—those I liked best! To make a long story short, I worried through the year happily enough, and received my degree on that occasion construed by many a college girl as the end of all things, known ironically as Commencement. . . .

. . . I was . . . grateful when I was taken to Europe in the autumn for the completion of a cure already well under way, my mother and I never to separate again till the Great Parting, thirty-five years later. . . .

Our destination was Oxford, where Clara [a Smith classmate] had serious study in view. Privileges there were just being tentatively opened to women; and if I am not mistaken, we were the first American girls to enjoy them. I went, not intending to study, being still supposed to be an invalid, but because I might as well go there as anywhere else. We four settled in lodgings opposite Worcester College Gardens, and since I was myself, I inevitably resumed a student life. . . .

. . . it was at Oxford that I woke up to the realities of modern civilization, and decided that I did not like them. I went there with an intellectual life vague and empty. . . .

I came away, not a convinced socialist—that was for five or six years later—but with a social radicalism nebulous enough, yet thundery and intense, a good bit of lightning playing about in it.

John Ruskin was largely responsible. We heard the last course of lectures he was to give, and that our privilege was great we were well aware. . . .

"Laissez Faire" was in its hey-day then; it is deliquescent now, though it lingers in the liking for "Rugged Individualism." But the bitter feeling aroused by that book of Ruskin's, presenting social ideas boldly founded on the Bible, would be incredible today, had not Roosevelt's New Deal, based on many of the same ideas, met in some quarters with the same reception. In any case, Ruskin, a hypersensitive man, had suffered keenly,—less from any fall into personal disfavor than from the public hostility to his thinking. . . .

This awakening was, I suppose, a major event in my inner life. It had a queer episodic expression. I was impelled—in Oxford, of all places!—to join the Salvation Army, which was leading a fervent semi-underground existence among those historic streets. Fifty years later I presume it would have been the communists whom I should have wished to join; but their day was not yet. . . .

As I said, I was not working for academic status, or facing any test. Had I gone to Oxford some fifteen or twenty years later, I should probably have done so; and, to be candid, my lack of a Ph.D. has mortified me at times. But, just as the thought of earning money did not occur to me till my life's purpose had been pretty well determined, so study to the end of a degree never at that time crossed my mind. Study was an end in itself, as my teaching was to be.

[On Scudder's return in 1886] my little doctor aunt ... had bought and furnished a pretty house, No. 250 Newbury Street, in the Back Bay of Boston, and had arranged for my mother and me to share it. It was taken for granted that we three belonged together. So there we were, settled in what was to be my home for twenty-five years. ...

I led outwardly a pleasant life, but it was aimless and groping. ...

For lack of anything better to do, I worked on a thesis which was to win me the M.A. at Smith College. The paper, bearing on science as a feeder to modern poetry, was later incorporated in my first book, *The Life of the Spirit in the Modern English Poets*. ...

It was Professor George Herbert Palmer who came to the rescue, putting my feet, as he put the feet of so many other young people, in the appointed path. ...

Perhaps such insight guided his suggestion to my mother that I apply for a position to teach English literature at Wellesley College. ...

So came the sudden call to a profession which, curiously enough, had never occurred to me. I had tried to be an artist, and failed; I had dreamed of being an author, and made no headway. Marriage, as I had always serenely suspected, without regrets, was not for me. ...

I was to teach at Wellesley, as instructor, associate professor and professor, till my retirement in 1927. As I went back for some special work in the spring of 1934, and still meet a class now and then, I might say that my academic career lasted nearly half a century. Till 1927, Wellesley was the center of my energy. This was partly because I loved my teaching so well, but also partly for the salutary reason that, when other interests clamored at my door and inevitable periods of weariness and revulsion came, this was the work I was paid to do. ...

The practical side of me was pleased when at the end of the academic year I was told that I had made good and was invited to return on a three-year appointment. An uneasy sense of future choice haunted me. But this work fitted admirably into my duties toward my mother. ...

It was at this time that I became a member of the Society of Companions of the Holy Cross. The act did not mean that my religious vision had cleared; my faith was still provisional. . . .

The Companionship of the Holy Cross when I entered it was a small group of perhaps forty or fifty women, members of the Protestant Episcopal Church, pledged to the Way of the Cross and to the practice of intercessory prayer. . . .

[At Wellesley] the modern field was for some time assumed to be mine, but before long instincts and tastes drove me irresistibly backward. . . .

I slipped away from desire to teach the nineteenth century. Friends are justified, I suspect, who tell me laughing that my real home is either in the Middle Ages or in the Utopian future; I know that in both the nineteenth and the twentieth century, I have often felt homesick enough. . . .

Very pleased I was . . . to offer work in Arthurian romance, centered in Sir Thomas Malory's *Morte d'Arthur*. Such a course is common now but I think it was seldom given anywhere at that time. . . .

Arthurian romance spans the Middle Ages, from the twelfth century to the fifteenth. . . . When first I offered my course, I was living my mental life, as shall be told, chiefly in the fourteenth century, with hankerings after the thirteenth; Malory led me back to the twelfth through his sources, and onward to the edge of the Renaissance through his tone and quality. . . .

The other course I founded faced toward the future. . . . It bore the title: "Social Ideals in English Letters." I first offered it in spite of administrative disapproval and departmental indifference, in the later Nineties, as a one-hour lecture course.

Ever since my Oxford days, I had been beating my wings against the bars,—the customs, the assumptions, of my own class. I moved in a garden enclosed, if not in a hothouse, an enclosure of gracious manners, regular meals, comfort, security, good taste. I liked the balmy air. Yet sometimes it suffocated me. I wanted to escape, where winds buffeted, blowing free. The spirit of adventure drives some men to explore the Gobi desert, or to seek the Pole; others to research in the buried past, or to travel among alien races. Me, it filled with a biting curiosity about the way the Other Half lived, and a strange hunger for fellowship with them. Were not the workers, the poor, nearer perhaps than we to the reality I was always seeking? . . .

To rouse the coming generation to know and feel that justice could only be won at cost of a tremendous crusade of social upheaval: that was my first hope in drawing people into settlements. And the fact that as a college teacher I held a position of vantage served as partial compensation for my own inability to live in one of our Houses. Nevertheless, that inability was bitter to me. . . .

Helena Stuart Dudley . . . abandoned the career full of promise on which she was happily embarked and for which she had prepared at a sacrifice: that of a scientist, a teacher of biology. Resigning her position at Packer Institute in Brooklyn, she offered herself to our Eastern settlement movement. After one year in Philadelphia, she came to Denison House in the autumn of 1893.

There, until my mother and I moved away from Boston in 1912, was the center of my social interests and was also, I may almost say, my spiritual home. . . .

. . . my interests at the College were purely academic, and I would hurry home as soon as classes and office hours were over, and speed me whenever strength allowed to Tyler Street. I can truly say that I knew the life of Denison House from within and shared all its developments. . . .

It was a grief to me that I could not share the community life at the College; and the loss was real. But one has to choose, and the center of my social living was at that dear House at the South End, where fifteen hundred people a week were presently passing through our pretty Green Room. I had wanted to escape from my class prison; and I did. . . .

Living among those very poor people, my sense of values changed curiously. I was used to hard self-respecting New England, insensibly dominated by the fundamental duty of paying one's debts, after which, if one had a fairly safe bank balance, the luxury of charity might be enjoyed. I found, half a mile away, a different psychological make-up. The patience of the poor! Their amiability, crowded as they were into those mean tenements! Their extraordinary hospitality! I thought how carefully we planned our guests for our one dainty guest-room. . . . Here, with matter-of-fact readiness, in time of need, one more child, a derelict friend out of work, any neighbor in distress, would be added to the cramped quarters. . . . Untidiness, of course. Smells, hitherto unknown. What did it matter? . . .

What settlements could accomplish in helpful ministration among "the submerged tenth" would, I perceived from the outset, amount to precious little. What we could achieve was next to nothing. But women who entered into settlement residence would be transformed and enlightened. . . .

Certainly, in those early days, settlements meant for many among the young intelligentsia what membership in the communist party means today. . . .

Was I hoping for further change in attitude, besides making people face the situation? Yes, I was. Early in this phase of my life, I became ardently and definitely a socialist; though I cannot remember when I took out my red card. I did not see how any one could live among poor working people for even a short time, and be anything else; wherein my youthful intolerance was all too evident. . . .

Bureaucratic, limited, the conceptions of those Fabians? Never looking beyond the horizons of state socialism and a municipal milk supply? Well, perhaps. I read Marx a little later, carefully, and to great profit. And of course we have moved on and penetrated deeper. . . . Moreover, I was a Fabian with a difference. For the ultimate source of my socialist convictions was and is Christianity. Unless I were a socialist, I could not honestly be a Christian, and although I was not sure I dared call myself by that name, I could use no other. . . .

But in my modest home on the Boston Back Bay, my mother, aunt, and I lived simply indeed but in dainty peace. . . .

[My mother] would gladly have spared me to the mission field, but she never understood my radicalism, and I did not force it on her. Now a certain text, "Whoso loveth father or mother more than Me," always tormented me; and had I been of more heroic fiber, I might have behaved differently. But common sense came to my aid. To abandon my profession for the undefined realm of social activities, would have meant exchange of sure usefulness for doubtful values. . . .

The time had come when to reach distinction in the academic world I should have secured a Ph.D. My first interlude, when in '93–'95 I took two years away from the College, gave me opportunity. But I devoted the first half of that period chiefly to settlements; in the second half, I got over to France for courses at the Sorbonne, but I ignored systematic study for a degree. Truth to tell,

I was impatient then, as sometimes now, with Ph.D. research. What I cared for was to keep my students as well as myself in the presence of significant racial experience, embedded in forms of undying beauty; I thought that was what America needed, and I was indifferent to rummaging about in literary byways in pursuit of unimportant information. . . .

As for social activities, they demand the whole of you. Didn't I know it? My best impulses, compounded of shame and of adventurous urge toward trail-making, pointed that way. . . .

When the time came to retire on a Carnegie pension, the old problem, quiescent but never solved, was acutely renewed for me. I wanted to refuse that money, and I could have done so and not starved. But I took it. I decided that my legal claim on it involved moral responsibility for its use. So I spend it year by year, on radical social causes mostly religious in character and inspired if not endorsed by the Church; thereby seeking to hack off the branch I sit on. I have been amused, and easy in my conscience; only, if the Revolution proceeds with quickened tempo, and dividends continue to crumble, I may be forced any day to the sad expedient of endowing myself as a revolutionary force. . . .

Perplexities, and opportunities, came to a head toward the end of the years I am reviewing, in the famous Lawrence strike of 1912. . . .

I went to Lawrence. I attended strike meetings, and was tremendously impressed by the able leadership which secured unity of action in that seething ferment where cross currents of racial and religious antagonism constantly interfered below the surface—I forgot how many languages were spoken by the strikers. I visited the workers' homes, bad enough to justify almost any revolt in my indignant eyes. I lunched at the Franco-Belge Co-operative, recognizing in that group, well versed as they were in revolutionary technique, the most competent among the strikers. And recognition grew on me of the amazing disciplines in comradeship and corporate action afforded to wage-earners by such grim warfare, offering as it does release from tread-mill monotony and sordid individual interests, into that consciousness of group life.

. . . in March 1901: . . . on the train one evening, returning from college where I had been hostess to some distinguished guest, something crashed in my head. I was used to severe headaches; this was different. I staggered home, and for many weeks lay sleepless in a darkened room, with explosions of such pain as I didn't know possible going on inside my brain. . . .

The doctors diagnosed no organic trouble, but deep exhaustion which would be slow to conquer; and, forced into this unknown sphere of passive suffering, I found myself not wholly unreconciled, when once adjustments involving other people had been made. I must here, however, reluctantly, write a little about my religious life.

Yearly my respect grew for Catholic theology. Every article in the historic creeds, with the exception of that postulating personal survival, held for me suggestion of something revealed not by thinking, but by life. I was no literalist; the Latin term for the creed, *Symbolum*, has always been a comfort to me; but the Christian "Symbol" reflected deeper as well as wider experience than any other of which I was cognizant. Ancient formulae may, of course, fall dead on the ear as cultures change; the language of the past seems alien to the unthinking. But I am cautious about rejecting such language lightly, for the reason that it brings report from a plane where neither need nor perception alters much from age to age. Religious formulae, far more than scientific, enshrine permanent, I dare to say eternal, values; and to refuse to use formulae at all in religion was not to be honest but to capitulate to the principle of isolation, which is death. I thought sadly at times that honesty was impossible to me; but neutrality is impossible in these matters; and I was inwardly assured that it would be less honest for me to range myself with those who denied than with those who affirmed.

[While in Europe recovering from her emotional collapse, Scudder began to study the lives of St. Francis of Assisi and St. Catherine of Siena.]

I do not think that I went to Assisi with any definite purpose, though my mood was that of the pilgrim rather than the tourist; for in Assisi, as in Palestine, many a traveler can say

The earth did undertake
The office of a priest.[1]

---

1. Thomas Traherne, *The Poetical Works of Thomas Traherne with Poems of Felicity*, edited with a preface and notes by Gladys I. Wade, P.J. and A.E. Dobell, London, 1932, p. 159.

... People were no longer driving to Assisi for an hour; they were realizing that the little town was not only holy ground, but also a treasure house of Italian art. Quite outgrown was the attitude of Goethe, who visited the place to see the Temple of Minerva, and never mentioned the Lower Church. Most visitors now stayed, as I did, at the old Hotel Subasio, next the *piazza* of the church and overlooking the wide Umbrian plain. ...

Catherine knew greater strain on her loyalty than we, for the Church in her day tolerated not only diffused worldliness but shocking corruptions. ... When Urban VI, that fierce fanatic, replaced the cultured, ineffective Gregory XI, whom she had persuaded to leave his pleasant exile in Avignon, we find Catherine writing: "It seems our new Christ-on-earth is a terrible man." He was; she served him faithfully; but pain struck deep. She knew the deathly apathy engendered by the sense of defeat at the heart of life. "Oh me, oh me," she wrote; "I see the Christian religion lying dead, and I neither mourn nor weep over it." ...

So, through my fellowship with her and her disciples, I finally worked out the answer to my old sorrowful question as to honest adherence to institutional religion. Loyalty was hard for one who had always sought reality in the positive, the assured. But it was the most sincere thing possible to me, and I deemed it worth the price of freedom.

In the autumn of 1912, my mother and I moved from Boston to Wellesley, where we had built us the house from which I am writing. To globe-trotters the change may seem like that of the Vicar of Wakefield, from the blue room to the brown, but to us it was momentous. It meant, for me, the surrender of some cherished interests, but it also offered new freedom.

The World War broke in August 1914. ... The war was not only a world event of the first magnitude; it was also an interior event to every one then living. No one emerged from those war years quite the same person as entered them. ...

I was writing my book on Malory's *Morte d'Arthur*, and my spirit responded to the challenge in the great oath of Arthur's knights with its code for the Christian fighter, to which they were sworn every year at the high Feast of Pentecost, the Festival of the Holy Spirit.

My apologia for war was contained in one word: chivalry. That word connotes heroism raised to the nth degree of sacrifice; it connotes the defense of the weak, and it implies a world which is a battlefield. Fighting is the condition of real living; and where fighting goes on, some one must be defeated. . . .

Already I had turned from aggressive war, waged on whatever provocation. But I had gone further: I did not believe in personal self-defense. I had read my Tolstoy too long, not to speak of my New Testament.

On the surface, our Wellesley life flowed serene, clear, and not without sparkle; but there were dark undercurrents. Helena Dudley, with all her Christian courage and wide personal sympathies, was a sorrowful woman; we all found it hard to maintain steady faith, in those post-war years. There is a worse type of Depression than the economic; such was shared by most people who in the pre-war period had joyously hailed what seemed the rising forces of social redemption. The Great War had not made the world safe for democracy; intelligent reformers had never expected it to do so, yet it was not easy to watch the surging flood of disillusion which threatened to submerge the idealism and drown the hopes of the world, nor to see the reforms on which hope and effort had centered, hardly with exception halted or destroyed. Those ten exhausted years were the most discouraged I have known, and I say this in 1936. . . .

In 1927 the natural term of professional life was reached, and I retired from teaching, though I continued to make my home in Wellesley. St. Francis used to say gaily to his brothers in the last months of his life: "Now let us begin to be Christians." I had a like sense of beginning; an exhilarating and absurd feeling of youth overswept me. . . .

So, with grateful encompassing sense of leisure, I completed my book at last. For twelve years I had been working on it, through interruptions and at intervals; since my retirement in 1927 it had been central not only in my purpose but in my activity. . . .

Most lovers of Francis paused with the saint himself; I, however, continually thought of Christianity in terms not only of personal but of social salvation. . . .

But my devotion to him, at first rather vaguely religious and wholly private, became a sharp-pointed instrument of inquiry into the whole relation of Christianity to the ethics of private ownership.

It is in my two romances, *The Disciple of a Saint* and *Brother John*, that I have come nearest to self-expression. . . .

This book has . . . at least aimed at being an accurate transcript of my adventures, spiritual and otherwise, in this maze of a world. . . .

Reality, like beauty, is in relationship and there only. I am no Berkeleian. The seeing eye does not invent the landscape. Something is there, though it is never what I see. At some point in the union of my faculty of sight with external nature, reality occurs; I would better say my reality, as opposed to yours, which can never be the same. . . .

Reality, I said, is in relationship alone. This is true, not only on the natural and sensible plane, but on that other plane, where consciousness, forever baffled, yet persists in contemplating one or another spiritual landscape, and in endeavoring to report and verify what is revealed. I know God only as I know the view; and your view can not be mine. Yet the vision vouchsafed to you and me by "sight of soul," to use the beautiful medieval phrase, is authentic, and summoning. That it is ultimate reality, no one dares assume. But it has reality for me. And the landscape beckons. Laus Deo!

Janet Scudder

(*1869–1940*)

Janet Scudder was the third daughter and fifth child of a Terre Haute, Indiana, confectioner and his first wife, a woman of impeccable Puritan lineage. Sent to the Cincinnati Academy of Art at age eighteen, Scudder discovered her talents as sculptor and wood-carver. Moving to Chicago in 1891, she found her way to the studio of the sculptor Lorado Taft, then at work on the extensive monuments planned for the World's Columbian Exposition in 1893.

Work in Taft's studio and the sight of the fountain sculpted by Frederick MacMonnies for the Honor Court of the exposition convinced Scudder of her vocation and prompted her, despite her penniless state, to set out for Paris in 1893. Here she quickly persuaded MacMonnies to take her on as a pupil, and within months she was one of his assistants.

When her critical eye and lack of tact aroused the jealousies of MacMonnies's other assistants in 1894, Scudder fled precipitously back to New York, where she experienced some grim months of little shelter and less food before securing her first commission through the intercession of a friend. A stream of commissions enabled her to return to Paris in 1896. While technically proficient, Scudder did not discover her métier as a sculptor until a trip to Italy enabled her to see the work of Donatello and Verrocchio, and to view sculpture as an expression of the drive to decorate and amuse.

Thereafter, whether in New York or in her Paris studio, Scudder worked in partnership with architects (the most distinguished being Stanford White) to enhance and decorate public space. She also earned much recognition for her portrait medallions, accents on the living, rather than the funerary monuments she saw as distorting the sculptor's calling in the United States.

A resident of France from 1909 until the year before her death, Scudder served energetically with the YMCA and the Red Cross to bring comforts and entertainment to the troops in France in 1917–18 while completing many of her own projects, ten of which were exhibited at the Pan-Pacific Exposition of 1915.

An extremely prolific artist, Scudder achieved her professional success with habits of discipline and with her determination to gain recognition for her work. Her autobiography reveals a narrator with a granite will and a passion for beauty which would not go unsatisfied. Her father's second marriage and her subsequent distance from her family left Scudder free to set out for Paris at age twenty-four unimpeded by genteel conventions about unchaperoned travel and able to live there unconstrained by family pressures to return.

MODELING MY LIFE

W hat do you think it was that made you decide to devote your life to art?" a friend once asked me.

This friend knew something about me, that I was born in Terre Haute, Indiana, in the '70's [sic], in surroundings utterly devoid of any artistic traditions and made dismal by poverty—all tremendous burdens for a young woman determined to hitch her wagon to a star.

The question sent my thoughts wandering back through the past for an answer until they stopped before the tiny figure of myself when I was about six years old. I had been out in the garden playing with the flowers. The colors evidently stirred something latent in me for I can remember, as distinctly as though it had happened yesterday, the feeling of intense excitement that swept over me and carried me into the house and up to my grandmother. . . .

"How did they ever get these beautiful colors?" I demanded breathlessly, holding a small bunch of flowers out towards her.

She put out her hand and touched me and then the flowers—for she had been blind for many years—and very solemnly and impressively explained that colors were given flowers by God.

"He painted them!" I gasped.

She nodded, still very solemn.

"How?"

At this she laid down her knitting and her voice came a bit uneasily. "Why do you ask that, my child?"

"Because I want to paint some just like them. I've got to! I must!"

I am sure the creative instinct was born at that moment. . . .

It was my father who realized, though he never admitted it, that I hated the idea of having to become a school teacher, . . . following the footsteps of my eldest sister Martha, who had undertaken that profession. . . .

I'm sure he chuckled to himself when I deliberately failed in the high school examinations, writing all the foolish answers I could think of to the questions so that I could not possibly be given a teacher's certificate.

The excitement of arriving in Cincinnati had nothing to do with the fact that it was my first visit to a large city; it was all due to that Academy of Art. All the details of being met by an uncle I had never seen and taken to a boarding house on Walnut Hills, where arrangements had been made for me to stay, made no impression. My eyes and my heart were straining in the direction of that seat of learning where something within me—I wasn't yet quite sure what—was going to burst into full bloom.

The first glimpse of the building sent a chill through me; I suppose it would even now if I should see it again; it was of gray stone, ominous, cold—exactly the sort of building you see from train windows and are told is the state penitentiary or lunatic asylum. . . .

There is something fundamental about drawing from geometrical solids; you are working from the outside in—not from the inside out. Somehow it rather suggests to me the need of a writer to know how to spell and punctuate before he can compose a really finished sentence.

From these solids I went on to drawing detached features—feet, hands, ears, noses, eyes—all from plaster casts; then came anatomical figures eight feet high. Three months were supposed to be spent on each anatomical drawing; three months on the front view, three months on the back view, and three months on the profile—the drawings being eight feet in length, as the figure. Every subcutaneous muscle was shown on the plaster figure, and we were supposed to reproduce them in the drawing. Connected with this work were other studies of anatomy. We had to read books on the subject and attend lectures; we even had to be present at the dissecting of a corpse, at which time we were shown muscles and ligaments and layers of flesh as they actually exist.

I studied anatomy prodigiously and have found sculpture immeasurably more alluring in consequence. I understand subcutaneous muscles now, know their sources and their effect upon each other. I learned all their names and could rattle them off without an effort. . . .

I entered every class in existence and was working every hour of the day and often in the evening; and yet, for some strange reason, I had not discovered the one class that was to mean so much to me.

This discovery came about quite casually. I had noticed from time to time very untidy-looking students going in and out of a room on the basement floor; I hadn't an idea what the white stuff was that covered their aprons nor what the work was that they were doing—plaster and clay meant nothing to me then. One day, seeing all these strange-looking students go out and leave the door open after them, I crept in to see what on earth could have been going on in that room. It was a bare room with high windows, much like all the others; but what caught my attention at once was that the floor and tables and walls were covered with plaster casts. Another drawing class, I thought; but there were no easels or quantities of paper and pencils about. It must be some form of art that I had not heard about. I approached an object covered with a damp cloth. I gingerly raised the cloth and found a wet clay bust in the process of formation. I next found a mound of soft clay. I picked up a handful, rolled it between my fingers and suddenly felt an almost overwhelming delight course through me. The feel of that clay in my hand was entirely different from anything I had ever experienced before. Just the mere sensual part of it, the touch, seemed to fire me with something tremendously stimulating.

Gradually it came over me that I was standing in the sculpture class room; and with this knowledge came a flaring resentment that no one had ever told me it existed. There I had been studying all those other things for months and not even hearing about this branch of art. I rushed upstairs, entered the secretary's room and spent an impatient half hour awaiting his return in order to announce that I wanted to enter the modeling class at once. . . .

I was told to begin modeling—copying—a plaster cast of a foot, always a difficult thing to do even after years of experience. But the feel of that wet clay in my hands was sufficient joy to overcome any moments of discouragement. I neglected everything else—even the money-making wood-carving—to work in the modeling room. I spent weeks on that foot, glancing only now and then at some shelves which were piled up with casts of faces and one or two figures. When, oh, when, would I be allowed to copy them! Two of them held special inspiration for me—a mask of a smiling boy and the head of a man. When I eventually copied these two favorites and carried them home with me, I told my friends that the boy had no name, but the head of the man was a portrait of King Lear. I didn't know any better—and no one in the class apparently did; at least no one took the trouble to tell me what these casts were. It was not until several years later, when I was wandering through the Louvre, that I recognized the boy as being Rude's Neapolitan Fisher Boy; and still later, when standing spellbound before the Arc de Triomphe in Paris, whom should I meet looking down at me from the Victory group, by the same artist, but that face that I had so long thought was a portrait of King Lear! . . .

I worked on that clay foot for weeks and weeks; as a matter of fact I very likely would still be working on it if it hadn't been for the appearance one day of a most perfectly tailor-made girl with a really lovely head. She blew into the class room one afternoon when I was there entirely alone, asked for the instructor and was on the point of going out when she happened to glance at the foot I was still struggling over.

"How long did it take you to do that?" she asked.

"I've been at it three weeks," I replied.

"Three weeks! Aren't you ever going to cast it?"

I blushed furiously. To be perfectly honest, I didn't know what she meant. I took refuge in saying I didn't know how to cast it.

"Would you like me to show you?"

"But—ought I? Would they let me?"

She glanced round and smiled. "No one's here. Let's do it."

She picked up a blouse some one had left hanging over a chair, carefully covered her pretty dress and went efficiently to work to cast my foot. She evidently knew what she was about, so I stood off and stared at her in amazement.

She first looked about for a long piece of stout thread, which, when found, she laid very carefully down the center of my clay foot. Then she went to a corner of the room where basins and barrels of plaster and water were kept, filled a basin half full of water, dropped a small blue ball in it which colored the water lightly, sifted into this several handfuls of plaster which she let flow slowly through her fingers. When the plaster had settled down under the water, she took a large spoon and began stirring it from the bottom. After the bubbles had all disappeared, the basin was carried to my clay foot and my new and most capable friend—much to my consternation—began throwing little handfuls of the plaster between the toes, and finally all over the foot, until my work of weeks was entirely hidden from view in a thin coat of blue plaster. While this was hardening she very carefully pulled up the thread so that a small open seam was made, running down the center of the plaster. The process was continued with another mixture of clay, this time white, though in adding this second coat the seam was never covered. When this second coat was quite hard, she took a chisel and worked gently along the edges of the seam until the plaster fell apart leaving two empty parts—the mold of my foot. These pieces were washed thoroughly, soaked, oiled, tied together with an opening left at the top and finally another mixture of quite liquid plaster was poured in until the empty center was filled.

"Now—we'll leave it until to-morrow," my amazingly accomplished friend said, covering the whole mass with a cloth. "I'll drop in about noon and we'll see what luck we've had." And before I could say anything or thank her or tell her how wonderful I thought she was, she had disappeared.

The next morning I was afraid to remove the cloth by myself. I awaited impatiently the arrival of what I was sure now was a famous sculptor who had appeared out of the void and so suddenly returned to it. She came at noon, soon found a hammer and chisel and began chipping away the white plaster and then, more carefully, the blue; there, at last, gleaming at me in all the glory of fresh white plaster was my first piece of sculpture.

There are no words that would express convincingly my sensations when I saw a plaster cast of my work there before me.

I thought my father's death would surely mean the end of all my ambitions, so far as further study in Cincinnati went; how he was ever able to send me there was never explained; but now that he was gone I supposed I must abandon all hope of returning to the Academy that autumn. But though life may be a fairly continuous gray, it is rarely all black, as that summer was. I still look back on it with a shudder. Then, as is invariably the case, the silver lining began to show through ominous clouds. My eldest brother, now married and living in Chicago, took pity on me and offered to pay for my next season at the Academy in Cincinnati.

This third year probably I made some progress—one usually advances in some direction—though now that I think of it, it seems to have been almost a waste of time. I really learned very little. Everything there must have been frightfully dull and wanting in anything that developed originality or personality. Perhaps this was due to the fact that the Academy was run and directed almost entirely on Munich art school traditions. I went on modeling, with now and then help and encouragement from Professor Ribisso; but on the whole it seems to have been a time given in great measure to that ever-present wood-carving which helped out my living expenses. I was sure the fates or the devil, or whatever my evil influences are, were determined to make and keep me a wood-carver.

At the end of the second term and with another ghastly summer facing me, my brother once more came to the rescue. He wrote that if I would come to Chicago, help his wife a bit with the housekeeping and the new baby, I could live with them and surely find something to do in my chosen profession. . . .

Again a silver lining, this time in the form of Lorado Taft, who I heard was employing assistants in his studio! It took me about ten minutes after I had heard this to reach the top story of an office building, where I was immediately admitted into what turned out to be a series of studios filled with clay figures in all sizes and conditions, scaffolds, ladders and a group of several young women working under the direction of Mr. Taft, who himself was just then modeling from life the figure of a nude girl. The whole scene was filled with enthusiasm and energy and concentration. I felt I had suddenly stepped into Paradise.

When Mr. Taft came towards me, tall, bearded, with clear blue eyes and dark hair, and asked what I wanted, I came right out with it and said I wanted a job in his studio.

"Have you had any experience in modeling?"

I stretched the blanket somewhat and painted my experience in the Academy in Cincinnati with glowing colors, being careful not to admit that I had never modeled from life.

He waited until I had finished and then glanced towards one end of the studio where strange-looking wooden cages and iron frames were standing.

"Can you point up small models?"

I hadn't the slightest idea what he meant; but I nodded convincingly.

"Good! Can you start in building up that group at once? I've got to get it along as soon as possible." . . .

The design for a group or statue is first made in a small sketch; from this sketch the sculptor models a very careful study in clay, usually one-fourth the size the finished work is to be; this is cast; over the plaster model is built a wooden frame, and from the top crosspieces strings are attached which fall to the floor. Beside this

caged-in model is built another frame containing the iron armature—the framework on which the enlarged statue is to be built
up. Then, by means of a compass, the distance from the strings to
the clay model is measured, multiplied by four, and sticks reproducing this measurement are attached to the armature and extend
to the point which is to be covered with clay. These sticks, with
small metal points at the end, serve as guides and are left uncovered
until the work is finished, thus aiding in rectifying all mistakes and
miscalculations. This so-called "pointing up" need not necessarily
be done by an artist; in fact the best "metteurs au point"—as the
French call them—often haven't the slightest idea about modeling
and are just careful mechanics. After the armature is covered with
the first application of clay, thus making a working foundation,
little sharp-pointed wooden pegs with heads are stuck into the
plaster, these heads at exactly the distance where the surface of the
finished statue will end. When all the necessary points are established, the strings and the wooden frame are removed, and the work
of building out the statue to the points indicated is commenced. . . .

Mr. Taft was very kind to me that morning. . . .

As soon as I had been furnished with a sculptor's apron, he
led me to that bewildering armature from which all sorts of points
and indications were coming from every direction and explained
very carefully what he wanted me to do. He never said that he was
a little doubtful of my ability to do the work, but his detailed
directions rather suggested it; and while he explained the work to
me he told me what the group I was to enlarge represented. It was
one of the four groups he was doing for the Horticultural Building
of the World's Fair. "Now—go ahead," he ended, "and be very
careful not to bury any of those sign posts in the clay."

I went ahead, and in a few minutes was hard at it getting some
of that ugly armature covered with clay. Soon Mr. Taft was back,
suggesting that I use butterflies, and—fortunately for me—picking
up a lot of those little pieces of crossed bits of wood and fastening
them here and there to the armature to help hold the clay together;
otherwise I should not have known what he meant. But I was so
enthralled in seeing something actually coming out of all that clay
and iron and wood—something that was slowly taking form—that
I soon forgot all about my uncertainty over this new work. I ran
up and down the ladder and piled on quantities of clay, quite un-
noticed by all the others in the studio, who were too occupied with
what they were doing to bother with me.

When evening came on and the studio was to be closed, I was still racing up and down that ladder, unaware that Mr. Taft and his assistant—Charlie Mulligan by name—were standing there watching me at work.

"That's enough for today," Mr. Taft said, a pleasant note of approval in his voice. "You're getting on famously. Only"—and he made some comments and corrections and ended by saying he would expect me the next morning.

I worked there many weeks and earned the reputation of being the most industrious and hard-working assistant in the studio. . . .

In the midst of this work [Mr. Taft] called us all together one day and said he had something important to tell us. My heart sank. I felt sure that he was about to say that his own studio was to be closed and that I was again to find myself without work—losing a job that was exactly what I had been longing for.

He began very solemnly to tell us that he had just had a talk with the architect-in-chief of the Fair, Mr. Burnham, who wished him to take charge of all the sculpture enlargements for the exposition buildings. The Horticultural Building, now completed, would be turned over to him for a studio. He was authorized to engage as many people as he could find capable of doing the work. The important thing was to get the work done within a year; nothing else mattered.

"When I told Mr. Burnham that I had several young women whom I would like to employ," he went on, a twinkle now in his eyes, "he said that was all right, to employ any one who could do the work—white rabbits, if they would help out. So you might begin right now calling yourself white rabbits—the kind that will receive five dollars for every week day and seven-fifty on Sundays. What do you all think of it?"

What did we all think of it! I don't know what the others thought, but when I realized that I was going to have a job that would last a whole year I left the studio with the feeling that I was either dreaming or had gone entirely out of my head.

That wonderful year! Filled with work, filled with accomplishment and filled with what was considered in those days a very fat salary! Taft's studio was moved out en bloc to the Horticultural Building and the white rabbits moved in. We were ten by this time, including the men assistants, and we all took up residence in a small hotel near the Fair grounds. . . .

It was tremendously thrilling to see statues and groups put into place on buildings and stand before them and know that I had spent hours working over them. My energy was inexhaustible. No scaffold was too high for me to mount, carrying a pail of plaster in one hand and tools in another. . . .

All through those months, out of dank marshes and a neglected wilderness, the most amazing city of lagoons and palaces was rising about us. It was all pure magic. One day I would be passing hideous iron girders and shapeless masses of sticks and mud; and seemingly the next day I would be standing spellbound before an edifice that fabulous princes were surely to inhabit. . . .

Towards the latter part of the year, I used to prolong my walk to the Horticultural Building by wandering through the grounds to see the new marvels that had sprung up. One day, passing before what was later to be the Court of Honor, I saw a number of men placing a plaster boat in the center of a large basin. The lines of the boat caught my attention. It had the grace and sweep of a gesture—the gesture of a master of line. The next day the workmen had placed four figures of women at the sides of the boat. Their plaster draperies seemed to float in the breeze. The next day they had oars in their hands. I could feel them leaning their weight against these oars, the muscles of their arms pleasantly taut, their heads thrown back, their nostrils extended with deep breathing—and more wonderful than anything else, under their force the boat seemed to move. I was late that day in arriving at work; and after I arrived I couldn't do anything but think of those living women of plaster and that marvelous boat. A few days later a figure of "Father Time" was placed at the prow; and a woman, "Victory," blowing a resounding blast on a trumpet, stood in the center of the barge.

That morning I stood there rooted to the spot, forgetting all about the timekeeper who had twice before docked me for being late at work. I might have stood there all day if it hadn't been for a burly Irishman, one of the workmen putting the fragments of the fountain together, speaking to me.

"Sorry, miss, but you're in the way. Would you mind moving?" . . .

"Who did it?" I went on. "Who could have done it?"

"A gent in Paris. MacMonnies is the name." . . .

When the World's Fair closed and I could no longer spend the days there, I turned away reluctantly—a vastly different young woman from the one who had left Terre Haute two years before.

The wonderful, enthralling, suggestive art of the world had been spread before me; and I had thirstily drunk it in. And as for having had ambition before—that was like groping in the dark; my ambition now was reaching out into light that was fairly blinding.

I came home late one evening, that autumn after the Fair had closed, and threw myself across the bed. Zulh Taft came into my room, glanced at me curiously and asked what was the matter.

I looked at her with what she afterwards said was the expression of a saint seeing some beatific vision.

"It's all settled," I told her. "I've just bought my ticket [for Paris] and paid for it. I haven't got but three hundred and fifty dollars left—but that's enough. It will keep me going for a while."

The tall white figure opened the door wider, ushered me in and showed me across a large studio to a small room which I took to be a sort of office, as it was furnished with desk and chairs. Here I was asked to sit down and wait a few minutes. This I did with considerable satisfaction. I was in the sacred precincts at last; and I had evidently impressed that white-clothed, masked figure, with the importance of my mission.

In a few minutes he was back again, . . . showing a very attractive, pleasant face, rather thin and long with a humorous twist to mouth and nose, gray-blue eyes, yellow hair and mustache, and a funny little tuft of hair growing straight out from the chin—all features that had impressed me when I saw him standing before his own work at the World's Fair.

He lighted a cigarette, sat down comfortably and crossed his legs.

"Well—fire away! What's it all about?"

I tried to keep my voice steady. "I saw your fountain in the Court of Honor at the World's Fair. It was the most beautiful thing I had ever seen. As soon as I found out you had done it I began planning and saving to come over here and ask you to let me study with you. Well—here I am."

"I don't take pupils."

"But—please—can't I do something here? I'm willing to work at anything. I'm not inexperienced. I worked a whole year with Mr. Taft on the World's Fair statues. I'm sure I could do something useful about the studio. I'll promise not to be in the way if—if you'll only let me come for a little while. I haven't money enough to stay long."

He went on smoking, inhaling deeply and sitting there as if he had not heard a word I said while I watched him eagerly to see what his decision was going to be.

"Done much drawing?" he suddenly asked me.

I told him of my work in the Academy at Cincinnati, all about my drawings from geometrical solids and detached features and the mammoth anatomical figure.

"Never drawn from life?"

"No."

"You must begin that at once. You must draw, draw, draw— all the time—all day—all night—until you know you can draw to the very best of your ability. You can never be a sculptor until you know how to draw." . . .

That first encounter with MacMonnies was somewhat characteristic of my subsequent relations with him. . . . At the time I met him he was about thirty and had got safely by those days of struggle and discouragement that everybody must pass through to achieve something. He had begun to study sculpture with Saint-Gaudens in America, and being very poor at the time, he had slept on a shelf in that sculptor's studio in lieu of anywhere else to go. When he arrived in Paris he went straight to Falguière and studied with him before entering the Ecole des Beaux Arts; and almost immediately he began to be noticed. His first year in Paris he carried off the prize of the atelier, even over the heads of many who had been there several years. Lack of funds soon drove him back to America, but he returned to Paris within a year. From then on his success had come very fast. His "Diana" brought him praise and honor at the Paris Salon; his "Pan" became known internationally; his statue of Stranahan, a most lovely portrait statue, placed in Prospect Park, Brooklyn, was one of the first sculpture figures of our day to wear modern clothes, even to an overcoat over one arm and a silk hat in the hand, a triumph of art over matter. But there is no need of citing the work that has made MacMonnies famous; any one interested in the development of art in America is familiar with his important contributions to it. . . .

To be told by MacMonnies that my work was worth anything to him—the man to whom I would have paid any amount that I might have had just for the privilege of studying with him—created a feeling of gratitude that has ever since been constantly with me; and not only did I feel gratitude but tremendously stimulating encouragement. I hadn't been in Paris a year and the master I had picked out of the whole world had told me that my work was worth something to him! No wonder, from that moment on, I spent every waking hour trying to do something that would be really important and useful to him—a desire that eventually led me into making an enemy who caused me to leave Paris much sooner than I could have wished.

The fact that MacMonnies fell ill soon after I was put on the salaried list made me all the more anxious to prove myself worthy of that fifty francs a week. Though the master came almost daily to the studio and spent a short time there, he was not able to work and he did not take his usual keen interest in everything that was going on. During this time a statue of Victory—now at West Point— was being enlarged in clay by one of his French assistants. I had often stood in rapt admiration before the plaster model of this statue—a model about two feet high; and what had particularly caught my attention were the wings, which were very long and perfectly flat—very much like the wings of the Pompeian Victory in the Naples Museum—and had great style. I noticed, as the assistant progressed with the enlargement, that he had lost sight of the fact that the wings were flat; or else he had decided to improve on the master's design; at any rate it seemed to me that he was working entirely in the wrong direction; and one day I saw him holding a pigeon's wing in his hand and using it as a model. The result was lacking entirely in the dashing effect of the little cast; the wings were becoming concave and weak. I resented this change immensely. Besides, a real Victory wouldn't be able to fly at all with pigeon wings; she wouldn't be able to rise from the ground.

MacMonnies, being ill all the weeks this work was progressing, had never taken the trouble to look up as high as those wings and had not yet climbed the scaffolding to examine them. Anyhow, he expected his assistants to follow closely his models. Once having assigned them a piece of work, he allowed them to go as far as they could without much comment on his part. When it seemed that the work was at a standstill, the assistant having gone as far as he could from the plaster model, MacMonnies would say: "That's enough. Work on something else." And then he would complete the work himself. No assistant was ever allowed to touch a statue or group after the master had taken it over. . . .

All this worked on my mind until watching the changes going on in those wings became a sort of obsession with me; I couldn't think of anything else; I thought the statue was going to be ruined, and yet what could I do! I had been told to work on the surface of the Bacchante and not on the wings of the Victory.

Finally I could stand it no longer; and finding MacMonnies wandering listlessly about the studio one day, I asked him what I was going to do when I finished the Bacchante.

"Anything you wish," he answered indifferently.

"I'd like so much to work a bit on those wings!" I pointed up to the Victory.

"All right. Why not! Anything you please."

The next day was Sunday. I always worked in the studio on Sundays as I then had the place to myself and enjoyed a whole day without anything to distract my attention. I got there early the next morning—I had been given a key to let myself in with—impatient and excited with the idea of getting those wings into shape before any one could stop me. I looked about for the largest and sharpest modeling tool I could find, mounted the scaffolding and spent two heavenly hours scraping and cutting off plasteline from one of the wings, unconscious of the fact that the floor, twenty feet below, was rapidly becoming littered with chunks and mounds of chipped-off plasteline feathers. Those weeks and weeks of the assistant's work were ruthlessly being demolished; my own idea was to get it completely obliterated before evening so that no one would know how many layers I had sliced away; nothing must stop me from flattening out those wings until they resembled the original model.

In the midst of my frantic efforts I heard a key turned in the studio door. I stood quite still, petrified with fear. I felt sure that if the assistant came in at that moment he wouldn't hesitate to murder me right there and entomb my body in one of the plaster casts— as had recently been done in one of the Grand Guignol horrors. But luck was with me. The door opened slowly and disclosed MacMonnies. He looked at the floor, now piled high with plasteline, started and leaned against the wall, evidently thinking the whole statue had fallen and broken into fragments; then his glance traveled up the scaffolding until it reached me.

"What in the name of God has happened?" he exclaimed.

Terror or excitement or embarrassment invariably makes me a bit shrill. I called down to him in a loud voice:

"It just had to be done, Mr. MacMonnies! Come up here and see for yourself! You haven't looked at the enlargement of these wings. That man has been putting pigeon wings on your wonderful Victory. Come up and look at them!"

He came up very slowly, a step at a time, for he was still quite weak; and as he drew nearer and nearer my fright increased. What if he should say the assistant had done right and I all wrong! He walked slowly round the platform, looked carefully at the wing I had demolished—at least flattened out—and then at the other large pigeon wing which I hadn't had time to touch. After this he looked at his little plaster model that was standing beside me—in more ways than one as its flat wings spoke convincingly of what I had been trying to do—threw another glance at the enlarged wings, said nothing, climbed down the scaffolding, went to his desk to get a letter he had come for, crossed to the door, fitted his key in the lock, held the door open and then, for the first time, met my agonized eyes. I may have passed through moments equally terrifying—but I don't seem to recall them.

"All right, Miss Scudder," he said quietly. "Go on—just as you have been doing."

The rest of the day was pure bliss, spent in getting both those wings perfectly flat and putting into them the style of the original little model. Before I left that night I got a shovel and carefully piled all the telltale plasteline into barrels; and the next morning, you may be sure, I avoided meeting that assistant as long as possible.

It was a great satisfaction to have gained my point; and more important still, to be allowed to finish those wings myself—not a very difficult work, as the model had been so carefully executed by the master. I only had to copy what had already been so precisely done. But the assistant! Of course, after that he only bided his time to get his revenge. I don't blame him. Any one would have resented such interference. But I bear him no grudge. Years later, when we met in New York, we always talked of the jolly times we had in "Mac's" studio.

When the Victory was completed, MacMonnies took me with him to the studio in the rue de l'Arrivée, where the enlargement of his Quadriga for the arch that now stands at the entrance of Prospect Park, Brooklyn, was being done. I had seen the designs and some of the work for this group of four horses, chariot, and three women; but it was a revelation to find all the horses enlarged to their huge size and standing about the large studio awaiting the final work of the master.

While I was gazing at them, MacMonnies picked up a tool, told me to watch what he was doing, began working on one of the horses and told me to reproduce on the other three horses what he was doing. His confidence in me during those days had made me a perfect tool to repeat whatever he did. I never thought of trying any tricks of my own—as that assistant had; I was too completely imbued with admiration and appreciation of the master's work to think of anything but reproducing it as exactly as I could.

[After Scudder returned to New York from Paris, her career proved difficult to launch.]

It was another one of those definitely black periods which I hadn't experienced since childhood. If there had been some sort of a students' club, some meeting place where I should have had at least the comfort of exchanging a few words with another human being, it would have been much easier for me to get along; but there was no place of the kind that I knew of. . . .

On the whole it was not the struggle to keep alive that I now look back on as being so dreary; it was the utter loneliness of those days. I hadn't a soul to say good-morning or good-night to; I might have been living on a desert island so far as companionship went; and the experience suggested to me something that I have never forgotten—that loneliness is the root of almost all evils. . . .

By the time Matilda Brownell [a fellow art student] and her family returned to town, I was facing a complete disappearance of funds; and during my first dinner with the family—only those who have lived for weeks and weeks on baked beans can realize what sitting at a table with flowers and candles and eating a delicious dinner perfectly served meant to me—I made a full confession of my discouraging situation. Mr. Brownell immediately took an interest in my problem, told me he admired pluck more than anything in the world and said he was going to make it his special work to see that it was rewarded—a promise that he fulfilled with amazing rapidity.

At that time he was secretary of the New York Bar Association, which had just decided to have a seal made. He mentioned me as an applicant for the work and in spite of objections against an unknown sculptor—and especially a woman—being given such an important work, he won out by guaranteeing that I could do the seal to the satisfaction of the association, saying he would refund the money if my work was unsuccessful.

This was my first really serious commission—for which I was paid seven hundred and fifty dollars in four installments. . . .

My first encounter with the committee that was to choose a design for the seal almost ended disastrously. They gave me the dimensions they had decided on and a photograph of a Minerva who held a spear in one hand, while the other quite empty, was outstretched as if clutching for something. I tried to persuade the committee that the subject was not very original. When asked to express my ideas, I suggested several ideas, but to no avail; they must have a Minerva; their minds were made up to that.

"But surely not with that outstretched, clutching hand!" I protested.

"What's the matter with that hand?" they demanded.

"Somehow it's unpleasantly suggestive for a lawyers' association. It looks as if she were reaching out frantically for her fee and backing up her demands with a spear."

The committee laughed and compromised, allowing me to model a small victory in the empty hand—this no doubt symbolic that the fee had been paid; and the next day I left that studio on 17th Street and moved into a real one farther uptown, having received the first installment on the work for the seal and feeling like nothing less than a millionaire with one hundred and eighty-seven dollars and fifty cents in my pocket. . . .

. . . after the first thrill of finding that I could support myself, I began to realize that making a living was not everything; and, most of all, I had no intention of wasting my life doing odd jobs and merely looking on while well-known sculptors got all the commissions for important work. Wire-pulling was always impossible for me; I couldn't help feeling a very deep contempt for it; it took all the dignity and sincerity out of one's work and out of one's life. It *was* possible for an artist to be independent, I kept repeating to myself; but of course to be independent one had to make a name; that would take time; and the question was: Could I afford to take the time? I decided in the affirmative.

I was in the midst of considering a proposed memorial that had been brought to me by Mr. Brownell—a portrait medallion with inscription for the founder of some small college in New York State. There was no photograph of the gentleman in existence and as he had died many years before, there was no clue to work on except the tradition that he was supposed to resemble Benjamin Franklin. I think it must have been the name of Franklin and the recollection of his little house in Passy that I had once seen that sent my thoughts racing back to Paris.

"Do you think I might do this memorial in Paris?" I asked Mr. Brownell.

"I see no objection," he replied. "But why Paris?"

"Because I've saved up enough money to return there now. I

can live in Paris much cheaper than in New York and I can continue my studies, which I left rather abruptly."

Mr. Brownell consented to the memorial being done in Paris and also decided to send his daughter back to continue her studies in painting. He asked me to dine with the family that evening and we were in the midst of discussing plans, all of us very happy and excited, when a servant came into the drawing-room and announced in a frightened voice that the French femme de chambre was having a fit. Mrs. Brownell rushed to the rescue and, after calming the woman to some extent, demanded the cause of her trouble, which was due, it seems, to hearing talk about going to Paris while she had to remain in New York. The thought was unbearable to her and had brought on hysterics. Mr. Brownell, hearing the groans and wails of the home-sick woman—and always sympathetic and kind—quieted her completely by telling her he would send her along as maid to his daughter and myself; and so Parot, wreathed in smiles, pulled herself together and began instant preparations for our departure.

When I was once more on a boat, steaming down the harbor and watching New York rise out of the dusk with its millions of electric lights, I nodded at it, smiled and waved my hand.

"On the whole," I said to it, "you haven't been so bad to me—not nearly as bad as you have been to lots of others, though you did try pretty hard to get the best of me. But you haven't given me yet what I want. You will though. Just wait and see!"

Matilda Brownell found me leaning on the rail, mumbling to myself.

"What's the matter?" she asked. "Already regretting leaving New York?"

"I was just telling it"—with a wave of the hand towards the now fading city—"that it has something I want—something that I'm going to make it give me."

We celebrated the first evening in our little Paris home with more color than we had intended, because of Parot's exuberance at finding herself once more in her native city. When we went down to the dining room there were no signs of dinner; and when we penetrated to the kitchen there were still fewer evidences of anything to eat. However, we did find Parot, overstimulated with red wine, vigorously painting the kitchen walls with a mixture of olive oil and vinegar and mustard. . . .

The life we led in that little house would have been a great comfort to those nervous mothers who think, when their daughters have gone to Paris to study art, that they have gone straight to the devil. It might almost have been called humdrum—made up, as it was, entirely of routine and hard work. Matilda went off in the morning and spent the day painting and I remained in the studio on the ground floor; in the evenings after dinner we went to Collarossi's Academy and drew from life for three hours; then back again to gather up energy for the next day. . . .

By the time I arrived in Paris for the second time I had reached the point where I was beginning to wonder what *kind* of sculpture I was going to do. I knew I could make a living; that was most satisfactorily demonstrated by having made enough money to return to Paris and not be worried for a long time about expenses. But beyond that—what could I do? Did I have a flair for any special branch of sculpture? Did I have ideas of making literature of sculpture, as a woman I knew did—every piece of her work was so cluttered up with symbolism that she had very little strength left, after she had composed her message to the world, to do the modeling? Did I believe that sculpture should teach lessons as those paintings that are supposed to tell stories do? Did I feel that art should be grave or gay—pagan or Christian—spiritual or sensual? But why go on with the endless questions that faced me! I didn't know at all what I wanted to do—and it took me three whole years to find out.

I did know, though, some of the things I did not want to do— and at the head of this list came equestrian statues; and this, too, in spite of a fleeting ambition while in Cincinnati to make this my life work. I think it was that winter in Washington, while I was doing two portrait medallions, when I realized that equestrian statues could come very near to ruining a beautiful city. It seems quite impossible to avoid running bang into one of these monster-pieces everywhere you turn in Washington. Thank Heaven I resisted adding to the number! And I think I deserve credit for being brave enough to refuse to do a portrait statue at a time when I was sadly in need of a commission.

[Before Scudder completed a commission for a cinerary urn, she decided to visit Italy to study classical monuments.]

Italy was calling me and . . . it was calling Matilda, too, and though she had been there several times. . . . she grew enthusiastic over the idea of personally conducting some one—and especially a sculptor—who had never seen Italy. . . .

I began sniffling as soon as I had spent an hour in the Milan cathedral; I continued sniffling when I stood before the Colleoni statue in Venice and almost changed my mind about equestrian statues; and by the time I had shivered for hours before the tombs of the Medicis in Florence, I was well on the way towards fatal influenza. Some one in the pension suggested that I drink hot cognac steadily and thus cure a cold that was becoming as objectionable to others as to myself; and accepting this advice, I went out and bought a large bottle of the believed-to-be curative liquor. Returning to the pension with the intention of spending the rest of the day in bed with a hot water bottle and frequent hot toddies, I happened to pass the Bargello and suddenly remembered I had not yet seen anything of Donatello's. . . .

I gathered together my rapidly failing forces, struggled up the famous staircase and at last reached the bas-reliefs of the singing boys. Suddenly I experienced a tremendous thrill. I forgot I was in a dying condition, I forgot I held the bottle of cognac in my hand, I forgot everything but the amazing realization that I had found the sort of sculpture that appealed to me in a way nothing else had ever done. But my exaltation was short-lived. It was completely dispelled by a furious guard who came up, spoke to me in a far from reassuring way and pointed accusingly at the broken bottle on the stone floor and the compromising streams of cognac which by this time were filling the whole room with strong fumes.

I always look back on that incident as being my first libation to Donatello and to the inspiration that later pointed out my way to me. And the second libation—if I had had any cognac left— would have been poured before Verrocchio's Boy and Fish which I discovered a day or two later in the Palazzo Vecchio. Somehow, the work of these two artists seemed to me to be exactly what I had been waiting for; they explained to me in a flash why I had so long felt a horror and aversion to bronze gentlemen in Prince Alberts.

I knew now what I wanted to do; and a visit the next week to the Naples Museum and to Pompeii settled the matter. The Pompeians understood perfectly the real personal use of sculpture. Their houses were built round a bronze statuette and the house was given its name from the name of that statuette—the House of Narcissus, the House of the Faun, etc. I filled my brain and my sketch book to overflowing with all those gay pagan figures and then and there decided never to do stupid, solemn, self-righteous sculpture—even if I had to die in a poorhouse. . . .

But, alas—I had that cinerary urn awaiting me in Paris! But even when I was once more at work on it I wasn't very solemn; I hummed gay little tunes; and the urn itself soon began to reflect my happiness and turned out to be a rather cheerful sort of an affair—which I don't think, after all, has done any harm to Wood-lawn Cemetery. . . .

Still working on that cinerary urn and thinking of the joyousness of Donatello and Verrocchio, I used to stop often in the street before Collarossi's Academy and find myself surrounded by fifty or more little children, ranging from one year up, who immediately set up a howl to be employed as models. . . .

These little tots knew they appealed to me and when they found out where I lived came in hordes to my door and had great fun with the bell, making Parot furious—though they invariably assumed most serious faces and asked if a model was wanted when the door was opened. . . .

. . . one day even her heart was touched by one of them and, opening the door noiselessly to my studio, she thrust a little boy of four into the room. He stood there timidly, looking at me through anxious, pleading eyes, dressed in the most absurd little uniform of a Paris coachman—red waistcoat, blue coat and trousers and white top hat. He was so cunning and so appealing that I didn't know whether I wanted to laugh or be sad. In the end I smiled at him and called him to me. His little face lit up with an extraordinarily happy expression and he ran to me with outstretched arms—sure at last that I was going to let him pose for me. How little I knew at that moment that he was Fate in disguise—rushing straight into my arms! . . .

In that moment a finished work flashed before me. I saw a little boy dancing, laughing, chuckling all to himself while a spray of water dashed over him. The idea of my Frog Fountain was born. It was only necessary now to get to work and make it reality.

[After her return to New York for a second lengthy stay, Scudder began to seek decorative commissions.]

One day I sat down and wrote a letter to Stanford White. I told him I had had the pleasure of meeting him in MacMonnies' studio in Paris—that threadbare form of beginning such a letter; then I went on to say that I had come to New York to get something to do in the way of sculpture, that my studio was only a few blocks from his office and that I would appreciate it very much if he would come and see the things I had with me.

I didn't have to wait very long for his reply. As a matter of fact it came the very next day, a short and curt reply, in which he said that he was far too busy a man to go round visiting studios, that he was rushed to death, had a thousand calls in every direction and hadn't a free moment.

This indifference hurt me very deeply and then made me furious. I worked up a very strong case against Mr. White and wrote it out to him in a letter I sent off in reply to his. I told him I didn't think my request was nearly so extraordinary as he had found it; and that furthermore I did not think the most important architect in New York had the moral right to refuse to investigate the work of young sculptors about him—no matter how busy he might be. . . .

A month later I was trying to cross Forty-second Street at that congested hour between noon and one o'clock. . . . I hurried out into the middle of the street and crashed straight into a very large man coming my way. . . .

I looked up and found myself staring at a very red, vexed face that was in some way familiar to me. I continued to stare, trying all the time to recall who it was, and finally heard my name spoken.

"Oh—you are Miss Scudder!"

I nodded and suddenly remembered. "Yes—Mr. White," I answered a bit breathlessly. . . .

"I saw that little figure of yours the other day in the Emmetts' studio. What do you call it?"

"Frog Fountain," I murmured.

"I like it. How much do you want for it?" . . .

"A thousand dollars," I answered with a calm that took so much nervous energy to produce that I was a wreck for days afterwards.

"All right," said Stanford White. "I'll take it. Send it to my office. Good-by." . . .

You may be sure I lost no time in getting my Frog Fountain out of the Emmetts' studio and into Mr. White's office. I even went to the extravagance of hiring a hansom cab. . . .

. . . and carried it there myself that same afternoon and waited an interminably long time for him to appear. In the end I had to leave without seeing him; but the next morning a check for one thousand dollars was in the post. . . .

It is really wonderful what a difference in one's outlook on the world a thousand dollars can make. With that check in hand I immediately gave up that horribly unsympathetic office-building-imitation-studio and moved into one I had been looking at with longing eyes for some time—the Gibson Studios on Thirty-third Street. . . .

I had a private staircase that gave on the street so that I was free from all communication with the rest of the house; and the bedroom and bath and most sympathetic, well-lighted studio made up a little suite that suited me perfectly. Of course there were some draw-backs, among them the rats, whose hunger made them very insistent at night, but an equally hungry gray cat soon managed to get them under control. . . .

As I have said, I have always found New York too exciting a place to produce my best work there. There is so much to do, there are so many amusements, so many surprises, so many adventures and so much telephoning that concentration for me is quite impossible. Affairs move too fast in New York; vital changes take place in people's lives often in a few hours; one may be as poor as a church mouse one moment and as rich as Croesus the next. It is all extremely exhilarating—which makes it one of the most fascinating places in the world to go to; but for a calm, definite pursuit of an idea, I have found Paris a much better place in which to work. In Paris there are few changes; one always finds one's niche there when one returns—no matter how long one may have been away. In New York one seems to begin life all over again upon each arrival.

I have had my present studio in Paris for ten years; and when I return from trips home I invariably find the same concierge to greet me, the same little restaurants near by, everything the same and always a pleasant greeting on all sides. I have employed the same coiffeur in Paris for years and when I return after a long absence the whole family comes forth to greet me. Having been in Paris during the war, my relations with the people in the Latin Quarter are very close. If I stayed away twenty years, I feel perfectly sure I would find my niche awaiting me when I got back. In a way it has something very closely akin to the personality and intimacy of small-town life.

Art is one of the mysteries of life and no rules can be made about it. During the great movement of art among the Greeks, sculpture was looked upon as a simple profession that any child could be apprenticed to and no more difficult than any other calling. That is perhaps the reason that the Greeks produced so many masterpieces; and it rather strengthens me in my theory that every child in the public or private schools should study art—not from the "flat" but from nature. A child should be taught to draw the object that he is learning to spell. Often quite intelligent people say they have no talent because they cannot draw a line. Not being able to "draw a line" is not an indication of lack of talent; it is a confession of a stupid education. Just think how much more difficult it is to learn to write letters and to form them into words and sentences than it is to sit down before a teapot and draw it on paper! This inclusion of drawing and painting and modeling in the education of every child naturally would not make of every child an artist, but it would result in the development of many more artists than we have now; and it would certainly give a greater and wider appreciation of things artistic to the general public.

I have often been asked why sculpture is considered one of the most difficult of all the professions and why it is that comparatively few students who undertake it arrive. It is a fact that, while there are hundreds of painters who make distinguished successes in America—where success in every human effort is open to the ambitious—the number of well-known sculptors can be counted on the fingers of two hands. I am almost inclined to say on the fingers of one hand. Why is this? The reason is perfectly simple and expressed in one word—memorials. The popular use of sculpture in America takes the form of commemorating our dead—our war heroes, our poets, our philanthropists, etc. In no country in the world is more honor paid to dead celebrities. But why wait until they are dead to begin honoring them? Why should our famous statesmen, generals, poets, and philanthropists not pose themselves for their portrait statues? Whatever these national heroes may have done to win the right to stand forth immortalized has, in most cases, been done long before their death. But it is a tradition that a memorial should not even be whispered about until long after the death of the distinguished person. The sculptor is then selected, and after a mad scramble to gather together photographs and old clothes, he begins his work under the most disheartening circumstances—and the result is usually another bronze horror which more often than not arouses public disfavor. Often, after several such experiences, the discouraged sculptor gives up his profession and turns to something else.

Ellen Anderson Gholson Glasgow

(1873–1945)

Ellen Anderson Gholson Glasgow, novelist, was born the fourth daughter and eighth of ten children to a Richmond, Virginia, industrialist and his Tidewater aristocrat wife. Morbidly sensitive as a child and subject to crippling headaches, Glasgow could not face the rigors of attendance at the private schools to which she was briefly sent. Instead she became self-educated, pursuing a breadth of reading unavailable to the conventionally schooled southern girl.

Clearly an intellectual from young girlhood, Glasgow read widely in history and the emerging social sciences and steeped herself in the British and American literary tradition. These pursuits made her recognize and wish to celebrate the emergence of the New South and the achievements of its rising capitalist entrepreneurs. Yet she was neurotically attached to her mother, a delicate and traditional southern belle who embodied the values of the old southern aristocracy.

Glasgow's passion for writing emerged in childhood, although many of her early efforts were destroyed. Distant in her relationships with her large family, except for her brother Frank and her younger sister Rebe, Glasgow inwardly rebelled against her proper southern family while outwardly accepting its comfortable standard of life.

Her two major love affairs were with successful businessmen, representatives of the economic energy and liberal values Glasgow admired. They were bons vivants, dedicated to economic success and the enjoyment of its rewards, secure enough to take pleasure in Glasgow's own success. Her first affair cured Glasgow of her feelings of unattractiveness, compared with her mother and sisters, and of her sense of gaucherie because of increasing deafness. This reassurance vanished with the failure of her second affair, leaving her worldview bleaker and her inner resources diminished.

When she began her adult writing career, Glasgow chronicled the rise of the southern middle class and the decline of the old southern elite. The unresolved conflicts in her family loyalties lent energy to her literary imagination, while her admiration for Tolstoy and Zola shaped her gemlike prose style. Critics have varied in their assessment of her extensive oeuvre. At the turn of the century she was praised as one of the proponents of a new southern realism. More psychologically inclined critics held her novels less satisfactory because of their unresolved social and political tensions. Later feminist critics have found much to praise in her steel magnolia heroines and her outspoken hatred of male dominance.

In *The Woman Within* we see and hear a narrator who insists on depicting the real tensions between men and women, the secret and deadly battles for power within families, the joys of love returned, and the despair of the creative woman confined within rigid social conventions. Glasgow's defiance of her stern Presbyterian father, her happiness in an illicit love affair with a married man, her zest for beauty, her coolly critical social gaze, and her limpid prose delight the reader, who is allowed to see how a seemingly conventional woman has actually lived life on a heroic scale. We know that, despite her ironic bows to convention, she *lived* a liberated life.

THE WOMAN WITHIN

This is my earliest impression: a face without a body hanging there in the sunset, beyond the top windowpanes. All the rest comes in fragments. I scream; I struggle; but my screams and my struggles tell them nothing. I cannot, even now, divide the aftergrowth from the recollection. Only one thing remains, unaltered and vivid as fear: a bodiless apparition, distorted, unreal, yet more real to me than either myself or the world.

My mother and my colored mammy bend over me. I have no words. I cannot tell them. I am too little. My cries choke me. But I remember a cluster of images. . . .

My mother was the center of my childhood's world, the sun in my universe. She made everything luminous—the sky, the street, the trees, the house, the nursery. Her spirit was the loveliest I have ever known, and her life was the saddest. I have two images of her, one a creature of light and the other a figure of tragedy. One minute I remember her smiling, happy, joyous, making gaiety where there was no gaiety. The next minute I see her ill, worn, despairing, yet still with her rare flashes of brilliance. I am as old now as she was when she died; yet my heart breaks again whenever I remember her life. A tragic shape dims her light. Then it passes as the drift of cloud over a star, and she shines there, in solitary radiance, unalterably fixed in my memory.

As life goes on her face becomes clearer and more youthful. I look beyond the misery of her later years, and see her smiling at me from between the blossoming oleanders, on the steps of the porch. Her face was oval, with so fair and fine a skin that she was called "the lily" in her girlhood, old ladies have told me. Her hair was as soft as spun silk, of a light chestnut shade, and very lustrous where it was parted over her wide beautiful brow and delicately arched eyebrows, over eyes that were blue when she smiled and gray when she was sad. She loved life until it bore down upon her, and she suffered the long anguish of a nervous illness. When I was a baby she lost her eldest son, my brother Joseph Reid, and though she was never really happy again, she recovered her gaiety and her laughing spirit. . . .

My father had little compassion for the inarticulate, and as his Calvinistic faith taught him, the soulless; and because of this and for many other reasons, including this iron vein of Presbyterianism, he was one of the last men on earth that she should have married. Though he admired her, he never in his life, not for so much as a single minute, understood her. Even her beauty, since he was without a sense of beauty, eluded him.

When I look back now, after time has softened my long perspective, I can see plainly and do proper justice to my father's character. His virtues were more than Calvinistic; they were Roman. With complete integrity, and an abiding sense of responsibility, he gave his wife and children everything but the one thing they needed most, and that was love. Yet he was entirely unselfish, and in his long life (he lived to be eighty-six, surviving my mother by a quarter of a century) he never committed a pleasure. . . .

When or where or how I learned to read, I could never remember. When I look back, it seems to me that one day the alphabet was merely a row of black or red marks on paper, and the next day I was earnestly picking out the letters in *Old Mortality*. I must have taught myself, for the doctors had warned my mother not to begin teaching me, and had prophesied that it was unlikely I should ever live to grow up. There were few things one would need less in Heaven than a command of the alphabet. "Don't push her, whatever you do. Let her take her own time about learning." But the trouble was that my own time was quick time. After hearing dear old Aunt Rebecca, my father's elder sister, and the perfect story-teller, relate the plots of *The Waverley Novels,* I resolved, apparently, that as soon as possible, I would read them for myself in my own way, which meant spelling out the words, letter by letter, as I went on. All that I now remember clearly is that *Old Mortality* and a little blue book called *Reading Without Tears* were the beginning of my serious education, and that, so far as I am aware, nobody ever taught me to read. "As soon as I learn my letters, Mammy, I'm going to teach you yours," I promised. But I never taught her, and to this day, I regret that I did not.

At this age, the monosyllable Why? Why? Why? was on my lips so often that my father, worn out after a day at the Tredegar, would pay me a new penny to stop asking questions, just as years later, anticipating the principle of the New Deal, he offered to pay me not to read Lecky's *European Morals* and *Rationalism in Europe*. I must have been a tiresome and exhausting child; yet never again in my life, perhaps, have I had so wide a circle of friends and admiring acquaintances. . . .

That morbid shyness combined with almost constant headaches, had not yet overcome my natural exuberance, and set me apart from the well and happy in childhood. Not until I was eight or nine years old was I driven to unchildlike brooding over my sense of exile in a hostile world, and back again to that half-forgotten presence of the evil face without a body. . . .

When I was very small, my father bought a farm, and, a little later, he sold the old house on Cary Street, and moved his family into a still older and larger house on the corner of Foushee and Main Streets. This is the square gray house where I have lived for the rest of my life, and where I have written all my books, with the exception of *Life and Gabriella*. The many tragedies of my life, and a fair measure at least of the happiness, have come to me in this house. The fibers of my personality are interwoven, I feel, with some indestructible element of the place; and this element is superior to time and chance, as well as to the material substance of brick and mortar.

But, before I came to this house, I loved, as a child, the farm of Jerdone Castle, in the way one loves not only a place but a person. In the first summers Mammy was with me, and we ranged over the wide fields, some plowed and planted in corn or tobacco, but the greater part of them left to run wild in broomsedge, and scrub pine, and life-everlasting. Farther away, there was a frame of virgin woods, where small wild violets and heartsease and a strange waxen blossom pushed up from under the dead leaves of last winter. Every vista in the woods beckoned me; every field held its own secret;

every tree near our house had a name of its own and a special identity. This was the beginning of my love for natural things, for earth and sky, for roads and fields and woods, for trees and grass and flowers; a love which has been second only to my sense of an enduring kinship with birds and animals, and all inarticulate creatures. . . .

I was five that first summer; and it was not until a year or so later that my mother gave Rebe and me each a tiny garden to work; and we planted a Safrano rose-bush, mother's favorite, and slips of heliotrope, sweet alyssum, and lemon verbena. Until Father sold the farm, and left us broken-hearted, we raised our flowers every spring in our own little gardens, just inside the big garden where the flowering shrubs had been uprooted by the overseer, to make way for the plow.

For the first few summers we had no dogs; but when I was older my "bosom friend," Lizzie Patterson, gave me a beautiful pointer puppy, and I learned what the companionship of a dog can mean to a child. After Mother and Mammy, Pat came nearest to me; and I never forgave Father, who did not like dogs, because, when he sold the farm, he would not let me bring Pat to town and gave him to an indifferent overseer whom I disliked. For years I agonized over Pat's fate; and that incident was one of the things, but not the only thing, that encouraged a childish affliction of nervous sensibility. . . .

In my seventh summer I became a writer. As far back as I remember, long before I could write, I had played at making stories, and, in collaboration with Mammy, I had created Little Willie and his many adventures. But not until I was seven or more, did I begin to pray every night, "O God, let me write books! Please, God, let me write books!"

One summer day, lying on the blue grass at Jerdone Castle, beneath sweeping boughs of the "old elm," which was so large that it took five of us to measure its bole, I found myself singing aloud in time with the wind in the leaves. Beyond the clustering leaves, I could see the sky as blue as the larkspur in the field below the garden fence, and over the blue a fleet of small white clouds was sailing.

"I would that I with the clouds could drift" I began to sing under my breath. "Quietly, happily onward—" And then suddenly, with a start of surprise, I exclaimed aloud, "But that's po'try! That's po'try! And I made it!" . . .

One morning, seeking more paper and a sharpened pencil in my sister's room, I heard her voice reading my precious verses aloud to her guests, and I overheard, too, the burst of kindly ridicule and amusement. Noiselessly, without the flutter of a curtain, I fled back through the window, and down the columns of the porch to the shelter of the big box-bush beneath. My skin felt naked and scorched, as if a flame had blown over it. . . .

After this bitter humiliation, I wrote only in secret; and I began to live two lives twisted together. One was my external life, delicate but intense, devoted to my few friends. . . .

My interior world was thickly woven of recollections, but these recollections had no part in the remote, hidden country of the mind. In that far republic of the spirit I ranged, free and wild, and a rebel. . . . Until my first book was finished no one, except my mother, who suspected but did not speak of it, was aware that, below the animated surface, I was already immersed in some dark stream of identity, stronger and deeper and more relentless than the external movement of living. It was not that I had so early found my vocation. At the age of seven my vocation had found me. The one permanent interest, the single core of unity at the center of my nature, was beginning to shape itself, and to harden. I was born a novelist, though I formed myself into an artist. Looking back on my life I can see that a solitary pattern has run through it, from earliest childhood. Always I have had to learn for myself, from within. Always I have persevered in the face of an immense disadvantage—in the face of illness, of partial deafness, which came later, of the necessity to blaze my own trail through the wilderness that was ignorance. To teach one's self is to be forced to learn twice. . . .

I must have been seven or eight years old when I was sent to school for my first term, which lasted less than a day. Although I was innocent of arithmetic and geography, I was well acquainted with English literature and with English history. It was my father's habit to read aloud to us every evening, and since we had a good old library, and no money to spend on current books, my taste was already formed. Or perhaps, as I have felt, I was born with an appreciation of the best, and an equal aversion from the second best. I was, even at that age, a social rebel. I cannot recall the time when the pattern of society as well as the scheme of things in general, had not seemed to me false and even malignant. Later on, I read widely in Adam Smith, Malthus, John Stuart Mill, Henry George.

I was a radical when everyone else I knew was conservative, and now I am conservative when most other people appear to be radical. This, of course, is merely the inevitable recoil from youth to age. If I were still one and twenty, I suppose I should continue to believe in both romantic love and the theory of collectivism. So it was, a little later, with votes for women. At eighteen, after discovering John Stuart Mill, I was an ardent suffragist, and the only one, except my sister Cary, in our circle of acquaintances. Years afterwards, when the cause had triumphed and attained respectability, I lost interest, and regarded it merely as one more reform that had ceased too soon to be exciting. The whole design of my life ran like that, in a rhythm and pause, forward and backward. By the time an idea has won its way in the world, I have rushed ahead to another....

But even an unhappy childhood life has its moments. My escape from hostile circumstances—from school and fear and God all together—came in the summer. On the farm, I was free, I was alive within, I even knew happiness. My headaches disappeared, when I roamed all day out of doors, and I have wondered whether my early frailty was imposed by conditions, or at least increased by the perpetual conflict between my nature and my surroundings....

I could not have been more than ten years old when I was overtaken by a tragic occurrence which plunged my childhood into grief and anxiety, and profoundly affected, not only my mind and character, but my whole future life. In a single night, or so it seemed to us, my mother was changed from a source of radiant happiness into a chronic invalid, whose nervous equilibrium was permanently damaged. A severe shock, in a critical period, altered her so completely that I should scarcely have known her if I had come upon her after a brief absence. She, who had been a fountain of joy, became an increasing anxiety, a perpetual ache in the heart. Although she recovered her health, in a measure, her buoyant emotion toward life was utterly lost. Even now, when she has been dead so long, I cannot write of these things without a stab of that old inarticulate agony....

At Jerdone Castle, when my father was away, Rebe and I slept in small twin beds in Mother's big airy room; but at the week end, when Father returned, we moved into the adjoining room with the door between left open. Night after night, we would lie awake, listening to Mother's voice, as she walked the floor in anguish, to and fro, back and forth, driven by a thought or a vision, from which she tried in vain to escape. After I was in bed, before I could fall asleep, I would draw the sheet over my head, holding it fast to the pillow, in a fruitless effort to shut out the sound of her voice, and to ease the throbbing pain in my throat, that unavailing passion of sympathy. In those years, the most impressionable of our lives, Rebe and I knew scarcely a night that was not broken by a sudden start of apprehension, or by a torment of pity and terror which was as physical as the turn of a screw in our flesh. All through her nervous illness Mother refused steadfastly to take even a mild sleeping potion. Her horror of drugs was inborn, and there was no one in our world who understood either the cause or the inevitable course of her malady. Her mind remained clear, brilliant, and reasonable, and she kept to the end an extraordinary sense of humor. No visitor, hearing her merry laugh, or listening to her gay stories, would have suspected the constant pain hidden under her sparkling vivacity.

I have wondered since why she was allowed to suffer without the slightest alleviation. The physicians she consulted were as helpless as the rest of us. One after another, they solemnly advised her to divert her mind by cheerful thoughts, or to try a change of scene. It was the ancient superstition that unhappiness resides in the country without, not within, and that one may cure a broken heart by a simple change of address.

Rebe and I, and through the day, Frank, who was the finest of us all, lived and breathed and moved, for months at a time, in the atmosphere of despair. The very bread we ate tasted of hopelessness. Not always, not without brief interludes of brightness and joy, and a renewal of vital expectancy. For weeks, perhaps, my mother would again become her radiant self. She would recover her cheerfulness, her look of effervescent delight, and sometimes she would join with us in our games, or dance with us in the immense hall at Jerdone Castle. Then, by magic it would seem, our whole world would be suffused with light. As she changed, so we changed with her. Even school would appear less threatening when the intolerable burden of anguish was lifted. If only the change could have lasted! But it was barely more than a semblance of brightness. Inevitably, the glow would fade from life, and the air of melancholy wash over us. This was our actual life, beneath the smooth conventional surface. A fate such as my mother's has been called, by one of the wisest of all philosophers, unbearable even as a subject of drama:—the spectacle of an innocent soul suffering an undeserved tragedy. . . .

My mother was married at twenty-one, and she bore ten children, not including one that came prematurely, and died stillborn.

Two of her children were born immediately before the Civil War, two came into the devastated Valley of Virginia, in the midst of the conflict, when there was not bread enough for the other babies, and the rest followed a sudden descent from affluence to comparative poverty, and the bitter struggle to build a home, and to bring up a family, among ruins. My mother, who in her youth, as the Negroes were fond of saying, "had never stooped to pick up a handkerchief," braced her strength for the long struggle, and worked harder, during her childbearing period, than any servant had been allowed to work for her in the past. Her courage never failed, but her delicate physical constitution, and her heightened sensibilities, reached the breaking-point, before her nervous system was injured by an emotional shock. . . .

From the mist and sunshine of those years a few stark shapes emerge. We had moved, now, into the big gray house on the corner of Main Street, and after my mother's nervous breakdown, we left Jerdone Castle forever. Mother had conceived a horror of the place I loved, and she could not stay on there without greater anguish of mind.

For Rebe, and for me, leaving the farm was like tearing up the very roots of our nature. This was the only place where I found health, where I had known a simple and natural life. It was the place where I had begun to write, and had discovered an object, if not a meaning, in the complicated pattern of my inner world. It was the place, too, where I had felt hours and even days of pure happiness, where I had rushed down the road to meet the advancing storm, while I felt in my heart the fine, pointed flame that is ecstasy.

All this was distressing, but far worse even than this was the enforced desertion of Pat, my beautiful pointer. For years, the memory of Pat, left with an overseer who might not be kind to him, would thrust up, like a dagger, into my dreams. What would they do with Pat when they moved? What would happen to him when he grew old? Why was it people made you do things that would break your heart always? Even now, I sometimes awake with a regret, that is half for Pat himself, and half a burning remorse for some act I have committed but cannot remember. . . .

Only a delicate child, rendered morbid by circumstances, could have suffered as I suffered from that change to the city in summer. Though I went to school for a few months each year, until my health grew frail again and my nervous headaches returned, I would wonder all the way home whether I should find my mother cheerful or sad. Usually, she sent us off brightly; but the brightness would fade as soon as we turned the corner, and the deep despondency would creep over her. Once in those years she went away on her only visit to her brother, whom she had adored since she was a baby. He lived in Holly Springs, Mississippi, and the doctors advised the long trip as a diversion. Rebe went with her, and they were away several months. It was my first long separation from them, and I missed them both with an ache that was like physical pain. . . .

I still had little Toy, [Glasgow's small pet dog] but, in Mother's absence, he was set apart, though I did not suspect this, as another victim. One afternoon, I could not find him when I was urged by my father to go to walk with Lizzie Patterson, and that night, after I had looked for him in vain, one of the servants told me that Father had had him put into a bag, and had given him to two men who worked at the Tredegar. They told me fearfully, wondering what "Miss Annie" (my mother) "would say when she came back"; but, without a word, I turned away and went straight to Father.

Rage convulsed me, the red rage that must have swept up from the jungles and the untamed mind of primitive man. And this rage— I have not ever forgotten it—contained every anger, every revolt I had ever felt in my life. . . .

If I spoke words, I cannot recall them. I remember only that I picked up a fragile china vase on the mantelpiece and hurled it across the room. It shattered against the wall, and I can still hear the crash it made as it fell into fragments. Then I rushed into my room and locked the door on my frightened sisters and the more frightened servants. I should never see Toy again, I knew. I had never seen Pat again. My father would not change his mind. Not once in my knowledge of him had he ever changed his mind or admitted that he was wrong—or even mistaken. . . .

The remembrance of children is a long remembrance, and the incidents often make milestones in a personal history. In those months of Mother's absence, I know that I broke forever with my childhood. For the first time I was standing alone, without the shelter and the comfort of her love and her sympathy. Her silence, inexplicable and utterly unlike her, seemed to thrust me still farther and farther into loneliness, until at last—for months may have the significance of years when one is very young—I began to love, not to fear, loneliness. . . . For weeks I hated them all. I hated the things they believed in, the things they so innocently and charmingly pretended. I hated the sanctimonious piety that let people hurt helpless creatures. I hated the prayers and the hymns, and the red images that colored their drab music, the fountains filled with blood, the sacrifice of the lamb.

And, then, much to Father's distress, and to my sisters' consternation, I refused to attend divine service—and there was nothing left that they could do about it. My will, which was as strong as Father's, plunged its claws into the earth. Nothing, not lectures, not deprivations, not all the pressure they could bring, could ever make me again go with them to church.

If I had won nothing else, I had won liberty. Never again should I feel that I ought to believe, that older people were wiser and better than I was. Never again should I feel that I ought to pretend things were different. Dumbly, obstinately, I would stare back at them when they talked to me. I could not answer them. I could not refute my father when he opened the Bible, and read aloud, in his impressive voice, the sternest psalms in the Old Testament. All I could do was to shake my ignorant head, and reply that, even if all that was true, it made no difference to me. I was finished with that way of life before I had begun it.

And, then, in the midst of it all, while my mother was still away, I was seized, I was overwhelmed by a consuming desire to find out things for myself, to know the true from the false, the real from the make-believe. The longing was so intense that I flung myself on knowledge as a thirsty man might fling himself into a desert spring. I read everything in our library. History, poetry, fiction, archaic or merely picturesque, works on science, and even *The Westminster Confession of Faith*. Lizzie Patterson and Carrie Coleman came frequently in the afternoon; but even with them, my two closest friends, I felt that I had changed beyond understanding and recognition. They lived happy lives on the outside of things, accepting what they were taught, while I was devoured by this hunger to know, to discover some meaning, some underlying reason for the mystery and the pain of the world.

For I had ceased to be a child. My mind and the very pit of my stomach felt empty. I needed the kind of reality that was solid and hard and would stay by one.

When, at last, Mother and Rebe returned, I felt shy with them and vaguely uncomfortable. It seemed to me, for the first few days at least, that they had changed, that they had seen things I had not seen, that they treasured recollections I could not share. Or perhaps I was the one who had changed. Something had gone out of me for good, and, in exchange, I had found something that, to me, was more precious. I had found the greatest consolation of my life; but I had found also an unconquerable loneliness. I had entered the long solitude that stretches on beyond the vanishing-point in the distance. . . .

At that time, I was looking forward to the normal life of a Southern girl in my circle. Yet my vital interests were not objective, and I put aside, indifferently, the offer of the usual "coming-out party" and the "formal presentation to Richmond society." For I was writing, or had already written, a long novel, of some four hundred pages, entitled *Sharp Realities,* a name borrowed from Beaumont and Fletcher; and in the year between the burning of this manuscript and the beginning of *The Descendant,* it had dawned upon me that I was gradually attaining a culture before I had acquired what we have agreed to call an education.

Guided by chance or inspired by my instructor, Walter McCormack, I had found, on the dusty shelf of a second-hand book shop, a copy of *Progress and Poverty.* After buying it for thirty cents, I had brought home my discovery, and I had plunged, eagerly, into the absorbing first chapters, with their able analysis of social conditions. As I read, I was impressed by Henry George's review of the world's poverty, and by his logical and unrelenting inferences from the facts. He may or may not have influenced my theme when I began my crude first book, *The Descendant.* I was striving more for art than for inspiration, which, as a beginning author, I needed far less; but, at least, he encouraged the revolutionary slant in my point of view. Why did not people rebel when they had nothing to lose? I wanted to know why. I wanted to discover what it was that kept the poor in their place. Was it merely the pressure from without? Or was it that still more demoralizing pressure from within? I had none of the early Christian belief that poverty was eternally blest. Only when it was chosen as a symbol of compassion had it ever blest anybody. The shaved head and the yellow bowl were the outward signs, not of material destitution, but of spiritual abundance.

Nevertheless, I might learn the effect of poverty on the will to live while I investigated the actual lives of the poor. . . .

A little later, at seventeen, I gave my first party, and, in the same winter, I joined the City Mission, and became the youngest "visitor" in its membership. Though my health was frail, my mental energy was inexhaustible, and I was eager to test life on every side

and in every situation. The squalor I saw horrified me, and, in the
majority of cases, I felt that I was dealing with inanimate matter. . . .

All that winter I worked with the City Mission, but I learned
so little that I decided the independent poor, the poor who were
"too proud to beg," must be different. The next year I went once
or twice a week to The Sheltering Arms, a private charity which
well merited its romantic name. That was a small hospital, down
on Governor Street, with no winding of red tape, but a pitifully
small income. . . .

Then, just as I was turning from the knowledge in books, and
eagerly grasping at the careless youth I had never known, life struck
again, and the blow left me writhing in anguish. My mother became
ill with typhoid fever, and died after a week's suffering. . . . To her
three younger children, it was as if the world rocked suddenly, and
fell to pieces. Well or ill, she had been the supreme figure in our
universe.

It is more than forty years now since she died, yet a part of me
seems still to live on, in that hour, in that moment. A part of me,
buried but alive, was held there, imprisoned and immovable, while
the rest of my being flowed on as time flows, relentlessly. . . .

Early that spring, Cary and Walter [McCormack, Cary's hus-
band] sent me a subscription to the Mercantile Library in New
York, and then the doors of a new world were flung back. When I
pause to think, now, of the way I waste money on books I can never
read—that I give away, merely to have them out of the house—I
am touched by the recollection of what that library and those weekly
or fortnightly parcels of books meant in my life. I had no money
to buy books; but I had all the time in the world to read them, and
I begrudged the hours I spent asleep or talking to my acquaintances,
who regarded books as not only unnecessary in well-bred circles,
but as an unwarranted extravagance. Besides, did not everybody
know what happened to bluestockings? Was not New England full
of them? And did not they invariably end as abolitionists—or, since
abolition was itself ended, did not they become either temperance
workers or women's rights advocates? "You are too attractive to
be strong-minded," they would remark, reassuringly.

When the first parcel came, I opened it eagerly. After this, I
would read all day, stopping only for a cup of tea or a plate of
soup, which Emily would send me in the hope of "tempting my
appetite." I was supposed to go to bed early; but after Rebe had

fallen asleep, I would slip from the adjoining bed, and steal down the dark stairs, feeling my way to the library, or—but this was after I had published a book and had been given a place to write in—I groped through the hall to the tiny study, which is now a bathroom, between the two rooms at the front. Here I would light the "students'" lamp, for this was before we had electricity in the house, and I would read, breathlessly, searching always for something I never found, until two o'clock in the morning. The only sounds that reached me were the rumble of occasional wheels in the street, or, if the windows were open, the slow, even tramp of a policeman's walk on the pavement.

From the Mercantile, I borrowed the works of all German scientists I had heard mentioned, or had seen quoted in books. Not until long afterwards did it occur to me that the German philosophers, especially Schopenhauer, would have been better reading, and that they possessed more of the hard truth I required—more, too, of that intellectual fortitude I was seeking. A few years later I read Kant and (though I could never read Hegel) the whole wide group of idealists, which included Fichte and Schelling. Of the German philosophy, only *The World as Will and Idea* stayed with me, until, by pure accident, I discovered the great prose-poem, *Thus Spake Zarathustra*. But we are in the early 'nineties, and I am running entirely too far ahead.

[After completing her second novel (her first having been destroyed), Glasgow went to New York in search of a publisher.]

No sooner had I settled myself [in New York] than I addressed my letter of introduction to Mr. Collier. After I had stolen down three flights of stairs to the post-box on the corner, I crept up again to my hall bedroom, where I waited, in anxious expectancy, for the next turn of the wheel, which so frequently, in my small affairs, revolved backward.

But, forward or backward, the wheel turned with promptness. By the next post, I received a note from Mr. Collier, who asked me to lunch with him at Delmonico's. The lunch, I recall, was delectable, and the wine all that artless ignorance, nourished on Father's temperance views and the rare mint juleps of neighbors, could imagine. Price Collier was pleasant, friendly, attractive, and patronizing, without offense, to a Southern girl who believed that she could break into American letters. I felt that in his heart, he esteemed

American letters, barring Henry James, his close friend, as lightly as I did; but, in any case, he wanted no more writing from women, especially from women young enough to have babies. . . .

. . . he told me frankly that there was no hope for me with Macmillan. No, it would not do the slightest good if he read my manuscript; he could tell, without reading it, that there was not a chance of Macmillan's accepting the book.

"The best advice I can give you," he said, with charming candor, "is to stop writing, and go back to the South and have some babies." . . . I was not made that way, and I did not see why I should pretend to be what I wasn't, or to feel what I couldn't. At that age I suspected, and later I discovered, that the maternal instinct, sacred or profane, was left out of me by nature when I was designed. I sometimes think that a hollow where it might have been was filled by the sense of compassion; but even of this, I am not entirely sure. All I know is that, at any time in my life, it would have seemed to me an irretrievable wrong to bring another being into a world where I had suffered so many indignities of the spirit. After my deafness, this became a moral conviction. . . .

But I did not like to be patronized, and I had not come so far from home in search of benevolent old gentlemen. That was a product in which the South was never found wanting. What I needed was to find higher intelligence than any I had ever known, a way of reason better than any I could invent for myself. And, more than anything else, I wanted the right to be heard. . . .

At last—at last the manuscript came back to me, and I tucked it under my arm and went down to see Mr. Lawrence, of the University Publishing Company. As a contemporary of Dr. Holmes, I had expected him to be eighty or more, and he was, indeed, a kindly, charming, and distinguished old gentleman. No one could have been more sympathetic, but he told me he published only textbooks, and he did not know, personally, any of the younger publishers in New York. "The best thing I can do for you," he said, "is to turn you over to one of the younger men in the firm. I'll ask Mr. Patton what he can do for you." He touched the bell, said: "Tell Mr. Patton I'd like to speak to him," and in less than a minute, a man of middle age came into the room, and all my helpless waiting on publishers was ended forever. The fate of my first book was whisked, as if by magic, into Mr. Patton's kind and competent hands. At first, he did not appear overeager, but after Mr. Lawrence had talked to him, he consented to read the manuscript, and to do what he could.

Publishers were not interested in first books, he said; they liked writers who were already established, and too many Southerners, he thought, were trying to write the same thing. . . .

He went out with my manuscript, and, in a few minutes, I parted from pleasant Mr. Lawrence, and returned to my boarding-house. All the afternoon and night I was seeing a sharp, wise face bending down over my book. I was too excited to sleep. I could only lie awake and wonder what passages he would like best as he went on.

The next evening after dinner, Mr. Patton came to see me, and fortunately, for a little while, the drawing room was empty of boarders. For an instant he looked at me without speaking, while my heart, as they say, seemed to miss a beat. Then he said slowly and gravely, for he was a silent man, "I read the manuscript last night without putting it down until I finished it at dawn. Don't worry, my child. That book shall be published if I have to build a publishing house in order to publish it." Then while I was groping for words, he saw tears in my eyes, and he added impulsively, "I haven't been so moved since I was a boy and read Victor Hugo."

Victor Hugo! Well, well—But I had won my first convert, and I knew that everything would be easier, now, because somebody, besides my two sisters and one friend, believed in me.

Again that night I could not sleep. For hours, until a glimmer of day extinguished the white glare in the street, and splashed like water over the bulging clothes on the fire escapes, I lay awake and tried to imagine what the world would be like when one had published a first book, and had found recognition. I had known few of what we call the natural pleasures of childhood and girlhood. Fear and illness and heartbreak had pursued me as far back as I could remember.

Well, I had had one book published, and I was not happy, I was not even appeased. *The Descendant* was somewhat of a success, and more of a little sensation. Published anonymously, it had excited curiosity among reviewers, who hesitated either to praise or to blame, because, after all, it might turn out to have been written by somebody.

But one novel, as I had long since observed, does not make a novelist. . . . I wanted not an inspiration (wasn't my mind bubbling with inspiration?); I wanted an art. I wanted a firm foundation; I wanted a steady control over my ideas and my material. What I understood more and more was that I needed a philosophy of fiction, I needed a technique of working. Above all, I felt the supreme necessity of a prose style so pure and flexible that it could bend without breaking. . . .

My second book was unfortunately brought out when the publishers were on the brink of failure and reorganization. It was written when I was still under the influence of Maupassant as a supreme craftsman, if not a supreme novelist. I read every line of his novels and short stories, and I yearned to write a novel as perfect in every sentence as *Une Vie*. Just as *Madame Bovary* had seemed to me the most flawless, so *Une Vie* seemed to me to be the most beautiful novel in all literature. Yet, even here, after the first wild enthusiasm had worn off, I felt that something was missing. As I studied Maupassant's short stories, phrase after phrase, I was conscious of an inner recoil from the world as art made it. Surely the novel should be a form of art—but art was not enough. It must contain not only the perfection of art, but the imperfection of nature. . . .

Then, suddenly, in the midst of my confusion, I happened, quite by accident, to read *War and Peace,* and . . . I knew what I wanted. Life must use art; art must use life. My first reading of Tolstoy affected me as a revelation from heaven, as the trumpet of the Judgement. What he made me feel was not the desire to imitate, but the conviction that imitation was futile. . . .

I had learned from Maupassant the value of the precise word, of the swift phrase, of cool and scrupulous observation. . . . My old childish pleasure in singing words came back to me, and I passed on from Flaubert's theory of the one, the only, the exact word for every object, to a wider range and an increasing delight in the rhythms and the minor cadences of English prose. But it was not until I came to write *Barren Ground* and my later books that I felt an easy grasp of technique, a practiced authority over style and material. I had worked too hard for this to be modest about it. I had found that French sentences had a way of going to one's head too quickly, and I had turned from Flaubert and Maupassant to the sobering English tradition. Always, I have felt by intuition when I needed an author. I may not have thought of him for years, but, suddenly, his name will spring into my mind, and I will say to myself, "I must read Bacon now," or "I must read Swift or Sterne, for a change."

In those first few years of partial deafness, I would never see strangers, and not even my former friends, except in the presence of Cary, who would know by intuition the words that I missed and would hasten to snatch up the broken thread. . . .

But it was a blessed relief to find that I appeared to hear better in New York. Twice a year I went on to be treated by one aurist or another, and as soon as I received a sufficient income from my books, I began a pilgrimage all over the world, as patient as, and more hopeless than, the pilgrimages to shrines of saints in the Dark Ages. I went everywhere I could perceive the faintest gleam of light. I was treated, not only in America, but in Europe, by every specialist who had distinguished himself in work for the ears. And it was all as futile as the quest for miracles, and far more expensive. In my case, which was a common, and very simple, hardening in the Eustachian tube and the middle ear, there was no cure to be found anywhere. Science had failed my body as ruinously as religion had failed my soul. . . .

After this, my point of view changed so completely that I was able to build a wall of deceptive gaiety around me. There was a surer refuge in mockery, I found, than in too grave a sincerity. It was then that I began to cultivate the ironic mood, the smiling pose, which I have held, without a break or a change, for almost forty years. "You are the only one of my patients who is not depressed by deafness," one of the leading aurists in New York said to me a few years ago. I smiled that faintly derisive smile. If only he could know! If only anyone in the world could know! That I, who was winged for flying, should be wounded and caged! . . .

But to return to the American scene in the last years of the century. Literature, too, has passed on. I have watched so many literary fashions shoot up and blossom, and then fade and drop, that I have learned to recognize a new movement while it is still on the way. Yet with the many that I have seen come and go, I have never yet encountered a mode of thinking that regarded itself as simply a changing fashion, and not as an infallible approach to the right culture. For my part, I could observe and ponder, because I also was sure of my own special pursuit. I knew that I craved the best amid a chaos of second bests. What astonished me most, I think, was the general lack of disinterested effort, and the lack, too, of the feeling that one's work was something larger and more important than one's private aims or ambitions. It may be that literary circles are perpetually closing in toward the center of gravity. Log-rolling was a prevalent pastime then, as it is nowadays; for that is always the case, I suppose, where reputations are made easily, and without merit. Never, in all the years since then, have I lost that sense of unreality, of insincerity, and of time-serving, in much, but by no means the greater part, of American culture. I had no place in any coterie, or in any reciprocal self-advertising. I stood alone. I stood outside. I wanted only to learn. I wanted only to write better.

Without warning, a miracle changed my life. I fell in love at first sight. Though I had had my casual romances, and even a rare emotional entanglement, I had not ever been in love with my whole being. One major obstacle was a deep conviction that I was unfitted for marriage. Loneliness had exercised a strange fascination; and I felt that I could not surrender myself to constant companionship, that I could not ever be completely possessed. It is true that I was both temperamental and imaginative, lightly disposed to cherish unreal and airy romances; but, apart from the lack in me of what people call the maternal instinct, I felt that my increasing deafness might be inherited, and that it would be a sin against life to pass on an affliction which even while it was scarcely noticeable, had caused such intense suffering. . . .

It was the winter after our return from abroad, . . . in New York. . . .

While we were there we went often to the play and the opera; and, among our friends, one we loved very much would ask us to drop in for tea on our way home from a matinée. It was in her charming drawing room (how vividly I can still see it!) that the flash came from an empty sky, and my whole life was transfigured.

Like all other romantic episodes, great or small, in my life, this began with a sudden illumination. Or, rather, it did not begin at all; it was not there, and then it was there. One moment the world had appeared in stark outlines, colorless and unlit, and the next moment, it was flooded with radiance. I had caught that light from the glance of a stranger, and the smothered fire had flamed up from the depths. And this first love, as always, created the illusion of its own immortality. When I went out into the street, after that accidental meeting, I felt that I was walking, not in time, but in eternity. I moved amid values that had ceased to be ephemeral, and had become everlasting.

I remember shrinking back, as I entered the room; and when

we were introduced, I scarcely distinguished him from the man with whom he was talking. Then, gradually, I noticed that he kept his eyes on me while he was speaking to someone else, and, in my shyness, I became faintly uncomfortable. Still, however hard I tried, I could not keep my glance from turning in his direction. I felt my gaze drawn back to him by some invisible thread of selfconsciousness. I was aware of his interest, and I was aware, too, of his tall thin figure and his dark keen face, with hair which was slightly gray on the temples. What I did not know, at the time, for his name meant nothing to me, was that he had been married for years, and was the father of two sons, already at school or at college. What I knew, through some vivid perception, was that the awareness was not on my side alone, that he was following my words and my gestures, that a circle of attraction divided us from the persons around us. Most women, I suppose, have lived through such moments, but with most women this emotional awakening, as intangible as air, and as life-giving, must come, I think, earlier in youth. For I was twenty-six, and my twenty-seventh birthday would come in April. In the years before my youth was clouded by tragedy, I had known an attraction as swift and as imperative; but not ever the permanence, and the infallible certainty, as if a bell were ringing, "Here, now, this is my moment!"

Looking back, over the flat surface of experience, the whole occurrence appears incredibly wild and romantic. It does not belong to life; yet it remains, after all the years between, intensely alive. It is the one thing that has not passed; for not ever again, in the future, could I see my life closing as if it had not once bloomed and opened wide to the light.

After a little while, he broke away from the group, and crossed the room to join me by the window. I remember the window, the street outside, the carriages that went by; and I remember, too, the look of the room behind him, and even the shadows of firelight on his face, as he paused for an instant on his way toward me. We talked first of my two books, and, crude as they were, he liked them, because, he said, "there is something, I don't know what, but there is something." While I listened to him, not wondering whether I could hear his voice, I found, with a shock of pleasure, that his clear, crisp tones were distinct, without straining, without effort. The one tremendous obstacle to a natural association did not exist at all, or existed but slightly, when I was with him. Even when, as occasionally happened, I had to ask him to repeat what he said, he replied as if this touch of dependence were an added attraction. Out of the whole world of men, I had met the one man who knew, by sympathy, or by some other instinct, the right way of approach, who could, by his simple presence, release me from my too sensitive fears. I shall call him Gerald B——, because this name will do as well as another.

Of this, I knew nothing at that moment. All I felt was a swifter vibration, a quivering joy, as if some long imprisoned stream of life were beginning to flow again under the open sky. His eyes were gay, searching, intensely alive. Though I felt, or found, that we had scarcely an intellectual interest in common, the difference seemed only to increase his imperative charm over my heart and my senses. For, through that difference, he had recognized something in me— that mysterious something—which was akin to his own nature.

Months afterwards, an unsuspecting friend said to me: "One miracle in life I have seen, without knowing the cause. I saw your whole life change in a single spring. Everything about you, even the way you looked, came to life. I saw radiance stream under your skin. I saw the stricken look leave your eyes. I saw the bronze sheen return to your hair. No one could miss it who watched you. A month before you had been cold and reserved. Then suddenly, you bloomed again, and everyone felt your charm. I used to see people look at you, and think to myself, 'They feel something about her.' "

If these were not her exact words, they are near enough to express her meaning and her surprise. What she did not know was that this passionate awakening to life had restored my lost faith in myself. Love had proved to me that my personality, or my charm, could overcome, not only my deafness, but the morbid terror of that affliction, and, especially, of its effect upon others. . . . But of the many ties between us, I think the strongest was a kind of intimate laughter. It began at that first meeting, and it endured until the end of his life, seven years later. This laughter, springing from a kindred sense of humor, with a compelling physical magnetism, was to thrust itself, as a memory, between me and the fulfillment of any future emotion. . . .

On the way home that afternoon, Cary told me what she had heard of Gerald B——. Of all the incredible pursuits, it appeared that he was engaged in high finance, with a firm in or near Wall Street. Several times, rumor reported, his wife had been on the point of seeking a divorce, and had been prevented only by his devotion to their two sons. Now, though they occupied the same house, it was common knowledge that they were barely more than strangers to each other.

But all these truths, or half-truths, were without validity. The look in his eyes was the only reality. Some essence of joy had passed between us at our first glance; and I knew that he had perceived this more quickly than I. Only the old or the loveless, I told myself, could deny this affirmation of life. It must mean less to him, naturally, but it must mean something. Even if I never saw him again, I could hold fast to this one moment. Yet, deep in my unconscious mind or heart, I knew that I should see him again.

The next afternoon, before sunset, he came to see how we were settled, or so he remarked lightly. We were staying in an old apartment house, the Florence, and the rooms were large, with high ceilings and wide windows. A friend was in our living room when he came. I cannot recall how it happened, but when I left the room to find something, she showed him a photograph I had just given to her. She told me he looked at it until they heard me returning, and he had said then, as he gave it back to her: "She is so lovely, how could anyone help loving her?" The words shone in my mind, ringed with light, when they were repeated. Even now, they gleam with a faint incandescence, and I shall always remember and treasure them. For it was not until long afterwards that I made a curious discovery. Although I was not beautiful, I created the semblance of beauty for everyone who has ever loved me. This may be true of other women. I do not know, I know it has been true of me, not only with the men who have cared for me, but also with many of the women who were my closest friends. . . .

The next day I left off the half-mourning I had worn since Mother's death, and I went out eagerly to buy dresses that were gay and youthful and becoming. There is much to be said, I feel now, for the modern fashion of taking death so simply that nobody stays at home, not even the corpse, which often stops in a funeral room on the way to the grave. But to us of Southern blood, in the eighteen-nineties, death and dying and burial were still solemn occasions. We could not put one we loved into the earth as soon as the heart had stopped beating, and the custom of mourning meant, for us, long remembrance. It was not reasonable, that lost habit of fidelity, but in its very unreasonableness it was impressive. I saw, now, that those years of prolonged sorrow were wasted years. They had helped no one, least of all the dead, for whom I went in black, and sacrificed, unconsciously, what should have been the happiest years of my youth. Mother would not have wanted this sacrifice, nor would Walter have wanted it; for both Mother and Walter wished us to be happy; and this pall of Cary's grief, and of mine, bore as heavily upon Rebe, who was just growing up into her saddened girlhood. She and I had always been inseparable, and we remained so until her marriage in December, 1906. Shadow, I had called her.

But now, in this lost and recovered April of my life, I longed for vivid colors, and, wearing them, I became, myself, vivid. I bought the smartest hats from Paris, and, as my books were bringing in a little money, I went, for my clothes, to fashionable dressmakers. In a few weeks, I was so changed that Rebe was writing home, "I wish you could see Ellen. I don't know what has happened to her. After all those years in black, she is buying the gayest and brightest clothes, and you can't imagine how becoming they are to her. She looks years younger. You ought to see the admiring way people look after her."

Whether it was the gay clothes or the demolished inhibitions, I do not know; but that spring, for the first time, I felt that it was possible to overcome what I had regarded as an insurmountable impediment. The great discovery that my own identity, that I, myself, could triumph over brute circumstances, had destroyed and then re-created the entire inner world of my consciousness. "I will make myself well," I resolved. "I will make myself happy. I will make myself beautiful." For years, after that, I plunged, once a day, into the coldest water, winter or summer. I played golf, or walked miles, in all weathers. I slept, on stormy nights, with the snow drifting in over me. Little by little, I won back at least moderate health and nervous equilibrium. I looked better than I had looked at sixteen. "To me, you will always be the youngest thing in the world," he said.

For the next seven years I lived in an arrested pause between dreaming and waking. All reality was poured into a solitary brooding power, a solitary emotion. I use the word "solitary" with meaning, because this intense secret life was lived almost, if not entirely, alone, and under the surface. So little happened in the concrete to exert so tremendous an influence. We were apart so much, and together so little. Several months each year, I spent in New York; and then we saw each other in the evening, whenever it was possible. But, in those seven years, though my two sisters must have suspected, I confided in no one.

It is more than difficult to write, literally, of those years. Yet no honest story of my life could be told without touching upon them, and the only reason for this memoir is the hope that it may shed some beam of light, however faint, into the troubled darkness of human psychology. Outwardly, there was little to record, little to keep for remembrance. Inwardly, the impression spread in my unconscious mind, like the circle made by a stone flung into deep water. Since I had absorbed it into the elements of my nature, not as a passion, but as a transfiguring power, I could escape from its control only by escaping from my own personality.

I cannot ever, at night, walk through the streets of New York without remembering and forgetting all over again. Forgetting and remembering! The little cares, the little anxieties, the little joys. There were dozens of small, foreign restaurants he had known of, or we had stumbled upon almost by accident. Sometimes, in summer or on mild spring evenings, we would take a boat to Coney Island, where we could lose ourselves completely among the four elements. Yet a few memories start out more vividly. Going out with him the first time he drove his small racing car. An evening in the country, when we sat on a bench before a tiny tavern, waiting for the car to be mended, and wondered what would happen if we never went back. And, more vividly still, the many dinners in an obscure Hungarian restaurant, tucked away at the end of a strange street smelling of crushed apples. Again and again, we went there, urged by some instinct for the alien and the remote. Over and over, a sad violinist played a nameless Hungarian air; and this air is woven and interwoven, like a thread of song, through every recollection of those seven years. I never knew what it was, yet I can still hear it, filled with longing and very far-off in space. Like the "little phrase" from a sonata that Proust recalls in *A la Recherche du Temps Perdu,* this thread of song was wound, not through external scenes and episodes, as in the life of Swann, but, deeper still, through all the after memories of joy or of pain. At the time I had never heard of Proust; but years later, I discovered, with a startled surprise, that "little phrase" from the sonata.

All that spring, and all through our other springs and autumns, the nameless Hungarian air followed us; and, frequently, I, who have no ear for music, would hear him humming it, without words, as we sat together. Spring passed. Time passed. Life passed. Then, suddenly, one day, long after he was dead, when I was engaged to be married to another man, I felt a quiver of desire, and I heard again, rippling very faint and far away, scarcely more real than a vibration of memory, that sad, gay, nameless little song. So closely intertwined was that music with my emotional responses that a fragile wisp of sound could rise from out the past, and hold me back from surrender to another, and a newer, impulse. After those years, I felt love again, but never again could I feel ecstasy, never again the rush of wings in my heart. Several times I was in love with love. Twice I was engaged to be married. Always, when my senses were deeply stirred, some ghost of recollection would float between me and perfect fulfillment. I would feel a chill of disillusion; the joy would darken, the vital impulse would fail. "This isn't real," would whisper that malicious demon of irony, who had been driven but once out of my mind. "This is only pretending."

All this, it must be remembered, occurred, not in the mental upheaval of the Freudian era, but in that age of romantic passion, the swift turn of the century. If only we had read Freud and the new wisdom, we might have found love a passing pleasure, not a prolonged desire. Yet even this is uncertain. Of one thing alone I am very sure: it is a law of our nature that the memory of longing should survive the more fugitive memory of fulfillment. The modern adventurers who imagine they know love because they have known sex may be wiser than our less enlightened generation. But I am not of their period. I should have found wholly inadequate the mere physical sensation, which the youth of today seek so blithely. If I were young, now, I might feel differently. It is possible that I may have been only another victim of the world's superstitions about women. Perhaps. I do not know. Yet I am so constituted that the life of the mind is reality, and love without romantic illumination is a spiritless matter.

Since that decade, many standards have fallen, and most rules of conduct have altered beyond recognition. I was always a feminist for I liked intellectual revolt as much as I disliked physical violence. On the whole, I think women have lost something precious, but have gained, immeasurably, by the passing of the old order.

From those seven years, I saved these two indestructible memories. Time has flowed over them, but they are still there, in the past, changeless, steadfast, hollowed out of eternity.

A summer morning in the Alps. We are walking together over an emerald path. I remember the moss, the ferny greenness. I remember the Alpine blue of the sky. I remember, on my lips, the flushed air tasting like honey. The way was through a thick wood, in a park, and the path wound on and upward, higher and higher. We walked slowly, scarcely speaking, scarcely breathing in that brilliant light. On and upward, higher, and still higher. Then, suddenly, the trees parted, the woods thinned and disappeared. Earth and sky met and mingled. We stood, hand in hand, alone in that solitude, alone with the radiant whiteness of the Jungfrau. From the mountain, we turned our eyes to each other. We were silent, because it seemed to us that all had been said. But the thought flashed through my mind, and was gone, "Never in all my life can I be happier than I am, now, here, at this moment!"

God must find the soul, for the soul alone cannot find God. All religion, for me, was a more or less glorified mythology, and, too often, a cruel mythology. Christ, I told myself, had been crowded out of Christianity. The inn at Bethlehem was the world's symbol. Divinity flamed up, here and there, like a wandering light; but underneath, there remained the unyielding heart of African darkness.

Gerald died before I sailed for America, and I knew it only from a newspaper (the Paris edition of the *New York Herald*) that I read on a train. So that was finished, that was over forever. . . .

But nothing lasts. This passed with everything else. After a period of death-in-life, my mind slowly became alive again, and took up the old search for reality. . . .

After Cary's death, I left Richmond, hoping and thinking that I should never again see the city and the old gray house, behind magnolias and boxwood trees, on that forsaken corner. In that agonized recoil, my flight was the instinctive flight of a wounded animal from the trap. Almost blindly, I went, with Caroline Coleman, my most faithful friend, to New York; and, in an utterly vain effort to forget, we tramped for miles, in that August weather, over the scorched pavements. We were looking for an apartment, and, finally, I leased one, with a beautiful view, high up on Central Park West. I did not want people; I did not want sympathy. I wanted only to lose myself in a strange place, where nothing would remind me of grief or of joy or of any life I had known. . . .

But this could not last. In the autumn my mind awakened from sleep, and strangely enough, I found that my imagination was more active than ever. The long vacancy, the fallow season, had increased its fertility. The idea for *Virginia* pushed its way to the surface of thought; but I soon discovered that the characters would not come to life in New York. They needed their own place and soil and atmosphere; and after a brief and futile resistance, I went back, for a visit to old Petersburg, which is the Dinwiddie of my novel. There, I found not only Virginia herself, but the people and the houses, and the very essence of time and place. My social history had sprung from a special soil, and it could grow and flower, naturally, in no other air. For the same reason, perhaps, I could not write in New York. So I lived there for a few months at a time. Then, when the mood for work seized me, I would go back to the upstairs study in my old house, where I would stay hidden, until the mood for work changed into the impulse to wander. Most of my summers were spent abroad, but wherever I was, whether in the actual world or in the old world of imagination, I was driven, consciously or unconsciously, by my old antagonist, a past from which I was running away. But, even then, there was no escape from that closing barrier of deafness which held me, imprisoned, with my sorrow and my memories. Not for a solitary minute in time could that wall of silence be broken through or pushed back into nothingness. . . .

The gift of imagination has been, with me, a divided endowment, and has run in two separate and dissimilar veins. Whenever I have worked one vein to the end, I find myself recoiling upon the other and seeking a fresh stimulus. This double system has prevented my "writing out," as so many novelists, particularly American novelists, have done after their earlier books. *Barren Ground* left me drained, but only in one capacity. Immediately, my imagination reacted from the novel of character into the mood of polite comedy. It required three comedies of manners to exhaust this impulse toward ironic humor, and not one of these books betrays, I think, the slightest sign that I had burned up my energy. After the long emotional strain of *Barren Ground,* my first comedy, *The Romantic Comedians,* seemed to bubble out with an effortless joy.

An unsentimental republic might have discovered the moron, as it discovered sex, with more understanding and less romance. But America has enjoyed the doubtful blessing of a single-track mind. We are able to accommodate, at a time, only one national hero; and we demand that that hero shall be uniform and invincible. As a literate people we are preoccupied, neither with the race nor the individual, but with the type. Yesterday, we romanticized the "tough guy"; today, we are romanticizing the under-privileged, tough or tender; tomorrow, we shall begin to romanticize the pure primitive.

The result of this tendency has been, of course, the general softening and weakening of our national fiber. One may share the generous wish that all mankind should inherit the world's beauty, without consenting to destroy that beauty because it is beyond the reach and the taste alike of the vast majority. For beauty, like ecstasy, has always been hostile to the commonplace. And the commonplace, under its popular label of the normal, has been the supreme authority for *Homo sapiens* since the days when he was probably arboreal.

But all memories return, especially the sharp-set memories of youth. For more than twenty years I had not thought of Gerald. He had ceased, even as a recollection, to have a part in my life. He was gone. He was finished, with my first love, with my girlhood. If he were to come back to me, I should scarcely recognize him, for he would be old. Once he had meant to me all the youth of the world; and, now, he would be old, and forgotten by time. So much had happened since I had known him. So much substance and illusion, so many figures and shadows, had come and gone in my mind, in my heart. . . . Then, when I was nearing sixty, I went out, one evening in New York, to a foreign restaurant in a strange street, which was yet vaguely familiar. I smelt the scents of crushed apples and crowded places; and, suddenly, I remembered. I saw him again, clearly; I heard again, from very far off, that little nameless Hungarian song. For one moment alone; not ever, not ever again, after that evening. . . .

It was nothing. It meant nothing. But that Hungarian air was the only music that I, who am not musical, have ever remembered. Or did I remember it? How can one tell where memory ends and imagination begins?

A friend said to me this summer: "The people here think you so gay and attractive that they wonder why you write such sad books."

I laughed. "But my books are not sad! And there will always be, if God permits, a last laugh at the end." In the life of the mind, glad or sad, there will always be laughter, and the life of the mind alone, I have found, contains an antidote to experience. . . .

Yes, I have had my life. I have known ecstasy. I have known anguish. I have loved, and I have been loved. With one I loved, I have watched the light breaking over the Alps. If I have passed through "the dark night of the soul," I have had a far-off glimpse of the illumination beyond. For an infinitesimal point of time or eternity, I have caught a gleam, or imagined I caught a gleam, of the mystic vision. . . . It was enough, and it is now over. Not for everything that the world could give would I consent to live over my life unchanged, or to bring back, unchanged, my youth. . . .

Only on the surface of things have I ever trod the beaten path. So long as I could keep from hurting anyone else, I have lived, as completely as it was possible, the life of my choice. I have been free. Yet I have not ever stolen either the ponderable or the imponderable material of happiness. I have done the work I wished to do for the sake of that work alone. And I have come, at last, from the fleeting rebellion of youth into the steadfast—or is it merely the seasonable—accord without surrender of the unreconciled heart.

Louise Bogan

(1897–1970)

Louise Bogan, poet and critic, was the second child and only daughter of lower-middle-class parents in Livermore Falls, Maine. Her parents' marriage was marked by violent quarrels, tensions over money, frequent sudden moves to escape creditors or to seek new employment, and finally separation. Bogan's education was episodic until the family moved to Boston in 1909, when she was enrolled in Girls' Latin School and began to demonstrate the intellectual brilliance and creative energy characteristic of her later life.

Like many daughters of troubled and violent marriages, Bogan early sought a family of her own through marriage. Although she supported herself entirely after her first year in college, life alone did not appeal to her. After enrolling in Boston University in 1915, she dropped out to marry Curt Alexander, a career man in the army by whom she had a child in 1917. The marriage was troubled from the start, but Bogan began writing poetry and saw her first work published the year of her daughter's birth.

Separating from her husband in 1919, Bogan settled in New York, where she took clerical jobs allowing her time to focus on her own writing and later worked for intervals at branches of the New York Public Library. In 1923 her first volume of verse, *Body of This Death*, was published to critical acclaim. The same year Bogan began a tempestuous relationship with Raymond Holden, whom she married in 1925.

Bogan's literary career gained momentum as she became a reviewer for *The New Republic* and was invited to the newly founded writers' colony Yaddo in 1926. *Dark Summer*, her second volume of verse, appeared in 1929, and the next year Bogan received the John Reed Memorial Prize for her poetry. The following year she became a reviewer for *The New Yorker,* a position she held for thirty-eight years. But this success was accompanied by the onset of severe depression requiring inpatient treatment at the New York Neurological Institute. In 1933, confident of recovery, she applied for and received a Guggenheim Fellowship to support her work abroad, but she was forced to return by the declining value of her dollar-denominated award. She entered New York Hospital's Westchester Division for further psychiatric treatment before the year ended.

After separating from her second husband, Bogan began an

affair with Theodore Roethke, an affair accompanied by another burst of creativity, work which was published as *The Sleeping Fury* in 1937. The same year she took up her interrupted Guggenheim Fellowship and while traveling abroad began a satisfactory affair, which provided stability and reassurance in her life. *Poems and New Poems,* published in 1941, established her as a major figure in American letters, and her work earned her an appointment as consultant in poetry to the Library of Congress, a fellowship in American letters at the Library of Congress, the Harriet Monroe Award from the University of Chicago, and numerous invitations to teach at American universities.

From the mid fifties Bogan was awarded every major prize for poetry available to an American poet except the Pulitzer, together with several honorary doctorates. Yet she was haunted by recurrent depression and fearful that her poetic powers had dried up. With great personal courage, she kept laboring, despite another hospitalization for depression, publishing *The Blue Estuaries: Poems 1923–1968* in 1969.

The narrative fragments which appear here are drawn from Bogan's short autobiographical essay published in *The New Yorker* in January 1933 and from selections of her letters and diary entries, edited posthumously by a friend. These fragments chronicle her troubled childhood, the sources of her poetry, and the purgatory of depression. While they cannot be called an autobiography, the narrator's voice within each fragment is so powerful that no anthology of American women's autobiographical writing can be satisfactory without including Bogan's ironic and witty voice.

JOURNEY AROUND MY ROOM:
The Autobiography of Louise Bogan

The most advantageous point from which to start this journey is the bed itself, wherein, at midnight or early in the morning, the adventurous traveller lies moored, the terrain spread out before him. The most fortunate weather is warm to cool, engendered by a westerly breeze, borne from the open window toward the ashes in the grate. At midnight, moonlight lies upon the floor, to guide the traveller's eye; in the early morning, the bleak opacity that serves the traveller in this region as sun brightens the brick wall of the house across the yard, and sheds a feeble reflected glow upon all the objects which I shall presently name.

This is a largish room, almost square in shape. It faces east and west, and is bounded on the north by the hall, which leads, after some hesitation, to the kitchen; on the south by someone's bedroom in the house next door; on the west, by backyards and the Empire State Building; on the east, by Lexington Avenue, up and down which electric cars roll with a noise like water running into a bottle. Its four walls are chastely papered with Manila paper. Its floor is inadequately varnished. Its ceiling bears all the honors away: it is quite lofty in pitch, and it is clean, absolutely unspotted, in fact, save for a little damp over the fireplace, which, from some angles, looks like a fish. A fireplace, resembling a small black arch, occupies a middle position in the south wall. Above it, a plain deal mantelpiece of ordinary design supports a row of books, a photograph of the News Building taken from the Chanin Building, four shells from a Maine beach, and a tin of Famous Cake Box Mixture. Above these objects hangs a Japanese print, depicting Russian sailors afflicted by an angry ocean, searchlights, a burning ship, and a boatload of raging Japanese.

The initial mystery that attends any journey is: how did the traveller reach his starting point in the first place? How did I reach the window, the walls, the fireplace, the room itself; how do I happen to be beneath this ceiling and above this floor? Oh, that is a matter for conjecture, for argument pro and con, for research, supposition, dialectic! I can hardly remember how. Unlike Livingstone, on the verge of darkest Africa, I have no maps to hand, no globe of the terrestrial or the celestial spheres, no chart of mountains, lakes, no sextant, no artificial horizon. If ever I possessed a compass, it has long since disappeared. There must be, however, some reasonable explanation for my presence here. Some step started me toward this point, as opposed to all other points on the habitable globe, I must consider; I must discover it.

And here it is. One morning in March, in the year 1909, my father opened the storm door leading from the kitchen to the backsteps, on Chestnut Street, in Ballardvale, a small town in Massachusetts, on the Boston & Maine Railroad. . . .

Although the houses stood securely fastened to the ground, as always, everything in the town went wild in autumn and blew about the streets. Smoke blew wildly from chimneys and torrents of leaves were pulled from the trees; they rushed across the sidewalks and blew against wagons and people and trains; they blew uphill and fell from great heights and small ones; they fell to the ground and into the river. Clouds rode high in the sky; the sun shone brilliantly everywhere. Or else half the town would lie in the shadow of a long cloud and half the town would stand shining bright, the weathervanes almost as still in a strong blast coming from one quarter as in no wind at all, the paint sparkling on the clapboards. Sometimes in the late afternoon the full sun came from two directions at once, from the west and reflected in a full blaze from the windows of houses looking westward.

The children were blown home from school, shouting and running, along with the leaves. They were blown up paths to side doors, or through orchards, or into back yards, where perhaps their mothers stood, taking the last clothes in off the line, apron strings flying out from their waists. The children rushed into kitchens that smelled of baking or of ironed clothes. The doors swung behind them; some of the wind came in, and some of the leaves.

The best time to write about one's childhood is in the early thirties, when the contrast between early forced passivity and later freedom is marked; and when one's energy is in full flood. Later, not only have the juices dried up, and the energy ceased to be abundant, but the retracing of the scene of earliest youth has become a task filled with boredom and dismay. The figures that surrounded one have now turned their full face toward us; we understand them perhaps still partially, but we know them only too well. They have ceased to be background to our own terribly important selves; they have irremediably taken on the look of figures in a tragi-comedy; we now look on them ironically, for we know their end, although they themselves do not yet know it. And now—in the middle fifties—we have traced and retraced their tragedy so often that, in spite of the understanding we have, it bores and offends us. There is a final antidote we must learn: to love and forgive them. This attitude comes hard and must be reached with anguish. For if one is to deal with the people in the past—of one's past—at all, one must feel neither anger nor bitterness. . . .

For people like myself to look back is a task. It is like re-entering a trap, or a labyrinth, from which one has only too lately, and too narrowly, escaped.

I used to think that my life would be a journey from the particular squalor which characterized the world of my childhood to another squalor, less clear in my mind, but nevertheless fairly particularized in my imagination. When I see some old building—one of those terrible rooming houses with a milk bottle and a brown paper bag on nearly every windowsill—being demolished, I say to myself, in real surprise: "Why, I have outlasted it!" For it was these old brick hotels and brownstone lodging houses that I early chose, consciously as well as subconsciously, as the dwelling of my old age. I saw them, moreover, as they were in my childhood, with the light of a gas mantle making their dark green and brown interiors even more hideous; with the melancholy of their torn and dirty lace-curtained windows intact. . . . all were there, behind some ragged curtain, waiting for me to return—to relive, in poverty-stricken old age, my poverty-stricken youth *in Ballardvale, a small town in Massachusetts, on the Boston & Maine Railroad*. . . .

We had come to Ballardvale from Milton, with no house ready for us to live in, and began by boarding at the Gardners'. My father must have been away, during those first few weeks, for I see only my mother and myself in the big guest bedroom, one window of which looked straight into the leaves of a tall tree. It must have been June or July, for I remember my mother sending me out to the little fruit store, down the hill, for a pound of cherries. . . . I was seven that summer. . . .

I can only express my delight and happiness with the Gardners' way of living by saying that they had one of everything. Up to that time (except for a short period before Milton) I had lived in the Milton Hotel; I had seen normal households only on short visits; I had no idea of ordered living. . . .

But with the Gardners it was different. Order ran through the house. There were no bare spaces, or improvised nooks and corners; the kitchen shone with paint and oilcloth; the parlor, although minuscule, was a parlor through and through. The dining room, with its round table always ready for a meal (the turning castor-set in the center, the white damask cloth), was used to eat in, three times a day, and the meals were always on time. There was a delightful little sitting room, off the front porch. And beyond the sitting room, in one of the ells (our bedroom was above it), ran Mrs. Gardner's workroom (she sewed), with a long bare table, a dress form, and a cabinet-like bureau where she kept her materials. This was the first workroom I had ever seen. I used to dream about it for years. . . .

Later, during the winter when my mother was away and I was in the convent, it was the parlor which enchanted me. . . .

One of everything and everything ordered and complete: napkins in napkin rings; plants in jardinieres; blankets at the foot of the beds, and an afghan on the sofa. Pills in little bottles in the sideboard drawer (the Gardners believed in homeopathic medicine). Doilies on the tables; platters and sauce boats and berry dishes and differently shaped glasses and crescent-shaped bone dishes and cups and saucers and cake plates in the dining-room china cabinet. A brightly polished silver card-receiver on the table in the hall. A hat rack. An umbrella stand. And, in the kitchen, black iron pans and black tin bread pans; a kettle; a double boiler; a roaster; a big yellow mixing bowl; custard cups; pie tins; a cookie jar. Mrs. Gardner often made, for midday dinner or for supper, *one* single large pie. . . .

Blessed order! Blessed thrift. . . .

People lived in intense worlds beyond me.

So that I do not at first see my mother. I see her clearly much later than I smell and feel her—long after I see those solid fractions of the houses and fields. She comes in frightfully clearly, all at once. But first I have learned the cracks in the sidewalk, the rain in the gutter, the mud and the sodden wayside leaves, the shape of every plant and weed and flower in the grass.

The incredibly ugly mill towns of my childhood, barely dissociated from the empty, haphazardly cultivated, half wild, half deserted countryside around them. Rough stony pastures, rugged woodlots, lit up and darkened by the clearly defined, pale, lonely light and shadow of weather that has in it the element of being newly descried—for a few hundred years only—by the eye of the white man. The light that falls incredibly down through a timeless universe to light up clapboard walls, old weathered shingles as well as newly painted, narrow-faced cottages, adorned with Victorian fretwork. In Ballardvale, the mill, warm, red brick, with small-paned windows (an example of good proportion, as I afterwards discovered); on side streets the almost entirely abandoned wooden tenements of the early mill town; on the main streets the big white or yellow houses with high, square parlors and bedrooms; the occasional mansard roof. . . .

The people can only be put down as they were *found* by the child, misunderstood by, and puzzling to, the child; clumsy beings acting seemingly without purpose or reason. The grain in a plank sidewalk certainly came through more clearly to me at first than anything grownups, or even other children, did. . . .

I must have experienced violence from birth. But I remember it, at first, as only bound up with *flight*. I was bundled up and carried away. . . .

In the town of Milton violence first came through. I remember getting there with my mother by train; the name of the town was planted out in coleuses and begonias on a bank beside the station. I was four or five. We lived in a hotel, a long drive back through the streets of the town from the station. The hotel faced the river and the mill; a long rough pasture ran behind it. I played with the rough Yankee and French-Canadian children in this field. We ate rhubarb with salt, and an occasional raw potato. Downstairs in the hotel was some kind of barroom and café. The man's collar with a stain of blood on it, on the sidewalk, one Sunday morning. . . .

We ate in the dining room. My mother soon became friendly with the waitresses. She wore white starched shirtwaists with gold cufflinks, and sometimes drove over in a buggy to a dressmaker in a neighboring town; she handled horses well. A long, high blue mass rose above the trees. "Is it the sea?" I asked. "No," she said. "It is the mountains." . . .

How ugly some of the women were! And both men and women bore ugly scars—of skin ailments, of boils, of carbuncles—on their faces, their necks, behind their ears. Sometimes their boils suppurated. All this I marked down with a clinical eye. Then, their bodies were often scarecrow thin, or monstrously bloated. Mrs. X (one of my mother's "familiars") was a dried up, emaciated woman with a sharp nose and ferret eyes: a little horror. Later, I learned that she had carried on a clandestine love affair, for years, with the hotel's proprietor. I must put down his name: Bodwell. Like every other woman in these towns, at that time, she had a house full of veneered furniture, plush, and doilies; and she kept her sewing machine (again a custom) in the bay window of the dining room. . . .

The secret family angers and secret disruptions passed over my head, it must have been for a year or so. But for two days, I went blind, I remember my sight coming back, by seeing the flat forked light of the gas flame, in its etched glass shade, suddenly appearing beside the bureau. What had I seen? I shall never know.

But one (and final) scene of violence comes through. It is in lamplight, with strong shadows, and an open trunk is the center of it. The curved lid of the trunk is thrown back, and my mother is bending over the trunk, and packing things into it. She is crying and she screams. My father, somewhere in the shadows, groans as though he has been hurt. It is a scene of the utmost terror. And then my mother sweeps me into her arms, and carries me out of the room. She is fleeing; she is running away. Then I remember no more, until a quite different scene comes before my eyes. It is morning—earliest morning. My mother and I and another woman are in a wooden summerhouse on a lawn. The summerhouse is painted white and green, and it stands on a slight elevation, so that the cool pale light of a summer dawn pours around it on all sides. At some distance away the actual house stands, surrounded by ornamental shrubs which weep down upon the grass, or seem to crouch against it. The summerhouse itself casts a fanciful and distorted shadow. Then we are in the actual house, and I am putting my hands on a row of cold, smooth silk balls, which hang from the edge of a curtain. Then someone carries me upstairs. The woman goes ahead with a lamp. . . .

Then I see her again. Now the late sun of early evening shoots long shadows like arrows, far beyond houses and trees: a low, late light, slanted across the field and river, throwing the shade of trees and thickets for a long distance before it, so that objects far distant from one another are bound together. I never truly feared her. Her tenderness was the other side of her terror. Perhaps, by this time, I had already become what I was for half my life: the semblance of a girl, in which some desires and illusions had been early assassinated: shot dead.

In Ballardvale a long path led up to the side door of the house, which led into the kitchen. At night, as you sat beside the table and the lamp, in the dining room, you could hear for a moment or two the footsteps of someone coming to that door, and, in the autumn, you could hear leaves scurrying down the path. You sat beside the lamp, which burned, without a shade, with a wide, flat flame.

My father's steps, coming home to supper, were reassuring.

Why do I remember this house as the happiest in my life? I was never really happy there. But now I realize that it was the house wherein I began to read, wholeheartedly and with pleasure. It was the first house where bookshelves (in a narrow space between the dining room and the parlor) appeared as a part of the building; they went up to the ceiling, and were piled with my brother's books, mixed with the books my mother had acquired in one way or another: from itinerant book salesmen, mostly, who in those days, in the country, went from door to door.

It is a house to which I return, in a recurrent dream. The dream is always the same. I go back to the house as I now am. I put into it my chairs, my pictures, but most of all my books. Sometimes the entire second floor has become a library, filled with books I have never seen in reality but which I have close knowledge of in the dream. I rearrange the house from top to bottom: new curtains at the windows, new pictures on the walls. But somehow the old rooms are still there—like shadows, seeping through. Indestructible. Fixed.

I began to read comparatively late, and I did not teach myself: I had to be taught my letters in school. I remember the summer I was seven staring at pages of print in bafflement and anger, trying to shake out some meaning from the rows of printed words, but it was no good: I could not read. But books were read to me, and I can remember the last occasion when this was done: it was during our first (and last) winter in the house on Oak Street, when I had scarlet fever, and was bedded down in the parlor for the length of the illness. My brother was home from school that winter and had not begun to work—he was nineteen or twenty. He and my mother were closer to one another, and gayer, than at any other time. They made a cookbook out of large sheets of brown paper, copying in the *receipts* by hand; and they laughed because so many directions ended by being placed under the heading *Miscellaneous*. My brother had been born when my mother was nineteen, and they had grown up together like brother and sister. He, too, had suffered his minor death, before I was born; he had been set apart from normal love long ago. Now he was a handsome young man, with great dark eyes; and that year, and for a few years thereafter, he was still capable of lightheartedness.

After my illness, I went back to school, and suddenly could read. I remember that early reader which was given to some of us, in the afternoon, as a sort of reward for a morning's good work. It was called *Heart of Oak,* and its contents were as delicious as food. They *were* food; they were the beginning of a new life. I had partially escaped. Nothing could really imprison me again. The door had opened, and I had begun to be free. . . .

Later, when we moved to the house opposite the Gardners', I had worked out my escape with some care. The stove in the dining room stood out from the wall, and behind it, on the floor, with an old imitation astrakhan cape of my mother's beneath me (as a rug to discourage drafts), I began to read everything in the house. First came my brother's books—books whose names and whose substance I can never forget. *Cuore: An Italian School Boy's Journal; Cormorant Crag; The Young Carthaginian.* The coal in the stove burns steadily, behind the mica door; I remember the feel of the ingrain carpet against the palms of my hands, and the grain of the covers of the books, and the softness of the woolen cape against my knees.

I am going away. I shan't ever see old Leonard . . . or the mill dam, or the mill, or the swing in Gardners' yard, or the maple tree in my own, or the hedge of arbor vitae around the Congregationalist church. Or hear, in the night, the express whistling for the crossing, or, in the daytime, the Boston train, and the train for Lawrence and Lowell, braking down for the stop, ringing its bell around the curve.

Now, this morning, the Boston train is coming in from the fields beyond the river, and slows and brakes and stops. The steam shrieks out of the engine and smoke trails out, into the clear morning, from the smokestack, blotting out the willows and the mill dam. The conductor lifts me up to the step. That is the reason for my presence here. I took the Boston train in March 1909.

Our house, built to accommodate three families, one to a floor, was perhaps two years old. Carpenters hammered new three-family houses together continually, on all sides of it. For several of my adolescent years, until the street was finally given up as completed,

I watched and heard the construction of these houses. Even when finished, they had an extremely provisional look, as though a breath of wind could blow them away.

Perhaps the beginning of my "depression" can be located at the occasion (a fall-winter morning and early afternoon) when I went back to the earliest neighborhood we lived in after coming to Boston. It was always a good distance away, in one of the drearier suburbs, to be reached by trolley car from Dudley Street. But in those days (1909) the red brick block of an apartment house (with stores below) was surrounded by empty lots, and even, at the back, within view of a wooden veranda, by a scrubby overgrown field, filled with underbrush and a few trees. A large, sunken field was visible from the row of windows, on the apartment's long side; and here boys played baseball all spring and summer. The front windows (two in the parlor, and one in the adjoining "alcove") faced the openings of two or more streets, rather nicely kept, with single wooden houses—and even some white-washed stones outlining pathways. The brand-new apartment house, more than a block long, abutted on a small, older region, with some stores and a general run-down air. A steep street forked off to the right, downhill; and at the bottom of this hill stairs went up (v. close to house-walls) to the local railway station, with infrequent trains. I sometimes walked down this unfrequented stretch of tracks, on the way to school. The neighborhood finally reached by such a walk was already a semi-slum: depressing by reason of single houses needing paint, as much as by a scattering of those three-decker wooden apartment buildings, with front and back porches, which were becoming so usual in the outer Boston suburbs.

Our own apartment was of the "railroad" kind: a center hall ran from the front door to the kitchen, with parlor, parlor alcove, the large bedroom, and dining room opening out from it. Beyond the kitchen (and its large pantry), to its right, and with the windows at the side (and at the back?), was a smaller bedroom, partially unfurnished, and dreary to a degree. My father and, often, my brother slept here. I slept with my mother, in the other bedroom, which had some respectable furniture in it, and a view over the open sunken field.

My father and mother, after a period of ghastly quarrels (and one long separation), at this time were making some effort to re-establish themselves, as a couple and as a family. New furniture and rugs had been bought for the front rooms; the piano was open and used; pictures were hung, and lace curtains veiled the windows. The woodwork of the place was, of course, dark brown, and dark green wallpaper predominated (although not in the bedroom, as I remember). There was a new brass bed. The dining room, where I came to do my lessons, had its square center table, its elaborate sideboard, a couch, and another largish table, which held some books and papers. The kitchen table was scrubbed pine. Was there a gas stove? The big black iron range functioned for major cooking—for those meals which often appeared at irregular intervals. I distinctly remember the taste of thin pieces of steak, kept warm in the overhead heating compartment, together with fried potatoes. Sunday dinner and the evening meals could be counted on to appear on time.

When I went back to this region, last fall, the whole area had slipped into true slumhood. The open field was gone; a large garage stood on its site; gray, metallic, forbidding. And the houses had crowded into the back scrubby field: a row of three-family structures, crowded as close to one another as possible. The air of a crowded necessitous place hit me like a breath of sickness—of hopelessness, of despair. The stores which had once existed in our block were gone: their windows cracked and broken. Only the old bakery, down the street, still persisted. . . . I had walked down from Codman Square—the cross streets here had lost all vestige of the openness and quiet which I remembered; again crowded with run-down stores, with only the Public Library branch (where I had read my first books, in 1909) keeping a certain dignity. A large school building also abutted on the Square. This is not the Girls' Latin School, which when I graduated from it, in 1915, was situated on the edge of the Boston Fenway.

A wave of despair seized me, after I had walked around the Library (now bedizened with cheap signs and notices but still keeping its interesting curved walls). No book of mine was listed in the catalogue. (A slight paranoid shudder passed over me.) —I felt the consuming, destroying, deforming passage of time; and the spectacle of my family's complete helplessness, in the face of their difficulties, swept over me. With no weapons against what was already becoming an overwhelming series of disasters—no insight, no self-knowledge, no inherited wisdom—I saw my father and mother (and my brother) as helpless victims of ignorance, wilfulness, and temperamental disabilities of a near-psychotic order—facing a period (after 1918) where even this small store of pathetic acquisitions would be swept away. The anguish which filled my spirit and mind may, perhaps, be said to have engendered (and reawakened) poisons long since dissipated, so that they gathered, like some noxious gas, at the v. center of my being. The modern horrors of the district also became part of this miasma; certainly the people in these newly overcrowded streets were as lost as those members of generations preceding them. . . . But those were my first years of adolescence—and of the creative impulse—and of hard and definitive schooling. And, as I remember, in spite of the growing sense of crisis by which I was continually surrounded, they were years of a beginning variety of interests—of growth and of hope.

The thing to remember, and "dwell on," is the extraordinary *courage* manifested by those two disparate, unawakened (if not actually *lost*) souls: my mother and father. I cannot bring myself to describe the horrors of the pre-1914 lower-middle-class life, in which they found themselves. My father had his job, which kept him in touch with reality; it was his life, always. My mother had nothing but her temperament, her fantasies, her despairs, her secrets, her subterfuges. The money—every cent of it earned by my father, over all the years—came through in a thin stream, often blocked or actually exhausted. Those dollar bills—so definitive! Those quarters and ten-cent pieces—so valuable. (I went to school on a quarter a day.) Those terrible splurges on her clothes, which kept my mother going! How did they manage to keep a roof over their heads! With absolutely no plans for the future—no foresight—no practical acumen of any kind.

Yet out of this exiguous financial situation came my music lessons—my music—my Saturday money (50¢, often) for movies and even the theatre; what clothes I had—that we all had—and food. Even a woman to help with the wash. Little excursions to the beach in the summer.

No books (the library supplied those). No social expenditures. Those two people, literally cut off from any social contacts, with the exception of one or two neighbors—often as eccentric as my parents themselves. —No invitation to classmates—or perhaps one or two—in all those years. Cut off. Isolated. Strung up with a hundred anxieties. And yet they survived—and I went through my entire adolescence—in this purgatory—with an open hell in close relation. A hell which tended to blow into full being on all holidays—when my mother's multiple guilts towards her treatment of her foster mother tended to shake loose. . . .

I cannot describe or particularize. Surely all this agony has long since been absorbed into my work. Even then, it was beginning to be absorbed. For I began writing—at length, in prose—in 1909; and within a year (my last in elementary school) I had acquired the interest of one of those intelligent old maids who so often showed talented children their earliest talents—opened up their earliest efforts by the application of attention and sympathy. I went to the Girls' Latin School in the autumn of 1910, at the age of thirteen, for five most fruitful years. I began to write verse from about fourteen on. The life-saving process then began. By the age of 18 I had a thick pile of manuscript, in a drawer in the dining room—and had learned every essential of my trade.

Beneath this truly horrifying array of literature is situated a large and comparatively unused desk, on which stand displayed pictures of myself and several other people, a pot of pencils, largely decayed, a cashbook that serves as a bill file, an inkstand that serves as a letter file, and a letter file that serves as a bill file. Also a lamp, an ashtray, a stamp box (empty), two postcards, a paper knife made out of a cartridge and bearing the arms of the city of Verdun, and a large quantity of blank paper. . . .

August 1933

My ability to write poetry comes to this: that I can write now only when in a rage (of anger or of hatred), or in a state which I can only describe as malicious pity. And the emotion that writes tender and delicate poetry is so much akin to the emotion of love that it *is* love, to all intents and purposes.

Yes, I remember very clearly the emotions, and their extraordinary resemblance to one another. The letting go, the swoon, the suffused eyes, the loose hand, the constriction in the throat, the abasement, the feeling of release.

Perfectly, perfectly, I remember them! But it would be a peculiar combination of overwhelming circumstances that could overcome my reluctance toward feeling either of them once more.

Abasement in religious poetry.

What one needs, when one has come to a state of this sort, is a bang up love affair that one can enjoy, and that one need not draw back from, or continually back and fill in. That's what one needs.

Otherwise, there's no hope, save a sourly smiling vigil waiting for the next rage to come on.

A dull life, really!

Going in is like this: one morning you finally make up your mind that no one in the world, with the single and certain exception of yourself, has a problem, utters a groan, or sheds a tear. The entire habitable globe, to your distraught imagination, is peopled by human beings who eat three meals a day, surrounded by smiling faces, work with a will in offices, fields, factories, and mines, and sleep every hour of the night. All the young human beings are in love; all the middle-aged are either charmingly drunk or soberly busy; all the old are reading memoirs or knitting or whittling wood, completely jolly and resigned. The animal world, as well, gambols about in jungle and over llano and crag; happy bright-eyed sheep crop grass; the gay cow chews its cud; the laughing crow swoops over the cornfield, fish and mussel, ant and peacock, woodchuck and mole, rabbit and cuttlefish go their several ways rejoicing. The cat on the hearth conceals no tattered heart beneath its fur, and the dog on the leash is ravaged by neither remorse nor despair.

You look back over history and it presents to your biased eye nothing but records of glamour and triumph. O happy happy Aztecs; O splendid Punic Wars; O remarkably situated medieval serfs; O Renaissance figures, armed to the teeth and glowing with inward delight; O fortunate members of the Children's Crusade; O jolly dwellers in the fifteenth, sixteenth, seventeenth, and eighteenth centuries! O Athenians, O Mongols, O Seljuk Turks, Semites, Visigoths, Manchus, Moors, and paleolithic woman and man! Happy, happy they!

As for you, the most miserable person in any age, you sob and clutch your breast and reject with a sneer all consolations of religion and philosophy. You kick, you snarl, you spit, and you scream. Outside your horrid home the peaceful world flows serenely by: traffic lights change, and the streetcars, instead of swerving off the tracks under the influence of a motorman in the throes of anguish, stop quietly at a lifted hand. People go from one place to another and seem equally pleased with either. Men and women, living their lives neatly and with hellish certainty and precision, rise in the morning, bathe, dress, eat breakfast, lunch, and dinner, smoke cigarettes, earn their livings, drink cocktails, brush their teeth; and, after a well-spent day, finally retire. Looms chatter, turbines whir, and automobiles consume gasoline (for, to your disordered mind, even the machines are happy). In the bowels of the earth miner does not attack miner with shovel and pick; sanely, and in an orderly fashion, all miners attack the coal, iron, or other mineral which they are expected to attack. The captains of ships do not furiously hurl their instruments of navigation clear across the bridge. No barricades are thrown up in the streets, and, in motion-picture and other theatres, the imperturbable patrons would never think of breaking into a howl and charging, in a body, the stage or screen.

Elsewhere, all is mild. But for you there is no hope. Your nervous system yawns before you like the entrance to the pit and you are going in.

The period of time over which you harbor these mistaken ideas about yourself and the rest of the world varies greatly. If your constitution is good, you may easily growl and snarl for the rest of your life. If you are of feeble stamina, you may sob and scratch for perhaps two months or two years. In order to give this article some point, let us assume that, after a reasonable lapse, you finally recover. A remnant of your life lies before you. You can choose several roads to happiness and a useful career. Let us examine these roads as briefly as possible.

You may, with great rapidity, start hating or loving. Your love may be of the Shelleyan or of the Christian variety: you may, on the one hand, sink infatuate on the breast of one individual (or, progressively, upon the breasts of several, in a series); on the other, you may figuratively embrace all mankind. Hate does not present many choices; if hate is your solution, you are fairly certain to hate all phenomena with equal joy and intensity, without troubling to drag into prominence any one feature from the loathsome whole. Or you may feel very noble or very powerful. Feeling noble or powerful also defies analysis; when one feels noble or powerful in any degree, one feels noble or powerful, and there's nothing more to say.

But no matter how rapidly you manage to go into your adjustment, no matter how eagerly you grab at the sops of love, hate, nobility, or the mission of personal dominance, you are certain to see, for one lucid moment, one clear flash of that world formerly thought so serene. For one split second you are upheld in a dead calm. You are no longer the world's lost child or the universe's changeling. You are a normal person, ready to join your fellows.

Standing on the latest point reached in the long and unbroken graph of lunacy that rises from the eoliths and culminates, for the time being, in the general situation at whatever day, hour, minute it happens to be, you may survey those fellows from whom you have long felt yourself estranged. You will survey them, I trust, with affection, or with malicious pity; it is not the part of a noble and newly normal soul to survey them with contempt. You will survey the intelligent unhinged, the unenlightened witless, and the plain cracked. And you will realize (only for a moment, you understand) that if you took to eating blotting paper, painting things green, living in trees, or indulging in frequent, piercing maniacal cries, you could not exceed the high average of oddity and derangement that you perceive all about you.

Having had your moment, you no longer have anything to fear. Crawl in and out of your nervous system as you will, you are an initiate. You are among friends. You are cured. You may again take your place as a normal person in a normal world.

What makes a writer? Is it the love of, and devotion to, the actual act of writing that makes a writer? I should say, from my own experience, NO. Some of the most untalented people *adore* writing; some have elaborate set-ups for the ritual: enormous desks, boxes of various kinds of paper; paper clips; pencil-sharpeners; several sorts of pen; erasers, ink, and whatnot. In the midst of all this they sit and write interminably. I suppose they *could* be called writers; but they should not be.

Is it intellectual power? Yes, I suppose so: of a kind. But it is sometimes the kind of intellect that is not fitted to pass examinations. It need not include, for example, the kind of photographic memory that produces a school career of straight A's. It is certainly not intellectual power functioning in an abstract way.

A writer's power is based on what we have come to call *talent,* which the dictionary describes first off as "a special natural ability or aptitude." Later on in this definition, talent is described as a *gift.* It is as a gift that I prefer to think of it. The ancients personified the giver of the gift as the Muse—or the Muses: the Daughters of Memory. The French use the word *souffle* figuratively for what passes between the Muse and the artist or writer—*le souffle du génie*—the breath of inspiration; and any writer worth his salt has felt this breath. It comes and goes; it cannot be forced and it can very rarely be summoned up by the conscious will.

The writer's gift usually manifests itself fairly early. The adolescent writer-to-be finds himself or herself *compelled* to write. These young people also are usually voracious readers. First they read everything that comes to hand; soon they find themselves seeking out what they feel to be *theirs*. In spite of all obstacles, they track down what they feel to be their own: from all periods of written literature, and often in several languages. *Words* are their passion; they intoxicate themselves with words. And almost immediately they begin to find their own idiosyncratic rhythm and pulse, to which the words may be fitted. They imitate others, naturally. But what they are looking for is their own voice and their own words. So, very naturally, they come upon the writer's second necessity: the mastering of technique. That battle never ends.

Talent and technique: the basic needs of a writer. For, as the talent, the gift, grows, it begins to absorb the other more usually human attributes. It draws intuition, intellect, curiosity, observation to itself; and it begins to absorb emotion as well. For a writer's power is based not upon his intellect so much as upon his intuition and his emotions. All art, in spite of the struggles of some critics to prove otherwise, is based on emotion and projects emotion.

The process by which emotion is translated into a pattern of words is unknowable. The emotion must be strong enough not only to produce the initial creative impulse, but to prefigure, in part, the structure of the poem as a whole. Not everything is "given," but enough of the design should come through to determine the poem's shape, direction, and speed. The rest must be filled in by the conscious mind, which, ideally, knows all the artful devices of language.

The gift comes and goes. As W. H. Auden remarked, a poet can never be certain, after writing one poem, that he will ever be able to write another. Training and experience can never be completely counted on; the "breath," the "inspiration" may be gone forever. All one can do is try to remain "open" and hope to remain sincere. Openness and sincerity will protect the poet from giving in to fits of temper; from small emotions with which poetry should not, and cannot deal; as well as from imitations of himself or others. The interval between poems, as poets have testified down the ages, is a lonely time. But then, if the poet is lucky and in a state of grace, a new emotion forms and a new poem begins, and all is, for the moment, well.

You can think of me spending days in perfectly unprofitable idleness. Perhaps I can write poetry again, I think, if the timetable can be completely upset for a time. So I read cookbooks and play the music I knew as a child, and try to raise petunias and morning glories in the windows. (Trivial pastimes; but so many people are making an inhuman job of being "useful" and "serious.")

Music in those days belonged to its own time and place. No one today can remember with the same nostalgia (my generation is the last to remember) the sound of music on the water (voices and a mandolin or guitar); of band concerts in town squares or in Army parade grounds, in the twilight or early evening, with a string of lights in the distance marking the line of the bay; or under trees in what was actually, then, a romantic "gloaming."

I'm really very proud of myself that I've managed to do "journalism" all these years. I'm a professional: I can turn it out. But I'm such a slow writer, and there's no one lazier than I. No one. I hate every minute of it.

First I read, then I take notes—sometimes too many—on yards of yellow foolscap; then I write a first draft, then a second. But I know now that it's possible. I remember, in the beginning, sitting at that desk with the tears pouring down my face trying to write a notice. Edmund Wilson would pace behind me and exhort me to go on. He taught me a great deal, at a period when I needed a teacher.

(Edmund speaks of Emerson's lack of real intellectual power: the essays are flashes, held together by no structure of "fundamental brainwork." And the thought struck me that I should take notes happily all my life, not ever troubling to put them into form. I am a woman, and "fundamental brainwork," the building of logical structures, the abstractions, the condensations, the comparisons, the reasonings, *are not expected of me*. But it is only when I am making at least an imitation of such a structure that I am really happy. It is only when the notes fall into form, when the sentences make *at least the sound of style,* that my interest really holds.)

It is sometimes a good thing—a fortunate development—when a piece of writing turns out to be quite different from what its author originally planned. Change of direction, even after a paper is well started, is, at best, a sign that the facts involved—and the

writer's feeling about the facts—are fairly lively; are not merely a
series of clichés or a file of dead notions. They move and breathe,
and given their head, often combine and re-combine in interesting
and unexpected ways.

How can we explain the places where we finally land, after
inexplicable journeys, long boring holidays, years of misapprehen-
sion? How do we finally find them—or do they find us, like a
happening coming after a dream, which follows the dream's speech
and action, so that we say it is our "dream out" ... It is only
infrequently that I now feel that wave of mysterious joy go over me
that I once felt in all meetings, partings, chance displays of natural
or manmade beauty, accidental losses or gains. . . .

Saturday 28 August/65
I am now taking 2 pills in the A.M.—one at 7:30 and one around
10:30. This morning I thought that the 1st pill was going to see
me through; a clear, untroubled interval would show up (take over)
every so often—perhaps because I was moving around in the open
air, having a *later* breakfast at the restaurant (dump!) and buying
things at Sloane's. But soon that secondary sort of *yearning hunger*
(which is not real hunger, but is in some way attached to the drug)
began again. Heart bumps also slightly involved.
    Of course I interpret everything in as black a way as possi-
ble.—(My left eye, incidentally, according to the eye man, is holding
its own against the vascular difficulty—and the actual sight is not
impaired. But, if left to myself, my own diagnosis would have been
exceedingly gloomy.)
    I *must* get someone to look at my teeth!
    And my business affairs must be elucidated. —Some afternoon
next week!
    A deep-seated masochism? Surely I have acted in a consistently
optimistic fashion, ever since the 1933 breakdown. —I have sur-
mounted one difficulty after another; I have *worked* for life and
"creativity"; I have cast off all the anxieties and fears I could; I
have helped others to work and hold on. Why this collapse of
psychic energy? Granted that my demands upon both physical and
psychic endurance during those last spring weeks in Waltham and
Cambridge were clearly excessive—why can't I refuel—recover?
    Of course, I must have improved to some degree. My afternoons
now (after lunch)—after a (usually) unplanned nap—are nearly

normal. The evenings, too—especially after the two drinks I am allowed. —At the moment (11:25) I am hoping to level off after the 2nd pill. Yesterday, I took *three*, in the A.M., including one just after lunch. I nodded off at the eye-doctor's—waiting for him between 12:30 and 1:00. Thereafter I was v. nearly normal, with another pill at supper. (But I was with Ruth from 3:20 on—at a movie.)

How am I going to stand further isolation?

Any *true* writing . . . will have to be done in the *afternoon*. The scraps of stories which I must finally get out of my memory can be attempted in the mornings.

The mere feel of the pen moving across the paper should be curative. That and *some* attempts to listen to music. —*Who* have I become? *What* has me in hand?

Deliver me!

Let me be strong and free once more.

Or at least *free*—and out of these waves of *malaise*. —For what am I berating myself? What am I afraid of?

Death—for one thing. Yes, that is part of it. —These deaths that are reported in the newspapers seem to be all my age—or younger.

But people keep hopeful and warm and *loving* right to the end—with much more to endure than I endure. —I see the old constantly, on these uptown streets—and they are not "depressed." Their eyes are bright; they have bought themselves groceries; they gossip and laugh—with, often, crippling handicaps evident among them.

Where has this power gone, in my case?

I weep—but there's little relief there.

How can I break these mornings?

Tomorrow I must write another "story." The revelation at Bass Point. . . . (But can I tell the whole truth? I never have, even to Dr. Wall. Is the emotional festering begun that far back? —Surely, farther back. . . . The early blows somehow *endured* . . .)

   . . . It is at this point, precisely when the end is in sight, and the starting point almost gained, that the catastrophe of the journey invariably occurs.

   For it is here, as I nearly complete the circle set, that at midnight and in the early morning I encounter the dream. I am set upon by sleep, and hear the rush of water, and hear the mill dam, fuming with water that weighs itself into foam against the air, and see the rapids at its foot that I must gauge and dare and swim. Give over, says this treacherous element, the fear and distress in your breast; and I pretend courage and brave it at last, among rocks along the bank, and plunge into the wave that mounts like glass to the level of my eye. O death, O fear! The universe swings up against my sight, the universe fallen into and bearing with the mill stream. I must in a moment die, but for a moment I breathe, upheld, and see all weight, all force, all water, compacted into the glassy wave, veined, marbled with foam, this moment caught raining over me. And into the wave sinks the armoire, the green bureau, the lamps, the shells from the beach in Maine. All these objects, provisional at best, now equally lost, rock down to translucent depths below fear, an Atlantis in little, under the mill stream (last seen through the steam from the Boston train in March 1909).

Margaret Bourke-White

(1904–1971)

Margaret Bourke-White, photographer and photojournalist, was the second child of a successful New York engineer and designer and his socially progressive wife. Both parents instilled intellectual honesty and physical courage in their children and encouraged their lifelong interest in nature and the natural world.

Bourke-White's academic career was checkered and marked by frequent transfers. She studied her first interests, engineering and biology, at Rutgers University, took up photography the next year at Columbia, shifted to herpetology at the University of Michigan, and returned to general studies at Case Western Reserve and Cornell, where she finally received her B.A. Along the way she married a University of Michigan sweetheart and divorced him after two years. The divorce meant that she had to support herself during her senior year at Cornell, and, because there was no university job available, she began photographing the campus and selling the results to classmates as a way of earning her living.

Her father shared his passion for design with his gifted daughter, so that, after graduating from Cornell, Bourke-White launched her photographic career by capturing the grandeur and power of the industrial landscape of Cleveland.

Her totally original and technically dazzling photographs of industrial America earned Bourke-White a place on the staff of the newly launched *Fortune* magazine in 1929, beginning a connection with Henry Luce's publications that she retained for the rest of her working life. The Depression and the tragic drought of the mid-thirties redirected her attention from machines to people, giving her the sense of human subjects and the capacity to depict them against a complex social and economic context upon which her subsequent career throve.

In 1935 Bourke-White joined the staff of *Life* magazine and provided the photographs for its first cover story. The same year she began a collaboration with the southern writer Erskine Caldwell, which produced the landmark exposé of the sufferings of southern sharecroppers *You Have Seen Their Faces* (1937). Bourke-White's pictures capture environmental, economic, and personal tragedy, combining relentless realism and deep human sympathy.

Bourke-White's subsequent collaborations with Caldwell,

whom she married briefly, were not so successful; the stormy relationship prevented her from giving her work the total concentration it required. Following her decision to divorce Caldwell, shortly after the U.S. entry into World War II, Bourke-White was accredited as an official Army Air Force photographer under an arrangement whereby her work could be used jointly by *Life* and the Air Force. Here began her legendary career as a war correspondent, always in the thick of the fighting, fearless in her efforts to record great events. A stunned witness as the survivors of Nazi concentration camps were freed, she took a series of photographs, "The Living Dead of Buchenwald." These probably represent the peak of her artistic achievement and are classic in the photographer's capacity to render tragedy and infamy in a single series of frames.

Postwar assignments in India and Korea enhanced her reputation as a photojournalist, while her participation in great international events prompted her to accompany her photographs with prose exposition. By her midfifties Bourke-White stood at the peak of her profession, unrivaled in her ability to find the story, capture it, and deliver it in flawless photographs. Her active career was brought suddenly to a close by Parkinson's disease, against which she fought unquenchably, using photographs of her efforts at rehabilitation to encourage fellow sufferers from the disease.

Bourke-White had become a skilled writer by the time she tackled *Portrait of Myself,* published in 1963. Her narrative blends the professional and personal with great success, especially when she speaks about the conflicts between the life of a professional journalist, whose time belongs to her employer, and the life of a married woman, on whom others must depend for emotional support. Her visual sense infuses her writing, so that the reader understands exactly why she was an early proponent of the aesthetic of the machine and how the human dimensions of her work evolved. The form of the narrative matches her life of adventure; romantic conventions are ironically set aside as she thanks her first mother-in-law for releasing her from a conventional marriage, setting her free to live life on her own terms.

PORTRAIT OF MYSELF

My father was an abnormally silent man. He was so absorbed in his own engineering work that he seldom talked to us children at all, but he would become communicative in the world of out-of-doors. . . .

Learning to do things fearlessly was considered important by both my parents. Mother had begun when I was quite tiny to help me over my childish terrors, devising simple little games to teach me not to be afraid of the dark, encouraging me to enjoy being alone instead of dreading it, as so many children and some adults do.

Father's contribution to the anti-fear crusade met with complete and unexpected success. With Father's introduction to snake lore, I decided to be a herpetologist and become so much of an expert that I would be sent on expeditions and have a chance to travel. I knew I *had* to travel. I pictured myself as the scientist (or sometimes as the helpful wife of the scientist), going to the jungle, bringing back specimens for natural history museums, and "doing all the things that women never do," I used to say to myself. . . .

Father was the personification of the absent-minded inventor. I ate with him in restaurants where he left his meal untouched and drew sketches on the tablecloth. At home he sat silent in his big chair, his thoughts traveling, I suppose, through some intricate mesh of gears and camshafts. If someone spoke he did not hear. . . . On Sundays, only his back was visible as he stooped over his drawing board. . . .

Now and then Father put the drafting tools aside and took me with him on trips to factories where he was supervising the setting up of his presses. One day, in the plant in Dunellen, New Jersey, where for many years his rotary presses were built, I saw a foundry for the first time. I remember climbing with him to a sooty balcony and looking down into the mysterious depths below. "Wait," Father said, and then in a rush the blackness was broken by a sudden magic of flowing metal and flying sparks. I can hardly describe my joy. To me at that age, a foundry represented the beginning and end of all beauty. Later when I became a photographer, with that instinctive desire that photographers have to show their world to others, this memory was so vivid and so alive that it shaped the whole course of my career. . . .

If Father had been money-minded, he might have become quite wealthy, but he paid no attention to money, was essentially the inventor and researcher, and made some unsound investments along the way—just how unsound they were came out only when he died. I was seventeen then, just starting college, and I know now that if we had been wealthy, and I hadn't had to work my way through college as I did after his death, I would never have been a photographer. . . .

It is odd that photography was never one of my childhood hobbies when Father was so fond of it. I hardly touched a camera and certainly never operated one until after he died. Yet he was always tinkering with lenses and working on devices to make exposure settings simpler for the amateur, some of which he had patented. He experimented with three-dimensional moving pictures long before their time, and what a thrill it was when he used us children as guinea pigs for trying out prisms and viewing lenses which created magic effects of depth illusion. . . .

Everything that had to do with the transmission and control of light interested my father, and I like to think that this keen attention to what light could do has influenced me. . . .

That, and the love of truth, which is requisite No. 1 for a photographer. And in this training Mother shared.

Once off to college . . . I was invited to dances. Lots of dances. Soon I was going to dances with just one man. . . .

Chappie was six feet tall with the shoulders of a football player, black snapping eyes, and a delightful sense of whimsy. He was a graduate electrical engineering student, working on his doctor's thesis in his specialty of electric welding. He played traps in a college dance band to pay his way through school.

One hears that a girl falls in love first with a man who reminds her of her father. Chappie—with his gaiety, his sense of fun—was unlike my father, but when I saw him at his bench in the engineering lab, I knew here was someone who was just the same. . . .

We chose Friday the thirteenth of June for our wedding day. . . .

If there was a portent in our wedding date, there was an omen in our wedding ring also. . . .

Chappie fashioned the ring charmingly, with tiny hammer strokes making a beaten pattern over the surface. The night before our wedding he took me to the lab to give me a last fitting. He laid the lovely circle on the anvil to round it out, gave it one light tap with his tiny hammer, and our wedding ring broke into two pieces.

In two years our marriage had broken to pieces also. . . .

The situation rose to a swift peak early in our honeymoon. The crisis broke in a single day—the black day of my life—the day my mother-in-law decided to clean house.

We were honeymooning in a cottage on one of the lovely Michigan lakes, close enough to the University so that Chappie could drive in and play in summer-school dance bands. My mother-in-law arrived for a visit of uncertain duration. On the momentous day, Chappie had left the house very early to go to the University and do some lab work, and I was still in my room when the mopping and sweeping began. Feeling that I should be "helping," I dressed hastily, and slipped into the kitchen. Hesitating to stop for breakfast in the face of the vigorous scrubbing I could hear from the next room, I plunged into some ironing I saw waiting to be done.

"Well, Margaret," my mother-in-law's rich contralto sounded from the next room, "how did your mother feel when she heard you were going to be married?"

I tried to answer, knowing how different would be the point of view of the two mothers. "Mother was very concerned at first because she wanted us to finish school, and because she thought we were both so young. But when she saw Chappie and me together and could see we were truly in love, she was glad."

"She's gained a son and I've lost a son."

I could picture my mother-in-law through the wall. She would be regal and beautiful always—even with a mop in her hand—with her silver hair piled duchess-high on her head and her deep-set black eyes flashing. The rich-timbred voice continued through the wall. "You got him away from me. I congratulate you. I never want to see you again."

Taking the speaker at her word, I carefully unplugged the iron, left the cottage, and walked seventeen miles to Ann Arbor to find my husband. It would have been wondrous luck if I had happened to have a nickel in my pocket, so as to shorten by streetcar some of those dusty miles. It would have been better, too, if I had had breakfast. But somehow, I was sure, when I found my husband everything would be all right. . . .

Things were never all right. . . . we were unhappily involved in a classic entanglement that neither of us was sagacious enough to cut through. . . .

"Everyone says the first year of married life is the hardest," I reminded myself. I had not expected it to be so hard as this, but surely the second year would be better. The second year was better only because we learned to face the facts more squarely and we recognized the marriage as a failure.

And now that I was facing life again as an individual, I made a great discovery. I had been through the valley of the shadow. I had lived through the loneliness and the anguish, It was as though everything that could really be hard in my life had been packed into those two short years, and nothing would ever seem so hard again. I had risen from the sickbed, walked out into the light, and found the world was green again.

I owe a peculiar debt to my mother-in-law. She left me strong, knowing I could deal with a difficult experience, learning from it, and leaving it behind without bitterness, in a neat closed room.

People seem to take it for granted that a woman chooses between marriage and a career as though she were the stone statue on the county courthouse, weighing one against the other in the balance in her hand. I am sure this is seldom so. Certainly in my own case there was no such deliberate choice. Had it not been for a red-gold ring that broke into two pieces, I would never have been a professional photographer.

It was sheer luck I still had that old secondhand camera when my marriage went on the rocks and I returned to college for my senior year. My mother had bought it for me when I was a freshman at Columbia and shortly after my father's death, when it was difficult for her to afford. The camera was a 3 1/4 × 4 1/4 Ica Reflex, modeled like a Graflex. It cost twenty dollars and had a crack straight through the lens. . . .

So here I stood, with my first marriage behind me and my seventh university ahead, poring through the college catalogs. I chose Cornell, not for its excellent zoology courses but because I read there were waterfalls on the campus.

Arriving in Ithaca, I did what other college students do who are broke. I tried to get a job as a waitress. Luckily for my photographic future, the waitress jobs were all taken. By the time I got to the student library to apply for a tempting forty-cents-an-hour job there, that was snapped up too. I wept some secret tears, and turned to my camera.

I believe it was the drama of the waterfalls that first gave me the idea I should put that old cracked lens to work. Here I was in the midst of one of the most spectacular campus sites in America, with fine old ivy-covered architecture and Cayuga Lake on the horizon and those boiling columns of water thundering over the cliffs and down through the gorges. Surely there would be students who would buy photographs of scenes like these. . . .

I belonged to the soft-focus school in those days: to be artistic, a picture must be blurry, and the exact degree of blurriness was one of the features over which I toiled during the long nights in Mr. Head's darkroom, diffusing, printing those celluloids. Ralph Steiner, whom I had met at the Clarence H. White School, a superbly sharp honest craftsman, caustically talked me into a fierce reversal of the viewpoint that a photograph should imitate a painting. . . .

I must get an unbiased opinion of my work, I told myself. . . . I would go to New York during Easter vacation, walk in on some architect cold, and base my momentous decision on his opinion. . . .

Someone gave me the name of York & Sawyer, a large architectural firm, and suggested asking for Mr. Benjamin Moskowitz. Arriving unwisely late in the day, I went into the upper reaches of the New York Central Office Building, entered a frighteningly spacious lobby, and asked to see Mr. Moskowitz. The tall dark man who came out in response to this request was plainly a commuter on his way to the train. As I outlined my problem, he was unobtrusively though steadily edging his way toward the elevator. I did not realize he had not taken in a word when he pushed the down button, but I was chilled by the lack of response. If the elevator had arrived immediately, I am sure that the next morning would have found me on the doorstep of the Museum of Natural History, but as we waited, the silence became so embarrassing that I opened my big portfolio. Mr. Moskowitz glanced at the picture on top, a view of the library tower.

"Did you take this photograph?"

"Yes, that's what I've been telling you."

"Did you take it yourself?"

I repeated my little tale, how I was considering becoming an architectural photographer, but first I wanted the unbiased opinion of an architect as to whether I had the ability for the work.

"Let's go back into the office and look at these," said the unpredictable Mr. Moskowitz.

He let his train go, stood up the photographs against the dark wood paneling of the conference room and called in the other members of the firm to look them over. After the kind of golden hour one remembers for a lifetime, I left with the assurance of Messrs. York, Sawyer, and associates that I could "walk into any architect's office in the country with that portfolio and get work."

Everything was touched with magic now. The Cornell pictures, both the blurry and the in-focus ones, sold out in the commencement rush. College over, I took the Great Lakes night boat from Buffalo to Cleveland and rising early, I stood on the deck to watch the city come into view. As the skyline took form in the early morning mist, I felt I was coming to my promised land: columns of masonry gaining height as we drew toward the pier, derricks swinging like living creatures—deep inside I knew these were my subjects.

One personal task remained to be completed. Cleveland was my legal "place of residence"—that was why I had returned to it—and on a rainy Saturday morning I slipped down to the courthouse, quietly got my divorce, and resumed my maiden name. I used my full name, with the addition of a hyphen. Bourke had been my mother's choice for my middle name, and she always like me to use it in full.

To me, fresh from college with my camera over my shoulder, the Flats were a photographic paradise. The smokestacks ringing the horizon were the giants of an unexplored world, guarding the secrets and wonder of the steel mills. When, I wondered, would I get inside those slab-sided coffin-black buildings with their mysterious unpredictable flashes of light leaking out the edges? . . .

. . . women were unwelcome in steel mills, especially in these particular mills, where they had been prohibited ever since a visiting schoolteacher twenty years earlier had inconsiderately fainted from the heat and fumes. . . .

. . . my wardrobe consisted of a gray suit, which I wore with red hat and red gloves or with blue hat and blue gloves. . . . it was a great morale factor with me to know that any given prospect was going to see me on a follow-up visit in a fresh color scheme. . . .

On a red-glove day I got my first job. This was to photograph a new school, just finished, which had been designed by Pitkin & Mott, architects and Cornell alumni. Messrs. Pitkin and Mott were almost as new in their business as I was in mine, and therefore it meant a good deal to them to get their school house published in a national architectural magazine. The editors of *Architecture* had expressed an interest in printing the school if good pictures could be obtained, but those already submitted had been rejected as not up to publication standards. . . .

A visit to the school revealed why my predecessor had had difficulty with the pictures. The building stood in the midst of a wasteland, littered with unused lumber, gravel dug out of the foundations, and withering remnants of workmen's lunches. As I walked around to look it over, the mud squished over my shoetops, but the lines of the school were good. The solution was to photograph it in silhouette against the sunset. . . .

On the first afternoon that a sunset seemed to be shaping up satisfactorily, I went back to the school, only to find that the sun set on the wrong side of the building. I would try for a sunrise. For four successive mornings I arose before dawn, hurried to location and found the stubborn sun rising behind overcast. On the fifth morning the sunrise was everything a photographer could ask, but the whole idea proved fruitless because heaps of refuse in strategic places blotted out the best angles on the school.

If only I could supply a few softening touches of landscaping! I ran to the nearest florist, invested in an armful of asters, carried them to the schoolhouse and stuck them in the muddy ground. Placing my camera low, I shot over the tops of the flowers, then moved my garden as I proceeded from one viewpoint to the next. By the time my asters had given up, exhausted, I had completed the photographs of the school from all points of view.

When I delivered the pictures (which of course I took care to do in blue gloves), I don't know who was the more amazed—Mr. Mott or Mr. Pitkin—at the miraculous appearance of landscaping. Publication of the pictures brought more work and a tinge of prestige to the Bourke-White Studio. . . .

Each trip to the Flats gave me new viewpoints on bridges: it might be the abstract construction pattern of a trestle, the cathedral-like arches of concrete piers which would carry railroad tracks, or the main traffic span of the High Level Bridge like a drawn bow reaching through the sky. It never occurred to me that I could sell these pictures, or that I was doing anything new. These were things I was impelled to take because they were close to my heart, so close that for some little time I was too shy about the photographs even to show them. . . .

Then, unexpectedly, I sold my first industrial picture. A friend urged me to take a portfolio to one of the banks. . . . Gus Handerson, the public relations officer of the Union Trust Company, needed covers for the bank's monthly magazine *Trade Winds*. . . . He turned rapidly through my photographs, picked a shot of the High Level Bridge, said "Make us a glossy of this," and with magnificent fairness added, "Send us a bill for fifty dollars." . . .

John Sherwin, president of Union Trust, was puzzled that a "pretty young girl should want to take pictures in a dirty steel mill " But he was quite willing to send a letter of introduction to his friend Elroy Kulas at Otis Steel.

Mr. Kulas was forceful, short of stature, able. In the twelve years since he had become president, his company's output of steel ingots had quadrupled. . . .

I remember standing there by his massive carved desk, trying to tell him of my belief that there is a power and vitality in industry that makes it a magnificent subject for photography, that it reflects the age in which we live, that the steel mills are at the very heart of industry with the most drama, the most beauty—and that was why I wanted to capture the spirit of steelmaking in photographs. . . .

To me these industrial forms were all the more beautiful because they were never designed to be beautiful. They had a simplicity of line that came from their direct application to a purpose. Industry, I felt, had evolved an unconscious beauty—often a hidden beauty that was waiting to be discovered. And recorded! . . .

I climbed up the hanging ladder into the overhead crane so I could shoot directly down into the molten steel during the pour. During some shots, bursts of yellow smoke at the height of the pour blotted out everything in front of the lens; during others, the crane cab started trembling during the vital moments, and all my pictures were blurred. . . .

[Bourke-White solved the severe lighting difficulties of photographing at Otis Steel by using flares intended for lighting movie sets.]

. . . we roamed the windy catwalks, climbed up and down ladders with the sleet driving through, and planned our shots. I was eager to work out a side lighting which would emphasize the great hulk and roundness of the ladles and molds, and still not flatten and destroy the magic of the place. . . .

Then in a great rush the pour began. With the snow at our backs and the heat in our faces, we worked like creatures possessed. The life of each flare was half a minute. During those thirty seconds

I steadied my reflex camera on a crossrail, made exposures of eight seconds, four seconds, two seconds, dashed to a closer viewpoint, hand holding the camera for slow instantaneous shots until the flare died. . . .

The next night we developed the films, and there it all was: the noble shapes of ladles, giant hooks and cranes, the dim vast sweep of the mill. There was one moment of anxiety, when we developed the negative we had taken with the eleventh flare. It was filled with black curving lines, as though someone had scratched it deeply with his fingernails. . . .

And suddenly I knew. I had photographed the actual path of the sparks. . . .

I remember waiting inside Mr. Kulas's office, but standing near the entrance and behind a screen, while he finished with some other people. Then my turn came. I remember his surprise and pleasure in the pictures. He said there had never been such steel mill pictures taken. He wanted to buy some of them. . . .

He picked eight photographs, commissioned me to make eight more, and laid plans for a privately printed book on *The Story of Steel*, which would be sent to his stockholders and would contain my photographs. . . .

In the late spring of 1929, I received a telegram from New York: HAVE JUST SEEN YOUR STEEL PHOTOGRAPHS. CAN YOU COME TO NEW YORK WITHIN WEEK AT OUR EXPENSE. It was signed: HENRY R. LUCE and under his name: TIME, THE WEEKLY NEWS MAGAZINE. I very nearly did not go. The name of Luce meant nothing to me. Of course I knew *Time,* which was then five years old. A trip to the public library to look through back files confirmed my impression that the only important use *Time* made of photographs was for the cover, where the portrait of some political personage appeared each week. I was not the least bit interested in photographing political personages. The whole dynamic world of industry lay before me. My discoveries had just begun. All over America were railroads, docks, mines, factories waiting to be photographed—waiting, I felt, for *me.* . . .

With the inevitable portfolio of my most recent work under my arm, I arrived in Manhattan and hunted up the small and rather drab office building on 42nd Street near Second Avenue where *Time Inc.* occupied a modest section of floor space. . . .

I was received by two very tall and distinctly unusual-looking young men. Both seemed to radiate an extraordinary quality of restless imagination, although in other ways I guessed their personalities were quite dissimilar. . . . One I judged was as young as I. . . . He was introduced to me as Parker Lloyd-Smith.

The other was Henry Luce. He was perhaps a year or two under thirty, strikingly powerful in build, with a large head over large shoulders. His words tumbled out with such haste and emphasis that I had the feeling he was thinking ten words for every one that managed to emerge. He began questioning me at once. Who was I and what was I? Why was I taking these industrial pictures? Was it just for fun? Was it my vocation? Or was it my profession? I solemnly assured Mr. Luce it was my profession, and a very serious one. . . .

Mr. Luce and his associates were planning to launch a new magazine, a magazine of business and industry. They hoped to illustrate it with the most dramatic photographs of industry that had ever been taken. . . .

An important item, and an exciting one, in planning a new magazine is the choice of the first story for the first issue. I am very lucky to have had the chance to take the photographs for this keynote spot twice in my lifetime, . . . with *Fortune,* and six years later with *Life.*

With *Fortune,* the decision for the lead was made very carefully. Essentially it must be an industry at the heart of American life and economy. Photographically it must be an eye-stopper—an industry where no one would dream of finding "art." . . .

Our first candidate was International Harvester. . . . When the tractor company proved "stuffy," as Parker expressed it, we switched from wheat to hogs.

Hogs were a wonderful choice. Certainly most of our readers would not expect to find beauty in the Chicago stockyards. But to Parker and me, the interior of the Swift meat-packing plant, where we spent a week, had a Dantesque magnificence. Daily some twenty thousand pigs went the way of all pork flesh, and were carried in solemn procession along the assembly line. Parker called it the "disassembly line" and pointed out in the piece he wrote for *Fortune* that "each pig was divided and subdivided as exactly as a suburban real estate development."

As I made pattern pictures of giant hog shapes passing through a corona of singeing flames, or under the flashing knives, Parker Lloyd-Smith, looking like a London fashion plate that had been set down in the most incongruous place possible, gathered his research. . . .

I was living a sort of double life now. As always, half of my time each year went to *Fortune* through an arrangement which I had asked for from the very beginning so I could do other jobs, and which had worked out most satisfactorily for both *Fortune* and myself. During the other half of the year I wrestled my way through the mad world of advertising. I was always glad when *Fortune*'s time rolled around again. . . .

In the early thirties, when *Fortune* was in its infancy, the land of tantalizing mystery was Russia. No foreign photographers had been allowed across Russian borders to take a direct look at what was going on under the Soviet Five-Year Plan. Foreign engineering consultants—mostly Americans—came and went with comparative freedom. But for the professional photographer from the outside world, it was a closed country. Nothing attracts me like a closed door. I cannot let my camera rest until I have pried it open, and I wanted to be first.

With my enthusiasm for the machine as an object of beauty, I felt the story of a nation trying to industrialize almost overnight was just cut out for me. . . .

The idea of running photographs of the sprouting industries of the U.S.S.R. intrigued *Fortune*'s editors, but they had grave doubts whether I could get anything done. They were sending me to Germany to take pictures of industry, and I decided to push on from there. . . .

I bought a cheap trunk and filled it with canned food. I had been warned that if I traveled off the beaten path, I would find near famine conditions. That night I left for Moscow. . . .

When I reached Berlin, on my way home, transatlantic phone calls started coming from New York. A transatlantic call was a great rarity in those days. The first call was from Fox-Movietone, offering to buy my film "sight unseen." This was followed by similar offers from other film companies. I should have placed it then and there, while the excitement was running high. But no, I was a perfectionist. I was going to supervise the cutting and editing of the film myself; then I would see about marketing it. . . .

I was left with my films and my bills. I had been hiring expensive help, professional film cutters and editors, each one supposed to be that "wonder boy" who could give a touch of greatness to any film footage. I could afford it no longer. I put the films back in their round tin boxes and decided to write them off as a loss. . . .

Then, the wheels of history turned. The U.S. recognized the U.S.S.R. There was a sudden wave of interest in Russia. The motion-picture companies began calling again. When a subsidiary of R-K-O made an offer, I jumped at it without delay. The film was made into two shorts called *Eyes on Russia* and *Red Republic*. My movie fever had burned itself out. I have never touched a motion-picture camera from that day to this.

One story which *Fortune* sent me out to cover was in a sphere quite new to me and left a very deep impression on me. This was the great drought of 1934. Word of its severity came so suddenly, and the reports we had were so scanty, that *Fortune* editors didn't know exactly where the chief areas of the drought were. Omaha, Nebraska, seemed as good a starting point as any, since it was in the middle of the corn belt. I left on three hours' notice and on arrival in Omaha found that the drought extended over a vastly greater area than we had known when I was in New York. It ran from the Dakotas in the North to the Texas panhandle. I was working against a five-day deadline, and it was such an extensive area to cover that I chartered a plane to use for the whole story. . . .

I had never seen landscapes like those through which we flew. Blinding sun beating down on the withered land. Below us the ghostly patchwork of half-buried corn, and the rivers of sand which should have been free-running streams. Sinister spouts of sand wisping up, and then the sudden yellow gloom of curtains of fine-blown soil rising up and trembling in the air. Endless dun-colored acres, which should have been green with crops, carved into dry ripples by the aimless winds.

I had never seen people caught helpless like this in total tragedy. They had no defense. They had no plan. They were numbed like their own dumb animals, and many of these animals were choking and dying in drifting soil. I was deeply moved by the suffering I saw and touched particularly by the bewilderment of the farmers. I think this was the beginning of my awareness of people in a human, sympathetic sense as subjects for the camera and photographed against a wider canvas than I had perceived before.

The drought had been a powerful eye-opener and had shown me that right here in my own country there were worlds about which I knew almost nothing. *Fortune* assignments had given me a magnificent introduction to all sorts of American people. But this time it was not the cross section of industry I wanted. Nor was it the sharp drama of agricultural crisis. It was less the magazine approach and more the book approach I was after. It was based on a great need to understand my fellow Americans better. I felt it should not be an assignment in the ordinary sense but should be as independent of any regular job as my steel mill pictures had been.

What should be the theme, the spine, the unity? I did not consider myself a writer. I felt this book had to be a collaboration between the written word and the image on the celluloid. I needed an author. . . .

It seemed a miracle that within a week or two I should hear of an author in search of a photographer. He had a book project in mind in which he wanted to collaborate with a photographer. I gathered he had paid little attention to the possibility that there might be mediocre or gifted photographers in the world. He just wanted to find the right one—someone with receptivity and an open mind, someone who would be as interested as he was in American people, everyday people. . . .

He was the author of an exceedingly controversial book. . . . He wanted to take the camera to *Tobacco Road*. His name was Erskine Caldwell. . . .

I could hardly believe this large shy man with the enormous wrestler's shoulders and quiet coloring could be the fiery Mr. Caldwell. His eyes were the soft rinsed blue of well-worn blue jeans. His hair was carrot—a subdued carrot. The backs of his hands were flecked with cinnamon freckles—cinnamon which had stood long on the kitchen shelf. . . .

His seeming mildness and gentleness came as a surprise against the turbulence of his writings. . . .

I was equally surprised that, humorist though Caldwell was known to be, his tight-locked face suggested a man who rarely laughs. . . .

I was informed in confidence . . . that Mr. Caldwell did not like the idea of working with a woman. . . .

Erskine had a gift, over and above the Southern tongue with which he was born, for picking up the shade and degree of inflection characteristic of the state in which we were working. His proficiency surprised me because he was uninterested in music. But in this he had a musician's ear. . . .

The people we were seeking out for pictures were generally suspicious of strangers. They were afraid we were going to try to sell them something they didn't want and fearful we were taking their pictures only to ridicule them. Reassuring them was a very important part of our operations, and a reassuring voice in their own mode of speech eliminated many a barrier. Of course, no amount of doctoring could disguise my mode of speech. I was unmistakably a Yankee, "down South on her vacation," Erskine would say. I could be labeled only as a foreigner and sometimes I am afraid I acted like one.

I remember one occasion when we went into a cabin to photograph a Negro woman who lived there. She had thick, glossy hair, and I had decided to take her picture as she combed it. She had a bureau made of a wooden box with a curtain tacked to it and lots of little homemade things. I rearranged everything. After we left, Erskine spoke to me about it. How neat her bureau had been. How she must have valued all her little possessions and how she had them tidily arranged *her* way, which was not my way. This was a new point of view to me. I felt I had done violence. . . .

I began watching for the effect of events on human beings. I was awakening to the need of probing and learning, discovering and interpreting. I realized that any photographer who tries to portray human beings in a penetrating way must put more heart and mind into his preparation than will ever show in any photograph. . . .

We plunged into writing captions for the book, and ours was a real collaboration. We did not want the matter of whether the pictures "illustrated" the text, or the words explained the pictures, to have any importance. We wanted a result in which the pictures and words truly supplemented one another, merging into a unified whole. . . .

"This book has to have a title, you know," Skinny [Caldwell] said one day.

I had been so deep in finishing the pictorial touches that actually I had never given any thought to the title. But Skinny had. In fact, the title came to his mind two years before he met me. I learned what it was only when we went to see Viking Press, the publishers. I still recall the little scene vividly: the rather severe vestibule of the office, the exhilaration of completing a big piece of work which was a milestone in my life.

"The title is *You Have Seen Their Faces,*" said Skinny. "How do you like it?"

The name implied just what I had been searching for as I worked. Faces that would express what we wanted to tell. Not just the unusual or striking face, but *the* face that would speak out the message from the printed page.

"The first issue of a magazine is not the magazine. It is the beginning."

With these words of introduction from the editors, *Life*'s Vol. I, No. 1, came into existence on November 23, 1936. A few weeks before the beginning, Harry Luce called me up to his office and assigned me to a wonderful story out in the Northwest. . . .

Harry's idea was to photograph the enormous chain of dams in the Columbia River basin that was part of the New Deal program. I was to stop off at New Deal, a settlement near Billings, Montana, where I would photograph the construction of Fort Peck, the world's largest earth-filled dam. Harry told me to watch out for something on a grand scale that might make a cover.

"Hurry back, Maggie," he said, and off I went. . . .

I had never seen a place quite like the town of New Deal, the construction site of Fort Peck Dam. It was a pinpoint in the long, lonely stretches of northern Montana—so primitive and so wild that the whole ramshackle town seemed to carry the flavor of the boisterous Gold Rush days. It was stuffed to the seams with construction men, engineers, welders, quack doctors, barmaids, fancy ladies, and, as one of my photographs illustrated, the only idle bedsprings in New Deal were the broken ones. People lived in trailers, huts, coops—anything they could find—and at night they hung over the Bar X bar. . . .

During the mornings I worked on the inspiring high earthworks of the dam. At noon when the light was too flat for photographs, I rode off on horseback through the endless level stretches which would be reservoir when the work was finished. When I had used the sun's last rays to the utmost, I would turn up at Bar X or the Buck Horn Club. . . .

These were the days of *Life*'s youth, and things were very informal. I woke up each morning ready for any surprise the day might bring. . . .

When the editors called me in on a story which they referred to as the "Bourke-White" type of story, this made me very proud. . . .

Up to now I had never worked on stories where the news timing was of paramount importance, but my next batch of assignments had to do with people and events in Washington. . . .

For photographers, this was a world of its own, or rather, a war of its own, with added stress when the target had something to do with Washington, or the administration, or, most backbreaking of all, with the President himself. For picture sessions, a very limited amount of time was rigidly set, and photographers of all kinds were rabidly intent on squeezing every usable second out of the meager allotment.

Usually I was the only woman photographer, and the technique I followed was to literally crawl between the legs of my competitors and pop my head and camera up for part of a second before the competition slapped me down again. At least, the point of view was different from that of the others whose pictures were, perforce, almost identical, and, anyway, I've always liked "the caterpillar view."

[Against her better judgment, Bourke-White began to consider marriage with her collaborator, Erskine Caldwell.]

We had talked this over so often. I did not want to marry again. It was not that I was against marriage, despite my initial unhappy experience. But I had carved out a different kind of life now. To me it was of the utmost importance to complicate my living as little as possible. The very secret of life for me, I believed, was to maintain in the midst of rushing events an inner tranquility. I had picked a life that dealt with excitement, tragedy, mass calamities, human triumphs and human suffering. To throw my whole self into recording and attempting to understand these things, I needed an inner serenity as a kind of balance. This was something I could not have if I was torn apart for fear of hurting someone every time an assignment of this kind came up. . . .

There was a puzzling insecurity in this withdrawn man which I was sure held a threat to my future work. I wanted no conflict of loyalties—that would be too painful. My first loyalty was to *Life*. There was no secret about it. My professional work came first. This is certainly not a unique problem, and I'm sure that many professional women, and men too, have had this difficulty in one form or another. How they resolve it is a highly personal thing. Dashing off at a moment's notice around the globe is wonderful if you are doing the dashing yourself. But if you are the one who stays behind, it must be hard to bear. . . .

Erskine had a very difficult attitude toward my magazine, a kind of jealousy, not toward any man, but concentrated on *Life* magazine itself. Our friendship had been strewn with danger signals—the unpredictable, frozen moods that seemed to have no traceable cause in a world of reality, the unfathomable silences ending only in violent tempests. . . .

It is often said that a woman is most strongly drawn to the man who needs her the most. I had always considered myself too selfish to be governed by such a motive. But there must be something to it. Perhaps if I became his wife, it would lighten the burden of insecurity which he seemed unable to cast off. I would not be satisfied until I had explored all possibilities thoroughly. If marriage would help, I was willing to try.

I had a plan. If Erskine would consent to it, I felt that our marriage would have a chance. He did consent to it and we boarded a plane for Nevada. Erskine chose this state because it issues wedding licenses immediately.

Once on the airplane, I worked on the plan and drew up a sort of marriage contract. The first point was that if some difficulty arose between us, we must talk it out before midnight; two, he should treat my friends as courteously as his own; he must attempt to realize and control his fluctuating moods, and there must be no attempts to snatch me away from photographic assignments.

We were flying over the great desert reaches of Utah and Nevada when Skinny signed this formidable document, and at least that was behind us.

Exactly one month after Erskine and I entered the country [in 1939], war broke out between Germany and Russia. . . . Immediately on the outbreak of hostilities, the military authorities issued a ukase forbidding the use of cameras; anyone seen with a camera ran the risk of being seized and imprisoned. Here was I, facing the biggest scoop of my life: the biggest country enters the biggest war in the world and I was the only photographer on the spot, representing any publication and coming from any foreign country. I felt sure I could cope with the anti-camera law somehow. But the first problem was to be allowed to stay on the scene of action. . . .

On previous trips to Russia, I tried in a routine way to get

permission to photograph Stalin. I had never had even an acknowledgment of my request.

Success came finally shortly after Russia entered the war, when
she felt she needed American good will. It was during this brief
honeymoon period that President Roosevelt sent Lend-Lease Administrator Harry Hopkins to Russia as his personal envoy. Hopkins
really went to bat for me and prevailed upon Molotov to get permission to photograph Stalin. . . .

I go to every important portrait appointment with a conviction
that my cameras are going to cease functioning—a dread that never
leaves me, even after years of experience, and this time I was certain
that nothing would work when I was face to face with Stalin. During
the wait, I polished my lenses, checked my synchronizers, powdered
my nose, glanced in my mirror to make sure the little red bow was
on at just the right angle. At last a Red Army officer, wearing an
impressive collection of medals, came for me.

I had just time to remind myself not to be nervous when I was
whirled through door No. 1 into a long, bare room. There was little
furniture except a long table, covered with green felt, and a large
globe of the world on a pedestal. I was conscious of Mr. Hopkins
standing at my side, but it took me a moment to find Stalin. I had
seen so many giant statues of him that I had come to think of him
as a man of superhuman size. I looked instinctively toward the
ceiling, then lowered my eyes and saw Stalin. He was standing very
stiff and straight in the center of the rug. His face was gray, his
figure flat-chested. He stood so still he might have been carved out
of granite. . . .

. . . Stalin spoke never a word. His rough, pitted face was as
immobile as ice. . . .

As I sank down to my knees to get some low viewpoints, I
spilled out a pocketful of peanut flashbulbs, which went bouncing
all over the floor. The Kremlin interpreter and I went scrambling
after them. I guess Stalin had never seen an American girl on her
knees to him before. He thought it was funny, and started to laugh.
The change was miraculous! It was as though a second personality
had come to the front—genial and almost merry. The smile lasted
just long enough for me to make two exposures, and then, as though
a veil had been drawn over his features, again he turned to
stone. . . .

It was almost half past nine when I left the Kremlin, and the
Luftwaffe had been calling regularly at ten o'clock each night. I

couldn't take a chance on developing my precious films at the hotel; to have an air-raid warden break into my bathroom and tear me away from a half-developed negative of Stalin was more than I could risk. I drove to the American Embassy where I would not be interrupted. The alarm sounded just as I drove through the gates. The Embassy was deserted. Everyone had gone off to shelters. The Ambassador and Mr. Hopkins were Stalin's guests for the air raid that night in the super-deep shelter far under the subway, reserved for the highest Soviet officials.

The chauffeur helped me set up my laboratory in the servants' bathroom in the Embassy cellar. The negatives of Stalin were so irreplaceable—should anything go wrong—that I did not have the courage to plunge them in, sink or swim, a whole film pack at a time. I began processing them one by one.

It was a busy night outside, and I could hear the rhythmic booming of the guns as I worked. And when finally long descending shrieks began, I was glad the cellar window was sandbagged. Wouldn't it be fantastic, I thought, if Uncle Joe got fogged by a fire bomb? After four hours, the raid ended.

As the night wore on, I grew hungry. In the excitement of the appointment, I had entirely forgotten to have supper, and I couldn't remember whether I had eaten any lunch. It should be easy to get something to eat in your own Embassy, I thought, but the steward had gone off with all the pantry keys in his pocket. One rarely used icebox in the basement had been left unlocked, but it contained only a bowl of rice of doubtful date.

At 5:00 A.M., it occurred to me that I should send *Life* some kind of description of my remarkable evening, since my editors would hardly be familiar with the inside of the Kremlin. I searched throughout the cellar for something to write on, and found a big, brown paper marketing bag. I was dazed with sleepiness, but I managed to scribble a short account of my exciting appointment. I was so weary that the words must have been almost illegible, and yet somehow, the editors back in New York made sense out of it.

Mr. Hopkins had promised to take the films back to Washington on the plane with him. I found him upstairs in the Embassy having breakfast, where I turned over the precious package to him. In less than two days, the films were in *Life*'s hands. . . .

. . . after each of these long journeys to distant countries or to the war, I came back so crowded with impressions that had to be shared that I would have thrown them out to a convenient taxi driver or the corner policeman if I had not had lectures coming up.

The first lecture after a big trip told me what I wanted to know—the relative importance of the events I had been through, the human beings who stood out as the most vivid or moving, the details I could draw on to make my points come alive. Once I made the discovery that my experiences would unfold of themselves on the platform, I never allowed myself to prepare too specifically. I wanted to be surprised, too. . . .

On a photographic assignment, I threw myself so intensely into the business of taking photographs that I could not have done it, year in and year out, without growing stale. Instead of taking a vacation in the usual sense of the word, which interested me very little, I liked throwing myself just as wholeheartedly into a field completely different from photography. Lecturing meant I was building on my experiences, but in another dimension. . . .

In my book *Shooting the Russian War,* published after our wartime trip, words and pictures began to be more evenly balanced. In two later war books, *Purple Heart Valley* and *Dear Fatherland, Rest Quietly,* about Italy and Germany respectively, the writing became a more important part of the book. . . .

It was about ten years before the outbreak of World War II that Erskine's powerful writings threw the searchlight on a hitherto ignored segment of American life. His book *Tobacco Road,* made into a play, had brought home to millions the plight of sharecroppers and tenant farmers in the South. . . . At the end of ten years . . . it seemed to me that Erskine was writing new books of old stories— a repetition of earlier Tobacco Road themes—that he was barricading himself from new experiences. Though there was still much warmth between us, Erskine's frozen moods were just as unaccountable and difficult as in the beginning. . . .

It took the war actually to separate us. The attack on Pearl Harbor took place and our country was in the war. For me, there was no other choice than to offer my special skills wherever they might be useful. I wanted to go overseas. Erskine wanted to accept a Hollywood offer. He saw to it that I had a very profitable offer, too. He bought a house in a lovely part of Arizona as a present for me. I wouldn't accept the Hollywood offer; I couldn't accept the house, which I felt was another set of golden chains.

I believe by this time both of us began to realize we were leading two separate lives that no longer fitted together. We had had five good, productive years—with occasional tempests, it's true, but with some real happiness. I was relieved when it was all over and glad we parted with a mutual affection and respect which still endures.

Now I could put personal problems behind me and get back to work. *Life* worked out a wonderful arrangement with the Pentagon in which I would be accredited to the U.S. Air Forces. With my love for taking pictures from airplanes and of airplanes, it was perfect. Both the Air Force and *Life* would use my pictures. . . .

During all this work with the U.S. Air Forces overseas, I was given extraordinary assistance. My accreditation was a unique one, as war photographer directly assigned to the Air Force, with the Pentagon as well as *Life* using my pictures. I was allowed to do everything I required to build up my picture story: photograph the early dawn briefings, go on practice flights, whatever I needed except the one thing that really counted. I was not allowed to go on an actual combat mission. . . .

In the early weeks of my work with the heavy bombers, no one from the press was allowed to go on missions. Then the ban was lifted, as it obviously had to be. There was not a whisper of a double standard in the directive, but as though written in invisible ink, it was there for all Air Force officers to read. Male correspondents who applied got permission. My requests got me nowhere. Yet I was fully qualified to cover a mission—perhaps more than they— not in the sense of woman against man, but because the Air Force was my explicit assignment, my special job and trust. I had to go on an actual combat mission. This was the heart and core of it all. On the first day the ban was lifted, two newspapermen flew the mission. They went in two different airplanes to the same target. Only one came back. This did not help my chances any. . . .

The war was soon to open on another front with an invasion of the North African coast. This plan was one of the best-kept secrets of the entire war. On the American side of the Atlantic, few people knew; even my home office did not know. I was assuming a great responsibility to jump to another continent without consulting my editors in New York. But I had not an instant of doubt. If the Air Force would have me, I wanted to come right along.

For the invasion, I yearned and prayed that being a woman would make no difference. Then one evening, Gen. Jimmy Doolittle, recently appointed Commanding General of the Eighth Air Force, turned up in the officers' lounge.

I had met him through Eddie Rickenbacker on the Indianapolis

Speedway some years earlier. His wife Jo had embroidered my name on her famous tablecloth on which she worked the signatures of scores and scores of Doolittle friends. I knew Jimmy well enough to be sure my sex would not prejudice him against my request to go along on the coming invasion. He gave me permission to go, without any red tape.

I assumed I would fly to the African front with the heavy bomb group—going in the *Flitgun* would be perfect. But no—the high brass were determined on one point. No one could tell what kind of resistance we would meet. I should be sent by sea in convoy—the nice safe way.

The upshot of that was that those who flew—and this included most of the brass—stepped out on the African continent with their feet dry. I had to row part of the way. . . .

The torpedo came almost softly, penetrating the ship with a dull blunt thud. Yet I am sure everyone aboard said inwardly as I did, "This is it." We knew our ship was gravely wounded. We believed she would die. She had been a person to us—a friend who had protected us as long as she could. And now we were preparing to desert her as quickly as possible.

The sudden sharp list catapulted me out of my bunk into the shambles of a stateroom. One of the sisters found her flash and switched it on, and by its wavering beam we raced into our clothes. (We had been ordered to sleep fully dressed, but few people did.) I remember having to make trivial choices. Should it be the olive-drab work slacks or the dress pinks? Should I wear the trench coat, which was waterproof, or my beautifully tailored officer's greatcoat, which was warmer? I chose the dress coat and the work pants. All this seemed to take a year, but it must have been only a few seconds. The sisters too were leaping into their slacks—and even in our haste the slacks impressed me. The girls were dressing correctly for the torpedoing! Wishing them luck, I threw my musette bag with its camera over my shoulder and dashed out. . . .

Later, when I had time to think about it, I marveled at the change in me the instant thoughts of work gave way to thoughts of survival. With the possibility of work, nothing seemed too dreadful to face, but now lifeboat station No. 12 suddenly became the most desirable place in the world to be. My journey down the long sloping deck seemed interminable. I kept barking my shins on metal debris and running into piles of wreckage which I had to scramble over. I dreaded to find my lifeboat already launched. And but for a special difficulty, it would have been. Our lifeboat had been flooded with the torpedo splash, and there was some doubt whether it would stay afloat. As crew members discussed this problem in low anxious tones, my boatmates held strict formation in total silence exactly as we had all been taught in boat drills. I slid gratefully into my place and stood in silence with my companions while the moon beat down on us all. . . .

. . . my Air Force friends . . . took me for a drying out to an exotic villa overlooking the Mediterranean and with a brook running right through the house. This architectural triumph in tiled gingerbread had been requisitioned by the Allied Air Command for such topflight air officers as the American General Spaatz, the British Air Chief Marshal Tedder and other transient brass.

Right inside the front door I collided with the air officer I wanted most to see: Gen. Jimmy Doolittle. His first words were "Maggie, do you still want to go on a bombing mission?"

"Oh, you know I do," I gasped. "I had given up asking, because I didn't want to make a nuisance of myself all the time."

"Well, you've been torpedoed. You might as well go through everything," said General Jimmy.

In the next minute he was on a field telephone calling through to the 97th Bomb Group—my bomb group—and conveying the glad news that I had permission to fly a combat mission at the discretion of the C.O.

I was flown in a cargo plane to "a secret air base in an oasis in the Sahara Desert." It sounded glamorous, and to me it was.

The oasis was called romantically "the Garden of Allah" and was windswept with stinging sands, hot and chilly by turns, its few buildings in ruins. But to me, with my precious permission I had gone through literal fire and water to obtain, and with my wonderful story ahead to work on, the Garden of Allah had that touch of enchantment the name implies. . . .

This was a Garden of Allah where I got the sniffles. Overnight this blew up into a roaring cold, and the flight surgeon grounded me for two weeks. This was standard practice for fliers. In the unpressurized planes of those days, the descent from the rarefied atmosphere of high altitude could cost an airman his eardrums, if he flew a mission with a cold.

I welcomed the fortnight's delay because I had a great deal to do in preparation for the mission. . . .

During the two weeks I was grounded with my cold, I learned

as much as I could about working inside the big bomber under conditions I had never met before. As for cameras, the Signal Corps generously—for they were short themselves—offered to lend me any equipment I could use. . . .

I had to choose, on consultation with the crew, the most important viewpoint of all—the spot to work during the few vital moments when we flew the bomb run over the target. The unanimous decision was the left waist window. This was a spacious opening in the side of the ship, but, like everything else, so filled with its machine gun and other bulky structures that it left just a few chinks through which to work. I did not know till later that the crew members had placed bets on me. If we were attacked, would the waist gunner knock me out so that he could defend our airplane, or would I knock out the waist gunner so I would have room to take pictures? . . .

Today for our mission to Tunis we were still in the great Stone Age of bombing. We were packing old-fashioned bombs in old-fashioned bombers—our trusty B-17s with their defensive cross fire and long offensive range, the planes which our airmen swore by. . . .

The crossing of the invisible boundary line was a signal for the bombardier to disappear into the bomb bay. I knew he was going to remove the safety pins which were installed to keep our bombs from exploding on our friends, in case we were shot down or crash-landed over our own territory. The idea of holding a bomb together with a safety pin intrigued me. I followed him to the great black cave of the bomb bay and squeezed in between the rows of bombs. When my eyes grew accustomed to the dim light, I could just make out the bomb racks stacked neatly like bookshelves in a public library, and amidst them the bombardier, who was pulling the safety devices out of the bombs. From all of them he removed the yellow tags, which bombardiers always saved as souvenirs, and stuck them in his cap. When he started stuffing them in his mouth, I decided this was the point to take a picture. I checked focus, slipped in a flashbulb and made my shot. To our eyes, which had become adjusted to the darkness in the bomb bay, the flash seemed blinding. Through the interphone strapped to my ears, I could hear the bombardier crying out, "Jesus Christ! They're exploding in my hands!" . . .

An hour later . . . we were sweeping toward the Mediterranean coast. We had made our feint toward Bizerte. We had passed the ancient city of Carthage, a white smudge on the edge of the sea.

The watery cross that marked the Tunis lagoon was plainly visible below. We were roaring to our goal, along that invisible road through the air which had been the center of all the planning, the calculations, the guesses, the hopes. Our formation swung into the bomb run, grouped in position to drop its bombs in a preconceived pattern and then take to evasive action.

During the handful of minutes over the target when the interphones were kept clear for only the most urgent directives, the men heard over their earphones a string of high-pitched squeaks unlike anything they had ever heard on a mission before, a voice crazily and indisputably feminine: "Oh, that's just what I want, that's a beautiful angle! Roll me over quick. Hold me just like this. Hold me this way so I can shoot straight down." Airplane photography has been part of my working life for so long, and operating with a pilot who will put you in position to photograph is such an integral part of it, that for a short time I had the illusion that the weaving flight of evasive action was carried on just to help me take pictures— which, in fact, is exactly what it did. . . . I was far too excited about the photographs I was getting to realize I was speaking out loud. Talking to myself meant talking to the entire ship, with all of us united by the throat mikes, earphones, communication lines which bound us together. Later, on the ground, the men told me they had nearly fainted when they heard my pipsqueak voice come through. Again, flattering or unflattering, they had completely forgotten there was a woman on board. . . .

I left the Garden of Allah and started home by way of Oran, the Gold Coast and South America. Messages from my New York office reached me along the way. It warmed my heart to be in direct communication with them again. By now wraps had been taken off, and they knew where I was and the stories I had been covering. The Pentagon had received some of my negatives by army courier pouch, and my editors had already started laying out the story, which was to be a lead. I was to learn later that they were topping the story with high letters like the marquee of a movie theater: "LIFE'S BOURKE-WHITE GOES BOMBING."

Six months after my return from covering the Air Force in North Africa, I asked to be sent overseas again to the Italian campaign. This time I wanted to record the war on the ground. . . .

My assignment to Italy was an unusual one. A request for my services came from the Pentagon to Wilson Hicks, then picture editor of *Life*. I thought this was a great honor, and so did Hicks.

There had been considerable concern in Army circles because while the heroes in the air had been deservedly glamorized, not much attention had been given to the man on the ground and to his importance to the war effort. . . . This was particularly true of . . . the Services of Supply. . . .

One day I flew in the observer's seat with Capt. Jack Marinelli from Ottumwa, Iowa, who was going to search for Screaming Meemie—a German mortar that had been harassing our troops. . . . all at once we were high over Cassino Valley. I was struck by the polka-dotted effect of the valley, with hundreds of thousands of shell holes filled with rainwater and shining in the sun. It seemed impossible that so many shells could fall in a single valley. It was as though this valley, in which so many had suffered and died, was clothed in a sequined gown.

"It's been so rough down there," said Captain Marinelli, "the boys are calling it 'Purple Heart Valley.' " (Thereby naming my book, although I did not know it at the time.) . . .

The Captain found his Screaming Meemie despite its camouflage. He spotted it by the bushes around it, which blew back violently with each gun blast.

From now on, it was a two-way radiophone conversation between the pilot and the artillery gun crew back on the ground. The pilot gave the command to fire, and the answer would come back: "Eighty-eight seconds. On the way." Those 88 seconds were the time it took the shell to travel its fourteen-mile journey from the muzzle of the Long Tom to the enemy mortar. Those 88 seconds were precious nuggets of time for me, because I could use my cameras while the pilot watched his watch. "We're going to be hanging around here for a while," said Captain Marinelli, "so speak up if you want to be put into position for anything special. . . ."

Several times I saw other planes in the sky and called out to Captain Marinelli, but each time, they were friendly planes. The Captain said, "That's all right. Just tell me anything you see."

What I missed seeing was a group of four German fighters. The Captain went into the steepest dive I had ever experienced. It was the neatest maneuver imaginable—diving to shake the Focke-Wulfs, then wriggling our way through a stream bed so we were actually below the treetops, then back to friendly territory and to our own airstrip.

————

I was with General Patton's Third Army when we reached Buchenwald, on the outskirts of Weimar. Patton was so incensed at what he saw that he ordered his police to get a thousand civilians to make them see with their own eyes what their leaders had done. The MPs were so enraged that they brought back two thousand. This was the first I heard the words I was to hear repeated thousands of times: "We didn't know. We didn't know." But they did know.

I saw and photographed the piles of naked, lifeless bodies, the human skeletons in furnaces, the living skeletons who would die the next day because they had had to wait too long for deliverance, the pieces of tattooed skin for lampshades. Using the camera was almost a relief. It interposed a slight barrier between myself and the horror in front of me.

Buchenwald was more than the mind could grasp. It was as though a busy metropolis had frozen in attitudes of horror. But even Buchenwald paled before some of the smaller, more intimate atrocity camps.

I remember one we stumbled on just as our Army was in the act of capturing Leipzig: the labor camp of the Leipzig-Mochau airplane small-parts factory. The camp was a modest little square of ground enclosed by barbed wire. The bodies were still smoldering when we got there, terribly charred but still in human form. We learned the ghastly details from one of the few survivors. The SS had made use of a simple expedient to get rid of the inmates all at once. The SS guards made pails of steaming soup, and as soon as the inmates were all inside the mess hall, the SS put blankets over the windows, threw in hand grenades and pailfuls of a blazing acetate solution. The building went up in sheets of flame. Some escaped, only to die, human torches, on the high barbed-wire fence. Even those who were successful in scaling the fence were picked off as they ran across an open field by savage youngsters of the Hitler *Jugend* shooting from a tank. There had been three hundred inmates; there were eighteen who miraculously survived.

To me, those who had died in the meadow made the most heartbreaking sight of all. To be shot down when they were so close to freedom, when the Allied armies were at the gates of the city. It was understandable that the Germans destroyed their bridges to slow up our advance. But to destroy these miserable people—what sense was there in that?

A final touch was added by the retreating Germans. On a flagpole set to one side they had run up a white surrender flag over the acre of bones.

People often ask me how it is possible to photograph such atrocities. I have to work with a veil over my mind. In photographing the murder camps, the protective veil was so tightly drawn that I hardly knew what I had taken until I saw prints of my own photographs. It was as though I was seeing these horrors for the first time. I believe many correspondents worked in the same self-imposed stupor. One has to, or it is impossible to stand it.

My house on a rocky Connecticut hill, which my lectures had helped me buy, means a great deal to me as a home base. . . .

This house, isolated by surrounding woods, is the best place I know for writing and for restoration of the spirit. Solitude is a precious commodity when a book is being written. I am a morning writer. The world is all fresh and new then, and made for the imagination. I keep an odd schedule that would be possible only for someone with no family demands—to bed at eight, up at four. I love to write out of doors and sleep out of doors, too. In a strange way, if I sleep under open sky, it becomes part of the writing experience, part of my insulation from the world. . . .

I'm afraid my closely guarded solitude causes some hurt feelings now and then. But how to explain, without wounding someone, that you want to be wholly in the world you are writing about, that it would take two days to get the visitor's voice out of the house so that you could listen to your own characters again? . . .

I think with every major photographic story there has been some man who, in his way, opened up his world for me and somehow stands for it in my mind. A man of stature from whom I could absorb a great deal. . . . The lasting quality of some of these friendships has been a source of great happiness to me. Long after the job which brought us together is over, we are bound by deep ties of affection. A happy twist of circumstances brings us together, and time raises no barriers. The intervening years fall away, and we pick up the friendship where we left off.

Some of these men have meant more to me than either of my husbands. Perhaps fliers have meant the most, particularly certain of the seasoned ones whose early work meant pioneering in one way or another, and called for great daring and imagination. With men like this there was always a quick understanding, and if the work meant danger shared, that was always a bond. . . .

Mine is a life into which marriage doesn't fit very well. If I had had children, I would have charted a widely different life, drawn creative inspiration from them, and shaped my work to them. Perhaps I would have worked on children's books, rather than going to wars. It must be a fascinating thing to watch a growing child absorb his expanding world. One life is not better than the other; it is just a different life. . . .

I have always been glad I cast the die on the side I did. But a woman who lives a roving life must be able to stand alone. She must have emotional security, which is more important even than financial security. There is a richness in a life where you stand on your own feet, although it imposes a certain creed. There must be no demands. Others have the right to be as free as you are. You must be able to take disappointments gallantly. You set your own ground rules, and if you follow them, there are great rewards.

Maxine Hong Kingston

(*1940–*   )

Maxine Hong Kingston was born in Stockton, California, the eldest of her Chinese immigrant parents' four children. As a child she worked in a succession of family laundries, experiencing the typical immigrant conflicts between her parents' culture and the California youth culture she learned in public school. Making a definitive step toward American culture, Kingston enrolled in 1958 in the University of California, Berkeley, where she majored in English. The year after her graduation she married Earll Kingston, with whom she has a son, Joseph.

Kingston taught English at high schools in California and Hawaii from 1965 to 1970, then at the Mid-Pacific Institute in Hawaii from 1970 to 1977. She was a visiting professor at Eastern Michigan University, Ypsilanti, in 1986, before becoming distinguished professor at her alma mater in 1990.

A prolific writer, Kingston has published *China Men* (1980), *Hawaii: One Summer* (1987), *Through the Black Curtain* (1988), and *Tripmaster Monkey: His Fake Book* (1989). Her work has won critical acclaim and a broad readership. The recipient of awards from the National Endowment for the Arts, the Guggenheim Foundation, and the National Book Critics Circle, Kingston was named a Living Treasure of Hawaii in 1980.

The Woman Warrior won the National Book Critics Circle Award the year of its publication and established Kingston's reputation as writer, feminist, and interpreter of the Asian-American experience.

THE WOMAN WARRIOR:
Memoirs of a Girlhood Among Ghosts

You must not tell anyone," my mother said, "what I am about to tell you. In China your father had a sister who killed herself. She jumped into the family well. We say that your father has all brothers because it is as if she had never been born.

"In 1924 just a few days after our village celebrated seventeen hurry-up weddings—to make sure that every young man who went 'out on the road' would responsibly come home—your father and his brothers and your grandfather and his brothers and your aunt's new husband sailed for America, the Gold Mountain. It was your grandfather's last trip. Those lucky enough to get contracts waved goodbye from the decks. They fed and guarded the stowaways and helped them off in Cuba, New York, Bali, Hawaii. 'We'll meet in California next year,' they said. All of them sent money home. . . .

"Don't let your father know that I told you. He denies her. Now that you have started to menstruate, what happened to her could happen to you. Don't humiliate us. You wouldn't like to be forgotten as if you had never been born. The villagers are watchful."

Whenever she had to warn us about life, my mother told stories that ran like this one, a story to grow up on. She tested our strength to establish realities. Those in the emigrant generations who could not reassert brute survival died young and far from home. Those of us in the first American generations have had to figure out how the invisible world the emigrants built around our childhoods fit in solid America.

The emigrants confused the gods by diverting their curses, misleading them with crooked streets and false names. They must try to confuse their offspring as well, who, I suppose, threaten them in similar ways—always trying to get things straight, always trying to name the unspeakable. The Chinese I know hide their names; sojourners take new names when their lives change and guard their real names with silence.

Chinese-Americans, when you try to understand what things in you are Chinese, how do you separate what is peculiar to childhood, to poverty, insanities, one family, your mother who marked your growing with stories, from what is Chinese? What is Chinese tradition and what is the movies?

If I want to learn what clothes my aunt wore, whether flashy or ordinary, I would have to begin, "Remember Father's drowned-in-the-well sister?" I cannot ask that. My mother has told me once and for all the useful parts. She will add nothing unless powered by Necessity, a riverbank that guides her life. She plants vegetable gardens rather than lawns; she carries the odd-shaped tomatoes home from the fields and eats food left for the gods.

Whenever we did frivolous things, we used up energy; we flew high kites. We children came up off the ground over the melting cones our parents brought home from work and the American movie on New Year's Day—*Oh, You Beautiful Doll* with Betty

Grable one year, and *She Wore a Yellow Ribbon* with John Wayne another year. After the one carnival ride each, we paid in guilt; our tired father counted his change on the dark walk home.

Adultery is extravagance. Could people who hatch their own chicks and eat the embryos and the heads for delicacies and boil the feet in vinegar for party food, leaving only the gravel, eating even the gizzard lining—could such people engender a prodigal aunt? To be a woman, to have a daughter in starvation time was a waste enough. My aunt could not have been the lone romantic who gave up everything for sex. Women in the old China did not choose. Some man had commanded her to lie with him and be his secret evil. I wonder whether he masked himself when he joined the raid on her family. . . .

She may have gone to the pigsty as a last act of responsibility: she would protect this child as she had protected its father. It would look after her soul, leaving supplies on her grave. But how would this tiny child without family find her grave when there would be no marker for her anywhere, neither in the earth nor the family hall? No one would give her a family hall name. She had taken the child with her into the wastes. At its birth the two of them had felt the same raw pain of separation, a wound that only the family pressing tight could close. A child with no descent line would not soften her life but only trail after her, ghostlike, begging her to give it purpose. At dawn the villagers on their way to the fields would stand around the fence and look.

Full of milk, the little ghost slept. When it awoke, she hardened her breasts against the milk that crying loosens. Toward morning she picked up the baby and walked to the well.

Carrying the baby to the well shows loving. Otherwise abandon it. Turn its face into the mud. Mothers who love their children take them along. It was probably a girl; there is some hope of forgiveness for boys.

"Don't tell anyone you had an aunt. Your father does not want to hear her name. She has never been born." I have believed that sex was unspeakable and words so strong and fathers so frail that "aunt" would do my father mysterious harm. I have thought that my family, having settled among immigrants who had also been their neighbors in the ancestral land, needed to clean their name, and a wrong word would incite the kinspeople even here. But there is more to this silence: they want me to participate in her punishment. And I have.

In the twenty years since I heard this story I have not asked for details nor said my aunt's name; I do not know it. People who can comfort the dead can also chase after them to hurt them further—a reverse ancestor worship. The real punishment was not the raid swiftly inflicted by the villagers, but the family's deliberately forgetting her. Her betrayal so maddened them, they saw to it that she would suffer forever, even after her death. . . .

My aunt haunts me—her ghost drawn to me because now, after fifty years of neglect, I alone devote pages of paper to her, though not origamied into houses and clothes. I do not think she always means me well. I am telling on her, and she was a spite suicide, drowning herself in the drinking water. The Chinese are always very frightened of the drowned one, whose weeping ghost, wet hair hanging and skin bloated, waits silently by the water to pull down a substitute.

When we Chinese girls listened to the adults talking-story, we learned that we failed if we grew up to be but wives or slaves. We could be heroines, swordswomen. Even if she had to rage across all China, a swordswoman got even with anybody who hurt her family. Perhaps women were once so dangerous that they had to have their feet bound. It was a woman who invented white crane boxing only two hundred years ago. She was already an expert pole fighter, daughter of a teacher trained at the Shao-lin temple, where there lived an order of fighting monks. She was combing her hair one morning when a white crane alighted outside her window. She teased it with her pole, which it pushed aside with a soft brush of its wing. Amazed, she dashed outside and tried to knock the crane off its perch. It snapped her pole in two. Recognizing the presence of great power, she asked the spirit of the white crane if it would teach her to fight. It answered with a cry that white crane boxers imitate today. Later the bird returned as an old man, and he guided her boxing for many years. Thus she gave the world a new martial art.

This was one of the tamer, more modern stories, mere introduction. My mother told others that followed swordswomen through the woods and palaces for years. Night after night my mother would talk-story until we fell asleep. I couldn't tell where the stories left off and the dreams began, her voice the voice of the heroines in my sleep. And on Sundays, from noon to midnight, we went to the movies at the Confucius Church. We saw swordswomen jump over houses from a standstill; they didn't even need a running start.

At last I saw that I too had been in the presence of great power, my mother talking-story. After I grew up, I heard the chant of Fa Mu Lan, the girl who took her father's place in battle. Instantly I remembered that as a child I had followed my mother about the house, the two of us singing about how Fa Mu Lan fought gloriously and returned alive from war to settle in the village. I had forgotten this chant that was once mine, given me by my mother, who may not have known its power to remind. She said I would grow up a wife and a slave, but she taught me the song of the warrior woman, Fa Mu Lan. I would have to grow up a warrior woman.

My American life has been such a disappointment.

"I got straight A's, Mama."

"Let me tell you a true story about a girl who saved her village."

I could not figure out what was my village. And it was important that I do something big and fine, or else my parents would sell me when we made our way back to China. In China there were solutions for what to do with little girls who ate up food and threw tantrums. You can't eat straight A's.

When one of my parents or the emigrant villagers said, "Feeding girls is feeding cowbirds," I would thrash on the floor and scream so hard I couldn't talk. I couldn't stop.

"What's the matter with her?"

"I don't know. Bad, I guess. You know how girls are. 'There's no profit in raising girls. Better to raise geese than girls.'"

"I would hit her if she were mine. But then there's no use wasting all that discipline on a girl. 'When you raise girls, you're raising children for strangers.'"

"Stop that crying!" my mother would yell. "I'm going to hit you if you don't stop. Bad girl! Stop!" I'm going to remember never to hit or to scold my children for crying, I thought, because then they will only cry more.

"I'm not a bad girl," I would scream. "I'm not a bad girl. I'm not a bad girl." I might as well as have said, "I'm not a girl."

"When you were little, all you had to say was 'I'm not a bad girl,' and you could make yourself cry," my mother says, talking-story about my childhood.

I minded that the emigrant villagers shook their heads at my sister and me. "One girl—and another girl," they said, and made our parents ashamed to take us out together. The good part about my brothers being born was that people stopped saying, "All girls," but I learned new grievances. "Did you roll an egg on *my* face like that when *I* was born?" "Did you have a full-month party for *me*?" "Did you turn on all the lights?" "Did you send *my* picture to Grandmother?" "Why not? Because I'm a girl? Is that why not?" "Why didn't you teach me English?" "You like having me beaten up at school, don't you?"

"She is very mean, isn't she?" the emigrant villagers would say.

I went away to college—Berkeley in the sixties—and I studied, and I marched to change the world, but I did not turn into a boy. I would have liked to bring myself back as a boy for my parents to welcome with chickens and pigs. That was for my brother, who returned alive from Vietnam.

If I went to Vietnam, I would not come back; females desert families. It was said, "There is an outward tendency in females," which meant that I was getting straight A's for the good of my future husband's family, not my own. I did not plan ever to have a husband. I would show my mother and father and the nosey emigrant villagers that girls have no outward tendency. I stopped getting straight A's.

And all the time I was having to turn myself American-feminine, or no dates.

There is a Chinese word for the female *I*—which is "slave." Break the women with their own tongues!

I refused to cook. When I had to wash dishes, I would crack one or two. "Bad girl," my mother yelled, and sometimes that made me gloat rather than cry. Isn't a bad girl almost a boy?

"What do you want to be when you grow up, little girl?"

"A lumberjack in Oregon."

Even now, unless I'm happy, I burn the food when I cook. I do not feed people. I let the dirty dishes rot. I eat at other people's tables but won't invite them to mine, where the dishes are rotting.

If I could not-eat, perhaps I could make myself a warrior like the swordswoman who drives me. I will—I must—rise and plow the fields as soon as the baby comes out.

Once I get outside the house, what bird might call me; on what horse could I ride away? Marriage and childbirth strengthen the swordswoman, who is not a maid like Joan of Arc. Do the women's work; then do more work, which will become ours too. No husband of mine will say, "I could have been a drummer, but I had to think about the wife and kids. You know how it is." Nobody supports me at the expense of his own adventure. Then I get bitter: no one supports me; I am not loved enough to be supported. That I am not a burden had to compensate for the sad envy when I look at women loved enough to be supported. Even now China wraps double binds around my feet.

When urban renewal tore down my parents' laundry and paved over our slum for a parking lot, I only made up gun and knife fantasies and did nothing useful. . . .

To avenge my family, I'd have to storm across China to take back our farm from the Communists; I'd have to rage across the United States to take back the laundry in New York and the one in California. Nobody in history has conquered and united both North America and Asia. A descendant of eighty pole fighters, I ought to be able to set out confidently, march straight down our street, get going right now. There's work to do, ground to cover. Surely, the eighty pole fighters, though unseen, would follow me and lead me and protect me, as is the wont of ancestors. Or it may well be that they're resting happily in China, their spirits dispersed among the real Chinese, and not nudging me at all with their poles. I mustn't feel bad that I haven't done as well as the swordswoman did; after all, no bird called me, no wise old people tutored me. I have no magic beads, no water gourd sight, no rabbit that will jump in the fire when I'm hungry. I dislike armies.

I've looked for the bird. I've seen clouds make pointed angel wings that stream past the sunset, but they shred into clouds. Once at a beach after a long hike I saw a seagull, tiny as an insect. But when I jumped up to tell what miracle I saw, before I could get the words out I understood that the bird was insect-size because it was far away. My brain had momentarily lost its depth perception. I was that eager to find an unusual bird.

I live now where there are Chinese and Japanese, but no emigrants from my own village looking at me as if I had failed them. Living among one's own emigrant villagers can give a good Chinese far from China glory and a place. "That old busboy is really a swordsman," we whisper when he goes by. "He's a swordsman who's killed fifty. He has a tong ax in his closet." But I am useless, one more girl who couldn't be sold. When I visit the family now, I wrap my American successes around me like a private shawl; I *am* worthy of eating the food. From afar I can believe my family loves me fundamentally. They only say, "When fishing for treasures in the flood, be careful not to pull in girls," because that is what one says about daughters. But I watched such words come out of my own mother's and father's mouths; I looked at their ink drawing of poor people snagging their neighbors' flotage with long flood hooks and pushing the girl babies on down the river. And I had to get out of hating range. I read in an anthropology book that Chinese say, "Girls are necessary too"; I have never heard the Chinese I know make this concession. Perhaps it was a saying in another village. I refuse to shy my way anymore through our Chinatown, which tasks me with the old sayings and the stories.

The swordswoman and I are not so dissimilar. May my people understand the resemblance soon so that I can return to them. What we have in common are the words at our backs. The ideographs for *revenge* are "report a crime" and "report to five families." The reporting is the vengeance—not the beheading, not the gutting, but the words. And I have so many words—"chink" words and "gook" words too—that they do not fit on my skin.

Whenever my parents said "home," they suspended America. They suspended enjoyment, but I did not want to go to China. In China my parents would sell my sisters and me. My father would marry two or three more wives, who would spatter cooking oil on our bare toes and lie that we were crying for naughtiness. They would give food to their own children and rocks to us. I did not want to go where the ghosts took shapes nothing like our own.

As a child I feared the size of the world. The farther away the sound of howling dogs, the farther away the sound of the trains, the tighter I curled myself under the quilt. The trains sounded deeper and deeper into the night. They had not reached the end of the world before I stopped hearing them, the last long moan diminishing toward China. How large the world must be to make my grandmother only a taste by the time she reaches me.

Quite often the big loud women came shouting into the house, "Now when you sell this one, I'd like to buy her to be my maid." Then they laughed. They always said that about my sister, not me because I dropped dishes at them. I picked my nose while I was cooking and serving. My clothes were wrinkled even though we owned a laundry. Indeed I was getting stranger every day. I affected a limp. And, of course, the mysterious disease I had had might have been dormant and contagious.

But if I made myself unsellable here, my parents need only wait until China, and there, where anything happens, they would be able to unload us, even me—sellable, marriageable. So while the adults wept over the letters about the neighbors gone berserk turning Communist ("They do funny dances; they sing weird songs, just syllables. They make us dance; they make us sing"), I was secretly glad. As long as the aunts kept disappearing and the uncles dying after unspeakable tortures, my parents would prolong their Gold Mountain stay. We could start spending our fare money on a car and chairs, a stereo. Nobody wrote to tell us that Mao himself had been matched to an older girl when he was a child and that he was freeing women from prisons, where they had been put for refusing the businessmen their parents had picked as husbands. Nobody told us that the Revolution (the Liberation) was against girl slavery and girl infanticide (a village-wide party if it's a boy). Girls would no longer have to kill themselves rather than get married. May the Communists light up the house on a girl's birthday.

I watched our parents buy a sofa, then a rug, curtains, chairs to replace the orange and apple crates one by one, now to be used for storage. Good. At the beginning of the second Communist five-year plan, our parents bought a car. But you could see the relatives and the villagers getting more worried about what to do with the girls. We had three girl second cousins, no boys; their great-grandfather and our grandfather were brothers. The great-grandfather was the old man who lived with them, as the river-pirate great-uncle was the old man who lived with us. When my sisters and I ate at their house, there we would be—six girls eating. The old man opened his eyes wide at us and turned in a circle, surrounded. His neck tendons stretched out. "Maggots!" he shouted. "Maggots! Where are my grandsons? I want grandsons! Give me grandsons! Maggots!" He pointed at each one of us, "Maggot! Maggot! Maggot! Maggot! Maggot! Maggot!" Then he dived into his food, eating fast and getting seconds. "Eat, maggots," he said. "Look at the maggots chew."

"He does that at every meal," the girls told us in English.

"Yeah," we said. "Our old man hates us too. What assholes."

Third Grand-Uncle finally did get a boy, though, his only great-grandson. The boy's parents and the old man bought him toys, bought him everything—new diapers, new plastic pants—not homemade diapers, not bread bags. They gave him a full-month party inviting all the emigrant villagers; they deliberately hadn't given the girls parties, so that no one would notice another girl. Their brother got toy trucks that were big enough to climb inside. When he grew older, he got a bicycle and let the girls play with his old tricycle and wagon. My mother bought his sisters a typewriter.

"They can be clerk-typists," their father kept saying, but he would not buy them a typewriter.

"What an asshole," I said, muttering the way my father muttered "Dog vomit" when the customers nagged him about missing socks. . . .

Now again plans were urgently afoot to fix me up, to improve my voice. The wealthiest villager wife came to the laundry one day to have a listen. "You better do something with this one," she told my mother. "She has an ugly voice. She quacks like a pressed duck." Then she looked at me unnecessarily hard; Chinese do not have to address children directly. "You have what we call a pressed-duck voice," she said. This woman was the giver of American names, my parents gave the Chinese names. And she was right: if you squeezed the duck hung up to dry in the east window, the sound that was my voice would come out of it. She was a woman of such power that all we immigrants and descendants of immigrants were obliged to her family forever for bringing us here and for finding us jobs, and she had named my voice.

"No," I quacked. "No, I don't."

"Don't talk back," my mother scolded. Maybe this lady was powerful enough to send us back.

I went to the front of the laundry and worked so hard that I impolitely did not take notice of her leaving.

"Improve that voice," she had instructed my mother, "or else you'll never marry her off. Even the fool half ghosts won't have her." So I discovered the next plan to get rid of us: marry us off here without waiting until China. . . .

I learned that young men were placing ads in the *Gold Mountain News* to find wives when my mother and father started answering them. Suddenly a series of new workers showed up at the laundry; they each worked for a week before they disappeared. They ate with us. They talked Chinese with my parents. They did not talk to us. We were to call them "Elder Brother," although they were not related to us. They were all funny-looking FOB's, Fresh-off-the-Boats, as the Chinese-American kids at school called the young immigrants. FOB's wear high-riding gray slacks and white shirts with the sleeves rolled up. Their eyes do not focus correctly—shifty-eyed—and they hold their mouths slack, not tight-jawed masculine. They shave off their sideburns. The girls said *they'd* never date an FOB. My mother took one home from the laundry, and I saw him looking over our photographs. "This one," he said, picking up my sister's picture.

"No. No," said my mother. "This one," my picture. "The oldest first," she said. Good. I was an obstacle. I would protect my sister and myself at the same time. As my parents and the FOB sat talking at the kitchen table, I dropped two dishes. I found my walking stick and limped across the floor. I twisted my mouth and caught my hand in the knots of my hair. I spilled soup on the FOB when I handed him his bowl. "She can sew, though," I heard my mother say, "and sweep." I raised dust swirls sweeping around and under the FOB's chair—very bad luck because spirits live inside the broom. I put on my shoes with the open flaps and flapped about like a Wino Ghost. From then on, I wore those shoes to parties, whenever the mothers gathered to talk about marriages. The FOB and my parents paid me no attention, half ghosts half invisible, but when he left, my mother yelled at me about the dried-duck voice, the bad temper, the laziness, the clumsiness, the stupidity that comes from reading too much. The young men stopped visiting; not one came back. "Couldn't you just stop rubbing your nose?" she scolded. "All the village ladies are talking about your nose. They're afraid to eat our pastries because you might have kneaded the dough." But I couldn't stop at will anymore, and a crease developed across the bridge. My parents would not give up, though. "Though you can't see it," my mother said, "a red string around your ankle ties you to the person you'll marry. He's already been born, and he's on the other end of the string." . . .

Maybe because I was the one with the tongue cut loose, I had grown inside me a list of over two hundred things that I had to tell my mother so that she would know the true things about me and to stop the pain in my throat. When I first started counting, I had had only thirty-six items: how I had prayed for a white horse of my own—white, the bad, mournful color—and prayer bringing me to the attention of the god of the black-and-white nuns who gave us "holy cards" in the park. How I wanted the horse to start the movies in my mind coming true. How I had picked on a girl and made her cry. How I had stolen from the cash register and bought candy for everybody I knew, not just brothers and sisters, but strangers too and ghost children. How it was me who pulled up the onions in the garden out of anger. How I had jumped head-first off the dresser, not accidentally, but so I could fly. Then there were my fights at Chinese school. And the nuns who kept stopping us in the park, which was across the street from Chinese school, to tell us that if we didn't get baptized we'd go to hell like one of the nine Taoist hells forever. And the obscene caller that phoned us at home when the adults were at the laundry. And the Mexican and Filipino girls at school who went to "confession," and how I envied them their white dresses and their chance each Saturday to tell even thoughts that were sinful. If only I could let my mother know the list, she—and the world—would become more like me, and I would never be alone again. I would pick a time of day when my mother was alone and tell her one item a day; I'd be finished in less than a year. If the telling got excruciating and her anger too bad, I'd tell five items once a week like the Catholic girls, and I'd still be through in a year, maybe ten months. My mother's most peaceful time was in the evenings when she starched the white shirts. The laundry would be clean, the gray wood floors sprinkled and swept with water and wet sawdust. She would be wringing shirts at the starch tub and not running about. My father and sisters and brothers would be at their own jobs mending, folding, packaging. Steam would be rising from the starch, the air cool at last. Yes, that would be the time and place for the telling. . . .

"What's it called, Mother"—the duck voice coming out talking to my own mother—"when a person whispers to the head of the sages—no, not the sages, more like the buddhas but not real people like the buddhas (they've always lived in the sky and never turned into people like the buddhas)—and you whisper to them, the boss of them, and ask for things? They're like magicians? What do you call it when you talk to the boss magician?"

" 'Talking-to-the-top-magician,' I guess."

"I did that. Yes. That's it. That's what I did. I talked-to-the-top-magician and asked for a white horse." There. Said.

"Mm," she said, squeezing the starch out of the collar and cuffs. But I had talked, and she acted as if she hadn't heard.

Perhaps she hadn't understood. I had to be more explicit. I hated this. "I kneeled on the bed in there, in the laundry bedroom, and put my arms up like I saw in a comic book"—one night I heard monsters coming through the kitchen, and I had promised the god in the movies, the one the Mexicans and Filipinos have, as in "God Bless America," that I would not read comic books anymore if he would save me just this once; I had broken that promise, and I needed to tell all this to my mother too— "and in that ludicrous position asked for a horse."

"Mm," she said, nodded, and kept dipping and squeezing.

On my two nights off, I had sat on the floor too but had not said a word.

"Mother," I whispered and quacked.

"I can't stand this whispering," she said looking right at me, stopping her squeezing. "Senseless gabbings every night. I wish you would stop. Go away and work. Whispering, whispering, making no sense. Madness. I don't feel like hearing your craziness."

So I had to stop, relieved in some ways. I shut my mouth, but I felt something alive tearing at my throat, bite by bite, from the inside. Soon there would be three hundred things, and too late to get them out before my mother grew old and died.

I had probably interrupted her in the middle of her own quiet time when the boiler and presses were off and the cool night flew against the windows in moths and crickets. Very few customers came in. Starching the shirts for the next day's pressing was probably my mother's time to ride off with the people in her own mind. That would explain why she was so far away and did not want to listen to me. "Leave me alone," she said.

The hulk, the hunching sitter [a retarded person who pursued Kingston; she feared her parents planned to marry her to him], brought a third box now, to rest his feet on. He patted his boxes. He sat in wait, hunching on his pile of dirt. My throat hurt constantly, vocal cords taut to snapping. One night when the laundry was so busy that the whole family was eating dinner there, crowded around the little round table, my throat burst open. I stood up, talking and burbling. I looked directly at my mother and father and screamed, "I want you to tell that hulk, that gorilla-ape, to go away and never bother us again. I know what you're up to. You're thinking he's rich, and we're poor. You think we're odd and not pretty and we're not bright. You think you can give us away to freaks. You better not do that, Mother. I don't want to see him or his dirty boxes here tomorrow. If I see him here one more time, I'm going away. I'm going away anyway. I am. Do you hear me? I may be ugly and clumsy, but one thing I'm not, I'm not retarded. There's nothing wrong with my brain. Do you know what the Teacher Ghosts say about me? They tell me I'm smart, and I can win scholarships. I can get into colleges. I've already applied. I'm smart. I can do all kinds of things. I know how to get A's, and they say I could be a scientist or a mathematician if I want. I can make a living and take care of myself. So you don't have to find me a keeper who's too dumb to know a bad bargain. I'm so smart, if they say write ten pages, I can write fifteen. I can do ghost things even better than ghosts can. Not everybody thinks I'm nothing. I am not going to be a slave or a wife. Even if I am stupid and talk funny and get sick, I won't let you turn me into a slave or a wife. I'm getting out of here. I can't stand living here anymore. It's your fault I talk weird. The only reason I flunked kindergarten was because you couldn't teach me English, and you gave me a zero IQ. I've brought my IQ up, though. They say I'm smart now. Things follow in lines at school. They take stories and teach us to turn them into essays. I don't need anybody to pronounce English words for me. I can figure them out by myself. I'm going to get scholarships, and I'm going away. And at college I'll have the people I like for friends. I don't care if their great-great-grandfather died of TB. I don't care if they were our enemies in China four thousand years ago. So get that ape out of here. I'm going to college. And I'm not going to Chinese school anymore. I'm going to run for office at American school, and I'm going to join clubs. I'm going to get enough offices and clubs on my record to get into college. And I can't stand Chinese school anyway; the kids are rowdy and mean, fighting all night. And I don't want to listen to any more of your stories; they have no logic. They scramble me up. You lie with stories. You won't tell me a story and then say, 'This is a true story,' or, 'This is just a story.' I can't tell the difference. I don't even know what your real names are. I can't tell what's real and what you make up. Ha! You can't stop me from talking. You tried to cut off my tongue, but it didn't work." So I told the hardest ten or twelve things on my list all in one outburst.

My mother, who is champion talker, was, of course, shouting at the same time. "I cut it to make you talk more, not less, you dummy. You're still stupid. You can't listen right. I didn't say I was going to marry you off. Did I ever say that? Did I ever mention that? Those newspaper people were for your sister, not you. Who would want you? Who said we could sell you? We can't sell people. Can't you take a joke? You can't even tell a joke from real life. You're not so smart. Can't even tell real from false."

"I'm never getting married, never!"

"Who'd want to marry you anyway? Noisy. Talking like a duck. Disobedient. Messy. And I know about college. What makes you think you're the first one to think about college? I was a doctor. I went to medical school. I don't see why you have to be a mathematician. I don't see why you can't be a doctor like me."

"I can't stand fever and delirium or listening to people coming out of anesthesia. But I didn't say I wanted to be a mathematician either. That's what the ghosts say. I want to be a lumberjack and a newspaper reporter." Might as well tell her some of the other items on my list. "I'm going to chop down trees in the daytime and write about timber at night."

"I don't see why you need to go to college at all to become either one of those things. Everybody else is sending their girls to typing school. 'Learn to type if you want to be an American girl.' Why don't you go to typing school? The cousins and village girls are going to typing school."

"And you leave my sister alone. You try that with the advertising again, and I'll take her with me." My telling list was scrambled out of order. When I said them out loud I saw that some of the items were ten years old already, and I had outgrown them. But they kept pouring out anyway in the voice like Chinese opera. I could hear the drums and the cymbals and the gongs and brass horns.

"You're the one to leave your little sisters alone," my mother was saying. "You're always leading them off somewhere. I've had to call the police twice because of you." She herself was shouting out things I had meant to tell her—that I took my brothers and sisters to explore strange people's houses, ghost children's houses, and haunted houses blackened by fire. We explored a Mexican house and a redheaded family's house, but not the gypsies' house; I had only seen the inside of the gypsies' house in mind-movies. We explored the sloughs, where we found hobo nests. My mother must have followed us.

"You turned out so unusual. I fixed your tongue so you could say charming things. You don't even say hello to the villagers."

"They don't say hello to me."

"They don't have to answer children. When you get old, people will say hello to you."

"When I get to college, it won't matter if I'm not charming. And it doesn't matter if a person is ugly; she can still do school-work."

"I didn't say you were ugly."

"You say that all the time."

"That's what we're supposed to say. That's what Chinese say. We like to say the opposite."

It seemed to hurt her to tell me that—another guilt for my list to tell my mother, I thought. And suddenly I got very confused and lonely because I was at that moment telling her my list, and in the telling, it grew. No higher listener. No listener but myself.

"Ho Chi Kuei," she shouted. "Ho Chi Kuei. Leave then. Get out, you Ho Chi Kuei. Get out. I knew you were going to turn out bad. Ho Chi Kuei." My brothers and sisters had left the table, and my father would not look at me anymore, ignoring me.

Be careful what you say. It comes true. It comes true. I had to leave home in order to see the world logically, logic the new way of seeing. I learned to think that mysteries are for explanation. I enjoy the simplicity. Concrete pours out of my mouth to cover the forests with freeways and sidewalks. Give me plastics, periodical tables, t.v. dinners with vegetables no more complex than peas mixed with diced carrots. Shine floodlights into dark corners: no ghosts.

I've been looking up "Ho Chi Kuei," which is what the immigrants call us—Ho Chi Ghosts. "Well, Ho Chi Kuei," they say, "what silliness have you been up to now?" "That's a Ho Chi Kuei for you," they say, no matter what we've done. It was more complicated (and therefore worse) than "dogs," which they say affectionately, mostly to boys. They use "pig" and "stink pig" for girls, and only in an angry voice. . . .

What I'll inherit someday is a green address book full of names. I'll send the relatives money, and they'll write me stories about their hunger. My mother has been tearing up the letters from the youngest grandson of her father's third wife. He has been asking for fifty dollars to buy a bicycle. He says a bicycle will change his life. He could feed his wife and children if he had a bicycle. "We'd have to go hungry ourselves," my mother says. "They don't understand that we have ourselves to feed too." I've been making money; I guess it's my turn. I'd like to go to China and see those people and find out what's a cheat story and what's not. Did my grandmother really live to be ninety-nine? Or did they string us along all those years to get our money? Do the babies wear a Mao button like a drop of blood on their jumpsuits? When we overseas Chinese send money, do the relatives divide it evenly among the commune? Or do they really pay 2 percent tax and keep the rest? It would be good if the Communists were taking care of themselves; then I could buy a color t.v.

Pioneers and Reformers

The seven women whose life stories appear in this section were all rebels, high-achieving leaders, individuals of extraordinary energy, possessed from childhood with a drive for adventure, their lives fueled by strong moral purpose. Most rejected conventional marriage as an unwelcome constraint which would subtract from their inner urge to achieve.

Anna Howard Shaw (1847–1919) and Jane Addams (1860–1935), feminists of the early Progressive era, described their lives in romantic terms. Shaw literally trusted the Lord to feed her during her unsupported theological studies in Boston. When the quality of her preaching brought her a gift of desperately needed money, she attributed the gift to divine intervention. This attitude is, however, contradicted many times in her narrative when Shaw left nothing to divine providence, as, for example, when she pulled a revolver on a threatening attacker in the Northern Michigan woods. Addams likewise transformed her unrelenting quest for a creative role for educated American women—in reality pursued with tireless intellectual and physical energy and an iron will—into a romantic conversion experience. Her account of life at Hull-House shows us a woman who is a born leader forging an institution, but her narrative is in the first person plural, and the events which made Hull-House a thriving institution seem just to have happened, without Addams's agency.

Anne Walter Fearn (1865–1939) and Margaret Sanger (1879–1966) represent two generations in the movement for health reform for women. Fearn uprooted herself from her conventional Mississippi Delta childhood to become a woman physician and then a health reformer associated with Protestant missions in China. Her love of travel and sense of adventure transform what might have been a routine description of good works into a moving evocation of another culture. Her phenomenal energy was celebrated by her Chinese name, "the Great Wind."

Fearn was frank about the conflicts in her marriage but otherwise sexually conventional. Sanger, the product of a new generation, exposed to radical socialist critiques of middle-class culture, dedicated her life to securing women's ability to control their fertility. Steeped in romanticism about sexuality, Sanger celebrated marital love in her writing but lived according to a male ethic of sexual freedom. A transitional figure, she narrated her life in semiromantic terms. She portrayed herself as drawn by the fates to the Lower East Side and overwhelmed by personal responsibility for the suffering and death of poor women killed by botched abortions or repeated childbirth. The conventions of the romantic heroine were, however, abandoned as Sanger narrated her leadership of the birth control movement. The I who speaks is a powerful leader, with unfaltering vision.

Anna Louise Strong (1885–1970), one of the first generation of American women to enter graduate school, told her life story as a quest for a true egalitarian community and as a progressive unlearning of her privileged American education. Like Fearn's, her memoir, potentially the wooden narrative of the convinced ideologue, becomes three-dimensional as it describes central Asia, her arrival at the Chinese Communist camp in Yenan in 1946, and other moments of high adventure. An outspoken critic of bourgeois marriage, Strong was antiromantic yet permanently in search of the excitement which she found as a mountain climber. From the moment we see her on a famine relief train, headed across the Russian steppes to Samara, we know she will find her way to excitement, more important to her than any settled home.

Babe Didrikson Zaharias (1914–1956), an athlete of genius with an unfaltering desire to win, created women's professional golf and thereby opened new opportunities for other women athletes. Her narrative is disarmingly uncomplicated, yet the reader knows that this woman's drive to excel her most recent performance, or to set another record, made her a leader from her earliest childhood. An inheritor of the women's health reform movement, Didrikson was born at a time when it was possible for a woman to be proud of her physical strength and endurance. Her narrative shows some sensitivity to the popular perception that women athletes are unfeminine, but nothing, including cancer and a colostomy, contained her determination to win or her joy at turning in a stellar performance. Later generations of feminists have come to understand the importance of athletic competition for developing women's sense of self. Didrikson was no theorist, but her athletic ability and personal discipline transformed women's competitive athletics. Contemporaries considered her brash for announcing the targets she set herself or rejoicing in a flawless win. But, as was true of Margaret Sanger, these were qualities considered normal for men in her field. Didrikson's unself-conscious joy in athletics was a significant aspect of her legacy to future generations.

Although Gloria Steinem (1934–   ) has written only autobiographical fragments, her essay in memory of her mother is a classic. The earlier autobiographical writings in this section pay little attention to mother-daughter relationships. We know Shaw and Fearn were daughters of sharply critical mothers; Addams, Sanger, and Strong lost their mothers during girlhood; and Didrikson's mother was her model athlete. But these relationships do not take center stage in the daughters' accounts of their lives. Steinem set out to understand her troubled mother and, in the process, herself. Her narrative doesn't stop to tell us that her precocious responsibility for her mother made her a leader, but we know it. What it does make us understand is that this relationship has been central to the unfolding of her own life, that she has grown to respect the frail woman for whom she cared as a child, and that the respect she accords her mother she also accords herself.

Anna Howard Shaw

(1847–1919)

Anna Howard Shaw was born in England, the youngest daughter and sixth of seven children of Scottish parents. Her parents were staunch Unitarians, part of the reformist culture of mid-nineteenth-century industrial England, which met with stern repression from established authority. Shaw's father, trained as a craftsman, did not fare well when he abandoned his craft for trading in flour and grain. Like many similar families, the Shaws sought economic opportunity in America, to which Thomas Shaw emigrated in 1850, followed by his wife and children in 1851.

The family settled in Lawrence, Massachusetts, where they quickly joined the reform movements of the 1850s while Thomas Shaw's enthusiasms for unsuccessful ventures were repeated. In 1859 he took up a 350-acre claim in Michigan, hoping to join other reform-minded settlers in establishing a frontier community.

Ever the enthusiast, Thomas Shaw traveled west to clear a patch of woods and build a ramshackle cabin, without doors, windows, or caulking to protect against the Michigan winters. There he sent his wife and four youngest children to settle, accompanied by James, the eldest son, no more experienced in backwoods life than the rest of the family.

When James became ill and left to seek medical care in Massachusetts, Anna, at age twelve, worked with her younger brother to trap food and split logs for fuel, while the older sisters struggled with household chores and the care of their critically depressed mother, who became an invalid when faced with her husband's abandonment.

Abandonment by the male members of the family became a recurring theme in Shaw's life when, in 1861, her father and adult brothers all enlisted in the Union army, leaving the female branch of the family to cope with the battle against the Michigan wilderness.

Mainly self-taught, Shaw had two years in a one-room country school before she became a schoolteacher to earn the cash income her family desperately needed. When she looked for larger economic opportunity in the nearby town of Big Rapids, Shaw met her first woman preacher and recognized her own passion to preach. To seek such a career within the Methodist, trinitarian Christian church was to contradict her family's beliefs and to ensure a certain confrontation with her parents. This Shaw did, seeking further high school education and supporting herself as an itinerant preacher, securing her license to preach in the Methodist church in 1871.

Two years later Shaw enrolled at the Methodist Albion College, supporting her studies by preaching and delivering temperance lectures. After two years of college, she made her greatest gamble with fate by enrolling in the divinity school of Boston University. She was replicating the extremes of her early life in Michigan, because women were not eligible for scholarships to the school, and she had no means of support.

Her graduation won her a license to preach, but Shaw was determined to secure ordination and to administer the sacraments to her flock. Refused by the Methodist Episcopal Church, she won ordination in the Methodist Protestant Church in 1880. Thereafter she served as pastor to two Cape Cod churches but still craved more active service. In 1883, with the agreement of her congregations, she enrolled in Boston University's medical school as a part-time student. By the time of her graduation as a physician in 1886, she had become deeply committed to the suffrage movement.

Resigning her two pastor's positions, Shaw worked first for the Massachusetts Woman Suffrage Association, then for the suffrage department of the National Woman's Christian Temperance Union, and finally for the National American Woman Suffrage Association, of which she became vice president in 1891 and president in 1904. Now a national figure, Shaw had found the cause to which she could dedicate her extraordinary powers as an orator. It brought an essentially solitary woman the friendship of outstanding peers, Frances Willard, head of the women's temperance movement, and Susan B. Anthony, the redoubtable pioneer of the suffrage struggle.

THE STORY OF A PIONEER

On landing [in America, when Shaw was four years old] a grievous disappointment awaited us; my father did not meet us. He was in New Bedford, Massachusetts, nursing his grief and preparing to return to England, for he had been told that the *John Jacob Westervelt* had been lost at sea with every soul on board. One of the missionaries who met the ship took us under his wing and conducted us to a little hotel, where we remained until father had received his incredible news and rushed to New York. He could hardly believe that we were really restored to him; and even now, through the mists of more than half a century, I can still see the expression in his wet eyes as he picked me up and tossed me into the air.

I can see, too, the toys he brought me—a little saw and a hatchet, which became the dearest treasures of my childish days. They were fatidical gifts, that saw and hatchet; in the years ahead of me I was to use tools as well as my brothers did, as I proved when I helped to build our frontier home.

We went to New Bedford with father, who had found work there at his old trade; and here I laid the foundations of my first childhood friendship, not with another child, but with my next-door neighbor, a ship-builder. Morning after morning this man swung me on his big shoulder and took me to his shipyard, where my hatchet and saw had violent exercise as I imitated the workers around me. Discovering that my tiny petticoats were in my way, my new friends had a little boy's suit made for me; and thus emancipated, at this tender age, I worked unweariyingly at his side all day long and day after day. . . .

We remained in New Bedford less than a year, for in the spring of 1852 my father made another change, taking his family to Lawrence, Massachusetts, where we lived until 1859.

The move to Michigan meant a complete upheaval in our lives. In Lawrence we had around us the fine flower of New England civilization. We children went to school; our parents, though they were in very humble circumstances, were associated with the leading spirits and the big movements of the day. When we went to Michigan we went to the wilderness, to the wild pioneer life of those times, and we were all old enough to keenly feel the change.

My father was one of a number of Englishmen who took up tracts in the northern forest of Michigan, with the old dream of establishing a colony there. None of these men had the least practical knowledge of farming. They were city men or followers of trades which had no connection with farm life. They went straight into the thick timber-land, instead of going to the rich and waiting prairies, and they crowned this initial mistake by cutting down the splendid timber instead of letting it stand. Thus bird's-eye maple and other beautiful woods were used as fire-wood and in the construction of rude cabins, and the greatest asset of the pioneers was ignored.

Father preceded us to the Michigan woods, and there, with his oldest son, James, took up a claim. They cleared a space in the wilderness just large enough for a log cabin, and put up the bare walls of the cabin itself. Then father returned to Lawrence and his work, leaving James behind. A few months later (this was in 1859), my mother, and two sisters, Eleanor and Mary, my youngest brother, Henry, eight years of age, and I, then twelve, went to Michigan to work on and hold down the claim while father, for eighteen months longer, stayed on in Lawrence, sending us such remittances as he could. His second and third sons, John and Thomas, remained in the East with him.

Every detail of our journey through the wilderness is clear in my mind. At that time the railroad terminated at Grand Rapids, Michigan, and we covered the remaining distance—about one hundred miles—by wagon, riding through a dense and often trackless forest. My brother James met us at Grand Rapids with what, in those days, was called a lumber-wagon, but which had a horrible resemblance to a vehicle from the health department. My sisters and I gave it one cold look and turned from it; we were so pained by its appearance that we refused to ride in it through the town. Instead, we started off on foot, trying to look as if we had no association with it, and we climbed into the unwieldy vehicle only when the city streets were far behind us. Every available inch of space in the wagon was filled with bedding and provisions. As yet we had no furniture; we were to make that for ourselves when we reached our cabin; and there was so little room for us to ride that we children walked by turns, while James, from the beginning of the journey to its end, seven days later, led our weary horses.

To my mother, who was never strong, the whole experience must have been a nightmare of suffering and stoical endurance. . . .

Our first day's journey covered less than eight miles, and that night we stopped at a farm-house which was the last bit of civilization we saw. Early the next morning we were off again, making slow progress due to the rough roads and our heavy load. At night we stopped at a place called Thomas's Inn, only to be told by the woman who kept it that there was nothing in the house to eat. Her husband, she said, had gone "outside" (to Grand Rapids) to get some flour, and had not returned—but she added that we could spend the night, if we chose, and enjoy the shelter, if not food. We had provisions in our wagon, so we wearily entered, after my brother had got out some of our pork and opened a barrel of flour. . . . When the meal was eaten she broke the further news that there were no beds.

"The old woman can sleep with me," she suggested, "and the girls can sleep on the floor. The boys will have to go to the barn."

She and her bed were not especially attractive, and mother decided to lie on the floor with us. . . .

At dawn the next morning we resumed our journey, and every day after that we were able to cover the distance demanded by the schedule arranged before we started. This meant that some sort of shelter usually awaited us at night. . . .

In that fashion we made our way to our new home. The last day, like the first, we traveled only eight miles, but we spent the night in a house I shall never forget. It was beautifully clean, and for our evening meal its mistress brought out loaves of bread which were the largest we had ever seen. She cut great slices of this bread for us and spread maple sugar on them, and it seemed to us that never before had anything tasted so good.

The next morning we made the last stage of our journey, our hearts filled with the joy of nearing our new home. We all had an idea that we were going to a farm, and we expected some resemblance at least to the prosperous farms we had seen in New England. My mother's mental picture was, naturally, of an English farm. Possibly she had visions of red barns and deep meadows, sunny skies and daisies. What we found awaiting us were the four walls and the roof of a good-sized log-house, standing in a small cleared strip of the wilderness, its doors and windows represented by the square holes, its floor also a thing of the future, its whole effect achingly forlorn and desolate. It was late in the afternoon when we drove up to the opening that was its front entrance, and I shall never forget the look my mother turned upon the place. Without a word she crossed its threshold, and, standing very still, looked slowly around her. Then something within her seemed to give way, and she sank upon the ground. She could not realize even then, I think, that this was really the place father had prepared for us, that here he expected us to live. When she finally took it in she buried her face in her hands, and in that way she sat for hours without moving or speaking. For the first time in her life she had forgotten us; and we, for our part, dared not speak to her. We stood around her in a frightened group, talking to one another in whispers. Our little world had crumbled under our feet. Never before had we seen our mother give way to despair.

Night began to fall. The woods became alive with night creatures, and the most harmless made the most noise. The owls began to hoot, and soon we heard the wildcat, whose cry—a screech like that of a lost and panic-stricken child—is one of the most appalling sounds of the forest. Later the wolves added their howls to the uproar, but though darkness came and we children whimpered around her, our mother still sat in her strange lethargy.

At last my brother brought the horses close to the cabin and built fires to protect them and us. He was only twenty, but he showed himself a man during those early pioneer days. While he was picketing the horses and building his protecting fires my mother came to herself, but her face when she raised it was worse than her silence had been. She seemed to have died and to have returned to us from the grave, and I am sure she felt that she had done so. . . .

That night we slept on boughs spread on the earth inside the cabin walls, and we put blankets before the holes which represented our doors and windows, and kept our watch-fires burning. Soon the other children fell asleep, but there was no sleep for me. I was only twelve years old, but my mind was full of fancies. . . .

. . . to-night that which I most feared was within, not outside of, the cabin. In some way which I did not understand the one sure refuge in our new world had been taken from us. I hardly knew the silent woman who lay near me, tossing from side to side and staring into the darkness; I felt that we had lost our mother. . . .

We held a family council after breakfast, and in this, though I was only twelve, I took an eager and determined part. I loved work—it has always been my favorite form of recreation—and my spirit rose to the opportunities of it which smiled on us from every side. Obviously the first thing to do was to put doors and windows into the yawning holes father had left for them, and to lay a board flooring over the earth inside our cabin walls, and these duties we accomplished before we had occupied our new home a fortnight. . . .

We began by making three windows and two doors; then, inspired by these achievements, we ambitiously constructed an attic and divided the ground floor with partitions, which gave us four rooms. . . .

No doubt we would have worked more thoroughly if my brother James, who was twenty years old and our tower of strength, had remained with us; but when we had been in our new home only a few months he fell ill and was forced to go East for an operation. He was never able to return to us, and thus my mother, we three young girls, and my youngest brother—Harry, who was only eight years old—made our fight alone until father came to us, more than a year later. . . .

The division of labor planned at the first council was that mother should do our sewing, and my older sisters, Eleanor and Mary, the housework, which was far from taxing, for of course we lived in the simplest manner. My brothers and I were to do the work out of doors, an arrangement that suited me very well, though at first, owing to our lack of experience, our activities were somewhat curtailed. . . .

Even during the second summer plowing was impossible; we could only plant potatoes and corn, and follow the most primitive method in doing even this. We took an ax, chopped up the sod, put the seed under it, and let the seed grow. The seed did grow, too—in the most gratifying and encouraging manner. Our green corn and potatoes were the best I have ever eaten. But for the present we lacked these luxuries. . . .

We had, however, in their place, large quantities of wild fruit— gooseberries, raspberries, and plums—which Harry and I gathered on the banks of our creek. Harry also became an expert fisherman. We had no hooks or lines, but he took wires from our hoop-skirts and made snares at the end of poles. My part of this work was to stand on a log and frighten the fish out of their holes by making horrible sounds, which I did with impassioned earnestness. When the fish hurried to the surface of the water to investigate the appalling noises they had heard, they were easily snared by our small boy, who was very proud of his ability to contribute in this way to the family table. . . .

Such furniture as we had we made ourselves. In addition to my mother's two chairs and the bunks which took the place of beds, James made a settle for the living-room, as well as a table and several stools. At first we had our tree-cutting done for us, but we soon became expert in this gentle art, and I developed such skill that in later years, after father came, I used to stand with him and "heart" a log. . . .

During the winter life offered us few diversions and many hardships. Our creek froze over, and the water problem became a serious one, which we met with increasing difficulty as the temperature steadily fell. We melted snow and ice, and existed through the frozen months, but with an amount of discomfort which made us unwilling to repeat at least that special phase of our experience. In the spring, therefore, I made a well. Long before this, James had gone, and Harry and I were now the only outdoor members of our working-force. Harry was still too small to help with the well; but a young man, who had formed the neighborly habit of riding eighteen miles to call on us, gave me much friendly aid. We located the well with a switch, and when we had dug as far as we could reach with our spades, my assistant descended into the hole and threw the earth up to the edge, from which I in turn removed it. As the well grew deeper we made a half-way shelf, on which I stood, he throwing the earth on the shelf, and I shoveling it up from that point. Later, as he descended still farther into the hole we were making, he shoveled the earth into buckets and passed them up to me, I passing them on to my sister, who was now pressed into service. When the excavation was deep enough we made the wall of slabs of wood, roughly joined together. I recall that well with calm content. . . .

During our first year there was no school within ten miles of us, but this lack failed to sadden Harry or me. We had brought with us from Lawrence a box of books, in which, in winter months, when our outdoor work was restricted, we found much comfort. They were the only books in that part of the country, and we read them until we knew them all by heart. Moreover, father sent us regularly the *New York Independent,* and with this admirable literature, after reading it, we papered our walls. Thus, on stormy days, we could lie on the settle or the floor and read the *Independent* over again with increased interest and pleasure. . . .

Our modest library also contained several histories of Greece and Rome, which must have been good ones, for years later, when I entered college, I passed my examination in ancient history with no other preparation than this reading. There were also a few arithmetics and algebras, a historical novel or two, and the inevitable copy of *Uncle Tom's Cabin,* whose pages I had freely moistened with my tears.

When the advantages of public education were finally extended to me, at thirteen, by the opening of a school three miles from our home, I accepted them with growing reluctance. . . . My reading and my Lawrence school-work had already taught me more than Prudence [Duncan, the teacher] knew—a fact we both inwardly admitted and fiercely resented from our different viewpoints. . . .

After I became a wage-earner I lost my desire to make a fortune, but the college dream grew with the years; and though my college career seemed as remote as the most distant star, I hitched my little wagon to that star and never afterward wholly lost sight of its friendly gleam.

When I was fifteen years old I was offered a situation as school-teacher. By this time the community was growing around us with the rapidity characteristic of these Western settlements, and we had nearer neighbors whose children needed instruction. I passed an examination before a school-board consisting of three nervous and self-conscious men whose certificate I still hold, and I at once began my professional career on the modest salary of two dollars a week and my board. The school was four miles from my home, so I "boarded round" with the families of my pupils, staying two weeks in each place, and often walking from three to six miles a day to and from my little log school-house in every kind of weather. During the first year I had about fourteen pupils, of varying ages, sizes, and temperaments, and there was hardly a book in the school-room except those I owned. . . .

When the news came that Fort Sumter had been fired on, and that Lincoln had called for troops, our men were threshing. There was only one threshing-machine in the region at that time, and it went from place to place, the farmers doing their threshing whenever they could get the machine. I remember seeing a man ride up on horseback, shouting out Lincoln's demand for troops and explaining that a regiment was being formed at Big Rapids. Before he had finished speaking the men on the machine had leaped to the ground and rushed off to enlist, my brother Jack, who had recently joined us, among them. In ten minutes not one man was left in the field. A few months later my brother Tom enlisted as a bugler—he was a mere boy at the time—and not long after that my father followed the example of his sons and served until the war was ended. . . .

Between those years I was the principal support of our family, and life became a strenuous and tragic affair. For months at a time we had no news from the front. The work in our community, if it werewas done at all, was done by despairing women whose hearts were with their men. When care had become our constant guest, Death entered our home as well. My sister Eleanor had married, and died in childbirth, leaving her baby to me; and the blackest hours of those black years were the hours that saw her passing. . . .

The problem of living grew harder with every day. We eked out our little income in every way we could, taking as boarders the workers in the logging-camps, making quilts, which we sold, and losing no chance to earn a penny in any legitimate manner. Again my mother did such outside sewing as she could secure, yet with every month of our effort the gulf between our income and our expenses grew wider, and the price of the bare necessities of existence climbed up and up. The largest amount I could earn at teaching was six dollars a week, and our school year included only two terms of thirteen weeks each. It was an incessant struggle to keep our land, to pay our taxes, and to live. . . .

I was walking seven and eight miles a day, and doing extra work before and after school hours, and my health began to fail. Those were years I do not like to look back upon . . . years in which life had degenerated into a treadmill whose monotony was broken only by the grim messages from the front. . . .

I gave up teaching, left our cabin in the woods, and went to Big Rapids to live with my sister Mary, who had married a successful man and who generously offered me a home. There, I had decided, I would learn a trade of some kind, of any kind; it did not greatly matter what it was. The sole essential was that it should be a money-making trade, offering wages which would make it possible to add more rapidly to my savings. In those days, almost fifty years ago, and in a small pioneer town, the fields open to women were few and unfruitful. The needle at once presented itself, but at first I turned with loathing from it. I would have preferred the digging of ditches or the shoveling of coal. . . .

Before I had been working a month at my uncongenial trade Big Rapids was favored by a visit from a Universalist woman minister, the Reverend Marianna Thompson, who came there to preach. Her sermon was delivered on Sunday morning, and I was, I think, almost the earliest arrival of the great congregation which filled the church. It was a wonderful moment when I saw my first woman minister enter her pulpit; and as I listened to her sermon, thrilled to the soul, all my early aspirations to become a minister myself stirred in me with cumulative force. . . .

. . . when she was alone and about to leave, I found courage to introduce myself and pour forth the tale of my ambition. Her advice was as prompt as if she had studied my problem for years.

"My child," she said, "give up your foolish idea of learning a trade, and go to school. You can't do anything until you have an education. Get it, and get it *now*." . . .

. . . the next morning I entered the Big Rapids High School, which was also a preparatory school for college. There I would study, I determined, as long as my money held out, and with the optimism of youth I succeeded in confining my imagination to this side of that crisis. My home, thanks to Mary, was assured; the wardrobe I had brought from the woods covered me sufficiently; to one who had walked five and six miles a day for years, walking to school held no discomfort. . . .

The preceptress of the high school was Lucy Foot, a college graduate and a remarkable woman. I had heard much of her sympathy and understanding; and on the evening following my first day in school I went to her and repeated the confidences I had reposed in the Reverend Marianna Thompson. My trust in her was justified. She took an immediate interest in me, and proved it at once by putting me into the speaking and debating classes, where I was given every opportunity to hold forth to helpless classmates when the spirit of eloquence moved me. . . .

From that night Miss Foot lost no opportunity of putting me into the foreground of our school affairs. I took part in all our debates, recited yards of poetry to any audience we could attract, and even shone mildly in our amateur theatricals. It was probably owing to all this activity that I attracted the interest of the presiding elder of our district—Dr. Peck, a man of progressive ideas. There was at that time a movement on foot to license women to preach in the Methodist Church, and Dr. Peck was ambitious to be the first presiding elder to have a woman ordained for the Methodist ministry. He had urged Miss Foot to be this pioneer, but her ambitions did not turn in that direction. Though she was a very devout Methodist, she had no wish to be the shepherd of a religious flock. She loved her school-work, and asked nothing better than to remain in it. Gently but persistently she directed the attention of Dr. Peck to me, and immediately things began to happen. . . .

Miss Foot finally arranged a meeting at her home by inviting Dr. Peck and me to dinner. Being unconscious of any significance in the occasion, I chatted light-heartedly about the large issues of life and probably settled most of them to my personal satisfaction. Dr Peck drew me out and led me on, listened and smiled. When the evening was over and we rose to go, he turned to me with sudden seriousness.

"My quarterly meeting will be held at Ashton," he remarked, casually. "I would like you to preach the quarterly sermon."

For a moment the earth seemed to slip away from my feet. I stared at him in utter stupefaction. Then slowly I realized that, incredible as it seemed, the man was in earnest.

"Why," I stammered, "*I* can't preach a sermon!"

Dr. Peck smiled at me. "Have you ever tried?" he asked.

I started to assure him vehemently that I never had. Then, as if Time had thrown a picture on a screen before me, I saw myself as a little girl preaching alone in the forest, as I had so often preached to a congregation of listening trees. I qualified my answer.

"Never," I said, "to human beings."

Dr. Peck smiled again. "Well," he told me, "the door is open. Enter or not, as you wish." . . .

Miss Foot could only advise me to put the matter before the Lord, to wrestle and to pray; and thereafter, for hours at a time, she worked and prayed with me, alternately urging, pleading, instructing, and sending up petitions in my behalf. . . . With all my heart I wanted to preach, and I believed that now at last I had my call. The following day we sent word to Dr. Peck that I would preach the sermon at Ashton as he had asked, but we urged him to say nothing of the matter for the present, and Miss Foot and I also kept the secret locked in our breasts. I knew only too well what view my family and my friends would take of such a step and of me. To them it would mean nothing short of personal disgrace and a blotted page in the Shaw record. . . .

It was not until three days before I preached the sermon that I found courage to confide my purpose to my sister Mary, and if I had confessed my intention to commit a capital crime she could not have been more disturbed. We two had always been very close, and the death of Eleanor, to whom we were both devoted, had drawn us even nearer to each other. Now Mary's tears and prayers wrung my heart and shook my resolution. But, after all, she was asking me to give up my whole future, to close my ears to my call, and I felt that I could not do it. My decision caused an estrangement between us which lasted for years. On the day preceding the delivery of my sermon I left for Ashton on the afternoon train; and in the same car, but as far away from me as she could get, Mary sat alone and wept throughout the journey. She was going to my mother, but she did not speak to me; and I, for my part, facing both alienation from her and the ordeal before me, found my one comfort in Lucy Foot's presence and understanding sympathy.

There was no church in Ashton, so I preached my sermon in its one little school-house, which was filled with a curious crowd, eager to look at and hear the girl who was defying all conventions by getting out of the pew and into the pulpit. There was much whispering and suppressed excitement before I began, but when I gave out my text silence fell upon the room, and from that moment until I had finished my hearers listened quietly. . . .

. . . the next day he [Dr. Peck] invited me to follow him around in his circuit, which included thirty-six appointments; he wished to preach in each of the thirty-six places, as it was desirable to let the various ministers hear and know me before I applied for my license as a local preacher. . . .

The members of my family, meeting in solemn council, sent for me, and I responded. They had a proposition to make, and they lost no time in putting it before me. If I gave up my preaching they would send me to college and pay for my entire course. They suggested Ann Arbor, and Ann Arbor tempted me sorely; but to descend from the pulpit I had at last entered—the pulpit I had visualized in all my childish dreams—was not to be considered. We had a long evening together, and it was a very unhappy one. At the end of it I was given twenty-four hours in which to decide whether I would choose my people and college, or my pulpit and the arctic loneliness of a life that held no family circle. It did not require twenty-four hours of reflection to convince me that I must go my solitary way. . . .

. . . the following spring, at the annual Methodist Conference of our district, held at Big Rapids, my name was presented to the assembled ministers as that of a candidate for a license to preach. There was unusual interest in the result, and my father was among those who came to the Conference to see the vote taken. During these Conferences a minister voted affirmatively on a question by holding up his hand, and negatively by failing to do so. When the question of my license came up the majority of the ministers voted by raising both hands, and in the pleasant excitement which followed my father slipped away. . . .

In the mean time my preaching had not interfered with my studies. I was working day and night, but life was very difficult;

for among my schoolmates, too, there were doubts and much head-shaking over this choice of a career. I needed the sound of friendly voices, for I was very lonely; and suddenly, when the pressure from all sides was strongest and I was going down physically under it, a voice was raised that I had never dared to dream would speak for me. Mary A. Livermore came to Big Rapids, and as she was then at the height of her career, the entire countryside poured in to hear her. Far back in the crowded hall I sat alone and listened to her, thrilled by the lecture and tremulous with the hope of meeting the lecturer. When she had finished speaking I joined the throng that surged forward from the body of the hall, and as I reached her and felt the grasp of her friendly hand I had a sudden conviction that the meeting was an epoch in my life. I was right. Some one in the circle around us told her that I wanted to preach, and that I was meeting tremendous opposition. She was interested at once. She looked at me with quickening sympathy, and then, suddenly putting an arm around me, drew me close to her side.

"My dear," she said, quietly, "if you want to preach, go on and preach. Don't let anybody stop you. No matter what people say, don't let them stop you!" . . .

When the time came to enter college I had exactly eighteen dollars in the world, and I started for Albion with this amount in my purse and without the slightest notion of how I was to add to it. The money problem so pressed upon me, in fact, that when I reached my destination at midnight and discovered that it would cost fifty cents to ride from the station to the college, I saved that amount by walking the entire distance on the railroad tracks, while my imagination busied itself pleasantly with pictures of the engine that might be thundering upon me in the rear. I had chosen Albion because Miss Foot had been educated there, and I was encouraged by an incident that happened the morning after my arrival. I was on the campus, walking toward the main building, when I saw a big copper penny lying on the ground, and, on picking it up, I discovered that it bore the year of my birth. That seemed a good omen, and it was emphatically underlined by the finding of two exactly similar pennies within a week. Though there have been days since then when I was sorely tempted to spend them, I have those three pennies still, and I confess to a certain comfort in their pos-session! . . .

Naturally, I soon plunged into speaking, and my first public speech at college was a defense of Xantippe. I have always felt that the poor lady was greatly abused, and that Socrates deserved all he received from her, and more. I was glad to put myself on record as her champion, and my fellow-students must soon have felt that my admiration for Xantippe was based on similarities of temperament, for within a few months I was leading the first college revolt against the authority of the men students.

Albion was a coeducational institution, and the brightest jewels in its crown were its three literary societies—the first composed of men alone, the second of women alone, and the third of men and women together. Each of the societies made friendly advances to new students, and for some time I hesitated on the brink of the new joys they offered, uncertain which to choose. A representative of the mixed society, who was putting its claims before me, unconsciously helped me to make up my mind.

"Women," he pompously assured me, "need to be associated with men, because they don't know how to manage meetings."

On the instant the needle of decision swung around to the women's society and remained there, fixed.

"If they don't," I told the pompous young man, "it's high time they learned. I shall join the women and we'll master the art."

I did join the women's society, and I had not been a member very long before I discovered that when there was an advantage of any kind to be secured the men invariably got it. While I was brooding somberly upon this wrong an opportunity came to make a formal and effective protest against the men's high-handed methods. The Quinquennial reunion of all the societies was about to be held, and the special feature of this festivity was always an oration. The simple method of selecting the orator which had formerly prevailed had been for the young men to decide upon the speaker and then announce his name to the women, who humbly confirmed it. On this occasion, however, when the name came in to us, I sent a message to our brother society to the effect that we, too, intended to make a nomination and to send in a name.

At such unprecedented behavior the entire student body arose in excitement, which, among the girls, was combined with equal parts of exhilaration and awe. The men refused to consider our nominee, and as a friendly compromise we suggested that we have a joint meeting of all societies and elect the speaker at this gathering; but this plan also the men at first refused, giving in only after weeks of argument, during which no one had time for the calmer pleasures of study. When the joint meeting was finally held, nothing was accomplished; we girls had one more member than the boys had, and we promptly re-elected our candidate, who was as promptly declined by the boys. Two of our girls were engaged to two of the boys, and it was secretly planned by our brother society that during a second joint meeting these two men should take the girls out for a drive and then slip back to vote, leaving the girls at some point sufficiently remote from college. We discovered the plot, however, in time to thwart it, and at last, when nothing but the unprecedented tie-up had been discussed for months, the boys suddenly gave up their candidate and nominated me for orator.

This was not at all what I wanted, and I immediately declined to serve. We girls then nominated the young man who had been first choice of our brother society, but he haughtily refused to accept the compliment. The reunion was only a fortnight away, and the programme had not been printed, so now the president took the situation in hand and peremptorily ordered me to accept the nomination or be suspended. . . .

To my family that oration was the redeeming episode of my early career. For the moment it almost made them forget my crime of preaching.

My original fund of eighteen dollars was now supplemented by the proceeds of a series of lectures I gave on temperance. The temperance women were not yet organized, but they had their speakers, and I was occasionally paid five dollars to hold forth for an hour or two in the little country school-houses of our region. As a licensed preacher I had no tuition fees to pay at college; but my board, in the home of the president and his wife, was costing me four dollars a week, and this was the limit of my expenses, as I did my own laundry-work. . . .

My most dramatic experience during this period occurred in the summer of 1874, when I went to a Northern lumber-camp to preach in the pulpit of a minister who was away on his honeymoon. The stage took me within twenty-two miles of my destination, to a place called Seberwing. To my dismay, however, when I arrived at Seberwing, Saturday evening, I found that the rest of the journey lay through a dense woods, and that I could reach my pulpit in time the next morning only by having some one drive me through the woods that night. It was not a pleasant prospect, for I had heard appalling tales of the stockades in this region and of the women who were kept prisoners there. But to miss the engagement was not to be thought of, and when, after I had made several vain

efforts to find a driver, a man appeared in a two-seated wagon and
offered to take me to my destination, I felt that I had to go with
him, though I did not like his appearance. He was a huge, muscular
person, with a protruding jaw and a singularly evasive eye; but I
reflected that his forbidding expression might be due, in part at
least, to the prospect of the long night drive through the woods, to
which possibly he objected as much as I did.

It was already growing dark when we started, and within a
few moments we were out of the little settlement and entering the
woods. With me I had a revolver I had long since learned to use,
but which I very rarely carried. I had hesitated to bring it now—
had even left home without it; and then, impelled by some impulse
I never afterward ceased to bless, had returned for it and dropped
it into my hand-bag.

I sat on the back seat of the wagon, directly behind the driver,
and for a time, as we entered the darkening woods, his great shoulders blotted out all perspective as he drove on in stolid silence.
Then, little by little, they disappeared like a rapidly fading negative.
The woods were filled with Norway pines, hemlocks, spruce, and
tamaracks—great, somber trees that must have shut out the light
even on the brightest days. . . . I could see neither the driver nor his
horses. I could hear only the sibilant whisper of the trees and the
creak of our slow wheels in the rough forest road.

Suddenly the driver began to talk, and at first I was glad to
hear the reassuring human tones, for the experience had begun to
seem like a bad dream. I replied readily, and at once regretted that
I had done so, for the man's choice of topics was most unpleasant.
He began to tell me stories of the stockades—grim stories with
horrible details, repeated so fully and with such gusto that I soon
realized he was deliberately affronting my ears. I checked him and
told him I could not listen to such talk.

He replied with a series of oaths and shocking vulgarities, stopping his horses that he might turn and fling the words into my face.
He ended by snarling that I must think him a fool to imagine he
did not know the kind of woman I was. What was I doing in that
rough country, he demanded, and why was I alone with him in
those black woods at night?

Though my heart missed a beat just then, I tried to answer him
calmly.

"You know perfectly well who I am," I reminded him. "And
you understand that I am making this journey to-night because I

am to preach to-morrow morning and there is no other way to keep my appointment."

He uttered a laugh which was a most unpleasant sound.

"Well," he said, coolly, "I'm damned if I'll take you. I've got you here, and I'm going to keep you here!"

I slipped my hand into the satchel in my lap, and it touched my revolver. No touch of human fingers ever brought such comfort. With a deep breath of thanksgiving I drew it out and cocked it, and as I did so he recognized the sudden click.

"Here! What have you got there?" he snapped.

"I have a revolver," I replied, as steadily as I could. "And it is cocked and aimed straight at your back. Now drive on. If you stop again, or speak, I'll shoot you."

For an instant or two he blustered.

"By God," he cried, "you wouldn't dare."

"Wouldn't I?" I asked. "Try me by speaking just once more."

Even as I spoke I felt my hair rise on my scalp with the horror of the moment, which seemed worse than any nightmare a woman could experience. But the man was conquered by the knowledge of the waiting, willing weapon just behind him. He laid his whip savagely on the backs of his horses and they responded with a leap that almost knocked me out of the wagon.

The rest of the night was black terror I shall never forget. He did not speak again, nor stop, but I dared not relax my caution for an instant. Hour after hour crawled toward day, and still I sat in the unpierced darkness, the revolver ready. I knew he was inwardly raging, and that at any instant he might make a sudden jump and try to get the revolver away from me. I decided that at his slightest movement I must shoot. But dawn came at last, and just as its bluish light touched the dark tips of the pines we drove up to the log hotel in the settlement that was our destination. Here my driver spoke.

"Get down," he said, gruffly. "This is the place."

I sat still. Even yet I dared not trust him. Moreover, I was so stiff after my vigil that I was not sure I could move.

"You get down," I directed, "and wake up the landlord. Bring him out here."

He sullenly obeyed and aroused the hotel-owner, and when the latter appeared I climbed out of the wagon with some effort but without explanation. That morning I preached in my friend's pulpit as I had promised to do, and the rough building was packed to its doors with lumbermen who had come in from the neighboring camp. Their appearance caused great surprise, as they had never attended a service before. They formed a most picturesque congregation, for they all wore brilliant lumber-camp clothing—blue or red shirts with yellow scarfs twisted around their waists, and gay-colored jackets and logging-caps. There were forty or fifty of them, and when we took up our collection they responded with much liberality and cheerful shouts to one another.

"Put in fifty cents!" they yelled across the church. "Give her a dollar!"

The collection was the largest that had been taken up in the history of the settlement, but I soon learned that it was not the spiritual comfort I offered which had appealed to the lumber-men. My driver of the night before, who was one of their number, had told his pals of his experience, and the whole camp had poured into town to see the woman minister who carried a revolver.

"Her sermon?" said one of them to my landlord, after the meeting. "Huh! I dunno what she preached. But, say, don't make no mistake about one thing: the little preacher has sure got grit!"

Possibly it was some inheritance from my visionary father which made me . . . pack my few possessions, and start for Boston, where I entered the theological school of the university in February, 1876. . . .

My class at the theological school was composed of forty-two young men and my unworthy self, and before I had been a member of it an hour I realized that women theologians paid heavily for the privilege of being women. The young men of my class who were licensed preachers were given free accommodations in the dormitory, and their board, at a club formed for their assistance, cost each of them only one dollar and twenty-five cents a week. For me no such kindly provision was made. I was not allowed a place in the dormitory, but instead was given two dollars a week to pay the rent of a room outside. Neither was I admitted to the economical comforts of the club, but fed myself according to my income, a plan which worked admirably when there was an income, but left an obvious void when there was not.

With characteristic optimism, however, I hired a little attic room on Tremont Street and established myself therein. In lieu of a window the room offered a pale skylight to the February storms, and there was neither heat in it nor running water; but its possession gave me a pleasant sense of proprietorship, and the whole experience seemed a high adventure. I at once sought opportunities to preach and lecture, but these were even rarer than firelight and food. In Albion I had been practically the only licensed preacher available for substitute and special work. In Boston University's three theological classes there were a hundred men, each snatching eagerly at the slightest possibility of employment; and when, despite this competition, I received and responded to an invitation to preach, I never knew whether I was to be paid for my services in cash or in compliments. . . .

There was no help in sight from my family, whose early opposition to my career as a minister had hotly flamed forth again when I started East. I lived, therefore, on milk and crackers, and for weeks at a time my hunger was never wholly satisfied. . . .

There is a special and almost indescribable depression attending such conditions. No one who has not experienced the combination of continued cold, hunger, and loneliness in a great, strange, indifferent city can realize how it undermines the victim's nerves and even tears at the moral fiber. The self-humiliation I experienced was also intense. . . .

The day dawned when I had not a cent, nor any prospect of earning one. My stock of provisions consisted of a box of biscuit, and my courage was flowing from me like blood from an opened vein. Then came one of the quick turns of the wheel of chance which make for optimism. Late in the afternoon I was asked to do a week of revival work with a minister in a local church, and when I accepted his invitation I mentally resolved to let that week decide my fate. My shoes had burst open at the sides; for lack of car-fare I had to walk to and from the scene of my meetings, though I had barely strength for the effort. If my week of work brought me enough to buy a pair of cheap shoes and feed me for a few days I would, I decided, continue my theological course. If it did not, I would give up the fight.

Never have I worked harder or better than during those seven days, when I put into the effort not only my heart and soul, but the last flame of my dying vitality. We had a rousing revival—one of the good old-time affairs when the mourners' benches were constantly filled and the air resounded with alleluias. . . . Then, the service over and the people departed, I sank, weak and trembling, into a chair, trying to pull myself together before hearing my fate in the good-night words of the minister I had assisted. When he came to me and began to compliment me on the work I had done,

I could not rise. I sat still and listened with downcast eyes, afraid
to lift them lest he read in them something of my need and panic
in this moment when my whole future seemed at stake.

At first his words rolled around the empty church as if they
were trying to get away from me, but at last I began to catch them.
I was, it seemed, a most desirable helper. It had been a privilege
and a pleasure to be associated with me. Beyond doubt, I would
go far in my career. He heartily wished that he could reward me
adequately. I deserved fifty dollars.

My tired heart fluttered at this. Probably my empty stomach
fluttered, too; but in the next moment something seemed to catch
in my throat and stop my breath. For it appeared that, notwithstanding the enthusiasm and the spiritual uplift of the week, the
collections had been very disappointing and the expenses unusually
heavy. He could not give me fifty dollars. He could not give me
anything at all. He thanked me warmly and wished me good night.

I managed to answer him and to get to my feet, but that journey
down the aisle from my chair to the church door was the longest
journey I have ever made. During it I felt not only the heart-sick
disappointment of the moment, but the cumulative unhappiness of
the years to come. I was friendless, penniless, and starving, but it
was not of these conditions that I thought then. The one overwhelming fact was that I had been weighed and found wanting. I
was not worthy.

I stumbled along, passing blindly a woman who stood on the
street near the church entrance. She stopped me, timidly, and held
out her hand. Then suddenly she put her arms around me and wept.
She was an old lady, and I did not know her, but it seemed fitting
that she should cry just then, as it would have seemed fitting to me
if at that black moment all the people on the earth had broken into
sudden wailing.

"Oh, Miss Shaw," she said, "I'm the happiest woman in the
world, and I owe my happiness to you. To-night you have converted
my grandson. He's all I have left, but he has been a wild boy, and
I've prayed over him for years. Hereafter he is going to lead a
different life. He has just given me his promise on his knees."

Her hand fumbled in her purse.

"I am a poor woman," she went on, "but I have enough, and
I want to make you a little present. I know how hard life is for you
young students."

She pressed a bill into my fingers. "It's very little," she said, humbly; "it is only five dollars."

I laughed, and in that exultant moment I seemed to hear life laughing with me. With the passing of the bill from her hand to mine existence had become a new experience, wonderful and beautiful.

"It's the biggest gift I have ever had," I told her. "This little bill is big enough to carry my future on its back!" . . .

I had a good meal that night, and I bought the shoes the next morning. Infinitely more sustaining than the food however, was the conviction that the Lord was with me and had given me a sign of His approval. The experience was the turning-point of my theological career. When the money was gone I succeeded in obtaining more work from time to time—and though the grind was still cruelly hard, I never again lost hope. . . .

. . . we students climbed three flights of stairs to reach our classrooms. Through lack of proper food I had become too weak to ascend these stairs without sitting down once or twice to rest, and within a month after my experience with the appreciative grandmother I was discovered during one of these resting periods by Mrs. Barrett, the superintendent of the Woman's Foreign Missionary Society, which had offices in our building. . . .

She let me leave without much comment, but the next day she again invited me into her office and came directly to the purpose of the interview.

"Miss Shaw," she said, "I have been talking to a friend of mine about you, and she would like to make a bargain with you. She thinks you are working too hard. She will pay you three dollars and a half a week for the rest of the school year if you will promise to give up your preaching. She wants you to rest, study, and take care of your health."

I took the money very gratefully, and a few years later I returned the amount to the Missionary Society; but I never learned the identity of my benefactor. Her three dollars and a half a week, added to the weekly two dollars I was allowed for room rent, at once solved the problem of living; and now that meal-hours had a meaning in my life, my health improved and my horizon brightened. . . .

During my vacation in the summer of 1876 I went to Cape Cod and earned my expenses by substituting in local pulpits. Here, at East Dennis, I formed the friendship which brought me at once the greatest happiness and the deepest sorrow of that period of my life. . . .

I . . . graduated—clad in a brand-new black silk gown, and with five dollars in my pocket, which I kept there during the graduation exercises. I felt a special satisfaction in the possession of that money, for, notwithstanding the handicap of being a woman, I was said to be the only member of my class who had worked during the entire course, graduated free from debt, and had a new outfit as well as a few dollars in cash. . . .

Naturally, I missed a great deal of class fellowship and class support, and throughout my entire course I rarely entered my classroom without the abysmal conviction that I was not really wanted there. But some of the men were good-humoredly cordial, and several of them are among my friends to-day.

On my return from Europe . . . I took up immediately and most buoyantly the work of my new parish. My previous occupation of various pulpits, whether long or short, had always been in the role of a substitute. Now, for the first time, I had a church of my own, and was to stand or fall by the record made in it. The ink was barely dry on my diploma from the Boston Theological School, and, as it happened, the little church to which I was called was in the hands of two warring factions, whose battles furnished the most fervid interest of the Cape Cod community. But my inexperience disturbed me not at all, and I was blissfully ignorant of the division in the congregation. . . .

My appointment did not cause even a lull in the warfare among my parishioners. Before I had crossed the threshold of my church I was made to realize that I was shepherd of a divided flock. . . . As soon as I arrived in East Dennis each faction tried to pour into my ears its bitter criticisms of the other, but I made and consistently followed the safe rule of refusing to listen to either side. . . . As I steadily declined to listen to complaints, they devised an original method of putting them before me. . . .

During the regular Thursday-night prayer-meeting, held about two weeks after my arrival, and at which, of course, I presided, they voiced their difficulties in public prayer, loudly and urgently calling upon the Lord to pardon such and such a liar, mentioning the gentleman by name, and such and such a slanderer, whose name was also submitted. . . .

I was still young, and my theological course had set no guideposts on roads as new as these. To interfere with souls in their communion with God seemed impossible; to let them continue to utter personal attacks in church, under cover of prayer, was equally impossible. Any course I could follow seemed to lead away from my new parish, yet both duty and pride made prompt action necessary. By the time we gathered for the third prayer-meeting I had decided what to do, and before the services began I rose and addressed my erring children. I explained that the character of the prayers at our recent meetings was making us the laughing-stock of the community, that unbelievers were ridiculing our religion, and that the discipline of the church was being wrecked; and I ended with these words, each of which I had carefully weighed:

"Now one of two things must happen. Either you will stop this kind of praying, or you will remain away from our meetings. We will hold prayer-meetings on another night, and I shall refuse admission to any among you who bring personal criticisms into your public prayers."

As I had expected it to do, the announcement created an immediate uproar. Both factions sprang to their feet, trying to talk at once. The storm raged until I dismissed the congregation, telling the members that their conduct was an insult to the Lord, and that I would not listen to either their protests or their prayers. . . .

At the end of my first six months in East Dennis I was asked to take on, also, the temporary charge of the Congregational Church at Dennis, two miles and a half away. I agreed to do this until a permanent pastor could be found, on condition that I should preach at Dennis on Sunday afternoons, using the same sermon I preached in my own pulpit in the morning. The arrangement worked so well that it lasted for six and a half years—until I resigned from my East Dennis church. During that period, moreover, I not only carried the two churches on my shoulders, holding three meetings each Sunday, but I entered upon and completed a course in the Boston Medical School, winning my M.D. in 1885, and I also lectured several times a month during the winter seasons. . . .

I have said that at the end of two years from the time of my appointment the long-continued warfare in the church was ended. I was not immediately allowed, however, to bask in an atmosphere of harmony, for in October, 1880, the celebrated contest over my ordination took place at the Methodist Protestant Conference in Tarrytown, New York; and for three days I was a storm-center around which a large number of truly good and wholly sincere men fought the fight of their religious lives. Many of them strongly believed that women were out of place in the ministry. I did not blame them for this conviction. But I was in the ministry, and I was greatly handicapped by the fact that, although I was a licensed preacher and a graduate of the Boston Theological School, I could not, until I had been regularly ordained, meet all the functions of my office. I could perform the marriage service, but I could not baptize. I could bury the dead, but I could not take members into my church. That had to be done by the presiding elder or by some other minister. I could not administer the sacraments. So at the New England Spring Conference of the Methodist Episcopal Church, held in Boston in 1880, I formally applied for ordination. At the same time application was made by another woman—Miss Anna Oliver—and as a preliminary step we were both examined by the Conference board, and were formally reported by that board as fitted for ordination. Our names were therefore presented at the Conference, over which Bishop Andrews presided, and he immediately refused to accept them. Miss Oliver and I were sitting together in the gallery of the church when the bishop announced his decision, and, while it staggered us, it did not really surprise us. We had been warned of this gentleman's deep-seated prejudice against women in the ministry.

After the services were over Miss Oliver and I called on him and asked him what we should do. He told us calmly that there was nothing for us to do but to get out of the Church. We reminded him of our years of study and probation, and that I had been for two years in charge of two churches. He set his thin lips and replied that there was no place for women in the ministry, and, as he then evidently considered the interview closed, we left him with heavy hearts. While we were walking slowly away, Miss Oliver confided to me that she did not intend to leave the Church. Instead, she told me, she would stay in and fight the matter of her ordination to a finish. . . . I, however, felt differently. I had done considerable fighting during the past two years, and my heart and soul were weary. I said: "I shall get out. I am no better and no stronger than a man, and it is all a man can do to fight the world, the flesh, and the devil, without fighting his Church as well. I do not intend to fight my Church. But I am called to preach the gospel; and if I cannot preach it in my own Church, I will certainly preach it in some other Church!" . . .

As if in response to this outburst, a young minister named Mark Trafton soon called to see me. He had been present at our Conference, he had seen my Church refuse to ordain me, and he had come to suggest that I apply for ordination in his Church—the Methodist Protestant. To leave my church, even though urged to do so by its appointed spokesman, seemed a radical step. Before taking this I appealed from the decision of the Conference to the General Conference of the Methodist Episcopal Church, which held its session that year in Cincinnati, Ohio. Miss Oliver also appealed, and again we were both refused ordination, the General Conference voting to sustain Bishop Andrews in his decision. Not content with this achievement, the Conference even took a backward step. It deprived us of the right to be licensed as local preachers. After this blow I recalled with gratitude the Reverend Mark Trafton's excellent advice, and I immediately applied for ordination in the Methodist Protestant Church. My name was presented at the Conference held in Tarrytown in October, 1880, and the fight was on.

During these Conferences it is customary for each candidate to retire while the discussion of his individual fitness for ordination is in progress. When my name came up I was asked, as my predecessors had been, to leave the room for a few moments. I went into an anteroom and waited—a half-hour, an hour, all afternoon, all evening, and still the battle raged. I varied the monotony of sitting in the anteroom by strolls around Tarrytown, and I think I learned to know its every stone and turn. The next day passed in the same way. At last, late on Saturday night, it was suddenly announced by my opponents that I was not even a member of the Church in which I had applied for ordination. The statement created consternation among my friends. None of us had thought of that! The bomb, timed to explode at the very end of the session, threatened to destroy all my hopes. Of course, my opponents had reasoned, it would be too late for me to do anything, and my name would be dropped.

But it was not too late. Dr. Lyman Davis, the pastor of the Methodist Protestant Church in Tarrytown, was very friendly toward me and my ordination, and he proved his friendship in a singularly prompt and efficient fashion. Late as it was, he immediately called together the trustees of his church, and they responded. To them I made my application for church membership, which they accepted within five minutes. I was now a member of the Church, but it was too late to obtain any further action from the Conference. The next day, Sunday, all the men who had applied for ordination were ordained, and I was left out.

On Monday morning, however, when the Conference met in its final business session, my case was reopened, and I was eventually called before the members to answer questions. . . . Still, many unpleasant things were said, and too much warmth was shown by both sides. We gained ground through the day, however, and at the end of the session the Conference, by a large majority, voted to ordain me.

The ordination service was fixed for the following evening, and even the gentlemen who had most vigorously opposed me were not averse to making the occasion a profitable one. . . .

When the great night came (on October 12, 1880), the expected crowd came also. And to the credit of my opponents I must add that, having lost their fight, they took their defeat in good part and gracefully assisted in the services. Sitting in one of the front pews was Mrs. Stiles, the wife of Dr. Stiles, who was superintendent of the Conference. She was a dear little old lady of seventy, with a big, maternal heart; and when she saw me rise to walk up the aisle alone, she immediately rose, too, came to my side, offered me her arm, and led me to the altar.

The ordination service was very impressive and beautiful. Its peace and dignity, following the battle that had raged for days, moved me so deeply that I was nearly overcome. Indeed, I was on the verge of a breakdown when I was mercifully saved by the clause in the discipline calling for the pledge all ministers had to make—that I would not indulge in the use of tobacco. When this vow fell from my lips a perceptible ripple ran over the congregation.

I was homesick for my Cape Cod parish, and I returned to East Dennis immediately after my ordination, arriving there on Saturday night. I knew by the suppressed excitement of my friends that some surprise awaited me, but I did not learn what it was until I entered my dear little church the following morning. There I found the communion-table set forth with a beautiful new communion-service. This had been purchased during my absence, that I might dedicate it that day and for the first time administer the sacrament to my people. . . .

After I had been in East Dennis four years I began to feel that I was getting into a rut. It seemed to me that all I could do in that particular field had been done. My people wished me to remain, however, and so, partly as an outlet for my surplus energy, but more especially because I realized the splendid work women could do as physicians, I began to study medicine. The trustees gave me permission to go to Boston on certain days of each week, and we soon found that I could carry on my work as a medical student without in the least neglecting my duty toward my parish.

I entered the Boston Medical School in 1882, and obtained my diploma as a full-fledged physician in 1885. During this period I also began to lecture for the Massachusetts Woman Suffrage Association, of which Lucy Stone was president. Henry Blackwell was associated with her, and together they developed in me a vital interest in the suffrage cause, which grew steadily from that time until it became the dominating influence in my life. I preached it in the pulpit, talked it to those I met outside of the church, and carried it into my medical work in the Boston slums when I was trying my prentice hand on helpless pauper patients.

Here again, in my association with the women of the streets, I realized the limitations of my work in the ministry and in medicine. . . .

I was in Boston three nights a week, and during these nights subject to sick calls at any hour. . . .

I was quite famous in three Boston alleys—Maiden's Lane, Fellows Court, and Andrews Court. It most fortunately happened that I did not lose a case in those alleys, though I took all kinds, as I had to treat a certain number of surgical and obstetrical cases in my course. . . .

It would have been pleasant to go on almost indefinitely, living the life of a country minister and telling myself that what I could give to my flock made such a life worth while.

But all the time, deep in my heart, I realized the needs of the outside world, and heard its prayer for workers. My theological and medical courses in Boston, with the experiences that accompanied them, had greatly widened my horizon. . . .

So it was that, in 1885, I suddenly pulled myself up to a radical decision and sent my resignation to the trustees of the two churches whose pastor I had been since 1878. . . .

Of course I had to earn my living; but, though I had taken my medical degree only a few months before leaving Cape Cod, I had no intention of practising medicine. I had merely wished to add a certain amount of medical knowledge to my mental equipment. The Massachusetts Woman Suffrage Association . . . offered me a salary of one hundred dollars a month as a lecturer and organizer. . . . The amount seemed too large, and I told Mrs. Stone as much, after which I humbly fixed my salary at fifty dollars a month. At the end of a year of work I felt that I had "made good"; then I asked for and received the one hundred dollars a month originally offered me.

During my second year Miss Cora Scott Pond and I organized and carried through in Boston a great suffrage bazaar, clearing six thousand dollars for the association—a large amount in those days. Elated by my share in this success, I asked that my salary should be increased to one hundred and twenty-five dollars a month—but this was not done. Instead, I received a valuable lesson. It was freely admitted that my work was worth one hundred and twenty-five dollars, but I was told that one hundred was the limit which could be paid, and I was reminded that this was a good salary for a woman.

The time seemed to have come to make a practical stand in defense of my principles, and I did so by resigning and arranging an independent lecture tour. The first month after my resignation I earned three hundred dollars. Later I frequently earned more than that, and very rarely less. Eventually I lectured under the direction of the Slaton Lecture Bureau of Chicago, and later still for the Redpath Bureau of Boston. . . . It may be worth while to mention here that through my lecture-work at this period I earned all the money I have ever saved. I lectured night after night, week after week, month after month, in "Chautauquas" in the summer, all over the country in winter, earning a large income and putting aside at that time the small surplus I still hold in preparation for the "rainy day" every working-woman inwardly fears. . . .

. . . in 1888 Miss [Susan B.] Anthony persuaded me to drop my temperance work and concentrate my energies on the suffrage cause. For a long time I hesitated. I was very happy in my connection with the Woman's Christian Temperance Union, and I knew that Miss [Frances] Willard was depending on me to continue it. But Miss Anthony's arguments were irrefutable, and she was herself, as always, irresistible.

"You can't win two causes at once," she reminded me. "You're merely scattering your energies. Begin at the beginning. Win suffrage for women, and the rest will follow." As an added argument, she took me with her on her Kansas campaign, and after that no further arguments were needed. From then until her death, eighteen years later, Miss Anthony and I worked shoulder to shoulder. . . .

A certain amount of independent lecturing was necessary for me, for I had to earn my living. The National American Woman Suffrage Association has never paid salaries to its officers, so, when I became vice-president and eventually, in 1904, president of the association, I continued to work gratuitously for the Cause in these positions. . . . I decided that I could earn my bare expenses by making one brief lecture tour each year, and I made an arrangement with the Redpath Bureau which left me fully two-thirds of my time for the suffrage work I loved.

This was one result of my all-night talk with Miss Anthony in Chicago, and it enabled me to carry out her plan that I should accompany her in most of the campaigns in which she sought to arouse the West to the need of suffrage for women. From that time on we traveled and lectured together so constantly that each of us developed an almost uncanny knowledge of the other's mental processes. At any point of either's lecture the other could pick it up and carry it on—a fortunate condition, as it sometimes became necessary to do this.

In 1908 I built the house I now occupy (in Moylan, Pennsylvania), which is the realization of a desire I have always had—to build on a tract which had a stream, a grove of trees, great boulders and rocks, and a hill site for the house with a broad outlook, and a railroad station conveniently near. . . . I have only eight acres of land, but no one could ask a more ideal site for a cottage; and on the place is my beloved forest, including a grove of three hundred firs. From every country I have visited I have brought back a tiny tree for this little forest, and now it is as full of memories as of beauty. . . .

Every suffragist I have ever met has been a lover of home; and only the conviction that she is fighting for her home, her children, for other women, or for all of these, has sustained her in her public work. . . .

As for life's other gifts, I have had some of them, too. I have made many friendships; I have looked upon the beauty of many lands; I have the assurance of the respect and affection of thousands of men and women I have never even met. Though I have given all I had, I have received a thousand times more than I have given.

Jane Addams

(1860–1935)

Jane Addams was born the eighth of nine children of a prosperous miller, banker, and Republican political leader in Rockford, Illinois. Both her parents had roots in colonial Pennsylvania, in the Quaker faith, and in its abolitionist reform tradition.

At the age of two, Addams witnessed her mother's death in childbirth, a loss which made her emotionally dependent on her father. This dependence was complicated by his second marriage when she was seven. Introspective and deeply influenced by her family's abolitionist sentiments, Addams possessed an active intellect stimulated by the new aspirations for higher education for women.

Although she wanted to go east to the recently founded Smith College, Addams was sent to Rockford Female Seminary, an institution modeled on Mount Holyoke College, which aimed to prepare its students for missionary work.

Graduated in Rockford's first college class in 1882, Addams faced the dilemma of a prosperous young woman who wanted to put her education to use in serious work while family pressures dictated marriage. This crisis was deepened by her father's sudden death and more exigent claims by her stepmother.

Addams sidestepped efforts to arrange her marriage by several years of genuine and occasionally neurotic illness, and she extended the conventional American girl's tour of Europe to two years of travel and study, from 1883 to 1885. Unable to settle on a vocation and determined to dodge her family's marriage plans, Addams returned to Europe with a group of college friends in 1887.

Her years of study and apparent paralysis of the will came to an end in 1889, when she returned to the United States and opened the first settlement house in Chicago's slums, Hull-House. Settlements elsewhere in the United States were distinctly Christian and sectarian, but Addams founded hers as a secular enterprise, committed to building community and providing opportunities for moral action for the overprivileged college-educated women and men of her generation.

Hull-House was a success from its first day, offering service to its immigrant neighbors and a highly charged intellectual life for its residents. It became a kind of social laboratory, in which efforts to bridge the gaps between native born Americans and immigrants, workers and the propertied classes, the middle-class values of philanthropists and the objects of their gifts were carried on in a spirit of pragmatic inquiry.

The settlement was a magnet for talented women, drawing residents who all subsequently played key roles in national and international reform movements. Unlike many counterparts, it was never hampered by financial constraints because of Addams's talents as a fund-raiser and considerable managerial ability.

Addams quickly became a leader in philanthropic and governmental efforts to deal with the problems of America's sprawling industrial cities, with their ethnic tensions and potentially explosive class conflicts. By the early twentieth century she was publishing one best-selling book after another, based on the speeches and talks she delivered to diverse audiences, all of them eloquent, moving, didactic, and superbly written.[1]

Addams became a national political figure in 1912, when she backed Theodore Roosevelt's Bull Moose campaign and toured the country speaking on T.R.'s behalf. Dedicated to internationalism and aware of the potential for massive destruction inherent in the weapons of industrial society, Addams also became a committed pacifist and a spirited participant in the efforts of various volunteer organizations to mediate between the warring powers in World War I.

As an opponent of the entry of the United States into the world conflict in 1917, Addams experienced her first disillusionment with popular sentiment in her native America and with the international women's movement, both of which proved susceptible to wartime propaganda. Forced back to her base in Hull-House for some years after her opposition to the war, Addams entered another period of prolific writing before being recruited to work on a national scale as the Hoover and Roosevelt administrations struggled to deal with the Great Depression.

At her death at age seventy-four, Addams was again the preeminent woman leader in the United States, the voice of its democratic

---

1. Addams's principal publications were *Democracy and Social Ethics* (1902), *Newer Ideals of Peace* (1907), *The Spirit of Youth and the City Streets* (1909), *Twenty Years at Hull-House* (1910), *A New Conscience and an Ancient Evil* (1911), *The Long Road of Woman's Memory* (1916), *Peace and Bread in Time of War* (1922), *The Second Twenty Years at Hull-House* (1930), *The Excellent Becomes the Permanent* (1932), and *My Friend Julia Lathrop* (1935).

conscience, and the experienced pioneer of many of the efforts at
welfare intervention adopted by the New Deal administration. Her
opposition to America's involvement in the First World War was
also vindicated by the exposés in the late 1920s of the role of
American banks and armaments manufacturers in the decision to
enter the war.

A brilliant writer, an inspired but moderate social activist, a
feminist, a dedicated peace worker, a civil rights worker, a pioneer
in social work, Addams defies brief summation. Her autobiography,
aimed at recruiting support for her social and political goals, falls
into the romantic style of women's narrative, describing her key
decisions as conversion experiences, presenting herself as the em-
bodiment of maternal instincts. The truth is far more complex,
although Addams became so famous and so crucial to the causes
she had launched that she lived her later life as a prisoner of the
mystique created by her public's response to her intellect and moral
character.

TWENTY YEARS AT HULL-HOUSE

I begin this record with some impressions of my childhood.
All of these are directly connected with my father, although
of course I recall many experiences apart from him. I was one of
the younger members of a large family and an eager participant in
the village life, but because my father was so distinctly the dominant
influence and because it is quite impossible to set forth all of one's
early impressions, it has seemed simpler to string these first memories on that single cord. . . .

[I associated the family] mill with my father's activities, for
doubtless at that time I centered upon him all that careful imitation
which a little girl ordinarily gives to her mother's ways and habits.
My mother had died when I was a baby and my father's second
marriage did not occur until my eighth year. . . .

I . . . contributed my share to that stream of admiration which
our generation so generously poured forth for the self-made man.
I was consumed by a wistful desire to apprehend the hardships of
my father's earlier life in that faraway time when he had been a
miller's apprentice. I knew that he still woke up punctually at three

o'clock because for so many years he had taken his turn at the mill in the early morning. . . .

. . . a little later . . . I held a conversation with my father upon the doctrine of foreordination, which at one time very much perplexed my childish mind. After setting the difficulty before him and complaining that I could not make it out, although my best friend "understood it perfectly," I settled down to hear his argument, having no doubt that he could make it quite clear. To my delighted surprise, for any intimation that our minds were on an equality lifted me high indeed, he said that he feared that he and I did not have the kind of mind that would ever understand foreordination very well and advised me not to give too much time to it; but he then proceeded to say other things of which the final impression left upon my mind was, that it did not matter much whether one understood foreordination or not, but that it was very important not to pretend to understand what you didn't understand and that you must always be honest with yourself inside, whatever happened. Perhaps on the whole as valuable a lesson as the shorter catechism itself contains. . . .

These early recollections are set in a scene of rural beauty, unusual at least in Illinois. The prairie round the village was broken into hills, one of them crowned by pine woods, grown up from a bag full of Norway pine seeds sown by my father in 1844, the very year he came to Illinois, a testimony perhaps that the most vigorous pioneers gave at least an occasional thought to beauty. The banks of the mill stream rose into high bluffs too perpendicular to be climbed without skill, and containing caves of which one at least was so black that it could not be explored without the aid of a candle; and there was a deserted limekiln which became associated in my mind with the unpardonable sin of Hawthorne's "Lime-Burner." . . .

Although I was but four and a half years old when Lincoln died, I distinctly remember the day when I found on our two white gate posts American flags companioned with black. I tumbled down on the harsh gravel walk in my eager rush into the house to inquire what they were "there for." To my amazement I found my father in tears, something that I had never seen before, having assumed, as all children do, that grown-up people never cried. The two flags, my father's tears and his impressive statement that the greatest man in the world had died, constituted my initiation, my baptism, as it

were, into the thrilling and solemn interests of a world lying quite
outside the two white gate posts. . . .

Thousands of children in the sixties and seventies, in the simplicity which is given to the understanding of a child, caught a
notion of imperishable heroism when they were told that brave men
had lost their lives that the slaves might be free. At any moment
the conversation of our elders might turn upon these heroic
events. . . .

We felt on those days a connection with the great world so
much more heroic than the village world which surrounded us
through all the other days. My father was a member of the state
senate for the sixteen years between 1854 and 1870, and even as
a little child I was dimly conscious of the grave march of public
affairs in his comings and goings at the state capital. . . .

As my three older sisters had already attended the seminary at
Rockford, of which my father was trustee, without any question I
entered there at seventeen, with such meager preparation in Latin
and algebra as the village school had afforded. I was very ambitious
to go to Smith College, although I well knew that my father's theory
in regard to the education of his daughters implied a school as near
at home as possible, to be followed by travel abroad in lieu of the
wider advantages which an eastern college is supposed to afford. I
was much impressed by the recent return of my sister from a year
in Europe, yet I was greatly disappointed at the moment of starting
to humdrum Rockford. After the first weeks of homesickness were
over, however, I became very much absorbed in the little world
which the boarding school in any form always offers to its students. . . .

The school in Rockford in 1877 had not changed its name from
seminary to college, although it numbered, on its faculty and among
its alumnae, college women who were most eager that this should
be done, and who readily accomplished it during the next five years.
The school was one of the earliest efforts for women's higher education in the Mississippi Valley, and from the beginning was called
"The Mount Holyoke of the West." It reflected much of the missionary spirit of that pioneer institution, and the proportion of
missionaries among its early graduates was almost as large as Mount
Holyoke's own. In addition there had been thrown about the founders of the early western school the glamour of frontier privations,
and the first students, conscious of the heroic self-sacrifice made in
their behalf, felt that each minute of the time thus dearly bought

must be conscientiously used. This inevitably fostered an atmosphere of intensity, a fever of preparation which continued long after the direct making of it had ceased, and which the later girls accepted, as they did the campus and the buildings, without knowing that it could have been otherwise. . . .

As I attempt to reconstruct the spirit of my contemporary group by looking over many documents, I find nothing more amusing than a plaint registered against life's indistinctness. . . .

At one time five of us tried to understand De Quincey's marvelous "Dreams" more sympathetically, by drugging ourselves with opium. . . .

There were practically no Economics taught in women's colleges—at least in the fresh-water ones—thirty years ago, although we painstakingly studied "Mental" and "Moral" Philosophy, which, though far from dry in the classroom, became the subject of more spirited discussion outside, and gave us a clew for animated rummaging in the little college library. Of course we read a great deal of Ruskin and Browning, and liked the most abstruse parts the best; but like the famous gentleman who talked prose without knowing it, we never dreamed of connecting them with our philosophy. My genuine interest was history, partly because of a superior teacher, and partly because my father had always insisted upon a certain amount of historic reading ever since he had paid me, as a little girl, five cents a "Life" for each Plutarch hero I could intelligently report to him, and twenty-five cents for every volume of Irving's *Life of Washington.* . . .

. . . this early companionship showed me how essentially similar are the various forms of social effort, and curiously enough, the actual activities of a missionary school are not unlike many that are carried on in a Settlement situated in a foreign quarter. . . .

The régime of Rockford Seminary was still very simple in the 70's. Each student made her own fire and kept her own room in order. Sunday morning was a great clearing up day, and the sense of having made immaculate my own immediate surroundings, the consciousness of clean linen, said to be close to the consciousness of a clean conscience, always mingles in my mind with these early readings. I certainly bore away with me a lifelong enthusiasm for reading the Gospels in bulk, a whole one at a time, and an insurmountable distaste for having them cut up into chapter and verse or for hearing the incidents in that wonderful Life thus referred to as if it were merely a record. . . .

Throughout our school years we were always keenly conscious of the growing development of Rockford Seminary into a college. The opportunity for our Alma Mater to take her place in the new movement of full college education for women filled us with enthusiasm, and it became a driving ambition with the undergraduates to share in this new and glorious undertaking. We gravely decided that it was important that some of the students should be ready to receive the bachelor's degree the very first moment that the charter of the school should secure the right to confer it. Two of us, therefore, took a course in mathematics, advanced beyond anything previously given in the school, from one of those early young women working for a Ph.D., who was temporarily teaching in Rockford that she might study more mathematics in Leipsic. . . .

Towards the end of our four years' course we debated much as to what we were to be, and long before the end of my school days it was quite settled in my mind that I should study medicine and "live with the poor." . . .

As our boarding-school days neared the end, in the consciousness of approaching separation we vowed eternal allegiance to our "early ideals," and promised each other we would "never abandon them without conscious justification," and we often warned each other of "the perils of self-tradition."

We believed, in our sublime self-conceit, that the difficulty of life would lie solely in the direction of losing these precious ideals of ours. . . .

The year after I had left college I came back, with a classmate, to receive the degree we had so eagerly anticipated. Two of the graduating class were also ready and four of us were dubbed B.A. on the very day that Rockford Seminary was declared a college in the midst of tumultuous anticipations. Having had a year outside of college walls in that trying land between vague hope and definite attainment, I had become very much sobered in my desire for a degree, and was already beginning to emerge from that rose-colored mist with which the dream of youth so readily envelops the future. . . .

Whatever may have been the perils of self-tradition, I certainly did not escape them, for it required eight years—from the time I left Rockford in the summer of 1881 until Hull-House was opened in the autumn of 1889—to formulate my convictions even in the least satisfactory manner, much less to reduce them to a plan for action. During most of that time I was absolutely at sea so far as any moral purpose was concerned, clinging only to the desire to live in a really living world and refusing to be content with a shadowy intellectual or aesthetic reflection of it. . . .

The winter after I left school was spent in the Woman's Medical College of Philadelphia, but the development of the spinal difficulty which had shadowed me from childhood forced me into Dr. Weir Mitchell's hospital for the late spring, and the next winter I was literally bound to a bed in my sister's house for six months. In spite of its tedium, the long winter had its mitigations, for after the first few weeks I was able to read with a luxurious consciousness of leisure, and I remember opening the first volume of Carlyle's *Frederick the Great* with a lively sense of gratitude that it was not Gray's *Anatomy,* having found, like many another, that general culture is a much easier undertaking than professional study. The long illness inevitably put aside the immediate prosecution of a medical course, and although I had passed my examinations creditably enough in the required subjects for the first year, I was very glad to have a physician's sanction for giving up clinics and dissecting rooms and to follow his prescription of spending the next two years in Europe.

Before I returned to America I had discovered that there were other genuine reasons for living among the poor than that of practicing medicine upon them, and my brief foray into the profession was never resumed. . . .

One of the most poignant of these experiences, which occurred during the first few months after our landing upon the other side of the Atlantic, was on a Saturday night, when I received an ineradicable impression of the wretchedness of East London, and also saw for the first time the overcrowded quarters of a great city at midnight. A small party of tourists were taken to the East End by a city missionary to witness the Saturday night sale of decaying vegetables and fruit, which, owing to the Sunday laws in London, could not be sold until Monday, and, as they were beyond safe keeping, were disposed of at auction as late as possible on Saturday night. On Mile End Road, from the top of an omnibus which paused at the end of a dingy street lighted by only occasional flares of gas, we saw two huge masses of ill-clad people clamoring around two hucksters' carts. They were bidding their farthings and ha'pennies for a vegetable held up by the auctioneer, which he at last scornfully flung, with a gibe for its cheapness, to the successful bidder. . . .

For the following weeks I went about London almost furtively, afraid to look down narrow streets and alleys lest they disclose again this hideous human need and suffering. I carried with me for days at a time that curious surprise we experience when we first come back into the streets after days given over to sorrow and death; we are bewildered that the world should be going on as usual and unable to determine which is real, the inner pang or the outward seeming. . . .

During the following two years on the continent, while I was irresistibly drawn to the poorer quarters of each city, nothing among the beggars of South Italy nor among the saltminers of Austria carried with it the same conviction of human wretchedness which was conveyed by this momentary glimpse of an East London street. . . .

I gradually reached the conviction that the first generation of college women had taken their learning too quickly, had departed too suddenly from the active, emotional life led by their grand-mothers and great-grandmothers; that the contemporary education of young women had developed too exclusively the power of ac-quiring knowledge and of merely receiving impressions; that some-where in the process of "being educated" they had lost that simple and almost automatic response to the human appeal, that old health-ful reaction resulting in activity from the mere presence of suffering or of helplessness; that they are so sheltered and pampered they have no chance even to make "the great refusal." . . .

I remember a happy busy mother who, complacent with the knowledge that her daughter daily devoted four hours to her music, looked up from her knitting to say, "If I had had your opportunities when I was young, my dear, I should have been a very happy girl. I always had musical talent, but such training as I had, foolish little songs and waltzes and not time for half an hour's practice a day."

The mother did not dream of the sting her words left and that the sensitive girl appreciated only too well that her opportunities were fine and unusual, but she also knew that in spite of some facility and much good teaching she had no genuine talent and never would fulfill the expectations of her friends. She looked back upon her mother's girlhood with positive envy because it was so full of happy industry and extenuating obstacles, with undisturbed opportunity to believe that her talents were unusual. The girl looked wistfully at her mother, but had not the courage to cry out what was in her heart: "I might believe I had unusual talent if I did not know what good music was; I might enjoy half an hour's practice a day if I were busy and happy the rest of the time. You do not know what life means when all the difficulties are removed! I am simply smothered and sickened with advantages."

It is hard to tell just when the very simple plan which afterward developed into the Settlement began to form itself in my mind. It may have been even before I went to Europe for the second time, but I gradually became convinced that it would be a good thing to rent a house in a part of the city where many primitive and actual needs are found, in which young women who had been given over too exclusively to study, might restore a balance of activity along traditional lines and learn of life from life itself; where they might try out some of the things they had been taught and put truth to "the ultimate test of the conduct it dictates or inspires." . . .

I can well recall the stumbling and uncertainty with which I finally set it forth to Miss Starr, my old-time school friend, who was one of our party. I even dared to hope that she might join in carrying out the plan, but nevertheless I told it in the fear of that disheartening experience which is so apt to afflict our most cherished plans when they are at last divulged, when we suddenly feel that there is nothing there to talk about, and as the golden dream slips through our fingers we are left to wonder at our own fatuous belief. . . .

A month later we parted in Paris, Miss Starr to go back to Italy, and I to journey on to London to secure as many suggestions as possible from those wonderful places of which we had heard, Toynbee Hall and the People's Palace. So that it finally came about that in June, 1888, five years after my first visit in East London, I found myself at Toynbee Hall equipped not only with a letter of introduction from Canon Fremantle, but with high expectations and a certain belief that whatever perplexities and discouragement concerning the life of the poor were in store for me, I should at least know something at first hand and have the solace of daily activity. I had confidence that although life itself might contain many difficulties, the period of mere passive receptivity had come to an end, and I had at last finished with the everlasting "preparation for life," however ill-prepared I might be. . . .

The next January found Miss Starr and myself in Chicago, searching for a neighborhood in which we might put our plans into execution. In our eagerness to win friends for the new undertaking, we utilized every opportunity to set forth the meaning of the settlement as it had been embodied in Toynbee Hall, although in those days we made no appeal for money, meaning to start with our own slender resources. From the very first the plan received courteous attention, and the discussion, while often skeptical, was always friendly. . . .

. . . time has also justified our early contention that the mere foothold of a house, easily accessible, ample in space, hospitable and tolerant in spirit, situated in the midst of the large foreign colonies which so easily isolate themselves in American cities, would be in itself a serviceable thing for Chicago. . . .

Hull-House was soberly opened on the theory that the dependence of classes on each other is reciprocal, and that as the social relation is essentially a reciprocal relation, it gives a form of expression that has peculiar value.

In our search for a vicinity in which to settle we went about with the officers of the compulsory education department, with city missionaries and with the newspaper reporters. . . .

One Sunday afternoon in the late winter a reporter took me to visit a so-called anarchist sunday school, several of which were to be found on the northwest side of the city. . . .

Another Sunday afternoon in the early spring, on the way to a Bohemian mission in the carriage of one of its founders, we passed a fine old house standing well back from the street, surrounded on three sides by a broad piazza which was supported by wooden pillars of exceptionally pure Corinthian design and proportion. I was so attracted by the house that I set forth to visit it the very next day, but though I searched for it then and for several days after, I could not find it, and at length I most reluctantly gave up the search. . . .

Three weeks later . . . we decided upon a location somewhere near the junction of Blue Island Avenue, Halsted Street, and Harrison Street. I was surprised and overjoyed on the very first day of our search for quarters to come upon the hospitable old house, the quest for which I had so recently abandoned. . . .

The fine old house responded kindly to repairs, its wide hall and open fireplaces always insuring it a gracious aspect. Its generous owner, Miss Helen Culver, in the following spring gave us a free leasehold of the entire house. Her kindness has continued through the years until the group of thirteen buildings, which at present comprises our equipment, is built largely upon land which Miss Culver has put at the service of the Settlement which bears Mr. Hull's name. In those days the house stood between an undertaking establishment and a saloon. "Knight, Death, and the Devil," the three were called by a Chicago wit. . . .

We furnished the house as we would have furnished it were it in another part of the city, with the photographs and other impedimenta we had collected in Europe, and with a few bits of family mahogany. While all the new furniture which was bought was enduring in quality, we were careful to keep it in character with the fine old residence. Probably no young matron ever placed her own things in her house with more pleasure than that with which we first furnished Hull-House. . . .

On the 18th of September, 1889, Miss Starr and I moved into it, with Miss Mary Keyser, who began by performing the housework, but who quickly developed into a very important factor in the life of the vicinity as well as in that of the household, and whose death five years later was most sincerely mourned by hundreds of our neighbors. . . .

Volunteers to the new undertaking came quickly; a charming young girl conducted a kindergarten in the drawing-room, coming regularly every morning from her home in a distant part of the North Side of the city. . . .

In spite of these flourishing clubs for children early established at Hull-House, and the fact that our first organized undertaking was a kindergarten, we were very insistent that the Settlement should not be primarily for the children, and that it was absurd to suppose that grown people would not respond to opportunities for education and social life. . . .

On our first New Year's Day at Hull-House we invited the older people in the vicinity, sending a carriage for the most feeble and announcing to all of them that we were going to organize an Old Settlers' Party.

Every New Year's Day since, older people in varying numbers have come together at Hull-House to relate early hardships, and to take for the moment the place in the community to which their pioneer life entitles them. Many people who were formerly residents of the vicinity, but whom prosperity has carried into more desirable neighborhoods, come back to these meetings and often confess to each other that they have never since found such kindness as in early Chicago when all its citizens came together in mutual enterprises. . . .

In those early days we were often asked why we had come to live on Halsted Street when we could afford to live somewhere else.

I remember one man who used to shake his head and say it was "the strangest thing he had met in his experience," but who was finally convinced that it was "not strange but natural." In time it came to seem natural to all of us that the Settlement should be there. If it is natural to feed the hungry and care for the sick, it is certainly natural to give pleasure to the young, comfort to the aged, and to minister to the deep-seated craving for social intercourse that all men feel. . . .

From the first it seemed understood that we were ready to perform the humblest neighborhood services. We were asked to wash the new-born babies, and to prepare the dead for burial, to nurse the sick, and to "mind the children." . . .

The Ethical Culture Societies held a summer school at Plymouth, Massachusetts, in 1892, to which they invited several people representing the then new Settlement movement. . . .

I venture to produce here parts of a lecture I delivered in Plymouth, . . . because I have found it impossible to formulate with the same freshness those early motives and strivings. . . .

We have in America a fast growing number of cultivated young people who have no recognized outlet for their active faculties. They hear constantly of the great social maladjustment, but no way is provided for them to change it, and their uselessness hangs about them heavily. Huxley declares that the sense of uselessness is the severest shock which the human system can sustain, and that if persistently sustained, it results in atrophy of function. These young people have had advantages of college, of European travel, and of economic study, but they are sustaining this shock of inaction. They have pet phrases, and they tell you that the things that make us all alike are stronger than the things that make us different. They say that all men are united by needs and sympathies far more permanent and radical than anything that temporarily divides them and sets them in opposition to each other. If they affect art, they say that the decay in artistic expression is due to the decay in ethics, that art when shut away from the human interests and from the great mass of humanity is self-destructive. They tell their elders with all the bitterness of youth that if they expect success from them in business or politics or in whatever lines their ambition for them has run, they must let them consult all of humanity; that they must let them find out what the people want and how they want it. . . .

Our young people feel nervously the need of assumption that Christianity is a set of ideas which belong to the religious con-

sciousness, whatever that may be. They insist that it cannot be proclaimed and instituted apart from the social life of the community and that it must seek a simple and natural expression in the social organism itself. . . .

It is quite impossible for me to say in what proportion or degree the subjective necessity which led to the opening of Hull-House combined the three trends: first, the desire to interpret democracy in social terms; secondly, the impulse beating at the very source of our lives, urging us to aid in the race progress; and, thirdly, the Christian movement toward humanitarianism. . . .

The Settlement, then, is an experimental effort to aid in the solution of the social and industrial problems which are engendered by the modern conditions of life in a great city. . . .

Its residents must be emptied of all conceit of opinion and all self-assertion, and ready to arouse and interpret the public opinion of their neighborhood. They must be content to live quietly side by side with their neighbors, until they grow into a sense of relationship and mutual interest. Their neighbors are held apart by differences of race and language which the residents can more easily overcome. They are bound to see the needs of their neighborhood as a whole, to furnish data for legislation, and to use their influence to secure it. In short, residents are pledged to devote themselves to the duties of good citizenship and to the arousing of the social energies which too largely lie dormant in every neighborhood given over to industrialism. They are bound to regard the entire life of their city as organic, to make an effort to unify it, and to protest against its over-differentiation. . . .

Of course, many people were indifferent to the idea of the Settlement; others looked on with tolerant and sometimes cynical amusement which we would often encounter in a good story related at our expense; but all this was remote and unreal to us and we were sure that if the critics could but touch "the life of the people," they would understand.

The situation changed markedly after the Pullman strike, and our efforts to secure factory legislation later brought upon us a certain amount of distrust and suspicion; until then we had been considered merely a kindly philanthropic undertaking whose new form gave us a certain idealistic glamour. . . .

. . . the memory of the first years at Hull-House is more or less blurred with fatigue, for we could of course become accustomed only gradually to the unending activity and to the confusion of a house constantly filling and refilling with groups of people. The little children who came to the kindergarten in the morning were followed by the afternoon clubs of older children, and those in turn made way for the educational and social organizations of adults, occupying every room in the house every evening. All one's habits of living had to be readjusted, and any student's tendency to sit with a book by the fire was of necessity definitely abandoned.

To thus renounce "the luxury of personal preference" was, however, a mere trifle compared to our perplexity over the problems of an industrial neighborhood situated in an unorganized city. . . .

. . . we were often bitterly pressed for money and worried by the prospect of unpaid bills, and we gave up one golden scheme after another because we could not afford it; we cooked the meals and kept the books and washed the windows without a thought of hardship if we thereby saved money for the consummation of some ardently desired undertaking. . . .

But more gratifying than any understanding or response from without could possibly be, was the consciousness that a growing group of residents was gathering at Hull-House, held together in that soundest of all social bonds, the companionship of mutual interests. These residents came primarily because they were genuinely interested in the social situation and believed that the Settlement was valuable as a method of approach to it. A House in which the men residents lived was opened across the street, and at the end of the first five years the Hull-House residential force numbered fifteen, a majority of whom still remain identified with the Settlement. . . .

This spirit of generalization and lack of organization among the charitable forces of the city was painfully revealed in that terrible winter after the World's Fair, when the general financial depression throughout the country was much intensified in Chicago by the numbers of unemployed stranded at the close of the exposition. When the first cold weather came the police stations and the very corridors of the city hall were crowded by men who could afford no other lodging. They made huge demonstrations on the lake front, reminding one of the London gatherings in Trafalgar Square. . . .

A beginning . . . was then made toward a Bureau of Organized Charities, the main office being put in charge of a young man recently come from Boston, who lived at Hull-House. But to employ scientific methods for the first time at such a moment involved difficulties, and the most painful episode of the winter for me came from an attempt on my part to conform to carefully received instructions. A shipping clerk whom I had known for a long time had lost his place, as so many people had that year, and came to the relief station established at Hull-House four or five times to secure help for his family. I told him one day of the opportunity for work on the drainage canal and intimated that if any employment were obtainable, he ought to exhaust that possibility before asking for help. The man replied that he had always worked indoors and that he could not endure outside work in winter. I am grateful to remember that I was too uncertain to be severe, although I held to my instructions. He did not come again for relief, but worked for two days digging on the canal, where he contracted pneumonia and died a week later. I have never lost trace of the two little children he left behind him, although I cannot see them without a bitter consciousness that it was at their expense I learned that life cannot be administered by definite rules and regulations; that wisdom to deal with a man's difficulties comes only through some knowledge of his life and habits as a whole; and that to treat an isolated episode is almost sure to invite blundering. . . .

I . . . longed for the comfort of a definite social creed, which should afford at one and the same time an explanation of the social chaos and the logical steps towards its better ordering. I came to have an exaggerated sense of responsibility for the poverty in the midst of which I was living and which the socialists constantly forced me to defend. . . .

The Pullman strike afforded much illumination to many Chicago people. Before it, there had been nothing in my experience to reveal that distinct cleavage of society, which a general strike at least momentarily affords. Certainly, during all those dark days of the Pullman strike, the growth of class bitterness was most obvious. The fact that the Settlement maintained avenues of intercourse with both sides seemed to give it opportunity for nothing but a realization of the bitterness and division along class lines. . . .

A very intimate and personal experience revealed, at least to myself, my constant dread of the spreading ill will. At the height of the sympathetic strike my oldest sister, who was convalescing from a long illness in a hospital near Chicago, became suddenly very much worse. While I was able to reach her at once, every possible obstacle of a delayed and blocked transportation system interrupted the journey of her husband and children who were hurrying to her bedside from a distant state. As the end drew nearer and I was obliged to reply to my sister's constant inquiries that her family had not yet come, I was filled with a profound apprehension lest her last hours should be touched with resentment towards those responsible for the delay; lest her unutterable longing should at the very end be tinged with bitterness. She must have divined what was in my mind, for at last she said each time after the repetition of my sad news; "I don't blame anyone, I am not judging them." . . .

When I returned to Chicago from the quiet country I saw the Federal troops encamped about the post-office; almost every one on Halsted Street wearing a white ribbon, the emblem of the strikers' side; the residents at Hull-House divided in opinion as to the righteousness of this or that measure; and no one able to secure any real information as to which side was burning the cars. . . .

The administration of charity in Chicago during the winter following the World's Fair had been of necessity most difficult for, although large sums had been given to the temporary relief organization which endeavored to care for the thousands of destitute strangers stranded in the city, we all worked under a sense of desperate need and a paralyzing consciousness that our best efforts were most inadequate to the situation.

During the many relief visits I paid that winter in tenement houses and miserable lodgings, I was constantly shadowed by a certain sense of shame that I should be comfortable in the midst of such distress. This resulted at times in a curious reaction against all the educational and philanthropic activities in which I had been engaged. In the face of the desperate hunger and need, these could not but seem futile and superficial. . . .

The dealing directly with the simplest human wants may have been responsible for an impression which I carried about with me almost constantly for a period of two years and which culminated finally in a visit to Tolstoy, —that the Settlement, or Hull-House at least, was a mere pretense and travesty of the simple impulse "to live with the poor," so long as the residents did not share the common lot of hard labor and scant fare.

Actual experience had left me in much the same state of mind I had been in after reading Tolstoy's *What to Do,* which is a description of his futile efforts to relieve the unspeakable distress and want in the Moscow winter of 1881, and his inevitable conviction that only he who literally shares his own shelter and food with the needy, can claim to have served them. . . .

Doubtless it is much easier to see "what to do" in rural Russia, where all the conditions tend to make the contrast as broad as possible between peasant labor and noble idleness, than it is to see "what to do" in the interdependencies of the modern industrial city. But for that very reason perhaps, Tolstoy's clear statement is valuable for that type of conscientious person in every land who finds it hard, not only to walk in the path of righteousness, but to discover where the path lies.

I had read the books of Tolstoy steadily all the years since *My Religion* had come into my hands immediately after I left college. . . .

But I was most eager to know whether Tolstoy's undertaking to do his daily share of the physical labor of the world, that labor which is "so disproportionate to the unnourished strength" of those by whom it is ordinarily performed, had brought him peace!

I had time to review carefully many times in my mind during the long days of convalescence following an illness of typhoid fever which I suffered in the autumn of 1895. The illness was so prolonged that my health was most unsatisfactory during the following winter, and the next May I went abroad with my friend, Miss Smith, to effect, if possible, a more complete recovery.

The prospect of seeing Tolstoy filled me with the hope of finding a clew to the tangled affairs of city poverty. I was but one of thousands of our contemporaries who were turning towards this Russian, not as to a seer—his message is much too confused and contradictory for that—but as to a man who has had the ability to lift his life to the level of his conscience, to translate his theories into action. . . .

We had letters of introduction to Mr. and Mrs. Aylmer Maude of Moscow. . . .

We gladly accepted Mr. Maude's offer to take us to Yasnaya Polyana and to introduce us to Count Tolstoy, and never did a disciple journey towards his master with more enthusiasm than did our guide. When, however, Mr. Maude actually presented Miss Smith and myself to Count Tolstoy, knowing well his master's attitude toward philanthropy, he endeavored to make Hull-House appear much more noble and unique than I should have ventured to do.

Tolstoy, standing by clad in his peasant garb, listened gravely but, glancing distrustfully at the sleeves of my traveling gown which unfortunately at that season were monstrous in size, he took hold of an edge and pulling out one sleeve to an interminable breadth, said quite simply that "there was enough stuff on one arm to make a frock for a little girl," and asked me directly if I did not find "such a dress" a "barrier to the people." I was too disconcerted to make a very clear explanation, although I tried to say that monstrous as my sleeves were they did not compare in size with those of the working girls in Chicago and that nothing would more effectively separate me from "the people" than a cotton blouse following the simple lines of the human form; even if I had wished to imitate him and "dress as a peasant," it would have been hard to choose which peasant among the thirty-six nationalities we had recently counted in our ward. . . .

. . . neither Countess Tolstoy nor any other friend was on hand to help me out of my predicament later, when I was asked who "fed" me, and how did I obtain "shelter"? Upon my reply that a farm a hundred miles from Chicago supplied me with the necessities of life, I fairly anticipated the next scathing question: "So you are an absentee landlord? Do you think you will help the people more by adding yourself to the crowded city than you would by tilling your own soil?" This new sense of discomfort over a failure to till my own soil was increased when Tolstoy's second daughter appeared at the five-o'clock tea table set under the trees, coming straight from the harvest field where she had been working with a group of peasants since five o'clock in the morning, not pretending to work but really taking the place of a peasant woman who had hurt her foot. She was plainly much exhausted but neither expected nor received sympathy from the members of a family who were quite accustomed to see each other carry out their convictions in spite of discomfort and fatigue. The martyrdom of discomfort, however, was obviously much easier to bear than that to which, even to the eyes of the casual visitor, Count Tolstoy daily subjected himself, for his study in the basement of the conventional dwelling, with its short shelf of battered books and its scythe and spade leaning against the wall, had many times lent itself to that ridicule which is the most difficult form of martyrdom.

That summer evening as we sat in the garden with a group of visitors from Germany, from England and America, who had traveled to the remote Russian village that they might learn of this man, one could not forbear the constant inquiry to one's self, as to why he was so regarded as sage and saint that this party of people should be repeated each day of the year. It seemed to me then that we were all attracted by this sermon of the deed, because Tolstoy had made the one supreme personal effort, one might almost say the one frantic personal effort, to put himself into right relations with the humblest people, with the men who tilled his soil, blacked his boots, and cleaned his stables. . . .

Miss Smith and I took a night train back to Moscow in that tumult of feeling which is always produced by contact with a conscience making one more of those determined efforts to probe to the very foundations of the mysterious world in which we find ourselves. A horde of perplexing questions, concerning those problems of existence of which in happier moments we catch but fleeting glimpses and at which we even then stand aghast, pursued us relentlessly on the long journey through the great wheat plains of South Russia, through the crowded Ghetto of Warsaw, and finally into the smiling fields of Germany where the peasant men and women were harvesting the grain. . . .

I may have wished to secure . . . solace for myself at the cost of the least possible expenditure of time and energy, for during the next month in Germany, when I read everything of Tolstoy's that had been translated into English, German, or French, there grew up in my mind a conviction that what I ought to do upon my return to Hull-House, was to spend at least two hours every morning in the little bakery which we had recently added to the equipment of our coffee-house. Two hours' work would be but a wretched compromise, but it was hard to see how I could take more time out of each day. I had been taught to bake bread in my childhood not only as a household accomplishment, but because my father, true to his miller's tradition, had insisted that each one of his daughters on her twelfth birthday must present him with a satisfactory wheat loaf of her own baking, and he was most exigent as to the quality of this test loaf. What could be more in keeping with my training and tradition than baking bread? I did not quite see how my activity would fit in with that of the German union baker who presided over the Hull-House bakery but all such matters were secondary and certainly could be arranged. It may be that I had thus to pacify my aroused conscience before I could settle down to hear Wagner's "Ring" at Bayreuth; it may be that I had fallen a victim to the phrase, "bread labor"; but at any rate I held fast to the belief that I should do this, through the entire journey homeward, on land and sea, until I actually arrived in Chicago when suddenly the whole scheme seemed to me as utterly preposterous as it doubtless was. The half dozen people invariably waiting to see me after breakfast, the piles of letters to be opened and answered, the demand of actual and pressing human wants, —were these all to be pushed aside and asked to wait while I saved my soul by two hours' work at baking bread? . . .

Throughout the history of Hull-House many inquiries have been made concerning the religion of the residents, and the reply that they are as diversified in belief and in the ardor of the inner life as any like number of people in a college or similar group, apparently does not carry conviction. I recall that after a house for men residents had been opened on Polk Street and the residential force at Hull-House numbered twenty, we made an effort to come together on Sunday evenings in a household service, hoping thus to express our moral unity in spite of the fact that we represented many creeds. But although all of us reverently knelt when the High Church resident read the evening service and bowed our heads when the evangelical resident led in prayer after his chapter, and although we sat respectfully through the twilight when a resident read her favorite passages from Plato and another from Abt Vogler, we concluded at the end of the winter that this was not religious fellowship and that we did not care for another reading club. . . .

The majority of the present corp of forty residents support themselves by their business and professional occupations in the city, giving only their leisure time to Settlement undertakings. This in itself tends to continuity of residence and has certain advantages. Among the present staff of whom the larger number have been in residence for more than twelve years, there are the secretary of the City club, two practicing physicians, several attorneys, newspaper men, business men, teachers, scientists, artists, musicians, lecturers in the School of Civics and Philanthropy, officers in The Juvenile Protective Association and in The League for the Protection of Immigrants, a visiting nurse, a sanitary inspector, and others.

We have also worked out during our years of residence a plan of living which may be called cooperative, for the families and individuals who rent the Hull-House apartments have the use of the central kitchen and dining room so far as they care for them; many of them work for hours every week in the studios and shops; the theater and drawing-rooms are available for such social organization as they care to form; the entire group of thirteen buildings is heated and lighted from a central plant. During the years, the common human experiences have gathered about the House; funeral services have been held there, marriages and christenings, and many memories hold us to each other as well as to our neighbors. Each resident, of course, carefully defrays his own expenses, and his relations to his fellow residents are not unlike those of a college professor to his colleagues. The depth and strength of his relation to the neighborhood must depend very largely upon himself and upon the genuine friendships he has been able to make. His relation to the city as a whole comes largely through his identification with those groups who are carrying forward the reforms which a Settlement neighborhood so sadly needs and with which residence has made him familiar.

Life in the Settlement discovers above all what has been called "the extraordinary pliability of human nature," and it seems impossible to set any bounds to the moral capabilities which might unfold under ideal civic and educational conditions. But in order to obtain these conditions, the Settlement recognizes the need of cooperation, both with the radical and the conservative, and from the very nature of the case the Settlement cannot limit its friends to any one political party or economic school. . . .

The educational activities of a Settlement, as well as its philanthropic, civic, and social undertakings, are but differing manifestations of the attempt to socialize democracy, as is the very existence of the Settlement itself.

Anne Walter Fearn

(1865–1939)

Anne Walter Fearn, the second daughter of a rich southern lawyer and his plantation-born wife, was one of ten children raised in Holly Springs, Mississippi, and on her mother's Delta plantation. Fearn's father and three older brothers perished in the yellow fever epidemic of 1878, and, although the pattern of her life continued externally as that of a southern belle, she became determined to live a more serious life.

While on a visit to her brother in San Francisco, Fearn met several women physicians and settled on medicine as her career. Graduating from the Women's Medical College of Philadelphia in 1893, Fearn indulged her lively spirit of adventure by agreeing to substitute for a classmate scheduled to go to Soochow as a medical missionary. Thus, while not herself a church member, she traveled to China in the employ of the Women's Board of Foreign Missions of the Methodist Episcopal Church, South.

For three years Fearn worked for the mission hospital, her energy and high spirits earning her the name Tai Foong, or Great Wind, from the Chinese. She served as a surgeon, midwife, pediatrician, and medical educator who loved the Chinese and the city of Soochow.

In 1896 she married a fellow medical missionary, John Burrus Fearn, a strict Southern Methodist and child of dirt farmers from Yazoo City, Mississippi. Fearn then entered private practice, her life briefly suffused with happiness at the birth of a daughter, who died of amoebic dysentery in her fifth year. The marriage was occasionally happy but frequently fraught with conflict; its battles are freely acknowledged in Fearn's autobiography. Fearn was not deeply religious and did not share her husband's strict religious codes. She was also a cheerful and adventurous entrepreneur, a role her more cautious husband distrusted and sought ineffectually to curb.

The pair were united by their love for China. A brief trip back to the United States in 1907 left them both longing for China, to which they returned the next year, when Fearn's husband was appointed business manager for the Associated Protestant Missions in China. She lived for most of the next thirty years in Shanghai, active in a variety of educational and philanthropic causes and, for ten years, operating the Fearn Sanatorium, her own private hospital.

Following her husband's death in 1926, Fearn came back to the United States but was unable to settle happily there. After her return to Shanghai in the 1930s, she worked with the national government on child welfare and served on a variety of relief committees for refugees from war and natural disaster. A beloved figure in Shanghai's vibrant international community, she was an unofficial hostess for visiting Americans and a willing ambassador for Chinese causes. Some of the finest writing in her autobiography comes from her loving evocation of the sounds, colors, smells, and light of South China, for which she shows a sense of place never demonstrated for her Mississippi home.

MY DAYS OF STRENGTH:
An American Woman Doctor's
Forty Years in China

A small girl with cropped, curly hair was perched precariously on the edge of the veranda. . . .

Half hidden by a pillar she listened to the strange sounds; she heard the rush of many feet, the rising murmur of the confused crowd that filled the yard. She watched the townspeople mill around the man on the steps, imploring him to stay with them. . . .

I was that eleven-year-old child, and the man was my father, Colonel Harvey Washington Walter. That was my last sight of him, standing there with his three grown sons behind him, and telling his neighbors that as long as life lasted he and his sons would remain there with them. . . .

That was the summer of 1878, the never-to-be-forgotten year, when the terror of the South—yellow fever—raged all around us. . . .

The morning after the meeting on our front lawn my mother, with the younger children, took "the last train that stopped." It was all very thrilling to a little girl who liked things to happen, whose mind was stirred by adventure then and always, and who didn't realize the seriousness of that trip or the tragedy left behind. . . .

But it was not until the frost had fallen, the greatest danger past, and the end of the epidemic in sight that my father and brothers fell ill with the fever. Then, within one week, all four were dead.

My mother was left desolate. Of our homecoming I cannot speak. . . .

Just about this time I had a severe attack of malaria, which altered the entire course of my life. I went to California in the summer of 1889 to recuperate and visit my brother Harvey, who was then in business in San Francisco. On the train I was attracted by a lovely looking woman and although I never spoke to her I overheard her brilliant conversation with others. I was told that she was a "woman physician." . . .

I never learned the name of the woman who made such a deep impression on me, but I never forgot her. . . .

In San Francisco . . . I met the orthopedic surgeon Dr. Harry Sherman. To him I poured out the story of my chance encounter and my enthusiasm for this unknown woman doctor. He suggested that it might interest me to meet a few of the women doctors of San Francisco and not long afterward he introduced me to Dr. Elizabeth M. Yates. Through her I met others.

A new world was opened to me. None of these women was a coarse-grained freak; they were fine, gentle and sensitive. . . .

Women in any profession were having a hard time in those days, but women physicians seemed particularly obnoxious to the average man and woman of the eighties and nineties. Study of the ills of the human flesh was a disgustingly unladylike occupation. The young woman student of medicine faced the reproaches of a "disgraced" family, social ostracism, and incalculable difficulties in the struggle to build up a practice.

All of this I knew quite well, but into my happy-go-luck life there suddenly came a purpose; and opposition served rather to spur me on than to deter me. . . .

I wrote to my mother, telling her I had decided to study medicine. She replied by wire:

"No disgrace has yet fallen upon your father's name. Should you persist in carrying out your mad determination to study medicine I shall never again recognize you as my daughter." . . .

My brother approved and encouraged my ambition but my mother's attitude was one of unmitigated reproach. It was no wonder, for if the women in this profession were looked on askance in other parts of the country they were distinctly taboo in the South. It was a question of propriety as to whether or not they should even be discussed in polite society. But I was in the freer air of the West, far from the staid old traditions. . . .

I had faith in my ability to swing Mother around to my way of thinking. This I set out to do during the next months, by means of tactful descriptions and suitable anecdotes about the various women physicians I was meeting. Eventually I won her over. . . .

The summer was coming to an end and I did not know what to do when Dr. Yates and Dr. Smiley suggested that I go to San Diego for a winter with Dr. Lucia Lane, Dr. Smiley's friend. I could begin my studies in her office under her wise direction. . . .

In San Diego I discovered that I did not know how to study. I didn't know anything! Many a night Gray's *Anatomy* was dashed to the floor, while I sobbed myself to sleep on a pillow wet with tears. Long bones, short bones, flat bones, articulations, muscular attachments—these were only on the edge of the morass of knowledge into which I stumbled and floundered.

An inherited obstinacy came to my rescue, and when the spring term of the Cooper Medical College in San Francisco opened I was one of the nine women who matriculated among hundreds of men. At Cooper women were not only admitted but welcomed. . . .

Money was scarce, as usual, and I did not know how I could complete the course. Again Dr. Smiley came to my rescue with the suggestion that I try for a scholarship in the Women's Medical College of Pennsylvania. . . .

I was immediately awarded a scholarship which included only tuition and laboratory fees. Dr. Yates advanced the money for expenses not covered by the scholarship. . . .

My first year at Women's Medical was a repetition of my previous work but I managed to find an outlet for my energy. Because of the work I had done at Cooper I was made curator of the museum and given the position of presector for the professor of anatomy. This latter job meant dissecting at various odd hours, but I had long ago acquired the matter-of-fact attitude of the medical student to such things. . . .

How I studied. For the first time I was awake to my responsibilities in life. Those were three happy years for me. For my mother they were by turns anxious and exultant ones. Having reconciled herself to having a woman doctor in the family, her revolutionary daughter became a matter of pride. At last the day for the final examinations came. We had agreed that the result would be wired her. It was long after midnight before the lists were out and the notice of success or failure alphabetically delivered. My name, Walter, coming so near the end of the list meant centuries before I could rush to the telegraph office.

My mother, rising with the dawn after an almost sleepless night, sat dressed in a fresh, cool morning gown, in an old rocking chair on the veranda, and waited for the message. Hours later she saw the messenger boy sauntering down the street. Seeing her he increased his gait, waving the telegram and shouting, "Good news, good news!" He handed her the folded slip and seeing that she could not read it for her tears opened it, and though he (and all Holly Springs he had met on the way) knew it by heart, read her the words:

"Hurray! I've won my degree!" . . .

. . . one noon shortly before commencement, when we were all gathered in the college mess hall, Dr. Margaret Polk, President of the College Association and one of my warmest friends, mentioned that if she had had my unusual advantages in hospital work she wouldn't mind going to China. She was then preparing for work in the mission field as physician in charge of the Women's Hospital in Soochow.

"I'll go in your place for a year, M.P.," I said, "while you take another year's work in the hospitals."

The twenty or thirty fledgling doctors seated around the table thought that was a grand idea and chipped in with suggestions. By the time the meal was over a plan had been evolved down to the most minute detail.

"I'll pay your expenses to China," said M.P., growing enthusiastic, "and the Women's Board of Foreign Missions can pay your salary for a year."

"All right," I said, "but I won't go as a missionary. I'm not even a church member. I'm a physician."

"That can be settled, I think," said Margaret, then suddenly practical. "The Board will have to pay my expenses out there. You must pay your own way back."

That was agreeable to me for then I could take up my postponed internship and when that was over settle down somewhere in the South. It was all only a lovely dream but it was fun dreaming. . . .

I was to work as a salaried employee, not as a missionary. . . .

It was in June, 1893 that I received my degree. I was so bursting with a desire to use my full title that stopping over several hours in Norfolk, on my way home from Philadelphia, I signed the hotel register with a flourish—"Dr. Anne Walter."

The news spread like wildfire and in short order curious people were hanging about the lobby and street, craning their necks for a glimpse of the creature who had disgraced her sex by becoming a doctor. That experience taught me a lesson; not for years did I use my title in registering at a hotel.

I spent a brief holiday in the big, high-ceilinged home of my childhood, recapturing my past but ever aware of my future. My precious medical degree aroused little enthusiasm or trust among my fellow-townsmen. I was forced to sit idly by while across the street a friend nearly died from a dangerous delivery, attended by doctors far older than I, but far less skilled in obstetrics.

My decision to go to China was a shock to my mother, but she conceded that it was a wonderful chance for me to see the world. Naturally I would return via Suez and Europe, thus encircling the globe, at that time a great event. When the hour of my departure came she pressed into my hand a ten-dollar gold piece, a coin never too plentiful in our household, insisting that with that special gold piece I should cable her the one word, "Safe," immediately on my arrival in Shanghai. . . .

And then came Shanghai with its wonderful Bund, its splendid buildings, its carriages, its rickshaws, and race course. It so filled me with amazement that no word so prosaic as "safe" satisfied me. The word I sent across the seas was "Delight." That alone could express the feeling that possessed me then, as it does now and will as long as I live. . . .

. . . to reach Soochow from Shanghai in the year 1893, one had to journey sixty miles by slow boat up the Soochow Creek Canal. Mrs. Josephine Campbell, the hospital matron and head of the private training school for nurses in Soochow conducted by the Women's Mission Board of the Methodist Episcopal Church, South, met me in Shanghai. On the Monday following my arrival we started out. For three days and nights the panorama of China spread itself before my eyes—my real introduction to the country, for Shanghai is something apart.

We passed water wheels, turned by patient blindfolded buffaloes; cormorant boats paddled slowly upstream, the birds sitting solemnly along each side with rings around their necks to keep them from swallowing the fish they had just caught; remarkably long bamboo rafts poled along with utter disregard of other traffic; farms clustered around huddled groups of village buildings. Once in a larger village we saw lively evidence of the weekly market day, that red-letter event in the monotonous life of the Chinese farmer. Frequently our boatman hopped off at some hamlet to buy eggs, fish, pork, and rice. Our boat was propelled by a *yuloh* which is a kind of oar but unlike any I had ever seen. It is shaped rather like a fishtail and fastened to the rear deck, extending out behind the boat. The boatmen sway rhythmically in unison with its motion, and croon strangely haunting minor airs whose tunelessness, to Western ears, is in fanastic harmony with the scene.

With the coming of evening that first day the head man or *laodah* came to us and squatting down, asked in a sepulchral whisper if they might tie up near a village, for the night was dark and before us lay the wilderness. This network of canals was in those days haunted by bandits and our boatmen were afraid to traverse it alone at night. When we gave our consent they tied up by sticking a long hook into the bank. All that night I lay sleepless, listening to the bullfrogs in the ponds near by, the three toads in the overhanging branches, the occasional twitter of wakeful birds, and the soft, mysterious thud, thud of oars as boats passed us in the darkness. All such familiar sounds I might have heard any similar night on my own plantation home, but now they were touched with an almost fearful strangeness.

In the early morning we were awakened by the deep tones of the temple bells. At noon of the fourth day we came to the walls of Soochow. . . .

Looking back after all that time I think it is the fragrance of the night and its sounds during that early period of my life in Soochow which linger most clearly in my memory.

A word, a sound, a fleeting perfume annihilates time and distance. Again I am sitting at my desk at one end of the large, pleasant living room of the Hospital Home. The air is heavy with the scent of sweet olive, of jasmine or tuberose, those heavily perfumed flowers of China. The school clock strikes nine; a bell sounds sending the boys to their dormitories. Ten o'clock, and the light appears on Dr. Parker's veranda across the street. I know that when he has taken the day's record for the Royal Asiatic Meteorological Bureau I shall be left all alone with the night sounds.

Eleven o'clock brings the shuffling, muffled sound of the water buffaloes, as the milkman leads them past the gates on their way to the pasture from which at five o'clock they will return. For everything in China is reversed. Even the cows are stabled during the day and pastured at night. A topsy-turvy, fantastic world it seems at first; a world that makes one's childhood speculations over the big globe and the Chinamen who must walk upside down seem quite reasonable.

At hour intervals all through the night I hear the night watchman beating his drum, blowing his horn and rattling his stick as he calls "coming, coming, coming," to frighten the thieves away and to avoid the embarrassment of being frightened himself.

An occasional Chinese passes by the window as speedily as possible, whooping and yelling at the top of his lungs to scare off all evil spirits as he nears the houses of the foreign devils. Upon the grave mounds in the lot in front of my window where for centuries coffins have been deposited, all the *wonks* (stray dogs) of the city collect night after night, to bark through the long darkness or to sit yapping at the moon.

But the noises and the pervasive smell of China soon ceased to disturb me. I was able to sleep serenely through it all, no longer feeling myself a stranger in an alien and rather terrifying land. . . .

. . . the Soochow Woman's Hospital . . . had been organized and built by Dr. Mildred Phillips. She had chosen a site next door to the Soochow Men's Hospital and near by was the Davidson School for Girls. All the buildings were close to the canal, spacious affairs, architectural hybrids of the East and West. When Dr. Phillips married and left Soochow the hospital was closed and unused for two or three years. . . .

The hospital was well equipped; and as we ordered drugs in large quantities from the leading wholesale druggists in the United States and paid no duty (the hospitals were under the Mission Board) there was no trouble on that score. . . .

When I arrived in Soochow I was one of a very small handful of foreign women doctors in all that huge country. . . .

The ignorance of the native physicians in their treatment of disease was remarkable. I was always stumbling over some queer treatment, and now and then, much to my surprise, discovering that these centuries-old ways were as effective as our modern methods; more often they were hideously primitive and immersed in superstition. . . .

All my experience with hospitals had been in San Francisco and Philadelphia where I had found them to be quiet and well-ordered places. I was totally unprepared for the daily disorder of a Chinese hospital. It is true that the doctors in charge were foreigners, but the nurses, the patients *and* the visitors were Chinese, and it was all new to them.

I started in a whirlwind of energy to open the hospital, establish some sort of system, clean up the building, the compound, the servants, the patients and the houses of the patients. I even had a few nebulous notions about cleaning up the city. My endeavors along these lines created considerable amusement among the Chinese who immediately gave me the nickname, *Tai Foong* (Great Wind or . . . Typhoon). They continued to call me this, behind my back, of course, for as long as I lived in Soochow.

The coming of the new year brought a change in the attitude of the people. They suddenly right-about-faced and grew confident. There were the usual percentages of success and failure but patients flocked to us and the fame of the hospital spread. Among my patients was the daughter of a *tao tai* [prefect] in Nganwui Province and from time to time the father sent a messenger two hundred miles to see and report the condition of his daughter.

The people permitted us to take many heretofore prohibited liberties. One little girl with tuberculosis of the hip joint consented to wear an extension apparatus, the first in Soochow. It was made at the hospital under my direction.

We were on our way at last. The first year there were twice as many patients as any other year in the history of the hospital and the second year there were three thousand more than the first. But I was not satisfied.

Hundreds and hundreds of children needed hospital care. Thousands of tortured feet were pleading for deliverance. Hundreds of thousands were doomed to lives of uselessness for the lack of a little medical aid. Day after day they came to us and we gave them cursory clinic care; then reluctantly sent them on their way. We had no place for them.

It finally reached the point where I couldn't stand it another minute. I decided that if it were at all possible I'd have a children's ward, and that it had to be possible. . . .

My request for a children's ward was endorsed by Bishop Galloway. He presented the project at the annual conference of the Women's Foreign Missionary Society of the Methodist Episcopal Church, South, who approved it. . . . The building was completed in the spring of 1895 but it could not be occupied until the following autumn when the beds and other furnishings arrived. . . .

With the beginning of the summer of 1895, my energy began to flag so seriously that I found it difficult to get through the necessary work; it was decided that it was time for me to take a rest. Sarah Poindexter came from her home and language study in Tsinanfu, and we started for our vacation in Japan. . . .

It was before Japan had become too Anglo-Japanese; and for a season we fell under the spell of its enchantment. Even then the cloven hoof was beginning to show in the many ceremonies and forms which, because of their newness, were done up with an extra amount of red tape and executed with a native tardiness. We waited a week for the necessary visas, obtained after arrival instead of before as they were necessary only for travel in the interior. But each day of that week was a joy, full of beauty and interest and vastly entertaining incongruities. . . .

I returned from my summer holiday in Japan refreshed and ready for my hospital work in Soochow, and looking forward to a busy year.

The first thing I did was to fall in love!

When Sarah and I, with the other missionaries who had joined us in Kobe, arrived in Shanghai we were met at the dock by the tall, handsome young man who had been left alone in charge of the hospital. This young man was John Burrus Fearn who had come out from America that spring, just a few weeks before my departure, to take charge of the Men's Hospital. He was replacing Dr. Edgerton H. Hart who had been substituting for Dr. Park during the latter's absence. He had been so lonely. He was glad to see us and welcome us home.

Less than one year later Dr. Fearn and I were married. This definitely settled my fate as far as my return to the United States was concerned for my husband expected to make China the field for his life work; as for me, I had grown to love the country so well that I welcomed the prospect of exile. But I am getting ahead of my story—

We all returned to Soochow and the very next day I remember going to the Men's Hospital to see the husband of one of my patients. As I passed an open room its disorderliness caught my eye. It was nearly noon but the bed was unmade and the unattractive red hospital blankets were in a heap, dragging the floor. Never, I thought, had I seen such an untidy room.

"Whose room is this?" I asked. "And why isn't the bed made at this time of the day?" I was ready to call the servants together for a scolding.

Dr. Fearn replied quietly that it was his room and that often the bed didn't get made at all. There was so much to be done for the sick.

I was surprised. "What, do you mean you live here in the hospital? Haven't you a house of your own?" We all had.

But it seemed there was no place for him. Suddenly I was filled with an overwhelming tenderness for this man who was so plucky and so uncomplaining, who had put in the whole hot summer working while we played, and who didn't even have a comfortable place to sleep. I scurried around and found a place for him with one of the missionary families and that was the beginning of a courtship which culminated in our marriage in Soochow on April 21, 1896.

It was odd that I had to go thousands of miles and across an ocean to meet a husband who was born in Jackson, Mississippi, and lived most of his life in Yazoo City, not far from my girlhood home of Holly Springs. As a matter of fact his sisters and I had been friends in those long ago debutante days when I was stealing jelly in the Governor's Mansion. . . .

Then came the day of my wedding, the one day I can't remember much about. I only know that it was a day of confusion. I delivered four babies to inconsiderate Chinese mothers who might have had them one day earlier—or later—before I could rush into my wedding gown and down into the parlor of my house. There missionaries, doctors and other foreign friends from as far away as Shanghai had already gathered to witness the ceremony—a very pretty one I've been told. And it must have been, with the flowers and the green grass, the cherry and peach trees blossoming, and one stately magnolia in full bloom in the front yard.

We went to Hangchow for our honeymoon and returned to take up our work in the adjoining hospitals as before, until the almost simultaneous arrivals of Dr. Park and Dr. Polk.

The beginning of our life together did not give promise of a useful happy marriage. For many years our attempts at adjustment seemed futile and many were the tempestuous disagreements from which we emerged with a courage born almost of despair. It could not have been otherwise, so different were the schools of life from which we have been graduated. My husband had grown up in the church. I had not. For every hour he had spent in Sunday School and church I had spent two in dancing and similar pleasures.

He was dominant and born to give orders just as definitely as I was born not to take them. I often told him that our life together would have been much happier had I been six thousand coolies. It took the Great War to make him realize that others had a right to their opinions even when those opinions were diametrically opposed to his. He became less critical of the "small sins" of his wife and friends.

I honestly endeavored to follow his wishes. One of his obsessions was that the day should begin with prayer and Bible reading, and that the Bible should be read through methodically once or twice a year. It was his desire to see me started on this course so we allotted ourselves five chapters daily and ten on Sunday, beginning with the first chapter of the Old Testament and not omitting a single begat.

This hour immediately after breakfast was to me the most important of the day. Wards had to be visited, the hospital inspected, operating room treatments given, and operations performed. While I read Isaiah, Jeremiah and other books of the Old Testament, all hospital work stopped. The nurses were annoyed, the Bible women (native teachers) lost control of the growing groups of clinic patients. The little child whose eyes fell out every time she sneezed or prayed, so slack were the muscles and ligaments, cried for me to come quickly for I had "magic" in my fingers and she would not let the nurses apply the packs. Patients pleaded frantically to see the doctor while the doctor read the Bible, wondering if any good could come from the reading at such a price.

One particular morning a Caesarean operation was set for eight o'clock. We began the reading of the five chapters of Isaiah while the patient was being prepared. With every nerve in my body on the jump we began our reading, and the nurses began coming for me. They stood outside the study door at my husband's unseeing back, but facing me.

I smiled as I nodded to them. "In a minute," I said, and asked my husband, "How many more chapters, dearest?"

At his reply, "Three," my heart almost jumped from its moorings.

Again a nurse appeared, adjuring me with clasped hands to come. "The patient is ready, Doctor."

Again I said, "In a minute," and to my husband, "Dearest, I

must go." His answer to the effect that the Bible reading was the most important duty of the day unloosed the rebellion in my heart, which even under ordinary circumstances was more like a repressed volcano than a normally functioning organ.

Springing up tempestuously I cried, "I can't bear it! I can't bear it! I wish I'd never seen the damned thing!" And flinging the Bible to the floor I rushed out, straight to the operating room where, after cleaning up, I got busy on one of the most vitally important of all abdominal operations. Fortunately the mother survived this combination of surgery and fury. The child had been dead several hours before the patient had been brought to us.

This little flare-up ended the Bible readings. The subject was never mentioned again but Dr. Fearn never forgave nor forgot, and I lost forever my taste, if I ever had any, for the Old Testament. . . .

Soon after this, my husband was transferred to Dzang Dzok, to open medical work there, and I accompanied him. It was the beginning of a period of confusion; of upheaval and tribulation for the Chinese; of travel, trial and great happiness for us. For during this time of chaos and change our child was to be born. It seemed a little strange but altogether delightful that I, who had delivered innumerable babies under every imaginable condition, should now be going to have one of my own.

Dzang Dzok was a city of wealth, aristocracy and great beauty, about a day's journey by boat from Soochow. . . .

Our experiences there were many-sided, for not only were we working hard to inaugurate hospital facilities, but our position as the only foreigners in the city made our home the center for great social activities and the meeting place for officials and the aristocracy. The people welcomed us at first with true Chinese hospitality and the clinic was well attended. Then fewer and fewer came; and finally the clinic was stopped entirely.

All over China at this time hostility to foreigners was increasing. Anti-foreign riots occurred frequently, and we came in for our share of the antagonism. We heard ugly rumors about ourselves; we were necromancers and worked only evil to people. When we passed children in their parents' arms their faces were covered with handkerchiefs to ward off the evils of our eyes. Constant and increasing reports reached us that we and all the Chinese who worked for us were to be killed.

Our old cook came back from market one day with word that our house was to be destroyed that night, and ourselves and our servants murdered. My husband called the servants together and told them that he had provided a boat for them; that they must leave at once for Soochow where they would find safety. They filed out silently. Ten minutes later they filed in again to say that they had talked it over and had decided that as we had been their friends in their hours of need they would remain with us in our trouble. In our over-wrought condition, this evidence of affection and loyalty almost brought us to tears, for the danger was far from imaginary.

Fortunately government troops arrived from Soochow in the later afternoon. In time the trouble blew over, but this was another experience which I'd rather not relive. . . .

I approached my confinement with the usual nervous trepidation of any normal expectant mother but I was not overly frightened. . . .

I had always considered birth a natural function of the female body and I had looked on it with a purely professional eye. I knew from actual experiences that the event of birth was never pleasant, the only variation being that some cases were worse than others. . . .

My own child was born on August 5, 1897, in the children's ward which I had built in the compound of the Soochow Woman's Hospital. I realized from my hemorrhagic condition, even before Dr. Polk and Dr. Poindexter were aware of it, that mine was a placenta praevia case, and I understood only too well what that meant. I had attended hundreds of these dangerous deliveries and I knew just what to expect, what should be done. They could not give me an anesthetic because that would increase the danger to mother and child, but if the doctors had not moved with such sure swiftness I would have died. I was conscious of each movement, and when a doctor's arm shot through the placenta to take the baby I suffered more than mere physical pain. I suffered the mental anguish that comes from too accurate a knowledge. Although my life hung in the balance for days both mother and baby survived. As a mother I forgot the momentary misery in the joy of the child; as a physician I remembered. The child was a girl, and we named her Elizabeth for my friend, Dr. Elizabeth Yates. . . .

I had always known that motherhood usually entailed sacrifices, but until Elizabeth's birth I had not realized how one's whole philosophy might be changed by a child. If Elizabeth's visit with us had not been so brief I might have been content to relinquish my practice and stay at home. I do not know. But I do know that if it had not been for Elizabeth I would have left undone many of the things that have been chalked up to my credit. I doubt if I would have contributed so much time and effort in later years to helping the children of China, both Chinese and foreign, if it had not been for her memory; nor would I have sought so hard to keep my days and nights filled with activity. . . .

At her birth the Chinese had brought us red eggs, symbol of good luck, and during her short life they were always her friends and willing followers.

Siau Sih Bah (Little Snow White) they called her and on more formal occasions *Fee Doo Siau Tia* (The Big Miss Fee). (The Chinese character most closely resembling Fearn is *Fee* and the "big" always is used to designate the first born.) . . .

Elizabeth . . . was . . . inordinately fond of the ragged urchins who played in and near our compound, bringing them in from the streets to have the midday meal with her. Her hospitality knew no bounds. One day when her tiffin party had grown to such enormous dimensions that it was impossible to crowd all the guests around our table we held a consultation with her and told her she could continue her daily tiffins on the one condition that she ask only as many guests as her special table would seat. She agreed. The table seated six and she almost always asked ten.

Like most foreign children born and raised in China she spoke the language of that country with greater fluency than she did her own and her tiffin parties were noisy affairs as chopsticks clicked and flew to hungry mouths and childish voices sing-songed in chatter. . . .

Elizabeth . . . , Dr. Fearn and I went to Kuling, high in the mountains, for a respite from the heat the summer of 1902. Elizabeth loved the gorgeous sunsets and always at sundown she was in a nervous state of excitement. She begged me to stay with her then to watch what she called "the opening of the gates of the sky." We returned to Soochow late in August and Elizabeth, never before sick a day in her life, fell ill with dysentery.

As I returned from my daily visits to patients one afternoon amah came to me. "Our baby is sick," she said.

"What is it?" I asked. She answered, "*Doo li za*" (diarrhea). But it wasn't, it was amoebic dysentery. Three days later she died in my arms as I sat in a rocking-chair by the window, just as the gates of the sky opened.

Ten years later Vedder discovered emetine as a specific cure for amoebic dysentery.

I was in a perfect frenzy after her death. I could not understand why death had passed by the beggars in their torn and filthy rags, the underfed who often went without their daily *san woen van*, the mentally afflicted, chained in some courtyard, and laid indiscriminate hands on my child, so protected, so well and so lovely. I decided that there must be some reason and until I found it—if ever I should—I could do no less than try to help those poor unfortunates. . . .

I had never been more unhappy in my heart, never happier in my work than at this time. We actually were accomplishing some of the things we had set out to do so long ago. During this period (1902–1907) the change in the attitude of the people toward surgery was surprising. It used to be that we had to cajole and connive to get them to let us perform the slightest operation; now they fairly beset us to do things that were nearly impossible. We had almost succeeded in rolling away that last obstacle; soon we should have dissecting taught in our medical college.

We had long ago outgrown the curtained hall which had served as our first medical college. By 1902 we were well on our way with a new building, already nearly fifty students were enrolled, and they were all from wealthy and hitherto decidedly anti-foreign families. I even had several applications from official families to take their daughters as medical students.

My husband resigned from the missionary board [in 1907] and we said good-by to China forever, or so we thought, and returned to America to spend the remainder of our days. But his heart was in China and I was more than willing to go back. So, in the face of many splendid opportunities in the United States, Dr. Fearn accepted an invitation to act as business manager of the Associated Protestant Missions in China. This time Shanghai, not Soochow, was to be our home. . . .

Shanghai is a city of hustling, bustling, hurrying, scurrying, jostling millions; a city of noise and confusion, tramcars clanging gongs, motor cars tooting horns, coolies sing-songing their interminable "ah ye—ah—yees." Chinese men walk the streets dressed in their traditional long silk gowns, blue cotton ones, or in the latest Western style. Some Chinese women are beautifully dressed, with smart waved heads, silk stockings and high-heeled shoes, and some cling to the divided skirts and embroidered jackets of tradition.

There are Japanese, Indians, Annamites and Europeans, a conglomeration of every nationality under the sun.

The traffic—foot, rickshaw, hand cart, wheelbarrow, bicycle, motor car, bus, tramcar—is stupendous.... There are crowds everywhere, not only hurrying and jostling crowds moving about the streets, but silent, gaping crowds....

Our new home was situated in Rue Palikao, number one hundred and twenty-two. The Chinese designated it as *Pah Sienjau*, or "At the Eight Fairy Bridge." The missionaries called it Poverty Flat. It was one of the first mission houses built in Shanghai, a large, rambling eight-room house in the same compound with old Trinity Church. We were in the French Concession, only a block or two from the race course and from Nanking Road, which the Chinese called *Tai Ma Loo* (Great Horse Road)....

We had so many rooms we didn't need that I furnished a few for the missionaries who came to Shanghai from Korea and the interior, and as long as we lived "At the Eight Fairy Bridge" the visiting missionaries were always welcome....

I was practically a stranger in Shanghai, and after the first excitement of settling a new home had subsided I found that I missed Soochow and my own work with a poignancy that made me restless and dissatisfied. A period of apparently aimless drifting was opening for me, although I was never without some work to do....

... all this time the seed of my pet idea was growing and growing. I wanted a hospital of my own. It became an obsession with me. I knew now, better than ever since encountering the snags in the way of a moderately successful private practice, the innumerable obstacles I must overcome before any such thing would be possible. But that did not prevent me from planning for it by day and dreaming of it by night until this wild idea became an integral part of my being.

[Fearn opened her private hospital on November 30, 1916.]

My great adventure had begun....

Two patients were staying in my house on Bubbling Well Road. By ten o'clock accommodations were ready for them and they were brought to the new sanatorium in ambulances. Between dawn and noon a small army of servants managed, by a magic known only to Chinese servants, to settle two rooms for my patients, to work wonders with the veranda and to bring the culinary department into running order....

For me the aftermath of that housewarming was deep despair. I had not seen the house, except in the most casual way, before deciding to take it. That day I had had a series of calamitous disappointments. By the time the last of my guests had departed I was limp and ragged with exhaustion, both mental and physical.

Out of the ten bedrooms at the disposal of patients, four were en suite, with no other entrance than through an adjoining room. I had horrible visions of stretchers being carried through rooms occupied by patients. There was no suitable room on the ground floor for a private office. I suddenly, and too late, awakened to the realization that beds, quantities of bed and table linen, towels, furniture, hospital accouterments, dishes, kitchen utensils, thousands of things, had to be purchased, and I had no money.

Where could I put the patients who had engaged rooms for the following week? How was I to manage the dietary kitchen, the very heart of a sanatorium such as I hoped to make mine? Who would I get for nurses? Must I depend on a kind providence and a few waifs and strays, wanderers to and from the Russian front? . . .

I found that by buying in small quantities, a bed at a time, I could avoid excessive outlay of expenditure and keep from running too deeply into debt. Everything I bought was of the best for I never believed in wasting money on makeshifts, and gradually my little plant grew into a well-organized, well-equipped, smoothly running sanatorium. But certainly I had never dreamed how many bills there would always be to pay.

In lieu of an office I placed my desk in an alcove in the entrance hall, well away from the staircase, and well lighted by a large bay window. I had my telephone by my side, bookcases behind me, and a Herring Hall combination safe within easy reach of my hand. At the start that safe was as empty as old Mother Hubbard's famous cupboard, but I sat there with great bravado and paid bills. I often wonder now what I paid them with.

Despite the bills I throve on the knowledge that I was responsible for the success or failure of this enterprise, and that what once had been a wild, impossible dream was now a reality. I vowed that no matter what obstacles were ahead I would make this thing a success. . . .

Chinese names have only one character, one syllable, while ours have several. Immediately upon a foreigner's arrival in China, his Chinese friends set about correcting this mistake, and a suitable character with a sound similar to the first syllable of the Western name is found. My husband's proper Chinese name became *Fee Ung*, which meant, according to the inflection, either "Dirty Dish Water" or "Prominent Front Tooth." Mine, *Wuan Me-tu*, almost forgotten because of my more appropriate nickname of *Tai Foong*, had come to mean only Dr. Walter but its real meaning was "Queen, Generous and Virtuous."

I often teased my husband about the difference in our names, his so funny and mine so flattering, and although he said little I am sure that he resented it. Indeed, all of our married life was tinged by the merest shadow of a professional jealousy. He had a strong sense of masculine protectiveness, just under the surface, and he was never so completely himself as when helping the sick and the weak. But in marrying a woman who took life with both hands and people as she found them, this protective instinct was more or less frustrated. He would much rather have had his wife sit at home and be managed by him. For her devotion to duty as a doctor, however, he had only admiration.

And now we were to become rivals in good earnest. He returned from France on October 1, 1919, to take up at once his appointment as medical superintendent and director of the Shanghai General Hospital. . . .

My husband had an apartment in the hospital, a corner suite on the fifth floor. The view from his window stretched out to that busiest of rivers, the Whangpoo, and over the surrounding city, of which the hospital seemed to be the center. At night it was like looking out over fairyland, with the lights of the tall buildings piercing the sky and the lower lights twinkling and blazing all around us.

When my husband became my professional rival I told him that I had no fear of him. His hospital was the largest in the Far East, but it was the most usual, it might be any hospital anywhere in the world; while mine, although it might be the smallest, certainly was the most unusual. I told him there was not another hospital like mine in the world. Laughingly he assured me that there wasn't; that there couldn't be anyone else quite so crazy as to attempt to run a hospital along the same extravagant lines.

We were friendly rivals, however, and I was genuinely glad to have his apartment to go to at night. It meant escaping from my own responsibilities for a few hours at least. He usually dined with me, or we dined out somewhere together, and returned to his rooms.

At seven o'clock in the morning my car was at the door of the General Hospital and half an hour later I was at the other end of town at my desk in the Fearn Sanatorium with the day's work begun. . . .

At eleven every morning, after the heavy work was done, clean white aprons, coats, gowns and caps were distributed among the staff. Altogether, there were usually fifty servants on the place, and the house servants in their immaculate uniforms were a joy to behold. Of course, all of the luxuries cost money but I managed to get all of the bills paid, although there was never much of a profit. . . .

Although the American flag flew over my sanatorium, it was as cosmopolitan as Shanghai itself. At one time, of my twelve trained nurses, two were American and the others Russian, Scotch, English, Swiss, Portuguese and Bohemian. The nationalities of my clientele varied quite as much. At one time, in sixteen beds I had sixteen patients of sixteen different nationalities.

My hospital *was* different. In the entire history of Shanghai there had never been one like it before, nor has there been one since.

One day as my husband was helping me struggle over my accounts he said, "Annie, if extravagance is a virtue you are indeed virtuous. The Chinese knew what they were about when they selected those particular characters to depict your name, for this is surely 'the hospital of the generous queen.' "

For some time the prospect of a country hospital had been brewing. . . .

When it finally opened [in 1926], the last word in magnificence and comfort, I realized that there was only one thing for me to do—close my hospital. . . .

The decision was made easier by two circumstances; one a happy instance, and the other the very serious illness of my husband.

At the beginning of his sickness, he had been asked to take over the medical superintendency and management of the new Country Hospital, a great tribute to him and to his work. . . .

Before putting this proposition to my husband, the Committee had obtained permission from the Shanghai Municipal Council for him to take over the work and still oversee the General Hospital. . . .

This evidence of the confidence of his confreres made those last weeks happier for us both.

As I look back over those seven weeks, it seems impossible that in his state of health he managed to carry out the work entrusted to him. . . .

I cannot speak of the last days of his illness. From the beginning we had known that his case was hopeless, but everything that kindness and friendship and medical knowledge could do was done. The last weeks of his life were spent in the work he loved and for which he had such great talent.

He possessed a rare administrative and executive ability, but because he had come to China as a missionary he had refused many attractive opportunities that would have taken him into business. . . .

For him, everything was made to serve a solemnly religious view of life. Yet there was a constant pull between the narrowness and intolerance of small town Southern Methodism . . . and the outward circumstances of his life, which constantly tended to liberate him. . . .

As for me, during the ten years that my sanatorium was in existence, there were frequent periods of utter discouragement, times when I seemed headed straight for financial ruin, when, but for friends and a native stubbornness which forced me to hang on, I would have given up the whole thing. Often now I wonder how I did it. But to whatever it was that upheld me I am grateful, for during those last sad weeks my husband often said to me,

"I didn't approve of your opening this hospital, Annie, but as I lie here I keep thinking how thankful I am for the care and comfort that surround me, and that it's all due to you."

He died on June 7, 1926. . . .

Those last days in Shanghai I remember as one remembers a horrible nightmare. . . .

. . . the mad turmoil of packing in the all-too-short intervals between farewell tiffins, teas, and dinners; saying good-by to friends; the empty rooms, the desolation, the awful, awful, anchorless feeling—

[Fearn returned to the United States in 1926.]

The thought of Shanghai pulled at me insistently, compellingly. I was restless and uprooted in the West; I had lost my place among my own people. . . .

One morning at breakfast I announced, "I'm going home." . . .

Almost shamefacedly I explained that I must finish out my cycle of Cathay. . . .

. . . it wasn't a mistake, my coming back. This was the same Shanghai I had pictured so often during my absence, the same bustling, thrilling city, busier than ever. Here were the hurrying pedestrians, charging from one side of the street to the other, oblivious of traffic; the same jostling mobs on the pavements and in the gutters; the same shops, the same sounds, the same smells! I had come home.

Margaret Sanger

(1879–1966)

Founder and leader of the American birth control movement, Margaret Sanger was born in Corning, New York, the third of four daughters of an Irish family of eleven children. Her mother, a devout Catholic, was exhausted by the births and the battle to raise the family on the income Sanger's freethinking father earned as a producer of stone monuments. From her father Sanger inherited her willingness to defy authority. From her mother, dead of tuberculosis at age forty-nine, Sanger inherited her sense of mission about women's need for reproductive freedom.

Sanger's choice of nursing as a career and her marriage to William Sanger, a handsome artist with progressive ideas, looked like conventional steps for one of the new breed of educated women emerging in American society at the turn of the century. What was different was that, when her husband introduced her to the avantgarde circles of bohemian New York in the early years of their marriage, she took the radical ideas seriously. And, when she attended poor women weakened by too frequent pregnancies, she was haunted by the memory of her mother's life and felt she had to do something about their dire need for birth control information. Moreover, when medical men brushed the need aside or laughed at the problem, Sanger was primed for rebellion.

Sanger's radical newspaper the *Woman Rebel*, launched in 1914, was a declaration of female independence based on her research on birth control techniques during a trip to Europe in 1913. It was also a classic radical action in the best tradition of leftist politics. Sanger printed material she knew would provoke prosecution, thereby giving publicity to her cause. Seven issues of the *Woman Rebel* came out before it was seized by the Post Office. Recognizing the value of the moment, Sanger prepared a pamphlet entitled *Family Limitation*, which gave detailed information on birth control techniques. She arranged for its distribution through the Industrial Workers of the World, then fled to Canada and Great Britain to escape her trial for sending forbidden material through the mails.

In Great Britain Sanger met and was influenced by the sex researcher Havelock Ellis, with whom she had an affair. Ellis toned down her radicalism and urged her to see sexual reform as a cause which could and should be pursued on its own merits, rather than as an aspect of socialism. By the time of her return to the United States in 1915, Sanger had become nationally famous for her work, her impending trial, and her widely distributed pamphlet.

She quickly organized her own clinic in the poor Brownsville section of Brooklyn and began demonstrating the use of diaphragms and advising her clients about birth control problems. The cause was publicized even more effectively when the clinic was raided and Sanger's sister and co-worker undertook a hunger strike in prison. Sanger herself served thirty days in jail, using her release as another opportunity for publicity.

Having mobilized and energized a grass-roots working-class birth control movement, Sanger found herself in the 1920s and 1930s obliged to fight in the courts for the right to distribute birth control information. The issues were constitutional and could not then be argued without convincing medical research. She was also involved in a bitter fight with the medical profession about whether birth control information could be made available through clinics or had to come only through medical consultation. Success in these battles was largely a matter of raising money, securing the most prestigious and effective legal help, and persuading middle-class supporters who influenced political parties that free access to birth control information was in their interests.

Sanger's later arguments for birth control stressed its eugenic value and linked its utility to happy family life. Middle-class support built her American Birth Control League into the national lobby which subsequently took on the name Planned Parenthood Federation of America. By 1923 she could back her arguments with solid medical research carried out under the auspices of her Birth Control Clinical Research Bureau in New York City. A network of some three hundred similar clinics across the country, staffed by women doctors and carrying out valuable research, followed.

During the 1920s and '30s Sanger had to smuggle European-made diaphragms into the country, and her final victory for the birth control movement was a decision from a federal court permitting the use of the mails to send contraceptive materials to physicians.

Unfailing in her concern for better contraceptive methods, Sanger raised money to fund research throughout her later years, and, at the end of her life, it was through her initiative that the work of the biologist Gregory Pincus was funded, leading to the develop-

ment of the Pill, Sanger's long-dreamed-of female-controlled physiological contraceptive.

In her youth a romantic radical, Sanger wrote her autobiography in the style of the romantic narrative, suppressing her insistence on sexual freedom and her liaisons with a number of
important lovers. Her papers show that she lived the life of freedom
she sought for all women, a freedom promised and respected by J.
Noah Slee, her second husband. Historians have been harsh with
Sanger for her determination to be recognized as *the* leader of the
birth control movement. However, her ambitions would be considered normal in a male reformer. Criticized by radicals for her shifting tactics, Sanger may be seen as a shrewd and practical strategist
who made sexual freedom possible for modern women, even though
political battles still rage about whether access to birth control may
be publicly funded.

MARGARET SANGER:
An Autobiography

I was the youngest of six, but after me others kept coming until
we were eleven. Our dolls were babies—living, wriggling bodies
to bathe and dress instead of lifeless faces that never cried or slept.
A pine beside the door was our Christmas tree. Father liked us to
use natural things and we had to rely upon ingenuity rather than
the village stores, so we decorated it with white popcorn and red
cranberries which we strung ourselves. Our most valuable gift was
that of imagination.

We had little time for recreation. School was five miles away
and we had to walk back and forth twice a day as well as perform
household duties. The boys milked the cow, tended the chickens,
and took care of Tom, the old white horse which pulled our sleigh
up and down the hill. The girls helped put the younger children to
bed, mended clothes, set the table, cleaned the vegetables, and
washed the dishes. We accepted all this with no sense of deprivation
or aggrievement, being, if anything, proud of sharing responsibility. . . .

We were all, brothers and sisters alike, healthy and strong,
vigorous and active; our appetites were curtailed only through ne-

cessity. We played the same games together and shared the same sports—baseball, skating, swimming, hunting. . . .

Father took little or no responsibility for the minute details of the daily tasks. I can see him when he had nothing on hand, laughing and joking or reading poetry. Mother, however, was everlastingly busy sewing, cooking, doing this and that. For so ardent and courageous a woman he must have been trying, and I still wonder at her patience. She loved her children deeply, but no one ever doubted that she idolized her husband, and through the years of her wedded life to her early death never wavered in her constancy. Father's devotion to mother, though equally profound, never evidenced itself in practical ways.

The relation existing between our parents was unusual for its day; they had the idea of comradeship and not merely loved but liked and respected each other. There was no quarreling or bickering; none of us had to take sides, saying, "Father is right," or, "Mother is right." We knew that if we pleased one we pleased the other, and such an atmosphere leaves its mark; we felt secure from emotional uncertainty, and were ourselves guided towards certainty in our future. . . . The century of the child had not yet been ushered in. . . .

Mother's loyalty to father was tested repeatedly. Hers were the responsibilities of feeding and clothing and managing on his income, combined with the earnings of the oldest children. But father's generosity took no cognizance of fact. Once he was asked to buy a dozen bananas for supper. Instead, he purchased a stalk of fifteen dozen, and on his way home gave every single one to schoolboys and girls playing at recess. On another occasion he showed up with eight of a neighbor's children; the ninth had been quarantined for diphtheria. They lived with us for two months, crowded into our beds, tucked in between us at the table. Mother welcomed them as she did his other guests. The house was always open. She was not so much social-minded as inherently hospitable. But with her frail body and slim pocketbook, it took courage to smile. . . .

Childhood is supposed to be a happy time. Mine was difficult, though I did not then think of it as a disadvantage nor do I now. . . .

Corning was not on the whole a pleasant town. Along the river flats lived the factory workers, chiefly Irish; on the heights above the rolling clouds of smoke that belched from the chimneys lived the owners and executives. The tiny yards of the former were asprawl with children; in the gardens on the hills only two or three played. This contrast made a track in my mind. Large families were associated with poverty, toil, unemployment, drunkenness, cruelty, fighting, jails; the small ones with cleanliness, leisure, freedom, light, space, sunshine.

The fathers of the small families owned their homes; the young-looking mothers had time to play croquet with their husbands in the evenings on the smooth lawns. Their clothes had style and charm, and the fragrance of perfume clung about them. They walked hand in hand on shopping expeditions with their children, who seemed positive in their right to live. To me the distinction between happiness and unhappiness in childhood was one of small families and of large families rather than of wealth or poverty.

In our home, too, we felt the economic pressure directly as-cribable to size. I was always apprehensive that we might some day be like the families on the flats, because we always had another baby coming, another baby coming. A new litter of puppies was interesting but not out of the ordinary; so, likewise, the cry of a new infant never seemed unexpected. Neither excited any more curiosity than breakfast or dinner. No one ever told me how they were born. I just knew.

I was little more than eight when I first helped wash the fourteen-and-a-half-pound baby after one of mother's deliveries. She had had a "terrible hard time," but father had pulled her through, and, in a few weeks, tired and coughing, she was going about her work, believing as usual that her latest was the prize of perfect babies. Mother's eleven children were all ten-pounders or more, and both she and father had a eugenic pride of race. I used to hear her say that not one of hers had a mark or blemish, although she had the utmost compassion for those who might have cleft palates, crossed eyes, or be "born sick." . . .

. . . we moved into town, still on the western hills. It marked the beginning of my adolescence, and such breaks are always dis-turbing. In the house in the woods we had all been children together, but now some of us were growing up.

Nevertheless, there were always smaller ones to be put to bed, to be rocked to sleep; there were feet and knees to be scrubbed and hands to be washed. Although we had more space, home study sometimes seemed to me impossible. The living room was usually occupied by the older members of the family, and the bedrooms were cold. I kept up in my lessons, but it was simply because I enjoyed them.

In most schools teachers and pupils then were natural enemies, and the one I had in the eighth grade was particularly adept at arousing antagonism. She apparently disliked her job and the youngsters under her care as much as we hated her. Sarcasm was both her defense and weapon of attack. One day in mid-June I was delayed in getting off for school. Well aware that being tardy was a heinous crime, I hurried, pulling and tugging at my first pair of kid gloves, which Mary had just given me. But the bell had rung two minutes before I walked into the room, flushed and out of breath.

The teacher had already begun the class. She looked up at the interruption. "Well, well, Miss Higgins, so your ladyship has arrived at last! Ah, a new pair of gloves! I wonder that she even deigns to come to school at all."

Giggles rippled around me as I went into the cloakroom and laid down my hat and gloves. I came back, praying the teacher would pay no more attention to me, but as I walked painfully to my seat she continued repeating with variations her mean comments. Even when I sat down she did not stop. I tried to think of something else, tried not to listen, tried to smile with the others. I endured it as long as I could, then took out my books, pyramiding arithmetic, grammar, and speller, strapped them up, rose, and left.

Mother was amazed when I burst in on her. "I will never go back to that school again!" I exclaimed dramatically. "I have finished forever! I'll go to jail, I'll work, I'll starve, I'll die! But back to that school and teacher I will never go!"

My sisters selected Claverack College and Hudson River Institute, about three miles from the town of Hudson in the Catskill Mountains. Here, in one of the oldest coeducational institutions in the country, the Methodist farmers of the Dutch valley enrolled their sons and daughters. . . . One sister paid my tuition and the other bought my books and clothes; for my board and room I was to work.

Going away to school was epochal in my life. The self-contained family group was suddenly multiplied to five hundred strangers, all living and studying under one roof. The girls' dormitory was at one end, the boys' at the other, but we shared the same dining room and sat together in classes; occasionally a boy could call on a girl in the reception hall if a teacher were present. I liked best the attitude of the teachers; they were not so much policemen as companions and friends, and their instruction was more individual and stimulating than at Corning. . . .

We scribbled during study periods, debated in the evenings. Without always digesting them but with great positiveness I carried over many of the opinions I had heard expounded at home. To most of the boys and girls those Saturday mornings when the more ambitious efforts were offered represented genuine torture. They stuttered and stammered painfully. I was just as nervous—more so probably. Nevertheless, I was so ardent for suffrage, for anything which would "emancipate" women and humanity, that I was eager to proclaim theories of my own.

Father was still the spring from which I drank, and I sent long letters home, getting in reply still longer ones, filled with ammunition about the historical background of the importance of women—Helen of Troy, Ruth, Cleopatra, Poppaea, famous queens, women authors and poets.

When news spread that I was to present my essay, "Women's Rights," the boys, following the male attitude which most people have forgotten but which every suffragette well remembers, jeered and drew cartoons of women wearing trousers, stiff collars, and smoking huge cigars. Undeterred, I was spurred on to think up new arguments. I studied and wrote as never before, stealing away to the cemetery and standing on the monuments over the graves. Each day in the quiet of the dead I repeated and repeated that speech out loud. What an essay it was!

"Votes for Women" banners were not yet flying, and this early faint bleating of mine aroused little enthusiasm. I turned then to an equally stern subject. The other students had automatically accepted the cause of solid money. I espoused free silver.

I spent three happy years at Claverack. The following season I decided to try my hand at teaching, then a ladylike thing to do. A position was open to me in the first grade of a new public school in southern New Jersey. The majority of the pupils—Poles, Hungarians, Swedes—could not speak English. In they came regularly. I was beside myself to know what to do with eighty-four children who could not understand a word I said. I loved those small, black-haired and tow-headed urchins who became bored with sitting and, on their own, began stunts to entertain themselves. But I was so tired at the end of the day that I often lay down before dressing for dinner and awakened the next morning barely in time to start the routine. . . .

I had been struggling for only a brief while when father summoned me home to nurse mother.

She was weak and pale and the high red spots on her cheek bones stood out startlingly against her white face. . . .

It was a folk superstition that a consumptive who survived through the month of March would live until November. Mother died on the thirty-first of the month, leaving father desolate and inconsolable. I came flying home. . . .

I had to take mother's place—manage the finances, order the meals, pay the debts. There was nothing left for my clothing nor for any outside diversions. All that could be squeezed out by making this or that do had to go for shoes or necessities for the younger brothers. Mend, patch, sew as you would, there was a limit to the endurance of trousers, and new ones had to be purchased.

To add to my woes, father seemed to me, who was sensitive to criticism, suddenly metamorphosed from a loving, gentle, benevolent parent into a most aggravating, irritating tyrant; nobody in any fairy tale I had ever read was quite so cruel. He who had given us the world in which to roam now apparently wanted to put us behind prison bars. His unreasonableness was not directed towards the boys, who were in bed as soon as lessons were done, but towards his daughters, Ethel and me. Whatever we did was wrong. He objected particularly to young men. . . .

Then came the climax. Ethel and I had gone to an open-air concert. On the stroke of ten we were a full block away from home running with all our might. When we arrived, three minutes late, the house was in utter darkness—not a sight nor sound of a living creature anywhere. We banged and knocked. We tried the front door, the back, and the side, then again the front. It opened part way; father looked out, reached forth a hand, and caught Ethel's arm saying, "This outrageous behavior is not your fault. Come in." With that he pulled her inside, and the door slammed, leaving me in the dark, stunned and bewildered. I did not know this monster.

Hurt beyond words, I sat down on the steps, worrying not only about this night but about the next day and the next, concerned over the children left at home with this new kind of father. I was sure if I waited long enough he would come out for me, but it was a chilly evening in October. I had no wrap, and began to grow very cold.

I walked away from the house, trying to decide where I should go and what I should do. I could not linger on the streets indefinitely, with the possibility of encountering some tipsy factory hand or drummer passing through. At first there seemed no one to turn to. Finally, exhausted by stress of emotion, I went to the home of the girl who had been with us at the concert. She had not yet gone to bed, and her mother welcomed me so hospitably that I shall be eternally grateful. The next morning she lent me carfare to go to Elmira, where I had friends with whom I could stay. . . .

Father and I tried to talk it over, but we could not meet on the old ground; between us a deep silence had fallen. . . .

Though the immediate occasion for reading medical books had ceased with mother's death, I had never, during these months, lost my deep conviction that perhaps she might have been saved had I had sufficient knowledge of medicine. This was linked up with my latent desire to be of service in the world. The career of a physician seemed to fulfill all my requirements. I could not at the moment see how the gap in education from Claverack to medical school was to be bridged. Nevertheless, I could at least make a start with nursing.

. . . father, though he proclaimed his belief in perfect independence of thought and mind, could not approve nursing as a profession, even when I told him that some of the nicest girls were going into it. "Well, they won't be nice long," he growled. "It's no sort of work for girls to be doing." My argument that he himself had taught us to help other people had no effect.

Father's notions, however, were not going to divert me from my intention; no matter how peaceful the home atmosphere had become, still I had to get out and try my wings. For six months more we jogged along, then, just a year after mother had died, Esther asked me to visit her in New York. I really wanted to train in the city, but her mother knew someone on the board of the White Plains Hospital, which was just initiating a school. There I was accepted as a probationer. . . .

Within a short period I considered myself thoroughly inured to what many look upon as the unpleasant aspects of nursing; the sight of blood never made me squeamish and I had watched operations, even on the brain, with none of the usual sick giddiness.

Then one day the driver of a Macy delivery wagon, who had fallen off the seat, was brought in with a split nose. I was holding the basin for the young doctor who was stitching it up, when one of the other nurses said something to tease him. He dropped his work, leaving the needle and cat-gut thread sticking across the patient's nose, and chased her out of the room and down the hall. The patient, painless under a local anesthetic, gazed mildly after them; but the idea that doctor and nurse could be so callous as to play jokes horrified me.

When pursuer and pursued returned they found me in a heap on the floor, the basin tipped over beside me, instruments and sponges scattered everywhere. The patient was still sitting quietly waiting for all the foolishness to stop. I am glad to say this was the one and only time I ever fainted on duty. . . .

Often I was called in the middle of the night on a maternity case, perhaps ten miles away from the hospital, where I had to sterilize the water and boil the forceps over a wood fire in the kitchen stove while the doctor scrubbed up as best he could. Many times labor terminated before he could arrive and I had to perform the delivery by myself.

To see a baby born is one of the greatest experiences that a human being can have. Birth to me has always been more awe-inspiring than death. As often as I have witnessed the miracle, held the perfect creature with its tiny hands and feet, each time I have felt as though I were entering a cathedral with prayer in my heart.

There is so little knowledge in the world compared with what there is to know. Always I was deeply affected by the trust patients, rich or poor, male or female, old or young, placed in their nurses. When we appeared they seemed to say, "Ah, here is someone who can tell us." Mothers asked me pathetically, plaintively, hopefully, "Miss Higgins, what should I do not to have another baby right away?" I was at a loss to answer their intimate questions, and passed them along to the doctor, who more often than not snorted, "She ought to be ashamed of herself to talk to a young girl about things like that."

All such problems were thus summarily shoved aside. We had one woman in our hospital who had had several miscarriages and six babies, each by a different father. Doctors and nurses knew every time she went out that she would soon be back again, but it was not their business or anybody's business; it was just "natural."

To be polished off neatly, the nurses in training were assigned to one of the larger city hospitals in which to work during the last three or six months of our course. Mine was the Manhattan Eye and Ear at Forty-first Street and Park Avenue, across the street from the Murray Hill Hotel, and I welcomed the chance to see up-to-date equipment and clockwork discipline. My new environment was considerably less harsh and intense, more comfortable and leisurely. . . .

At one of the frequent informal dances held there my doctor partner received a message—not a call, but a caller. His architect wanted to go over blueprints with him. "Come along," he invited. "See whether you think my new house is going to be as fine as I do."

The architect was introduced. "This is William Sanger."

The three of us bent over the plans. The doctor was the only one unaware of the sudden electric quality of the atmosphere.

At seven-thirty the next morning when I went out for my usual "constitutional," Bill Sanger was on the doorstep. He had that type of romantic nature which appealed to me, and had been waiting there all night. We took our walk together that day and regularly for many days thereafter, learning about each other, exploring each other's minds, and discovering a community of ideas and ideals. His fineness fitted in with my whole destiny, if I can call it such, just as definitely as my hospital training. . . .

Bill was an architect only by profession; he was pure artist by temperament. Although his heart was not in mechanical drawing, he did it well. Stanford White once told me he was one of the six best draftsmen in New York. He confided to me his dream of eventually being able to leave architecture behind and devote himself to painting, particularly murals. . . .

On one of our rambles he idly pulled at some vines on a stone wall, and then, with his hands, tilted my face for a kiss. The next morning, to my mortification, four telltale finger marks were outlined on my cheek by poison ivy blisters. The day after that, my face was swollen so that my eyes were tight shut, and I was sick for two months; since my training was finished, I was sent home to convalesce. . . .

For a while I stayed at Corning, and then went back to New York to start nursing in earnest. On one of my free afternoons in August, Bill and I went for a drive, and he suggested we stop in at the house of a friend of his who was a minister. All had been prepared. License and rice were waiting. And so we were married. . . .

In our case . . . obstacles arose with undue speed.

I was not well. I was paying the cost of long hours in mother's closely confined room and of continuous overwork in the hospital. Medical advice was to go West to live, but I would not go without Bill, and he had a commission which kept him in New York. Accordingly, I was packed off to a small semi-sanitarium near Saranac where the great Dr. Trudeau, specialist in pulmonary tuberculosis, was consulted. . . .

In this gloomy environment I rested, preparing myself for motherhood. . . .

Just before it was time for the baby to be born I returned to the little apartment on St. Nicholas Avenue at 149th Street, then practically suburban. . . .

When towards three o'clock one morning I felt the first thin, fine pains of warning, Bill tried one after the other of our obstetricians—not one could be located. He had to run around the corner to the nearest general practitioner. Due almost as much to this young doctor's inexperience as to my physical state, the ordeal was unusually hard, but the baby Stuart . . . was perfectly healthy, strong, and sturdy. . . .

I enjoyed my literary activities along with my children [Sanger had two other children—Grant and Peggy], and Bill encouraged me. "You go ahead and finish your writing. I'll get the dinner and wash the dishes." And what is more he did it, drawing the shades, however, so that nobody could see him. He thought I should make a career of it instead of limiting myself to small-town interests.

Both Bill and I were feeling what amounted to a world hunger, the pull and haul towards wider horizons. For him Paris was still over the next hill. I was not able to express my discontent with the futility of my present course, but after my experience as a nurse with fundamentals this quiet withdrawal into the tame domesticity of the pretty riverside settlement seemed to be bordering on stagnation. I felt as though we had drifted into a swamp, but we would not wait for the tide to set us free.

It was hopeless to emphasize the importance of practical necessities to an artist, and consequently I decided to resume nursing in order to earn my share. We had spent years building our home and used it only for a brief while. I was glad to leave when, in one of our financial doldrums, we plunged back into the rushing stream of New York life. . . .

We took an apartment way uptown. It was the old-fashioned railroad type—big, high-ceilinged, with plenty of room, air, and light. The children's grandmother came to live with us and her presence gave me ease of mind when I was called on a case; my children were utterly safe in her care.

Headlong we dived into one of the most interesting phases of life the United States has ever seen. Radicalism in manners, art, industry, morals, politics was effervescing, and the lid was about to blow off in the Great War. John Spargo, an authority on Karl Marx, had translated *Das Kapital* into English, thus giving impetus to Socialism. Lincoln Steffens had published *The Shame of the Cities*, George Fitzpatrick had produced *War, What For?* a strange and wonderful arraignment of capitalism, which sold thousands of copies.

The names of Cézanne, Matisse, and Picasso first became familiar sounds on this side of the Atlantic at the time of the notable Armory Exhibition, when outstanding examples of impressionist and cubist painting were imported from Europe. But there was so much of eccentricity—a leg on top of a head, a hat on a foot, the *Nude Descending a Staircase*, all in the name of art—that you had to close one eye to look at it. The Armory vibrated; it shook New York.

Although Bill had studied according to the old school, he could see the point of view of the radical in art, and in politics as well. His attitude towards the underdog was much like father's. He had always been a Socialist, although not active, and held his friend Eugene V. Debs in high esteem. . . .

Intellectuals were then flocking to enlist under the flag of humanitarianism, and as soon as anybody evinced human sympathies he was deemed a Socialist. My own personal feelings drew me towards the individualist, anarchist philosophy, and I read Kropotkin, Bakunin, and Fourier, but it seemed to me necessary to approach the ideal by way of Socialism; as long as the earning of food, clothing, and shelter was on a competitive basis, man could never develop any true independence.

Therefore, I joined the Socialist Party, Local Number Five, itself something of a rebel in the ranks, which, against the wishes of the central authority, had been responsible for bringing Bill Haywood East after his release from prison. The members—Italian, Jewish,

Russian, German, Spanish, a pretty good mixture—used the rooms over a neighborhood shop as a meeting place and there they were to be found every evening reading and discussing politics.

Somebody had donated a sum of money to be spent to interest women in Socialism. As proof that we were not necessarily like the masculine, aggressive, bulldog, window-smashing suffragettes in England, I, an American and a mother of children, was selected to recruit new members among the clubs of working women. The Scandinavians, who had a housemaids' union, were the most satisfactory; they already leaned towards liberalism. . . .

Everybody else was amused when the Sangers went to a Socialist meeting. If I had an idea, I leaned over and whispered it to Bill, who waved his hand and called for attention. "Margaret has something to say on that. Have you heard Margaret?" Many men might have labeled my opinions silly, and, indeed, I was not at all sure of them myself, but Bill thought if I had one, it was worth hearing.

John Block and his wife, Anita, were ardent workers for the cause. She was a grand person, a Barnard graduate and editor of the woman's page of the *Call*. She telephoned me one evening, "Will you help me out? We have a lecture scheduled for tonight and our speaker is unable to come. Won't you take her place?"

"But I can't speak. I've never made a speech in my life."

"You'll simply have to do it. There isn't anybody I can get, and I'm depending on you."

"How many will be there?" I asked.

"Only about ten. You've nothing to be frightened of."

But I was frightened—thoroughly so. I could not eat my supper. Shaking and quaking I faced the little handful of women who had come after their long working hours for enlightenment. Since I did not consider myself qualified to speak on labor, I switched the subject to health, with which I was more familiar. This, it appeared, was something new. They were pleased and said to Anita, "Let's have more health talks." The second time we met the audience had swelled to seventy-five and arrangements were made to continue the lectures, if such they could be called, which I prepared while my patients slept.

The young mothers in the group asked so many questions about their intimate family life that I mentioned it to Anita. "Just the thing," she said. "Write up your answers and we'll try them out in the *Call*." The result was the first composition I had ever done for publication, a series under the general title, *What Every Mother*

Should Know. I attempted . . . to introduce the impersonality of nature in order to break through the rigid consciousness of sex on the part of parents, who were inclined to be too intensely personal about it.

Then Anita requested a second series to be called *What Every Girl Should Know.* The motif was, "If the mother can impress the child with the beauty and wonder and sacredness of the sex function, she has taught it the first lesson."

These articles ran along for three or four weeks until one Sunday morning I turned to the *Call* to see my precious little effort, and, instead, encountered a newspaper box two columns wide in which was printed in black letters,

WHAT EVERY GIRL SHOULD KNOW

N
O
T
H
I
N
G
!

BY ORDER OF
THE POST-OFFICE DEPARTMENT

The words gonorrhea and syphilis had occurred in that article and Anthony Comstock, head of the New York Society for the Suppression of Vice, did not like them. By the so-called Comstock Law of 1873, which had been adroitly pushed through a busy Congress on the eve of adjournment, the Post Office had been given authority to decide what might be called lewd, lascivious, indecent, or obscene, and this extraordinary man had been granted the extraordinary power, alone of all citizens of the United States, to open any letter or package or pamphlet or book passing through the mails and, if he wished, lay his complaint before the Post Office. So powerful had his society become that anything to which he objected in its name was almost automatically barred; he had turned out to be sole censor for ninety million people.

During these years in New York trained nurses were in great demand. Few people wanted to enter hospitals; they were afraid they might be "practiced" upon, and consented to go only in desperate emergencies. Sentiment was especially vehement in the matter of having babies. A woman's own bedroom, no matter how inconveniently arranged, was the usual place for her lying-in. I was not sufficiently free from domestic duties to be a general nurse, but I could ordinarily manage obstetrical cases because I was notified far enough ahead to plan my schedule. And after serving my two weeks I could get home again.

Sometimes I was summoned to small apartments occupied by young clerks, insurance salesmen, or lawyers, just starting out, most of them under thirty and whose wives were having their first or second baby. They were always eager to know the best and latest method in infant care and feeding. In particular, Jewish patients, whose lives centered around the family, welcomed advice and followed it implicitly.

But more and more my calls began to come from the Lower East Side, as though I were being magnetically drawn there by some force outside my control. I hated the wretchedness and hopelessness of the poor, and never experienced that satisfaction in working among them that so many noble women have found. My concern for my patients was now quite different from my earlier hospital attitude. I could see that much was wrong with them which did not appear in the physiological or medical diagnosis. A woman in childbirth was not merely a woman in childbirth. My expanded outlook included a view of her background, her potentialities as a human being, the kind of children she was bearing, and what was going to happen to them.

The wives of small shopkeepers were my most frequent cases, but I had carpenters, truck drivers, dishwashers, and pushcart vendors. I admired intensely the consideration most of these people had for their own. Money to pay doctor and nurse had been carefully saved months in advance—parents-in-law, grandfathers, grandmothers, all contributing.

As soon as the neighbors learned that a nurse was in the building they came in a friendly way to visit, often carrying fruit, jellies, or gefüllter [sic] fish made after a cherished recipe. . . . Always back of the little gift was the question, "I am pregnant (or my daughter, or my sister is). Tell me something to keep from having another baby. We cannot afford another yet."

I tried to explain the only two methods I had ever heard of among the middle classes, both of which were invariably brushed aside as unacceptable. They were of no certain avail to the wife because they placed the burden of responsibility solely upon the husband—a burden which he seldom assumed. What she was seeking was self-protection she could herself use, and there was none. . . .

The utmost depression came over me as I approached this surreptitious region. Below Fourteenth Street I seemed to be breathing a different air, to be in another world and country where the people had habits and customs alien to anything I had ever heard about. . . .

Pregnancy was a chronic condition among the women of this class. Suggestions as to what to do for a girl who was "in trouble" or a married woman who was "caught" passed from mouth to mouth—herb teas, turpentine, steaming, rolling downstairs, inserting slippery elm, knitting needles, shoehooks. When they had word of a new remedy they hurried to the drugstore, and if the clerk were inclined to be friendly he might say, "Oh, that won't help you, but here's something that may." . . . On Saturday nights I have seen groups of from fifty to one hundred with their shawls over their heads waiting outside the office of a five-dollar abortionist.

Each time I returned to this district, which was becoming a recurrent nightmare, I used to hear that Mrs. Cohen "had been carried to a hospital, but had never come back," or that Mrs. Kelly "had sent the children to a neighbor and had put her head into the gas oven." Day after day such tales were poured into my ears—a baby born dead, great relief—the death of an older child, sorrow but again relief of a sort—the story told a thousand times of death from abortion and children going into institutions. I shuddered with horror as I listened to the details and studied the reasons back of them—destitution linked with excessive childbearing. . . .

Then one stifling mid-July day of 1912 I was summoned to a Grand Street tenement. My patient was a small, slight Russian Jewess, about twenty-eight years old, of the special cast of feature to which suffering lends a madonna-like expression. The cramped three-room apartment was in a sorry state of turmoil. Jake Sachs, a truck driver scarcely older than his wife, had come home to find the three children crying and her unconscious from the effects of a self-induced abortion. He had called the nearest doctor, who in turn had sent for me. Jake's earnings were trifling, and most of them had gone to keep the none-too-strong children clean and properly fed. But his wife's ingenuity had helped them to save a little, and this he was glad to spend on a nurse rather than have her go to a hospital.

The doctor and I settled ourselves to the task of fighting the septicemia. Never had I worked so fast, never so concentratedly. The sultry days and nights were melted into a torpid inferno. It did not seem possible there could be such heat, and every bit of food, ice, and drugs had to be carried up three flights of stairs.

Jake was more kind and thoughtful than many of the husbands I had encountered. He loved his children, and had always helped his wife wash and dress them. He had brought water up and carried garbage down before he left in the morning, and did as much as he could for me while he anxiously watched her progress.

After a fortnight Mrs. Sachs' recovery was in sight. Neighbors, ordinarily fatalistic as to the results of abortion, were genuinely pleased that she had survived. She smiled wanly at all who came to see her and thanked them gently, but she could not respond to their hearty congratulations. She appeared to be more despondent and anxious than she should have been, and spent too much time in meditation.

At the end of three weeks, as I was preparing to leave the fragile patient to take up her difficult life once more, she finally voiced her fears, "Another baby will finish me, I suppose?"

"It's too early to talk about that," I temporized.

But when the doctor came to make his last call, I drew him aside. "Mrs. Sachs is terribly worried about having another baby."

"She well may be," replied the doctor, and then he stood before her and said, "Any more such capers, young woman, and there'll be no need to send for me."

"I know, doctor," she replied timidly, "but," and she hesitated as though it took all her courage to say it, "what can I do to prevent it?"

The doctor was a kindly man, and he had worked hard to save her, but such incidents had become so familiar to him that he had long since lost whatever delicacy he might once have had. He laughed good-naturedly. "You want to have your cake and eat it too, do you? Well, it can't be done."

Then picking up his hat and bag to depart he said, "Tell Jake to sleep on the roof."

I glanced quickly at Mrs. Sachs. Even through my sudden tears I could see stamped on her face an expression of absolute despair. We simply looked at each other, saying no word until the door had closed behind the doctor. Then she lifted her thin, blue-veined hands and clasped them beseechingly. "He can't understand. He's only a man. But you do, don't you? Please tell me the secret, and I'll never breathe it to a soul. *Please!*"

What was I to do? I could not speak the conventionally comforting phrases which would be of no comfort. Instead, I made her as physically easy as I could and promised to come back in a few days to talk with her again. A little later, when she slept, I tiptoed away.

Night after night the wistful image of Mrs. Sachs appeared before me. I made all sorts of excuses to myself for not going back. I was busy on other cases; I really did not know what to say to her or how to convince her of my own ignorance; I was helpless to avert such monstrous atrocities. Time rolled by and I did nothing.

The telephone rang one evening three months later, and Jake Sachs' agitated voice begged me to come at once; his wife was sick again and from the same cause. For a wild moment I thought of sending someone else, but actually, of course, I hurried into my uniform, caught up my bag, and started out. All the way I longed for a subway wreck, and explosion, anything to keep me from having to enter that home again. But nothing happened, even to delay me. I turned into the dingy doorway and climbed the familiar stairs once more. The children were there, young little things.

Mrs. Sachs was in a coma and died within ten minutes. I folded her still hands across her breast, remembering how they had pleaded with me, begging so humbly for the knowledge which was her right. I drew a sheet over her pallid face. Jake was sobbing, running his hands through his hair and pulling it out like an insane person. Over and over again he wailed, "My God! My God! My God!"

I left him pacing desperately back and forth, and for hours I myself walked and walked and walked through the hushed streets. When I finally arrived home and let myself quietly in, all the household was sleeping. I looked out my window and down upon the dimly lighted city. Its pains and griefs crowded in upon me, a moving picture rolled before my eyes with photographic clearness: women writhing in travail to bring forth little babies; the babies themselves naked and hungry, wrapped in newspapers to keep them from the cold; six-year-old children with pinched, pale, wrinkled faces, old in concentrated wretchedness, pushed into gray and fetid cellars. . . .

As I stood there the darkness faded. The sun came up and threw its reflection over the house tops. It was the dawn of a new day in my life also. The doubt and questioning, the experimenting and trying, were now to be put behind me. I knew I could not go back merely to keeping people alive.

I went to bed, knowing that no matter what it might cost, I was finished with palliatives and superficial cures; I was resolved to seek out the root of evil, to do something to change the destiny of mothers whose miseries were vast as the sky. . . .

How were mothers to be saved? I went through many revolving doors, looked around, and, not finding what I was seeking, came out again. I talked incessantly to everybody who seemed to have social welfare at heart. . . .

In order to ascertain something about this subject which was so mysterious and so unaccountably forbidden, I spent almost a year in the libraries—the Astor, the Lenox, the Academy of Medicine, the Library of Congress, and dozens of others. Hoping that psychological treatises might inform me, I read Auguste Forel and Iwan Block. At one gulp I swallowed Havelock Ellis' *Psychology of Sex*, and had psychic indigestion for months thereafter. I was not shocked, but this mountainous array of abnormalities made me spiritually ill. So many volumes were devoted to the exceptional, and so few to the maladjustments of normal married people, which were infinitely more numerous and urgent. . . .

The pursuit of my quest took me away from home a good deal. The children used to come in after school and at once hunt for me. "Where's mother?" was the usual question. If they found me at my mending basket they all leaped about for joy, took hands and danced, shouting, "Mother's home, mother's home, mother's sewing." Sewing seemed to imply a measure of permanence.

I, too, wanted to drive away the foreboding barrier of separation by closer contact with them. I wanted to have them solely to myself, to feed, to bathe, to clothe them myself. I had heard of the clean, wind-swept Cape Cod dunes, which appeared to be as far from the ugliness of civilization as I could get. . . .

Big Bill [Haywood, the I.W.W. leader] was one of the few who saw what I was aiming at, although fearful that my future might involve the happiness of my children. Even he did not feel that the small-family question was significant enough to be injected into the labor platform. Nevertheless, as we rambled up and down the beach he came to my aid with that cheering encouragement of which I was so sorely in need. He never wasted words in advising me to "wait." Instead, he suggested that I go to France and see for myself the conditions resulting from generations of family limitation in that country. This struck me as a splendid idea, because it would also give Bill Sanger a chance to paint instead of continuing to build suburban houses.

The trip to Europe seemed so urgent that no matter what sacrifices had to be made, we decided to make them when we came to them. In the fall we sold the house at Hastings, gave away some of our furniture and put the rest in storage. Although we did not realize it at the time, our gestures indicated a clean sweep of the past. . . .

Bill found a studio on Montparnasse, just back of the Station. Again and again he came home aglow with news of meeting the great Matisse and other revolutionary painters barely emerging from obscurity. . . .

The parents of France . . . had settled the matter to their own satisfaction. Their one or two children were given all the care and advantages of French culture. I was struck with the motherly attention bestowed by our *femme de chambre* upon her only child. She came promptly to work, but nothing could persuade her to arrive before Jean had been taken to his school, and nothing could prevent her leaving promptly at noon to fetch him for his luncheon.

When Bill Hayward began taking me into the homes of the syndicalists, I found perfect acceptance of family limitation and its relation to labor. "Have you just discovered this?" I asked each woman I met.

"Oh, no, *Maman* told me."

"Well, who told her?"

"*Grandmère*, I suppose." . . .

Some of the contraceptive formulas which had been handed down were almost as good as those of today. Although they had to make simple things, mothers prided themselves on their special recipes for suppositories as much as on those for *pot au feu* or wine. . . .

Bill was happy in his studio, but I could find no peace. Each day I stayed, each person I met, made it worse. A whole year had been given over to this inactive, incoherent brooding. Family and friends had been generous in patience. I had added to my personal experience statistics from Glasgow and the little formulas I had gathered from the French peasants. With this background I had practically reached the exploding point. I could not contain my ideas, I wanted to get on with what I had to do in the world.

The last day of the year, December 31, 1913, Bill and I said good-by, unaware the parting was to be final. With the children I embarked at Cherbourg for home. . . .

I knew something must be done to rescue those women who were voiceless; someone had to express with white hot intensity the conviction that they must be empowered to decide for themselves when they should fulfill the supreme function of motherhood. . . . To this end I conceived the idea of a magazine to be called the *Woman Rebel*, dedicated to the interests of working women. . . .

I fully recognized I must refrain from acts which I could not carry through. So many movements had been issuing defiances without any ultimate goal . . .

With as crystal a view as that which had come to me after the death of Mrs. Sachs when I had renounced nursing forever, I saw the path ahead in its civic, national, and even international direction—a panorama of things to be.

A new movement was starting, and the baby had to have a name. It did not belong to Socialism nor was it in the labor field, and it had much more to it than just the prevention of conception. As a few companions were sitting with me one evening we debated in turn voluntary parenthood, voluntary motherhood, the new motherhood, constructive generation, and new generation. The terms already in use—Neo-Malthusianism, Family Limitation, and Conscious Generation seemed stuffy and lacked popular appeal.

The word control was good, but I did not like limitation—that was too limiting. I was not advocating a one-child or two-child system as in France, nor did I wholeheartedly agree with the English Neo-Malthusians whose concern was almost entirely with limitation for economic reasons. My idea of control was bigger and freer. I wanted family in it, yet family control did not sound right. We tried population control, race control, and birth rate control. Then someone suggested, "Drop the rate." Birth control was the answer; we knew we had it. Our work for that day was done and everybody picked up his hat and went home. The baby was named. . . .

I was solely responsible for the magazine financially, legally, and morally; I was editor, manager, circulation department, bookkeeper, and I paid the printer's bill. But any cause that has not helpers is losing out. So many men and women secretaries, stenographers, clerks, used to come in of an evening that I could not find room for all. Some typed, some addressed envelopes, some went to libraries and looked up things for us to use, some wrote articles, though seldom signing their own names. Not one penny ever had to go for salaries, because service was given freely.

In March, 1914, appeared the first issue of the *Woman Rebel*, eight pages on cheap paper, copied from the French style, mailed first call in the city and expressed outside. My initial declaration of the right of the individual was the slogan "No Gods, No Masters." Gods, not God. I wanted that word to go beyond religion and also stop turning idols, heroes, leaders into gods.

I defined a woman's duty, "To look the world in the face with a go-to-hell look in the eyes; to have an idea; to speak and act in defiance of convention." It was a marvelous time to say what we wished. All America was a Hyde Park corner as far as criticism and challenging thought were concerned. We advocated direct action and took up the burning questions of the day. . . .

My daily routine always started with looking over the pile of mail, and one morning my attention was caught by an unstamped official envelope from the New York Post Office. I tore it open.

Dear Madam, You are hereby notified that the Solicitor of the Post Office Department has decided that the *Woman Rebel* for March, 1914, is unmailable under Section 489, Postal Law and Regulations.

E. M. Morgan, Postmaster.

I reread the letter. It was so unexpected that at first the significance did not sink in. I had given no contraceptive information; I had merely announced that I intended to do so. Then I began to realize that no mention was made of any special article or articles. I wrote Mr. Morgan and asked him to state what specifically had offended, thereby assisting me in my future course. His reply simply repeated that the March issue was unmailable.

I had anticipated objections from religious bodies, but believed with father, "Anything you want can be accomplished by putting a little piece of paper into the ballot box." Therefore, to have our insignificant magazine stopped by the big, strong United States Government seemed so ludicrous as almost to make us feel important.

To the newspaper world this was news, but not one of the dailies picked it out as an infringement of a free press. The *Sun* carried a headline, " 'WOMAN REBEL' BARRED FROM MAILS." And underneath the comment, "Too bad. The case should be reversed. They should be barred from her and spelled differently."

Many times I studied Section 211 of the Federal Statutes, under which the Post Office was acting. This penal clause of the Comstock Law had been left hanging in Washington like the dried shell of a tortoise. Its grip had even been tightened on the moral side; in case the word obscene should prove too vague, its definition had been enlarged to include the prevention of conception and the causing of abortion under one and the same heading. To me it was outrageous that information regarding motherhood, which was so generally called sacred, should be classed with pornography. . . .

The *Woman Rebel* produced extraordinary results, striking vibrations that brought contacts, messages, inquiries, pamphlets, books, even some money. . . .

After the second number the focus had been birth control. Within six months we had received over ten thousand letters, arriving in accelerating volume. Most of them read, "Will your magazine give accurate and reliable information to prevent conception?" This I could not print. Realizing by now it was going to be a fairly big fight, I was careful not to break the law on such a trivial point. It would have been ridiculous to have a single letter reach the wrong destination; therefore, I sent no contraceptive facts through the mails. . . .

However, I had no intention of giving up this primary purpose. I began sorting and arranging the material I had brought back from France, complete with formulas and drawings, to be issued in a pamphlet where I could treat the subject with more delicacy than in a magazine, writing it for women of extremely circumscribed vocabularies. A few hundred dollars were needed to finance publication of *Family Limitation*, as I named it, and I approached Theodore Schroeder, a lawyer of standing and an ardent advocate of free speech. He had been left a fund by a certain Dr. Foote who had produced a book on *Borning Better Babies*, and I thought my pamphlet might qualify as a beneficiary. . . .

I took the manuscript to a printer well known for his liberal tendencies and courage. He read the contents page by page and said, "You'll never get this set up in any shop in New York. It's a Sing Sing job."

Every one of the twenty printers whom I tried to persuade was afraid to touch it. It was impossible ever, it seemed, to get into print the contents of that pamphlet.

Meanwhile, following the March issue the May and July numbers of the *Woman Rebel* had also been banned. In reply to each of the formal notices I inquired which particular article or articles had incurred disapproval, but could obtain no answer.

At that time I visualized the birth control movement as part of the fight for freedom of speech. How much would the postal authorities suppress? What were they really after? I was determined to prod and goad until some definite knowledge was obtained as to what was "obscene, lewd, and lascivious." . . .

One morning I was startled by the peremptory, imperious, and incessant ringing of my bell. When I opened the door, I was confronted by two gentlemen.

"Will you come in?"

They followed me into my living room, scrutinized with amazement the velocipede and wagon, the woolly animals and toys stacked in the corner. One of them asked, "Are you the editor and publisher of a magazine entitled the *Woman Rebel*?"

When I confessed to it, he thrust a legal document into my hands. I tried to read it, threading my way slowly through the jungle of legal terminology. Perhaps the words became a bit blurred because of the slight trembling of my hands, but I managed to disentangle the crucial point of the message. I had been indicted— indicted on no less than nine counts—for alleged violation of the Federal Statutes. If found guilty on all, I might be liable to forty-five years in the penitentiary.

I looked at the two agents of the Department of Justice. They seemed nice and sensible. I invited them to sit down and started in to explain birth control. For three hours I presented to their imaginations some of the tragic stories of conscript motherhood. I forget now what I said, but at the end they agreed that such a law should not be on the statute books. Yet it was, and there was nothing to do about it but bring my case to court.

When the officers had gone, father came through the door of the adjoining room where he had been reading the paper. He put both arms around me and said, "Your mother would have been alive today if we had known all this then." He had applied my recital directly to his own life. "You will win this case. Everything is with you—logic, common sense, and progress. I never saw the truth until this instant." . . .

My faith was still childlike. I trusted that, like father, a judge representing our Government would be convinced. All I had to do was explain to those in power what I was doing and everything would come right.

August twenty-fifth I was arraigned in the old Post Office way downtown. Judge Hazel, himself a father of eight or nine children, was kindly, and I suspected the two Federal agents who had summoned me had spoken a good word on my behalf. But Assistant District Attorney Harold A. Content seemed a ferocious young fellow. When the Judge asked, "What sort of things is Mrs. Sanger doing to violate the law?" he answered, "She's printing articles advocating bomb throwing and assassination."

"Mrs. Sanger doesn't look like a bomb thrower or an assassin."

Mr. Content murmured something about not all being gold that glittered; I was doing a great deal of harm. He intimated he knew of my attempts to get *Family Limitation* in print when he said, "She is not satisfied merely to violate the law, but is planning to do it on a very large scale."

Judge Hazel, apparently believing the charges much exaggerated, put the case over until the fall term, which gave me six weeks to prepare my answer, and Mr. Content concurred, saying that if this were not enough time, I could have more. . . .

I had many things to do which could not be postponed, the most important among them being to provide for the children's future. This occupied much of my time for the next few weeks. Temporarily, I sent the younger two to the Catskills and Stuart to a camp in Maine, arranging for school in the fall on Long Island. . . .

During what might be called my sleepwalking stage it was as though I were heading towards a precipice and nothing could awaken me. I had no ear for the objections of family or the criticism of friends. People were around me, I knew, but I could not see them clearly; I was deaf to their warnings and blind to their signs.

When I review the situation through the eyes of those who gave me circumspect advice, I can understand their attitude. I was considered a conservative, even a bourgeoise by the radicals. I was digging into an illegal subject, was not a trained writer or speaker or experienced in the arts of the propagandist, had no money with which to start a rousing campaign, and possessed neither social position nor influence.

In the opinion of nearly all my acquaintances I would have to spend at least a year in jail, and they began to condole with me. . . .

But I myself had no intention of going to jail; it was not in *my* program.

One other thing I had to do before my trial. *Family Limitation* simply must be published. I had at last found the right person— Bill Shatoff, Russian-born, big and burly, at that time a linotype operator on a foreign paper. So that nobody would see him he did the job after hours when his shop was supposed to be closed.

At first I had thought only of an edition of ten thousand. However, when I learned that union leaders in the silk, woolen, and copper industries were eager to have many more copies to distribute, I enlarged my plan. I would have liked to print a million but, owing to lack of funds, could not manage more than a hundred thousand. ˙

Addressing the envelopes took a lot of work. Night after night the faithful band labored in a storage room, wrapping, weighing, stamping. Bundles went to the mills in the East, to the mines of the West—to Chicago, San Francisco, and Pittsburgh, to Butte, Lawrence, and Paterson. All who had requested copies were to receive them simultaneously; I did not want any to be circulated until I was ready, and refused to have one in my own house. I was a tyrant about this, as firm as a general about leaving no rough edges.

In October my case came up. I had had no notice and, without a lawyer to keep me posted, did not even know it had been called until the District Attorney's office telephoned. Since Mr. Content had promised me plenty of time, I thought this was merely a formality and all I had to do was put in an appearance.

The next morning I presented myself at court. As I sat in the crowded room I felt crushed and oppressed by an intuitive sense of the tremendous, impersonal power of my opponents. Popular interest was now focused on Europe; my little defiance was no longer important. When I was brought out of my reverie by the voice of the clerk trumpeting forth in the harshly mechanical tones of a train announcer something about *The People v. Margaret Sanger*, there flashed into my mind a huge map of the United States, coming to life as a massive, vari-colored animal, against which I, so insignificant and small, must in some way defend myself. It was a terrific feeling.

But courage did not entirely desert me. Elsie Clapp, whose ample Grecian figure made her seem a tower of strength, marched up the aisle with me as though she, too, were to be tried. I said to Judge Hazel that I was not prepared, and asked for a month's adjournment. Mr. Content astonished me by objecting. "Mrs. Sanger's had plenty of time and I see no reason, Your Honor, why we should have a further postponement. Every day's delay means that her violations are increased. I ask that the case continue this afternoon."

A change in Judge Hazel's attitude had taken place since August. Instead of listening to my request, he advised me to get an attorney at once—my trial would go on after the noon recess.

I was so amazed that I could only believe his refusal was due to my lack of technical knowledge, and supposed that at this point I really had to have a lawyer. I knew Simon H. Pollock, who had represented labor during the Paterson strike, and I went to see him. He agreed with me that a lawyer's plea would not be rejected and that afternoon confidently asked for a month's stay. It was denied. He reduced it to two weeks. Again it was denied. At ten the following morning the case was to be tried without fail.

From the Post Office Department I received roundabout word that my conviction had already been decided upon. When I told this to Mr. Pollock he said, "There isn't a thing I can do. You'd better plead guilty and let us get you out as fast as we can. We might even be able to make some deal with the D.A. so you'd only have to pay a fine."

I indignantly refused to plead guilty under any circumstances. What was the sense of bringing about my indictment in order to test the law, and then admit that I had done wrong? I was trying to prove the law was wrong, not I. Giving Mr. Pollock no directions how to act, I merely said I would call him up.

It was now four o'clock and I sought refuge at home to think through my mental turmoil and distress. But home was crowded with too many associations and emotions pulling me this way and that. When my thoughts would not come clear and straight I packed a suitcase, went back downtown, and took a room in a hotel, the most impersonal place in the world.

There was no doubt in my mind that if I faced the hostile court the next morning, unprepared as I was, I would be convicted of publishing an obscene paper. Such a verdict would be an injustice. If I were to convince a court of the rightness of my cause, I must have my facts well marshaled, and that could not be done in eighteen hours.

Then there was the question of the children's welfare. Had I the right to leave them the heritage of a mother who had been imprisoned for some offensive literature of which no one knew the details?

What was I to do? Should I get another lawyer, one with personal influence who could secure a postponement, and should we then go into court together and fight it out? I had no money for such a luxury. Should I follow the inevitable suggestion of the "I-told-you-so's" and take my medicine? Yes, but what medicine? I would not swallow a dosage for the wrong disease.

I was not afraid of the penitentiary; I was not afraid of anything except being misunderstood. Nevertheless, in the circumstances, my going there could help nobody. I had seen so many people do foolish things valiantly, such as wave a red flag, shout inflammatory words, lead a parade, just for the excitement of doing what the crowd expected of them. Then they went to jail for six months, a year perhaps, and what happened? Something had been killed in them; they were never heard of again. I had seen braver and hardier souls than I vanquished in spirit and body by prison terms, and I was not going to be lost and broken for an issue which was not the real one, such as the entirely unimportant *Woman Rebel* articles. Had I been able to print *Family Limitation* earlier, and to swing the indictment around that, going to jail might have had some significance.

Going away was much more difficult than remaining. But if I were to sail for Europe I could prepare my case adequately and return then to win or lose in the courts. There was a train for Canada within a few hours. Could I take it? Should I take it? Could I ever make those who had advised me against this work and these activities understand? Could I ever make anyone understand? How could I separate myself from the children without seeing them once more? Peggy's leg was swollen from vaccination. This kept worrying me, made me hesitate, anxious. It was so hard to decide what to do.

Perfectly still, my watch on the table, I marked the minutes fly. There could be no retreat once I boarded that train. The torture of uncertainty, the agony of making a decision only to reverse it! The hour grew later and later. This was like both birth and death—you had to meet them alone.

About thirty minutes before train time I knew that I must go. I wrote two letters, one to Judge Hazel, one to Mr. Content, to be received at the desk the next day, informing them of my action. I had asked for a month and it had been refused. This denial of right and freedom compelled me to leave my home and my three children until I made ready my case, which dealt with society rather than an individual. I would notify them when I came back. Whether this were in a month or a year depended on what I found it necessary to do. Finally, as though to say, "Make the most of it," I enclosed to each a copy of *Family Limitation*.

Parting from all that I held dear in life, I left New York at midnight, without a passport, not knowing whether I could ever return. . . .

At Montreal I found comfort and refuge. In fact, on any road I took men and women who knew about the *Woman Rebel* came to my aid. . . .

Since I was charged with felony I could be extradited. I was obliged, therefore, in buying my passage, to choose a new name. No sooner had I selected the atrociously ugly "Bertha Watson," which seemed to rob me of femininity, than I wanted to be rid of it. But once having adopted it I could not escape.

I boarded the *RMS Virginian*, laden with munitions, food, Englishmen returning home for war duty, and Canadians going over. Even before the printing of *Family Limitation* had begun in August, I had arranged a key message which would release all the pamphlets simultaneously whenever it should be received by any of four trusted lieutenants. In case one should be arrested, another ill, or a third die, still everything would go forward as provided for. . . .

Three days out of Montreal I sent a cable and shortly had one in reply that the program was being executed as planned. . . .

The government official examining credentials at Liverpool said sternly, "England is at war, Madam. You can't expect us to let you through. We're sending back people without passports every day, and I can't make an exception in your case."

But I had Good Luck as an ally; she comes so often to help in emergencies. A shipboard acquaintance telephoned and pulled wires, a procedure not so common in England as in the United States. On his guarantee that I would get a passport from the American Embassy immediately on reaching London I was allowed to enter. . . .

Liverpool was only a junction; London was my terminus. There

I could study at the British Museum, and meet the Neo-Malthusians. Towards the end of the month I rolled up to London through miles of chimney-potted suburbs; it continued rainy and foggy, but still there was a friendly atmosphere in the air. I seemed to be coming to a second home. . . .

Each week day, however, found me at the British Museum, going in with the opening of the gates in the morning. . . . My aim was to present my case from all angles, to make the trial soundly historical so that birth control would be seriously discussed in America. Therefore, I read avidly and voluminously many weighty tomes, and turned carefully the yellowed, brittle pages of pamphlets and broadsides, finding much that was dull, much that was irrelevant, but also much that was amusing, if only for the ponderous manner of its expression. In the end I had a picture of what had gone before. . . .

As Christmas approached, my loneliness for the children increased. This was their particular time. I had messages from and about them, but these could not give the small, intimate details; the Atlantic was a broad span, seeming more vast to letter writers. I missed their voices, their caresses, even their little quarrels. I almost wondered whether solitary confinement in prison were not preferable to my present isolation.

In the midst of this stark yearning to be with them and share their tree I received a cordial note from Havelock Ellis asking me to come to tea. With kindly foresight he had given me explicit directions how to reach Fourteen Dover Mansions in Brixton across the Thames. I boarded a crowded bus at Oxford Circus. . . .

Looking askance at the police station which occupied the lower floor I climbed up the stairs, and, with the shyness of an adolescent, full of fears and uncertainties, lifted the huge brass knocker. The figure of Ellis himself appeared in the door. He seemed a giant in stature, a lovely, simple man in loose-fitting clothes, with powerful head and wonderful smile. He was fifty-five then, but that head will never change—the shock of white hair, the venerable beard, shaggy though well-kept, the wide, expressive mouth and deep-set eyes, sad even in spite of the humorous twinkle always latent.

I was conscious immediately that I was in the presence of a great man, yet I was startled at first by his voice as he welcomed me in. It was typically English, high and thin. . . .

When he asked me to describe the details of how I had locked horns with the law, I spoke glowingly of the heartening approval which the Drysdales [Dr. C. V. and Mrs. Bessie Drysdale, leaders of the British Neo-Malthusian Society] had just given me. He did not show the same enthusiasm; in fact he was rather concerned, and not so ready with praise for my lack of respect for the established order, believing so strongly in my case that he wanted me to avoid mistakes. I think his influence was always more or less subduing and moderating; he tried to get me, too, to take the middle road. Though he occasionally alluded to some of the more amusing phases of the trial of his own work, he had pushed it into the back of his mind. . . .

Since I am slow in my decisions and cannot separate myself from past emotions quickly, all breaches must come gradually. A measure of frustration is an inevitable accompaniment to endeavor. My marriage had not been unhappy; I had not let it be. It had not failed because of lack of love, romance, wealth, respect, or any of those qualities which were supposed to cause marital rifts, but because the interests of each had widened beyond those of the other. Development had proceeded so fast that our lives had diverged, due to that very growth which we had sought for each other. I could not live with a human being conscious that my necessities were thwarting or dwarfing his progress.

It had been a crowded year, encompassing the heights and depths of feeling. Christmas Eve was too much for me. I went back again and sat, wondering whether the children were well and contented. The next morning came a cable from them, flowers from Bill, and a nice note from Havelock Ellis. . . .

Thereafter Havelock aided me immensely in my studies by guiding my reading. Tuesdays and Fridays were his days at the British Museum, and he often left little messages at my seat, listing helpful articles or offering suggestions as to books which might assist me in the particular aspect I was then engaged upon. . . .

Day after day the attendants at the British Museum piled books and pamphlets on the table before my seat. As I pored over the vital statistics of Europe it seemed to me that chiefly in the Netherlands was there a force operating towards constructive race building. The Dutch had long since adopted a common-sense attitude on the subject, looking upon having a baby as an economic luxury— something like a piano or an automobile that had to be taken care of afterwards. . . .

Impatient to go to the Netherlands and dig out the real facts, not only from Dutch records but from personal observation, I de-

cided quietly—most of my decisions in those days were quiet ones—
to cross the Channel. . . .

After my morning's work with Dr. Rutgers I usually repaired
to the Central Bureau of Statistics with my three-in-one translator,
interpreter, and guide. My findings were that in all cities and districts
where [contraceptive] clinics had been established the figures
showed improvement—labor conditions were better and children
were going to schools, which had raised their educational standards. . . .

For two months I wandered about the Netherlands, visiting
clinics and independent nurses in the Hague, Rotterdam, and Amsterdam. In spite of the League propaganda against commerciali-
zation I found many shops in which a woman, if she so desired,
could purchase contraceptive supplies as casually as you might buy
a toothbrush. . . . Although fifty-four clinics were in operation,
many well-informed people did not know anything about them.
More surprising still, the medical profession as a whole appeared
to be utterly ignorant of the directed birth control work that was
going on. It did not, therefore, seem extraordinary that no inkling
of all this—either clinics or contraceptive methods—had ever
reached the United States, and practically no attempt to copy it
been made in England. . . .

Writing at this time was a means of expression much easier
than speaking. I had not forgotten my subscribers to the *Woman
Rebel*. I had to fulfill my obligations and supply something to take
the place of the three issues which I had been unable to furnish
them. Therefore, I wrote three pamphlets on methods of contraception in England, the Netherlands, and France respectively. Printing them cost me a considerable amount of money. My friends in
Canada, knowing I was not affluent, now and then when they had
a little windfall or unexpected dividend sent me small checks of
from five to ten pounds, saying, "To use for your work." These had
come in quite often. . . .

The War had sent many Americans back from Europe and Bill
had returned to New York. I had had a detailed letter from him
describing the stirring events of the previous December. A man
introducing himself as A. Heller had called upon him at his studio
and requested a copy of *Family Limitation*, pleading that he was
poor, had too large a family, and was a friend of mine. Bill said he
was sorry but we had agreed that I was to carry on my work
independently of him, and he did not even think he had any of the

pamphlets. However, the man's story was so pathetic that he rummaged around and by chance found one in the library drawer.

A few days later Bill opened the door to a gray-haired, sidewhiskered six-footer who lost no time in announcing, "I am Mr. Comstock. I have a warrant for your arrest on the grounds of circulating obscene literature." Accompanying him was the so-called Heller, who turned out to be Charles J. Bamberger, an agent of the New York Society for the Suppression of Vice. The three departed but Bill soon found himself in a restaurant instead of the police station. When he protested that he wished to consult a lawyer without delay, Comstock, between mouthfuls of lunch, offered advice. "Young man, I want to act as a brother to you. Lawyers are expensive and will only aggravate your case." Here he patted Bill on the shoulder. "Plead guilty to this charge, and I'll ask for a suspended sentence."

Bill's answer was that, though he had been in Europe when the pamphlet had been written, he believed in the principles embodied in it, and that, therefore, his own principles were at stake. He would not plead guilty. "You know as well as I do, Mr. Comstock, there's nothing obscene in that pamphlet."

"Young man, I have been in this work for twenty years, and that leaflet is the worst thing I have ever seen."

This sort of conversation went on all afternoon; Comstock even tried to bribe Bill to turn state's evidence by disclosing my whereabouts. It was his custom to arrive at the police station so late that his prisoner could not communicate with a lawyer or bonding office and had to spend the night in jail. He could then make a statement to the papers that his captive had been unable to secure bail.

When Comstock and Bill at last reached the Yorkville Police Court and the clerk had asked the latter how he wished to plead, Comstock spoke for him, "He pleads guilty."

"I do not," expostulated Bill. "I plead not guilty."

He was arraigned and bail fixed at five hundred dollars, but he was obliged to spend thirty-six hours in jail before it could be procured.

In September I had word that, after several postponements, his trial had finally come up before Justices McInerney, Herbert, and Salmon. He started to read his typewritten statement. "I admit that I broke the law, and yet I claim that in every real sense it is the law and not I that is on trial here today."

Justice McInerney interrupted him. "You admit you are guilty, and all this statement of yours is just opinions. I'm not going to have a lot of rigmarole on the record. We've no time to bother. This book is not only indecent but immoral. Its circulation is a menace to society. Too many women are going around advocating woman suffrage. If they would go around advocating bearing children we should be better off.

"The statute gives you the privilege of being fined for this offense, but I do not believe this should be so. A man, guilty as you are, ought to have no alternative from a prison sentence. One hundred and fifty dollars or thirty days in jail."

"Then I want to say to the court," shouted Bill, leaning forward and raising his hand for greater emphasis, "that I would rather be in jail with my self-respect than in your place without it!"

Although he was convinced of the justice of my cause, this was the first and only copy of the pamphlet he had ever given out. It was one of life's sharpest ironies that, despite our separation, he should have been drawn into my battle, and go to prison for it. . . .

The question before me was, "Should I go back?" As had gone Bill's trial so would probably go my own. I did not want to sacrifice myself in a lost cause. I was young, and knew I should be used for something. . . . I decided to return to the United States, but only long enough to survey the situation, to gather up my children. . . .

To see American faces again after the unutterable despair of Europe, to sense the rough democracy of the porters and of the good-hearted, hard-boiled taxi-drivers; to breathe in the crisp, electric autumn air of home—all these brought with them an irresistible gladness. Because I wanted the feeling to linger, I refused a taxi, picked up my small bag, and walked away from the pier, looking about.

At the first news stand I passed I caught sight of the words, "WHAT SHALL WE DO ABOUT BIRTH CONTROL?" on the cover of the *Pictorial Review*. It seemed strange to be greeted, not by friends or relatives, but by a phrase of your own carried on a magazine. I purchased it and, singing to myself, went on to a hotel where the children were brought to me. I cannot describe the joy of being reunited with them.

That evening I sat down at my desk and wrote several letters. I notified Judge Hazel and Assistant District Attorney Content that I was now back and ready for trial, and inquired whether the indictments of the previous year were still pending; I was politely informed that they were.

A note more difficult to compose went to the National Birth Control League, which had been re-organized in my absence under the leadership of Mary Ware Dennett, Clara Stillman, and Anita Block. To it had been turned over all my files, including the list of subscribers to the *Woman Rebel*. I asked them what moral support I could expect from the League, saying this would help to determine the length of my stay.

Mrs. Stillman, the secretary, invited me to call a few days later at her home, where an executive meeting was to convene. I went with keen anticipation, totally unprepared for the actual answer. The committee had met. Mrs. Dennett, Mrs. Stillman, and Anita were all there. Mrs. Dennett spoke for the group; the National Birth Control League disagreed with my methods, my tactics, with everything I had done. Such an organization as theirs, the function of which was primarily to change the laws in an orderly and proper manner, could not logically sanction anyone who had broken those laws. . . .

Dr. Abraham Jacoby, beloved dean of the profession, in accepting the presidency of the Academy of Medicine, had backed birth control, and through Dr. Robinson's endeavors a small committee had later been formed to look into it. From the reports that had come to me I could not discover whether any harmonious agreement that the subject lay within the province of medicine had been made. To my inquiry Dr. Robinson replied that the committee had met only once and he considered I could expect no support from them. He enclosed a check for ten dollars towards the expenses of my trial.

Here were two disappointments to face. Both these organizations had seemed so well suited to continue progress: one to change the laws, the other to take proper medical charge. Neither had fulfilled my hopes and therefore I felt I had to enter the fray again. My burning concern for the thousands of women who went unregarded could apparently find no official endorsement; birth control was back again where it had started. I was convinced I had to depend solely upon the compassionate insight of intelligent women, which I was certain was latent and could be aroused.

But these problems were suddenly swept aside by a crisis of a more intimate nature, a tragedy about which I find myself still unable to write, though so many years have passed.

A few days after my arrival Peggy was taken ill with pneumonia. When Mr. Content telephoned to say I had better come down and talk it over, I could not go. He was extremely kind, assuring me there was no hurry and he would postpone my trial until I was free. This allowed me to devote my whole attention and time to her.

Peggy died the morning of November 6, 1915.

The joy in the fullness of life went out of it then and has never quite returned. Deep in the hidden realm of my consciousness my little girl has continued to live, and in that strange, mysterious place where reality and imagination meet, she has grown up to womanhood. There she leads an ideal existence untouched by harsh actuality and disillusion. . . .

Public opinion had been focused on Comstock's activities by Bill's sentence, and the liberals had been aroused. Committees of two and three came to request me to take up the purely legislative task of changing the Federal law. Aid would be forthcoming—special trains to Congress, investigations, commissions, and victory in sight before the year was over! It was tempting. It seemed so feasible on the surface, so much easier than agonizing delays through the courts. Many others advised me just as before that in pleading guilty I was choosing the best field in which to make my fight. . . .

The law specified obscenity, and I had done nothing obscene. I even had the best of the Government as regarded the precise charge. I had not given contraceptive information in the *Woman Rebel,* and therefore had not violated the law either in spirit or principle. But I had done so in circulating *Family Limitation,* and that would inevitably be brought up. I really wanted this, so that birth control would be defined once and for all as either obscene or not obscene. . . .

. . . when I arrived at nine o'clock at the Federal Court building more than two hundred partisans were already in the corridors. A great corps of reporters and photographers was on hand. The stage had been set for an exciting drama.

Judge Henry D. Clayton and Assistant District Attorneys Knox and Content arrived at ten-thirty, apparently feeling the effects of the publicity of the night before.

The moment Knox moved to adjourn for a week I was on my feet asking immediate trial, but Judge Clayton postponed the case. Everybody went home disappointed.

February 18th the Government finally entered a nolle prosequi. Content explained there had been many assertions that the defendant was the victim of persecution, and that had never been the intent of the Federal authorities. "The case had been laid before the grand jurors as impartially as possible and since they had voted an indictment there was nothing that the District Attorney could do but prosecute. Now, however, as it was realized that the indictment was two years old, and that Mrs. Sanger was not a disorderly person and did not make a practice of publishing such articles, the Government had considered there was reason for considerable doubt." . . .

The Federal law concerned only printed literature. My own pamphlet had given the impression that the printed word was the best way to inform women, but the practical course of contraceptive technique I had taken in the Netherlands had shown me that one woman was so different from another in structure that each needed particular information applied to herself as an individual. Books and leaflets, therefore, should be of secondary importance. The public health way was through personal instruction in clinics. . . .

If I could start them, other organizations and even hospitals might do the same. I had a vision of a "chain"—thousands of them in every center of America, staffed with specialists putting the subject on a modern scientific basis through research. . . .

Once Amos Pinchot asked me how long it had taken me to prepare that first lecture I delivered on my three months' trip across the country in 1916.

"About fourteen years," I answered. . . .

I repeated the lecture over and over to myself before I tried it on a small audience in New Rochelle. I did not dare cut myself adrift from my notes; I had to read it, and when I had finished, did not feel it had been very successful. By the time I reached Pittsburgh, my first large city, I had memorized every period and comma, but I was still scared that if I lost one word I would not know what the next was. I closed my eyes and spoke in fear and trembling. The laborers and social workers who crowded the big theater responded so enthusiastically that I was at least sure their attention had been held by its content. . . .

I wanted the world made safe for babies. From a government survey significant conclusions had emerged as to how many babies lived to celebrate their first birthday. These were based largely on three factors: the father's wage—as it went down, more died, and as it rose, more survived; the spacing of births—when children were born one year apart, more died than if the mother were allowed a two- or three-year interval between pregnancies; the relative position in the family—of the number of second-born, thirty-two out of every hundred died annually, and so on progressively until among those who were born twelfth, the rate was sixty out of a hundred. . . .

In the fall of 1916 whoever walked along the corridor of the top floor of 104 Fifth Avenue could have seen the words "Birth Control" printed on the door leading to an office equipped in business-like, efficient manner with files and card catalogs. Presiding over it was Fred Blossom, the perfect representative. He had told me at Cleveland he was tired of ameliorative charity and, wanting to do something more significant, had offered six months for this work. Now indefatigably he wrote, spoke, made friends, and, most important, raised money. His meals were limited to an apple for luncheon and a sandwich for dinner; he seldom left the office until midnight.

Like a vacuum cleaner Blossom sucked in volunteers from near and far to help with the boxes and trunks of letters which had come to me from all over the country—one thousand from St. Louis alone. As long as I had had no stenographic aid I had been able only to open and read them and put them sadly away. At last with fifteen or twenty assistants the task began of sorting these out and answering them. The contents almost invariably fell into certain definite categories, and I instituted a system so that such and such a paragraph could be sent in response to such and such an appeal.

We had only one paid stenographer—little Anna Lifshiz, who soon became far more a co-worker than a secretary. If we had no money in the bank she waited for her salary until we did. When I met Anna's mother, who graced her hospitable home with an old world dignity, I realized that her daughter's fine character had been directly inherited. Every Christmas I used to receive a present of wine and cakes of Mrs. Lifshiz' own make, and Anna always said when she brought them, "My mother prays for your health, your happiness, and that you will keep well." . . .

The legislative approach seemed to me a slow and tortuous method of making clinics legal; we stood a better and quicker chance by securing a favorable judicial interpretation through challenging the law directly. I decided to open a clinic in New York City. . . . Section 1142 of the New York statutes was definite: *No one* could give contraceptive information to *anyone* for *any* reason.

On the other hand, Section 1145 distinctly stated that physicians could give prescriptions to prevent conception for the cure or prevention of disease. Two attorneys and several doctors assured me this exception referred only to venereal disease. In that case, the intent was to protect the man, which could incidentally promote immorality and permit promiscuity. I was dealing with marriage. I wanted the interpretation to be broadened into the intent to protect women from ill health as the result of excessive childbearing and, equally important, to have the right to control their own destinies.

To change this interpretation it was necessary to have a test case. This, in turn, required my keeping strictly to the letter of the law; that is, having physicians who would give only verbal information for the prevention of disease. But the women doctors who had previously promised to do this now refused. I wrote, telephoned, asked friends to ask other friends to help find someone. None was willing to enter the cause, fearful of jeopardizing her private practice and of running the risk of being censured by her profession; she might even lose her license. . . .

I did not wish to complicate the question of testing the law by having a nurse give information, because a nurse did not come under the Section 1145 exception. But since I could find no doctor I had to do without. Ethel, a registered nurse, had a readiness to share in helping the movement, though she did not belong to it in the same sense as I. Then, as long as I had to violate the law anyhow, I concluded I might as well violate it on a grand scale by including poverty as a reason for giving contraceptive information. I did not see why the hardships and worries of a working man's wife might not be just as detrimental as any disease. I wanted a legal opinion on this if possible. . . .

The two questions—where and how—were settled on one and the same day.

That afternoon five women from the Brownsville Section of Brooklyn crowded into my room seeking the "secret" of birth control. Each had four children or more, who had been left with neighbors. One had just recovered from an abortion which had nearly killed her. "Another will take me off. Then what will become of my family?"

They rocked back and forth as they related their afflictions, told so simply, each scarcely able to let her friend finish before she took up the narration of her own sufferings—the high cost of food, her husband's meager income when he worked at all, her helplessness in the struggle to make ends meet, whining, sickly children, the constant worry of another baby—and always hanging over her night and day, year after year, was fear.

All cried what a blessing and godsend a clinic would be in their neighborhood. . . .

I decided then and there that the clinic should open at Brownsville, and I would look for a site the next day. How to finance it I did not know, but that did not matter. . . .

Then suddenly the telephone rang and I heard a feminine voice saying she had just come from the West Coast bringing from Kate Crane Gartz, whom I had met in Los Angeles, a check for fifty dollars to do with as I wished. I knew what I should do with it; pay the first month's rent. I visualized two rooms on the ground floor, one for waiting and one for consultation, and a place outside to leave the baby carriages. . . .

The inhabitants were mostly Jews and Italians, some who had come to this country as children, some of the second generation. I preferred a Jewish landlord, and Mr. Rabinowitz was the answer. He was willing to let us have Number 46 Amboy Street at fifty dollars a month, a reduction from the regular rent because he realized what we were trying to do. Here in this Jewish community I need have no misgivings over breaking windows or hurling of epithets, but I was scarcely prepared for the friendliness offered from that day on.

I sent a letter to the District Attorney of Brooklyn, saying I expected to dispense contraceptive information from this address. Without waiting for the reply, which never came, we began the fun of fixing up our little clinic. . . . If I were to leave no loophole in testing the law, we could only give the principles of contraception, show a cervical pessary to the women, explain that if they had had two children they should have one size and if more a larger one. This was not at all ideal, but I had no other recourse at the time. . . .

Meanwhile we had printed about five thousand notices in English, Italian, and Yiddish:

MOTHERS!

Can you afford to have a large family?
Do you want any more children?
If not, why do you have them?

DO NOT KILL, DO NOT TAKE LIFE, BUT PREVENT
Safe, Harmless Information can be obtained of trained Nurses at
46 Amboy Street
Near Pitkin Ave.—Brooklyn

Tell Your Friends and Neighbors.   All Mothers Welcome.
A registration fee of 10 cents entitles any mother
to this information.

The morning of October 16, 1916—crisp but sunny and bright after days of rain—Ethel, Fania [Mindell, a key volunteer], and I opened the doors of the first birth control clinic in America, the first anywhere in the world except the Netherlands. I still believe this was an event of social significance.

Would the women come? Did they come? Nothing, not even the ghost of Anthony Comstock, could have kept them away. We had arrived early, but before we could get the place dusted and ourselves ready for the official reception, Fania called, "Do come outside and look." Halfway to the corner they were standing in line, at least one hundred and fifty, some shawled, some hatless, their red hands clasping the cold, chapped, smaller ones of their children.

Fania began taking names, addresses, object in coming to the clinic, histories—married or single, any miscarriage or abortions, how many children, where born, what ages. . . .

Children were left with her and mothers ushered in to Ethel or me in the rear room, from seven to ten at once. To each group we explained simply what contraception was; that abortion was the wrong way—no matter how early it was performed it was taking life; that contraception was the better way, the safer way—it took a little time, a little trouble, but was well worth while in the long run, because life had not yet begun. . . .

In the course of the next few days women appeared clutching minute scraps of paper, seldom more than an inch wide, which had crept into print. The Yiddish and Italian papers had picked up the story from the handbills which bore the clinic address, and the husbands had read them on their way from work and clipped them out for their wives. Women who had seen the brief, inconspicuous newspaper accounts came even from Massachusetts, Pennsylvania, New Jersey, and the far end of Long Island. . . .

Day after day the waiting room was crowded with members of every race and creed; Jews and Christians, Protestants and Roman Catholics alike made their confessions to us, whatever they may have professed at home or in church. I asked one bright little Catholic what excuse she could make to the priest when he learned she had been to the clinic. She answered indignantly, "It's none of his business. My husband has a weak heart and works only four days a week. He gets twelve dollars, and we can barely live on it now. We have enough children."

Her friend, sitting by, nodded approval. "When I was married," she broke in, "the priest told us to have lots of children and we listened to him. I had fifteen. Six are living. I'm thirty-seven years old now. Look at me! I might be fifty!"

That evening I made a mental calculation of fifteen baptismal fees, nine baby funerals, masses and candles for the repose of nine baby souls, the physical agonies of the mother, and the emotional torment of both parents, and I asked myself, "Is this the price of Christianity?" . . .

Then one afternoon when I, still undiscouraged, was out interviewing a doctor, a woman, large of build and hard of countenance, entered and said to Fania she was the mother of two children and that she had no money to support more. She did not appear overburdened or anxious and, because she was so well fed as to body and prosperous as to clothes, did not seem to belong to the community. She bought a copy of *What Every Girl Should Know* and insisted on paying two dollars instead of the usual ten-cent fee.

Fania, who had an intuition about such matters, called Ethel aside and said warningly she was certain this must be a policewoman. But Ethel, who was not of the cautious type, replied, "We have nothing to hide. Bring her in anyhow." She talked with the woman in private, gave her our literature, and, when asked about our future plans, related them frankly. The sceptical Fania pinned the two-dollar bill on the wall and wrote underneath, "Received from Mrs. —— of the Police Department, as her contribution." Hourly after that we expected trouble. We had known it must occur sooner or later, but would have preferred it to come about in a different way.

The next day Ethel and Fania were both absent from the clinic. The waiting room was filled almost to suffocation when the door opened and the woman who had been described to me came in.

"Are you Mrs. Sanger?"

"Yes."

"I'm a police officer. You're under arrest."

The doors were locked and this Mrs. Margaret Whitehurst and other plain-clothes members of the vice squad—used to raiding gambling dens and houses of assignation—began to demand names and addresses of the women, seeing them with babies, broken, old, worried, harrowed, yet treating them as though they were inmates of a brothel. Always fearful in the presence of the police, some began to cry aloud and the children on their laps screamed too. For a few moments it was like a panic, until I was able to assure them that only I was under arrest; nothing was going to happen to them, and they could return home if they were quiet. After half an hour I finally persuaded the policemen to let these frightened women go.

All of our four hundred and sixty-four case histories were confiscated, and the table and demonstration supplies were carried off through the patient line outside. The more timid had left, but many had stayed. This was a region where a crowd could be collected by no more urgent gesture than a tilt of the head skyward. Newspaper men with their cameras had joined the throng and the street was packed. Masses of people spilled out over the sidewalk on to the pavement, milling excitedly.

The patrol wagon came rattling up to our door. I had a certain respect for uniformed policemen—you knew what they were about—but none whatsoever for the vice squad. I was white hot with indignation over their unspeakable attitude toward the clinic mothers and stated I preferred to walk the mile to the court rather than sit with them. Their feelings were quite hurt. "Why, we didn't do anything to you, Mrs. Sanger," they protested. Nevertheless I marched ahead, they following behind. . . .

I stayed overnight at the Raymond Street Jail, and I shall never forget it. The mattresses were spotted and smelly, the blankets stiff with dirt and grime. The stench nauseated me. It was not a comforting thought to go without bedclothing when it was so cold, but, having in mind the diseased occupants who might have preceded me, I could not bring myself to creep under the covers. Instead I lay down on top and wrapped my coat around me. The only clean object was my towel, and this I draped over my face and head. For endless hours I struggled with roaches and horrible-looking bugs that came crawling out of the walls and across the floor. When a rat jumped up on the bed I cried out involuntarily and sent it scuttling. . . .

I went straight back to the clinic, reopened it, and more mothers came in. I had hoped a court decision might allow us to continue, but now Mr. Rabinowitz came downstairs apologetically. He said he was sorry, and he really was, but the police had made him sign ejection papers, on the ground that I was "maintaining a public nuisance."

In the Netherlands a clinic had been cited as a public benefaction; in the United States it was classed as a public nuisance.

Two uniformed policemen came for me, and with them I was willing to ride in the patrol wagon to the station. As we started I heard a scream from a woman who had just come around the corner on her way to the clinic. She abandoned her baby carriage, rushed through the crowd, and cried, "Come back! Come back and save me!" For a dozen yards she ran after the van before someone caught her and led her to the sidewalk. But the last thing I heard was this poor distracted mother, shrieking and calling, "Come back! Come back!" . . .

Out of the raid four separate cases resulted: Ethel was charged with violating Section 1142 of the Penal Code, designed to prevent dissemination of contraceptive information; Fania with having sold an allegedly indecent book entitled *What Every Girl Should Know;* I, first, with having conducted a clinic in violation of the same Section 1142, second, with violating Section 1530 by maintaining a public nuisance.

I claimed that Section 1142 which forbade contraceptive information to, for, and by anyone was unconstitutional, because no state was permitted to interfere with a citizen's right to life or liberty, and such denial was certainly interference. Experience had shown it did that case no good merely to defend such a stand in a lower court; it must be carried to a higher tribunal, and only a lawyer versed in whereases and whatsoevers and inasmuches could accomplish this. But I was still hopeful of finding one who was able to see that the importance of birth control could not be properly emphasized if we bowed too deeply before the slow and ponderous majesty of the law.

The attorney who offered himself, J. J. Goldstein, had a background which made him more sympathetic than other lawyers, even the most liberal. He was one of those young Jewish men of promise who had been guided through adolescence by Mary Simkhovitch, founder of Greenwich House, and Lillian Wald, founder of the Henry Street Settlement. The seeds of social service had been planted in him; his legal training only temporarily slowed down their growth. . . .

J.J. had placed himself in a difficult position for a youthful Tammany Democrat, some day to be a magistrate; he might have been forgiven more easily had he received a larger fee. Though he had to be convinced that we declined to have anything to do with political wire-pulling, he fought for us valiantly.

November 20th we pleaded not guilty and trial was set for November 27th. . . .

Evening after evening J.J. rehearsed the arguments he was going to present and directed me to respond to questioning. I did not understand the technicalities and begged to be allowed to tell the story in my own way, fearful lest the heartaches of the mothers be lost in the labyrinthine maze of judicial verbiage. But he maintained if the case were to be appealed to a higher court, it had to be conducted according to certain formalities.

"Why should it have to be in legal language?" I demanded. "I'm a simple citizen, born in a democratic country. A court should also listen to my plea expressed in plain language for the common people. I'm sure I can make them understand and arouse their compassion." . . .

Trial was marked for January 4, 1917, but the first case, that of Ethel, was reached so late in the afternoon it had been postponed. Four days afterwards, in spite of our attempts to be tried together, she appeared alone. She freely admitted she had described birth control methods but denied the District Attorney's accusation that our ten-cent registration fee made it a "money making" affair. . . .

Ethel was sentenced January 22nd to thirty days in the Workhouse on Blackwell's Island in the East River. In spite of our discussion over this possibility, she was utterly shocked, and exclaimed, "I'm going to go on that hunger strike."

After spending the night in the Tombs, she was returned the next morning to the Federal District Court of Brooklyn on a writ of habeas corpus as a means of suspending sentence pending appeal. Daylight had brought no change in her determination to continue with the hunger strike. "I haven't had anything to eat yet," she declared, and, remembering the tale that one hunger striker had received nourishment in her cups of water, she added, "and, if they send me back, I shan't drink anything either." . . .

. . . she was remanded to the Workhouse. On her way there she told the women with whom she shared the patrol wagon the salient facts of birth control. . . .

Ethel had gone one hundred and three hours without eating when Commissioner Lewis established a precedent in American prison annals by ordering her forcibly fed, the first woman to be so treated in this country. He stated optimistically to the press how simple the process was, consisting of merely rolling her in a blanket so she could not struggle, and then having milk, eggs, and a stimulant forced into her stomach through a rubber tube. He stressed how healthy she continued to be, how little opposition she offered, how foolish the whole thing appeared to him anyhow; he was going to charge her for the expense incurred in calling in an expert to feed her. . . .

Nobody was allowed to visit Ethel but J.J., who, as her lawyer, could not well be refused. But reporters have their own mysterious ways of getting what they want. The World man succeeded in reaching her. It was not on the whole a successful interview, because she did not know who he was, but it did have one important result—it confirmed at first hand our statements as to the seriousness of her condition. . . .

In the midst of my anxiety over Ethel, my own trial opened January 29th in the same bare, smoky, upstairs Brooklyn court in which she had appeared. Justices John J. Freschi, Italian, Moses Hermann, Jewish, and George J. O'Keefe, Irish, sat on the bench. Judge Freschi, a rather young man, presided, and on him we pinned our hopes. We did not expect anything of old Judge Herrmann [sic] except that, because he was Jewish, he might be broad-minded. As to Judge O'Keefe we had no illusions.

No less than thirty of the mothers of Brownsville had been subpoenaed by the prosecution, but about fifty arrived—some equipped with fruit, bread, pacifiers, and extra diapers, others distressed at having had to spend carfare, timid at the thought of being in court, hungry because no kosher food could be obtained near by. Nevertheless, all smiled and nodded at me reassuringly.

Formerly, a few women of wealth but of liberal tendencies had been actively concerned in the movement, but now some who were prominent socially were coming to believe on principle that birth control should not be denied to the masses. The subject was in the process of ceasing to be tagged as radical and revolutionary, and becoming admittedly humanitarian. . . .

It surprised me that in my trial the prosecution should be carried on so vehemently, because the prosecutor had little to prove. To me there seemed to be no argument at all; the last thing in my mind was to deny having given birth control advice. Certainly I had violated the letter of the law, but that was what I was opposing.

I grew more and more puzzled by the stilted language, the circumlocutions, the respect for precedent. These legal battles, fought in a curiously unreal world, intensified my defiance to the breaking point. I longed for a discussion in the open on merit and in simple, honest terms.

I thought I might have my wish when Judge Freschi, holding up a cervical cap which the prosecuting attorney had put in evidence, said, "Who can prove this is a violation; the law states that contraception is permitted for the prevention of disease. May it not be used for medical reasons?"

This question raised my hopes high. At last the law might be interpreted according to the definition I so desired; ill health resulting from pregnancy caused by lack of its use might be construed as disease.

Then one by one the Brownsville mothers were called to the stand to answer the District Attorney. "Have you ever seen Mrs. Sanger before?"

"Yess. Yess, I know Mrs. Sanger."

"Where did you see her?"

"At the cleenic."

"Why did you go there?"

"To have her stop the babies."

The witness bowed sweet acknowledgment to me until she was peremptorily commanded to address the court.

"Did you get this information?"

"Yess. Yess, dank you, I got it. It wass gut, too."

"Enough," the District Attorney barked, and called another.

Time after time they gave answers that were like nails to seal my doom, yet each thought she was assisting me.

J.J. saw how their testimony could be turned to our advantage. He asked, "How many miscarriages have you had? How much sickness in your family? How much does your husband earn?" The answers were seven, eight, nine dollars a week.

At last one woman more miserable and more poverty-stricken than the rest was summoned. "How many children have you?"

"Eight and three that didn't live."

"What does your husband earn?

"Ten dollars a veek—ven he vorks."

Judge Freschi finally exclaimed, "I can't stand this any longer," and the court adjourned over the week-end.

J.J. was jubilant, because he said there was nothing for him to do; the court was arguing his case for him. . . .

Being the real instigator, I had every reason to expect a longer term than Ethel. Logically, her hunger strike had served its purpose; that form of strategy was closed. But personally I decided that, if I should receive a year, I should do the same. On the other hand, if I were given three months or less, I could study and make use of my time. J.J. had heard on reliable authority that if I were to change my plea to guilty, I could have a suspended sentence. To his mind freedom alone meant victory, and he urged me to accept it if it were offered. . . .

I sat listening to what seemed an interminable discussion between J.J. and Judge Freschi over whether the appeal were going to be prosecuted in a quick and orderly fashion, until I was nearly lulled to sleep. Suddenly my attention was caught by hearing J.J. declare that I would "promise not to violate the law." . . .

THE COURT: All we are concerned about is this statute, and as long as it remains the law will this woman promise here and now unqualifiedly to respect it and obey it? Now, it is yes or no. What is your answer, Mrs. Sanger? Is it yes or no?

THE DEFENDANT: I can't respect the law as it stands today.

THE COURT: Margaret Sanger, there is evidence that you established and maintained a birth control clinic where you kept for sale and exhibition to various women articles which purported to be for the prevention of conception, and that there you made a determined effort to disseminate birth control information and advice. You have challenged the constitutionality of the law under consideration and the jurisdiction of this Court. When this is done in an orderly way no one can find fault. It is your right as a citizen. . . . Refusal to obey the law becomes an open defiance of the rule of the majority. While the law is in its present form, defiance provokes anything but reasonable consideration. The judgment of the Court is that you be confined to the Workhouse for the period of thirty days.

A single cry, "Shame!" was followed by a sharp rap of the gavel, and silence fell.

March 6, 1917, dawned a bitter, stinging morning. Through the metal doors I stepped, and the tingling air beat against my face. No other experience in my life has been like that. Gathered in front were my old friends who had frozen through the two hours waiting to celebrate "Margaret's coming out party." They lifted their voices in the *Marseillaise*. Behind them at the upper windows were my new friends, the women with whom I had spent the month, and they too were singing. Something choked me. Something still chokes me whenever I hear that triumphant music and ringing words, "Ye sons of freedom wake to glory!"

I plunged down the stairs and into the car which stood ready for me, and we swept out of the yard towards my apartment. At the entrance were Vito, the coal man, and his wife, beaming and proudly pointing to the blazing fire they had made on the hearth to welcome me home. . . .

. . . prison had been a quiet interim for reflection, for assembling past experiences and preparing for the future. The tempestuous season of agitation—courts and jails and shrieking and thumbing-the-nose—should now end. Heretofore there had been much notoriety and but little understanding. The next three steps were to be: first, education; then, organization; and, finally, legislation. All were clearly differentiated, though they necessarily overlapped to a certain extent.

I based my program on the existence in the country of a forceful sentiment which, if co-ordinated, could become powerful enough to change laws. . . .

The public had to be educated before it could be organized and before the laws could be changed as a result of that organization. I set myself to the task. It was to be a long one, because the press did not want articles stating the facts of birth control; they wanted news, and to them news still consisted of fights, police, arrests, controversy. . . .

. . . the *Birth Control Review*, . . . from 1917 to 1921, was the spearhead in the educational stage. . . .

For the purpose of having a more solid and substantial basis on which to operate the *Review*, the New York Women's Publishing Company was incorporated in May, 1918; shares were sold at ten dollars each. The women who gave both monetary and moral support were the wives of business men who advised them how to conduct this organization in the proper fashion. . . .

Inevitably I have been constantly torn between my compulsion to do this work and a haunting feeling that I was robbing my children of time to which they were entitled. Back in 1913 I had had some vague notion of being able to spend all my summers with them at Provincetown. That visionary hope had been immediately dissipated because too many painters began to discover it and the place became littered with easels and smocks. Gene O'Neill's plays were being produced on the wharf opposite Mary Heaton Vorse's house, and these brought many more people. I wanted to get away even further, and so did Jack Reed, who had also sought sanctuary there. A real estate agent took him to near-by Truro where the feet of New Yorkers had not yet trod, and I was invited to come along. We saw a little house on a little hill, one of the most ancient in the village. Below it the Pamet River wound like a silver ribbon to the ocean. An old sea captain had squared and smoothed and fitted the timbers, brought them up from the Carolinas in a sailing vessel, and fastened them tightly together with wooden pegs. The kitchen was bright and warm, and seemed as though many cookies and pies had been baked in it.

Jack bought the cottage, but he was never able to live there. As a staff correspondent of the *Metropolitan Magazine* he was dashing from the Colorado Fuel and Iron strike to the European War and back again to New York. In 1917, knowing I, too, had looked at it with longing eyes, he asked whether I would like to buy it; he was starting for Russia the next day and had to have ready money. By a lucky chance I had just received a check for a thousand dollars in payment for some Chicago lectures. We exchanged check and deed. . . .

Truro provided the children with three carefree months every summer in what still seems to me one of the most beautiful spots in the world. For several years I hung on to this dream of being with them constantly, but it was only a dream. I used to go down to open the house and perhaps snatch a week or so there before being obliged to hurry back, but father and my sister Nan were good foster-parents. This house was eventually to burn as had the one in Hastings; fate seemed to decree I should not be tempted to slip back into peaceful domesticity.

Nor did I have all those hoped for years of watching the boys grow from one stage to another. I had had to analyze the situation— either to keep them at home under the supervision of servants who might perhaps be incompetent, and to have no more than the pleasure of seeing them safely to bed, or else to sacrifice my maternal feelings and put them in country schools directed by capable masters where they could lead a healthy, regular life. Having come to this latter decision I sent them off fairly young, and thereafter could only visit them over week-ends or on the rare occasions when I was speaking in the vicinity. If the desire to see them grew beyond control, I took the first train and received the shock of finding them thoroughly contented in the companionship they had made for themselves; after the initial excitement of greeting had passed away they ran off again to their games.

At times the homesickness for them seemed too much to bear; especially was this true in the Fourteenth Street studio. When I came in late at night the fire was dead in the grate, the book open on the table, the glove dropped on the floor, the pillow rumpled on the sofa—all the same—just as I had left them a day, a week, or a month before. That first chill of loneliness was always appalling. I wanted, as a child does, to be like other people; I wanted to be able to sink gratefully into the warmth and glow of a loving family welcome. . . .

It became obvious that progress depended on finding a means of contraception, cheap, harmless, easily applied. Way back in 1914 Havelock had seen in some of the last medical journals to come out of Germany an advertisement of a chemical contraceptive. He had mentioned it to me, and ever since I had been eager to track it down. . . . Thus was inaugurated a new phase in the movement—the use of a chemical contraceptive. . . .

In confirming my conviction in 1918, Judge Frederick E. Crane of the Appellate Division of the Supreme Court of New York had for the first time interpreted the section of the state law which permitted a licensed physician to give contraceptive advice for the "cure or prevention of disease"; and, further, he had taken from *Webster's Dictionary* the broad definition of disease as any alteration in the state of body which caused or threatened pain and sickness, thus extending the meaning of the word far beyond the original scope of syphilis and gonorrhea. But, never satisfied, I wanted women to have birth control for economic and social reasons.

Therefore, in January, 1921, Anne Kennedy and I went to Albany to find a sponsor for a bill which was to change the New York law. It was not only a question of amending it, but also a means of educating the public, of explaining our cause through the medium of legislation. . . .

Since the hospitals were laggard in this matter, I decided to open a second clinic of my own. It was to be in effect a laboratory dealing in human beings instead of mice, with every consideration for environment, personality, and background. I was going to suggest to women that in the Twentieth Century they give themselves to science as they had in the past given their lives to religion. . . .

Because organized medical support was lacking, I tried to see what could be done with individuals, writing to various doctors to inquire whether they were willing to sponsor such an undertaking. . . .

Dr. Emmett Holt, then the outstanding pediatrician of New York, whose book, *The Care and Feeding of Children*, was the bible of thousands of mothers, invited me to come to his office; before making any endorsement he wanted to know more about it.

I packed up all my European supplies and showed them and explained them to Dr. Holt, who had called in also an obstetrician and a neurologist, Dr. Frederick Peterson, for the discussion. The usual attitude of the child specialist was, "Our living depends upon babies. Why should we advocate limiting the supply? The more the merrier. If you cut down, you're taking our maintenance from us." But Dr. Holt said, "A thoroughly reliable contraceptive would be a godsend to us. If the family cannot afford a nurse we must rely on the health and strength of the mother to keep her baby alive. If pregnancy can be postponed for a few years, not only the baby who has been born, but the baby who comes after is much more likely to survive."

Dr. Holt lent us his name, one of the first important physicians to do so, thus setting an example which eventually others followed. Five or six men and women doctors agreed to stand behind the clinic.

To every woman there comes the apprehension that marriage may not fulfill her highest expectations and dreams. If in the heart of a girl entering this covenant for the first time there are doubts, even in the slightest degree, they are doubled and trebled in their intensity when she meditates a second marriage.

J. Noah H. Slee, whom I had known for some time, was what the papers called "a staid pillar of finance." He was South African born but had made his fortune in the United States. In customs and exteriors we were as far apart as the poles; he was a conservative in politics and a churchman, whereas I voted for Norman Thomas and, instead of attending orthodox services, preferred to go to the opera.

An old-fashioned type of man, J.N. yearned to protect any type of woman who would cling. . . . Nevertheless, despite his foibles, he was generous in wanting me to continue my unfinished work, and was undeterred by my warning that he would always have to be kissing me good-by in depots or waving farewell as the gangplank went up.

I had to consider also that I had two boys to be educated, and that children were much more to a woman than to a man. Yet I knew he would be kind and understanding with them. Furthermore, he had faith both in individuals and in humanity; his naïve appearance of hardness was actually not borne out in fact. He kept his promises and hated debts; we attached the same importance to the spirit of integrity. . . .

In 1923, with stones gathered from the fields we built a house near Fishkill, New York, cradled in the Dutchess County hills, beside a little lake. On it we tried out swans, but they did not work; although they looked picturesque, they were too messy. So we changed to ducks and stocked the water with bass. I planned a blue garden which grew up and down and threw itself about the house and altered with the seasons. Pepper, a cocker spaniel puppy of two months, came the first year and bounced and leaped around us as we walked through the woods or rode horseback over the hills.

Willow Lake was only sixty miles from New York. I could make out the menus for a week ahead, leave directions for the gardening, be in my office fairly early and back again for dinner at night. Later, for working purposes, we built a studio among the treetops on the edge of a cliff from which I could look far off across the majestic valley of the Hudson.

Domesticity, which I had once so scorned, had its charms after all. . . .

The more I had studied, the more clearly I had recognized that it was not possible to advise a standard contraceptive for all women any more than it was possible to prescribe one set of eyeglasses for all conditions of sight. Only upon examination and careful check-up could you determine the most suitable method. No detailed statistics had ever been kept except at Brownsville, and those case histories had never been returned to me by the police. I wanted to collect at least a thousand such records for a scientific survey before any opposition could interfere with the plan.

Many women were still coming to me personally for information at 104 Fifth Avenue. The best thing to do was have a woman doctor right there to take care of them—a quiet way to begin. It was hard to locate one foot-loose and free; I could have no shying or running off at the first indication of trouble. In making inquiries I heard of Dr. Dorothy Bocker, who held a New York City license though she was at present in the Public Health Service of Georgia. This single, cordial, and enthusiastic young woman knew practically nothing about birth control technique, but was willing to learn. The difficulty was that she wanted five thousand dollars a year.

At first this appeared an almost unsurmountable obstacle. Here was just the person I had been looking for, but it seemed beyond my power to raise so large a sum. I was loaded with the financial weight of the *Review* and the League. That organization had been admitted as a membership corporation and hence could not secure a license to conduct a clinic, which in New York was synonymous with a dispensary. No clinic, therefore, could be included in its budget; it would remain a department of the League by courtesy only, being actually my private undertaking. Where could I find someone to donate such an enormous amount?

Then I remembered Clinton Chance, a young manufacturer of Birmingham, who had prospered exceedingly both before and during the War. He and his wife, Janet, had become good friends of mine during my 1920 visit to England. Having felt the need of a more sound and fundamental outlet for his riches than that provided by charity, he had come to see that birth control information was far better for his employees than a dole at the birth of every new baby. He was not in any sense a professional philanthropist, but only wanted to help them be self-sufficient.

Clinton had once offered me money to set the birth control movement going in England, but I had refused then because England had enough co-workers, who were handling the situation well, and, furthermore, my place was in the United States. He had then said to me, "I won't give you a contribution for regular current expenses, but if ever you see the necessity for some new project which will advance the general good, call on me."

Now I cabled Clinton at length, explaining my need. He promptly answered, "Yes, go ahead," and soon arrived an anonymous thousand pounds to cover Dr. Bocker's salary for the first year. I made out a contract for two. She was to come in January, 1923, and we were to shoulder the risks and responsibilities together.

Even to choose a name for the venture was not easy. I had been steadily advertising the term "clinic" to America for so long that it had become familiar and, moreover, to poor people it meant that little or no payment was required. But the use of the word itself was legally impossible, . . . and I was not certain that the same might not be true of "center" or "bureau." I wanted it at least to imply the things that clinic meant as I had publicized it, and also to include the idea of research.

Finally, one of the doors of the two rooms adjoining the League offices, readily accessible to me and to the women who came for advice, was lettered, Clinical Research.

It was still a clinic in my mind, though frankly an experiment because I was not even sure women would accept the methods we had to offer them. We started immediately keeping the records. Dr. Bocker wrote down the history of the case on a large card, numbering it to correspond with a smaller one containing the patient's name and address. Each applicant she suspected of a bad heart, tuberculosis, kidney trouble, or any ailment which made pregnancy dangerous, she informed regarding contraception and advised medical care at once.

In our first annual report, which attracted much attention, all our cases were analyzed. We said, "Here is the proof—nine hundred women with definite statistics concerning their ages, physical and mental conditions, and economic status." . . .

Dr. Hannah M. Stone, a fine young woman from the Lying-In Hospital, volunteered to take Dr. Bocker's place without salary. Her gaze was clear and straight, her hair was black, her mouth gentle and sweet. She had a sympathetic response to mothers in distress, and a broad attitude toward life's many problems. When the Lying-In Hospital later found she had connected herself with our clinic, it gave her a choice between remaining with us and resigning from the staff. She resigned. Her courageous stand indicated staunch friendship and the disinterested selflessness essential for the successful operation of the clinic. These qualities have kept her with us all this time, one of the most beloved and loyal workers that one could ever hope for. . . .

Meanwhile, between 1921 and 1926, I received over a million letters from mothers requesting information. From 1923 on a staff of three to seven was constantly busy just opening and answering them. Despite the limitations of the writers and their lack of education, they revealed themselves strangely conscious of the responsibilities of the maternal function.

Childbearing is hazardous, even when carried out with the advantages of modern hygiene and parental care. The upper middle classes are likely to assume all confinements are surrounded by the same attention given the births of their own babies. They do not comprehend it is still possible in these United States for a woman to milk six cows at five o'clock in the morning and bring a baby into the world at nine. The terrific hardships of the farm mother are not in the least degree lessened by maternity. If she and her infant survive, it is only to face these hardships anew, and with additional complications. . . .

To prove that the story could be told by the mothers themselves, ten thousand letters, with the assistance of Mary Boyd, were selected and these again cut to five hundred. Eventually this historical record appeared in book form as *Motherhood in Bondage*.

Whenever I am discouraged I go to those letters as to a well-spring which sends me on reheartened. They make me realize with increasing intensity that whoever kindles a spark of hope in the breast of another cannot shirk the duty of keeping it alive. . . .

The jelly I had found in Friedrichshaven had turned out to be too expensive, because it was made with a chinosol and Irish moss base, and the price of the former was prohibitive in preparing it for poor women. Dr. Stone and Dr. Cooper, therefore, devised a formula for a jelly with a lactic acid and glycerine base, which was within our means. Most of their cases, however, were sufficiently grave for them not to feel justified in using it alone experimentally. Consequently, they took the precaution of having a double safeguard by combining the chemical contraceptive with the mechanical—jelly with pessary—which proved ninety-eight percent efficacious.

At this time we could not import diaphragms directly. Although I had given various friends going to Germany and England the mission of bringing them in, this could not be done in sufficient quantity. Furthermore, since bootlegging supplies could not continue indefinitely I had to find out how they could legally be made here.

Two young men came to help in whatever way was most necessary. Herbert Simonds, who had been in advertising, began to investigate the possibility that some recognized rubber company should make our supplies. When one and all were fearful, he and Guy Moyston, who did some publicity for us, concluded they would form the Holland-Rantos Company, selling only to physicians or on prescription. They spent their own time and thousands of dollars personally on research, in the end perfecting a quality of rubber that could stand the variations of climate in the United States—hot houses and cold winters, Florida dampness and Western dryness.

Meanwhile, Julius Schmid, an old established manufacturer, had been importing from his own concern in Germany a few diaphragms, but only on a modest scale because he did not want to run afoul of the Comstock law. As soon as he saw a potential market in the medical profession he fetched from the Fatherland several families who had been making molds there, gave them places to live in, and set up a little center, expanding gradually until eventually he sold more contraceptive supplies than any firm in the world. . . .

As a cause becomes more and more successful, the ideas of the people engaged in it are bound to change. . . .

There is doubtless a place for organizations that restrict their scope to the status quo. Most charities are like that—they live on securities, install as officers those who keep pace with but are never in advance of general opinion. Two members of the Board, with League-of-Women-Voters training, saw the movement in the light of routine, annual membership dues and a budget, going through the same ritual year after year and remaining that way, performing a quiet service in the community. I looked upon it as something temporary, something to sweep through, to be done with and finished; it was merely an instrument for accomplishment. I wanted us to avail ourselves of every psychological event, to push ahead until hospitals and public health agencies took over birth control as part of their regular program, which would end our function. . . .

June 12, 1928, I resigned the presidency of the League. Because the majority of the Directors were against this, and because I wanted to make it easier for Mrs. Robertson-Jones to take over, I stayed on the Board and continued to edit the *Review*.

But the divergence of opinions rapidly crystallized in the next few months. This had to be pondered upon and wisely dealt with. The situation was going to mean constant friction, and the League might easily disintegrate into a dying, static thing. In any event, internal discord was abhorrent. I began to ask myself whether I could pass over the *Review*, which for eleven years had been a vital part of my own being.

Then came a meeting at which the question of the editorship arose. For the first time friend opposed friend. Three voted against me; the other nine were for me. But my mind was now made up.

I could fight outside enemies but not those who had been my fellow-workers; I would give complete freedom to others in order to obtain a new freedom for myself. Therefore, I surrendered the *Review* to the League as its private property. . . .

In the beginning of the birth control movement the main purpose had been the mitigation of women's suffering, Comstock law or no Comstock law. Its very genesis had been the conscious, deliberate, and public violation of this statute. Later, to change it became imperative, so that the millions who depended upon dispensaries and hospitals could be instructed by capable hands. . . .

Before you had seen it, the Congress of the United States loomed impressively in your consciousness; you had a feeling, "This is the greatest country in the world, this is its Government, I helped to send these men here." Then you watched Congress at work, listened to it, and were disillusioned. A few years of sitting in the gallery and looking down gave you less respect for the quality of our representatives, less faith in legislative action, and you wondered whether those who had already abandoned hope of obtaining relief in this way and resorted to direct action had not, perhaps, the right idea.

The same arguments went on from year to year. A certain amount of publicity was secured, a certain number were educated. Some of our followers, in face of the evidence to the contrary, still were confident that if the Catholics understood our bill they would not obstruct it. . . .

In 1934 identical bills were introduced in Senate and House. . . . For the first time the Senate sub-committee reported out the bill and it was put on the unanimous consent calendar. The last day of the session came, June 13th. Over two hundred were ahead of it, but there was always hope. One after another they were hurried through and then, miracle of miracles, ours passed with no voice raised against it. The next one came up, was also converted into law, another up for discussion, tabled. Twenty minutes went by. Suddenly Senator Pat McCarran from Reno, Nevada, famous divorce lawyer though an outstanding Catholic, came rushing in from the cloak room and asked for unanimous consent to recall our bill. As a matter of senatorial courtesy Senator Hastings granted his request; had he not done so Senator McCarran would have objected to every bill he introduced thereafter. It was summarily referred back to the committee and there died. . . .

In 1935 we took the fatal step of having it voted on early in the session and it was promptly killed. The whole year's labor was lost. . . .

Another line of attack on the Comstock law was to try for a liberal interpretation through the courts. Among the products shown at the Zurich Conference in 1930 had been a Japanese pessary. Pursuing the clinic policy of testing every new contraceptive that appeared, I ordered some of these from a Tokyo physician. When notified by the Customs that they had been barred entrance and destroyed, we sent for another shipment addressed to Dr. Stone in the hope that it would then be delivered to a physician. But this also was refused, and accordingly we brought suit in her name.

After pending two years the case finally came up for trial before Judge Grover Moscowitz of the Federal District Court of Southern New York. Morris Ernst conducted our claim brilliantly, and January 6, 1936, Judge Moscowitz decided in our favor—the wording of the statute seemed to forbid the importation of any article for preventing conception, but he believed that the statute should be construed more reasonably. The Government at once appealed and the case was argued in the Circuit Court of Appeals before Judges Augustus N. Hand, Learned Hand, and Thomas Swan, whose unanimous decisions were rarely reversed in the Supreme Court.

In the fall of 1936, while I was in Washington getting the Federal bill started again in advance of Congress' meeting, news came that the three judges had upheld the Moscowitz decision and had added that a doctor was entitled not only to bring articles into this country but, more important, to send them through the mails, and, finally, to use them for the patient's general well-being—which, for twenty years, had been the object of my earnest endeavor. . . .

The Government still had the right to appeal inside of ninety days. Therefore, I was not unduly jubilant. We had had so many seeming victories that melted away afterwards.

But long before the period of grace had expired, Attorney General Cummings announced to the press that the Government would accept the decision as law, and, with commendable consistency, the Secretary of the Treasury sent word to the Customs at once that our shipments should be admitted. It is really a relief to be able to say something good about the Government. . . .

I was at Willow Lake one June morning of 1937 when I saw spread across the newspaper in double column the glad tidings: the Committee on Contraception of the American Medical Association had informed the convention that physicians had the legal right to give contraceptives, and it recommended that standards be investigated and technique be taught in medical schools.

In my excitement I actually fell downstairs. To me this was really a greater victory than the Moscowitz decision. Here was the culmination of unremitting labor ever since my return from Europe in 1915, the gratification of seeing a dream come true.

These specific achievements are significant because they open the way to a broader field of attainment and to research which can immeasurably improve methods now known, making possible the spread of birth control into the forlorn, overpopulated places of the earth, and permitting science eventually to determine the potentialities of a posterity conceived and born of conscious love.

What I have been able to contribute to the birth control movement has been the result of forces which set a clear design almost from infancy, each succeeding circumstance tracing the lines more sharply: my being born into a family so large as to be in part responsible for my mother's premature death; my preparation as a nurse, which awoke me to the sorrows of women; the inspiration of having come into contact with great minds and having claimed many as friends. It may have been destiny as some have said—I do not know.

To have helped carry the cause thus far has been at times strenuous, but I have never considered it a sacrifice. Every conscious hour, night and day, in any city, in any country, has brought its compensations. My life has been joyous and exulting and full because it has touched profoundly millions of other lives. It is ever a privilege to be a part of something unquestionably proved of value, something so fundamentally right. . . .

In January, 1937, in that same Town Hall where fifteen years before I had been forbidden to speak, and whence I had been haled into court, I was honored with a medal. Pearl Buck said on one occasion, "The cause conquers because youth is for you. I have lived in China so long, and know what it is to wait until the old ones die and the young can do what is necessary to be done." I am glad both my sons are doctors with a background of human interest to which has been added a scientific quality of mind that can aid in pushing the horizon of service further into the future.

I am often asked, "Aren't you happy now that the struggle is over?" But I cannot agree that it is. Though many disputed barricades have been leaped, you can never sit back, smugly content, believing that victory is forever yours; there is always the threat of its being snatched from you. All freedom must be safeguarded and held. Jubilation is unwarranted while the world is in warring turmoil, each political unit trying to hold on to what it has—some threatening to take it away and others looking covetously towards outlets in countries not yet completely filled. The application of the movement to nations which should, in the interests of peace, control their populations, must endure.

Anna Louise Strong

(1885–1970)

Anna Louise Strong, radical journalist and writer, was born in Friend, Nebraska, the eldest daughter of a Congregational minister. She was a precocious child, educated in public schools until the family settled in Cincinnati in 1892. Graduated from high school at age fifteen, Strong studied at Oberlin College and Bryn Mawr, receiving her B.A. from Oberlin in 1905 and entering graduate study in philosophy at the University of Chicago, from which she received her Ph.D. in 1908, at the age of twenty-three.

The year 1915 found Strong in Seattle, where her father, now widowed, had settled. Here she wrote for progressive newspapers, won election to the school board, and organized antiwar rallies in the west. By 1918 her defense of opponents of the draft led to her recall from the school board and sent her to write under a pseudonym for the *Seattle Union Record,* a labor newspaper. Her editorials and feature articles helped build the climate for the Seattle General Strike, which gave her radical views wide publicity.

When the general strike collapsed, Strong, disillusioned, set out for Eastern Europe as an employee of the American Friends Service Committee, hoping that she could move on into Russia to see the new society being built by the Bolsheviks. Successful in getting to the Soviet Union, she remained to teach English, counting Trotsky among her pupils, and to write a spirited defense of Bolshevik economic policy (*The First Time in History,* 1924).

While she hoped to help the Revolution through work with the orphans of the Volga Famine and through the establishment of a trade school in Moscow, it was Strong's access to the press in the United States that most interested her Soviet colleagues. Her life became a pattern of travel to selected sites around the Soviet Union followed by lecture trips and fund-raising events in the United States.

Strong went to Soviet Asia and China in 1925, beginning the fascination with China which shaped the latter half of her life. In the Soviet Union she found the partner she had sought in life, not a romantic lover but a friend and co-worker, Joel Shubin, with whom she formed a common law union. In 1939 the two were together briefly in New York, where Shubin was in charge of the

Soviet Pavilion at the World's Fair, but Strong was trapped in the United States by the outbreak of the Second World War.

Strong wrote a series of books and film scripts publicizing Soviet heroism in the war, her most noted success being the MGM film *Song of Russia,* for which she was the technical adviser. Accredited by the *Atlantic Monthly* in 1944, Strong returned to Russia in time to follow the Red Army's drive across Poland to Berlin.

Footloose because of her husband's death in wartime Moscow, Strong left for the Chinese Communist headquarters in Yenan in 1946. There she met Mao Tse-tung and reported his famous dictum that all reactionaries are paper tigers. Her request to remain with the Communist Chinese was denied by Mao, who asked instead that she return to the West and publicize the Chinese Revolution. She did this so energetically in the Soviet Union that she was deported as a spy in 1949. After living in some obscurity in the United States, Strong traveled in 1958 to Peking, from whence she began to publish her famous *Letter from China* in 1962.

Her service to China was recognized by Mao in 1965, when on her eightieth birthday she was made an honorary member of the Red Guard. In failing health, she sought to return to the United States in 1969 to campaign against the Vietnam War, but she died in Peking and was buried in the National Memorial Cemetery of Revolutionary Martyrs.

Strong was probably the most effective publicist of the Soviet Union in the United States in the 1930s and '40s; her writing makes the collectivization of farming sound like the triumph of the serfs, and her romanticized portraits of Lenin and his associates make them sound like benevolent municipal planners. Yet she captured the diversity of the Soviet world, its vast land expanse, its Asian hinterland, its utopian hopes for a future shaped by industrial technology. Her *Letter from China* was one of the few sources of information in English about the Sino-Soviet dispute and daily life in Mao's China.

I CHANGE WORLDS:
The Remaking of an American

My father was the pioneer of his family; every American family in those days had one or more. It was he who went west. He went west spiritually also. . . .

My mother determined to make us fearless. The thunderstorms of the west, which rage across the prairie and are feared by many children and even by timid adults, were cleverly made by her our special treats for good behavior. We were allowed, as a great prize, to sit on the porch and watch the next thunderstorm. . . .

The northern part of Ohio, where my mother grew to womanhood, had led in the fight against Negro slavery; her college, Oberlin, held the proud tradition of being the first university to admit Negroes, as it had admitted women, on the basis of a common humanity. . . .

It was and is the theory of the American middle class that their children should see no evil in the world. None of the great battles of man should enter the home to "take the bloom from youth." . . .

From neither of my parents did I ever hear a harsh or unjust word: if they blamed or punished, it was only after careful inquiry showed me the reason for my punishment. I grew up expecting justice and kindness as natural rights of man: if anyone treated me with unkindness, I assumed it must be through my fault.

Whether through my own reputation for cleverness or the standing of my father's church or my mother's personal persuasiveness I was accepted as "guest pupil" in the best private school of Cincinnati where, with excellent individual instruction, I promptly finished eight grades in four years and even acquired a smattering of French. . . .

Not for nearly a lifetime did it occur to me that it may be a dangerous thing to launch into life expecting only kindness, and always inventing plausible good motives for acts that are clearly evil.

Even the family kindness which surrounded me could not protect me from the human loneliness which befell one day in a garden and which set a recurring problem for nearly forty years of life. For as I try to answer the question what took me to Moscow and what it is that I found, I seem to trace the beginning of all my conscious seeking in the little girl, eleven years old, who played on a perfect day in spring near lilac bushes on a parsonage lawn in Oak Park. . . .

. . . for one long eternal moment there was no living creature there at all. Then, whether it was the blue and gold perfection of the day, of the intoxication of the lilac-laden air, or the exquisite curve of one white spray against the purple blooms—suddenly the little girl knew that she was a hard, round soul and that all the spacious springtime was outside. . . .

I do not know what psychologists now teach about that loneliness of the human soul with which philosophers begin and poets end.

Our individuality is partial and restless; the stream of consciousness that we call "I" is made of shifting elements that flow from our group and back to our group again. Always we seek to be ourselves and the herd together, not One against the herd.

So at high moments, when our life is keenest, striving to lose itself in wider life beyond us—each in his own way by art, religion, patriotism, love, comradeship or work—we lose ourselves in something larger.

The way out of human loneliness—this was the search that began for me a lifetime ago in a garden. . . .

As adolescence deepened, heaven grew more personal. It acquired companionship more intimate and perfect than anything afforded by earth. My first contacts with the world outside my home had shown me that by no means everybody loved me.

A painful feeling began to grow of being generally not wanted. I felt in terms of great generalities. I wanted everybody to like me; I felt that nobody did.

From this haunting feeling of being not wanted, which remained a recurrent haunt through life, I found two ways of escape, both of which in changing form also persisted. One was the invention of gods, the other was personal efficiency in work. . . .

I was still in my early teens when I discovered the poverty of Chicago's west side; I went there to teach sewing in settlement classes. I was told that this poverty was due to ignorance; these people were not yet developed. I never thought of them as a different "class." They were just immigrants from a more backward world who had not yet attained the polished prosperity which America gave. . . .

. . . it was in my middle teens . . . that I read Bellamy's *Looking Backward*. Entranced by this Utopia of the year 2000, which bore marked resemblances to my early heaven, I was also impressed by its economic basis in publicly owned wealth and equal division of goods. . . .

My father . . . had become unusually broad-minded for his generation on the question of divorce and fallen women, for his own family he accepted the view that the first sexual experience of a girl either establishes her or ruins her. He had rejected property marriage with disdain, yet he cherished uncritically the ethics derived from it.

Nor did I myself escape those ethics. In spite of my protest that "nothing a man could do to me could permanently ruin me" I really thought of marriage as the great decisive choice of life which would determine all my future and to which any previous schemes of my own must be sacrificed.

I even chose my future work with reference to its possible subordination in marriage. Writing seemed to me an admirable occupation because it could be done in any part of the world to which my husband might take me, and could even be accomplished in odd moments at home. I tried to avoid having opinions which were too fixed and definite, which might some day have to be changed to fit a married state. I reasoned that I must have some work of my own and save a little money in order to be independent in case I should disagree with my husband, and not be a burden on him in case we happily agreed. If I did all these things then when the master of my fate at last arrived, I should be ready to adapt myself to anything he might demand. . . .

The paths of love and work are indeed the twin paths out of loneliness for all generations of men; but always they are conditioned by the environment of class and time. . . .

I finished high school so early that I spent a year in Germany and half a year in Switzerland studying languages before I was considered old enough for college. I studied a year in Bryn Mawr, graduated in Oberlin and took postgraduate work leading to a doctor's degree in the University of Chicago, partly because I finished so soon that I wasn't old enough for a good job. Yet none of all the courses I took was any very exact preparation for anything I might intend to do. None of us knew what the world would make us do (we called it "what we expect to do"). We knew only that we intended to get ahead in the world. This everyone in America intended. One got ahead by efficiency.

To make a little learning seem much; to sell ourselves to the world at a price higher than was justified by the quality of our goods—this salesman's ethic was our ethic. We called it "making the most of ourselves." . . .

I decided to specialize in philosophy chiefly because I had liked the religious emotions which accompanied that subject in Oberlin, where one got the sense of discovering an infinite world. After the first six months of the dry philosophy of the University of Chicago, with its logic and theory of knowledge, I knew that I hated it. Nevertheless I stuck; I was growing alarmed at my frequent shifting from school to school and from school to jobs. I wanted to prove to myself and the world that I could stick to something. This was the form my personal efficiency took; it led me even to do away with bluff. A doctorate of philosophy was a sure proof of efficiency; nobody could call you shallow after that. So I worked my brain till I could feel it ache, twisting around new problems which seemed to me to have no connection with life. . . .

I came to my last year of graduate study and took as subject for the thesis on which the granting of my degree of doctor of philosophy depended "A Study of Prayer from the Standpoint of Social Psychology." This emotional material attracted me. For a whole year I read and classified the devotional literature of the centuries. It was characteristic of the liberal theology around me that religion should not fear science.

I . . . classified prayers into "esthetic prayers" of the Christian mystics and the Buddhists, who seek oblivion in the infinite, and "practical prayers" in which more energetic people use God to get anything from a job to moral strength.

It never occurred to me that it was the suppressed peoples who tried to forget despair, and the imperialist peoples who asked God's blessing on their work. The thesis was published as a book by the University of Chicago Press. . . .

This was what the efficient American universities had made of that lonely girl in a garden. Her parents made her fearless and independent, yet wanting to win love by being good. Her gods made her a seeker for masters whom she was ready to serve and adore. Now her education made of her mind an efficient two-edged tool, able to cut in any direction but not to choose a direction. . . .

I discovered the world in the Child Welfare Exhibit of Kansas City, in 1911. I saw it forever after in terms of my first responsible job. The very same week I discovered socialism. . . .

I had known the word *socialism* from my brief youthful dream inspired by Bellamy's *Looking Backward*. But now in Kansas City

I came to socialism backward as an employer of labor. The architectural draftsman who helped draw plans for the booths and central court of our exhibit came to me in the midst of the crowds of the opening and asked how much longer we would need him. . . .

"Not that I want to leave but I ought to know. As far as I can see, there's nothing for me to do after Saturday."

"No, there's nothing after Saturday," I answered. Actually his work was already over; I was giving him the grace of an extra week. It was one of the forgotten details of the opening.

That night I found it was not forgotten. . . .

Joyously weary with the opening, I could not sleep. The words of the draftsman came back in their full meaning. I knew he had a wife and two small children and had been without a job for months. I knew the prospects for his future work were poor. How did it chance that I, a girl in my twenties and in no way related to this man, had the power to refuse him the right to a living? . . .

If I had ever heard of Marx at all, the whole set-up of my student life was arranged to make me minimize and forget him. They did not argue against him; they merely ignored him. If I ever had heard of the Paris Commune it can only have been by vague references to riots at the end of the Franco-German War of 1870–71; even years later when I heard of it in Russia, I thought they were talking of the French Revolution. Not only college but all American middle class life was thus protected against knowledge. I may have heard of socialism on the west side of Chicago; but if so, it passed lightly over an already insulated surface. . . .

I came to Seattle during the early years of the World War, while the peoples of Europe writhed in the agony of new forms of death, and America stood aloof. My father had gone there earlier, during my last year of graduate work in Chicago; my mother was long since dead. I had been organizing Child Welfare Exhibits around the country for years. But the exhibits were becoming standardized under the U.S. Children's Bureau and the Russell Sage Foundation, which told the folk of the provinces what to believe. The thrill of feeling a whole community come into organized life was gone. I ran one last exhibit of the U.S. Children's Bureau at the Panama Pacific Exposition in San Francisco in 1915, organized an "exhibit-investigation" of "Children's Interests" in Portland, Oregon, where children displayed toys, pets and hobbies, and then refused to return to the deadening life of Washington, D.C.

On the Pacific Coast to which my job had taken me, I had found a new solace for human isolation—the companionship of the hills. Long hikes on Tamalpais from San Francisco were followed in Portland by trips with the Mazamas, a mountaineering organization which conquered the tangled jungles of western forests and climbed the glaciers of Mt. Hood. This new-found wilderness became for me a passion; I began to seek more and more difficult climbs, new peaks to conquer. I organized in November the first winter climb of Mt. Hood, in which we four participants were all but swept away in an unexpected blizzard. All night under a starless sky we felt our way downward while storm clouds darkened the upper air and swept the peak which we had quitted just in time.

On our return to Portland less venturesome members of the Mazamas berated us for the foolhardy risking of lives. "If there had been a scientific end to be gained! What did you go for? Just a record!" I retorted that we had at least found out whether the upper slopes were snow or ice in winter, which had not been known before. But this was not the reason that had driven me. How could I explain that ecstasy that arose out of physical pain and exhaustion which the human will subdued, that new mysticism of the adventurer, conquering the unconquerable forces of desolate nature. . . .

I loved these savage wastes which the strength of my youth could conquer, and from which I wrung far vistas of blinding beauty; the knowledge that advancing age or weakness must in the end betray me to a death on some cliff or glacier only added to the fascination of these dark gods of nature. For the next five years this was my new form of opium. . . .

The Seattle to which I came in the second year of the World War rated as a progressive city. The populace invariably voted against the "reactionary interests" who represented capital imported from New York. . . .

The progressive forces asked me to run for the School Board; for many years they had wished to have a woman on that board, which had been for two decades a self-perpetuating committee of bankers and business men. The chief plank in our platform was the wider use of school buildings for all sorts of public meetings, a demand close to the heart of all small clubs, societies, coöperative organizations, liberal and radical associations, which wished a respectable and inexpensive place in which to meet.

Fresh from my work with the U.S. Children's Bureau, with the degree of doctor of philosophy and two or three books to my credit, I was easily the most acceptable candidate in town. University clubs supported "a really educated woman against those self-made men of business." Labor organizations supported "schools run by teachers and mothers, instead of by capitalists." I was not a little helped by the wide popularity of my father. He had induced the Ministers' Federation to exchange fraternal delegates with organized labor, and had supported certain local strikes. The school election was at that time a sleepy affair attended by a few citizens and usually controlled by the self-perpetuating board through their pressure on the teachers. I easily captured the election. . . .

Once by judicious use of publicity I succeeded in stopping the use of our high schools to recruit under-age volunteers for the war. Otherwise the machine rolled over me weekly, voting appropriations for matters about which I understood little. Questions of education they never dealt with; they referred them to the superintendent. The interest of the board members was in gas and heating contracts, new buildings for important new areas, the spending of public funds. . . .

. . . in larger commercial cities, like Seattle, there were many smaller business men who depended on the trade of the lumberjacks, and were themselves oppressed by big business. In such cities the fighting lumberjacks got a hearing. They carried on free speech fights, defying the lawless tactics of police by getting themselves arrested in such numbers that they flooded the local jails and broke the machinery of local courts with the number of cases. Such tactics brought grins of approval from large numbers of ordinary citizens who had not forgotten the courage and grimness of the pioneer. . . .

Towards the end of 1916 it became evident that strong forces were pushing America towards the battle trenches of Europe. Yet "our America's" pioneer traditions were against "entangling alliances." To supplement this negative aloofness we had a positive faith. Men of all nations and races, the best and most energetic, had come to our America seeking freedom. We must preserve freedom and democracy for the world.

I threw myself into the Anti-Preparedness League, the Union Against Militarism, the Emergency Peace Federation—all that rapidly shifting galaxy of organizations with which pacifists, liberals, radicals and progressives fought America's advance towards war. . . .

Then this America whose populace protested war and whose profiteers desired it, left us and marched into the war with all of Europe. As the war approached, our local branch of the Anti-Preparedness Committee, the American Union Against Militarism, the Emergency Peace Federation, dwindled; the respectable members were turning to war work. The presidents of women's clubs were "swinging in behind the President"; the head of the Parent-Teachers organizations, who spoke so valiantly for peace in the mass meeting which featured the flag, found other duties now. . . .

I was still secretary of the organization and I glanced bitterly at the empty tables. "Only a handful of socialists and wobblies left," I said. "All the people of prominence have deserted. Nobody left who can do anything."

The meeting reorganized as the "Anti-Conscription League," and voted to communicate with organizations of that name a-rising in the East. I asked them to elect another secretary. "Anti-conscription is a man's fight," I said. "My summer camps in the mountains are soon starting and I shall not be in town."

I drugged myself with forests, cliffs and glaciers. I exhausted myself with twenty-four-hour climbs. It was the end of youth, the end of belief, the end of "our America." I could not face the ruins of my world. . . .

The fall of the tsar passed lightly over me; I was chiefly annoyed at the way it was seized by our patriots to justify America's participation in the war. I was too far removed from any large Russian populations to note the flocking of revolutionists back to Petrograd, or to understand its importance. The first signal from the revolution which I caught was the call for a conference in Stockholm to discuss terms of "a democratic peace without annexations or indemnities."

It came to me in the mountain camps by the glaciers. Towards the end of summer a new newspaper began to appear in camp occasionally—the Seattle *Daily Call*. Four pages, poorly written, badly printed—it said what I wanted to say about the war. It said them in harsh words and poor English—the things that respectable folk had ceased to say. It jeered at the Wilson slogans, at "war to end war," at "world safe for democracy." It declared that America went into the war to protect her loans to the Allies and to make money for war profiteers. It demanded conscription of profits to balance conscription of men. It published the call to the Stockholm conference, from a land in revolution beyond both seas. "Let the workers of all lands get together and end this war," said that message. . . .

As soon as the summer camp season ended I found the office of the *Call* and offered them my services as a writer. Thereafter I wrote almost a page of the paper a day. I covered "class war" trials

in the courts; I already called it that when socialists and I.W.W.s
were railroaded to jail for demanding normal American rights. I
covered local city hall grafts, local jail conditions, local labor, the
newly forming Loyal Legion of Lumbermen, which was being organized to undercut the I.W.W. I covered also whatever we could
get of national and world affairs. . . .

Meantime class lines in Seattle were forming around a more
personal struggle. An anti-conscription leaflet which had been authorized in that last meeting I had attended after the declaration of
war had led to the arrest of four men, of whom the best known
was Hulet Wells, socialist, former president of the Seattle Central
Labor Council. . . . The defense intended to assert their right as
American citizens to oppose European entanglements and conscript
armies; they would list the many prominent Americans who had
openly agreed with them only a few months ago.

"If that is your method of defense," I said, "you should call
me as witness. I can connect you not only with people prominent
in Seattle, but with famous names in the East. I will tell of the
cafeteria meeting where we voted to print that dodger and show
that it was paid for by well-known Americans, from funds which
I personally handled."

Wells wanted to spare me; he knew better than I what would
be the result for me personally. We consulted Vanderveer, attorney
for the defense. He also displayed some conscience towards my
future. "Young lady," he said with a warning smile, "my advice to
you personally is that you need a guardian to keep you out of this;
but my statement as attorney for the defense is that you offer us
our best chance of winning."

Across eight columns of Seattle's front pages flamed the news
when the woman member of the School Board took the stand in
the "treason case." Vanderveer staged it well. He let the prosecutor
display the evidence of police court agents, creating an atmosphere
of cellar conspiracies. Then he called, as his unexpected first witness,
the best known among all the respectable women of Seattle, the
woman member of the School Board, connected with mothers and
children and with progressives. My connection with the Seattle
Daily Call was not yet widely known except among the workers
who read it.

This highly respectable young woman said: "Certainly we
printed that dodger! What's wrong with it except its rotten style?
Are you arresting for mistakes in grammar? I could have written it

better; but I only gave money to print it. All of us did. Who? The American Union Against Militarism, affiliated in the East with Jane Addams, Lillian Wald, all the real patriots who hated this war as un-American. What's unlawful about that dodger? Printed before the conscription law passed, wasn't it, when nine-tenths of this country thought conscription un-American? Even if it hadn't been, who prevents free-born Americans from attacking an oppressive law?"

. . . It finished the trial; it gave us a hung jury. It can be done once—that approach of outraged respectability; it can be done by the same person only once. After it I was the best-known woman in Seattle; I was no longer among the most respectable. . . .

For the defendants my testimony changed little in the end. The district attorney tried them again a few months later when we no longer had the weapon of surprise. He got his conviction easily the second time, and the socialists went to jail. The real result of that first trial lay in the agitation it caused, and in my own changed status. The political hangers-on of the Chamber of Commerce seized the chance to start a recall to remove me from the School Board. . . .

. . . though no word of our side was printed for three months by any newspaper except the Seattle *Daily Call,* yet when the votes were counted, the good citizens who had expected a ten to one victory over a "handful of traitors," won by only some two thousand votes in a total of eighty-five thousand. They actually lost the city council to the "reds" who had intelligently prepared a whole slate, while the patriots had emotionally concentrated on the recall and the mayor. The patriots were momentarily crushed into silence; they were actually worried. We celebrated our "victorious defeat" in the Central Labor Council. . . .

The general strike thus thrust upon unwilling leaders grew out of a strike of thirty-five thousand shipyard workers for wage adjustments. Throughout the war wages had been fixed by government boards in consultation with national presidents of craft unions. They bribed the highly skilled workers and cut the pay of the unskilled, which ran counter to the "solidarity" policy of our local Metal Trades Council. Discontent smoldered for a year and a half of war-time, ready to burst into flame when restraints should be removed. . . .

. . . swiftly union after union violated its constitution, flouted its national officers and sacrificed hard-won agreements to join the strike. . . .

Suddenly on the fourth morning the strike was called off by a resolution which declared that there had been no defeat but that everyone should return to work on the following day. It was a muddled resolution in which the only thing that was clear was that the strike was over, and that nobody could tell exactly why. Its confused tone was echoed almost exactly years later by the resolution which ended the British general strike. . . .

A history committee was elected to produce a collectively authenticated account of our experiences that "the workers of the world may learn from our mistakes as well as from our successes." I was historian, submitting everything first to the committee and then through the columns of the *Union Record* to the workers' comments. We tried to analyze what we had hoped to gain and how we should have gained it. Was it a strike to demonstrate solidarity? Then we should have fixed a definite termination. Was it a strike for shipyard wages? Then we should have made this clear. Was it a strike for revolution? Then we should have been prepared to hold and organize power. "But we did not have the past experience or the intentions on which revolution is built." . . .

There began to arise again in me the longing of the pioneer to escape from insoluble problems of the human society around me. Whither could I flee from the empty dissensions, from the deadening yet bitter reaction in which the exultant faith of our Seattle "revolution" so unaccountably had perished? . . .

. . . when my old friend [Lincoln] Steffens, the admired reporter of my youth who had covered the "shame of the cities" and all the muck-raking reforms which tried to keep America democratic, came back from the war-torn lands of Europe to lecture about the Bolshevik Revolution, it was to Blanc's I took him for those personal additions to his lecture which we merciless friends of the lecturer always exact. He had seen half a dozen revolutions from Mexico to Moscow; he had attended the making of the Versailles treaty of peace which was no peace, and, far more exciting to all of us, he had helped influence President Wilson to send a special emissary, Bullitt, to Russia on the first official quest to that Soviet land about which the whole world wondered. He himself had gone with Bullitt; he was lecturing about it across America and granted a day to Seattle. . . .

We began to talk of Moscow, which Steffens had recently seen, that glamorous, adventurous country which was building a new world behind the old world's blockade, Moscow, whose pamphlets

I had seized and reprinted yet which I had never thought of visiting. Now suddenly I cried, meaning it as much and as little as one always means such phrases: "Oh, I'd give anything if I could go there."

"Why don't you then?" asked Steffens calmly. It brought me up short. Were the words I had said just words or did I mean them? What was there to hold me in Seattle? Money? I had saved up enough from my salary to live anywhere for a couple of years. My job? But my job was now a disillusion. Family ties? My father's household wants were cared for by a Japanese school boy, and his reconciliation with old friends after the war-time separation caused by his pacifism, was retarded rather than helped by his radical daughter.

The American Friends Service ran a smooth, sophisticated office—idealism tempered to the methods of this world.

It was clear they expected me to stay chiefly in Poland and to use my writing talents for the raising of funds. It was equally clear that they would not say this explicitly, and that nothing in their letter forbade me to dream. Not that their forbidding would have stopped it; I had begun my preparations before I got their letter.

If I thus made use of the Friends' Service to reach in the end a purpose alien to their will, they similarly made use of me and of all their staff in Poland. Most of the members of their mission in Warsaw had originally applied to go to Russia, which to all us young left-wing idealists was our land of dreams. . . .

I had covered all their stations and was ready to leave the last one, Lodz, for Warsaw when there occurred the final chance which gave me Moscow. Into my room on the last evening in Lodz came an American Red Cross girl fresh from New York. She was frankly bored by her first ten days in Poland and was praying that a kind God would send her with the Hoover relief just organizing to carry food to the Volga famine in Russia.

"They are up at Riga now," she told me. "Americans are going in; I hope one of them will be me."

"What makes you want to go to Russia?" I asked her, since her conversation had shown not the slightest interest in labor problems or revolutions.

"It's so much bigger; there's so much more to do," she answered. "Here in Poland is no different from working in the slums at home. Only dirtier. Over there is a famine to fight—something big!" . . .

I asked for three weeks' leave of absence to go as far as the Volga; I asked the right to cable New York and form connections with a press agency. I brought out for all it was worth the promise of a Russian visa made by Rubenstein. "I can go more quickly than anyone else," I said. "There is no work holding me just now in Poland."

After a day Miss Barrow gave her decision. "You need not take a leave of absence. You can go for our Warsaw mission," she said. "We had determined to close our relief in eastern Poland. But the Volga famine is flooding us with refugees. We must know what to expect; will they come by hundreds of thousands or by millions? How fast and in what condition will they come? On this depends our future work in Poland.

"Go therefore as far as Moscow, and if you can manage it, as far as the famine areas. Report to the Friends Mission in Moscow; if they need you, their demands take precedence of ours. If they do not need you, do not bother them but carry out our assignment. I do not forbid your connection with any American press agency that will take your cables." . . .

. . . it worried our Philadelphia office when I suddenly appeared in Moscow, and traveled as far as the Volga, sending out daily cables to the Hearst papers, which had snatched at the chance to have me cover the famine. I made it quite plain that the Friends had done relief work in Moscow long before Hoover, and that the food I personally took to the Volga reached Samara two weeks before the Hoover shipments arrived. I made it equally plain that the Soviets themselves were contributing, by heroic sacrifice, far more relief to the famine than they got from abroad. I showed an orderly world of health departments, school departments, local authorities fighting a natural catastrophe, instead of anarchy brought into order by Americans. . . .

I had thought the revolution was loved by everyone; I had thought to find a brave new world beyond the border; I found the collapse of an old world under whose ruins men were dying. But living among those ruins were men who were building a new world from the broken pieces under which all the armies of earth had sought to bury them. The armies had made chaos; but there were creators in chaos! They were men like flames in the mist, signaling each other till fog dissolves in light!

My desire for this new land strengthened into a passion. Here was a real job, the biggest job in the world. I was going to be one of those creators in chaos; I had a chance to begin right away by taking food to the famine area. That was only the beginning; I must at once learn Russian and see what I could do next. . . .

The trains from Moscow to Samara take now some forty hours as normal schedule. In the famine year of 1921, the special health train on which I traveled took ten days. It was a wonderful train equipped with kitchen-car to prepare five thousand rations, with a bake-car that made a ton of bread at a baking, a dispensary car and a first-aid car, as well as living quarters for a fair-sized staff. It carried also some thirty cars of food materials, besides my two cars of Quaker food. It was one of many such trains operated by the Health Commissariat for the famine; it bore a special mandate instructing station masters to speed it on its way. But we spent our time waiting on sidings. We waited for engine repair, for the cutting of wood fuel, for trains of famine refugees, even more broken than our train, to drag themselves past towards Moscow. We made four hundred miles in the first five days! With my American impatience I went nearly crazy; I thought everyone would die before we got there! . . .

I knew the story I must send by cable to a full-fed land beyond the sea. I knew the wild tales spread in the press outside Russia of hospitals burned in panic, of peasants rioting as they fled. . . .

I must tell of a vast land—ruined by long war, by civil war in every city and village, where trains still halted on the emergency wood fuel enforced by the blockade, and moved forward with exasperating slowness on tracks not yet fully repaired—a land which nevertheless organized its cities and disciplined its peasants to concentrate what life was left on one united struggle, and whose fighting youth, even its girls, held nothing impossible. . . .

After the whirlwind of those four weeks in Samara, working as relief organizer by day and as correspondent by night, I was suddenly stricken with typhus which turned me from a would-be "creator in chaos" into a mere consumer of food and hospital space, the two most precious articles in Samara. . . .

I have often been asked what drew me back to Russia, which I saw first in its utterly darkest days. . . .

I had saved some lives in Samara and increased relief funds by my pamphlets and given a better picture of Soviet Russia in far-away America; but for months I had been a burden. . . .

Yet not for a moment did it occur to me that I could permanently leave this country, this chaos in which a world was being born. It was the chaos that drew me, and the sight of creators in chaos. I intended to have a share in this creation. The wrecked buildings, the pavements broken to dust, the ruined railroads stirred me to an angry lust of battle. America was no longer the world's pioneer. The World War had degraded her to be chief of imperial nations. It seemed to me—it still seems to me—that Russia was the advancing battlefront of man. . . .

I used the last few days of convalescence in Moscow, when the doctor allowed me to leave the house for an hour or two each day, to make connections which should bring me back when my agreement with the Quakers expired. . . .

Just before I left London for Moscow the International News Service (Hearst's) offered me a half-time job as their correspondent in the Soviet Union. "We have no objection to your writing also for the labor press under the name 'Anise,' " they added. I agreed to write for them unless the labor press objected or unless I found the double work too taxing. . . .

The joy that kept me awake under the northern lights of Karelia was no new emotion. It repeated the joy with which Ruth White and I had once discovered socialism. . . . It recalled the new reason for living which, after the loss of "my America," had brought me down from the mountains to the Seattle *Daily Call,* and when the Seattle labor movement crashed into discord, had taken me over the seas to Soviet Russia. For years this joy and desire had grown ever stronger.

Yet I was not always the same person; contradictory emotions swayed me. The sight of some injustice might suddenly make me see in Soviet Russia a new tyranny or an Asiatic market place. . . .

I saw that the building of socialism was no longer a dream, but real. There were greater difficulties than I had expected, but also greater power. This power I saw rather mystically, as a Common Consciousness coming into being to plan the future of mankind. . . .

The practical connection with this organized power was not so simple. My desire to be part of this country had received its first rude check on my day of arrival when the press representative in the Foreign Office advised me to eat Quaker food if I wished to be efficient. I received even ruder checks when I raised the question of joining the communist party. The first communists to whom I mentioned it laughed: "A sentimental bourgeois like you!"

That hurt; I was a woman who offered a life's devotion and had been laughed at. I grew more indirect, and asked like an inquiring journalist about conditions of entrance to this party. I learned that one joined at one's place of work, but I worked in a hotel room. I learned next that capitalist correspondents were barred. . . .

I was working chiefly for *Hearst's International Magazine*. Its editor, Norman Hapgood, liked my articles, and I liked the standards he set. "We want new, exhaustive information on events of historic importance. Then we want it written so simply and vividly that the milk-wagon driver in Kansas City and the drug-store clerk in St. Louis will find it interesting and important." To write for the great middle western masses of America intrigued me. So I dropped the daily grind of Internews cables to devote myself to long, vivid articles on various aspects of Soviet life: "The Fight for Russian Oil," "The War with Booze," "The Church Revolution," and many other topics. . . .

After nearly three years as correspondent for *Hearst's International Magazine* for Russia and Central Europe, I received a cablegram from Norman Hapgood canceling the work on which I was engaged, a study of Jewish settlement on farms in South Ukraine. . . .

Mr. Hapgood's efforts to build a popular international journal had raised circulation to a point where it began to cut into the sales of the *Cosmopolitan,* another Hearst publication. The great magnate decided to combine them; two "properties" were made one for greater profit. . . .

When I came to America soon afterwards, Hapgood sent me with a glowing letter of recommendation to the editor of the *Cosmopolitan* who had swallowed him. The new editor said: "No, we don't want Russia or Central Europe. We're going in for confessions. They thrill the readers more." . . .

My new plan was to make myself leading specialist on the Soviet Union for miscellaneous publications. I would come to America once a year on a lecture trip, renew connections with editors, and plan with them to what parts of Soviet Russia I should travel and on what subjects I should write. I should thus keep my freedom and would use my leisure time for John Reed Colony or for something else in Russia. . . .

I had written a book on the John Reed Colony, *Children of Revolution,* which I planned to sell to raise money for the work. I would use the trip to get mechanics and funds for the American

Educational Workshops. I asked the Concessions Committee what I should do for them in America.

They said: "Meet the business men of Wall Street and see what they say of us, what kind of concessions they want." . . .

It was a mad trip that I made to America that winter. Arriving in Seattle via China, . . . I had a triple task: to make my living for the coming year by lectures, to talk to Wall Street for the Concessions Committee, and to make the most serious drive yet attempted for funds and technical assistance to John Reed Colony and the American Educational Workshops. Out into Canada as far as Winnipeg, back to Seattle and down the coast, across by Kansas to the eastern cities, I gave that winter eighty-four lectures, sometimes as many as five a day.

A free, adventurous and lonely life now began for several years for me. I had lost my room in Moscow, and though Soviet Russia still remained the center of my plans, it was not easy for me to reside there. My connections with John Reed Colony, the American Educational Workshops, the Concessions Committee, had collapsed. I no longer believed that I could organize anything in Soviet Russia. . . .

I still intended to live in Moscow so I joined a housing cooperative and paid in advance for an apartment which I was to receive in two years. But I no longer dreamed of becoming a creator in chaos. I was broken; I would organize no more.

Well, I could always write. Everyone told me to do it. The other American correspondents never ceased saying that I was foolish to waste my time on all these projects. "They'll never let foreigners do anything here," they said. This seemed borne out by the similar advice of the Russian communists I met; they were always urging me to continue writing—for that very capitalist press they so denounced. . . .

Thus I began roving to revolutions, and writing about them for the American press. My job became a game between editors and myself; it amused me to see how much I could "put over" of what I wanted to say. I knew the "high-paying magazines" would not accept me; they paid high for subtle defense of capitalism in a vaudeville of tales and articles. But scores of other publications were accessible; I had learned the technique of my trade. I studied the special interests of editors; to one I sold articles because he wanted "travel" or "women"; to another because he was anti-

British in his policy on Asia. Some editors cursed my stuff as propaganda, yet took it because it was so vivid; then they would follow it by other articles which attacked the Soviets. They "gave all sides of the question." Some editors liked my stuff and helped me "put it over" on the owners of the papers; they didn't always last. But if one disappeared, others arose. The editors seemed to have the last word in this game; they changed my copy. Authors weren't supposed to object to being edited; hadn't they been paid? But I could always stop writing for editors who made annoying changes, as long as I could find others who changed me less. And if some day I should cease to find them? Why borrow trouble? For the moment I had the last word; I was "free."

What was this "freedom"? Sometimes in a lonely hotel room I would muse on its meaning. This freedom which everybody called desirable yet nobody defined. Those people who lauded freedom from their tight little nests of compulsion—would they like to be cast forth as I was, to wander across the earth? Free to say: "Shall I go next month to Mexico, Canton or Moscow; there is nobody in all the world who cares!" No confining job, no compelling dream of creation. Only my father's home, long since abandoned in Seattle, and in some future Moscow a flat not yet completed; otherwise a suitcase at the last hotel till the next lecture. It seemed to me at times that any bondage would be better than to be thus adrift upon the world. . . .

The hardest aspect of this enforced freedom of mine was not its loneliness but its lack of stability. The human mind demands a moving foam of choice on a great sea of habit; my habit was now in turmoil and I lived in a great sea of tossing choices. Any hour of any day a suggestion might impinge upon me that Canton or Samarkand was the next place to visit, or that lectures were more important than articles; or that a month in some friend's home on the seashore would perhaps be pleasanter than either. . . .

Outwardly I was becoming a writer of increasing fame and authority on Russia and on other revolutions which began to appear. Inwardly, and only half-consciously, I was seeking a successful revolution in which I might be reasonably important without having to endure the distressing preliminaries. Was I alone in this? Is not half America like me today? Any such revolution seemed then too far ahead in America; besides I was not sure that I wanted to take part in America; I had too many friends on the wrong side. Germany, Mexico, China—these were the places where I might become "chronicler of the revolution," in addition to writing about Soviet Russia. . . .

Thus in autumn of 1925 I took my first trip through China on my way from Moscow to Vancouver. I could give only a month from Mongolian blizzards to the heat of Canton. . . . Yet I found in that month that my four years' struggle in Soviet Russia—the famine, the John Reed Colony—had revealed to me the continent of Asia as an American seldom sees it. Instead of exotic culture of shrines and ancient palaces, amusing laws and quaint religions, I saw peasant populations, essentially similar over the greatest land area of earth. I began to see the Russian revolution not only as a pioneer land emerging from chaos but also as first stage in the awakening and industrialization of Asia.

Day by day on the trans-Siberian train I saw the plains unroll from Moscow over the Urals, across the rich Siberian lands to the great forests, down by the Khingan range to Harbin, Mukden, Peking. Russians, Tartars, Buriats, Chinese succeeded each other— all ancient peasant peoples left behind in the march of the world. The advancing, fighting tribes had poured westward by the black earth lands of Russia and Poland down to Rome and Spain. Breaking across the sea they had reached America—adventurous subduers of wildernesses. With inventive genius awakened by new conditions and rich, undeveloped lands they had built an ever-expanding industrial civilization.

Now this journey of man had come full circle; it was swinging round the world to Asia after three thousand years. It was crashing upon these peoples of earth's mother continent, huddled in villages, bound in a farm and family routine that had endured through centuries unchanged. To them now were coming the railroad, the factory, the industrial civilization of the west. They came in two forms between which was war irreconcilable: naked exploitation in the south by the world's imperialists and the Russian revolution in the north. . . .

A year later still, I went on May Day, 1930, to the opening of the Turkestan-Siberian Railway, of which I had heard three years before from the man who was purchasing its lumber. My old friend Bill Shatoff, veteran of a hundred free-speech fights in America, veteran also of the Russian civil war, was its director and builder. He had driven a thousand miles of railroad line north and south across plains and deserts of Asia, to connect Siberian wheat with Turkestan cotton and thus develop both regions.

"First of the Giants of the Five-Year Plan to Open"—thus the new railway celebrated itself on banners and in the press. . . .

Our train ran by no schedule. There was no schedule yet created; we were the first train. On new-laid rails our locomotive swayed drunkenly, a festival locomotive painted green. It was a present from the railway-repair shops at Aulie-Ata, repaired by volunteer workers in spare time without wages—their present to a great celebration. It flamed with banners and inscriptions. A shining steel star replaced the headlight, and over the star the words: "Daesh Sibir"—"Give us Siberia"—a battle-slang from the civil war. An engine crew selected from the volunteer repair gang had the honor of riding night and day on their engine. This was their new war, their victory—the opening of Turk-Sib!

"Nothing I ever did in all my life will hurt capitalism as much as this Turk-Sib railway," said Shatoff to me. Not the old, valiant free-speech fights, not the battles of civil war, not the organization of metal import and oil export. This railway united wheat and cotton, industrialized the farms of Central Asia and the nomad tribes of the great prairies, sent Soviet trade beyond her borders to Asia's backward peoples, and bound the far southeast frontier of the Soviet Union with a thin steel line of defense.

The workers on our special train knew it; they were delegates for half a hundred factories; chosen "champions" rewarded for good work by a trip to Turk-Sib. The foreign journalists on the train also knew it; thirty of them came from America, Germany, England, Italy. They knew this railway changed the history of Asia, joining two streams of life that had moved separately for ages, the life which flows along the forest rivers of the north and the caravan life across the plains of the south. They knew it fixed the grip of the Soviet power in the heart of Asia. They noted this and sent it in cables, cursing because for a thousand miles no telegraph operators could be found who even knew the Latin alphabet!

[In 1931, after the opening of the Trans-Siberian railroad, Strong visited the long-planned steel plants of Magnitogorsk.]

Forty Americans were on the job in Magnitogorsk, from the McKee Company and the Koppers Company. Many of them were making themselves popular by showing methods to the Russian workers. Yet none of them seemed quite adjusted; those who were most popular with the workers seemed to develop friction with their firms. . . .

It was clear from all my trips to the new giants, that few Americans felt themselves to be making good. Something had happened to their personal efficiency; it didn't work. This made them discontented. Most of the Russians had a simple, cynical cure. "Let them go if we don't need them. If we need them, offer more dollars."

This attitude outraged the Americans. "These guys say they're building socialism, but all they can think of is dollars! They could get a lot of good men cheaper, if they'd give them a chance to work. But God, how they squander the dollars. They'll save on a few men's salary and blow in millions on wrong equipment. I could have saved them a million on that machinery but their engineers were like drunken sailors. . . ." The American's deepest religion was outraged; waste was to him the devil, as it had been in the schools of my youth.

I protested often to Russians. "These men aren't just 'bought-and-paid-for.' They want to do good work."

"They're not interested in socialism," came the ready answer. "And we notice they take the dollars."

Yes, they did. What American refuses dollars? Dollars were to the American a token of worth. He came from a capitalism which standardizes men as "five-thousand-dollar men." His will to create, his craving to know himself efficient and his wish for dollars were so mixed in him that he didn't even try to tell them apart. Dollars made him feel successful, individually significant, personally worthy; the offer of more dollars reassured him when he worried that his work seemed bad. Didn't even I think in dollars, in an odd reversed way? My symbol of freedom had been the refusal of salary from the Concessions Committee; my flag of idealism had been the cutting of salary on *Moscow News;* my belief in my authority began when Ogonek gave out money. Was this all twisted? Didn't money really mean something?

To the Russians, dollars were not standards of worth, but bribes. In their swift leap from the ethics of the Asiatic market to those of socialism, they had not acquired that instinctive standardization of things and men in terms of money which a long period of efficient capitalism gave the Americans. Some of this standardization by money the Russians soon found it necessary to acquire; hordes of workers, recently peasants, needed the stimulus of differentiation in rewards based on standardized piece work. But basically the Russians classified men into those who worked from the will to socialism and those who had to be coerced or bribed. The

Americans weren't coerced, nor did they care about socialism. Clearly, reasoned the Russians, give them bribes!

Before going to Kuznetsk I was married. I met an old acquaintance whom I had not seen for several years. I told him my impression of Stalin, and ended enthusiastically: "I'd like to take orders from those men anywhere in the world. I feel they wouldn't give an order until I knew myself it was the thing I must do." I still thought in terms of "orders."

"I think," he smiled, "you must be getting ready to join our party." I nodded, but at once panic seized me, as it always did when I approached ultimate decision. I should like Stalin for a boss, but they wouldn't give me Stalin. I should have to obey some bureaucrat in an office. No, I couldn't! But here was the first responsible communist in ten years who had had such faith in me. I badly felt the need of such a comrade. Friendship resumed and deepened swiftly into marriage. The trip to Kuznetsk was made together.

Thus began to end for me that loneliness in the Soviet Union which had been for ten years more stormily painful than the quest for work which I have described in this book. After some months my husband gave me a clew to it. "You always attracted me," he said, "but in former years I never felt sure that we were on the same side of the barricades."

Barricades? Was that what those others had seen, both men and women, for whose comradeship I had hungered so long in vain. The many American idealists who wish to pioneer in this new land, to give their services, always tell me they are not afraid of hardship, by which they mean some trivial lack of housing or food. How can I tell them of the loneliness—they who expect their facile gesture of friendship to win great hosts of comrades, who think the land they deign to "love" will love them also. Let them look at the first generation of immigrants in America and tell themselves that the gulf they seek to cross is greater.

In ten years I attained in the Soviet Union two friends who had time to talk with me; they were non-party women of my own temperament, idealists working hard. Of the many communists whom I admired and from whom I hoped for friendship, some simply exploited me in passing while some took time to toss an encouraging word. Some sought from me the adventure of the alluring stranger, never companionship and home.

I learned to snatch enlightenment from brief contacts, to study in isolation fleeting words. From one I gained some understanding of the peasant, from another the need of careful analysis, while another suggested my letter to Stalin, which more than any one event changed my life. I learned to say, as each new hope for friends gave place to a new despair of isolation, "In all this land of comrades there seems to be for me no comrade, but the knowledge here is worth whatever I have to pay for it." Yet at times it seemed the price exacted would be ruined health, broken nerves, and emotional storms which shook the bounds of sanity.

I learned at last to understand my loneliness though never quite to endure it. We whose souls were formed by an old social system cannot pass to a new one without the change of every nerve-reaction, every habit, every "ideal." No single generation in all history has crossed so deep a gulf as our generation is crossing. It is crossed only in mortal combat and those who win across find on the far shore ruins to rebuild. Workers, fighting in compact ranks for life, cross most easily; their conflicts are outer ones. Capitalists never cross; they die when the old world dies. We intellectual idealists cross only when everything that the past has built is broken in us—everything that we ever called truth, virtue, friendship, freedom, and that made up our highly cherished "souls." Only then do we reach new truth, virtue, comradeship and freedom upon the barricades.

This crossing, painful and difficult for all who make it, is easier when we go forward with an army of marching workers in the scenes of our youth at the speed and with the thought-forms that we know. I challenged that crossing in a strange land whose habits, thought-forms, rate of movement derived from a different past. I gained a swifter but more shattering knowledge.

To a country where every person had been long tested and classified by conflict I came as stranger; not for many years does such a country accept strangers. I derived my concept of "friendship" from a land where we shared ideals and emotions by hours of vivid talk; I came to a land where even close comrades found one hour a year for talk. In the vast disorganization they rebuilt they had scarce time to snatch scant food and sleep; they shared not emotions but labor, danger and victory. In such a land I continued the divided purpose of a writer for American capitalist newspapers; what sharing of labor and danger arose from that?

One man, a worker from the Donetz coal-fields, sought of his own desire to cross the gulf between us. I met him in a workers' sanitarium where I never became for him a well-known foreign writer but just "a good-looking woman who wrote." He said: "I've left my first wife because she persisted in remaining a dark peasant, weeping every night when I went to party meetings. I've responsible tasks for the party and I want an intelligent wife who has work of her own. I don't know whether you could stand it on the Donetz but it wouldn't hurt you to try. At least you'd learn a lot about our workers while I'd learn culture and American efficiency." His realism shocked my American sentiment; I decided that I couldn't feel "in love" with him at all. I look back at it now as an honest, workmanlike proposal.

In choosing the Soviet Union for my residence I added to the perilous gulf another chasm, those early thought-forms which harden into the lifelong symbols of reality and desire. To the difficult analysis of class struggle, I added the difficulties of alien forms of expression. Our deep, unanalyzed feelings derive from a different past. Most intelligent Russian men of my generation feel life in terms of the 1905 barricades. That worker of the Donetz felt deepest desire as the old peasant hunger for culture. My husband's daughter and the Soviet youth of today find the deepest symbols of reality in steel mills and construction jobs. I have met a few people whose symbol of ultimate reality is some great festival in color, some harmony of the spheres in music. One old Bolshevik told me: "My deepest reality is still the developing human soul, but we shall have no time for that for many years."

These ultimate symbols of theirs are for me embroideries, which I note, analyze but do not deeply feel. My symbol of reality remains—whenever I feel most deeply—the unexplored trail in the untamed wilderness, the hiking into the West to undiscovered ranges, the glad adventure of man to conquer the stars! So feel the men from Chicago west to the Pacific; with them I might more easily have "held the barricades" or "dared the crossing." . . .

It was thus I chose the Soviet Union as environment that it might make of me what I wished to be. It was thus I chose my husband, not from any of those emotional flurries which American romanticists call love but from a need far deeper—the deep, instinctive need of my own future. American youth which wastes so much of life in bewildering emotion needs to be told what I took years to know. To fall in love is very easy, even to remain in it is not difficult; our human loneliness is cause enough. But it is a hard quest worth making to find a comrade through whose presence one becomes steadily the person one desires to be. This I have found and hold. . . .

I had been trained as a woman to "want to be wanted." I had been trained by one professor after another to "allow myself to be stirred." I had been trained by my religion to wait adoringly for a will that was "higher." Even as a child I had been trained to be "good" interesting yet never obtrusive—in the hope that everybody would like me. To be liked, desired, wanted by parents, playmates, sororities, men, editors, had been the goal of life. To desire, to want—food, sex or an evening's uninvited conversation—had been improper. I had been trained to expect a god and then serve him. And what a good little slave they had made of me! My earliest compliment had been that I could invent good excuses for mean girls and persuade myself that they meant to be kind. Able to justify petty tyrants!

It went further back, even before childhood. Wasn't that the function we all had, we intellectuals, makers of laws, art, ideals, governments, education? Didn't we spend our time inventing "excuses for mean girls," and "explaining how they meant to be kind"? We never were masters; we justified masters. We had our preference of course as to who should boss us. Those preferences we called "ideals"; tossing between them was "freedom." We prized ideals, for they distinguished us one from the other and made our value. . . .

Why this, I said in growing wonder, this is freedom! Not that endless fleeing from tyrants through the wilderness of one's soul, more and more alone in shrinking spaces. Not that endless finding and losing of editors who like my stuff till the editor changes his mind or the owner changes the editor. Not those scraps of life are freedom. But this conscious seeking and finding over wider and wider areas, for ever more complex creation, comrades with whom to consult and create.

It is more than freedom; it is an end forever to loneliness. Not to "be chosen," but to choose with others. Freedom and comradeship can grow wider always. Increasing organization does not squeeze out freedom, but multiplies its vast variety of choices!

What had I once meant when I said "freedom"? I could hardly now recall. It was as if I had come over a great divide and could no longer see that lower valley. Yet a moment before I had not seen these new horizons. As I went further into the range ahead it would grow ever harder to remember that past. . . .

Swiftly then I must seize this moment of passing; I must delay briefly on these ridges to chart the path by which I had come. A thousand ways rose to this high pass across the ranges, and all of them were new and steep. Every map sent back helped those who followed; I must mark down the steep bits and morasses and the places where I managed to get through. Then there would be no time for looking back. There was such a long trail ahead and such great mountains.

Mildred Ella (Babe) Didrikson Zaharias

(1914–1956)

Mildred Ella (Babe) Didrikson Zaharias, athlete and pioneer in women's sports, was born in Port Arthur, Texas, the fourth daughter and sixth of seven children of Norwegian immigrant parents. Her father was a carpenter, and her mother, an amateur athlete, was a practical nurse and occasionally a laundress.

Didrikson was an intensely competitive athlete in elementary and secondary school, working to improve her performance in any game to which she was introduced. While still an elementary school student, she watched the school basketball games and found ways to get advice from the team's coach. Her performance on the high school women's team in Beaumont, Texas, brought her to the attention of Melvin McCombs, the manager at a Dallas insurance company responsible for recruiting women athletes for the company's teams, which were maintained for public relations. In 1930 McCombs hired Didrikson as a typist and at once began to advance her athletic career.

The woman he had to work with was an athlete without equal. She led the company's team to a national basketball championship, and, once McCombs introduced her to track and field, she set American, Olympic, and world records in hurdles, javelin, high jump, broad jump, and baseball throw. In the 1932 Amateur Athletic Union championships, Didrikson competed as a one-woman track and field team, entering eight events, winning five, tieing for first in one, and finishing fourth in another, to win the championship.

At the 1932 Olympics, where she was limited to three events, Didrikson won javelin and hurdles, and took second place in the high jump. Still in her early twenties, she did not understand that her Olympic fame could not easily be translated into an athletic career because there was no competitive context for women in track and field. There followed a period in which she appeared in vaudeville and played with a mixed basketball team, and then with an all-male team, assignments she undertook to support her still poor family.

Didrikson took up golf, in which her strength and the length of her drive astonished coaches and public alike. After three years in the game she won her first state tournament and was immediately disqualified from further amateur competition. She returned to barnstorming and the endorsement of athletic goods.

Didrikson's career opportunities changed in 1938, when she married the wrestler George Zaharias. He was well enough off to support his wife while she regained amateur status. Once reinstated as an amateur, she won fourteen consecutive golf titles, culminating in the British Women's Open Championship in 1947. She was the first American to win this prestigious title.

Following this success, Didrikson turned professional and, drawing on her husband's advice and financial support, began to create the framework for professional women's competition in golf. She joined five other women golfers to establish the Ladies Professional Golf Association in 1948, recruiting an athletic goods company to provide the prize money for the first round of tournaments.

Her successful golf career was cut short by cancer of the rectum, requiring a colostomy. Never one to concede to circumstances, Didrikson came back to win her third U.S. Women's Open title in 1955, only fifteen months after her first surgery. Her cancer recurred the same year, and she died after a brief illness.

An athlete of genius, Didrikson created the environment for women's professional competition in golf, and, by extension, in other sports. She had the physical talent, the will, and the temperament to train well beyond established expectations for women's athletics, and as a result her career transformed expectations for women in all the sports in which she excelled.

THIS LIFE I'VE LED:
My Autobiography

My mother and father were both from Norway. They were already married and had three children when they came to this country. My dad was Ole Didrikson. . . . His own father was a cabinet maker in Oslo, but Poppa spent the first part of his life going to sea. He went around Cape Horn on sailing vessels something like seventeen times. . . .

Momma's maiden name was Hannah Marie Olson. She was the daughter of a shoemaker in Bergen, Norway. She was a little shorter than I am, about five feet four. You could tell by the way she handled herself that she was a natural athlete. . . .

When I got to be a sports champion, Poppa would kid around and say, "Well, she must get it from me." But I think that as far as athletics are concerned, I probably took after my mother. I understand she was considered the finest woman ice skater and skier around her part of Norway. . . .

After she and Poppa were married and raising a family in Oslo, one of his voyages was on an oil tanker that went to Port Arthur in Texas. He really liked it down there on the Gulf of Mexico. When he got back to Oslo, he told Momma that as soon as he could get enough money together, he was going to bring them all to Port Arthur to live.

Momma got excited about the idea too. Finally they saved enough money to come over. They landed in Port Arthur with their three kids, Dora and Esther Nancy and young Ole. . . .

The Didriksons settled right down in Port Arthur. Poppa gave up the sea and went into furniture refinishing, following his father's old trade. . . .

In Port Arthur the family increased. First there were the twins, Louis and Lillie. Then I arrived on June 26, 1914—Mildred Ella Didrikson. Finally there was Arthur. . . .

We picked up and moved seventeen miles from Port Arthur to Beaumont when I was about three and a half. . . .

Before I was even into my teens, I knew exactly what I wanted to be when I grew up. My goal was to be the greatest athlete that ever lived. I suppose I was born with the urge to get into sports, and the ability to do pretty well at it. And my dad helped to swing me in that direction. He followed the sports news in the papers, and he'd talk to us about it. I began reading the sports pages when I was very young myself; I can remember that even then I was interested in the famous golfers. . . .

Poppa kept reading about the Olympics in the newspapers, and telling us about the star athletes over there.

I got all steamed up. I was fourteen years old at the time. I said, "Next year I'm going to be in the Olympics myself."

Poppa said, "Babe, you can't. You'll have to wait four years."

I said, "Well, why? Why can't I be in it next year?" And he explained to me that the Olympic Games were held four years apart.

Lillie and I started in training for the Olympics right then and there.

. . . back in 1928 when we started thinking about the Olympics, Lillie was going to be a runner and I was going to be a hurdler and jumper. I never was too good at straightaway running. I didn't seem to want to stay on the ground. I'd rather jump some obstacle.

There were hedges in the yards along our block—seven of them between our house and the corner grocery. I used those hedges to practice hurdling. But there was one of them that was higher than the others. I couldn't get over it. That sort of messed up my practicing. So I went to the people who lived in that house. Their name was King. I asked Mr. King if he'd mind cutting his hedge down to where the rest of them were, and he did it.

You're supposed to put your leg out straight when you hurdle. But a regular hurdle is just half an inch or three-quarters of an inch thick. These hedges were about two feet across. So I had to crook my left knee—that was the leg I always took off on—or I'd scratch myself up. That style of hurdling stayed with me. When I did get to the Olympics they tried to have me change, but I wouldn't do it.

I'd go flying over those hedges, and Lillie would race alongside me on the pavement. She was a fast runner, and had an advantage anyway because I had to do all that jumping. I worked and worked, and finally got to where I could almost catch her, and sometimes beat her. . . .

In junior high school I made the basketball team, but when I got to Beaumont High they said I was too small. All of us Didrikson kids seemed to get our growth late. Even in the Olympics, when I was eighteen, I wasn't much over five feet tall, and weighed only 105 pounds.

I couldn't accept the idea that I wasn't good enough for the basketball team. I didn't think the girls who played on it were anything wonderful. I was determined to show everybody. To improve myself, I went to the coach of the boy's team, Lil Dimmitt. I said to myself, "The men know more about basketball than the women."

I'd use my study hours to go practice basketball. I'd show the teacher that I had my homework all done, and get excused from the study hall. I'd go where Coach Dimmitt was, and say, "Coach, how about watching me for a while?" I'd worry him to death with questions about how to pivot and shoot free throws and do this and that. He took the time to help me, because he could see I was interested. . . .

I was a junior before they finally gave me a chance on the Beaumont High girls' team. And I was the high scorer from the start. We went to different towns to play girls at other high schools, and we beat them all. I got my first newspaper write-up—a little item headed, BEAUMONT GIRL STARS IN BASKETBALL GAME. Then it was, BEAUMONT GIRL STARS AGAIN. I became all-city and all-state in basketball.

Down in Dallas, Col. M. J. McCombs saw those write-ups and decided to take a look at me. He's dead now. He was the boss of a department in an insurance firm, the Employers Casualty Company, and he also was director of the women's athletic program. . . .

He went to Houston one afternoon to watch us play the Houston Heights high-school girls. This was in February 1930. I wasn't sixteen yet. That Houston Heights team was made up of big, tall girls, like the name of the school. I was still small, but I was fast, and I could run right around those girls. I scored something like twenty-six points in that game. . . .

After the game Colonel McCombs came around and introduced himself, and asked if I'd like to play on a real big-time basketball team.

I said, "Boy, would I! Where?"

He said, "At the Employers Casualty Company in Dallas. We're getting ready to go into the nationals in March."

I told him that sounded great, and asked what I'd have to do. He said, "Well, see if you can arrange to get off from school, and get permission from your mother and dad to go." . . .

. . . after the first national tournament back there in 1930 I went home to finish up at Beaumont High, then came back to Dallas in June to go to work permanently for the Employers Casualty Company.

I was getting $75 a month salary, and sending $45 of it home. I paid about $5 a month for a room. I wasn't spending anything on clothes. I had just the one pair of shoes, and the leather was beginning to curl. Sometimes a girl would give me one of her old dresses, and I'd cut it up and make a skirt out of it for myself.

I lived on Haines Street in the Oak Cliff section of Dallas. The basketball girls all lived in that neighborhood. We ate at the same place, Danny Williams' house. He was the assistant coach. His wife did the cooking, and she was a good cook. I can still remember her pies with graham cracker crust.

We paid 15 cents for breakfast and 35 cents for dinner. For lunch I always had toasted cupcakes and a Coke down in the drugstore. The guy at the soda fountain would never charge me for my

Coke. He'd say, "How about another one, champ?" That made me feel good, because I wasn't any champ then.

Colonel McCombs would drive me to and from work, and any of the other girls that wanted to go, to save us carfare. One Saturday morning at the office early that first summer he said to me, "Babe, what are you doing to occupy yourself now that the basketball season's over?" I told him I wasn't doing anything much. He said, "Well, how would you like to go out to Lakeside Park with me this afternoon and watch a track meet?"

Here I'd been thinking about the Olympic Games since 1928, and yet I never had seen a track meet. So I went out there with him, and we stood around watching. I saw this stick lying on the ground, and I said, "What's that?" Colonel McCombs said, "It's a javelin. You throw it like a spear."

He went through the motions for me, and I picked it up and tried it. I got pretty good distance, but it was so heavy—it was a men's javelin—that I slapped my back with it as I threw it, and raised a welt. Four times I slapped myself on exactly the same spot. And that welt was really big.

Colonel McCombs took me around and explained some of the other events. He showed me the high jump and the hurdles and stuff like that. Those hurdles reminded me of all the hedge-jumping I'd done back home. I liked the looks of that event better than almost anything else.

By the time we left, Colonel McCombs was agreeing with me that it would be a good idea if Employers Casualty had a women's track and field team, so the girls would have some athletics during the summer. I'm sure that's what he'd had in mind all along. He said he'd take it up with Homer R. Mitchell, the president of the company. . . .

So we all got together and started talking about this track team we were going to organize. One girl said, "I'm going to throw the javelin." Another said, "I'm going to throw the discus." Another girl thought she'd like to do the hurdles.

When it came around to me, I said, "Colonel, how many events are there in this track and field?" He said, "Why, Babe, I think there are about nine or ten."

I said, "Well, I'm going to do them all." . . .

I really worked hard at that track and field. I trained and trained and trained. I've been that way in every sport I've taken up. After dinner I'd go out in my tennis shoes and run. They had a hill on

Haines Street that went down to a lake. I'd run all the way down there, and then I'd jog all the way back up. I'd jog my legs real high, and work my arms high, to get them in shape. Of course, they were already about as hard as they could be, but I thought they had to be better.

We had just a few days to get ready for our first meet. Our regular hour or two of practice in the afternoon wasn't enough to satisfy me. I'd go out to Lakeside Park at night and practice by myself until it got dark, which wasn't until nine or nine-thirty at that time of year. If there was good clear moonlight, I might keep going even longer.

The last night before that first track meet I went out and worked extra hard. I practiced my step timing for the broad jump and for the high jump. I put in about two hours at that, and then finished off by running the 440 yards. They'd told me to pace myself in that, but I was going to see if I couldn't sprint all the way.

Well, I just barely made it to the finish line. I fell face down on the grass. I was seeing stars. I must have laid there fifteen or twenty minutes before I could get up. . . .

I competed in my four events that afternoon, and I won all four. It was that last extra practice that did it, especially in the broad jumping and the high jump, where I had my steps down just right.

I eventually got to be pretty good at the high jump. I started out doing the old-style scissors jump. One afternoon I was working out, and I kept going higher and higher. Finally Colonel McCombs had the cross bar up to the women's world record. I believe it was five feet, three inches at that time.

He said, "Babe, tell you what. I'll buy you a chocolate soda if you can jump this."

I said, "Out of my way!" and sailed right over.

Then I said, "I think I can go higher." He told me to go ahead and try. I did, but I couldn't make it any more after that. So we decided that if I was ever going to get above the record, I'd have to switch from the scissors jump to the Western roll, which wasn't too common then. In the Western roll you kick up there and roll over the bar flat. Under the high-jump rules they had at that time, your feet had to go over the bar first.

I was the longest time mastering that Western roll. In the beginning I'd just dive. I'd go over head first and my feet would kick up in the air and my body would knock the bar off coming down. But Colonel McCombs kept working with me, and I kept practicing, until I was sliding laterally and bringing my whole body over just the way you were supposed to. . . .

But 1932 was the summer when I was really keyed up about track and field. That was an Olympic year. The national championships and the Olympic tryouts were being combined. So the ones who came out ahead in the nationals would also get to be in the Olympics. There were a lot of different events that I wanted to compete in.

I was sitting in the office one day thinking about it when Colonel McCombs buzzed for me.

Colonel McCombs buzzed for me often. He'd call me in to work out basketball plays with him and things like that.

So I went into his office. I said, "Colonel, will I get to go up to Chicago for the nationals this year?"

He said, "Yes. That's what I wanted to talk to you about. I've been studying the records of the girls on the other teams. I think if you enter enough different events, and give your regular performance, you can do something that's never been done before. I believe we can send you up there to represent the Employers Casualty Company, and you can win the national championship for us all by yourself." . . .

Some of the events that afternoon were Olympic trials. Others were just National A.A.U. events. But they all counted in the team point scoring. So they were all important to me if I was going to bring back the national championship for Employers Casualty.

For two-and-a-half hours I was flying all over the place. I'd run a heat in the eighty-meter hurdles, and then I'd take one of my high jumps. Then I'd go over to the broad jump and take a turn at that. Then they'd be calling for me to throw the javelin or put the eight-pound shot.

Well, there were several events I didn't figure to do too much in. One was the 100-meter dash, and I drew a blank there, although I just missed qualifying for the finals. I was edged out for third place in my semifinal heat.

But that was the only thing I got shut out in. Even in the discus, which wasn't a specialty of mine at all, I placed fourth to pick up an extra point. And I actually won the shot put, which was a big surprise. . . .

I won the championship in the baseball throw for the third straight year. My distance was 272 feet, two inches. Then in three Olympic trial events I broke the world's record. In two of them it was a case of beating a record that I already held myself. I threw the javelin 139 feet, three inches, which was nearly six feet better than my old mark of 133 feet, five-and-a-half inches. I won an eighty-meter hurdle heat in 11.9 seconds, a tenth of a second faster than my previous mark. In the finals of my eighty-meter hurdles I didn't do quite that well, but my time of 12.1 seconds was good enough to win. . . .

Colonel McCombs had that track meet doped out just about right. Of the eight events I entered, I placed in seven. I won five of them outright, and tied for first in a sixth. I scored a total of thirty points, which was plenty to win the national championship for Employers Casualty. The Illinois Women's Athletic Club was second with twenty-two points. . . .

It was a wonderful thrill to march into the Olympic Stadium in the parade on opening day, Monday, August first. To tell you the truth, though, I couldn't enjoy the ceremonies much after we got out there. We all had to wear special dresses and stockings and white shoes that the Olympic Committee had issued to us. I believe that was about the first time I'd ever worn a pair of stockings in my life; I was used to anklets and socks. And as for those shoes, they were really hurting my feet.

We had to stand there in a hot sun for about an hour and a quarter while a lot of speeches and things went on. My feet were hurting more and more. Pretty soon I slipped my feet out of my shoes. Then another girl did. By the end I think everybody had their shoes off.

They also issued us track shoes, but there I got permission to wear my own, which were all broken in and fitted me just right.

I was in the javelin throw that first day, and it didn't get started until late afternoon. Shadows were coming up over the stadium, and it was turning pretty cool. We all got out there to warm up. I was watching the German girls, because they were supposed to be the best javelin throwers. I could see that they'd been taught to loosen up by throwing the spear into the ground. I'd been told myself that this was the way to practice, but I never could agree. It seemed to me that this gave you the wrong motion. You'd feel a tug that wasn't right. I always thought you should warm up with the same swing you used in competition.

There were too many of us around for me to risk throwing any spears up into the air the way I wanted to. Rather than have no warm-up at all, I thought I'd practice that other way, throwing the javelin into the ground. I tried it, and I almost put it in a German girl's leg. I decided I'd better stop.

The event started. They had a little flag stuck in the ground out there to show how far the Olympic record was. It was a German flag, because a German girl had set the record. It was some distance short of my own world's record.

When my first turn came, I was aiming to throw the javelin right over that flag. I drew back, then came forward and let fly. What with the coolness and my lack of any real warm-up, I wasn't loosened up properly. As I let the spear go, my hand slipped off the cord on the handle.

Instead of arching the way it usually did, that javelin went out there like a catcher's peg from home plate to second base. It looked like it was going to go right through the flag. But it kept on about fourteen feet past it for a new Olympic and world's record of 143 feet, four inches. . . .

The finals of the eighty-meter hurdles followed. . . . I was so anxious to set another new record that I jumped the gun, and they called us all back. Now in Olympic competition, if you jump the gun a second time they disqualify you. I didn't want that to happen, so I held back on the next start until I saw everybody taking off. It wasn't until the fifth hurdle that I caught up, and I just did beat out Evelyne Hall of Chicago. If it was horse racing, you'd say I won by a nose. Even with the late start, I set another new record with a time of 11.7 seconds. . . .

. . . another time after I first came to Dallas, Colonel McCombs drove me home one Saturday afternoon, the way he so often did. I'd been practicing basketball or track—I forget which. I remember I was still in my sweat suit and tennis shoes. Anyway, Colonel McCombs said, "Babe, do you mind if I stop at a driving range on the way home and hit a few golf balls?"

I told him to go right ahead. I believe I added something about how silly I thought it was for people to hit a little white ball and then chase it.

We stopped at the driving range, and Colonel McCombs hit a few drives. Finally he invited me to try one. Or maybe I asked him to let me do it. I took my stance in front of a light post. I reared back and swung with all my might. I caught that ball square, but I came around so hard that the club hit the light post on the follow through and broke in two.

The little Scotsman who ran the driving range came running

up to us. He was shouting. I thought he was mad because I'd broken the club. But instead of that he was yelling, "Wow! Look at that! See where she hit the ball!" They measured it, and it was about 250 yards. . . .

Well, after the Olympics and the post-Olympics and all that were over, I got back into the old office and basketball routine at Employers Casualty. I was still liking it. But the pressure got pretty heavy on me during the fall of 1932. People kept telling me how I could get rich if I turned professional. That big-money talk sounds nice when you're just a kid whose family has never had very much.

What I really wanted to do at this point was to become a golfer. I was going to make an appearance at the Dallas ball park, and they were going to present me an expensive watch. I went by the Cullum and Boren sporting-goods store there in Dallas one day, and saw this beautiful set of golf clubs in the window. It was like a girl seeing a mink coat. I was just dying to have those golf clubs, but I couldn't possibly afford to buy them.

I went in and handled the clubs and everything. I know they'd have been glad to present me the golf clubs at the ball-park ceremony instead of the watch, which cost just about as much. But it might impair my amateur standing in golf if I accepted those clubs. So I took the watch instead. . . .

These years I'm talking about were a mixed-up time for me. My name had meant a lot right after the Olympic Games, but it had sort of been going down since then. I hadn't been smart enough to get into anything that would really keep me up there.

I had to find some way to build my name up again, so I could make some money. There had to be money—not just for me but for the family. At one point I thought maybe tennis would be the answer. I figured there could be money in that—it's a sport where you can sell tickets and people can sit down and watch you play. If I got good enough at the game, I thought perhaps a lot of people would pay to see me play tennis matches.

I don't know whether it would have worked out like that, because I never got a chance to try it. I started practicing tennis. I was learning the forehand stroke, and the backhand. Then we began on the serve, and I found I couldn't do it right. I couldn't raise my arm properly. That cartilage I'd torn in my right shoulder, throwing the javelin at the Olympic Games, still hadn't healed quite right. . . .

The shoulder didn't interfere with my golf swing. . . . And golf was still my real objective. All I wanted to accomplish with these other things was to get in a financial position where I could concentrate on golf. That was my big sports love now. . . .

Employers Casualty helped to make it possible for me to get going on golf again. They not only gave me my job back one more time, they got me a membership at the Dallas Country Club and paid for my lessons there with George Aulbach.

I spent practically all my spare hours out there. In November of 1934 I decided to find out how much progress I was making by entering my first golf tournament—the Fort Worth Women's Invitation.

I went out there for the qualifying round. Somebody asked me how I thought I'd do, and I said, "I think I'll shoot a seventy-seven." I said things like that in those days, and I wasn't trying to be smart—it was just what was in my mind at the time. And that's the sort of thing that can make you famous—if it comes true.

It came true that day. I played eighteen holes, and my score was exactly seventy-seven. That made me the medalist for the tournament—the next best score was eighty-two.

It did me good to see the headlines in the Texas newspapers the next day: WONDER GIRL MAKES HER DEBUT IN TOURNAMENT GOLF: TURNS IN 77 SCORE. It was like 1932 all over again. . . .

Then it was winter. I was already thinking about the Texas state women's championship in the spring of 1935. That would be my next chance to establish myself as a golfer. It was terribly important to me to win that tournament. I started getting ready for it about three-and-a-half months beforehand. . . .

. . . no prize I've won, either before or since, looked any bigger to me than the Texas state women's golf championship did when I took aim on it in 1935. . . .

Weekends I put in twelve and sixteen hours a day on golf. During the working week I got up at the crack of dawn and practiced from 5:30 until 8:30, when I had to leave for the office. I worked until lunch time, then had a quick sandwich and spent the rest of my lunch hour practicing in the boss's office, which was the only one that had a carpet. He told me it was all right to do it.

I practiced putting on the carpet, and I chipped balls into his leather chair. They moved the chair over into a corner for me, away from the window. And I stood in front of the mirror on his closet door and practiced my grip. I watched to see whether I had it exactly the way Stan Kertes and George Aulbach had told me.

When the lunch hour was over, I went back to work until 3:30.

After that I was free to go out to the golf course. George Aulbach would give me an hour's instruction. Then I'd drill and drill and drill on the different kinds of shots. I'd hit balls until my hands were bloody and sore. I'd have tape all over my hands, and blood all over the tape.

After it got too dark to practice any more, I went home and had my dinner. Then I'd go to bed with the golf rule book. I'll bet I have read that book through twenty-five times, line by line. . . .

When the United States Golf Association declared me ineligible for the women's amateur golf tournaments back there in the spring of 1935, they never did announce the reasons why they had decided I was a pro. I know that complaints by certain Texas women entered into it. Anyhow, Archie M. Reid of the USGA was the fellow who issued the ruling, and all he said for publication was that they were doing it "for the best interest of the game."

When George [Zaharias] and I decided not to go through any more delays on getting married, Tom Packs, the St. Louis wrestling promoter, volunteered to hold the wedding at his house. So we arranged to get married there on December 23, 1938. . . .

We got back home to California in the fall of 1939. And George began to do some heavy thinking about my golf future. It was something that had worried me, too. Here I'd been practicing all the time, and developed this fine golf game, and about all I could do with it was play exhibition matches. I wasn't getting a chance to show whether I was the best woman player, because I was barred from practically all the women's tournaments as a professional.

At the time when they'd declared me a professional in the spring of 1935, there was only one tournament of any importance that I could enter. That was the Western Women's Open. Then my friend Bertha Bowen, of Fort Worth, helped get a Texas Women's Open going, which made two.

But two a year isn't enough to give you tournament sharpness.

I had to stay professional, because I needed the money. But when I married George, that problem ended. He was a top bean in the wrestling business. He was one of the wealthy wrestlers. . . .

. . . and he'd been making good business investments. George could see that what I really wanted in golf was to compete and win championships. So he set out to see if we could get my amateur standing back. . . .

We found out that I'd have to apply for reinstatement before

I'd been a professional five years. This meant I had to do it before May of 1940. Then I'd have to go through a three-year grace period, laying out of all professional things. That wouldn't be easy, but I was willing to go through with it. I was ready to do whatever it took to get me eligible for all those golf tournaments. . . .

The USGA agreed to restore my amateur standing if I went through the three-year waiting period. I settled down to sweat it out. I dropped all my professional contracts and appearances, and when I entered the occasional open tournaments that I was eligible for, I told them to count me out on any prize money. . . .

On January 21, 1943, my amateur standing came back in golf. I don't think I've ever been happier in my life. Of course, most of the big tournaments had been suspended for the duration of the war. But from now on, I was eligible to enter all the tournaments there were.

My first appearance as an amateur was in a special thirty-six-hole charity match they arranged the next month between me and the California state women's champion, Clara Callender. It was held at the Desert Golf Club in Palm Springs. I couldn't have asked for a better start. Clara scored a pair of seventy-twos, which is real fine shooting. But I had a seventy in the morning round and a sixty-seven in the afternoon, which broke the course record. I took the match by a margin of four-and-two. . . .

Although I didn't know it, 1946 was going to be my one and only chance to take the National Women's Amateur championship. Well, my performance that week was everything I could have hoped for. There was a thirty-six-hole qualifying round, in which I placed third, and my game just built up from there. I didn't have a single narrow squeak in working my way to the finals, although I had to get past some tough competitors. . . .

On the last day I was opposed by the girl I'd had those two close matches with in California right after my amateur standing came back in 1943. She was Clara Callender then; now she was Mrs. Sherman.

This time it wasn't close. I was hot. She wasn't. We were even through the first six holes. After that I was ahead all the way. At lunch time I was five up. It only took nine more holes in the afternoon to finish things. I won the eighth with an eagle—my 130-yard second shot went in the cup for a two. I took the ninth with a par to end the match. My winning margin of eleven-and-nine was the second biggest in the history of the tournament.

What gave me the most satisfaction, next to winning my first national championship, was that I hadn't played any bad golf at all that week. I don't really enjoy a tournament, even if I win, unless I play well. Sometimes you hit a ball, and you don't hit it the way you wanted to, but it goes on the green anyhow. You were lucky. I don't like it that way. I'm never really satisfied unless I can feel that I'm hitting the ball just right. . . .

When I came back there at the end of the tournament season in October, I was ready to take a long layoff from golf competition and just enjoy my home for a while. But George had other ideas. He said, "Honey, you've got something going here. You've won five straight tournaments. You want to build that streak up into a record they'll never forget. There are some women's tournaments in Florida at the start of the winter. I think you should go down there."

I got out early the morning of my first match in the British Women's Amateur tournament. I expected to see a crowd already gathering, the way it does for an American tournament. But there was hardly a soul in sight.

I said to the club secretary, "I thought Scotland was golf country. Where are all the people?"

He said, "They'll be here." And sure enough, all these buses began coming in, and by the time I teed off there must have been several thousand people there. . . .

The crowd gave me a wonderful ovation when it was over. It seemed like they stood for fifteen minutes and applauded. Then there was more picture-taking and dancing the Highland Fling and signing autographs and everything.

During the autographing I took the glove off my left hand. That was the first time I'd done it. Nobody had seen the bandage on my left thumb until now. It caused something of a sensation. Then the photographers had me go over to the area in front of the clubhouse for pictures, and I hurdled the brown brick wall that ran around it. There was another uproar over that.

Finally there was the presentation of the championship trophy. I sang a little Highland song I'd learned from some of the Scottish golf pros in the Untied States—hoping I'd have this occasion to use it. And everybody seemed to like that touch.

———————

When George set out to get the ball rolling for a women's pro golf tour late in 1948, he had himself an uphill roll. One big problem was that there were so few women golf professionals. In addition to myself, there was only Patty Berg, Helen Dettweiler, Betty Jameson, Betty Hicks, Bea Gottlieb and one or two others. Patty Berg was about the only one who was really active. Like me, she was working for the Wilson Sporting Goods Company, and giving exhibitions all over the country. . . .

Things went along pretty slowly at the start, but eventually it started to snowball, both in numbers of tournaments and numbers of players. At first we'd play for anything we could get. The total purses for 1949 didn't come to more than $15,000. By 1955 the minimum per tournament was $5000, and the total prize money for the year was around $200,000.

Meanwhile I kept on making plenty of money from nontournament stuff. And I was working hard for it. To give you one example, there was a weekend in June of 1948 when I started out playing in New Canaan, Connecticut. Then we got in the car and drove to Detroit to play there on a Sunday. And from Detroit we went right on to Chicago for the Western Women's Open that coming week.

I've never been one to worry much about my health, but I'd been feeling so low for several months in 1953 that I couldn't help thinking once in a while that I just might have cancer. I was pretty sure of it from the way Doctor Tatum suddenly went white while he was examining me.

But when I asked him straight out if I had cancer, he said, "Now, Babe, we don't know that. But here's what I want you to do. I want you to go to Fort Worth and see a specialist there, a proctologist, and have him make some tests."

I said, "Can't I see him when I come back this way to play in the Texas Women's Open in October?"

He said, "No, you'll have to go down there today. I'll phone ahead and make the arrangements."

This was on a Monday morning, April sixth. George and I had planned to go from Beaumont to San Antonio, where Betty Dodd lived with her family. We were going to spend the night there, and then caravan it with Betty to Phoenix in time for the start of the Phoenix Women's Open on Thursday.

I came back from Doctor Tatum's office and told George that we'd have to change our plans and go to Fort Worth, because I was supposed to see a specialist there. We set off in the car, and got to the specialist's office in Fort Worth in the early evening.

He was Dr. William C. Tatum—no relation to the Doctor Tatum in Beaumont. He did what they call taking some biopsies for analysis. He said he'd have the result for us at eleven o'clock Wednesday morning.

We waited it out at the home of R. L. and Bertha Bowen, the close friends we always visit when we're in Fort Worth. . . .

The doctor didn't do any hemming or hawing. "Babe," he said, "you've got cancer." I thought I was prepared for it, but that report just hit me like a thunderbolt. George too. His hand shot out and grabbed mine.

The doctor went straight on talking, I suppose to get us started right in thinking about what could be done. He said my cancer was in the rectum, and that I needed a colostomy. He brought out pictures and diagrams to show us what kind of operation that was— how they'd cut off part of the lower intestine, and reroute it, and make a new outlet in the left side of the abdomen.

I guess he talked to us there for about two hours. He told me I'd be able to play golf again after the operation, although probably not tournament golf. He said to go ahead and get other medical opinions if we wanted.

We left his office, and I was crying when we went down on the elevator. George was all distressed. He had never seen me cry before, and I don't believe he saw me do it any more after that. . . .

I went off by myself for a while and lay on a bed, thinking, "What in the world have I done wrong in my life to deserve this?" I'd always tried to do right, and help other people. I'd played in I don't know how many benefits for the American Cancer Society. I kept saying to myself, "God, why did I have to have this? Why does anybody have to have it?" But my idea has always been that whatever God intended for me in this life, I'd go along with. . . .

We got ready to leave the Bowens. It didn't take much preparation, because we'd hardly unpacked the car at all since we got there. I get plenty of golf supplies, since I'm under contract to a sporting-goods company, and every time we visited the Bowens, I used to give R.L some of my practice balls.

This time when we got out to the car, I saw my golf clubs sitting in it, and that was one of the few moments I let myself give in to despair. I grabbed the bag and handed it to R.L. and said, "Here! I want you to have these, because I won't be needing them any more."

George snatched the bag and said, "No, honey, no! You'll play again!" . . .

George was . . . worried a short time later when I told him I was going to enter the Tam o' Shanter "All-American" at the end of July. But the doctors said this was all right. In fact, they told both George and Betty Dodd to encourage me on playing golf, and on getting out in public again. They said the biggest problem with colostomy patients was to get them back into normal living. They're sometimes too self-conscious about their changed condition to want to go anywhere or do anything.

Well, a colostomy is a big change, but the body can adjust to it. It's a wonderful thing the way the human body will correct itself if you give it a chance.

Anyway, on July thirty-first, about three-and-a-half months after the operation, I put myself to the test at the Tam o' Shanter Country Club in Niles, Illinois. They had promised in advance to pair Betty Dodd with me. She was familiar with my condition, and could step in and help if I had any trouble.

I got up there on the first tee with a big crowd of people watching me. The question in everybody's mind, and in my mind too, was "Is Babe still capable of tournament golf?" To me, shooting tournament golf doesn't just mean getting a respectable score and finishing up among the leaders. It means being able to win. That's the standard the public has come to judge me by. It's the standard I set for myself. I wouldn't want it to be any other way.

Well, I hit that opening drive, and it sailed 250 yards straight down the middle. Those people screamed as if it was a football game. But that was about the end of my good golf for a while. I could still bang out some long ones, but I didn't seem to have the control and the touch that you need, especially on the short game. . . .

I wound up down in fifteenth place in the "All-American." . . .

Only two days later I came back and played in the second Tam o' Shanter tournament, the "World Championship," and after three-and-a-half rounds I was ahead. Then I ran out of gas and took forty-three strokes to get around the last nine holes. My back was killing me, and it was an effort to swing the club. I sat down between shots and everything to rest, but it was no use. Patty Berg picked up seven strokes on the back nine to win the tournament with a 300 score. Louise Suggs was second with 303. I wound up third with 304. . . .

It was disappointing to lose out at the end, and yet I was encouraged that I could stay up there as long as I did that soon after the operation. My performance brought me a great many inspiring letters. Those letters sort of built up my determination to continue in golf. It meant a lot to know that so many people were rooting for me in my comeback. . . .

People would say to me when I came back to the tournament circuit after my cancer operation, "Why don't you just take life easy?" My doctors would tell me not to drive myself so hard. George would say, "You've proved everything. You don't have to prove anything more."

There are several reasons why I didn't retire from golf after that 1953 cancer business—and still don't intend to retire, in spite of my 1955 ailments. One reason is that every time I get out and play well in a golf tournament, it seems to buck up people with the same cancer trouble I had. I can tell that from the letters I keep getting. . . .

Another reason why I've kept coming back to the golf circuit is that I helped start the Ladies' Professional Golf Association, and I want to help it keep on growing. The Ladies' PGA has been building up right along in tournaments and purses and good players. At first there were just six or seven of us. Now we've got about twenty-five or thirty girls who are very fine golfers. I know the tournaments draw better when all of us are in there than when some of us aren't.

Finally, there's this. Since I began having my medical troubles, any time I've played two or three tournaments in a row without winning, people have started saying, "What's the matter with Babe? Is she through?" And then I get back to where I don't want to get beat. I get that old desire to win. I want to go out and prove all over again that I'm still a championship golfer.

Gloria Steinem

(1934–   )

Gloria Steinem was born in Toledo, Ohio, the second daughter of ill-matched parents. Her mother gave up her career in journalism for marriage to a man of marginal economic talents; she sank into depression and neurotic illness as the marriage crumbled and the family endured a series of failed business ventures.

Steinem won a scholarship to Smith College, graduating in 1956 and departing almost immediately for postgraduate work in India. This year of study led to the publication of *The Thousand Indias* in 1957 and to several years of foundation work in Cambridge, Massachusetts, and New York.

Steinem's real vocation was as a writer, and by 1960 she was supporting herself as a free-lance journalist. The story of her assignment to write on the life of a bunny in the New York Playboy Club is now legendary. She was radicalized by her research, becoming the principal feminist leader of her generation.

In the late 1960s and early 1970s Steinem played a critical role in publicizing feminist ideas as cofounder of *New York* magazine and then founder and editor of *Ms.* magazine. Her work as a journalist and feminist placed her at the center of Democratic politics; she was involved in the presidential campaigns of Adlai Stevenson, Robert Kennedy, Eugene McCarthy, Shirley Chisholm, and George McGovern. She was a prominent figure in the Vietnam War protest movement and a supporter of the efforts to organize migrant labor through the United Farm Workers.

Steinem's influence as a speaker, on television, testifying before Congress, at countless feminist events, on college campuses, and for the political causes she supported reached well beyond the readership of her books, making her a cultural icon of the 1960s and '70s. Her humor, high spirits, and inexhaustible energy made her a warm and positive platform presence. Her intellectual brilliance and way with words made her effective even before hostile audiences.

Steinem wrote regularly for national magazines, producing a collection of her essays, *Outrageous Acts and Everyday Rebellions,* in 1983. Like many in her generation, Steinem was fascinated by Marilyn Monroe, a powerful symbol of the exploitation of women's sexuality by the media. Her biography of Monroe, *Marilyn: Norma*

Jeane (1986), was an effort to highlight the reality of Monroe's life as an exploited and abused child and painfully vulnerable adult woman against the Hollywood myth of the sex goddess.

Steinem's account of her life with her mother has been reproduced in many anthologies and stands as a classic in narratives of mother-daughter relations. It is unusual for its fairness, its deep compassion, and the moral Steinem is able to draw from her mother's years of mental illness and dependency.

OUTRAGEOUS ACTS AND EVERYDAY REBELLIONS: Ruth's Song (Because She Could Not Sing It)

For many years I . . . never imagined my mother any way other than the person she had become before I was born. She was just a fact of life when I was growing up; someone to be worried about and cared for; an invalid who lay in bed with eyes closed and lips moving in occasional response to voices only she could hear; a woman to whom I brought an endless stream of toast and coffee, bologna sandwiches and dime pies, in a child's version of what meals should be. She was a loving, intelligent, terrorized woman who tried hard to clean our littered house whenever she emerged from her private world, but who could rarely be counted on to finish one task. In many ways, our roles were reversed: I was the mother and she was the child. Yet that didn't help her, for she still worried about me with all the intensity of a frightened mother plus the special fears of her own world full of threats and hostile voices.

Even then I suppose I must have known that, years before she was thirty-five and I was born, she had been a spirited, adventurous young woman who struggled out of a working-class family and into college, who found work she loved and continued to do, even after she was married and my older sister was there to be cared for. Certainly, our immediate family and nearby relatives, of whom I was by far the youngest, must have remembered her life as a whole and functioning person. She was thirty before she gave up her own career to help my father run the Michigan summer resort that was the most practical of his many dreams, and she worked hard there as everything from bookkeeper to bar manager. The family must have watched this energetic, fun-loving, book-loving woman turn into someone who was afraid to be alone, who could not hang on to reality long enough to hold a job, and who could rarely concentrate enough to read a book.

Yet I don't remember any family speculation about the mystery of my mother's transformation. To the kind ones and those who liked her, this new Ruth was simply a sad event, perhaps a mental case, a family problem to be accepted and cared for until some natural process made her better. To the less kind or those who had resented her earlier independence, she was a willful failure, someone who lived in a filthy house, a woman who simply would not pull herself together.

. . . exterior events were never suggested as reason enough for her problems. Giving up her own career was never cited as her personal parallel of the Depression. (Nor was there discussion of the Depression itself, though my mother, like millions of others, had made potato soup and cut up blankets to make my sister's winter clothes.) . . . The real influence of newspaper editors who had praised her reporting was not taken as seriously as the possible influence of one radical professor.

Even the explanation of mental illness seemed to contain more personal fault when applied to my mother. She had suffered her first "nervous breakdown," as she and everyone else called it, before I was born and when my sister was about five. It followed years of trying to take care of a baby, be the wife of a kind but financially irresponsible man with show-business dreams, and still keep her much-loved job as reporter and newspaper editor. After many months in a sanatorium she was pronounced recovered. That is, she was able to take care of my sister again, to move away from the city and the job she loved, and to work with my father at the isolated rural lake in Michigan he was trying to transform into a resort worthy of the big dance bands of the 1930s.

But she was never again completely without the spells of depression, anxiety, and visions into some other world that eventually were to turn her into the nonperson I remember. And she was never again without a bottle of dark, acrid-smelling liquid she called "Doc Howard's medicine": a solution of chloral hydrate that I later learned was the main ingredient of "Mickey Finns" or "knockout drops," and that probably made my mother and her doctor the pioneers of modern tranquilizers. Though friends and relatives saw this medicine as one more evidence of weakness and indulgence, to me it always seemed an embarrassing but necessary evil. It slurred her speech and slowed her coordination, making our neighbors and my school friends believe she was a drunk. But without it, she would not sleep for days, even a week at a time, and her feverish eyes began to see only the private world in which wars and hostile voices threatened the people she loved.

Because my parents had divorced and my sister was working in a faraway city, my mother and I were alone together then, living off the meager fixed income that my mother got from leasing her share of the remaining land in Michigan. I remember a long Thanksgiving weekend spent hanging on to her with one hand and holding my eighth-grade assignment of *Tale of Two Cities* in the other, because the war outside our house was so real to my mother that she had plunged her hand through a window, badly cutting her arm in an effort to help us escape. Only when she finally agreed to swallow the medicine could she sleep, and only then could I end the terrible calm that comes with crisis and admit to myself how afraid I had been.

No wonder that no relative in my memory challenged the doctor who prescribed this medicine, asked if some of her suffering and hallucinating might be due to overdose or withdrawal, or even consulted another doctor about its use. It was our relief as well as hers.

But why was she never returned even to that first sanatorium? Or to help that might come from other doctors? It's hard to say. Partly, it was her own fear of returning. Partly, it was too little money, and a family's not-unusual assumption that mental illness is an inevitable part of someone's personality. Or perhaps other family members had feared something like my experience when, one hot and desperate summer between the sixth and seventh grade, I finally persuaded her to let me take her to the only doctor from those sanatorium days whom she remembered without fear.

Yes, this brusque old man told me after talking to my abstracted, timid mother for twenty minutes: She definitely belongs in a state hospital. I should put her there right away. But even at that age, *Life* magazine and newspaper exposés had told me what horrors went on inside those hospitals. Assuming there to be no other alternative, I took her home and never tried again.

In retrospect, perhaps the biggest reason my mother was cared for but not helped for twenty years was the simplest: Her functioning was not that necessary to the world. Like women alcoholics who drink in their kitchens while costly programs are constructed for executives who drink, or like the homemakers subdued with tranquilizers while male patients get therapy and personal attention instead, my mother was not an important worker. She was not even the caretaker of a very young child, as she had been when she was hospitalized the first time. My father had patiently brought home the groceries and kept our odd household going until I was eight or so and my sister went away to college. Two years later when wartime gas rationing closed his summer resort and he had to travel to buy and sell in summer as well as winter, he said: How can I travel and take care of your mother? How can I make a living? He was right. It was impossible to do both. I did not blame him for leaving once I was old enough to be the bringer of meals and answerer of my mother's questions. ("Has your sister been killed in a car crash?" "Are there German soldiers outside?") I replaced my father, my mother was left with one more way of maintaining a sad status quo, and the world went on undisturbed.

That's why our lives, my mother's from forty-six to fifty-three, and my own from ten to seventeen, were spent alone together. There was one sane winter in a house we rented to be near my sister's college in Massachusetts, then one bad summer spent house-sitting in suburbia while my mother hallucinated and my sister struggled to hold down a summer job in New York. But the rest of those years were lived in Toledo where both my mother and father had been born, and on whose city newspapers an earlier Ruth had worked.

First we moved into a basement apartment in a good neighborhood. In those rooms behind a furnace, I made one last stab at being a child. By pretending to be much sicker with a cold than I really was, I hoped my mother would suddenly turn into a sane and cheerful woman bringing me chicken soup à la Hollywood. Of course, she could not. It only made her feel worse that she could not. I stopped pretending.

But for most of those years, we lived in the upstairs of the house my mother had grown up in and that her parents left her—a deteriorating farm house engulfed by the city, with poor but newer houses stacked against it and a major highway a few feet from its sagging front porch. For a while, we could rent the two downstairs apartments to a newlywed factory worker and a local butcher's family. Then the health department condemned our ancient furnace for the final time. . . .

In that house, I remember:

. . . lying in the bed my mother and I shared for warmth, listening on the early morning radio to the royal wedding of Princess Elizabeth and Prince Philip being broadcast live, while we tried to ignore and thus protect each other from the unmistakable sounds of the factory worker downstairs beating up and locking out his pregnant wife.

. . . hanging paper drapes I had bought in the dime store; stacking books and papers in the shape of two armchairs and covering them with blankets; evolving my own dishwashing system (I waited until all the dishes were dirty, then put them in the bathtub); and listening to my mother's high praise for these housekeeping efforts to bring order from chaos, though in retrospect I think they probably depressed her further.

. . . coming back from one of the Eagles' Club shows where I and other veterans of a local tap-dancing school made ten dollars a night for two shows, and finding my mother waiting with a flashlight and no coat in the dark cold of the bus stop, worried about my safety walking home.

. . . in a good period, when my mother's native adventurousness came through, answering a classified ad together for an amateur acting troupe that performed Biblical dramas in churches, and doing several very corny performances of *Noah's Ark* while my proud mother shook metal sheets backstage to make thunder.

. . . on a hot summer night, being bitten by one of the rats that shared our house and its back alley. It was a terrifying night that turned into a touching one when my mother, summoning courage from some unknown reservoir of love, became a calm, comforting parent who took me to a hospital emergency room despite her terror at leaving home.

. . . coming home from a local library with the three books a week into which I regularly escaped, and discovering that for once there was no need to escape. My mother was calmly planting hollyhocks in the vacant lot next door.

But there were also times when she woke in the early winter dark, too frightened and disoriented to remember that I was at my usual after-school job, and so called the police to find me. Humiliated in front of my friends by sirens and policemen, I would yell at her—and she would bow her head in fear and say "I'm sorry, I'm sorry, I'm sorry," just as she had done so often when my otherwise-kindhearted father had yelled at her in frustration. Perhaps the worst thing about suffering is that it finally hardens the hearts of those around it.

And there were many, many times when I badgered her until her shaking hands had written a small check to cash at the corner grocery and I could leave her alone while I escaped to the comfort of well-heated dime stores that smelled of fresh doughnuts, or to air-conditioned Saturday-afternoon movies that were windows on a very different world.

But my ultimate protection was this: I was just passing through, a guest in the house; perhaps this wasn't my mother at all. Though I knew very well that I was her daughter, I sometimes imagined that I had been adopted and that my real parents would find me, a fantasy I've since discovered is common. (If children wrote more and grown-ups less, being adopted might be seen not only as a fear but also as a hope.) Certainly, I didn't mourn the wasted life of this woman who was scarcely older than I am now. I worried only about the times when she got worse.

Pity takes distance and a certainty of surviving. It was only after our house was bought for demolition by the church next door, and after my sister had performed the miracle of persuading my father to give me a carefree time before college by taking my mother with him to California for a year, that I could afford to think about the sadness of her life. Suddenly, I was far away in Washington, living with my sister and sharing a house with several of her friends. While I finished high school and discovered to my surprise that my classmates felt sorry for me because my mother *wasn't* there, I also realized that my sister, at least in her early childhood, had known a very different person who lived inside our mother, an earlier Ruth.

She was a woman I met for the first time in a mental hospital near Baltimore, a humane place with gardens and trees where I visited her each weekend of the summer after my first year away in college. Fortunately, my sister hadn't been able to work and be our mother's caretaker, too. After my father's year was up, my sister had carefully researched hospitals and found the courage to break the family chain.

At first, this Ruth was the same abstracted, frightened woman I had lived with all those years; though now all the sadder for being approached through long hospital corridors and many locked doors.

But gradually she began to talk about her past life, memories that doctors there must have been awakening. I began to meet a Ruth I had never known.

. . . A tall, spirited, auburn-haired high-school girl who loved basketball and reading; who tried to drive her uncle's Stanley Steamer when it was the first car in the neighborhood; who had a gift for gardening and who sometimes, in defiance of convention, wore her father's overalls; a girl with the courage to go to dances even though her church told her that music itself was sinful, and whose sense of adventure almost made up for feeling gawky and unpretty next to her daintier, dark-haired sister.

. . . A very little girl, just learning to walk, discovering the body places where touching was pleasurable, and being punished by her mother who slapped her hard across the kitchen floor.

. . . A daughter of a handsome railroad-engineer and a school-teacher who felt she married "beneath her"; the mother who took her two daughters on Christmas trips to faraway New York on an engineer's free railroad pass and showed them the restaurants and theaters they should aspire to—even though they could only stand outside them in the snow.

. . . A good student at Oberlin College, whose freethinking traditions she loved, where friends nicknamed her "Billy"; a student with a talent for both mathematics and poetry, who was not above putting an invisible film of Karo syrup on all the john seats in her dormitory the night of a big prom; a daughter who had to return to Toledo, live with her family, and go to a local university when her ambitious mother—who had scrimped and saved, ghostwritten a minister's sermons, and made her daughters' clothes in order to get them to college at all—ran out of money. At home, this Ruth became a part-time bookkeeper in a lingerie shop for the very rich, commuting to classes and listening to her mother's harsh lectures on the security of becoming a teacher; but also a young woman who was still rebellious enough to fall in love with my father, the editor of her university newspaper, a funny and charming young man who was a terrible student, had no intention of graduating, put on all the campus dances, and was unacceptably Jewish.

I knew from family lore that my mother had married my father twice: once secretly, after he invited her to become the literary editor of his campus newspaper, and once a year later in a public ceremony, which some members of both families refused to attend as the "mixed marriage" of its day.

And I knew that my mother had gone on to earn a teaching certificate. She had used it to scare away truant officers during the winters when, after my father closed the summer resort for the season, we lived in a house trailer and worked our way to Florida or California and back by buying and selling antiques.

But only during those increasingly adventurous weekend outings from the hospital—going shopping, to lunch, or the movies—did I realize that she had taught college calculus for a year in deference to her mother's insistence that she have teaching "to fall back on." And only then did I realize she had fallen in love with newspapers along with my father. After graduating from the university paper, she wrote a gossip column for a local tabloid, under the name "Duncan MacKenzie," since women weren't supposed to do such things, and soon had earned a job as society reporter on one of Toledo's two big dailies. By the time my sister was four or so, she had worked her way up to the coveted position of Sunday editor.

It was a strange experience to look into those brown eyes I had seen so often and realize suddenly how much they were like my own. For the first time, I realized that she might really be my mother.

I began to think about the many pressures that might have led up to that first nervous breakdown: leaving my sister whom she loved very much with a grandmother whose values my mother didn't share; trying to hold on to a job she loved but was being asked to leave by her husband; wanting very much to go with a woman friend to pursue their own dreams of New York; falling in love with a co-worker at the newspaper who frightened her by being more sexually attractive, more supportive of her work than my father, and perhaps the man she should have married; and finally, nearly bleeding to death with a miscarriage because her own mother had little faith in doctors and refused to get help.

Did those months in the sanatorium brainwash her in some Freudian or very traditional way into making what were, for her, probably the wrong choices? I don't know. It almost doesn't matter. Without extraordinary support to the contrary, she was already convinced that divorce was unthinkable. A husband could not be left for another man, and certainly not for a reason as selfish as a career. A daughter could not be deprived of her father and certainly not be uprooted and taken off to an uncertain future in New York. A bride was supposed to be virginal (not "shopworn," as my euphemistic mother would have said), and if your husband turned out to be kind, but innocent of the possibility of a woman's pleasure, then just be thankful for kindness. . . .

At the hospital and later when Ruth told me stories of her past, I used to say, "But why didn't you leave? Why didn't you take the job? Why didn't you marry the other man?" She would always insist it didn't matter, she was lucky to have my sister and me. If I pressed hard enough, she would add, "If I'd left you never would have been born."

I always thought but never had the courage to say: *But you might have been born instead.*

I'd like to tell you that this story has a happy ending. The best I can do is one that is happier than its beginning.

After many months in that Baltimore hospital, my mother lived on her own in a small apartment for two years while I was in college and my sister married and lived nearby. When she felt the old terrors coming back, she returned to the hospital at her own request. She was approaching sixty by the time she emerged from there and from a Quaker farm that served as a halfway house, but she confounded her psychiatrists' predictions that she would be able to live outside for shorter and shorter periods. In fact, she never returned. She lived more than another twenty years, and for six of them, she was well enough to stay in a rooming house that provided both privacy and company. Even after my sister and her husband moved to a larger house and generously made two rooms into an apartment for her, she continued to have some independent life and many friends. She worked part-time as a "salesgirl" in a china shop; went away with me on yearly vacations and took one trip to Europe with relatives; went to women's club meetings; found a multi-racial church that she loved; took meditation courses; and enjoyed many books. She still could not bear to see a sad movie, to stay alone with any of her six grandchildren while they were babies, to live without many tranquilizers, or to talk about those bad years in Toledo. The old terrors were still in the back of her mind, and each day was a fight to keep them down.

It was the length of her illness that had made doctors pessimistic. In fact, they could not identify any serious mental problem and diagnosed her only as having "an anxiety neurosis": low self-esteem, a fear of being dependent, a terror of being alone, a constant worry about money. She also had spells of what now would be called agoraphobia, a problem almost entirely confined to dependent women: fear of going outside the house, and incapacitating anxiety attacks in unfamiliar or public places.

Would you say, I asked one of her doctors, that her spirit had been broken? "I guess that's as good a diagnosis as any," he said. "And it's hard to mend anything that's been broken for twenty years."

But once out of the hospital for good, she continued to show flashes of the different woman inside; one with a wry kind of humor, a sense of adventure, and a love of learning. Books on math, physics, and mysticism occupied a lot of her time. ("Religion," she used to say firmly, "begins in the laboratory.") When she visited me in New York during her sixties and seventies, she always told taxi drivers that she was eighty years old ("so they will tell me how young I look"), and convinced theater ticket sellers that she was deaf long before she really was ("so they'll give us seats in the front row"). She made friends easily, with the vulnerability and charm of a person who feels entirely dependent on the approval of others. After one of her visits, every shopkeeper within blocks of my apartment would say, "Oh yes, I know your mother!" At home, she complained that people her own age were too old and stodgy for her. Many of her friends were far younger than she. It was as if she were making up for her own lost years.

She was also overly appreciative of any presents given to her— and that made giving them irresistible. I loved to send her clothes, jewelry, exotic soaps, and additions to her collection of tarot cards. She loved receiving them, though we both knew they would end up stored in boxes and drawers. She carried on a correspondence in German with our European relatives, and exchanges with many other friends, all written in her painfully slow, shaky handwriting. She also loved giving gifts. Even as she worried about money and figured out how to save pennies, she would buy or make carefully chosen presents for grandchildren and friends.

Part of the price she paid for this much health was forgetting. A single reminder of those bad years in Toledo was enough to plunge her into days of depression. There were times when this fact created loneliness for me, too. Only two of us had lived most of my childhood. Now, only one of us remembered. But there were also times in later years when, no matter how much I pled with reporters *not* to interview our friends and neighbors in Toledo, *not* to say that my mother had been hospitalized, they published things that hurt her very much and sent her into a downhill slide.

On the other hand, she was also her mother's daughter, a person with a certain amount of social pride and pretension, and some of her objections had less to do with depression than false pride. She complained bitterly about one report that we had lived in a house trailer. She finally asked angrily: "Couldn't they at least say 'vacation mobile home'?" Divorce was still a shame to her. She might cheerfully tell friends, "I don't know *why* Gloria says her father and I were divorced—we never were." I think she justified this to herself with the idea that they had gone through two marriage ceremonies, one in secret and one in public, but been divorced only once. In fact, they were definitely divorced, and my father had briefly married someone else.

She was very proud of my being a published writer, and we generally shared the same values. After her death, I found a mother-daughter morals quiz I once had written for a women's magazine. In her unmistakably shaky writing, she had recorded her own answers, her entirely accurate imagination of what my answers would be, and a score that concluded our differences were less than those "normal for women separated by twenty-odd years." Nonetheless, she was quite capable of putting a made-up name on her name tag when going to a conservative women's club where she feared our shared identity would bring controversy or even just questions. When I finally got up the nerve to tell her I was signing a 1972 petition of women who publicly said we had had abortions and were demanding the repeal of laws that made them illegal and dangerous, her only reply was sharp and aimed to hurt back. "Every starlet says she's had an abortion," she said. "It's just a way of getting publicity." I knew she agreed that abortion should be a legal choice, but I also knew she would never forgive me for embarrassing her in public.

In fact, her anger and a fairly imaginative ability to wound with words increased in her last years when she was most dependent, most focused on herself, and most likely to need the total attention of others. When my sister made a courageous decision to go to law school at the age of fifty, leaving my mother in a house that not only had many loving teenage grandchildren in it but a kindly older woman as a paid companion besides, my mother reduced her to frequent tears by insisting that this was a family with no love in it, no home-cooked food in the refrigerator; not a real family at all. Since arguments about home cooking wouldn't work on me, my punishment was creative and different. She was going to call up

The New York Times, she said, and tell them that this was what feminism did: It left old sick women all alone.

Some of this bitterness brought on by failing faculties was eventually solved by a nursing home near my sister's house where my mother not only got the twenty-four-hour help her weakening body demanded, but the attention of affectionate nurses besides. She charmed them, they loved her, and she could still get out for an occasional family wedding. If I ever had any doubts about the debt we owe to nurses, those last months laid them to rest.

When my mother died just before her eighty-second birthday in a hospital room where my sister and I were alternating the hours in which her heart wound slowly down to its last sounds, we were alone together for a few hours while my sister slept. My mother seemed bewildered by her surroundings and the tubes that invaded her body, but her consciousness cleared long enough for her to say: "I want to go home. Please take me home." Lying to her one last time, I said I would. "Okay, honey," she said. "I trust you." Those were her last understandable words.

The nurses let my sister and me stay in the room long after there was no more breath. She had asked us to do that. One of her many fears came from a story she had been told as a child about a man whose coma was mistaken for death. She also had made out a living will requesting that no extraordinary measures be used to keep her alive, and that her ashes be sprinkled in the same stream as my father's.

Her memorial service was in the Episcopalian church that she loved because it fed the poor, let the homeless sleep in its pews, had members of almost every race, and had been sued by the Episcopalian hierarchy for having a woman priest. Most of all, she loved the affection with which its members had welcomed her, visited her at home, and driven her to services. I think she would have liked the Quaker-style informality with which people rose to tell their memories of her. I know she would have loved the presence of many friends. It was to this church that she had donated some of her remaining Michigan property in the hope that it could be used as a multiracial camp, thus getting even with those people in the tiny nearby town who had snubbed my father for being Jewish.

I think she also would have been pleased with her obituary. It emphasized her brief career as one of the early women journalists and asked for donations to Oberlin's scholarship fund so others could go to this college she loved so much but had to leave.

I know I will spend the next years figuring out what her life has left in me.

I realize that I've always been more touched by old people than by children. It's the talent and hopes locked up in a failing body that gets to me; a poignant contrast that reminds me of my mother, even when she was strong. . . .

I'm no longer obsessed, as I was for many years, with the fear that I would end up in a house like that one in Toledo. Now, I'm obsessed instead with the things I could have done for my mother while she was alive, or the things I should have said.

I still don't understand why so many, many years passed before I saw my mother as a person and before I understood that many of the forces in her life are patterns women share. Like a lot of daughters, I suppose I couldn't afford to admit that what had happened to my mother was not all personal or accidental, and therefore could happen to me.

One mystery has finally cleared. I could never understand why my mother hadn't been helped by Pauline, her mother-in-law; a woman she seemed to love more than her own mother. This paternal grandmother had died when I was five, before my mother's real problems began but long after that "nervous breakdown," and I knew Pauline was once a suffragist who addressed Congress, marched for the vote, and was the first woman member of a school board in Ohio. She must have been a courageous and independent woman, yet I could find no evidence in my mother's reminiscences that Pauline had encouraged or helped my mother toward a life of her own.

I finally realized that my grandmother never changed the politics of her own life, either. She was a feminist who kept a neat house for a husband and four antifeminist sons, a vegetarian among five male meat eaters, and a woman who felt so strongly about the dangers of alcohol that she used only paste vanilla; yet she served both meat and wine to the men of the house and made sure their lives and comforts were continued undisturbed. After the vote was won, Pauline seems to have stopped all feminist activity. My mother greatly admired the fact that her mother-in-law kept a spotless house and prepared a week's meals at a time. Whatever her own internal torments, Pauline was to my mother a woman who seemed able to "do it all." "Whither thou goest, I shall go," my mother used to say to her much-loved mother-in-law, quoting the Ruth of the Bible.

In the end, her mother-in-law may have added to my mother's burdens of guilt.

Perhaps like many later suffragists, my grandmother was a public feminist and a private isolationist. That may have been heroic in itself, the most she could be expected to do, but the vote and a legal right to work were not the only kind of help my mother needed.

The world still missed a unique person named Ruth. Though she longed to live in New York and in Europe, she became a woman who was afraid to take a bus across town. Though she drove the first Stanley Steamer, she married a man who never let her drive.

I can only guess what she might have become. The clues are in moments of spirit or humor.

After all the years of fear, she still came to Oberlin with me when I was giving a speech there. She remembered everything about its history as the first college to admit blacks and the first to admit women, and responded to students with the dignity of a professor, the accuracy of a journalist, and a charm that was all her own.

When she could still make trips to Washington's wealth of libraries, she became an expert genealogist, delighting especially in finding the rogues and rebels in our family tree.

Just before I was born, when she had cooked one more enormous meal for all the members of some famous dance band at my father's resort and they failed to clean their plates, she had taken a shotgun down from the kitchen wall and held it over their frightened heads until they had finished the last crumb of strawberry shortcake. Only then did she tell them the gun wasn't loaded. It was a story she told with great satisfaction.

Though sex was a subject she couldn't discuss directly, she had a great appreciation of sensuous men. When a friend I brought home tried to talk to her about cooking, she was furious. ("He came out in the kitchen and talked to me about stew!") But she forgave him when we went swimming. She whispered, "He has wonderful legs!"

On her seventy-fifth birthday, she played softball with her grandsons on the beach, and took pride in hitting home runs into the ocean. . . .

My father was the Jewish half of the family, yet it was my mother who taught me to have pride in that tradition. It was she who encouraged me to listen to a radio play about a concentration camp when I was little. "You should know that this can happen," she said. Yet she did it just enough to teach, never enough to frighten.

It was she who introduced me to books and a respect for them, to poetry that she knew by heart, and to the idea that you could never criticize someone unless you "walked miles in their shoes."

It was she who sold that Toledo house, the only home she had, with the determination that the money be used to start me in college. She gave both her daughters the encouragement to leave home for four years of independence that she herself had never had.

After her death, my sister and I found a journal she had kept of her one cherished and belated trip to Europe. It was a trip she had described very little when she came home: She always deplored people who talked boringly about their personal travels and showed slides. Nonetheless, she had written a descriptive essay called "Grandma Goes to Europe." She still must have thought of herself as a writer. Yet she showed this long journal to no one.

I miss her, but perhaps no more in death than I did in life. Dying seems less sad than having lived too little. But at least we're now asking questions about all the Ruths and all our family mysteries.

If her song inspires that, I think she would be the first to say: It was worth the singing.

EDITIONS CITED

Jane Addams, *Twenty Years at Hull House* (Macmillan Publishing Company, Inc., New York, 1938).

Marian Anderson, *My Lord, What a Morning* (The Viking Press, New York, 1956).

Maya Angelou, *I Know Why the Caged Bird Sings* (Random House, New York, 1968).

S. Josephine Baker, *Fighting For Life* (Macmillan Publishing Company, Inc., New York, 1939).

Louise Bogan, *Journey Around My Room*, compiled and edited by Ruth Limmer (The Viking Press, New York, 1980).

Anne Walter Fearn, *My Days of Strength* (Harper & Brothers, New York, 1939).

Cecilia Payne Gaposchkin, *An Autobiography and Other Recollections* (Cambridge University Press, 1984).

Ellen Anderson Gholson Glasgow, *The Woman Within* (Harcourt Brace & Company, New York, 1954).

Zora Neale Hurston, *Dust Tracks on a Road* (J. B. Lippincott and Company, Philadelphia, 1942).

Harriet Ann Jacobs, *Incidents in the Life of a Slave Girl* (Boston, 1861).

Maxine Hong Kingston, *The Woman Warrior* (Alfred A. Knopf, New York, 1976).

Lucy Larcom, *A New England Girlhood* (Houghton, Mifflin Company, Boston and New York, 1889).

Margaret Mead, *Blackberry Winter* (Angus and Robertson, London, 1972).

Dorothy Reed Mendenhall's Unpublished Memoir is part of the Sophia Smith Collection at Smith College, Northhampton, Massachusetts.

Margaret Morse Nice, *Research Is a Passion with Me* (Consolidated Amethyst Publications, Toronto, Ontario, 1970).

Hortense Powdermaker, *Stranger and Friend* (W. W. Norton & Company, New York, 1966).

Margaret Sanger, *Margaret Sanger: An Autobiography* (W. W. Norton & Company, New York, 1938).

Janet Scudder, *Modeling My Life* (Harcourt, Brace & Company, New York, 1925).

Vida Dutton Scudder, *On Journey* (E. P. Dutton & Company, Inc., New York, 1937).

Anna Howard Shaw, *The Story of a Pioneer* (Harper & Brothers, Publishers, New York, 1915).

Gloria Steinem, *Outrageous Acts and Everyday Rebellions* (Holt, Rinehart, and Winston, New York, 1983).

Anna Louise Strong, *I Change Worlds* (Garden City Publishing Company, New York, 1937).

Margaret Floy Washburn, *A History of Psychology in Autobiography*, edited by Carl Murchison (Clark University Press, Worcester, Massachusetts, and Oxford University Press, 1932).

Margaret Bourke-White, *Portrait of Myself* (Simon and Schuster, New York, 1963).

Mildred Ella (Babe) Didrikson Zaharias, *This Life I've Led*, as told to Harry Paxton (A. S. Barnes & Co., New York, 1955).